INSIDE
THE
MIDDLE
EAST

INSIDE
THE
MIDDLE
EAST
ENTERING A NEW ERA

AVI MELAMED
WITH MAIA HOFFMAN

Skyhorse Publishing

Skyhorse Publishing books may be purchased in bulk at special discounts for sales promotion, corporate gifts, fund-raising, or educational purposes. Special editions can also be created to specifications. For details, contact the Special Sales Department, Skyhorse Publishing, 307 West 36th Street, 11th Floor, New York, NY 10018 or info@skyhorsepublishing.com.

Skyhorse® and Skyhorse Publishing® are registered trademarks of Skyhorse Publishing, Inc.®, a Delaware corporation.

Visit our website at www.skyhorsepublishing.com.

10 9 8 7 6 5 4 3 2 1

Library of Congress Cataloging-in-Publication Data is available on file.

Cover design by Didier Bodin, DiCi Design
Maps by Didier Bodin, DiCi Design

Cover description: The Middle East is a multi-dimensional game of chess. What happens in one place impacts what happens in another. And what happens in the Middle East does not stay in the Middle East.

Print ISBN: 978-1-5107-6933-5
Ebook ISBN: 978-1-5107-6934-2

Printed in the United States of America

CONTENTS

PREFACE

THE SIXTH DECADE OF MY LIFE unfolded precisely between the years 2010 and 2020. It just so happened that the same decade witnessed tremendous upheaval in the Middle East. I have devoted most of my life and professional career to expanding my knowledge and understanding of the Middle East. Having a front-row seat to history in the making was a rare and unique opportunity. Moreover, being privileged to be an educator as the region goes through such a fierce upheaval has been incredibly challenging and rewarding.

My bio lists my background—counterterrorism professional, intelligence official, Middle East expert, policy advisor, senior official on Arab Affairs, social entrepreneur, etc. But to me, the most important title I have is "educator."

Over the last two decades, I have had the opportunity to combine my professional background and skills and fulfill my purpose as an educator.

I became an independent intelligence analyst in the mid-2000s. Intelligence analysis, which provides the basis of my educational efforts, is extraordinarily demanding—emotionally, intellectually, and physically. It requires the constant, persistent, and unrelenting pursuit of information and knowledge. And at the same time demands the unwavering practice of consistently evaluating my observations and predictions and testing and evaluating them against the on-the-ground reality.

I cannot allow my narratives or my emotions to make the analysis. I cannot hide beyond general concepts, narratives, and theories that do not reflect reality. And the only way I can assess if my analysis is accurate is to put my neck on the line and make predictions. That is the reason you will notice I have included predictions throughout the book. I resolutely practice what I preach.

Since entering the private sector, I have presented analysis in private and public forums, written articles, and provided briefings and lectures that outlined my predictions regarding various regional events.

I named my 2009 North American lecture tour "The Middle East: Smoking Volcanoes, Fertile Ground." The tour's theme centered on my prediction that the Arab world was on the verge of an outbreak of widespread social and political protests. Toward the end of 2010, my prediction "came true," with the explosion of protests in the Arab world that came to be known as the "Arab Spring" or, as I prefer to call it, "the Arab Awakening."

My ability to foresee the Arab Spring was one in a long line of documented accurate predictions throughout my career. This includes the inability to reach an Israeli-Palestinian peace agreement; the deepening of the internal Palestinian split; the resilience of the Arab monarchies in the face of the "Arab Spring"; the crisis and split within Political Islam and the Muslim Brotherhood—including their trend toward pragmatism; the growing Iranian threat; the disintegration of Lebanon; the war in Syria; the consequences of the war in Yemen; the rapprochement between Israel and Arab states; and more.

I mention this not to brag, but rather because I believe these facts validate the reliability of my book's analysis. In this book, like in all my writings and teaching, I have tried my best to present the Middle East's current geopolitical environment. I believe the analysis and predictions I offer accurately dialogue with the Middle Eastern reality. Therefore, in my estimation, this book—like the previous one—will be relevant for years to come.

The goal of my previous book, *Inside the Middle East: Making Sense of the Most Dangerous and Complex Region on Earth* (2016, Skyhorse Publishing, NY), was to provide the Western audience with the database necessary to understand the contemporary Middle East. To that end, I provided the historical background to build that database.

My 2016 book offered the reader a basic GPS to navigate the Middle East. I dedicated a large portion of the 2016 book to what, in my professional analysis, were (and still are) the core issues that influence the present and future of this region. This includes the struggle for identity, path, and direction in the Middle East; the Iranian-Arab power struggle; the strengthening of civil society; and the growing influence of social media. And finally, I had to be true to my roots as an educator and intelligence professional. And that meant I had to make predictions. I am humbly proud to say that, as of the summer of 2021—well over five years after the book was published—the picture I painted regarding the Middle East's course and direction has proven to be very accurate.

Writing my previous book occurred parallel to another exciting chapter in my personal and professional career. Between 2013 and 2018, I had the honor to serve as the Eisenhower Institute's Salisbury Fellow of Intelligence and Middle East Affairs.

At this point, I would like to express my gratitude to Jeffery Blavatt. Jeff was, at the time, the visionary executive director of the Eisenhower Institute. As the executive director, he asked me to build an educational program for undergraduate students at Gettysburg College. I designed a curriculum and taught a sixty-hour undergraduate course that offered an apolitical non-partisan education about the Middle East. And I created a praxis that used intelligence methodology to teach critical thinking and media literacy. My goal was to equip young people with the knowledge, skills, and tools to accurately interpret the Middle East and predict the direction of future events. The program would come to be called Inside The Middle East | Intelligence Perspectives (ITME).

During my tenure, I was fortunate to teach five cohorts at Gettysburg College. My wife and business partner, Maia Hoffman, Jeff Blavatt, and myself take pride in the fact that many ITME alumni have been accepted to competitive positions in government, intelligence, national security, research, public policy positions, and more. Each graduate is a source of great pride to our generous donors and ourselves.

I am grateful for the opportunity I had at the Eisenhower Institute and Gettysburg College. The experience offered me the platform to build a program that has grown exponentially and allowed me to reach a broad and varied audience.

In 2018, I left the Eisenhower Institute, and ITME became an independent 501(c)(3). For over a decade, due to the grace and generosity of our visionary donors, friends, and supporters, I have had the honor of educating thousands of current and future leaders from high school students attending

Catholic schools in the South Bronx, to college students at Gettysburg College, to senior congressional staffers on Capitol Hill, as well as current and future community leaders across the United States.

The Middle East of 2021 is not the Middle East of 2016. *Inside the Middle East: Entering a New Era* offers an advanced GPS and additional lenses to navigate the Middle East. In this new volume, I examine and analyze what has happened in the region since 2016. And I look ahead and offer my predictions as to where the area is going as we enter the third decade of the twenty-first century.

I would like to thank you for choosing this book, thank you for taking the time to read this book, and thank you for trusting me. I am profoundly grateful, honored, and humbled for each and every platform, stage, or venue that I am offered to share my knowledge, analysis, and predictions about the Middle East. Having the opportunity to provide people with knowledge, insights, perspectives, and reflections is an incredible privilege.

In closing, I would like to thank a few people.

I am grateful to Skyhorse, who decided to publish another one of my books. And I am particularly thankful to Caroline Russomanno, editor at Skyhorse publishing. She was instrumental in making this book happen in the shadow of the challenges and difficulties of COVID-19 and other unanticipated hiccups. Maia and I are profoundly grateful for Caroline's commitment, dedication, patience, and unwavering professionalism over the course of this project and throughout the development and publication of this volume. Thank you, Caroline. Through writing this book, we not only had the honor to work with an exceptional editor, but we also gained a valued friend.

I would like to thank Didier Bodin, the Design Director of DiCi Consulting & Design. Didier is a good friend, an extraordinarily talented and committed professional who has been our marketing and branding consultant over the past year and a half. Little did he know when he began working with us that he would become an integral part of this project. He painstakingly worked with Maia to create the maps and all the artwork in the book. And Didier worked with Maia and me to create the compelling and distinct cover of this book. Didier, we are profoundly grateful to you and your wife and business partner, Adi Zilbershten, the branding director for DiCi Consulting, for your uncompromising dedication to our work and all of our projects. Thank you. We are incredibly fortunate to have the opportunity to work with you.

I would like to thank Mohamed Zalabia for his work in transcribing all of the endnotes. Given the scope of this book, his contribution and work were invaluable.

And I would like to express my deep gratitude to two people.

One is Jeffery Blavatt. I mentioned Jeff earlier, but it is worth mentioning him twice. I am proud to continue to call Jeff a friend and a colleague as he continues to pioneer his unique brand of interactive education. In his current position as the executive director of the Insight Israel Forum, an initiative of The Associated: Jewish Federation of Baltimore, Jeff continues to be a trailblazer with the same zest and fervor and an uncompromising dedication to impactful and unique sustainable educational opportunities of uncompromising quality.

The other person is Maia Hoffman, my partner for life since 2006. I don't have enough room to describe Maia's central place and the very important role she plays in my private and professional life. In Maia, a native of Baltimore, the daughter of Sandy Hoffman who helped us with some of the proofreading (may she live until 120) and the late professor and scholar, Dr. Ronald Hoffman, there is a combination of the core qualities of an authentic educator: intellectual curiosity, meticulous observation to every sentence and every word, uncompromising professionalism, constant striving for improvement, self-criticism, and most importantly, a deep personal commitment to the great responsibility and privilege to educate, to offer knowledge, insights, and perspectives. Whether it is strategizing about how to maximize our impact, editing movies, writing and editing articles, working with high school students in the Bronx, college students at Gettysburg College, senior congressional staffers on the Hill as well as in Israel and the Palestinian Territories, or writing and editing, and writing and editing, and writing and editing, this book as well as the 2016 book—Maia demonstrates the same deep and uncompromising commitment to making sure we do our utmost to fulfill our responsibility and great privilege to educate and influence. Maia is a full partner with equal rights in our joint and growing educational endeavors. I am incredibly fortunate to have Maia in my life, and I am deeply grateful for everything she brings to our relationship, work, and life.

I would like to celebrate the memory of my beloved and deceased parents Yardena and Joseph Melamed. Both were born in Jerusalem. They gave me the values and skills without which I could not overcome the challenges of being an educator.

I dedicate this book to my children, Sapir and Nimrod—the fourth generation of my family born in Jerusalem. The main principle that guided me in educating my children as a parent is not to decide for them or force my will upon them. As I see it, my role is to explain to them the implications and possible consequences of the choices and decisions they make. It makes me happy to know my children think that this approach was the right one.

And a final, personal comment. I feel blessed and fortunate. That is because I am fulfilling my destiny in my personal path and professional activities. It is a notion for which I am deeply grateful. Some people would call that notion happiness.

~Avi Melamed
August 2021

INTRODUCTION

ALMOST SIX YEARS HAVE PASSED SINCE the publication of *Inside the Middle East: Making Sense of the Most Dangerous and Complicated Region on Earth*. My goal in the 2016 book was to provide the database to understand the contemporary Middle East.

The Middle East of 2022 is not the Middle East of 2016. However, I believe the 2016 book provided a road map to help us understand where we are today. And I hope this volume will provide a reliable guide as we move into a new era in the region.

At the beginning of the third decade of the twenty-first century, as the book title emphasizes, the Middle East is entering a new era.

Ancient and modern, domestic, regional, and international factors, forces, and underlying currents have joined together not coincidentally to create that new era in the Middle East. These forces are reshaping the labyrinthine geostrategic contours of this ancient landscape and are redesigning the geopolitical map.

The new era we are entering is fraught with challenges and full of opportunities. Is it a new dawn? Or is it a setting sun?

A complex and intricate pluri-dimensional equilibrium will write the next chapter of this region. In this book, I hope to help you connect the dots and build a multidimensional picture. We will explore each of the factors that I believe will create a new era. And we will look ahead to see what the future might bring.

In this book, I will update you on the region's significant developments since 2016. I will also provide insights, observations, and predictions. I hope the analysis, information, knowledge, and perspectives I offer will be a GPS to help you navigate the Middle East.

Let me begin by providing you a roadmap of the book, *Inside the Middle East | Entering a New Era.*

• **CHAPTERS 1–3**

Ancient Rivalries Are Alive and Well and Iran's and Turkey's Hegemonic Ambitions

In the first three chapters of this book, we will begin by taking a deep dive into the two regional powers pursuing hegemony: Iran and Turkey.

We will explore the ancient and modern motivations of their aggressive policies. We will understand their current strategies, examine their actions, and explore the immediate, possible, and projected implications of their hegemonic aspirations on the Middle East.

To right an ancient historical wrong and regain—what it sees—as its rightful place as the leader of the Muslim world, Iran pursues an aggressive and destructive strategy.

From the Arabian/Persian Gulf through the Arabian and Red Seas, Iran, directly and indirectly, terrorizes vital maritime arenas critical to regional and global commerce, trade, and security. Iranian-backed armies of terror from the Gaza Strip through Lebanon, Syria, Iraq, and Yemen spread death and destruction and inflict havoc on the region.

In a bid to revive the Ottoman Empire and position Turkey—and especially its current president Recep Tayyip Erdoğan—as the leader of the Sunni camp in the region. Erdoğan looks for every opportunity to secure his interests and expand and increase Turkey's reach and power.

Turkey deploys its military and a network of armed proxies in northern Syria, northern Iraq, the Arab/Persian Gulf, south Yemen, the Red Sea, Somalia, Libya, and throughout Africa.

I devote so much time to Iran and Turkey because, in a plethora of ways, their pursuit of hegemony, through a mixture of hard and soft power, plays a pivotal role in creating the new era in the Middle East.

Understanding their actions, motivations, and strategies is essential to accurately interpret the Middle East today and navigate the new era.

• **CHAPTERS 4–7**

The Struggle Over Path, Identity, and Direction—On the Way to a New Nation-State Model?

By the time we get to Chapter 4, it will be apparent that the Middle East is experiencing very turbulent times.

We will learn how Iran and Turkey simultaneously foment and capitalize on the unstable environment in the first chapters.

In Chapters 4–7, we will focus much more on the second factor that will shape the new era.

The twentieth-century nation-state model in the Arab world has failed or at least encountered severe difficulties. The traditional core building blocks of individual and collective identity—ethnicity, geographical location, religion, tribalism, and narrow particularistic interests and politics—have been much more powerful than the core values which are critical to the existence of a functioning nation-state: civic responsibility, shared destiny, governmental accountability, mutual responsibility, and the rule of law.

The notion of "statehood," although it existed, was a secondary component of people's individual and collective identity.

The failure of the statehood model has resulted in autocracies and dictatorships in many Arab countries. Rulers were, first and foremost, focused on brutally and oppressively securing their power. The well-being of the people was a secondary objective. The combination led to growing socio-economic hardships that in turn fueled increasing rage and unrest in Arab countries.

The escalating anger and frustration led to the outbreak of mass protests across the Arab world in 2010, known as the "Arab Spring."

A decade has passed since the Arab Spring. People often attribute the current chaos in the Arab world to the Arab Spring. I argue, as I often do *that it is the other way around.* The volcano that exploded in 2010 is not the cause of the chaos. *It was the result of the chaos.*

Over the past decade, the Arab world has experienced tremendous upheaval. And the aftershocks will continue. Amid this deepening chaos and instability, I identify an interesting process that could potentially lead to the emergence of a new, perhaps more stable, nation-state model.

In Chapters 4, 5, and 6, we will take a multidimensional look at a number of countries to assess where they are today. And we will try to determine if they are on a path to a new and more healthy and stable state or if they are on the path to disintegration and increasing instability.

In Chapter 4, we begin looking at Libya. An oil-rich country, uniquely located, steeped in a complex civil war for a decade. The war in Libya has also become a platform for a local and international power struggle.

In Chapter 5, we begin to focus on the forces and trends underlying a process that I believe may lead to a new, stable nation-state model in some Arab countries. We will visit Egypt, Algeria, Sudan, and Tunisia. We will discuss the struggle between dogmatism and pragmatism and the evolving impact of civil society. We will look at a rising sense of nationalism in some sectors and consider if a pact of accountability and responsibility between citizens and government may be leading to a healthier nation-state.

As of 2021, for five Arab countries, Libya (that we visit in Chapter 4); Lebanon, Syria, Iraq (that we visit in Chapter 6); and Yemen (that we do not specifically visit, but that is interwoven throughout the book), the road toward a possible new statehood model is even more challenging.

In Chapter 6, we will take an in-depth look into three of these five countries—Syria, Lebanon, and Iraq. In 2021, the Lebanese, Syrians, and Iraqis are not only struggling to have a better state model. They are actually fighting for their independence. Two common denominators have brought these three countries to their bleak circumstances. One is the failure of the modern nation-state. The other is that they have become victims of Iran's hegemonic ambitions. In this chapter, we will explore the complex struggles each of these countries is experiencing. And we will try to evaluate their path ahead.

Unexpected events have a way of accelerating and compressing extended processes into a short period of time. The COVID-19 pandemic that is gripping the world in 2020 and 2021 has the potential to be such an event. The COVID-19 pandemic caught the Middle East at a particularly critical and delicate juncture. In Chapter 7, I consider whether COVID-19 strengthened or weakened the potential for the emergence of a new nation-state model in the Arab world.

- **CHAPTER 8**

The Alliance of Moderation

Over the past seven chapters, we have looked at Iran's and Turkey's policies. We have explored the escalating political struggle over the path, identity, and direction in the Arab world. We have pondered the future of Arab states as people ask themselves, what course do we as individuals, a society, country, want to take? What do we want our future to look like?

In Chapter 8, we continue to connect the dots and build our multidimensional picture.

Everything we have discussed until now—Iran's and Turkey's hegemonic ambitions, combined with the increasing challenges of Arab countries—have resulted in two epic developments. Both of which define the new era.

One is the formation of a new geopolitical construct I call the Alliance of Moderation. I foresaw this evolution in my previous book when I outlined the accelerating rapprochement between Israel and Arab states. The alliance of moderation includes major Arab countries like Egypt, Saudi Arabia, and the UAE. But there is another significant partner, Israel. The confederation is based on a conjunction of long-term strategic interests.

The second development, which is directly related to the first, is the Abraham Accords. A set of peace treaties signed in 2020 between Israel and the United Arab Emirates and normalization agreements between Israel and three Arab countries—Bahrain, Sudan, and Morocco.

In Chapter 8, we begin to examine the alliance of moderation members' interests. What brought them together? What does the current cooperation look like? What are the future possibilities? What are the implications on the Middle East ecosystem? How does the alliance impact the current and future geopolitical climate?

The alliance of moderation set the stage for the historic Abraham Accords. We will begin looking at the Abraham Accords and the normalization agreements through the lenses of the region. How has the Arab world reacted to this groundbreaking event? We will then examine how the Abraham Accords is impacting collaboration, communication, and partnerships. And we will, of course, ponder if other countries may join the normalization train.

• **CHAPTERS 9–10**

The Changing Middle East | And Its Impact on the Trajectory of the Israeli-Palestinian Conflict

By this time in the book, you will notice that I challenge many Western narratives when it comes to the Middle East.

In Chapters 9 and 10, I challenge one of the most central and incorrect narratives. The common refrain is that the Israeli-Palestinian conflict is what shapes the Middle East.

Throughout these two chapters, we will look at the local and regional players that positively and negatively influence the Israeli-Palestinian arena. We will trace the evolution of the conflict and the Palestinian issue, or as it is called in Arabic, *al Qadiyah al-Filastiniyah*. We will connect the dots and understand how the struggle for path, identity, and direction of the nation-state in the Arab world influences the Israeli-Palestinian conflict. We will learn how the hegemonic aspirations of Iran and Turkey impact the course of the Israeli-Palestinian conflict. We will learn about the relationship between the Israeli-Palestinian conflict, the alliance of moderation, the Abraham Accords, and the normalization agreements. And we will look at these issues through the eyes of Arab commentators, influencers, and thinkers from across the Arab world.

From the beginning of my career, I have maintained that peace between Israel and the Palestinians is not feasible. That statement does not reflect an emotional or political outlook. It is based on my professional and accurate assessment of reality. I have said this for decades, and I stand by that statement today. However, I do believe that immediate arrangements can be made that will benefit Israelis and Palestinians.

In these two chapters, I provide insights and a concrete framework to put us on a constructive, productive, and sustainable path toward a better future.

I hope influencers and leaders who honestly want to build a better future for Israelis and Palestinians—and the region—will consider my analysis and suggestions helpful.

I believe by the end of these two chapters, my opening statement in which I challenge the standard narrative will make sense. The Israeli-Palestinian conflict does not shape the Middle East. It is the Middle East that shapes the trajectory of the Israeli-Palestinian conflict.

• **CHAPTER 11**
A Late Addition—The Taliban Retakes Afghanistan

As the final manuscript was being prepared, a pivotal event occurred in the Middle East, which truly has significant regional and global ramifications. The United States began leaving Afghanistan, the Afghan President Ashraf Ghani fled, and the Taliban reclaimed Afghanistan. All of this happened a few days short of the tenth commemoration of the September 11, 2001, attacks that precipitated what is called "America's Longest War"—the war in Afghanistan.

Unfortunately, as I say in the book, given the timing, I cannot provide a comprehensive analysis of the situation in Afghanistan. Nor can I offer a full in-depth estimation of what I believe this means for Afghanistan and the region.

However, I do offer a few preliminary thoughts and observations regarding what I see as the immediate and possible ramifications, at least in the short term, of the US withdrawal from Afghanistan and the Taliban regaining control of the country. I offer my analysis on the impact of the event on several key players such as Iran, China, Pakistan, and Russia.

And there is another aspect of the withdrawal of the United States from Afghanistan that I explore in this chapter. And that is the threat of militant Islam.

In my 2016 book, *Inside the Middle East: Making Sense of the Most Dangerous and Complicated Region on Earth,* I explored at length the cultural, ideological, political, and social background to the phenomenon of militant Islam. In this book, however, I examine the issue of militant Islam mainly through the prism of the Taliban and what their victory means for militant Islam.

The Taliban regaining control of Afghanistan has repercussions, both negative but perhaps positive as well.

But what is important to remember is that what happens in the Middle East does not stay in the Middle East.

• **CHAPTER 12**

The End of Western Hegemony in the Middle East

So far in this book, we have examined what, in my estimation, will define the new era of the Middle East.

One of the historical transitions we will experience in the new era is the sunset of Western hegemony.

In Chapter 12, I examine how evolving tensions between realpolitik and idealpolitik, combined with a very fragmented understanding of Western policymakers regarding the multifaceted complexity of the Middle East, have made it increasingly difficult for Western policymakers to formulate a coherent Middle East policy.

Western policy in the Middle East has failed because of a 'looping echo chamber' in which *Concepts* became "*Facts.*" *Narratives* became "*Reality.*" *Theories* exempted from the test of validity became "*Truth.*" Critical thinking and media literacy are not encouraged, and conveyors of knowledge are exempt from professional accountability for the validity of their theories and analyses.

Nonetheless, based upon these almost non-controversial "Facts," "Realities," and "Truths," policies were created. The challenge is that the concepts and narratives were based upon a false reading of reality. The reality on the ground was quite different. Therefore, inevitably, the policies failed.

The Western failure to formulate effective policies in the Middle East has profound ramifications. One, the West has failed to stabilize the Middle East. Two, the West has failed to secure its own interests.

These failures put the new era of the Middle East and the West into question.

• **CHAPTER 13**

The Democrats Are Back in the White House

As I write this book, President Joe Biden, the forty-sixth president of the United States, is eight months in office.

In Chapter 13, I look at regional reactions to Biden's election and Biden's presidency. Throughout this chapter, we will look at President Biden's relationship with various Middle East players. In my analysis, in that regard, there are two distinct periods. November 2020 to February 2021 and February 2021 to August 2021.

In this chapter, I will offer my analysis. And we will look at the current administration through the lenses of Middle East commentators, journalists, thinkers, etc.

• CHAPTER 14
The Rise of China

In Chapter 12, I maintain Western hegemony in the Middle East comes to an end.

In Chapter 14, we will look east to the rising powers. Mainly China, and behind China will be India.

In the new era, China will be a key, perhaps the key powerbroker, in the Middle East.

China's laser-focused foreign policy is the total opposite of Western policy. In this chapter, we look at China's interest in the region from Haifa Bay to Pakistan. We will get a sense of the scale of China's involvement in the region. And we will discuss the role China can play in the evolving complex regional equilibrium.

• CHAPTER 15
2021 | The Middle East Is Entering a New Era

The Middle East as is a multidimensional game of chess. A complex, multifaceted, and intricate pluri-dimensional equilibrium will write the next chapter of this region.

In Chapter 15, I outline the factors that, in my analysis, will characterize and define the new era.

- A triangular power struggle between Iran, Turkey, and the alliance of moderation.
- A rough and turbulent road that may lead to the emergence of a new, hopefully, healthier, solid, and stable model of statehood in the Arab world.
- The evolving battle for the independence and sovereignty of Iraq, Lebanon, and Syria.

- Economic, environmental, political, and social challenges will further fuel radical extremist ideology and increase militant Islam terror activities.
- The end of Western hegemony and the rise of the giants from the East—China, and India—will define the new era in the Middle East.

I hope the information I have provided in this book will equip you with the knowledge and the lenses to navigate this fascinating and inherently dynamic region's endless dimensions.

A FEW DIDACTIC AND METHODOLOGICAL COMMENTS

Before we embark on our journey, I want to share a few thoughts to help you understand my approach to this book.

First and foremost, this is not a book on the history of the Middle East. Instead, I examine the features that, in my professional evaluation, are the most important things we need to understand if we genuinely want to decipher the current events and estimate the region's future trajectory at the beginning of the third decade of the twenty-first century.

Given that is my goal, there are a couple of historical milestones I have chosen to include because they play a central role in the current geopolitical fabric of the region. For example, the Sunni-Shi'ite split and the historic power struggle between three regional civilizations—Arab, Persian, and Turkish.

There are many other historical factors I have chosen not to bring in the book. I am aware that some will criticize me for the fact that I do not include, for example, the influence of colonialism and imperialism. I want to be clear that I consciously make this decision for two reasons.

One reason is that I can confidently demonstrate the relevance of the Sunni-Shi'ite rivalry and the Arab-Persian-Turkish power struggle on the current geopolitical construct and features of the Middle East. I cannot confidently illustrate the relevance of colonialism on the current geopolitical construct of the region.

The second reason is that the excessive weight attributed to colonialism and imperialism has, in my view, impaired the West's reading of the Middle Eastern reality. I know that in Western academic and intellectual circles, it is widely argued that the arbitrary borders drawn by the West to further the West's own interests and needs have doomed the people of the Middle East to a reality of violence, destruction, and systemic inequality. That outlook ignores the historical fact that inequality and violence stemming from rivalries between various regional groups, whether based on ethnic, economic, familial, geographical, religious, tribal, or other factors, existed in the area long before the current boundaries were drawn. Ultimately, human beings, not physical boundaries drawn on a map, shape their own reality.

In this book, I argue that the failed nation-state has significantly contributed to the current chaos in the region. That said, claiming that colonialism or imperialism caused the failure of the nation-state is wrong. This theory places the blame on the true causes of the failed states or the crisis in the Arab world elsewhere. And, as we will learn in the book, this is actually one of the underlying challenges of the Arab world. Arab leaders and rulers, to retain their own power, have encouraged the people they rule to look elsewhere for their problems to divert criticism and quiet the street. The fact is that Arab states have been independent states for at least fifty years or more. In 2021, Jordan, an artificial entity founded by the West, celebrated one hundred years of independence. Arab states have armed forces, constitutions, governments, police, security forces, etc. Failing Arab countries like Iraq, Libya, and Yemen have been blessed with vast natural resources such as oil and gas that could have been a source of growth and prosperity. First and foremost, Arab governments must be held accountable for their actions.

I want to emphasize two other guidelines I follow in my writing.

First, I go to great lengths to provide data and chronological documentation of various events, especially in the chapters discussing Iran and Turkey. I do this for two reasons. One of my goals is to provide as broad a factual basis as possible for the diagnoses and arguments I offer in the book. My second goal is to provide a reliable record of events and chronology for future generations. I make a great effort and go to great lengths to ensure that the information I provide is accurate and reflects reality. If incorrect or inaccurate information appears in this book, I take full responsibility for any errors.

Second, as an intelligence analyst, the only way to evaluate the accuracy of my analysis is to make a prediction. Predictions are a cornerstone of my work as an analyst. I cannot find shelter behind theories or arguments that are exempt from the test of reality. I make sure to uphold this principle in all my professional work, whether written or oral.

The criticism of certain people I put forth in this book reflects a difference in my worldview. I do not disparage or disregard the opinions of the people I criticize. If anyone thinks that my criticism has gone beyond legitimate criticism and critique, I apologize in advance.

An essential aspect of educational responsibility is the content and quality of knowledge and how it is transmitted. And I try very hard to practice what I preach. In the articles I write, the interviews I give, in my lectures, and my teaching, I believe delivering knowledge and insights in a restrained and carefully worded manner are more powerful and impactful than an aggressive and combative disposition. And I believe that this approach is needed today more than ever.

As I said, this book is not intended to be a history of the Middle East. But I do hope that it will be viewed, well into the future, as a book that reliably describes an important, and I believe, pivotal chapter in the history of the Middle East.

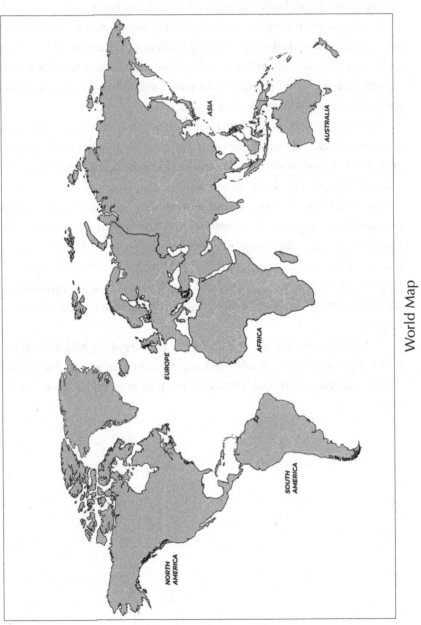

World Map

A NEW ERA | AND ANCIENT RIVALRIES ARE ALIVE AND WELL

To Understand the Present, We Need to Understand the Past

As we begin our journey, I would like to start by focusing on the two major historic rivalries that have played a central role in shaping the Muslim world and the Middle East. I begin with this because to accurately navigate the geopolitics of the contemporary Middle East, we need to understand the core power struggles that have shaped the region for centuries. These same rivalries will define and influence the region—and the world—for the foreseeable future.

The Sunni-Shi'ite Split

One axis is a religious and political divide within Islam between Sunnis and Shi'ites.

The Prophet Muhammad (570–632) founded Islam in the early seventh century. When Muhammad died, his successors were called *caliphs*. The term caliph is part of the Arabic term *Caliphat Rasul Allah*—translated as "the replacer of *Allah's* 'God's' messenger (Prophet Muhammad)." The first four caliphs in Islam are known as the *Four Rightly Guided Caliphs*—who were either nominated by their predecessor or elected by a religious advisory council.

The fourth caliph was 'Ali Bin Abi Talib. He was a cousin and the son-in-law of Muhammad. He ruled from 656 until he was assassinated in 661.

'Ali had nine wives and a total of twenty-one children. His first wife was Muhammad's daughter, Fatimah. Together they had four children—two boys, Hassan and Hussein. And two girls, Zaynab al-Kubra "elder Zaynab" and Zaynab al-Sughra "littler Zaynab," also known as Umm Kulthum. 'Ali and Fatimah's oldest son was Hassan. After 'Ali was assassinated, Hassan took his father's place and became the caliph. After a while, Hassan stepped down.

When Hassan abdicated the throne, his brother Hussein Bin 'Ali Bin Abi Talib said: "My grandfather was Prophet Muhammad, my father 'Ali was the caliph, my brother Hassan was the caliph, so I am the next one in line." His opponents disagreed. They argued that leading Islam is not about bloodline. It is about the most suitable person for the position.

The power struggle escalated. In 680, Hussein Bin 'Ali Bin Abi Talib—Muhammad's last grandson through direct bloodline—was slaughtered in a battle along with his followers. The battle took place in Karbala, which is modern-day Iraq. The slaughter of Hussein Bin 'Ali Bin Abi Talib at Karbala in 680 is when Islam split into *Sunnis* and *Shi'ites*.

The term *Sunnat al-Nabi* means "the Prophet's (Muhammad's) Path." Hence the term *Sunni*. *Sh'iat 'Ali* means "the political faction of 'Ali Bin Abi Talib"—the fourth Caliph in Islam. Hence the name *Shi'ite*. The overwhelming majority of Muslims—80 percent—are Sunnis. Less than 20 percent are Shi'ites.

The schism between the two is a difference of opinion regarding who is entitled to lead the Muslim empire. Sunnis believe the ruler of the Muslim world should be the most suitable person for the position. Shi'ites believe the leader of the Muslim should be a male descendant of the fourth Caliph, 'Ali Bin Abi Talib. Therefore, the Shi'ites argue that when Hussein Bin 'Ali Bin Abi Talib was killed, the crown of leadership was stolen from them.

The rivalry between the merit camp (the Sunnis) and the bloodline camp (the Shi'ites) has led to an unbridgeable gap of irreconcilable hatred and animosity since 680.

The Rivalry between the Arab, Persian, and Turkish Civilizations

The other axis that has shaped the region for centuries and will impact the Middle East—and the world—for the foreseeable future is the rivalry between

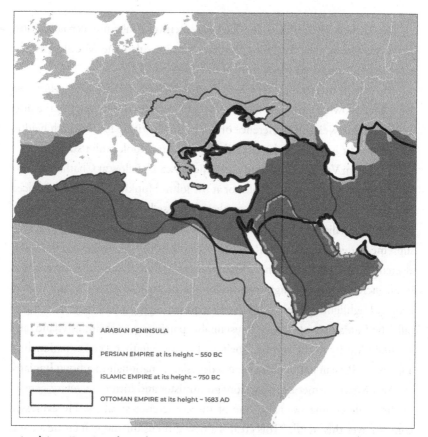

Arabian Peninsula, Islamic, Persian, Ottoman Empires (This map is in color on page A in the insert.)

three large regional civilizations: the Arab civilization, the Persian civilization, and, since the late Middle Ages, the Turkish civilization.

The Arab civilization. The Arab civilization gave birth to Islam. Arabs come from the Arabian Peninsula. The first Muslims were culturally and ethnically Arabs. Most Arabs are Sunnis. However, most Muslims are not Arabs.

The Persian civilization. The Persians are not Arabs. They do not come from the Arabian Peninsula. They come from Persia. They do not speak Arabic; they speak Farsi. Persians were pagans. As Islam rapidly spread, the Persian civilization adopted Sunni Islam. But in the Middle Ages, the Persian ruling dynasty adopted the Shi'ite orthodoxy, which has been the primary religion of Persia ever since.

The Turkish civilization. The Turks are neither Arabs nor Persians. Most Turks are Sunni. The Turkish Ottoman Empire ruled the Middle East for more than six hundred years, from about 1299 to 1922.

The title of this chapter is *A New Era | And Ancient Rivalries Are Alive and Well*. The following episode undoubtedly demonstrates the accuracy of the title.

At the thirty-eighth conference of the Beirut Institute for Research held in Abu Dhabi in July 2021, the Arab-Persian tensions took center stage.

Dr. Sanam Vakil, deputy head and senior research fellow at Chatham House in the United Kingdom and professor at the Johns Hopkins School of Advanced International Studies, and other speakers discussed the trend of the growth of Persian nationalism in Iran under the current regime. They explained that the supreme leader of the Islamic Republic, Ayatollah Ali Khamenei, and the newly elected (June 2021) president, Ebrahim Raisi Al-Sadati, are currently engaged in an increasingly challenging battle for the hearts and minds of the Iranian people. Highlighting their collective Persian heritage is a tool they are using to rally the Iranian people, create a sustainable patriotism to the motherland, and maintain loyalty to the regime. Their goal is to strengthen Persian nationalism and ensure Persian nationalism supersedes Islamic nationalism among Iranians.

Amr Musa, former Egyptian foreign minister and former secretary-general of the Arab League, was also one of the conference speakers. He expressed concern over this trend. "This creates a new dimension and will create a completely new game in the Middle East," and "will make it more difficult to reach understandings with Arab societies and governments." He said, "The Iranians have the right to adopt Persian nationalism. But they do not have the right to continue interfering in Iraq, Lebanon, Syria, and Yemen to say: we Persians have come to you to persecute you and impose our rule on you. This phenomenon is a dangerous thing that we must think about differently."[1] In other words—it is OK for the Iranians to take pride in their Persian heritage. But it is not OK for the Arab world to pay the price.

So, as you can see, ancient rivalries are very much alive and well.

Since 2016—Conflicts Escalate and Expand

Since 2016, the Sunni-Shi'ite and the Arab-Iranian power struggles have significantly escalated and expanded.

The Shi'ite mullah regime that has ruled the Islamic Republic of Iran since 1979 is determined to correct the historical injustice the Shi'ites believe they suffered in 680 when Hussein Bin 'Ali Bin Abi Talib was killed in Karbala. Guided by that narrative, the Shi'ite mullah regime is committed and determined to recapture the crown of leadership and regain its rightful place as the leaders of the Muslim world. To achieve this goal, Iran pursues an aggressive policy it calls "exporting the Iranian revolution." The goal of "exporting the Iranian revolution" is to spread and expand the Islamic Republic of Iran's control and influence and ensure that Iran becomes the dominant superpower in the Middle East. Since 2016, Iran has significantly increased its aggressive policies toward that end.

And an old player has aggressively entered the stage and added a new and further destabilizing twist. And that player is Turkey, led by President Recep Tayyip Erdoğan. Turkey's President Erdoğan is an Islamist committed to spreading Islam across the globe. He aspires to revive the glory days of the Ottoman Empire—and he wants to position himself as the leader of the Sunni camp in the region and as a frontline global leader. To achieve these goals, Erdoğan works tirelessly to extend his influence and power throughout the Middle East and Africa. Since becoming the twelfth president of Turkey in 2014 until this very day, Erdoğan has looked for and capitalized on any opportunity to achieve his objectives.

Iran and Turkey both seek regional domination, and both regimes want to be global powerbrokers. In pursuit of these ambitions, Iran and Turkey create and implement aggressive and disruptive expansionist policies throughout the region. Their calculated and sophisticated multipronged policies simultaneously fuel tensions, leverage instability, and capitalize on the chaos. Both are shrewd and calculated players that know how to skillfully use the existing and induced turbulence they themselves create in the Arab world for their own gain and to further their own hegemonic goals.

Throughout this book, we will see the current manifestations of the Arab-Iranian-Turkish power struggle.

In the following two chapters, I will focus on these two major regional players—Iran and Turkey.

Given their centrality and impact on the contemporary Middle East, both countries are interwoven throughout the book. However, from a methodological perspective, I believe it is most logical to begin the book by presenting Iran's and Turkey's motivations and goals, exploring their modus operandi, and understanding the ramifications and repercussions of their aspirations on the Middle East's geostrategic construct. Both are significant powers, and each will have a large part in defining the new era in the Middle East.

CHAPTER 2

IRAN'S QUEST FOR HEGEMONY | EXPORTING THE ISLAMIC REVOLUTION

The Islamic Revolution

The Iranian mullah regime came to power in 1979. In a series of events called the Islamic Revolution, Ayatollah Ruhollah Khomeini and his followers seized power from Shah Mohammad Reza Pahlavi. He ruled Iran from 1941 to 1979. The Pahlavi dynasty had ruled the Imperial State of Iran since 1925.

On April 1, 1979, Iranians approved a new constitution creating a theocratic republic named the Islamic Republic of Iran.

The Islamic Republic of Iran is an Islamic Shi'ite theocracy ruled by *mullahs*. The word mullah is an Islamic clerical term. A mullah is a learned scholar of Islamic theology who is authorized to share his knowledge.

The Shi'ite clerical order is hierarchical, and therefore the Iranian regime itself is hierarchical. The central figure of the Islamic Revolution and the supreme leader of the Iranian Islamic Republic until his death in 1989 was Ayatollah Ruhollah Khomeini. The title *ayatollah* is two words (pronounced as one word; however, it is made of two words—*aya* "sign, flag, verse" and *Allah* "The God") that together mean "sign of God." The current supreme leader since 1989 is Ayatollah Ali Khamenei. The most senior Shi'ite cleric is *ayatollah 'uzma*—"the grand ayatollah."

As we learned in the first chapter, one of the core Shi'ite narratives is that their God-given right to lead the Muslim world was stolen from them in 680 when Hussein Bin 'Ali Bin Abi Talib was killed in Karbala. Inspired, guided,

Iran

and motivated by that belief, the Iranian mullah regime is determined to take back its rightful place as the leader of the Muslim world.

To that end, since coming to power in 1979, Tehran has designed and pursued an aggressive foreign policy called "exporting the Islamic Revolution." The goal of "exporting the Islamic Revolution" is to spread Shi'ite *Twelver* orthodoxy, expand the Islamic Republic of Iran's control and influence, and ensure that Iran becomes the dominant superpower in the Middle East.

A note about Twelver orthodoxy. The largest denomination in Shia Islam is the Twelver branch, also known in Arabic as the *Imamiyyah*. About 85 percent of Shi'ites are Twelvers. Twelvers believe that twelve divinely ordained imams succeeded the Prophet Muhammad. The line starts with the fourth Caliph 'Ali Bin Abi Talib. A general definition of *imam* is one who leads Muslim worshippers in prayer. In a global sense, the term imam refers to the head of the Muslim congregation (the *ummah*). According to the Twelvers, the last imam, Imam al-Mahdi, disappeared as a small child in the ninth century. And he is waiting "outside of time" to come back as the *Mahdi* "The Rightly-Guided One." The Redeemer. When he returns, he will lead humanity to eternal prosperity and justice through a process in which most people in the world will perish.

To export the Islamic Revolution, one of the first things the mullah regime created was a military force that would function parallel to the Iranian Armed Forces.

The additional army it created in May 1979 was named the Islamic Revolutionary Guards Corps (IRG or IRGC). The IRG's mandate is to protect the mullah government and ensure it stays in power; to protect the government from external military threats; to develop and implement the strategy necessary to export the Islamic Revolution; and to secure Iran as the dominant force in the region.

The Islamic Revolutionary Guards Corps is enshrined in the constitution:

> In the formation and equipping of the country's defence forces, due attention must be paid to faith and ideology as the basic criteria. Accordingly, the Army of the Islamic Republic of Iran and the Islamic Revolutionary Guards Corps are to be organized in conformity with this goal, and they will be responsible not only for guarding and preserving the frontiers of the country but also for fulfilling the ideological mission of jihad in God's way; that is, extending the sovereignty of God's law throughout the world (this is in accordance with the Qur'anic verse.
>
> "Prepare against them whatever force you are able to muster, and strings of horses, striking fear into the enemy of God and your enemy, and others besides them" [8:60]).[1]

Since 1979, the IRG has evolved to become the most powerful political and military body in Iran and Iran's wealthiest entity.

In 2021, the IRG is the power center in Iran. The IRG commands many aspects of Iranian politics and controls all of Iran's critical economic sectors.

The commander-in-chief of the Islamic Revolutionary Guards Corps since the Spring of 2019 is IRG Major General Hossein Salami. As the commander of the IRG, he is under the direct command of Iran's Supreme Leader Ali Khamenei. On the other hand, the Iranian Armed Forces are under the command of the Ministry of Defense, which is a political appointment. Since 2016, the chief-of-staff of the Iranian army has been Major General Mohammad Bagheri. Major General Bagheri's power pales in comparison to the power and status of Major General Hossein Salami.

Within the IRG, there is an elite unit called the *al-Quds Force*. *Al-Quds* is the Arabic name for Jerusalem. The al-Quds force's specific mission is to spearhead Iran's goal of regional hegemony strategically and tactically. Its task is to develop, command, nurture, and manage a network of Iranian proxies, agents, and terror cells in the region and around the world to achieve this goal.

Another force under the command of the IRG is the *Basij Resistance Force* (usually just called *Basij*). The Basij is a volunteer paramilitary organization that includes children as young as twelve years old. The omnipresent organization known as "the eyes and ears" of the regime is spread throughout Iran. It is primarily responsible for internal security, law enforcement, morality policing, and maintaining law and order. The Basij is a vast and fierce force the mullah regime uses to oppress political demonstrations and suppress dissent.

Six-Pillar Strategy to Export the Islamic Revolution and Achieve Regional Hegemony

The Iranian regime employs a sophisticated six-pillar strategy to export the Islamic Revolution to spread Shi'ite orthodoxy, expand Iran's control and influence, and achieve regional dominance.

1. *International Relations and Diplomacy*
Diplomatic, commercial, and military relations with other states.

2. *Educational, Charitable, and Cultural Activities*

These are often used as shadow operations, money laundering mechanisms, or hidden channels that are actually put in place to finance and operate terror cells around the world, including Africa, the Arab Gulf Monarchies, Europe, Israel, the Palestinian territories in the West Bank, South America, and more.

3. *Agents & Proxies*

Iran has a network of agents and proxies—armies of terror—across the Middle East that are massively armed and financed by Iran. This network is Iran's most essential and powerful mechanism to expand its control and pave its way to regional hegemony.

Here is how the Iranian agent-proxy model works.

Iran identifies locations that can help the regime meet its hegemonic goals. Preferably areas with a large Shi'ite population that also suffer from chronic political instability and have a weak government.

Once Iran identifies such an arena, it either creates a proxy or cultivates and nurtures an existing force as an agent.

If Iran can find an existing entity that can help the regime further its goals, Iran will cultivate that agent.

Examples of agents are the Palestinian Sunni Islamist groups, *Hamas* and *Islamic Jihad in Palestine (IJIP)* in the Gaza Strip (though both are Sunni, not Shi'ite), and *Ansar Allah*, the military force of the Shi'ite *Houthi* tribes in Yemen.

If there is no existing Shi'ite or Sunni entity Iran can co-opt, Iran creates one to act as a proxy.

Examples of proxy Shi'ite militias Iran has created are the Afghani *Al-Fatemiyoun*, the Iraqi *Al-Badr, 'Asaib Ahl al-Haq, Harakat al-Nujaba, Kataib Hezbollah, Imam' Ali brigades, Liwa Abu al-Fadhal al-Abbas*, the Lebanese *Hezbollah*; Pakistani *Liwa Zainebiyoun*; and the Palestinian *Harakat as-Sabireen Nasran li-Filastin* in the Gaza Strip.

Iran's extensive military arsenal—including the largest missile force in the Middle East—is the backbone of Iran's agent and proxy militias. Iran cultivates its agents and proxies by supplying them with ammunition, financial support, manpower, technical assistance, training, weapons, etc.

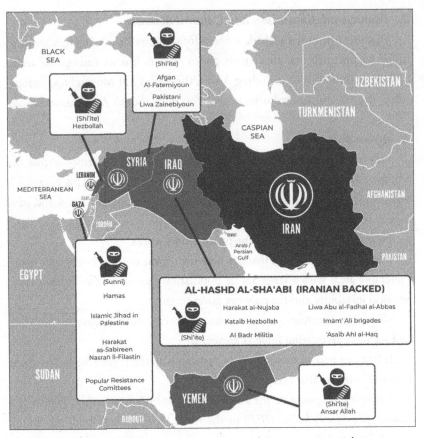

Sunni and Shi'ite Iran Agents and Proxies (Sample)

Iran has successfully leveraged the agent-proxy model to gain growing influence and control throughout the Middle East. Through its network of agents and proxies, Iran now:

- Dictates Lebanon's domestic and foreign policy through Hezbollah.
- Occupies parts of Syria via local and regional Iranian-backed Shi'ite militias, the Islamic Revolutionary Guards forces, and the IRG's elite al-Quds force.
- Significantly influences Iraqi domestic politics, regional policy, and the Iraqi economy via Iranian-backed Iraq-Shi'ite militias and political allies.

- Influences Yemenite politics and has a foothold on the ground in Yemen, on the Bab el-Mandeb Strait, and the Red Sea via the Yemenite Houthis.
- Influences the Gaza Strip, fuels the flames of the Israeli-Palestinian conflict, and has a foothold on the ground in Gaza via Hamas and Islamic Jihad in Palestine.

Each one of these achievements exceeds the specific country or territory. The locations Iran has chosen are not random. Each arena is part of a considered and calculated regional strategy with a very clear goal. To be the regional—and then, a global—superpower. Iran's agent-proxy model has secured strategic assets and geographic strongholds for Iran. And accordingly, it has increased its power.

Employing this strategy, Iran now has established:

- A partially Iranian-controlled land corridor from Iran through Iraq, Syria, and Lebanon to the Mediterranean Sea.
- A foothold in Iraq—one of the largest oil producers in the world.
- A stronghold on the Mediterranean Sea—the Gaza Strip, Lebanon, and Syria.
- A significant foothold on one of the most strategic spots on the planet— the Bab el-Mandeb Strait at the southern entrance of the Red Sea.

Through its network of proxies and agents, Iran continues to skillfully use these tried-and-true mechanisms of inciting violence and capitalizing on the chaos to advance its aggressive expansion policy and establish, deepen, and entrench its influence throughout the Middle East. And Tehran has been quite successful in its endeavor. So much so that Iranian leaders boast that they control four Arab state capitols—Baghdad, Beirut, Damascus, and Sana'a. And to a large extent, it does.

4. *Al-Muqawama w'al Muman'aah*—"The Resistance and Defiance"

You might wonder how Iran manages to recruit such disparate entities from different places with varying ideologies (including Sunni organizations like Hamas or IJIP) and missions to its cause. Well, here is the 'magic phrase'—which is the fourth pillar of 'exporting the Islamic Revolution'— *Al-Muqawama w'al Muman'aah*, which means "The Resistance and Defiance."

Al-Muqawama w'al muman'aah is a concept that became popular in the Muslim world's intellectual, political, and cultural discourse following World War II. At that time, *al-Muqawama,* "the Resistance," was primarily about the struggle to end Western control in North Africa.

In its essence, al-Muqawama's core philosophy is a blend of traditional Arab values and modern global aspirations. Advocates of al-Muqawama believe that the best way for Arabs and Muslims—as communities and as individuals—to live is by rejecting Western cultures and powers and creating a cultural and political life whose core is the noble tradition of Arab culture and Islam's enlightened moral values. But inherent in al-Muqawama are

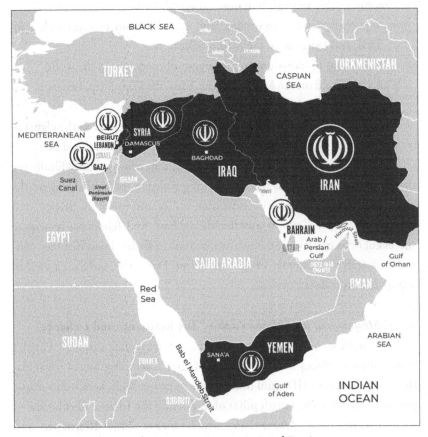

Mihwar al-Muqawama — Axis of Resistance

also modern political concepts, including emancipation, independence, and statehood.

The establishment of the State of Israel in 1948 and the evolving Israeli-Arab conflict added another layer to the concept of al-Muqawama. Al-Muqawama became the rallying cry calling to 'Liberate Palestine' and destroy the State of Israel.

The phrase, al-Muqawama, has become part and parcel of the vernacular of the modern Middle East. The successful branding of al-Muqawama has in many ways defined a generation of Muslims—both Sunni and Shi'ite— throughout the Middle East and around the world.

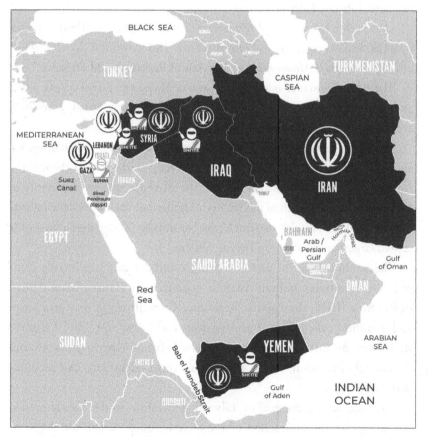

Axis of Resistance Including Shi'ite and Sunni Agents and Proxies

As I described in my 2016 book, and as we will see in this book, leaders throughout the Muslim world have used al-Muqawama to rally the masses.

The mullah regime understood the centrality of the Israeli-Palestinian conflict in the hearts and minds of the Arab world.

Most of the Palestinians—like most Muslims—are Sunni. The Shi'ite regime knew that if it positioned itself as the defender of the Palestinians, it would earn points in the Arab Sunni world and smooth over the resentments of Arabs toward their historical rival—the Shi'ite (Persian) Iranians. Building on the rallying cry to destroy Israel, the Iranians identified al-Muqawama as the narrative that could pave their path to regional supremacy. And so, the Iranian mullah regime decided to position itself as the spearhead of al-Muqawama to 'Liberate Palestine.'

Under the banner of al-Muqawama, Iran recruits, cultivates, trains, finances, and manages a global infrastructure. This network is called '*Mihwar al-Muqawama w'al Muman'aah*'—"The Axis of Resistance and Defiance."

The axis of resistance is a powerful web of Shi'ite and Sunni agents, allies, and proxies—non-state, semi-state, and state entities—cultivated, developed, armed, and sponsored by the Iranians.

The Shi'ite part of the axis of resistance and defiance is comprised of agents, allies and proxies, including Shi'ite militias in Iraq; Hezbollah in Lebanon; the Assad regime in Syria (Assad is Alawite; the Alawites, who are a minority in Syria, are a distant branch of the Shi'ites); Afghan and Pakistani Shi'ite militias in Syria; and the Houthis in Yemen (the Houthis are Zaidiyyah Shi'ites—the second largest group after the Twelver Shi'ites.)

The Sunni part of the axis of resistance and defiance is primarily comprised of Palestinian militant Islamist organizations Hamas, Islamic Jihad in Palestine (IJIP); the Popular Resistance Committees in the Gaza Strip; and a militia called *Saraya al-Muqawama al-Lubnaniya* "The Lebanese Resistance Brigades" located in southern Lebanon—particularly around the coastal city, Sidon, which is Lebanon's third-largest city, and predominantly Sunni.

For Iran, adding the goal of 'Liberating Palestine' to the already present cry calling for 'the destruction of the State of Israel' turned the slogan of al-Muqawama into a perpetually winning card for Iran.

The Iranian regime uses the slogan of al-Muqawama and the axis of al-Muqawama w'al muman'aah to fan the flames of the Israeli-Palestinian conflict. And this creates a permanent and continuous loop to advance its hegemonic vision. Here is how the mullah regime's strategy works:

Hamas and IJIP vow to destroy Israel. And they are committed to eliminating Israel through the use of military power. Therefore, their goals and interests overlap with Iran's. The mullah regime equips Hamas and IJIP with arms, military know-how, and financing, knowing it will further fuel the violence between Gaza and Israel. The escalating violence feeds hatred toward Israel in the Arab and Muslim world. That further injects and embeds the slogan of al-Muqawama into the hearts, minds, and public discourse of the Arab world.

And this is how Iran etches in the hearts and minds of the Arab and Muslim world that the mullah regime is leading the charge to eliminate Israel and liberate Palestine.

The concept of al-Muqawama, the axis of resistance and defiance, and the call to 'Liberate Palestine' is the perfect mechanism for Iran. They work hand in glove to continue to incite hatred of Israel, position Iran as the defender of the Palestinians, the patron of the axis of resistance, and the liberator of Palestine.

This triad—that Iran both controls and capitalizes on—ensures the Israeli-Palestinian conflict never ends. And that is good for the mullah regime.

5. Iran's Ballistic Missile Program

Iran has the most diverse missile arsenal in the Middle East. Tehran has a vast arsenal of long-range missiles (some capable of striking Israel and as far as southeastern Europe), rockets, attack drones, cruise missiles, and UAVs (unmanned aerial vehicles).

Over the past decade, Iran has invested significant resources to improve these weapons' precision and lethality. Such developments have made Iran's missile forces a potent tool for Iranian power projection and a credible threat to the United States and US partner military forces in the region.[2]

Iran has not yet tested or deployed a missile capable of striking the United States. Still, through its aerospace program, it continues to hone longer-range missile technologies.

Iran's extensive military arsenal and know-how are the backbones of Tehran's armies of terror that the mullah regime controls throughout the Middle East. Iran supplies its agents, allies, and proxies (such as Hamas and Islamic Jihad, Hezbollah, and the Assad regime in Syria) with a steady supply of missiles, rockets, attack drones, and intelligence gathering capacities, as well as the knowledge and materials they need to produce their own. Iran equips the Houthis with a steady supply of increasingly advanced ballistic and cruise missiles and long-range unmanned aerial vehicles. And Iran makes sure the Shi'ite militias in Iraq have enough rockets and other small projectiles to attack Iraqi and US military and diplomatic facilities.[3]

6. Nuclear Military Program

I am finalizing this book in August 2021, eight months after President Joe Biden has taken office as the forty-sixth president of the United States. One of the Biden administration's first orders of business was, together with members of the European Union, to launch rounds of talks with Iran in Vienna. The goal was to reenter the 2015 Joint Comprehensive Plan of Action (JCPOA).

Given the importance of this subject and its role in Iran's hegemonic strategy, I would like to overview Iran's nuclear program briefly.

The Iranian Nuclear Program—The Road to Sanctions

Iran began its nuclear program in the 1950s. But it was not until the late 1980s and early 1990s that the international community became concerned.

Iran was one of the original sixty-two countries to sign the 1970 Non-Proliferation Treaty (NPT). The NPT agreement banned all countries except China, France, Russia, the United Kingdom, and the United States from acquiring nuclear weapons. Non-nuclear signatories could develop peaceful nuclear programs for generating power and electricity.

In August 2002, a group of former Iranian generals exposed Iran's secret nuclear military program. It was then that the International Atomic Energy Agency (IAEA) began to monitor Iran's activity closely.

On December 18, 2003, Iran and the IAEA signed the Additional Protocol to the Non-Proliferation Treaty (NPT) Safeguards Agreement. The Additional

Protocol granted IAEA inspectors greater authority to monitor Iran's nuclear program. Including the right to conduct short-notice, strict, and thorough inspections at undeclared Iranian nuclear sites to determine if Iran was conducting secret nuclear activities.

Between 2002 and 2004, the IAEA released several reports revealing Iran concealed the actual dimensions and purpose of its nuclear program. Furthermore, the IAEA and the international community accused Iran of violating the terms of the Additional Protocol it signed in 2003. The reports also proved that, time and again, Iran had violated its obligation to cooperate with the IAEA and the international community. Nevertheless, Iran continued to lie and conceal its military nuclear program.

On September 18, 2004, fed up with Iran's lies and deception, the IAEA Board of Governors issued an ultimatum to Iran. By November 2004, Iran had to provide the board with a detailed report of its nuclear activities. Iran did not provide the requested information. In November 2004, under the threat of sanctions, Iran announced that it accepted the European Union's offer to negotiate. Furthermore, Iran promised to suspend its uranium enrichment activity as long as the negotiations continued. However, despite the regime's promises, according to the IAEA and the international community, Iran violated the international agreements it had signed, refused to cooperate with the IAEA and other international bodies, and continued to pursue an elusive, nontransparent policy regarding its nuclear activities.

Given this, on July 31, 2006, the United Nations Security Council (UNSC) passed its first resolution regarding Iran's nuclear ambitions. UNSCR 1696 called on the regime to suspend its enrichment program and comply with the IAEA Board of Governor's requirements. Iran refused to cooperate and comply with UNSCR 1696 as well as subsequent demands of the international community, including additional UNSC requests and resolutions. Therefore, in December 2006, the UNSC passed UNSCR 1737. UNSCR 1737 was the first international resolution that imposed sanctions on Iran for not complying with previous demands and continuing its uranium enrichment program.

Iran's continuing refusal to cooperate with the IAEA and international bodies is what has led the international community—since 2006—to impose sanctions on Iran.

Unruffled and indifferent, Iran continued to play 'hide and seek.' The regime continued to circumvent its commitments and refused to cooperate with the IAEA inspectors and the international community.

The 2015 JCPOA—An Iranian Victory Because It Was a Smokescreen to Protect the Most Important Pillars of Its Hegemonic Strategy

In July 2015, under the mounting pressure of sanctions, the mullah regime and the P5+1 (the five permanent members of the United Nations Security Council—China, France, Russia, the United Kingdom, and the United States, plus Germany)—together with the European Union, signed the Joint Comprehensive Plan of Action (JCPOA) with Iran.

The Joint Comprehensive Plan of Action (JCPOA) is a detailed, 159-page agreement with five appendices. The nuclear deal was endorsed by UN Security Council Resolution 2231 and adopted on July 20, 2015. Iran's compliance with the nuclear-related provisions of the JCPOA was to be verified by the International Atomic Energy Agency (IAEA) according to certain requirements outlined in the agreement.[4]

The deal is also known as the 'Vienna Agreement,' the 'Iran Nuclear deal,' or 'the Iran Deal.'

Whatever name you call it, the deal played right into the hands of the Iranian mullah regime. Why is that?

Because Iran's position throughout the negotiations with the P5+1 was a smokescreen.

Iran has a holistic and sophisticated strategy to achieve its objectives. Of all the six pillars of Iran's hegemonic policy strategy, the three most vital elements Iran uses to spread the Islamic Revolution, spread Shi'ite orthodoxy, expand its control and influence, and pursue regional dominance are Iran's agents and proxies, its ballistic missile program, and its nuclear program.

During the negotiations, the Iranians were less concerned about securing a deal about their nuclear project. The Shi'ite mullah regime that currently rules Iran is a marathon runner. The nuclear issue could wait.

What Tehran really wanted out of the 2015 negotiations was to sign a deal that would lift the sanctions and not impact its two most powerful cards. Iran's ballistic missile program and Tehran's armed network of agents and proxies that it has been nurturing and supporting for decades.

It is essential to understand that all of the six pillars of Iran's strategy work together. They are not separate. They are part of an ecosystem. Each element, together and as a whole, is meant to help Iran achieve its objectives. Iran's ballistic missile program and the armies of terror are supposed to deter attacks on Iran's nuclear program. And Iran's nuclear program is supposed to prevent attacks on its armies of terror. These strategic assets are the critical tools Iran needs to achieve its hegemonic ambitions.

Apparently, the Western negotiators failed to understand the Iranians' master plan.

The deal offered by the Western negotiators completely ignored Iran's very straightforward blueprint. Therefore, the West played into Tehran's hands and gave the Iranian negotiators precisely what they wanted. And more.

Apparently, the US administration under President Barack Obama and the European Union's premise was that the agreement would restrain Iran's aggressive regional and global policies and contribute to overall stability in the Middle East. This belief proved to be wishful thinking. The result of the JCPOA was the exact opposite. The 2015 JCPOA agreement did not restrain Iran. Instead—as I predicted at the time—it encouraged the regime to escalate and expand its aggression in the region.

This is important to understand because—contrary to what some Western circles argue—Iran's aggressive behavior after signing the JCPOA led the United States to withdraw from the JCPOA in May 2018.

I was in the throes of writing my 2016 book when the JCPOA was signed in 2015. I always emphasize to my audiences that the only way to evaluate your analysis's accuracy is to make a prediction and test your prediction. On page 111 of that book, I wrote, "As a result of these achievements (the articles of the JCPOA), Iran's geostrategic policy is, for now, enjoying significant momentum and marking important achievements. The mullah regime seems to be on a path to securing its strategic interests and marking another milestone on its way to fulfilling its vision of being the leading Middle East superpower."[5]

So, let's look to see if my prediction was accurate.

Following the JCPOA and Before US Withdrawal from the JCPOA—Iran Increased Its Aggression

Iran Increases Military Spending and Continues Funding Its Armies of Terror

In 2014, the year before Iran signed the JCPOA, Iran's official defense expenditure was $16.9 billion. In 2015, the year Iran signed the JCPOA, it spent $19.5 billion; in 2016, $19.9 billion; in 2017, $23.9 billion. In 2018, the year the United States left the JCPOA, Iran's official defense expenditure was $27.3 billion. So, between 2014 and 2018, Iran almost doubled the amount of GDP it invested in defense from 3.2 percent to 6.1 percent.[6]

Between 2012 and 2018, according to Iran's reported governmental budget allocations, Iran provided more than $16 billion to the Syrian regime, Hezbollah, Iraqi Shi'ite militias, the Houthis, and Palestinian groups.[7]

However, multiple sources fund the complete Iranian military posture. According to a 2018 report by the Foundation for Defense of Democracies, Iran provides its agents and proxies, including the Assad regime, $16 billion annually.[8] It is, therefore, reasonable to assume the actual military expenditures both at home and abroad are significantly higher.

Iran Escalates Its Aggression toward the Arab World and Israel

Since the JCPOA, in addition to—or because of—its increased investments, Iran has strengthened its hold on the Middle East. Emboldened by the deal, Iran became increasingly aggressive.

Most senior Iranian leaders speak openly of Iran's hegemonic ambition. In August 2016, not a year after signing the JCPOA, a senior officer of the IRG, identified as Mohammed Ali Filki, announced that Iran would establish a military force called the Shi'ite Liberation Army. Major-General Qasem Soleimani, the commander of the al-Quds Force (from 1998 until the United States eliminated him in 2020), was to head the Shi'ite Liberation Army. Ali-Filki stated that the Shi'ite Liberation Army's goal would be to fight in Iraq, Syria, and Yemen and establish a military presence on the Golan Heights bordering Israel.[9]

In September 2016, Mohammad Ali Jafari, the commander of the IRGC between 2007 and 2019, declared that Iran had no intention of relinquishing control of Yemen, Syria, and Iraq.[10]

In November 2016, Hossein Salami, who was at that time the deputy commander of the IRG under Ali Jafari (and since 2019 is the commander of the IRG), announced that once Iran crushes the Syrian rebels in Aleppo, it will focus on deepening its entrenchment in Bahrain and Yemen.[11]

In October 2017, Iran's President Hassan Rouhani announced that Iran has unprecedented power in Iraq, Lebanon, Syria, the Arab (Persian) Gulf, and Africa. He further explained that meant that no decision could be made in the region without Iran's approval.[12]

Iran vows to eliminate the state of Israel. In December 2017, and again in February 2018, overtly violating the 2006 UNSC Resolution 1701 (which ended the Second Lebanon War), Hezbollah toured the Israeli-Lebanese border with the leaders of two Iranian-backed Iraqi militias—'Asaib Ahl al-Haq and Harakat al-Nujaba. Overlooking Israel, the two leaders vowed their militants would join Hezbollah in the battle to eliminate Israel.

In January 2018, Ali al Akhbar Wilayati, senior advisor on International Affairs to Iran's Supreme Leader Ali Khamenei, said, "Iran's presence in the region is irreversible. Iran will be the most powerful factor in the region and will continue its agenda. And Iran supports the axis of resistance to eliminate the Zionist entity."[13]

Nayef bin Falah al-Hajraf, the secretary-general of the Cooperation Council for the Arab States of the Gulf (GCC), clearly described the Iranian threat. In an October 2020 article titled, "The Gulf Cooperation Council holds Iran responsible for the spread of violence in the region," he said, "Iran fuels instability in the region through violence in the service of its ideology and agenda. Iran must stop supporting armed militias."[14]

Following the JCPOA, Iran has expanded and strengthened its network of agents and proxies. Tehran—unabashedly, undeterred, and successfully—works to entrench itself further and increase its power throughout the region in Bahrain, the Gaza Strip, Iran, Iraq, Lebanon, Syria, and Yemen. The outcome is increasing violence, chaos, and instability.

Now that we see how Iran's military investment, aggression, and support for its armies of terror rose after signing the JCPOA and before the United States withdrew in 2018, let's look at Iran's behavior post-JCPOA regarding its nuclear program.

Iran Continues to Deceive and Build Its Nuclear Program

Since 2015, Iran has not become a more cooperative, responsible, or transparent international community member. Iran continues to be evasive about its nuclear program. And the regime refuses to fully cooperate with the United Nations and the International Atomic Energy Agency.

On January 31, 2018, the national intelligence agency of Israel, the Mossad, obtained Iran's nuclear program archives from a warehouse in Tehran. The Mossad brought thousands of documents and 163 disks of memos, videos, and plans. The Israeli government invited Western journalists to view the Iranian archives. The archives confirmed what inspectors from the International Atomic Energy Agency, in report after report, had suspected. Despite Iranian insistence that its program was for peaceful purposes, the country had worked to systematically assemble everything it needed to produce atomic weapons.[15]

At the November 2019 IAEA Board of Governors meeting, the IAEA's acting director-general, Cornel Feruta, said, "As I reported to the Board on November 7, the Agency has detected natural uranium particles of anthropogenic origin at a location in Iran not declared to the Agency. We have continued our interactions with Iran since then, but have not received any additional information, and the matter remains unresolved."[16] At that meeting, he reiterated his request that Iran provide complete and timely cooperation with the Agency in implementing its 2003 Safeguards Agreement and Additional Protocol.[17]

Reportedly, in early June 2020, the IAEA distributed a confidential memo that Iran continued to increase its stockpiles and remained in violation of its agreements with world powers.[18] And according to a November 2020 IAEA report, Iran had more than twelve times the amount of enriched uranium

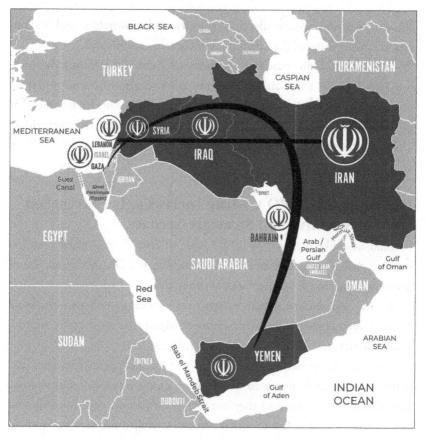

Iranian Crescent and Iranian Corridor

permitted under the 2015 Nuclear Deal. The IAEA also said Iran's explanation for the presence of nuclear material at an undeclared site was "not credible."[19]

On January 4, 2021, Iran announced that it had begun enriching uranium to a level of 20 percent. According to the JCPOA, Iran can have up to 300 kg of its self-enriched uranium at a level of 3.67 percent. According to Edwin Lyman, director of Nuclear Power Safety, Climate and Energy Program at the Union of Concerned Scientists, "Twenty percent is the lowest enrichment that is considered practical for making a nuclear weapon."[20] Nuclear weapons require three main components: fissile material, military-grade enriched uranium; a weapons system; and a platform for delivering the nuclear bomb. Iran already has platforms—missiles that can carry nuclear weapons. And Iran can produce fissile material (i.e., uranium enrichment capability).[21]

In a May 2021 interview with the *Financial Times*, Rafael Grossi, the director-general of the IAEA since December 2019, expressed alarm over Iran's nuclear program and Tehran's announcement that it was enriching uranium at 60 percent, saying that "A country enriching at sixty-percent is a severe thing. Only countries making bombs are reaching this level."[22]

Following the JCPOA—Iran Increasingly Entrenched Itself in Sensitive and Strategic Arenas

I would now like to zoom in on a couple of critical areas where Iran has become increasingly aggressive since signing the JCPOA that should be of particular concern to the international community.

Iran expands and strengthens its network by funding and massively arming its allies and subcontractors with advanced high-precision missiles, rockets, assault drones, and UAVs (Unmanned Aerial Vehicles).

Iran's armies of terror, which are all part of the axis of resistance and defiance, are what Iran uses to fuel growing chaos, instability, and violence throughout the region. And they use Tehran's advanced, sophisticated, and vast military arsenal to launch attacks, create instability, and secure a foothold in some of the most strategic waterways on the planet—the Arab-Persian Gulf, the Straits of Hormuz, the Bab el-Mandeb Strait, Yemen, and the Red Sea.

Let us look closely at those arenas.

The Arab-Persian[1] Gulf and the Hormuz Strait— Iran's Backyard

Bahrain, Iraq, Kuwait, Saudi Arabia, Qatar, the United Arab Emirates, and Iran flank the Gulf shores. For Bahrain, Iraq, Kuwait, and Qatar, the only maritime access they have is the Gulf.

The gateway that connects the Gulf and the Arabian Sea is the Hormuz Strait. Flowing between Iran and the United Arab Emirates, it is about

---

1   Please note that this body of water is called many names, including the Arab and the Persian Gulf. In this book, I will be using the word Gulf.

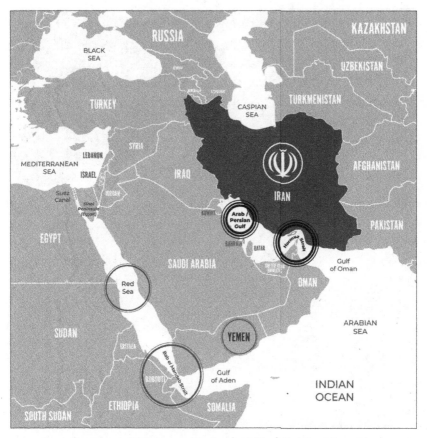

Iran Increases its Aggression in the World's Most Sensitive
Waterways—Arab/Persian Gulf, Hormuz Strait, Bab el-Mandeb
Strait, Yemen, and Red Sea.

twenty miles wide at its narrowest point. The Hormuz Strait is the busiest
passageway in the world for oil tankers. It is a vital corridor for container
ships and for global energy markets. Because of the large volume of oil that
flows through the strait, the Hormuz is the world's most important oil
chokepoint. In 2018, its daily oil flow averaged twenty-one million barrels
per day (b/d), equivalent to about 21 percent of global petroleum liquids
consumption.[23]

Since 2015, the mullah regime has been working to solidify its hold on
the Hormuz Strait. It has escalated its aggression in the Gulf—targeting its
neighbors, the Arab Gulf monarchies, and international actors.

Bahrain, Iraq, Kuwait, Saudi Arabia, Qatar, the United Arab Emirates, and Iran Flank the Gulf Shores. For Bahrain, Iraq, Kuwait, and Qatar, the Only Maritime Access They Have Is the Gulf.

In December 2015, the US military reported that in a test, Iran fired "several unguided rockets" about 1,370m (1,500 yards) from two US vessels and a French frigate in the Strait of Hormuz.[24] Iran denied the report.

In January 2016, the IRG seized two US Navy command boats near the Gulf's Farsi Island.

According to a 2019 memo from Lieutenant General Robert P. Ashley Jr, the director of the US Defense Intelligence Agency:

> Iran's substantial arsenal of ballistic missiles is designed to overwhelm US forces and our partners in the region. Its swarms of small boats,

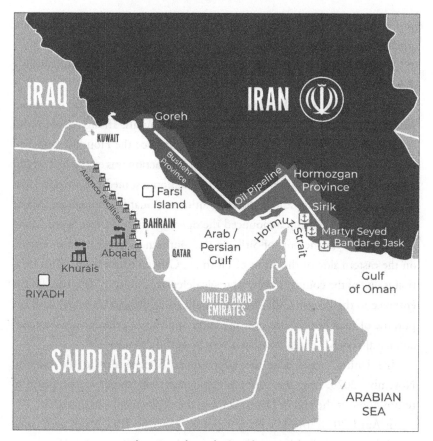

The Gorek-Jask Pipeline and
Some Locations of Suspected Iran Attacks in the Gulf (2019–2021)

a large inventory of naval mines, and an arsenal of anti-ship missiles can severely disrupt maritime traffic in the Strait of Hormuz—a strategic chokepoint critical to global trade. Each of these forces is becoming increasingly survivable, precise, and responsive.[25]

Though it did not claim responsibility, it is widely believed that Iran was behind a series of attacks in the Gulf over the past few years. These attacks were on Norwegian, Saudi, and UAE oil tankers in the Gulf in May and June 2019, Aramco oil production facilities in Saudi Arabia on May 14, 2019, and Saudi oil tankers near the Hormuz on June 13, 2019.

On June 20, 2019, Iran shot down a US drone over the Hormuz Strait, arguing the US had invaded its territory.

In July 2019, Iran detained two British oil tankers in the Hormuz, alleging they had infiltrated Iran's territorial waters.

On September 14, 2019, two swarms of at least twenty-five assault drones struck Saudi Arabia's oil facilities in Abqaiq and Khurais. Though the Houthis claimed responsibility, it is widely believed Iran, not the Houthis, launched the attack. As a result of the strike, Saudi oil production was cut by half (about 5 percent of the goal oil supply). Total production resumed a few weeks later.

On September 23, 2020, the Revolutionary Guards commander, Major General Hossein Salami, announced the opening of the Martyr Seyed Majid Rahbar base near the port of Sirik, in the southern province of Hormozgan, on the eastern side of the Strait of Hormuz. General Salami said, "This location is one of the country's most strategic defensive points ... This base [at the entrance to the Persian Gulf] has been built [over the past six years] with the purpose of total dominance over the entry and exit of extraterritorial aircraft and naval vessels ... Iran now has a very powerful naval base."[26]

The United States sent the USS *Nimitz* Supercarrier to the Gulf in November 2020. After a ten-month deployment, the carrier was supposed to return home at the end of December, but the deployment was extended.

In April 2021, the US Navy reported that the IRG Navy performed multiple aggressive actions and maneuvers in proximity to American navy vessels.

In May 2021, Pentagon Press Secretary John Kirby reacted to a May 10, 2021, US Navy 5th Fleet statement. A group of six US vessels had been escorting the guided-missile submarine USS *Georgia* into the strait when Iranian boats approached them. The US Navy reported that thirteen IRG Navy boats had broken up into two groups, with two of the ships approaching the US vessels at speeds in excess of 32 knots, "with their weapons uncovered and manned." Kirby reported that the Iranian vessels approached US assets "at a very fast speed ... acting very aggressively." The secretary called the high-speed encounter, involving thirteen Islamic Revolutionary Guard Corps Navy (IRGCN) boats, "significant" given that it took place in an area where movement is limited.[27]

According to the United States Defense Intelligence Agency,

> The regime seeks to develop its conventional military capabilities, particularly its missiles, naval forces, airpower, and air defense forces and will try to procure advanced technologies. The regime seeks to field "improved naval mines, faster and more lethal surface platforms, more advanced [anti-ship cruise missiles], larger and more sophisticated submarines, and new [anti-ship ballistic missiles]." Iran could become emboldened to take increasingly aggressive actions against the US and its allies as it consolidates strength around the Strait of Hormuz.[28]

On July 29, 2021, a drone attack on a Japanese-owned ship—the HV *Mercer Street*—in international waters off the coast of Oman killed two civilians on board. The US Central Command published an announcement that United States investigators concluded based on the evidence that the UAV was produced in Iran. Following the attack, the United States and the G7 condemned Iran, saying that "This was a deliberate and targeted attack and a clear violation of international law."[29]

Iran clearly was not deterred by the strong statement. On August 3, 2021, a Panama-flagged tanker was reportedly seized by Iranian-backed forces in the Gulf of Oman and was towed into Iranian waters.[30]

Iran is strengthening its strategic leverage over the Strait of Hormuz. It is laying the groundwork for more significant Iranian influence around the strait by expanding its military footprint and building critical infrastructure in the area.[31] One of the most significant and strategic projects in that regard is the Goreh-Jask pipeline, allowing Tehran to bypass the Strait of Hormuz. Iran currently exports around 90 percent of its oil from the Bushehr province via the Hormuz. The Goreh-Jask pipeline will allow Iran to export vast amounts of oil, and at the same time, cause chaos for a third of the rest of the world's oil shipments by blockading the Strait of Hormuz. Iran wants to use the threat—or reality—of closing the Strait of Hormuz for political reasons without also destroying its own oil exports revenue stream.

In May 2021, Iran started its first transfer of crude oil via the Goreh-Jask pipeline.

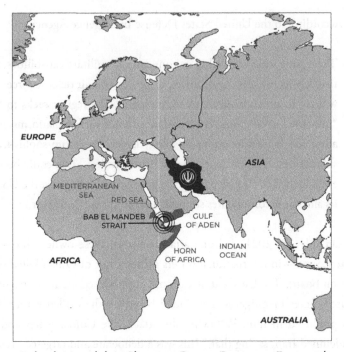

Bab el-Mandeb—Shortest Route Between East and
West. One of the Most Crucial Maritime Transport
Routes on the Planet.

The Bab el-Mandeb Strait, Yemen, the Red Sea, and the Suez Canal

The Hormuz Strait connects the Gulf with the world. There is another vitally strategic location directly southwest of the Hormuz, right on the other side of the Arabian Peninsula. And that is the Bab el-Mandeb Strait, "The Gate of Lamentation (or) Tears."

The Bab el-Mandeb is the chokepoint between the Horn of Africa and Asia. It is also the southern entrance to the Red Sea. This strait is one of the most strategic places in the world. Eighteen miles wide at its narrowest point, the Bab el Mandeb is flanked from the east by Yemen and from the west by Djibouti and Eritrea. The strait connects the Gulf of Aden and the Red Sea. It is the link between the Indian Ocean and the Mediterranean Sea. It is the shortest route between the Mediterranean, the Indian Ocean, and East Asia.

The Bab el-Mandeb is one of the most crucial maritime transport routes on the planet. Estimates are that 12 to 20 percent of the world's trade passes

Bab el-Mandeb—One of the Most Strategic Places
in the World. Eighteen Miles Wide at Its Narrowest
Point, Creating Two-Mile-Wide Shipping Lanes.

through this one strait. It is a vital trade and transportation link between Asia, the Mediterranean, Europe, and North America.

In June 2020, former Australian Defense official Elizabeth White wrote about the importance of the security of the Bab el Mandeb:

> The two-mile-wide shipping lanes of the BAM (Bab el Mandeb) also squeeze in local and international merchant shipping, military vessels, fishing trawlers, and cruise ships. The world cannot afford for the fourth busiest waterway to crumble into lawlessness and cripple a trading system and regional economy already teetering on the edge. Securing this chokepoint is vital to the US and its allies, but they are not the only ones seeking to gain the upper hand in this turbulent patch of ocean.[32]

Whoever sits on the shores of the Bab el-Mandeb Strait holds a staggeringly powerful card. It is one of Iran's strategic goals to control this area. And sitting right on the Bab el-Mandeb is Yemen.

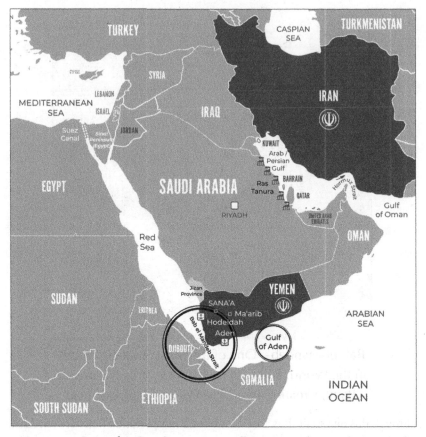

Yemen, a Stage for Saudi-Iranian Collision. And Sample Sites of Suspected Iranian Attacks on Saudi Arabia.

Yemen—A Stage for a Saudi-Iranian Collision

Yemen is one of the most strategically located countries on the planet. At the southwestern tip of the Arabian Peninsula, its 1,200-mile-long shoreline straddles the Arabian Sea, the Gulf of Aden, the Bab el-Mandeb Strait, and the Red Sea.

Yemen is a tribal society, a fact which dictates its society, politics, and economy. The Shi'ite Houthi tribes, traditionally based in northern Yemen, are 35 percent of Yemen's population and a significant political entity. Like all other players in Yemen, the Houthis are looking for the strongest cards to secure its political position.

The relationship between Iran and the Shi'ite Houthis accelerated after the Arab Spring when Iran began sending money and weapons to the Houthis. More specifically, Iran provides arms, financing, military hardware, training, and support to *Ansar Allah*, "The Supporters of God"—the Islamist military wing of the Houthis. Iran's support boosts the Houthis' political influence in Yemen and subsequently increases Iran's grip on Yemen.

In September 2014, the Houthis, backed by Iran, executed a coup in Yemen. They ousted the Yemenite government led by Sunni President Abd Rabbuh Mansur Hadi and took over Yemen's capitol, Sana'a. Hadi's ousted government relocated to Aden, the southernmost point in Yemen on the Gulf of Aden.

One of the reasons Iran supports the Houthis is to ensure a foothold on one of the most strategic locations on the planet.

One of the Houthis' first moves in the war was to take control of the Red Sea Al-Hodeidah Port. (We will explore Iran's activity in the Red Sea in depth later in this chapter.) Controlling Al-Hodeidah is part of Iran's strategy to continue to gain control over Yemen. Al-Hodeidah is the fourth largest city in Yemen and Yemen's main Red Sea port. It is also Iran's major supply pipeline to the Houthis. Arms, militants, money, narcotics, etc., all flow freely through the port.

In March 2015, concerned with an Iranian takeover of Yemen and following the failure to reach a diplomatic solution, Saudi Arabia and the UAE led a Sunni military coalition to restore Hadi as president and prevent Iran from taking control of Yemen.

In April 2015, UNSC Resolution 2216 demanded the Houthis withdraw from all areas seized during the conflict, relinquish the arms it took from military and security institutions, and restore the authority of the legitimate government of Yemen. The Houthis ignored the resolution.

Since 2015, Iran's agent, the Houthis, has launched countless attacks on Saudi Arabian cities using ballistic missiles and attacking drones. Since 2015, Iran has enabled the development of the Houthis' advanced attack capabilities. Iran has provided Yemen's Houthis with increasingly advanced ballistic and cruise missiles and long-range unmanned aerial vehicles.[33]

In October 2016, the Houthis shot a ballistic missile at Saudi Arabia for the first time. There had been cross-border attacks since 2015, but the ballistic missile attack marked an increase in the level of tensions.

In November 2017, the Houthis began attacking Saudi cities, airports, and oil facilities with missiles and attack drones supplied by Iran.

In December 2018, the UNSC unanimously passed Resolution 2451 endorsing an agreement between the Yemenite government and the Houthis, known as the Stockholm Agreement or the Al-Hodeidah Agreement. The goal of the 2018 deal was to stop the violence and alleviate the escalating humanitarian crisis. According to the agreement, Al-Hodeidah and the surrounding areas that the Houthis occupy were to be demilitarized, and all foreign forces must leave. And the United Nations was to monitor the Al-Hodeidah port. Thus far, the Stockholm Agreement and the UNSC Resolution 2451 have not been implemented.

In fact, the Houthis have escalated their attacks in the Yemen arena.

On June 23, 2020, the Houthis used drones and a cruise missile to target the King Khalid Airport and the Defense Ministry headquarters in Saudi Arabia's capitol of Riyadh.

A report by Missile Defense Project at the Center for Strategic and International Studies (CSIS) in June 2020 reads, "If unchecked, moreover, Houthi missile activity could inadvertently widen the conflict, possibly pulling in the United States or bringing the United States into direct conflict with Iran. Mitigating the Houthi missile threat, as such, will be a necessary component of any lasting peace."[34]

Between the summer of 2020 and January 2021, the Houthis attempted to attack Saudi Arabia with missiles, drones, and crewless vehicles on almost a monthly basis.

In January 2021, then US Secretary of State Mike Pompeo designated Yemen's Iranian-backed Houthi, including three of the group's leaders—Abdul Malik al-Houthi, Abd al-Khaliq Badr al-Din al-Houthi, and Abdullah Yahya al-Hakim—as foreign terrorists. On January 19, 2021, the designation went into effect one day before President Joe Biden's inauguration.

President Joe Biden, the forty-sixth president of the United States, put Yemen at the top of his list of priorities when he entered office in January

2021. He was resolute that he was determined to end the war and the severe humanitarian crisis in Yemen.

One of the first steps the Biden administration took in February 2021 was to overturn the Trump administration's decision to define the Houthis as a foreign terrorist organization. At the same time, the administration decided to freeze the delivery of offensive weapons to Saudi Arabia, but in parallel stressed that the United States was committed to the defense and security of Saudi Arabia. Through these actions, the administration sought to prepare the groundwork for ceasefire talks to end the war.

The new administration's efforts produced the opposite results. The war escalated. The Houthis launched a widespread offensive military attack on the oil-rich Yemenite city of Ma'rib (southeast of Sana'a). Ma'rib is one of Yemen's largest cities. And many of its 1.5 million residents are people who have been dislocated because of the war and sought refuge in the city. As of August 2021, one result of US policy is that the war and the humanitarian crisis in Yemen are escalating.

In parallel, Iran and the Houthis significantly escalated their aggression against Saudi Arabia.

Since February 2021, the Houthis increased their attacks on civilian targets in Saudi Arabia, emphasizing oil infrastructure facilities and domestic and international airports throughout the country.

In March 2021, the Houthis again significantly escalated their attacks on Saudi Arabia. They attempted a bold drone and ballistic missile attack on March 7 that targeted Saudi Aramco oil facilities in Ras Tanura on the Hormuz Strait. That was the second of many Houthi attacks on Saudi Arabia that month.

On March 23, 2021, Saudi Arabia announced it was ready for an unconditional ceasefire. The Saudi move coincided with Biden's effort to end the war. Therefore, I primarily attribute the Saudis' move to their interest in improving their relationship with the Biden Administration.

The Houthis response was a further escalation.

Reportedly, from March 23, 2021, until the end of April 2021, the Houthis launched thirty-seven attacks on Saudi territory using missiles and drones.[35]

On April 15, the Houthis announced launching another drone and ballistic missile attack on Jizan in southwestern Saudi Arabia. An al-Houthi spokesman alleged this attack targeted oil facilities and Patriot missile batteries. Saudi Arabia did not confirm strikes on these targets but reported that debris from intercepting the drones and missiles fell on the campus of a local university.[36]

The escalation caused the US special envoy to Yemen, Timothy Lenderking, to officially blame Iran and the Houthis for stirring up the war.[37]

Throughout 2021, the Houthis have expanded their attacks against Saudi Arabia on all levels. The attacks are more frequent. They are increasingly targeting civilians and civilian assets. The attack drones, ballistic missiles, marine vehicles, and UAVs are more sophisticated. And the targets the Houthis are choosing are increasingly sensitive.

In late July 2021, the Arab Interior Ministers Council (AIMC) strongly condemned the repeated terrorist operations carried out by the Houthis. In a statement, the council's general secretariat said: "The Iran-backed Houthi group aims to destabilize security and stability in the Arab region. The Houthis are armed, financed, and trained by external parties. They are deliberately pursuing aggressive practices that violate the rules of international humanitarian law. And they are ignoring all efforts to end the conflict in Yemen."[38] The AIMC called on the international community to hold the perpetrators accountable and reiterated its support for all the Kingdom's measures to protect its security, stability, and sovereignty. The council also supported the Arab coalition in confronting the Houthis' threats and hostilities.[39] (The AIMC plays an understated but important role in regional and international cooperation in the Arab world, in all areas related to the internal security of the Arab States, including criminal issues.)

In the same month, the Arab Parliament, the legislative body of the Arab League, reiterated its support for Saudi Arabia and described the Houthi militia as a "terrorist organization operated from Tehran to implement a policy of spreading chaos and terror in the region and the world."[40] It echoed the Interior Ministers Council's call. It urged the international community to assume its responsibilities in confronting Houthi attacks that threaten regional and international peace and security and take measures to deter these groups and those who finance and support them—Iran.

Throughout the summer of 2021, the Organization of Islamic Cooperation (OIC) strongly condemned the Houthis' attempts to target innocent civilians in Saudi Arabia. The secretary-general of the OIC, Yousef Bin Ahmad Al-Othaimeen, reiterated the OIC's condemnation of the Houthi terrorist militia's attempts by launching booby-trapped drones toward innocent civilians in the Kingdom, terming them "war crimes."[41] He stressed the OIC's firm solidarity with the Kingdom in all the measures it takes to protect its security and stability and the safety of its citizens and residents in its territories.

Throughout August 2021, in addition to formal Arab organizations condemning Iran, supporting Saudi Arabia's efforts to protect its land and citizens, and calling on the international community to hold the Houthis and Iran accountable for the Houthi attacks that threaten regional security and stability, individual countries including Bahrain, Jordan, Kuwait, and the UAE firmly echoed the same messages.

An analysis published by the Emirates Policy Center (EPC) in February 2021 predicted that the Biden administration's policy would encourage the Houthis and Iran and would therefore lead to an escalation in the war. As of the summer of 2021, events on the ground validate the EPC prediction.[42]

Iran's belligerence in Yemen is not limited to attacks on Saudi Arabia. The regime's increasingly aggressive behavior in Yemen's surrounding waterways attests to Iran's regional and global threat. Iranian control over two major maritime routes that are a lynchpin of the world's economy is an unbearable threat that the world must not tolerate.

The Bab el-Mandeb, Red Sea, and the Suez Canal

Yemen sits at the intersection of the Gulf of Aden and the Bab el-Mandeb Strait—the gateway to the Red Sea. The Red Sea countries are Djibouti, Egypt, Eritrea, Israel, Jordan, Saudi Arabia, Sudan, and Yemen.

At the northernmost point of the Red Sea lies the Suez Canal, one of the world's most important waterways. Located seventy-five miles east of Cairo, the Suez Canal connects the Red Sea and the Mediterranean Sea, allowing direct shipping from Europe to Asia. More than 12 percent of the world's shipping traffic flows through the Suez Canal. On average, about 10 percent of

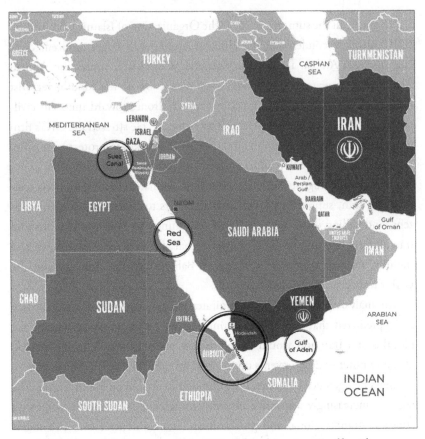

More than 12 Percent of the World's Shipping Traffic Flows
Through the Suez Canal.

the world's oil shipped by the sea travels through the canal—that equals about
three billion barrels a day. And it is one of Egypt's primary income sources.

In July 2015, Egypt widened the Suez Canal. The project's goal was to
increase revenue by allowing more—and larger—ships to pass through with
shorter waiting times and develop service and industrial zones around the
canal. According to an August 6, 2020, press conference given by Suez Canal
Authority (SCA) Chairman Osama Rabie, between 2015 and 2020, canal
revenues rose to $27.2 billion from $25.9 billion in 2010–2015.[43]

On June 30, 2021, Mr. Rabie reported that despite various challenges,
including the coronavirus pandemic's effect on world trade as well as a six-day

blockage at the end of March, revenues from the canal rose sharply in the fiscal year ending June 30, 2021. He reported that the Suez Canal netted a record $5.84 billion, the highest revenues in the canal's history, and an increase of more than 2 percent from 2019.[44]

The importance of the Suez Canal was underscored in March 2021 when the *Ever Given* cargo ship was lodged in the Suez Canal for six days. The immobilized 1,300-foot-long ship weighing 200,000 tons, carrying 18,300 shipping containers, brought the canal's cargo traffic to a standstill. The incident disrupted supply chains around the world. About $10 billion of daily marine shipping came to a halt.[45] Since the blockage, shipping costs have increased, and the event impacted everything from oil to food to clothing to semiconductors.

Alex Hersham, the CEO and co-founder of Zencargo, a London-based digital freight forwarder, said the pandemic and the Suez blockage, compounded by other global events, has created staggering delays and skyrocketing container rate costs. This is a nightmare for businesses because their profits are slashed, and it takes longer to receive parts or products. At the same time, consumers may face long wait times and could potentially end up having to pay more if companies end up passing on the cost. Industries will struggle to get the materials they need, while governments will need much more time to stock up on personal protective equipment (PPE). The effects are very tangible and will likely start to bleed over from the industry into the mainstream.[46]

The fact that five months after traffic in the Suez Canal was disrupted, the global supply chain has yet to recover underscores the international importance of the Bab el-Mandeb, the Red Sea, and the Suez Canal. The security of these waterways is not only a local issue. It is a global concern.

In addition to being a key source of revenue for Egypt and a vital strategic chokepoint for global trade and the worldwide economy, the Red Sea region also offers diverse economic and commercial opportunities and partnerships around tourism initiatives, infrastructure development, and transportation projects.

Since 2017, Saudi Arabia has been working on one of the most ambitious projects in the Middle East. It is called NEOM. And it will be in northwest Saudi Arabia (the Tabuk region) on the shore of the Red Sea. The $500 billion project aims to transform more than 11,000 square miles of desert into a futuristic sustainable mega-city boasting a wide range of renewable energy sources. NEOM is part of Saudi Arabia's attempt to diversify its income sources away from oil. In July 2021, NEOM CEO Nadhmi Al-Nasr said, "NEOM is meant to be a model where this region will be a semi-independent free zone, it will have its own laws, it will have its own regulations and its own authority as a semi-government."[47] NEOM's website describes the project accordingly: "NEOM is a new vision of what the future could be. It's an attempt to do something that's never been done before, and it's coming at a time when the world needs fresh thinking and new solutions. Put simply, NEOM will not only be a destination but a home for people who dream big and who want to be present. Within NEOM will be THE LINE, a city of a million residents with a length of 170 km that preserves 95 percent of nature within NEOM, with zero cars, zero streets, and zero carbon emissions. NEOM is a vision of what the future will be. A home for people who dream big and want to build a new model for sustainable living."[48]

Another massive international project underway is the King Salman Causeway—described as "the biggest project in the world"—which, when completed, will connect Egypt and Saudi Arabia.

The security of the waterways from Yemen to the Mediterranean is a priority for the region and the world.

From the Hormuz to the Red Sea—Iran Builds a Loop around Saudi Arabia's Neck and Holds the World Hostage

The map shows that Iran has built a loop around Saudi Arabia from the Hormuz Strait to Yemen to the Bab el-Mandeb and the Red Sea. This network is a noose the mullah regime has completed around Saudi Arabia's neck. The eastern edge of that loop is the Gulf and the Hormuz Strait, and the western edge of the loop is the Red Sea and the Bab el-Mandeb Strait.

We have explored how Iran uses the Gulf and Yemen to attack Saudi Arabia and international actors. This section will explore how Tehran uses the Red Sea to further threaten Saudi Arabia and international actors.

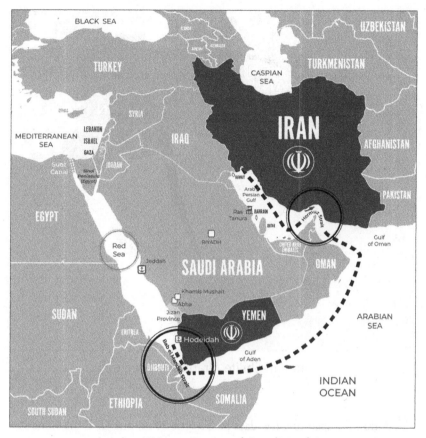

Iranian "Noose" around Saudi Arabia

As mentioned earlier, one of the first things the Iranian-backed Houthis did after overthrowing the Yemenite government was to seize control of Yemen's Red Sea Al-Hodeidah port.

Historically, Iran has used the Red Sea to smuggle arms, primarily to Hamas and Islamic Jihad in the Gaza Strip and Hezbollah in Lebanon. Since the Iranian-backed Houthis overthrew the government in Yemen, Iran has used Yemen and the war in Yemen to increase its presence and control of the waterways surrounding Yemen.

Since 2015, Iran has increased its control of Yemen and Al-Hodeidah. As a result, strategic sea trade routes near Yemen have come under increasing threats, and Houthi militants have attacked vessels near the coast of Yemen.

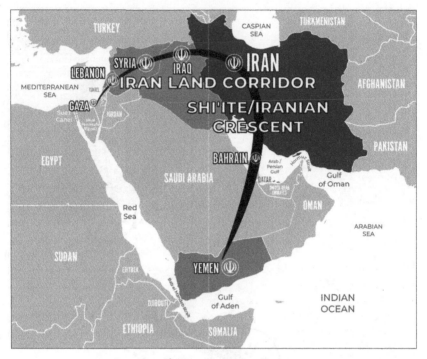

Iranian Shi'ite / Iranian Crescent

Within the span of a few days in October 2016, one UAE maritime vessel and two US navy ships, the USS *Mason* and the USS *Ponce,* were fired on in the Red Sea. In at least one instance, it was reported the missiles were launched from Houthi-held Al-Hodeidah port.[49] Later that month, a Spanish gas tanker was attacked.

In January 2017, a Saudi frigate was attacked by a Houthi speedboat killing two crew members and causing an explosion on the ship. In May 2017, the Houthis denied attacking a Marshall Islands–flagged vessel with RPGs. In July 2017, the Houthis attacked two Saudi oil tankers in the Red Sea. Since 2017, the Saudis have witnessed, intercepted, and destroyed several crewless remote-controlled explosive-laden speed boats that the Houthis have launched in the southern part of the Red Sea.[50]

Houthi attacks on the arena of the Red Sea have intensified since 2019. Between July and September 2019, water mines scattered by the Houthis damaged several ships in the Red Sea.

Throughout 2020, Saudi forces continued to struggle with similar incidents. In November 2020, the Houthis shot an Iranian-made missile at Saudi Arabia's Jeddah Red Sea oil refinery.

And the Houthi attacks on Saudi Arabia have intensified exponentially in 2021.

On January 15, 2021, the Saudis intercepted three suicide drones launched from Al-Hodeidah.

On February 27, 2021, the Houthis claimed to have launched several attacks using UAVs, attack drones, and a missile that was reportedly domestically manufactured, at Saudi Arabia. The targets were "sensitive targets" in Riyadh and military targets in western Saudi Arabia—close to the Red Sea, namely in Abha, Khamis Mushait, and the Jizan province. The Saudi military said that one missile and three weaponized UAVs had been used in the attacks.[51]

Throughout April, May, June, and July 2021, the Saudis reported more than a dozen successes in foiling Houthi attempts to attack Saudi Arabia from the Red Sea with bomb-laden crewless marine vessels and drones.

As of August, there have been more than forty Houthi attacks on Saudi Arabia in 2021.

Iran has demonstrated its ability to ratchet up aggression at any time and at its will. Iran increasing its dominance over waterways critical for regional and global security is one element of its hegemonically driven foreign policy. It is a danger to the Middle East and the world.

The Shi'ite Crescent and the Iranian Land Corridor

In addition to its maritime ambitions, Iran invests significant efforts in what has become a cornerstone of Iran's regional foreign policy and one of the most important keys to its hegemony: the Shi'ite Crescent and the Iranian Land Corridor.

In December 2004, King Abdullah II of Jordan warned that Iran was developing a Shi'ite Crescent—Lebanon, Syria, Iraq, Iran, Bahrain, and Yemen—to become the regional superpower. He warned that Iran would foment instability to achieve its objective and that it would be disastrous for the region if the Shi'ite Crescent were realized. As Iranian aggression has escalated, the king has used international forums, including the 2018 World Economic Forum in Davos,[52] as a platform to express his concern. And in a January

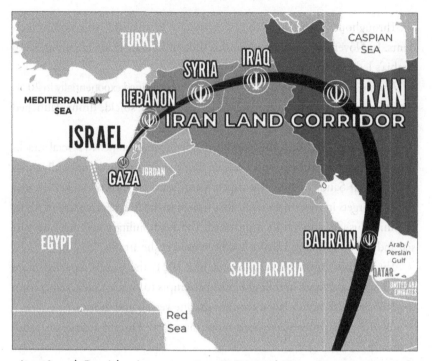

Iran Land Corridor Increases Iran's Control Over Iraq, Syria, and Lebanon; Creates a Militarized Noose Around Israel, Gives Iran Access to the Mediterranean and a Launchpad to Europe.

2020 interview with France24, he changed the term "Shi'ite Crescent" to the "Iranian Crescent."[53]

A large part of the crescent is an Iranian-controlled land corridor Iran has been building in recent years parallel to the war in Syria, which began in 2011. (We will explore the war in Syria further later in this chapter and Chapter 6.)

The land bridge begins in Iran and travels west, crosses through Iraq, Syria, and Lebanon, and ends in the Mediterranean Sea. The corridor is critical for Iran's hegemonic vision because:

- It increases and secures Iran's power and control in Iraq, Syria, and Lebanon.
- It creates a militarized corridor that forms a strangling "noose of militants, rockets, and missiles" around Israel's neck so Iran and its agents and proxies can easily target Israel's soft belly—cities and civilians.
- It gives Iran direct access to the Mediterranean Sea and a launchpad to Europe.

We just finished learning how Iran uses the regional and global vital waterways to foment and capitalize on the chaos and instability to meet its objectives.

When we look at the Shi'ite Crescent and the Land Corridor, we will see the same tactics. But we will also see something else.

We will see very clearly how the mullah regime strategically uses its own elite forces—the Islamic Revolutionary Guards and the al-Quds Force, and its network—the axis of resistance, its agents and proxies, and its military arsenal and soft power to secure the corridor and entrench itself as the power on the ground. And we will see how it uses all these assets to further its own mission to become the dominant force in the region.

Let's look at the corridor, beginning with Iraq.

The Iranian Land Corridor—Iraq

Iraq is of utmost strategic importance to Iran. Without Iraq, there is no Iranian land corridor.

Iran considers Iraq its jurisdiction. Many aspects of everyday life connect these two countries—commerce, religious observances, religious sites, tourism, trade, etc.—particularly in eastern Iraq that borders Iran. Iraq is primarily Shi'ite, and the most sacred shrines and spiritual centers of the Shi'ites—Najaf and Karbala—are in southern Iraq. These are important pilgrimage destinations that also provide economic and commercial opportunities for Iranian companies in many fields, from construction to transportation and tourism. Iraq is a significant customer of Iranian goods. And Iran and Iraq share five cross-border oil fields estimated to be the largest in the Middle East.

Since signing the JCPOA in 2015, Iran has been steadfast in increasing and expanding its influence in Iraq.

Iraqi Shi'ite Nationalists v. Iraqi Shi'ite Non-Nationalists

Iran's deepening grip in Iraq fuels a power struggle between Iraqi Shi'ite nationalists and Iraqi Shi'ite non-nationalists. It is a battle over Iraq's identity and trajectory (I discuss this in more detail in Chapter 6.)

Shi'ites are the majority in Iraq (about 65 percent). Iraqi Shi'ites are predominantly Arab in their ethnicity (and a small number of Iraqi Kurds are Shi'ite).

Without Iraq There Is No Iranian Land Corridor

Iraqi nationalists believe that the central component of Iraq's identity should be ethnic and not religious. Iraqi Shi'ite nationalists believe that being Arab—not Sunni, or Shi'ite, or Christian—should define Iraqi identity. Therefore, in their view, Iraq is and should be an independent Arab country that is part of the Arab world.

Iraqi Shi'ite non-nationalists believe that Iraq's central component should be religious (Shi'ite), not ethnic (Arab/Kurdish). Therefore, in their view, Iraq should not be a part of the Arab world (which is 80 percent Sunni). Iraq should be part of Shi'ite Iran and be under Iran's umbrella. Iranian-backed Shi'ite Iraqi political figures and Iranian-backed Iraqi Shi'ite militias support and advance Iranian intervention in Iraq.

Iranian-Backed Iraqi Shi'ite Militias, the Iranian Corridor, and the Iranian Crescent

As I said above, Iran considers Iraq its jurisdiction, particularly south Iraq. Iran has always had access to and a relationship with the communities in those areas. Being an integral part of the landscape provided the platform for Iran to develop relationships to serve its own goals.

One of the most significant things Iran did was to create its own militias in Iraq or establish a relationship with local militias. Beyond being military and logistical forces, these militias play a significant role in Iraqi politics. In fact, they are part of a formal Iraqi military structure that functions in parallel to the Iraqi armed forces, known as *Al-Hashd Al-Sha'abi*—the Popular Mobilization Units (PMU). (We will explore Iran's involvement in Iraq and the Iranian-backed *al-Wilaiyah* Iraqi Shi'ite militias, including the PMU, in-depth in Chapter 6.)

Iranian-backed Iraqi Shi'ite militias have become one of Iran's most productive assets.

The Iranian-backed Iraqi Shi'ite militias control the Iraq-Syria border crossings. For Iran, controlling the Iraqi-Syria border is a critical piece of the corridor and the crescent. Controlling the Iraqi-Syria border enables Iranian-backed Iraqi proxies to move freely from Iraq to Syria and back.

I opened this section by saying that without Iraq, there is no land corridor. I want to add that Syria (and we will discuss this further in the next section) is the lynchpin of the corridor and the cornerstone of the axis of resistance.

Controlling the Iraqi-Syria border helps Iran stream weapons and ammunition to Syria and then to Hezbollah in Lebanon over land. The land route is parallel to an already existing areal route that Iran operates in the corridor.

Iran's significant influence Iraq and Iran's control over the border crossing between Iraq and Syria is what has allowed Iran to establish a military stronghold in eastern Syria.

To secure its control over this pivotal crossing, Iran's Islamic Revolutionary Guards Corps and its elite unit, the al-Quds force, have been building a military installation in eastern Syria called the Imam 'Ali Compound. The Imam 'Ali Compound serves as a transition depot for Iranian-backed Iraqi militias heading to Syria. The passage's name on the Syrian side is Al-Bukamal, and the name of the crossing on the Iraqi side is Al-Qa'im. In addition to the sprawling warehouses it has built, reports are that Iran has built tunnels and bunkers in the compound that store missiles and rockets. The Imam 'Ali Compound is a keystone of the corridor. That is why it has been attacked several times by

Iraqi Iranian-Backed Shi'ite Militias (Sample)

the United States. Also, reportedly Israel has attacked the installation. Israel has never claimed responsibility for those attacks.

Iran wants US troops to leave Iraq. Getting the United States to leave Iraq is one of Iran's primary objectives. In the last section, we saw how Iran uses waterways to attack the United States and other international assets.

Iran's deepening grip in Iraq has turned Iraq into a stage of intensifying military friction between Iranian-backed Iraqi Shi'ite militias and the United States. The infrastructure—that includes both militias and physical structures and infrastructure—that Iran built from Iran through Iraq makes it easier for Iran to attack US and international troops inside Iraq. Under Iranian order, the Iranian-backed Iraq militias launch rocket and mortar shell attacks on US military and diplomatic facilities.[54]

On December 27, 2019, *Kataib Hezbollah*—"The Hezbollah Brigades," an Iranian-backed Iraqi proxy militia controlled by the Islamic Revolutionary Guards—launched rockets on a military base near Kirkuk that housed US military service and Iraqi personnel. Kataib Hezbollah's attack killed one US civilian contractor, injured four US service members and two Iraqis. The December attack sparked escalating military rounds between Iranian-backed

Iraqi Shi'ite militias and the United States. On December 29, 2019, the United States attacked a Kataib Hezbollah base. The US attack killed dozens of militants, apparently including several IRGC officers. On December 31, 2019, Iraqi protesters—Iranian-backed Iraqi militants dressed in civilian clothes—stormed the US Embassy in Baghdad and blocked it for several days.

This series of events resulted in a direct military collision between Iran and the United States.

On January 3, 2020, the United States eliminated Major-General Qasem Soleimani, the Iranian al-Quds Force commander. Another man killed in the attack, which took place near the Baghdad airport, was Abu Mahdi al-Muhandis, the deputy commander of al-Hashd al-Shaabi (the PMU). Iran retaliated by shooting missiles at bases in Iraq that house some five thousand US troops.[55] The Iranian retaliation did not cause any fatalities, but it did injure dozens of US military personnel. I want to make a note here that I will elaborate on later in the book. But it is critical to note. The elimination of Soleimani sent shock waves through the mullah regime. The assassination of Soleimani made Tehran question what they knew about their enemy. The act took them out of balance and made them question their tactics.

On March 11 and March 14, 2020, Kataib Hezbollah launched a rocket attack on the Camp Taji military base located fifteen miles north of Baghdad. The Camp Taji base is an Iraqi military base that also housed US-led international coalition forces until August 2020. Two American soldiers and one British soldier were killed, and dozens were injured in the attacks. In response, the United States attacked and reportedly did severe damage—almost completely destroying the Imam 'Ali military compound. The United States also struck five weapon storage facilities next to the installation that belong to Kataib Hezbollah. The continuing military attacks have reportedly resulted in US plans to eliminate the Iranian-backed Iraqi militia, Kataib Hezbollah.[56] As of August 2021, that has not happened.

The attacks of the Iranian-backed Shi'ite militias against US targets and assets—including the US Embassy in Baghdad—intensified and widened in the second half of 2020 and throughout 2021.

Syria is the Lynchpin of the Axis of Resistance and Creates an
Iranian "Noose" Around Israel

Iran's role in the attacks is increasingly brazen and overt. As recently as July 13, 2021, it was reported that a senior IRG commander went to Baghdad. While in the Iraqi capitol, he urged Iraqi Shi'ite militias to step up attacks on US targets and asked them to widen their attacks beyond Iraq and attack US assets in Syria.[57] Indeed his visit was bookended with drone and missile attacks on US military and diplomatic installations in Iraq. And following his visit, there were several attacks on US forces in Syria.

I opened this section by saying that Iran's grip on Iraq results in a growing power struggle between Iraq nationalists and Iranian-backed Iraqi Shi'ite militias. It is a battle over Iraq's identity and trajectory. However, it is also a battle over Iraqi sovereignty. (We will explore this in more detail in Chapter 6). An Iranian-controlled corridor through Iraq will guarantee that Iraq will continue to be a platform for Iran to advance its own hegemonic objectives, disregarding Iraq's policies and preferences as well as those of the Iraqi people.

The Corridor and the Crescent—A Noose Around Israel

Iran openly promises to eliminate Israel. To set the stage to advance this goal, Iran is creating a network surrounding Israel.

Since signing the JCPOA in 2015, far from becoming a more stabilizing factor, Iran has ramped up its efforts to entrench itself on Israel's borders by increasing its presence in Lebanon, Gaza, and Syria. That military infrastructure includes missiles and rockets as well as terror armies of tens of thousands of Shi'ite militants. One of Iran's core objectives is to create a "strangling noose of militants, rockets, and missiles around Israel's neck that target Israel's soft belly—cities and civilians." To build and secure this apparatus, Iran needs to create a passage that it can control that provides it an unfettered Iranian land bridge from Tehran to Beirut.

Lebanon and Syria, two Arab countries that border Israel from the north and northeast, make up the northern and northeastern parts of the noose. Both are located on the Iranian land corridor. Iran's proxies in both of those countries are part of the strangling noose. The southwest portion of this militarized loop is Iranian proxies in the Gaza Strip, not located on the land corridor.

In the previous section we began to discuss the corridor in Syria, and we will explore Syria in greater detail in this section. Syria is Israel's northeastern neighbor. Syria is the lynchpin of the axis of resistance.

But let's start with two other arenas bordering Israel that are very central components in Iran's Shi'ite Crescent blueprint. One is Lebanon, Israel's northern neighbor. The other is the Gaza Strip bordering Israel from the southwest.

Lebanon

Israel's northern neighbor is Lebanon. Though Lebanon has a government, ministers, a parliament, etc., Tehran calls the shots in Lebanon, not the Lebanese government. That is because *Hezbollah*—two words in Arabic that mean "Party of God" controls Lebanon.

Iran created Hezbollah in Lebanon in the early 1980s. Since then, Hezbollah has become Iran's most important and powerful proxy. Iran has used Hezbollah to kidnap Lebanon from within. (We will discuss Iran and Hezbollah's role in Lebanon in depth in Chapter 6.)

In 2018, the Trump administration began imposing increasing sanctions on Iran. Before that, Iran's annual allocation to Hezbollah was between $700 and $800 million a year. Iran has equipped Hezbollah with an arsenal of over 120,000 rockets (according to some estimations, the numbers exceed

150,000), including heavy missiles. Hezbollah can launch missiles on every corner of Israel. However, although Hezbollah's arsenal is currently massive, most of its rockets are short-range and not precise. Iran and Hezbollah want the organization to have high-precision missiles that can be accurate within a range of thirty feet.

Just as Iran provides the equipment and technology to its other proxies and agents, Iran equips Hezbollah with attack drones, advanced military communication and intelligence gathering systems, the most cutting-edge technology, and equipment to build high-precision missiles. In addition to hardware and know-how, Iran trains an elite ground force of Hezbollah called *Radwan*. In the *Qur'an* (the Islamic bible), Radwan is the name of the "Gatekeeper of Heaven."

For Israel, hundreds of thousands of rockets, high-precision heavy missiles, and swarms of attack drones sitting on Israel's northern border that can strike anywhere in Israel is an intolerable threat.

Another example of the threat Israel faces from Lebanon because of the Iranian corridor is not in the sky but rather under the ground.

On December 4, 2018, after years of surveillance, preparations, and intelligence gathering, Israel launched Operation Northern Shield to uncover attack tunnels dug by Hezbollah. The Israeli operation ended on January 13, 2019.

Operation Northern Shield exposed and neutralized six attack tunnels that crossed into Israeli territory from Lebanon. The deepest one was 180 feet deep. This tunnel had tracks to remove the debris created by the digging process, electricity, and communication systems. The soil on the Israeli Lebanese border is very rocky, so it took years and vast resources to dig such sophisticated tunnels. Iran planned, financed, and controlled the construction of the tunnels.

The tunnels played a pivotal role in Hezbollah's war plan against Israel. The tunnels' purpose was to flood the Israeli communities on the Lebanese border with thousands of Hezbollah militants to kidnap and kill Israelis and occupy Israeli territory.

An important point to note is that building these tunnels took place under the Lebanese government's nose, that—according to the August 2006 UNSC resolution 1701—together with UNIFIL units deployed in South Lebanon, is supposed to secure the Lebanese border with Israel.

Hezbollah's tunnel project is not confined only to the Lebanese-Israeli border. In August 2021, the Israeli-based Alma Research and Education Center published "Hezbollah's 'Land of Tunnels'—the North Korean-Iranian connection."

Here is a quote from the report:

> In our estimation, after the Second Lebanon War of 2006, Hezbollah, with the help of the North Koreans and the Iranians, set up a project forming a network of "inter-regional" tunnels in Lebanon, a network significantly larger than the "Hamas" metro (in our assessment, Hamas used Iranian and North Korean knowledge to build its tunnels as well). It is not merely a network of offensive and infrastructure local tunnels in or near villages. It's a network of tens of kilometers of regional tunnels that extend and connect the Beirut area (Hezbollah's central headquarters) and the Beqaa area (Hezbollah's logistical operational rear base) to southern Lebanon (which is divided into two staging areas named by Hezbollah "the lines of defense"). We call this inter-regional tunnel network "Hezbollah's Land of the Tunnels."[58]

The Gaza Strip

The southwest portion of this Iranian-mastered militarized noose is the Iranian proxies in the Gaza Strip. The Gaza Strip is not part of the corridor—but it is the southwestern edge of the crescent. Since Hamas gained control of Gaza in 2007, there have been ongoing attacks and counterattacks and escalating military rounds in 2008, 2012, 2014, and 2021 between Israel and Iranian agents, namely Hamas and Islamic Jihad in Palestine.

Hamas and Islamic Jihad in Palestine (IJIP) are Palestinian Sunni organizations armed and financed by the mullah regime. They have approximately 20,000 rockets aimed at Israel's cities, towns, and villages. Their military forces are thousands of militants strong.

Since 2007, the rounds of violence between Israel and Gaza-based Palestinian organizations have escalated. The militarization of the conflict has intensified—more weapons and more lethal weapons. Civilians on both sides—in Israel and Gaza are on the front lines and in the line of fire—it is a 'Lunatic Reality' for everyone involved.

On May 10, 2021, Hamas shot rockets toward Jerusalem. Hamas's attack ignited an eleven-day war with Israel. In those eleven days, Hamas fired 4,500 short-, mid-, and long-range rockets. They shot an unknown number of mortar shells, launched incendiary balloons and kites, tried to launch "Special Operations" using attack drones, mini-submarines, intrusive tunnels, etc., and utilized Anti-Tank-Ground Missiles (ATGM). (We will discuss the war in detail and explore Gaza further in Chapters 9 and 10.) Following this war, Hamas's leader Ismail Haniyeh, who lives in Qatar, expressed "gratitude to Iran for providing Hamas with missiles and weapons."[59]

Like Hezbollah in Lebanon, Hamas and Islamic Jihad also dig tunnels into Israeli territory. The purpose of the tunnels from Gaza into southern Israel is the same as the tunnels drilled into Israel from Lebanon in the north; to send an underground stream of thousands of Hamas and Islamic Jihad militants to occupy Israeli communities located near the Israel-Gaza border. Different from Lebanon, the soil around the Gaza Strip is soft. You can dig in it with an ice cream scooper. Taking advantage of the terrain, Hamas and Islamic Jihad built a network of dozens of very sophisticated border-crossing tunnels. Many are equipped with electricity, advanced communication systems, elevators to transfer militants and weapons, etc. You may remember that, in 2006, an Israeli soldier named Gilad Shalit was abducted by militants from Gaza. That is the way he was kidnapped.

The tunnels from Gaza, like Hezbollah's tunnels in Lebanon, are financed by Iran. Like it did in its northern border, Israel has exposed and neutralized many of the underground tunnels crossing from Gaza into Israel. To address the threat of the tunnels, Israel has developed technological and intelligence capacities that exposed and neutralized many underground tunnels crossing from Gaza into Israel. In addition, over the past few years, Israel has been building a barrier along its twenty-five-mile-long border with the Gaza Strip. The obstacle is meant to address the threat of intrusive tunnels from Gaza. The barrier consists of two major elements. An underground wall going as deep as 200 feet (that wall includes advanced technological capabilities to detect underground movement). And an above-ground, twenty-foot-high metal fence. The underground part of the barrier was concluded in March 2021. It is expected that the above-ground portion will be completed by the end of 2021.

In October 2020, Israel exposed a tunnel that was dug from the Gaza Strip. The tunnel crossed the line of Israeli fences located about one hundred yards west of its new underground barrier. Yet, the tunnel did not cross the new obstacle. The Israel Defense Forces (IDF) chief of staff, Lieutenant General Aviv Kochavi, described the specific tunnel discovered by Israel as a "very, very significant asset of the enemy."[60]

Egypt also struggles to stop the intrusive and border crossing smuggling tunnels. Egypt shares an eight-mile-long border with the Gaza Strip. Hamas and Islamic Jihad in Palestine have built a massive and intricate network of tunnels under the Egypt-Gaza border. Estimates are that they have created more than one thousand underground passages that are used to smuggle weapons, fuel, commodities, narcotics, etc. Since 2014, Egypt has taken various measures to put a stop to these tunnels. Their efforts have included flooding the tunnels with sewage water, razing communities and neighborhoods on the Egyptian side of the border so Egypt can create a wide buffer zone between Egypt and Gaza, and building concrete barriers and walls. Egypt is also building an additional layer—a massive iron fence along its border with Gaza.[61]

Syria

Syria is Israel's northeastern neighbor. As we have learned, Syria is the lynchpin of the axis of resistance. Syria is also pivotal to Iran's plan to eliminate Israel.

In the Iraq section of this chapter, we discussed Syria's importance to Iran in the context of the Imam 'Ali Compound. And we discussed the fact that Syria is a critical link in the land corridor from Iran to Lebanon. To complete the corridor and the loop around Israel's neck, Iran must control and militarize Syria. Securing a position in Syria with Hezbollah to the west and Hamas and IJIP to the southwest would create that reality.

To understand the Iranian corridor in Syria, we need to zoom out and look at the evolution of the war in Syria and Iran's engagement in the conflict.

The unrest leading to the war in Syria began in 2011. Iran intervened in the war in Syria almost from the outset. Tehran wanted to save the Assad regime and preserve the enormous resources it had poured into Syria. Iran's

Iranian Involvement in Syria

investment in Syria is decades-long. It is significant and has substantially increased since the war in Syria began. Ankara-based political analyst and researcher Ali Bakir estimated in 2019 that since the outbreak of the Syrian revolution in March 2011, Iran has spent around $15 billion annually to keep al-Assad in power.[62]

Iran has used the war in Syria as an opportunity to occupy and militarize Syria further, strengthen the corridor, and embed the mullah regime on Israel's northeastern border. In short, Iran has used the war in Syria as an opportunity to further its hegemonic vision.

This is why since the fall of 2011 until today—for its own gain and to further its own mission and ambitions—Tehran continuously floods Syria with

Iranian weapons and Iranian-backed militias, Lebanese Hezbollah, Iraqi Shi'ite militias, Syrian proxies that Iran recruits and nurtures in east and southwest Syria, and a small number of Iranian IRG specialists. In addition, the regime created new militias by promising citizenship to Iran's illegal residents. One of the militias, al Fatemiyoun (also written al-Fatimayoun), is made up of Shi'ite Afghans. It is named after Fatimah, the daughter of the Prophet Muhammad. Reportedly, Iran is also recruiting local Syrians to join the al-Fatemiyoun militias.[63] Another militia is al-Zainebiyoun (also written al-Zaynabiyoun), which is made up of Shia Pakistanis. It is named after the Prophet Muhammad's granddaughter Zaineb (also written Zaynab). As an aside, the names of those militias emphasize the validity of the name of the first chapter of this book *A New Era | And Ancient Rivalries Are Alive and Well.*

Over a decade after the war in Syria began, Iran has placed thousands of Shi'ite Iranian-backed militants in Syria. According to a January 2021 report published by the Jusoor Centre in Istanbul, Iran and its subordinate militias have 131 military sites in Syria scattered in ten districts, thirty-eight of them in and around Dara'a, twenty-seven in Damascus, fifteen in Aleppo, thirteen in Deir ez-Zor, twelve in Homs, six in Hama, six in Latakia, five in Suwayda, five in Quneitra, and four in Idlib.[64] Since then, Iran also has reportedly created an additional nine militias in the district of Deir ez-Zor. Those militias are mostly based on domestic Arab tribes and local warlords in eastern Syria. Reportedly they are thousands strong.[65] In addition, Hezbollah commands an additional 116 military points across Syria. It is estimated that Hezbollah and other Shi'ite militias control approximately 20 percent of Syria's borders.[66]

There are Iranian military bases and installations throughout Syria. Iran has moved heavy artillery and precision missiles into Syria stored in bunkers and tunnels throughout Syria. Reportedly, in 2021 Iran has deployed mid-range surface-to-surface missiles in eastern Syria.[67]

And a large concentration of Iranian or Iranian-controlled assets is in southwestern Syria near the Israeli border. In addition to headquarters, bunkers, military camps, artillery, and rocket launchers, Iran has deployed surveillance technology and conducts human intelligence operations on the Syrian side of the Golan Heights.

Iranian involvement in Syria extends beyond the military sphere. Since 2013, Iran has deepened its grip on Syria's civilian and economic sectors. Tehran's effort is intended to secure Iran's hold over Syria to ensure that it will be almost impossible to extricate Iran from Syria. We will further explore Iran's increasing entrenchment in Syria in Chapter 6. But here is an overview.

A June 2021 detailed report by the Moshe Dayan Center for Middle Eastern & African Studies presents a multipronged Iranian strategy. Tehran creates and builds institutions to promote Iranian culture and teach about the Shi'a religion and tradition, as well as Farsi. These efforts are particularly focused on the youth. The IRG has appropriated banks, purchased commercial and residential real estate—including entire neighborhoods. Tehran partially owns Syrian infrastructure—electricity, ports, railroads, etc. Furthermore, Iran is rewriting history, refurbishing and building new Shi'ite monuments and shrines, and renaming streets in Damascus after Shi'ite historical figures and contemporary martyrs. And the mullah regime is actively pursuing a policy to change the demographics of Syria, giving Syrian citizenship to foreign Shi'ites and encouraging their Iraqi and Lebanese militants to move to Syria with their families. And they are choosing where to settle the incoming Shi'ites. They are creating Shi'ite neighborhoods, including a neighborhood just for the Iranian Islamic Revolutionary Guards Corps and their families.

Remember, Syria is a Sunni country; about 80 percent of Syrians are Sunnis. Iran is in the midst of taking over Syria, rewriting history, and reengineering the Syrian population.[68]

All of this is to further Iranian hegemony from Iran to the Mediterranean Sea and to surround Israel from all sides.

The Crescent and the Corridor—An Intolerable Threat to Israel

In January 2017, I published an article predicting that Iran would use the military capacity it was building in Syria against Israel under the excuse of "liberating the occupied Golan Heights."[69] My prediction quickly came true. In late February 2017, Akram al Ka'abi, the leader of the Iranian-backed Iraqi Shi'ite militia Harakat al-Nujaba, announced that the militia will operate in Syria to liberate the Golan Heights.[70]

Shi 'ite / Iranian Crescent and the Corridor—
An Intolerable Threat to Israel

Since then, Iranian officials have repeated that statement. For example, in October 2020, the then- chief of Iran's Judiciary Authority, Ebrahim Raisi Al-Sadati (now president of Iran), told Syria's ambassador to Iran that it supports the "resistance" to retake the Golan Heights from Israel.[71] In December 2020, then-Iranian President Hassan Rouhani said his country will continue to support Syria, urging Damascus to confront Israel in the Golan Heights.[72]

As I said earlier, in the section *Iran Escalates Its Aggression toward the Arab World and Israel*, in December 2017 and February 2018, the leaders of 'Asaib Ahl al-Haq and Harakat al-Nujaba, escorted by Lebanese Hezbollah militants—toured the Lebanese-Israel border. Overlooking Israel, brazenly disregarding UNSC resolutions, the leaders of the Iranian-backed Iraqi militias vowed that their militants would join Hezbollah in the battle to eliminate Israel.

Later that month, in February 2018, the Islamic Revolutionary Guards launched an assault drone from the Syrian side of the Golan Heights. That attack was a significant milestone because it was the first time that Iran directly attacked Israel militarily. All previous Iranian military attacks against Israel were carried out by Iranian proxies like Hezbollah in Lebanon, Hamas, or Islamic Jihad in Palestine in the Gaza Strip.

The Iranian corridor is an existential threat to the State of Israel. The sophisticated and widespread infrastructure I have just described to you, a 'noose' as I call it, will offer Tehran a contiguous platform to attack Israel. One can imagine the death toll and destruction that will occur when hundreds of thousands of rockets and heavy high-precision missiles rain down on Israeli cities and infrastructure.

Israel is determined to intercept the Iranian threat. The Israeli air force has attacked Iran's military infrastructure in Syria hundreds of times to disrupt Iran from completing this land bridge. As discussed previously, Israel is reportedly responsible for a series of attacks against the Iranian military Imam 'Ali military infrastructure near the Iraqi-Syrian border. And there are also reports that Israel has attacked Iranian installations located inside Iraq. And in Lebanon, it was also reported that Israel launched an attack on a Hezbollah stronghold in southern Beirut. This location stored components necessary to build high-precision missiles. Throughout 2021 Israel continued its attacks on sites and compounds in Syria suspected to be part of the Iranian-Hezbollah heavy and precise missiles infrastructure.

In May 2020, some Israeli intelligence sources evaluated that Iran was recalculating its entrenchment in Syria in response to increasing Israeli pressure. One Israeli intelligence official was quoted as saying, "The octopus is starting to fold its tentacles."[73] However, other analysts—including myself—argued it was premature to conclude that Iran will leave Syria any time soon.[74]

The reality on the ground as of August 2021 proves my skepticism was accurate. Iran continues to work toward expanding and securing the crescent and the land corridor. And accordingly, Israel continues its attacks to intercept Iran's military threat. One should expect the Israeli-Iranian standoff in Syria to continue—and consequently, the potential for escalation grows.

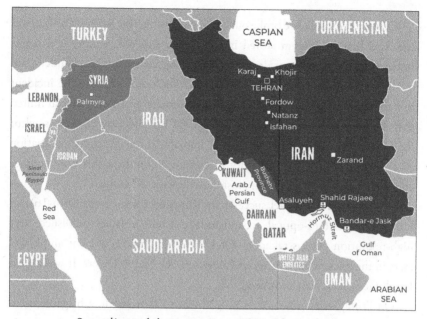

Sampling of the Locations of Incidents in the
Israel-Iran Shadow War (2020 and 2021)

Israel-Iran Shadow War

The growing Israeli-Iranian friction has extended into the shadows—assassinations, cyber-attacks, sabotage, as well as the waterways and naval routes throughout the Middle East.

On April 23, 2020, Israel reportedly intercepted a cyberattack that targeted Israel's water infrastructure. The Israel National Cyber Directorate (INCD) head said that the outcome could have been severe had Israel not thwarted the attack. Though he did not indicate who was behind it, reports attribute the cyberattack to Iran.

On May 18, 2020, the *Washington Post* reported that Israel was likely behind a hack that brought the "bustling Shahid Rajaee Port Terminal to an abrupt and inexplicable halt" on May 9, 2020.[75]

On June 26, 2020, an enormous blast occurred at the Khojir missile complex east of Tehran. The Iranian authorities attributed the explosion to a gas leak.

On July 2, 2020, a fire broke out at the Natanz nuclear facility. The Iranians admitted that equipment stored in the facility suffered significant damage. Apparently, the equipment destroyed was advanced centrifuges. Unidentified intelligence sources quoted on some media platforms attribute the incident to a massive Israeli cyberattack.[76] However, though an Iranian official hinted that the fire was caused by sabotage, Iran has not officially blamed Israel or the United States. In August 2020, the Iranian Atomic Energy Organization spokesperson stated that "Security investigations confirm this was sabotage and what is certain is that an explosion took place in Natanz."[77]

On July 6, 2020, Israel successfully launched Ofek-16 (or Ofeq-16), an Israeli-made electro-optical reconnaissance satellite. Israel published very high-resolution photos taken by Ofek-16 of the famous ancient amphitheaters in the ancient Syrian city of Palmyra in the Syrian Desert. It was a clear Israeli message to Iran and Assad.

On Friday, November 27, 2020, Mohsen Fakhrizadeh, a brigadier general in Iran's Islamic Revolutionary Guards Corps, Iran's top nuclear scientist, and the head of Iran's secret military nuclear program, was eliminated in Iran. Israeli Prime Minister Benjamin Netanyahu specifically named Mr. Fakhrizadeh in a briefing in April 2018 when Netanyahu unveiled the Iranian nuclear archives the Mossad had smuggled into Israel from Iran. Shortly after the assassination, Iranian Foreign Minister Javad Zarif tweeted that there was evidence linking Israel to the assassination. The *New York Times* also claimed that Israel was behind the assassination.[78] Israel and the United States remain silent on the matter. The assassination of Fakhrizadeh took place close to the anniversary of the assassination of Qasem Soleimani, commander of the al-Quds Force (January 3, 2020). The Islamic Revolutionary Guards vowed to avenge Fakhrizadeh's death. Iranian threats to take revenge met with US and Israeli signals that an Iranian attack will result in a military strike on Iran.

In 2021 there has seen a substantial uptick in incidents attributed to Israel and Iran's cyberwar.

In January, hackers linked to Hezbollah breached telecom companies, the Internet, and hosting service providers in many Middle Eastern and European countries, including Israel.

In February, hackers suspected of being Iranian targeted government agencies in the UAE as part of a cyber espionage campaign because of UAE normalizing relations with Israel.

In March, hackers suspected to be Iranians targeted government agencies, academia, and the tourism industry in Israel as part of a multi-nation cyber espionage campaign.

On April 11, there was a power failure at Iran's Natanz uranium enrichment site.

On May 7, a fire broke out in Bushehr in northwestern Iran, near Iran's only functioning nuclear power plant.

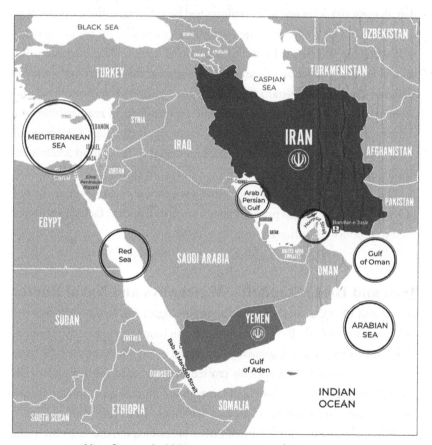

Key Strategic Waterways & Naval Routes—
Platforms for Attacks and Shadow Wars

On May 23, there was a blast at an Iranian plant that reportedly produces UAVs in Isfahan. On May 26, an explosion took place at a petrochemical complex in the city of Asaluyeh in southern Iran.

In June, the Iranian government launched a wide-scale disinformation campaign targeting WhatsApp groups, Telegram channels, and messaging apps in Israel. On June 2, there was a gas leak and a massive fire at an oil refinery in Tehran. On June 5, an explosion took place at the Zarand Iranian Steel Company in eastern Iran. On June 20, it was reported that Iran's sole nuclear power plant at Bushehr underwent an emergency shutdown that would last between three and four days. On June 23, Iran's Atomic Energy Agency said that an early attack on one of its facilities had been foiled, with no casualties or structural damage to the site. The agency's statement did not reveal the name of the site, but the targeted building was one of Iran's leading manufacturing centers for the production of the centrifuges used at the country's two nuclear facilities, Fordow and Natanz, according to a senior intelligence official and an Iranian familiar with the attack. While no one claimed responsibility, the centrifuge factory, known as the Iran Centrifuge Technology Company, or TESA, was on a list of targets that Israel presented to the Trump administration in early 2020.[79]

On July 5, a large fire was reported at a warehouse or factory near the city of Karaj, where an alleged previous attack targeted a nuclear facility reportedly used to produce centrifuges.

Iran and Israel Standoff—Waterways and Naval Routes

At the end of 2020, and again at the beginning of 2021, the United States sent assets to the Gulf. B-52 strategic American bombers appeared in the Gulf skies. An American attack submarine appeared in the waters of the Gulf. And an Israeli submarine also reportedly crossed the Red Sea in the direction of the Gulf. As tensions grew, at the end of December, a Houthi spokesperson threatened to attack Israeli targets in the Red Sea should Israel "act irresponsibly."[80]

But unfortunately, as we learned earlier in the chapter, the situation in the Red Sea and the waterways from the Gulf to the Mediterranean have been far from stable. For years, Iran and Israel have engaged in tit-for-tat attacks on each other's ships from the Hormuz Strait, the Gulf of Oman, the Red Sea, and the Eastern Mediterranean. Increasingly, these waterways have become another platform for the covert war between Iran and Israel.

The Red Sea is one of the routes through which Iran sends weapons to Gaza. Israel has more than once intercepted shipments of Iranian weapons.

The Israeli government acknowledges that since 2019 it has been conducting an ongoing campaign to counter Iranian arms flows and influence activities. Still, it has declined to confirm any specifics. The campaign aims to disrupt Iran's oil trade with Syria and intercept its arms shipments to its regional proxy forces.[81] Most of the ships Israel allegedly targeted were headed for Syria to deliver oil or were en-route to supply Iran's agents and proxies.

In 2021, several incidents have been recorded in these maritime arenas, including the Gulf of Oman, the Red Sea, and the Mediterranean Sea, where Iranian ships—including Iranian navy ships and Israeli-owned merchant ships—were damaged by explosions and mishaps apparently caused by deliberate attacks.

It is estimated that Iran has carried out about a dozen attacks on Israeli-owned ships. Israel has carried out dozens of attacks on Iranian ships. Naturally, neither Israel nor Iran claimed responsibility for the incidents.

Here is a glimpse of what has transpired so far in 2021.

On February 25, an Israeli-owned ship was damaged in an explosion in the Gulf of Oman.

On March 25, an Israeli-owned container ship was hit by an Iranian rocket in the Arabian Sea.

On April 6, an Iranian ship was damaged by landmines in the Red Sea. On April 13, an Israeli-owned ship was attacked next to the UAE. On April 24, an Iranian fuel tanker was reportedly attacked off the Syrian coast.

On May 9, an explosion occurred on an oil tanker off the coast of Syria.

On June 2, Iran's largest navy ship, the *IRIS Kharg*, sank after catching fire in the Gulf of Oman near the Port of Jask.

On July 3, a previously Israeli-owned commercial ship was attacked in the northern Indian Ocean. On July 29, a Japanese-owned commercial vessel, managed by an Israeli company, was attacked in the Gulf of Oman. The attack that was carried out by assault drones killed two crewmen, a British national and Romanian national.

Israel and Iran on Their Way to a Direct Military Collision?

Most senior Iranian leaders, including Supreme Leader 'Ali Khamenei, repeatedly vow to eliminate Israel.[82]

From Israel's perspective, the most severe threats to Israel's existence are: Iran achieving nuclear military capabilities and Iran completing a 'noose' of missiles and rockets around Israel's neck by securing its military infrastructure in Syria and completing the land corridor.

Therefore, it is not surprising that Israel has demonstrated, in word and deed, that the state will do whatever it takes to prevent Iran from achieving those goals.

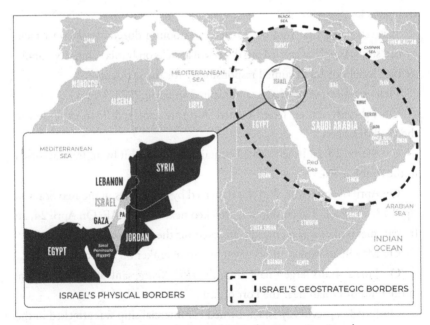

Israel's Physical Borders and Israel's Security Borders—
The "Battle Between the Wars"

In a speech he delivered on January 26, 2021, Israel Defense Forces Chief-of-Staff Lieutenant-General Aviv Kochavi said he ordered the IDF to prepare operational plans to address the Iranian threat of a nuclear weapon.[83]

One cornerstone of Israel's security strategy is a policy called 'the battle between the wars.' The purpose of this policy is to minimize the chances of an all-out war. The 'battle between the wars' is a multipronged approach that combines Israeli diplomatic, intelligence, and military actions and initiatives. These activities have two primary objectives. One is to neutralize and prevent developing threats against Israel. Another is to set national security red lines. Lines Israel will not allow anyone to cross because, in Israel's view, crossing those lines will be a *casus belli*. The second cornerstone of Israel's national security policy is defining the arenas that might be geographically distant from Israel but are legitimate and sometimes critical for implementing the 'battle between the wars' strategy.

Israel's physical borders are Lebanon in the north, Syria in the northeast, Jordan in the east, and Egypt and Gaza in the southwest.

However, in terms of Israel's national security, Israel's geopolitical borders do not physically border Israel and are sometimes thousands of miles away.

Thus, Israel's northern geopolitical border is Turkey. Its eastern border is Iran. Its southern border is Yemen. And its western border is North Africa.

As far as Israel is concerned, the areas stretching beyond its physical borders are legitimate territories to wage the 'battle between the wars.' Because what happens in those areas has a direct impact on Israel's security. Therefore, they are part and parcel of Israel's national security doctrine.

Given the severity of the threat, Israel is willing to risk an all-out total war to prevent Iran from building a nuclear weapon and completing the corridor. Such a battle, should it take place, will likely not be confined to the Syrian-Israeli arena. A fight between Israel and Iran and its proxies that begins in Syria may expand to other areas of the region—including remote theaters such as the Red Sea or the Gulf.

A conflict of this magnitude will inflict massive destruction and will result in powerful aftershocks.

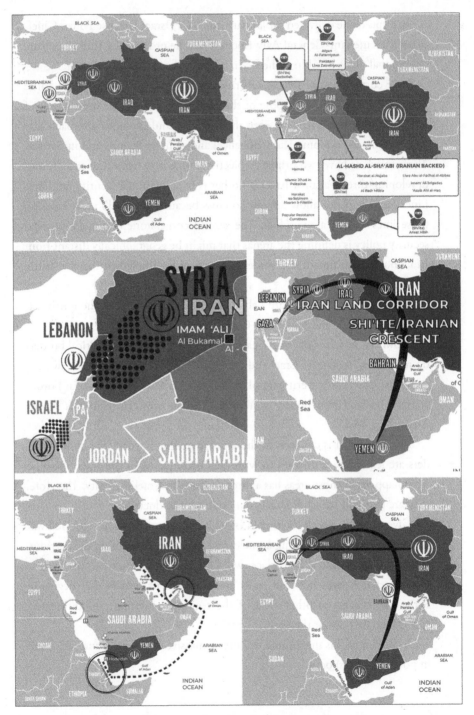

Summary Iranian Achievements

World leaders must understand that what happens in the Middle East does not stay in the Middle East. World leaders should make it a priority to:

- Prevent Iran from acquiring military nuclear capabilities.
- Prevent Iran from holding the most sensitive and strategic waterways on the planet hostage to Tehran and its proxies.
- Prevent Iran from permanently entrenching itself in Syria.
- Prevent Tehran from realizing its vision of a land corridor from Iran to the Mediterranean Sea.

What Does the Future Hold for Iran's Hegemonic Vision?

Iran's quest to be the regional superpower has inflicted death and destruction across the Middle East. For decades Iran has gladly sacrificed Afghans, Iraqis, Israelis, Lebanese, Palestinians, Syrians, Yemenites, and others on the altar of its hegemonic ambitions.

Iran's expansion policy, which is primarily dependent on agents, allies, proxies, its drone and missile programs, its nuclear program, and using the concept of al-Muqawama w'al Muman'aah, the resistance and defiance, has been a good strategy for Tehran. It has allowed the regime to gain power and wield influence. While, at the same time, Iranian leaders stay safely at home— far away from the death, destruction, and havoc that result from its determination for regional hegemony.

However, five things may be able to curb or prevent Iran from realizing its hegemonic dream.

- Growing challenges inside Iran.
- The Achilles heel of Iran's agent-proxy model.
- The fact that Iran's aggressive policies have resulted in the strengthening of nationalism and patriotism in Iraq, Lebanon, and Syria.
- The emerging counter alliances to block Iranian ambitions.
- The rise of the new power in the Middle East—China.

Growing Challenges inside Iran

One factor is the domestic situation inside Iran.

The enormous hardships of the Iranian people are causing increasing unrest. In mid-November 2019, a wave of public demonstrations spread throughout almost all of Iran's cities.

The reasons for the protests were Iran's crumbling economy, growing inflation, high unemployment, and rampant and systemic corruption. The Iranian people demanded that the billions of dollars their government allocates to arm and finance their agents, proxies, and militias in the Middle East instead be used at home to meet the needs of the Iranian people. The Iranian people are screaming, "We will die for Iran—not for Lebanon, Palestine, or Iraq."

There are two unique aspects of the November 2019 protests in Iran that I want to emphasize.

In November 2019, the Iranian protesters confronted the regime's oppressive Basij Resistance Force, who brutally and mercilessly squashed the 2009 protests. The fact that the protesters in 2019 were willing to confront the Basij indicated that the barrier of fear was breached. Another unique aspect was that the 2019 demonstrations were widespread and included practically all of Iran's cities. Protesters attacked and burned government facilities, banks, gas stations, and police stations and blocked roads. In response, the regime fiercely suppressed the protests. Hundreds (according to reports by the Iranian opposition, more than a thousand) of protesters were killed, thousands were wounded, and thousands were arrested. It is evident that the flames are there and that the unrest within Iran deepens. Most Iranians are young—the median age is thirty-two.[84] And the young generation demands to be released from the iron grip of the oppressive mullah regime.

Another interesting aspect of the 2019 protests were reports that among the protesters were young mullahs.[85] If this is true, the Iranian clergy's participation in demonstrations is not insignificant. The young mullahs are part of society. They are in tune with the people's hardships—who are often their own families and relatives. Growing criticism of the regime within the ranks of the young generation of mullahs is a process that could present a growing challenge to the government.

Elections to the Iranian Parliament were held in Iran in February 2020. The results illustrated two trends. First, the Iranian public does not trust the regime. Reportedly, about 42 percent of eligible voters participated in the election. Even if that number is accurate—and there is reason to doubt that it is the actual number—it is the lowest voter turnout since 1979. The low voter turnout reflects the lack of people's trust. Second, the IRG and the ultraconservative stream won in a landslide. Following the elections, they control 221 seats out of 290. The reformist wing—incorrectly described in the West as "moderate"—dropped from 121 seats in the 2016 elections to only nineteen seats in February's election. The drop is staggering. As a result of the February 2020 elections, the IRG and the ultraconservative groups tightened their grip on Iran and the Iranians.

In June 2021, Ebrahim Raisi Al-Sadati was elected president of Iran (he took office in August) in a "pre-determined" election. In response to his election, the US State Department spokesman, Ned Price, said the "US considers the election process to be pretty manufactured. This was not a free and fair election."[86] Raisi (born in 1960) is associated with the ultra-extremist current in Iran. He chaired the Judiciary Authority in Iran from March 2019 until he was elected president. He was also a member of a notorious four-member committee known as "The Death Committee"—an entity that sent thousands of Iranians to their deaths on charges of subversion against the regime. Raisi was also actively involved in the brutal oppression of the public protests in Iran in 2019. The United States imposed personal sanctions on Raisi for his actions. Given his background and following his election as president, Amnesty International said that Raisi must be investigated for crimes against humanity.[87]

The results of the 2020 elections increased the grip, power, and reach of the IRG and the ultraconservative wing. The 2020 elections, compounded by the 2021 victory of the ultraconservative Raisi, does not bode well for the Iranian people or the region.

The Iranian government oppresses its citizens and sacrifices their welfare for the mullah regime's aspirations of regional hegemony.

Another major factor that could spark wide-scale riots in Iran has to do with the environment—namely, the water crisis. Iran is drying up. The country is facing a severe water emergency. Eighty-five percent of Iran is arid or semi-arid. Reportedly, 97 percent of Iranians are struggling with a lack of water. Agriculture is crumbling, resulting in substantial migration waves inside Iran. Thirty percent of the people in Iran's second-largest province, Sistan-Baluchestan in southwestern Iran on the Gulf coast next to Afghanistan, have migrated to the cities.[88] The crisis is deepening, and accordingly, the anger and public outrage are intensifying. In July 2021, the water shortage ignited massive and violent riots in the district of Khuzestan in southwestern Iran. The protests echoed in Tehran as well. The regime sent IRG forces to restore control in Khuzestan in southern Iran. (We will talk more about Sistan-Baluchestan and Khuzestan in Chapter 11.)

These events combined with a very harsh socio-economic reality are enough to ignite a massive explosion in Iran. History teaches us that economic and social distress can lead to a tremendous eruption and a great fire.

The Achilles Heel of Iran's Agent-Proxy Model

A second factor that could disrupt Iran's modus operandi is that the agent-proxy model has an inherent weakness that could compromise Iran's ability to use its relationship with its agents and proxies to further its objectives.

The first weakness is that some of Iran's most powerful militias, including Hezbollah in Lebanon and the pro-Iranian Shi'ite militias in Iraq, have complicated relationships with the political entities in the countries in which they operate. And sometimes, the mullah regime's subcontractors prioritize domestic interests over Iranian interests.

In December 2020, when asked if he thought Iran would ask Hezbollah to avenge the killing of Soleimani or Fakhrizade, the secretary-general of Hezbollah in Lebanon, Hassan Nasrallah, said the revenge "is a matter for the Iranians to take care of."[89] Nasrallah did not want to execute the revenge because Lebanon is on the edge of a cliff. Should Hezbollah attack Israel, it risks a total war that would push Lebanon—and Hezbollah—over the edge. That was also the reason Hezbollah stayed out of the Hamas-Israel war in May 2021. (We will explore the war in Chapters 9 and 10.)

The multiple calculations and loyalties Iranian sub-contractors juggle were evident in Hamas senior leader Khaled Mashal's interview with the Saudi-owned *Al-Arabiya* news network following the May 2021 war. On the one hand, Mashal thanked his patron Iran for its support in supplying Hamas with weapons and missiles. However, he said that Hamas does not agree with the Iranian regional and international policy.[90]

The second flaw in the agent-proxy model is that it can cause tension among and between Iran's agents and proxies. This inner friction could weaken the power of the model that has been so successful for Tehran. Iraq is an excellent example of this.

As we learned earlier in this chapter, one of the major fault lines in Iraq is between Iraqi Shi'ite nationalists who believe that Iraq should be an independent Arab country. And Iraqi Shi'ite non-nationalists who want Iraq to be under Iran's umbrella. We also learned that the Iranian-backed Iraqi Shi'ite militias that Iran has created or cultivated have become one of Iran's most productive assets. And these militias play a significant role in Iraqi politics. I also mentioned that these forces are part of a formal Iraqi military structure that functions in parallel to the Iraqi armed forces, known as Al-Hashd Al-Sha'abi—the Popular Mobilization Units (PMU).

Some of the Shi'ite militias that make up Al-Hashd Al-Sha'abi (the PMU) are Iraqi nationalists, who want an independent Iraq, and some are loyal to Iran. This reality is naturally a source of multiple tensions. The duality of being both an Iraqi Arab and a Shi'ite Iraqi affiliated with Iran has a price. The Iranian-backed Iraqi militias sometimes find themselves in conflict with their own surroundings, including relatives. This multifaceted reality results in growing tensions within the ranks of the Iranian-affiliated Iraqi Shi'ite militias, which might compromise their effectiveness.

The Gaza Strip is also an excellent example that demonstrates the tension between Iranian subcontractors that can compromise the efficacy of the agent-proxy model. The two major forces in Gaza are Hamas and Islamic Jihad in Palestine.

Hamas has two meanings; the English translation is "zeal," but Hamas is the acronym for *Harakat al-Muqawama al-Islamia* or "The Islamic Resistance Movement."

Islamic Jihad in Palestine, *Harakat al-Jihād al-Islāmi fi Filastīn* is also known as IJIP or PIJ.

Both have a close relationship with Iran. Both Hamas and IJIP are members of the resistance axis. They both vow to eliminate Israel and are committed to using violence to destroy Israel.

Though traditionally, the two cooperate militarily, a difference between the two Palestinian groups sometimes overshadows their military cooperation and even raises the tensions between Gaza's two most powerful entities.

It is important to remember that Hamas governs the Gaza Strip. And as the Gaza government, Hamas has a responsibility to the 1.8 million Gazans that live there. Hamas has a broad and solid political power base in Gaza. One reason is that hundreds of thousands of people in Gaza benefit from Hamas's rule or are on the Hamas payroll. Examples are business people, government employees, judges, militants, military personnel, police and security services, teachers, and their families. Though they may identify with Hamas's militant way, Hamas's supporters expect Hamas to prioritize their interests over its militant agenda. Unlike Hamas, IJIP is not the government in Gaza, and it has no governmental responsibilities that it must consider. IJIP military action is not subdued to calculations of governmental accountability. IJIP has a core, dogmatic loyal political power base in Gaza that blindly supports the IJIP militant path.

This difference in agenda and priorities creates tension between Hamas and IJIP—the two most powerful forces in Gaza.

Here is an example of how that plays out: Hamas and IJIP have a joint operational headquarters to coordinate their attacks against Israel. However, throughout 2019, IJIP launched rockets and missiles on Israel without coordinating with Hamas beforehand. Hamas was neither interested in nor positioned to be engaged in a comprehensive military confrontation with Israel. Those attacks, however, threatened to drag Hamas into a war with Israel. Though the two organizations' differing priorities cause frictions between them from time to time, it is not likely to result in a massive direct collision between them. However, it can compromise Iran's ability to turn the conflict on and off at its will.

Iran's Hegemonic Vision Triggers a Counter Reaction of Arab Particular Nationalist Identity

The third factor that could limit Iran's hegemonic vision is that one of the responses to Iran's increasing hegemony is a strengthening particular nationalist identity.

This phenomenon is ironic because one of the causes of instability in the Middle East is the fact that the model of the nation-state in the Arab world has failed or faces severe challenges. And the reason for this is that ethnicity, geography, religion, sectarianism, and tribalism were more central to people's individual and collective identity than their connection to their "country" and their compatriots. In other words, traditional affiliations were more powerful than particularistic nationalism.

Iran understood this and has deliberately and strategically taken advantage of the states' failures to expand its influence and power. This is one of the cornerstones of Iran's expansionist strategy. Identify the struggling countries—the weaker and more chaotic the country is, the better. Instability makes it easier for Iran to gain allies, control and ultimately highjack the country or territory to advance Tehran's agenda.

By capitalizing on and creating instability, Iran has secured a foothold in Gaza, controls Lebanon, occupies parts of Syria, and maintains significant influence in Iraq and Yemen.

However, one of the results of Iran spreading its influence throughout the region and tightening its grip in pursuit of its own hegemonic ambitions has been strengthening a previously absent sense of national identity in the areas under its control.

Here is an example of what I mean.

During the fall of 2019, ongoing evolving public unrest evolved into mass protests in Lebanon and Iraq. In Lebanon, a common refrain was "we are Lebanese, not Iranian." Iraqis chanted "*Baghdad Hurra Hurra, Iran Barra Barra*," meaning "Baghdad free—Iran out." These sentiments are gaining traction and are widely expressed daily in the public discourse of the Arab world.

In an October 2019 article titled "The Slogan 'Iran Get Out' is the Next Stage," Bahraini liberal intellectual Sawsan al-Shaer wrote, "Sooner or later, Beirut, Damascus, Baghdad, and Sana'a will kick out Iran. The Arab traitors who sold their homeland to Iran are facing a dark fate. Their punishment will be a lesson for the next generations."[91]

In February 2020, Iraqi commentator Farouk Yousef penned a piece he called "Iran is a Cancer that Should be Eradicated, Not Dialogued With." Here is an excerpt: "Iran provides its servants in Iraq, Lebanon, and Yemen

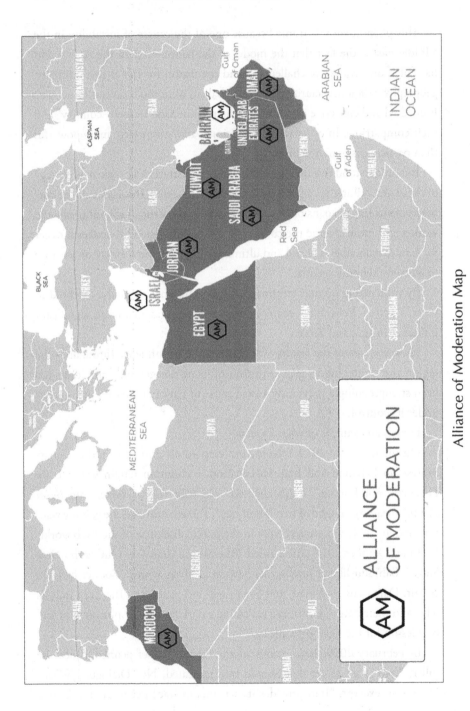

Alliance of Moderation Map

with nothing but explosives. Turning youth of these countries into landmines. And if they occupy high positions in a country, which is what is actually taking place in Iraq, then that country will be at risk of explosion."[92]

Some Middle East analysts argue that the Lebanese, Syrian, and Iraqi rejection of Iran's hegemonic plan will fuel opposition inside Iran to the mullah regime and eventually lead to the failure of Iran's hegemonic vision and possibly lead to the regime's collapse.[93]

In April 2021, Moroccan commentator Ali Anuzla wrote an article he called "Iran's Gain and Arab Losses." Iran, he maintains, "has defeated the Arabs in all aspects . . . the Iranian regime cleverly echoes the slogan of external enemies—Israel and the United States—to solidify its iron grip on the Iranian people . . . But what will destroy Iran is the inner conflict between the Iranian regime's deep state system and the Iranian society. No matter how long it takes, the day will come when the internal explosion occurs, just as it happened in the Soviet Union after seventy-four years of the complete control of the Soviet ideological machine over all the outlets of life in the most powerful military empire."[94]

I should note that this outlook is not new. And it is quite common in Arab media. As of 2021, however, it reflects mostly wishful thinking.

The Alliance of Moderation

A fourth factor that could block Iran's hegemonic vision is an entity that was born to a large extent for that exact purpose. It is a regional alliance I have described as the "Alliance of Moderation." The alliance of moderation is a coalition—including significant regional powers—that has evolved over the past decade around shared strategic interests, which are, above all, blocking Iran and its proxies. The coalition members (in alphabetical order) are Bahrain, Egypt, Jordan, Kuwait, Morocco, Oman, Saudi Arabia, and the United Arab Emirates (UAE). In essence, the alliance's primary goal is stability within their individual countries and stability throughout the region. And there is another silent yet significant member of this coalition. And that is Israel.

The alliance of moderation was the precursor to the Abraham Accords—a groundbreaking set of peace and normalization agreements signed between Israel and the UAE, Bahrain, Sudan, and Morocco. (We will delve into the alliance of moderation and the Abraham Accords in Chapter 8.)

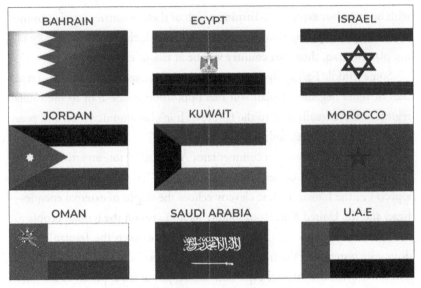

Flags of Alliance of Moderation

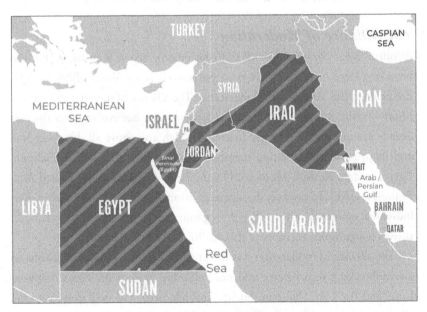

Egypt-Jordan-Iraq Alliance

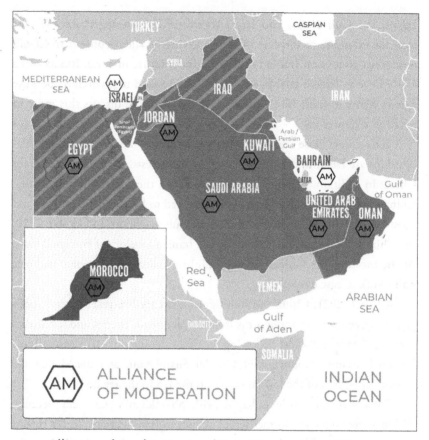

Alliance of Moderation and Egypt-Jordan-Iraq Alliance

And there is another potential coalition evolving—one that consists of Egypt, Iraq, and Jordan. Some analysts view this emerging alliance as a partnership aiming, among other common objectives, to thwart or block the Iranian attempt to expand its influence in those specific countries and surrounding territories.

China

And finally, the fifth factor that could compromise Iran's hegemonic ambitions is the growing engagement of China and Russia in the region.

Although both China and Russia enjoy close relations with Iran, they are very tuned to the acute concern of critical regional players such as

Egypt, the Gulf states, and Israel regarding Iranian aggression. We see this, for example, in the case of Russia giving its silent consent to Israel's numerous attacks on Iranian military infrastructure in Syria. Russia turns a blind eye to Israel's attacks on Iranian proxies and bases in Syria because Russia wants to limit Iran's influence in Syria. (I will discuss this more in detail in Chapter 6.)

China enjoys close relations with the Arab Gulf monarchies. These relationships are based upon long-term strategic interests. Arab oil is crucial for China. In addition, Beijing is deeply invested in the Arab Gulf monarchies. China sends clear signals to Iran about the need to build a more positive and good-neighborly relationship with its Arab Gulf neighbors. In October 2020, the Chinese foreign minister met with the Iranian minister of Foreign Affairs. At the meeting, the Chinese foreign minister called for a regional dialogue framework to ease tensions.[95]

In March 2021, China and Iran signed a twenty-five-year strategic cooperation agreement in various areas from development, energy, and infrastructure to military and trade. Following the deal's signing, the chairman of Iran's National Security Council (SNSC), 'Ali Shamkhani, announced that the agreement is "part of the resistance axis to the US in the region."

China was apparently unhappy with Shamkhani's statement because, within a few hours, the former senior adviser to Iran's supreme leader rushed to announce that "China is not interested in resistance but rather looking for its own interests."[96]

The Chinese message is clear. China's involvement in the Middle East is deepening. (We will explore this further in Chapter 14.) And China's global hegemonic vision requires stability. Iranian aggression produces instability, and that compromises China's interests. Therefore, if necessary, China will restrain Iran. And China has the tools and the power to do so.

These five factors: growing challenges inside Iran; the Achilles heel of the agent-proxy model; strengthening of particular nationalist identity; emerging and evolving regional alliances including the Alliance of Moderation, the Abraham Accords and the emerging coalition between Egypt, Iraq, and Jordan; and China are the significant factors presenting the Iranian mullah regime significant obstacles on its path to hegemony.

But, on the other hand, Iran's hegemonic vision has increasing support from a somewhat less expected direction.

Western Circles Protect the Mullah Regime

Some circles in the West believe Iran's aggression is because the United States withdrew from the JCPOA. But the opposite is true.

The withdrawal of former President Donald Trump from the agreement in May 2018 and the heavy economic sanctions on Iran are *because* of Iran's aggression and deception following the signing of the JCPOA.

I hope that in this chapter, I have adequately demonstrated Iran's growing aggression after signing the 2015 JCPOA.

From the most sensitive maritime arenas on the globe to the Shi'ite Crescent and the Iranian Corridor, instead of becoming a more reasonable country that contributes to stability in the Middle East, Iran ratcheted up its activities and continues to prove that it will do everything in its power to expand its control and sacrifice anyone necessary to achieve its own ambitions of exporting and expanding the Islamic Revolution and securing itself as the dominant superpower in the Middle East.

The mullah regime is a brutal, cynical, dangerous, sophisticated, and violent regime. The regime despises the West and every democratic value the West holds dear. Particularly progressive values.

Ibtihal al-Khatib, a Kuwaiti academic, journalist, and prominent advocate of secular liberal values in Arab society, observes in her August 2021 article, "Smile to the Camera," that the mullah regime is entirely male—women are out.[97]

The question then ultimately needs to be: Why is it that, unfortunately, and oddly, it is none other than the democratic and progressive circles in the United States and Europe that insist on protecting and supporting the regime?

The European Union looks for ways to bypass and alleviate US sanctions on Iran. Federica Mogherini, the European Union representative of the Union for Foreign Affairs and Security Policy (2015–2019), and one of the foremost advocates of the JCPOA, continues to side with Tehran even though the regime increases its aggression and its expansionist policy across the Middle

East and in Europe, and even though the government brutally violates human and civil rights in Iran against its own people.

The current United States deputy secretary of state, Wendy Sherman, was the undersecretary of state for Political Affairs when she was one of the chief negotiators that penned the JCPOA. In July 2018, Ms. Sherman said that "President Trump does not understand that Iran has a culture of resistance that equates giving in to those kinds of public threats as surrender, and they won't surrender."[98] I conclude from her observation that, unfortunately, one of the key US negotiators with Iran, who currently holds one of the most senior United States' policy positions, does not fully understand the meaning of the term 'resistance' and 'the axis of resistance.'

I cannot avoid the impression that Ms. Sherman expresses a very puzzling oblivion toward Iran's aggression in the region, which is profoundly alarming and disconcerting.

Continuing Secretary Sherman's line, some argue that pressuring Iran will strengthen the hardliners and lead to war. Barbara Slavin, the director of the Future of Iran Initiative at the Atlantic Council, echoes that argument. In an April 23, 2020, article titled "How the US Military Should Leave Iraq," she wrote:

> This author (herself) has argued elsewhere that the decision to kill Soleimani and Muhandis was an overreaction to Iranian provocations ... Ideally, the United States should re-examine its policy of "maximum pressure" towards Iran, which has not and will not achieve its stated goals. Iran is more, not less, aggressive in the region, continuing its development of ballistic missiles—including its first successful satellite launch—and has accelerated its nuclear program. More pressure will either lead to war, strengthen Iranian hardliners, or both. The United States could use the pandemic as an opportunity to make goodwill gestures toward Iran.[99]

I want to take this opportunity to contextualize her comment about Soleimani. On January 3, 2020, the United States eliminated the al-Quds Force commander, Major-General Qasem Soleimani. General Soleimani was the spearhead of Iranian aggression. In January 2021, there was a conference commemorating the one-year anniversary of Soleimani's death. Advisor to the supreme leader of the Islamic Revolution, Major-General Yahya Rahim-Safavi, said the following: "In Soleimani's life, he established twenty-two brigades of Shi'ite militants in Iraq (he provided no figures regarding the number of the Iraqi-based militants) and sixty brigades in Syria with 70,000 militants."[100] The blood of hundreds of thousands of people—Iraqis, Israelis, Lebanese, Palestinians, Saudis, Syrians, Yemenites, Jews, Christians, Sunnis, and Shi'ites in the region—was on his hands.

In another interview, Ms. Slavin said, "After the Joint Comprehensive Plan of Action (JCPOA) was reached, we optimistically thought that there was going to be a change in US-Iran relations. We believed that Iran would integrate with the international community . . . Needless to say, things changed when President Trump was elected, and he announced that he was going to leave the JCPOA in 2018."[101] In the same interview, when asked about the Trump legacy on US-Iran relations, she answered: "It is clearly not easy on the Iranian side after what they have been put through. Remember, they were essentially punished for reaching an agreement with the Obama administration. They were in full compliance with this agreement when President Trump scrapped it. The situation sends a very bad message that is certainly helping anti-US elements in the country who may very well take the Presidency in the elections this year. So, there may still be unforeseen consequences that will play out this year."[102]

Unfortunately, Ms. Slavin very conveniently prefers to ignore the facts presented in this book that clearly demonstrate that Iran increased its aggression and continued to deny IAEA access to its nuclear program and sites *before* former President Trump withdrew from the JCPOA.

Slavin's observation that "more pressure will either lead to war, strengthen Iranian hardliners, or both," or that "US actions are responsible for anti-US candidates winning the Iranian elections" is disturbingly misguided and demonstrates a startling and concerning misunderstanding of the mullah regime in Iran. From its inception and at its core, the Iranian mullah regime is an extreme, hardline regime. Furthermore, a cornerstone of Iran's foreign policy is expanding its control and becoming the regional superpower. Violence is one of the primary tools Iran uses to achieve its goals.

Ms. Slavin seems to be determined to paint a picture that portrays Iran's aggression as an outcome of US actions and sanctions.

Yet, the reality is the other way around. The increasing Iranian aggression following the signing of the JCPOA led the United States to withdraw from the agreement. The facts and the chronological timeline decisively speak for themselves. Iran's aggression is not the outcome of the sanctions. Iranian aggression is the *reason* for the sanctions.

Some Western leaders suggested the United States could use the COVID-19 pandemic as an opportunity to make some 'goodwill gestures' to Tehran. On March 26, 2020, eleven US Democratic senators wrote to US Secretary of State Mike Pompeo and Treasury Secretary Steven Mnuchin requesting that the Trump administration suspend sanctions on Iran and Venezuela. In their letter, they argue that "US sanctions are hindering the free flow of desperately needed medical and humanitarian supplies." They also argue that sanctions have "exacerbated the failing medical responses" and are increasing "anti-Americanism that is at the heart of both regimes' hold on power."[103]

I would like to question those who call for more Western goodwill gestures toward Iran. First of all, I cannot understand the argument that not giving Iran financial aid to confront COVID-19 results in "increasing anti-American sentiments." Are lawmakers unaware that since the mullah regime came to power in 1979, the government has referred to the United States as "the Big Satan" and Israel as "the Little Satan" and that they vow "death to America" and "death to Israel"? US and Israeli flags are burned in Iran's streets during mass ceremonies orchestrated and organized by the mullah regime. In September 2015, a few months after signing the JCPOA, Major General Mohammed 'Ali Jafari, who was then the commander of the IRGC, warned that America was still the "same Great Satan despite the nuclear deal."[104] Furthermore, while Washington was considering sending money to Tehran to help the regime, here is what was happening on the ground.

Throughout 2020 and 2021, as COVID-19 was spreading in Iran at a terrifying pace and the number of infected and dying Iranians soared, the mullah regime did not allocate funds to help the Iranian people to face the disease. The mullah regime was busy developing more weapons.

In April 2020, the IRG launched a military satellite. This was not Iran's first launch, but it was the first IRG launch and the first launch of a military satellite. The Noor-1 (Light) satellite was launched from an IRG base and unveiled Iran's EastMed military space program. This is significant because it was the first launch by the IRG instead of the Iran Space Agency (ISA). This was also the first time Iran had successfully used a three-stage rocket. Hossein Salami, the IRGC commander, called the launch a "leap" in Iran's space capabilities. "The world's powerful armies do not have a comprehensive defense plan without being in space," he said. "Achieving this superior technology that takes us into space and expands the realm of our abilities is a strategic achievement."[105]

In May 2020, the IRGC Navy received 112 new patrol and missile attack crafts from the Defense and Armed Forces Logistics Ministry.[106]

In June 2020, the Iranians introduced what they claim was a new cruise missile by test-firing missiles in a naval exercise in the Gulf of Oman and the northern Indian Ocean.[107]

In July 2020, the Islamic Revolutionary Guard Corps Navy (IRGCN) and Aerospace Force kicked off Iran's fourteenth Great Prophet naval drills (GP-14) by firing ballistic and anti-ship missiles and staging a swarm attack against a mockup of an American aircraft carrier (the USS *Nimitz*). Some of the ballistic missiles were fired into Persian Gulf waters in the general direction of two regional airbases with significant coalition military presence: al-Udeid in Qatar and al-Dhafra in the United Arab Emirates.[108]

In July 2020, the IRG announced it had built underground "missile cities" along the Gulf coastline, warning of a "nightmare for Iran's enemies."

In August 2020, Iran held its annual "Defense Industry Day." Iran showcased its progress on longer-range, more-versatile ballistic missiles, long-range cruise missiles, and high-performance jet engines.[109]

In January 2021, the IRG unveiled a massive underground missile base. It tested long-range missiles that it said could take out enemy vessels and aircraft carriers more than 1,800 km (1,118 miles) away.[110]

It was also in May 2021 that, as I mentioned earlier, IAEA Director General Rafael Grossi said, "A country enriching at sixty percent is a severe thing—only countries making bombs are reaching this level."[111]

In June 2021, the Islamic Revolutionary Guards unveiled an underground missile base at an undisclosed location in the Gulf. IRG commander, Major General Hossein Salami, is quoted as saying, "The base is one of several bases housing the Guards' Navy's strategic missiles. These missiles have ranges of hundreds of kilometers, enjoy pinpoint accuracy and huge destructive power, and can overcome the enemy's electronic warfare equipment." In the same month, Salami said Iran has crewless aerial vehicles with an extended range of 7,000 kilometers.[112]

In July 2021, the IRG unveiled new precision-guided missiles and various long-range combat and surveillance drones and upgraded anti-tank missiles capable of destroying stationary and moving targets within a range of ten kilometers using thermal and laser detectors. It added several combat helicopters equipped with Iranian-made Qaem-114 missiles to its arsenal. It received high-powered bombs and various types of artillery.[113]

Meanwhile, in August 2021, only 3.34 percent of the Iranian public has been vaccinated. There are currently 843,751 new cases in August, which is a record high since the pandemic began. The last record high was in July 2021, in which Iran officially recorded 666,451 new cases. So far in August, Iran has reported that 8,909 people have died. The highest death toll recorded from COVID-19 in Iran was in November 2020—13,382 people. So far, the official records show 94,603 people have died in Iran since the beginning of the pandemic.[114] I stress those are official numbers—various experts, government officials, and opposition leaders doubt the veracity of these numbers and estimate the numbers could exceed a half-million people.[115]

The Islamic Revolutionary Guards is an arm of the regime and the wealthiest and most powerful entity in Iran—some even say it is the most powerful entity in Iran period. The IRG controls Iran's aviation, oil, shipping, and transportation industries. The IRG manages Iran's legal and illegal international trade, including operating a global narcotics empire; it has created dozens of companies to smuggle oil and other resources. And all the money goes back to the IRG's budget. The IRG-owned company, Khatam al-Anbiya, established as the IRG's arm in the construction sector, currently controls 812 officially registered Iranian companies with some 1,700 governmental contracts. Another IRG-owned company has also recently bought a 51 percent stake in the Telecommunications Company of Iran that was privatized at a $5 billion value.[116] The Revolutionary Guards use an Iranian banking system called NIMA to acquire and transfer millions of dollars to fund their militias across the Middle East.[117]

In January 2021, IRG Brigadier General Mohamed Rida Naqdi announced that the IRG has spent a total of $17 billion on "defensive and cultural missions in the Middle East."[118] I hope that by now, you understand that the terms 'defensive and cultural missions' are the code name for arming and funding armies of terror and death in the region. I highly doubt the accuracy of these figures. Sources I evaluate as accurate and reliable report that the mullah regime spends upwards of $16 billion a year to fund its agents and proxies.[119] One explanation for the significant gap is that it does not serve the regime to disclose its actual investments in its armies of terror. The Iranian people are furious and resentful that their government funds their hegemonic ambitions while the Iranian people sink into poverty and despair.

In January 2021, the IRG unveiled a sprawling, underground missile base, tested long-range missiles.

Speaking at an event of the Iranian American Community in July 2018, then-Secretary of State Mike Pompeo said, "And not many people know this, but Ayatollah Khamenei has his own personal, off-the-books hedge fund called the Setad, worth $95 billion, with a B."[120]

So, given all these facts and figures, one must wonder: Why do Western countries, international organizations, and Western taxpayers need to pay for the well-being of the Iranian people who are neglected and oppressed by their own government, which is busy pouring billions of dollars into advancing its nuclear program, shoring up its military capabilities, arming and funding terror armies across the Middle East, and developing cross-continental missiles that jeopardize Western interests, global stability, and target the West itself?

A Word About Sanctions and Trump's Iran Policy

Former US President Donald Trump (2016–2020) conducted a very different Iranian policy than President Barack Obama (2008–2016). The Trump administration—rightly so—identified the Iranian mullah regime as a severe threat to the United States and the region and accordingly applied tough sanctions on Iran. This policy reflects the simple truth: You do not dialogue with thugs, and you do not—time and time again—offer them "goodwill gestures."

Instead, you make them understand that their bullying has severe ramifications that will hurt them. Trump's policy vis-à-vis the Iranian threat was welcomed by the United States' main allies in the Middle East—Egypt, the Gulf States, Israel, Jordan, and Saudi Arabia. Yet, Western leaders refused to back the Trump administration's efforts to restrain Iran.

Critics of Trumps' "Maximum Pressure" policy toward Iran—focusing on increasing sanctions—argue that it failed. Iran did not come back to the negotiating table, and they further breached the JCPOA. These are accurate arguments.

However, this is not the whole picture. I maintain that Trump's strategy was correct.

The maximum pressure policy did damage the operational capability of Iran's armies of terror. As a result of the sanctions, Iran had to reduce its allocation to finance its proxies. For example, Iran reportedly had to half its annual support of Hezbollah from $700 million to $350 million.[121] Hezbollah's leader, Hassan Nasrallah, has increasingly emphasized that Hezbollah suffers an acute financial crisis. The decreased Iranian support forced Hezbollah to decide what to fund, which compromises Hezbollah's operational capacities.[122]

The sanctions on Iran severely damaged Iran's economy. However, resolutely determined to achieve its objective, the mullah regime sacrifices its citizens on the altar of its hegemonic vision.

In this chapter, we have looked at Iran's armies of terror and destruction. The militias and the tens of thousands of militants well beyond Iran's borders require massive funding—ammunition, communication systems, healthcare, missiles, rockets, salaries, technology, training, transportation, etc.

Under biting sanctions, Iran and its proxies were still able to cause significant death and destruction. Without sanctions, Iran would be able to pour infinite and unbound resources to fund its military activities and regional aggression. Imagine Tehran's ability without sanctions and with billions of more dollars at their disposal.

But the most significant reason for my belief that Trump's policy on Iran was appropriate is the following. Because of Trump's withdrawal from the

JCPOA, Western leaders were given a second chance to correct the significant flaws of the 2015 agreement. As we will see in the next section, the Western powers acknowledge that themselves.

Its aggressive Middle East policy is causing increasing friction with its neighbors and with the international community. And the international community is also beginning to internalize the danger posed by the mullah regime to the region and the world.

Second and Last Chance for Western Diplomacy to Block Iran's Hegemonic Vision

In January 2021, Anthony Blinken (then secretary of state-designate) pledged that the Biden administration would reenter the 2015 Iran nuclear deal "if Tehran first rolled back its recent violations. But would then 'seek a longer and stronger agreement' in collaboration with the other five major powers. New diplomacy would address Iran's ballistic missile program and its destabilizing activities in the Middle East."[123] A statement published by the G7 NATO members in June 2021 reads, "We condemn Iran's support of proxy forces and non-state armed actors, including through financing, training, and the proliferation of missile technology and weapons. We call on Iran to stop all ballistic missile activities inconsistent with UNSCR 2231, refrain from destabilizing actions, and play a constructive role in fostering regional stability and peace."[124]

In an August 26, 2021, meeting with Israeli Prime Minister Naftali Bennett, US Secretary of Defense Lloyd Austin referred to the threat Iran presents to the region, saying, "Iran must be held accountable for acts of aggression in the Middle East and on international waters."[125]

Their statements explicitly reflect the understanding that the JCPOA was flawed for not including these central pillars of Iranian policy. This understanding is critical.

As of 2021, Western Diplomats Have a Very Strong Hand

There are three main reasons for their leverage.

First, the US withdrawal from JCPOA itself provides the Western negotiators a strong card. Now they can go back to negotiate the JCPOA and include as part of a new deal that which was alarmingly absent in the 2015 agreement: Iran's armies of terror and ballistic missile program.

Second, the impact of the Trump administration's 'maximum pressure policy.' The Iranian economy is shattered. There is increasing unrest in Iran. Continued sanctions will jeopardize the endurance of the mullah regime. Therefore, Iran is desperate to lift the sanctions. Most analysts agree that the Iranian economy is in a dire situation, and the mullah regime wants the sanctions to be lifted quickly.

Third, the impact of the compounding difficulties Iran is having in Iraq, Lebanon, and Syria. The challenges they face in this arena are due to a concurrence of two primary factors. One is an increasing nationalistic patriotism in Iraq and Lebanon in response to Tehran's takeover of these countries. The second is the rising Israeli-Russian-US interest, and possibly the Assad regime as well to end Iran's military presence in Syria. (We will explore this further in Chapter 6.)

Western Diplomats Should Reverse the JCPOA Flaws

When Iran signed the JCPOA, the sanctions were lifted, and the money flowed into Tehran's coffers. And we saw very clearly that as a result, Iran boosted its aggression and deepened its grip throughout the region.

One of the shortfalls of the JCPOA was the "sunset clause." In January 2031, the limit on Iran's stockpile of enriched uranium will expire. Iran will be permitted to enrich uranium to levels greater than 3.67 percent uranium-235. From that point onwards, Iran could theoretically sprint toward manufacturing a nuclear weapon.

The funds Iran received after signing the JCPOA allowed Iran to continue to fund and expand its militias and its non-nuclear military program. That coupled with the sunset clause meant that when JCPOA expires, the Iranian regime would be able to calmly and legally complete its military nuclear program. A nuclear Iran, supported by agents and proxies throughout the Middle East equipped with the largest and most sophisticated conventional military arsenal, means Iran will be completely immune. And the world—not only the Middle East—will be the mullah regime's hostage.

In August 2020, the UN Security Council rejected a draft resolution submitted by the United States to extend the embargo on arms sales to Iran, which were to expire on October 18, 2020. Major Western powers—the United Kingdom, France, and Germany—abstained. Following the United States' failure to extend the embargo, veteran Iraqi British journalist Mina al-Oraibi, editor-in-chief of *The National*, wrote, "the US failure is bad news for the region. Iran will boost the arming of its proxies and therefore deepen its grip and increase instability in the region."[126]

Following the embargo's expiration, in November 2020, in his annual speech at the eighth Shura Council session, King Salman of Saudi Arabia called on the international community "to take a firm stance towards Iran that guarantees to stop it from obtaining weapons of mass destruction, developing its ballistic missile program and threatening peace and security."[127]

Whatever the considerations and calculations of Western negotiators were, the reality since the JCPOA proves that JCPOA was an agreement that reflects staggering short-sightedness on behalf of the West. The JCPOA was one tremendous Western goodwill gesture toward Iran. We have seen the severe outcomes of that goodwill. I don't think any objective analyst truly believes that the mullah regime will make any concession just out of goodwill. The mullah regime reciprocates gestures and goodwill with more death, destruction, and terror. These are facts that we saw play out right in front of our eyes after the JCPOA during the Obama administration, before the sanctions under the Trump administration, and most recently as a response to the Biden administration's policy in Yemen.

We must remember that sanctions—not gestures and flowers—brought the mullah regime to the pre-JCPOA negotiations. Therefore, it is just puzzling why Western powers insist on sheltering the mullah regime. How many more "goodwill gestures" will be required to make the mullah regime abandon terror and destruction? And an even more significant question: Why would the mullah regime abandon terror and destruction when what it gets in return is more "goodwill gestures"? I have urged Western policymakers to develop a constructive policy to restrain the mullah regime for over a decade. In my 2016 book and countless articles, interviews, and briefings, I have painstakingly outlined that the Iranian mullah regime's hegemonic vision and the increasingly aggressive expansion policy will increase chaos, violence, and bloodshed. And that the ramifications will exceed the region. I have sounded the warning bells that

Western attempts to appease Iran do not tame the regime—instead, it fuels their aggression. These observations and predictions have proven to be accurate.

Unfortunately, it seems that Iran's determination, which is fueled by extremist ideology and is violently implemented on the ground snuffing out the lives, hopes, and dreams of hundreds of millions of people in the Middle East, is not enough to encourage the West to counter this dangerous regime. Sadly, the fact that Iran violates all fundamental principles of Western democracy and undermines Western countries' security and interests is not enough to motivate Western circles that insist on appeasing Iran to revise their approach.

Recommendations for Western Policy Makers and Influencers

It is essential to understand that the mullah regime sees itself as a revolutionary power destined to lead the world to redemption through a process called in Farsi *ashak and arak*—tears and sweat—in which most of humankind will die. And those that survive will be redeemed by Allah. It is a regime fueled by narratives of victimhood, motivated by an apocalyptic outlook on history, and propelled by a sense of moral and cultural superiority.

In 2021, Western leaders seem to finally recognize that Iranian aggression presents a significant global threat that jeopardizes the West's interests. Restraining Iran and putting an end to its aggression in the region is critical. Assuming that the West will not use military might to curb Iran's aggression, and assuming the West realizes that gestures and goodwill are counterproductive, what other tool does the West have to secure its interests other than sanctions? Keeping biting sanctions in place is the only thing that will force the Iranian regime to negotiate and compromise.

But in addition, Western leaders must internalize that the Iranian armies of terror, ballistic missiles, attack drones, and its nuclear program are integrated and based upon a guiding concept of 'mutual insurance.' Iran's missiles, drones, and armies of terror aim—among their other tasks—to deter an attack on Iran's nuclear program and vice versa; Iran's nuclear program aims to prevent attacks on Iran's armies of terror. This 'Iranian ecosystem' is why the JCPOA played into the hands of Iran.

The West must be sure that any deal with Iran—unlike the JCPOA—refers to all the pillars of Iran's hegemonic vision: its nuclear program, missile and drone program, and armed militant proxies. And the agreement must clearly define inspecting and monitoring mechanisms of each element—nuclear, missiles, and proxies. And it should clearly state that severe sanctions will be immediately implemented if Iran violates its commitment or fails to comply with the inspections' terms.

On the nuclear issue: As I mentioned earlier, one of the shortfalls of the JCPOA was the "sunset clause." When it comes to Iran's nuclear program, the next deal should not have a "sunset clause" at all. Full stop. Through a strict and precise set of conditions, the agreement must ensure that Iran will not have the ability to develop or own a nuclear weapon.

Regarding Iran's ballistic missile and drone program: The agreement should define the arsenal contents and the types of long-range and cruise missiles Iran can possess. The deal should define the mechanism to monitor Iran's drone and ballistic missile program, as well.

And then there are Iran's armed proxies. The agreement should fully enforce the United Nations Security Council resolutions in Lebanon, Syria, and Yemen. This should include eliminating Hezbollah's missile stockpile in Lebanon and following the UN resolutions road map to end the war in Syria, which emphasizes the evacuation of all foreign entities from Syria and the evacuation of all foreign entities from Yemen. Iran must be held accountable for the actions of its proxies.

In May 2021, US Secretary of State Antony Blinken outlined the preferred steps to return to an agreement with Iran. According to his plan, the first step will be going back to JCPOA and ensuring that Iran meets its commitments. Blinken noted that "then we can use that as a foundation both to look at how to make the deal itself potentially longer and stronger—and also engage on these other issues, whether it's Iran's support for terrorism . . . its destabilizing support for different proxies throughout the Middle East."[128]

On June 15, 2021, the leaders of the Group of Seven wealthy nations (the G7 nations are Canada, France, Germany, Italy, Japan, the United Kingdom, and the United States) and members of NATO made a formal statement reaffirming a commitment to stop Iran from producing nuclear weapons. The

NATO statement also chastised the Islamic Republic for supporting proxy terror groups and rebuked its ballistic missile program. "We condemn Iran's support to proxy forces and non-state armed actors, including through financing, training, and the proliferation of missile technology and weapons," the statement said. "We call on Iran to stop all ballistic missile activities inconsistent with UNSCR 2231, refrain from destabilizing actions, and play a constructive role in fostering regional stability and peace."[129]

On April 6, the P5+1 minus the US began talks with Iran in Vienna. The goal was to get the United States and Iran back into full compliance with the 2015 nuclear deal. Iran refused to negotiate directly with the US. On June 20, 2021, after six rounds of talks and two days after ultraconservative Ebrahim Raisi became president of Iran, Iran left the negotiations and has not returned.

In June 2021, Emirati political analyst, Salem Al-Ketbi, wrote an article, "Hezbollah has Kidnapped Lebanon." In it, he urges, "The global powers must join forces to prevent Iran from further arming and financing its proxies in the Middle East. This is the most serious issue that needs urgent solutions. And the solution will not be through dialogue with the mullah regime, as the West believes. The first thing to do is restrict Iran's movement and its ability to finance and arm its proxies. It will only be through a unified position of the major powers and the conviction of all that the continuation of this situation presents a danger whose negative repercussions will not be far from the interests of any of these powers."[130]

Western leaders should pen a new agreement with Iran. And the West, not Tehran, must dictate the terms of the deal. Western diplomats, negotiators, and officials must craft an agreement that addresses all the pillars of Iran's hegemonic strategy. Failing to do that will result in growing instability. But will Western leaders internalize this message and act firmly to restrict Iran for their own sake? I must admit I am skeptical.

If Western negotiators fail to negotiate an effective deal this time, in the trial of history, Western leaders will not be able to defend themselves by saying that they were unaware of the reality or that their failure was an outcome of poor judgment.

Turkey

CHAPTER 3

TURKEY'S QUEST FOR HEGEMONY—THE BLUE HOMELAND AND REVIVING THE OTTOMAN EMPIRE | RECEP TAYYIP ERDOĞAN AND HIS QUEST FOR POWER

Sunni Islam

Before we dive into this chapter, I want to explain several terms. Up until this point, we have focused on Shi'ite Islam. Now that we are discussing Turkey, we are shifting to Sunni Islam. I would like to introduce some central terms relevant to Sunni Islam.

First, just to refresh our memory. The overwhelming majority of Muslims follow Sunni orthodoxy. Sunnis believe that the leader of the Muslim world should be the best person for the position. Shi'ites believe the leader of the Muslim world must be a male descendant of Islam's fourth caliph 'Ali Bin Abi Talib.

Let me begin by distinguishing between two terms that are similar yet have different meanings. The words are Muslim and Islamist.

Muslim (Sunni or Shi'ite) is an individual whose religion is Islam.

Islamist is a Muslim (Sunni or Shi'ite) committed to spreading and implementing Islam through political, cultural, educational, or militant action. It can be different versions of Islam, according to their orthodoxy and ideology.

The *Muslim Brotherhood* (MB) is a Sunni Islamist political, religious, and social movement. It was founded in Egypt in 1928 by a Muslim scholar, Hassan al-Banna. The MB is the largest Sunni movement in the Muslim world, with over seventy branches worldwide.

The Muslim Brotherhood adheres to the Political Islam school of thought. The ultimate objective of political Islam is to create a global Islamic cultural, political, and religious entity—the *Caliphate*, in which no other independent or sovereign state exists. That Caliphate should be governed and ruled by the Islamic law, the *sharī'ah*—"the path."

Islamist theologists view the sharī'ah as the master plan given to human-kind by Allah. The sharī'ah, therefore, is perfect and flawless. Any other political philosophy or political system—communism, democracy, socialism, etc.—is unacceptable to Islamists because it is human-made. And therefore, it is imperfect, unjust, and doomed to fail. Moreover, adopting any of these systems defies Allah's will.

I also want to explain the term Islamic fundamentalism. Islamic fundamentalism shares the same ultimate vision of political Islam. Muslim fundamentalists want to create a Caliphate ruled by the strictest interpretation of the sharī'ah. Islamic fundamentalists entirely reject Western values and call for returning to the early years of Islam's pure ideals and laws.

Islamic fundamentalists that want to implement sharī'ah law according to the most puritan dogmatic interpretation are known as *Salafists*. The ideology they ascribe to is known as *Salafi*. The word *salaf* means "what has been previously." *Salafism*'s core ideology is that Islam will thrive and flourish again once Muslims return to the roots, to the origin of Islam, and adopt and apply the Islamic codes, law, norms, and values as they were in the time of the Prophet Muhammad and his first four successors.

Contemporary Islamic fundamentalism (called in Arabic *Usuliyah*, which means "going back to the origin or the roots") has two branches.

One branch is the non-militant Salafi Islamist fundamentalist camp. Non-militant Salafi Islamists are called *Usuliyun*. Usuliyun follow a strict interpretation of sharī'ah law. But they do not try to impose it on others forcefully. Instead, they use preaching, education, and political actions to try to gain followers, grow the movement, and fulfill their religious objectives. Some choose to isolate themselves and minimize their interaction with the surrounding society, state authorities, and institutions.

The other branch of contemporary Islamic fundamentalism is the militant camp—Militant Islam. Fundamental militant Islam adheres to the *Salafi-Jihadi* ideology.

The word *Jihad* in Arabic literally means "an effort." It comes from the widely known Arabic concept *Jihad fi Sabil Allah*, "an effort to implement Allah's way." In the very early days, Islam was on the run. Operating in a hostile environment, the prophet Muhammad and his first disciples had to exercise *jihad*—an intensive spiritual journey to reach a higher degree of inner purity in their beliefs and to try to be a purer worshipper of Allah.

Throughout the evolution and expansion of Islam, jihad has become much more associated with the Muslim's willingness to sacrifice materially—including sacrificing their lives—for the glory of Islam and Allah. *Salafi-jihadi* ideology's core belief is that Islam will thrive again once it adopts the codes, laws, and values as they were in the time of the Prophet Muhammad and his first four successors. However, to achieve this goal, Salafi-jihadists violently impose their ideology and rules.

Militant Islamists are often called *Usuliyun Mutashaddidun* or *al-Mutashaddidun al-Islamiyyun*. As we said earlier, the word *usilyun* or *usuliyah* means "the origin or the roots." The word *mutashaddidun* means "extremist."

Militant Islamists are what is often referred to in Western media as "extreme fundamentalists" or "extreme Islamic fundamentalists" or "radical fundamentalists." The West is most familiar with the following militant Islam Salafi-jihadi ideology groups *Al-Qaeda* "The Base," *Al-Shabab* "The Youth" in Somalia, African-based *Boko Haram* "Western Values are Forbidden," *Global Jihad, ISIS,* and *Islamic Jihad.*

A core value of all Salafi-jihadists is the concept of *Talb a-Shahada*—"the quest for martyrdom for the glory of Islam and Allah's rule." To summarize their value system: *It is good, necessary, and noble to kill and be killed for the sake of Allah.* For militant Islamist groups, violence is an essential tool that they must use to bring about the caliphate.

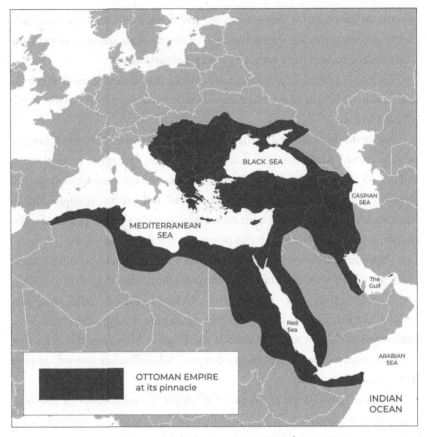

OTTOMAN EMPIRE
at its pinnacle

Ottoman Empire at its Height

The Ottoman Empire

For 600 years (1299–1923), the Ottoman Empire ruled large areas of Eastern Europe, the Middle East, and North Africa. It was the most powerful and longest-lasting dynasty in world history.

Turkey is a Sunni country. It is one of the largest and most important countries in the Middle East. Population-wise it is the second-largest country (Egypt is the largest) with eighty-four million people (the same as Iran). Turkey has the second-largest economy (after Saudi Arabia) with a GDP of $744 billion, which entitles it to membership in the G-20. Its army is the second largest in NATO, after the United States. Turkey is very strategically located. It is the westernmost point in Asia, the southeastern entrance to

Europe, and is on the eastern shores of the Mediterranean and the Black Sea. And its control of the Bosphorus Strait, which connects the Black Sea and the Mediterranean Sea, adds to its importance as a significant geopolitical actor.

Recep Tayyip Erdoğan Aspiring to Be the Sunni Sultan

Sunni Islamist Recep Tayyip Erdoğan was mayor of Istanbul from 1994 to 1998. He was prime minister of Turkey from 2003 to 2014. And he was elected president of Turkey in 2014—a position he still holds as of 2021. Under the tight dictatorship of Erdoğan, Turkey has become, in a way, a one-man show.

Since coming into power, Erdoğan has single-handedly changed Turkey's face from a secular democracy to an Islamist autocracy. Erdoğan wants to restore the glory days of the Ottoman Empire and position himself to be the leader of the Sunni Middle East and a Pan-Islamic first line leader. Inspired by the Muslim Brotherhood ideology, pursuing his pan-Islam, neo-Ottoman, hyper-nationalism, Erdoğan leverages collapsing governments, growing chaos, and spiraling instability in the Middle East, Africa, and beyond to spread his influence, power, and pave his path to supremacy. Erdoğan—a skillful, cynical, and driven leader—pursues every opportunity he can to amass power and influence.

When Erdoğan took office as the prime minister in March 2003, he pursued a "Zero Conflict" policy. Turkey was going to be friends with everyone. Yet Erdoğan's ideology, ambition, personality, and aggressive and provocative expansionist policies have pitted Turkey against regional and global players.

Five-Pillar Strategy to Revive the Ottoman Empire and Position Erdoğan as the Sultan of the Sunni World

Like Iran, Erdoğan capitalizes on chaos and instability to expand Turkey's influence and power. Like Iran, Erdoğan uses various tools and mechanisms to spread his control throughout the Middle East and Africa.

Erdoğan employs a sophisticated five-pillar strategy to spread Sunni orthodoxy, expand Ottoman influence and power, and position himself as the leader of the Sunni camp in the region and as a frontline leader of the Muslim world.

1. International Relations and Diplomacy

Diplomatic, commercial, and military relations with other countries.

2. Humanitarian Aid, Assistance, and Welfare Services

From the Levant to Africa, NGOs and organizations supported by the Turkish government like the Turkish Red Crescent, the Turkish Federation of Humanitarian Associations, and others build schools that teach a political Islam curriculum and build mosque complexes to spread Islamist ideology, expand political Islam, and increase Erdoğan's influence.

Most of the projects are funded by government agencies.

And other public and private initiatives—from education and training to military arms sales—are carried out by companies that present themselves as independent but are arms of the regime or closely affiliated with Erdoğan.

Like in the case of Iran, many are shadow operations for recruiting and financing terror organizations.

The Foundation for Human Rights and Freedoms and Humanitarian Relief (IHH) is one of the leading entities Erdoğan uses to further his political agenda and goals abroad. The IHH is a front charity that was accused of smuggling arms to al-Qaeda-affiliated jihadists in Syria. The IHH was also used to transport wounded ISIS and al-Qaeda fighters by ambulance from Syria to Turkey.[1] Erdoğan used the IHH to organize provocative flotillas to Israel under the guise of humanitarian activity. And the IHH is reportedly expanding its activities into south Yemen.[2]

3. Playing Both Sides of the Fence

Erdoğan is a calculated and shrewd politician who is always looking for opportunities to help him achieve his nationalist, religious, and political goals.

And that often means holding the stick at both ends. Erdoğan provides and sells intelligence and provides security and military hardware, know-how, and training to state and non-state actors and legitimate governments. And on the other hand, he arms, supports, aligns himself, cooperates, and often benefits from known terror organizations.

On the one hand, Turkey defines Salafi-jihadi groups as terror organizations. Yet, on the other hand, Erdoğan uses them as powerful pawns to further his own objectives. For example, Turkey supported the Islamic State ISIS established in eastern Syria because ISIS was fighting the Kurds in eastern Syria. And this served Turkish interests. So, the relationship was mutually beneficial.

And outside of the Middle East, Erdoğan nurtures a network of Islamic terror organizations in Africa.

The war in Syria is an excellent example of the nimble and cunning Erdoğan. Before the war in Syria, Erdoğan and Assad were close allies. As the war evolved into a Sunni-Shi'ite battle, Erdoğan wagered that it was beneficial to him and his greater ambition to line up against Assad.

And positioning himself on the Sunni side and as the Sunni patron has served him. He has leveraged the war in Syria to further his own hegemonic mission on many levels. He has gained territory—parts of northern Syria became a Turkish protectorate. And the war in Syria has helped him gain proxies.

And that brings us to the following tool Erdoğan uses to further his domestic priorities, such as preventing Kurdish autonomy in northern Syria or Iraq, advancing his hyper-nationalistic goals, and expanding the territory he controls or influences from Africa to the Gulf and beyond.

4. Agents and Proxies

Whereas Iran cultivates, develops, and supports mainly (but not only) Shi'ites to spread the Islamic Revolution and Twelver Shi'ism, Erdoğan focuses, of course, on Sunnis. Given that 80 percent of Muslims are Sunnis, this gives Erdoğan a large pool—from both the militant Islam camp (Salafi-jihadi) and political Islam camp (and mainly the Muslim Brotherhood).

And as Erdoğan's presence throughout the Middle East and Africa grows, so do his proxies. In Africa, Iraq, Lebanon, Libya, Syria, Yemen, etc., Erdoğan uses his growing presence to gain more subcontractors to help him spread his power and influence—culturally, militarily, politically, religiously, etc.

"Despite the time it took to get here, decision-makers in Ankara have grown increasingly amenable to the use of proxies, prompting a change in psychology and perception that represents a significant departure from Turkey's historic policy of relying on conventional forces," said Osman Sert, research director at the Ankara Institute. "Proxies are now perceived as being a critical component of Turkey's regional security interests."[3]

Let's look at some of Turkey's proxies.

A principal Turkish agent in Syria is the Free Syrian Army (FSA). The FSA was the primary Syrian rebel body in the first years of the war in Syria. Turkey has trained and equipped the FSA since 2016. In 2019, it renamed itself the Syrian National Army (SNA). The SNA has 22,000–35,000 fighters.[4]

Erdoğan's strongest proxy is in north Syria: the National Liberation Front (NLF) is a Turkish-sponsored network of twenty-two rebel militias. The dominant militias in the NLF are a Salafi militia—*Ahrar al-Sham* and a Muslim Brotherhood militia—*Faylak al-Sham*. Reportedly, the NLF has approximately 70,000 militants—including Muslim Brotherhood and Salafi-jihadi militias.[5]

The Salafi-jihadi *Hayat Tahrir al-sham* (HTS) is another example of a Turkish subcontractor. The HTS is a coalition made up of several Salafi-jihadi militias in Syria. HTS's early roots go back to 2012. Back then, al-Qaeda's branch in Syria was called *Jabhat al Nusrah (li) Ahl al-Sham,* "Supporters' Front for the People of ash-Sham." *Ash-Sham* is the Arabic name that, for centuries, referred to a geographic area of Mesopotamia—consisting of what is today Israel, Lebanon, Syria, Jordan, and Iraq. In July 2016, Jabhat al Nusrah (li) Ahl al-Sham split from al-Qaeda and called itself *Jabhat Fath al-Sham* "The Front for al-Sham's Triumph." In January 2018, Jabhat Fath al-Sham created a coalition with other Salafi-jihadi groups in Syria. The new alliance was named Hayat Tahrir al-Sham (HTS).

In addition to its Syrian Salafi-jihadi proxies, Turkey uses non-Syrian and non-Arab Sunni militias of Kazakhs, Turkmen, and Uighurs. They came to Syria to join the war and fight Assad, Iran, and their proxies.

5. *Al-Muqawama w'al Muman'aah*—"The Resistance and Defiance"

Like the mullah regime, Erdoğan understood the centrality of the Israeli-Palestinian conflict in the hearts and minds of the Muslim world.

Like Iran, Erdoğan also knew that using al-Muqawama and positioning himself as the defender of the Palestinians would earn him points throughout the Arab and Muslim world.

Hamas defines itself as the Muslim Brotherhood branch in Palestine. Coming from the same Islamist and ideological womb, Erdoğan supports Hamas primarily—but not solely—diplomatically and financially.

Erdoğan makes a concerted effort to position himself as the world leader that provides humanitarian aid to Gaza. Whether it is flotillas or trucks—the amount of support Turkey provides to the Palestinians is more symbolic—first aid supplies, food parcels, hygiene kits, toys for children, etc. Nonetheless, Erdoğan creates an entire marketing and public relations effort each and every time. The broad media exposure managed by Istanbul gives Erdoğan points in the Muslim—and partially Arab—public opinion.[6]

Here is an example.

During the May 2021 war, an article published in the Turkish state-run news organization the *Anadolu Agency* was called "Only Erdoğan Can Protect the Innocent Children of Palestine." The writer, Anisa Bahati, wrote:

> This crisis has only one solution. The only solution to the current crisis in Palestine is for Turkey and its President Recep Tayyip Erdoğan to take over the protection of civilians and children. Turkey is a NATO country with a powerful and robust army and a political, diplomatic, military regional power like no one else. Turkey is the only state that Israel really fears. The sooner Turkey intervenes to protect Palestinian civilians and children, the sooner this ridiculous and bloody conflict, which is likely to be avoided, will end. That's why everyone's eyes are on Turkey and President Erdoğan ... The Arabs in the region have forgotten Palestine ... The ten-year bloody war in Syria, the violent collapse of political systems in Egypt, the conflict and destruction in Yemen, and the three-year internal crisis in Lebanon made the Arabs forget about the Palestinians and the Palestinian issue, dealing only with their own internal problems.[7]

But Turkey's support for Hamas, the Palestinian Islamist movement that has ruled the Gaza Strip since 2007, is far from being confined to toys and medicine. Some of Hamas's senior officials—including senior military commanders and personnel—have been, or are, based in Turkey.[8]

Turkey in Gaza

Reportedly, Hamas has a secret cyberwarfare and counter-intelligence enterprise headquartered in Turkey. The operation is managed by the *Izz ad-Din al-Qassam Brigades*, the military wing of Hamas. Hamas's cyberwarfare and counter-intelligence organization coordinates cyber-operations against Hamas's enemies. Their targets include the Palestinian Authority and worldwide embassies of Saudi Arabia and the United Arab Emirates. The headquarters is also reportedly responsible for the purchasing of equipment to manufacture weapons. Turkish authorities were allegedly unaware of its existence. That is highly unlikely.

Erdoğan supports Hamas because of shared ideology. However, beyond that—just as in the case of the mullah regime in Iran—the continuation

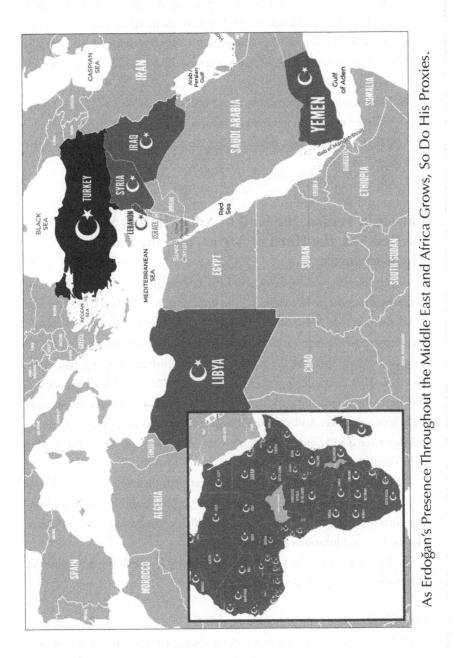

As Erdoğan's Presence Throughout the Middle East and Africa Grows, So Do His Proxies.

of the Israeli-Palestinian conflict serves Erdoğan's quest for domination. Through these five mechanisms, Turkey spreads political Islam, gains followers, creates loyalty to Turkey, foments anti-Western sentiments, advances Turkey's interests, and increases Ankara's power and reach. Yet, it comes with a price tag.

As I said earlier, when Erdoğan came into office, he had a "Zero Conflict Policy." Turkey was going to be friends with everyone.

Less than a decade later, these policies have put him on a collision course with almost everyone.

The Gulf, Yemen, the Gulf of Aden, Bab el-Mandeb, the Red Sea, the Horn of Africa, and the Eastern Mediterranean

In the previous chapter, we discussed the major maritime routes from the Gulf to the Mediterranean. We explored the importance of the Gulf, the Hormuz Strait, the Bab el-Mandeb Strait, the Red Sea, the Suez Canal, and the Eastern Mediterranean. We surveyed Iran's strategy to achieve dominance on land and sea—particularly through the war in Yemen and investing in its own infrastructure along the Gulf (Iran's Gulf coastline is 1,750 miles long). We learned how Iran uses the maritime routes to supply its agents and proxies and support the axis of resistance. And we saw the aggressive actions it pursues with its vast military arsenal and hardware to subdue its foes and ensure the mullah regime is the dominant power in the region.

Given what we learned about the significance of these waters, it should not surprise you that Erdoğan—like Iran—is trying to establish a military presence directly and/or indirectly through his allies, organizations, and proxies in a lot of the exact locations and more.

So, let's begin with the Gulf to see how Erdoğan is gaining a foothold in and around the Arabian Peninsula.

The Gulf

While Iran is Shi'ite, the Gulf monarchies (except Bahrain) are predominantly Sunni. Driven to be the leader of the Sunni camp in the region and determined

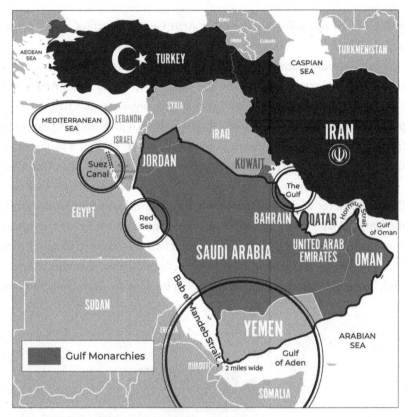

Erdoğan Trying to Gain Control in Gulf, Yemen, Gulf of Aden, Bab el-Mandeb, Red Sea, Horn of Africa, and the Eastern Mediterranean.

to secure Turkey as the regional superpower, Erdoğan is trying to increase his power and gain a foothold in the heartland of the Sunni monarchies.

However, his ambitions, provocative actions, partnership with the Muslim Brotherhood (which is defined by Saudi Arabia and Egypt as a terror organization), and Erdoğan's desire to usurp the traditional Sunni leaders irks the more considerable Sunni powers—specifically Egypt, Saudi Arabia, and the UAE.

The one Gulf exception is Qatar. Sitting on the southwest corner of the Gulf, almost right between Saudi Arabia and Iran, Qatar aspires to be a leader and a pivotal player in the region. Along the way, it annoys its brother monarchies by creating its own independent policies that often do not align with theirs. Qatar has long conducted a separate and independent regional

policy—often not following the other Arab Gulf monarchies' joint coordi-
nated policies.

Here are some examples. Qatar supports the Muslim Brotherhood and its
chapters throughout the region and the world. In contrast, Saudi Arabia and
Egypt define the Muslim Brotherhood as a terror organization. Qatar also supports Hamas, the Muslim Brotherhood's official branch in Palestine. Qatar is also
friendly with Iran, which threatens Saudi Arabia and the UAE. It is also reported
that Qatar secretly finances Iran's most important proxy, Hezbollah, in Lebanon.[9]

As a result of Qatar's policies, in June 2017, eight Muslim States—Bahrain,
Egypt, Libya, the Maldivian Islands, the Republic of Mauritius, Saudi Arabia,
the United Arab Emirates, and Yemen's ousted government led by the former
Sunni Yemeni President Abdrabbuh Mansur Hadi—announced that they were
cutting relations with Qatar. In an unprecedented move, a complete aerial,
land, and naval blockade and siege were imposed by the Arab Gulf States on

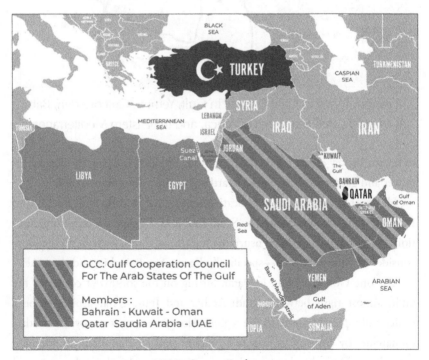

2017 Qatar Embargo

Qatar—except for Kuwait and the Sultanate of Oman, who abstained from the embargo. The main demands to end the embargo were, Doha should limit its engagement with Iran and Turkey and stop funding terror organizations, including the Muslim Brotherhood.

Erdoğan identified the rift between Qatar and the other Arab Gulf monarchies as an opportunity to deepen his presence and foothold in the Gulf. And he has worked hard to cultivate the relationship and cooperation with Qatar.

Qatar and Turkey have increasingly strengthened their relationship over the past decades. The two created a Turkish-Qatari axis to counter Saudi Arabia and the UAE as the Gulf leaders.

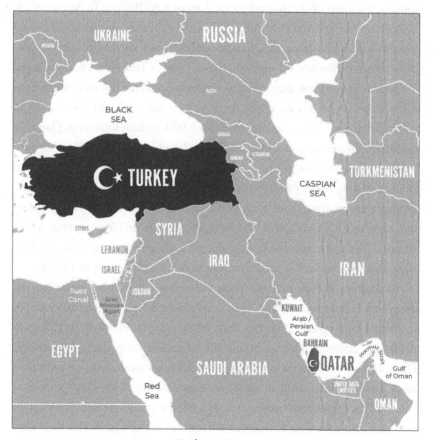

Turkey-Qatar

Ankara and Doha have penned several military training and arms sales agreements. And relations related to the military sphere intensified after 2014 when they established the High Strategic Committee, which brings together Turkey and Qatar annually to sign agreements and deepen collaboration[10] in areas of the defense industry, education, military, and trade. Though the exact scope of Turkey's military presence in Qatar is not clear, this is the picture to the best of my estimation.

Throughout 2015, several dozen Turkish soldiers were stationed at a Qatari military base, Tariq Bin Ziad, in Doha, Qatar. They were then moved to a nearby military base that Turkey built. That is significant because this is Turkey's first permanent military base in the Gulf. According to several Arab sources, the name of the military establishment is Al-Rayyan. In August 2019, Turkish media reported that in the fall of 2019, Turkey was going to open a second Turkish base in north Qatar. To the best of my knowledge, as of August 2021, this base has not yet opened. The number of Turkish soldiers stationed in Qatar is also unclear. According to various reports, the number ranges from a few dozen to several hundred. According to one report in January 2020, which I estimate to be excessive, there are 5,000 Turkish soldiers in Qatar.[11] I estimate there are around 3,000 Turkish soldiers based in Qatar.[12]

A military presence in Qatar solidifies Erdoğan's presence in the Gulf. But beyond existing bases, the military collaboration between the two is extensive. During the embargo, their relationship significantly increased. It was during that time that Qatar allowed Turkey to increase its military presence in the country. The two countries also conducted joint military exercises, and they signed agreements for Qatar to purchase military hardware from Turkey.

In addition to their military cooperation, their relationship expanded and deepened during the embargo. Qatari investments have exponentially grown in Turkey, topping $22 billion in 2019. More than five hundred Turkish companies are active in Qatar working on infrastructure projects. Meanwhile, Qatar and China were the only two countries to establish currency swap lines with Turkey to help with its ailing economy. In May 2020, Qatar tripled its previously set agreement, raising it to $15 billion to support financial stability and trade. The following November, during the emir of Qatar's visit to Turkey, the two countries signed ten new deals, which included economic agreements like Turkey selling Qatar 10 percent of shares in Borsa Istanbul, Turkey's stock exchange.[13]

In July and October 2020, Erdoğan visited Qatar. During his visit, he stated that Turkey's military presence in the Arab Gulf "serves the Gulf area's peace and stability."[14]

For Erdoğan, establishing a military foothold in the Gulf is a very significant achievement. And though Erdoğan's military presence in Qatar is more symbolic—unlike his proactive engagement, military and otherwise, in other arenas like Libya and Syria that we will learn about in Chapters 4 and 6—it still does not sit well with Saudi Arabia and the UAE.

In January 2021, the Gulf Cooperation Council ended its boycott of Qatar. The emir of Qatar, Sheikh Tamim bin Hamad al-Thani, attended the forty-first Gulf Cooperation Council (GCC) Summit held in the Saudi city of Al-Ula. Sheikh Tamim was personally and somewhat warmly welcomed by Crown Prince Mohammad bin Salman bin Abdulaziz Al-Saud—also known as MBS—the crown prince of Saudi Arabia. And on January 5, 2021, the GCC members—Bahrain, Kuwait, Oman, Qatar, Saudi Arabia, and the UAE—signed the "Al-Ula Declaration," expressing unity and the start of a new chapter in their relationship. Egypt (not a member of the GCC) also signed the declaration.

For Qatar, this was a material achievement, mainly because the boycott was lifted, and Qatar was reembraced without Doha having to meet any of the conditions set by the GCC and Egypt to end the embargo.

Qatar continues to maintain close ties with Iran, the Muslim Brotherhood, and Turkey. Lifting the boycott of Qatar is a bitter pill that Egypt and Saudi Arabia had to swallow. It seems to me that the background to the move lies in Saudi Arabia's relationship with the Biden administration. Although former President Trump was in office when the agreement was signed, the Saudis were already preparing themselves for the incoming president. And the Saudis knew there were three immediate issues on the table that would be flashpoints with the incoming Biden administration and would likely generate tensions and frictions in Saudi-US relations: violation of human rights in Saudi Arabia, the Khashoggi affair (we will discuss this issue more in Chapter 12), and the war in Yemen. In my analysis, the lifting of the boycott on Qatar was a Saudi move designed to meet US interests and soften tensions with the new administration.

By lifting the boycott, Saudi Arabia temporarily soured the Kingdom's relationship with Egypt. Cairo reluctantly followed the Saudis but was not happy that Qatar did not have to pay any price for reentering the GCC and having all sanctions rescinded.

The reason for Egyptian President Abdel Fattah al-Sisi's resentment is that Cairo is particularly disturbed by Qatar's support for the Muslim Brotherhood. Qatar is the home of Sheikh Yussuf al-Qardawi, a senior Islamic theologist of Egyptian origin who serves as the chairman of the International Union of Islamist Scholars. Al-Qardawi is the unofficial higher spiritual authority of the Muslim Brotherhood. He is known for his firm (sometimes rude) criticism of the Egyptian president. Expressing his discontent with al-Qardawis' position, Egyptian authorities arrested al-Qardawi's daughter and her husband (in 2017 and again in 2018), signaling Qatar to restrain al-Qardawi.

However, it does seem that in the summer of 2021, there is a warming of relations between Egypt and Qatar.

In early June 2021, Egypt's Foreign Minister Sameh Shoukry visited Doha. He delivered a letter from al-Sisi to the emir of Qatar Sheikh Tamim bin Hamad Al Thani, including an official invitation to visit Cairo.

Cairo withdrew its ambassador from Doha on June 5, 2017. On June 23, 2021, Egyptian President al-Sisi, for the first time since 2014, appointed Egyptian diplomat Amr Kamal Eddin al-Sherbiny ambassador extraordinary and plenipotentiary to the government of Qatar.

On July 3, 2021, there was another significant public step in Egyptian-Qatari relations. The commander of the Qatar Emiri Naval Force, Major General Abdullah bin Hassan al-Sulaiti attended President Abdel Fattah al-Sisi's inauguration of Egypt's newest naval base in the Gargoub area on the Egyptian northwestern Mediterranean coast near the border with Libya. The naval forces, equipment, and base are designed to secure Egypt's northern and western border and the shipping lanes.

Side by side with the warming of relations between Qatar and Egypt and the Gulf monarchies, it is essential to note that the major controversial issues that caused the Arab boycott in the first place—namely Qatar's relationship with Iran and Turkey and its support of Hamas and the Muslim Brotherhood—are still unresolved. So, as of the summer of 2021, it is premature to conclude

Turkey in Yemen

that the crisis is over. Qatar's policies still compromise Egypt's security and stability and the Arab world in general. Accordingly, one cannot rule out the resumption of the tensions between Qatar and Egypt and the GCC. However, the rapprochement between Qatar and Egypt and the Gulf monarchies—including Saudi Arabia's appointment of an ambassador to Qatar, Ambassador Prince Mansour bin Khalid bin Farhan Al-Saud, in late June 2021—does not necessarily compromise the relationship between Turkey and Qatar.

South Yemen and the Gulf of Aden
It will not surprise you that Erdoğan is trying to gain a foothold and establish a military presence in Yemen—specifically in south Yemen and the Gulf

Iran in Yemen

of Aden. We discussed Aden before, but I want to repeat the significance of it. In September 2014, the Houthi Shi'ite tribes in Yemen, backed by Iran, executed a coup in Yemen. They ousted the Yemenite government led by Sunni President Abd Rabbuh Mansour Hadi and took over Yemen's capitol, Sana'a. Hadi's ousted government relocated to Aden, the southernmost point in Yemen on the Gulf of Aden.

The Gulf of Aden connects the Indian Ocean and the Arabian Sea with the Mediterranean Sea. And Yemen sits at the intersection of the Horn of Africa, the Gulf of Aden, and the Bab el Mandeb Strait—the chokepoint of the maritime passage that physically connects the east and the west. This is one of the most strategic and sensitive points on the planet. Whoever controls Yemen and the surrounding waterways wields enormous power.

Turkey is trying to establish a military presence in three strategic points in southern Yemen.

The first point of interest for Erdoğan is a group of four islands, in the Arabian Sea, at the Gulf of Aden entrance, which is under Yemen's sovereignty. The largest of the islands is called Socotra.

The Socotra Archipelago sits right on one of the world's busiest shipping lanes. Turkey has enlisted a proxy in south Yemen, an Islamist Muslim Brotherhood party called *Al-Tajamm'u Al-Yamani L(il)-Islah,* "The Yemenite Reform Coalition"—often referred to as *Islah.* Islah is part of Hadi's government. According to sources, Turkey is increasingly providing Islah with financial and tactical support—intelligence, money, weapons, and military know-how.[15]

In June 2020, Islah battled a UAE-backed separatist Yemenite group—STC, the Southern Transitional Council—for control of Socotra. The clashes ended with STC in control of Hadiboh, the capitol of the archipelago.

The second point where Erdoğan is trying to gain influence and a foothold in this arena is a port city northwest of the Socotra Islands. This is a place called Qana, located in Bir 'Ali', a coastal town in south Yemen's Shabwah district. In January 2021, Qana reportedly started functioning as a launchpad for oil tankers. Sources claim Turkey operates the port and uses a Yemenite company called QYZ as its "cover."[16] Reports are that the governor of Shabwah district, Mohamad Saleh Bin Adiyu, has authorized Turkey's control of the port.[17] Reportedly, Islah supports Bin Adiyu. Turkey can use the Qana port to ship weapons from Turkey to supply Islah.[18]

And the final location Erdoğan is trying to position himself in Yemen is on the Red Sea on the other side of the Bab el Mandeb. And this is the strategically located city of Mocha. This port sits at the narrowest and northernmost point of the Bab el Mandeb Strait.[19]

If Turkey's attempts to secure a foothold in Socotra, Qana, and Mocha succeed, Turkey would be at the entrance to the Gulf of Aden and on either side of the Bab el Mandeb. That would be a staggeringly strategic position.

The Bab el Mandeb, the Red Sea, and the Horn of Africa

As we discussed in the last chapter, the Red Sea is a vital link between Asia, the Mediterranean, Europe, and North America. It is one of the world's most crucial maritime transport routes. The Red Sea's southern gate is the Bab el

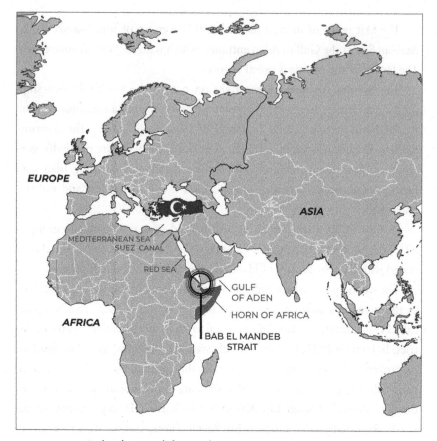

Bab el-Mandeb, Red Sea, Horn of Africa —
Physically Connects East and West

Mandeb Strait off the coast of Yemen, and the northern point of the Red Sea is Egypt's Suez Canal. The Red Sea physically connects the East and the West.

But this area is not only about shipping and trade. Erdoğan sees it as an excellent opportunity and platform to advance his hegemonic strategy to revive the great Ottoman Empire.

Turkey's expansion—which spans the continent—to Africa is multilayered. Erdoğan's engagement in Africa centers around four out of the five pillars we discussed at the beginning of the chapter: humanitarian assistance, expansion of diplomatic missions, playing both sides of the fence, and employing his proxies.

Erdoğan has visited Africa twenty-seven times.

His first visit was in 2011 to provide famine relief, marking the start of Turkey as a 'humanitarian actor' in Africa. Turkey has steadily spread its political, economic, and military foothold across Africa.

Between 2003 and 2021, Ankara has gone from having just twelve embassies to forty-two. Over the same period, direct foreign investment jumped from US$100 million to US$6.5 billion. And Turkish Airlines now flies to fifty-one African cities.[20] Turkey supports cultural activities and economic projects and runs schools. Turkey provides military know-how, training, and weapons to states, governments, and non-state actors, claiming they are helping to fight terror. And Turkey also maintains relations with Islamic terror groups in Africa like ISIS and Boko Haram.

Speaking of which, one major thing to watch is Erdoğan's engagement in Africa's military and defense sphere. Turkey's involvement in this sector on a state and private level is broad and deep. Turkey and Turkish companies train troops, build bases, and sell a wide array of defense equipment. Clearly, the defense and military industry is a significant pillar of Erdoğan's strategy to solidify his relationship and gain influence and power.

Given Erdoğan's keen interest in Africa, it would only make sense that he would look to secure a significant foothold at the intersection of the Bab el-Mandeb, the Red Sea, and the Horn of Africa. And sitting right at that intersection is Somalia.

A peninsula on the Horn of Africa, Somalia's northern, eastern, and southern coastlines are more than 2,000 miles long and span the Indian Ocean, the Arabian Sea, and the Gulf of Aden. Somalia sits right on the southern entrance to the Bab el Mandeb and the Red Sea. In addition to having an incredibly strategic maritime base, a foothold in Somalia positions Erdoğan at the eastern gateway to Africa. Somalia is an optimal location for Erdoğan to position himself to advance his hegemonic vision—economically, ideologically, militarily, and politically.

In addition to its location, other characteristics of Somalia are attractive to Erdoğan. Somalia—practically entirely Sunni—is a fractured country that suffers from chronic instability, decentralized government, economic hardship, and semi-autonomous regions, all looking to gain the upper hand. The

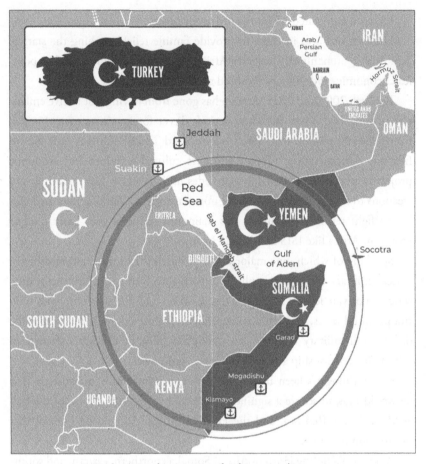

Turkey in the Horn of Africa and Yemen

Somali Federal Government (recognized by the international community as the legitimate government in Somalia) only controls the capitol of Mogadishu and its surrounding areas. The rest of Somalia is divided into five autonomous provinces.

Erdoğan first visited Somalia in 2011, and then again in 2016 when he personally attended the inauguration of the Turkish embassy in Mogadishu. In April 2017, Turkey opened a large military base in Mogadishu to help train the Somali army. Somalia is now home to Turkey's largest military installation outside of Turkey.

According to the Institute of Security Studies, Turkey's military base in Somalia and training of the Somali military are some signs of Turkish geopolitical efforts to establish Turkey as an important political and military power in the Horn of Africa. The study goes on to say that "Turkey aims to become an economic, humanitarian and military power in sub-Saharan Africa."[21] Somalia may also be the next oil frontier. Decades of unrest and economic instability have prevented Somalian oil exploration onshore as well as offshore. Seismic surveys conducted by two British companies, Soma Oil & Gas and Spectrum Geo, suggest that Somalia has promising oil reserves along the Indian Ocean coast, between the cities of Garad and Kismayo. Total offshore deposits could be as high as a hundred billion barrels.[22] In January 2020, Erdoğan announced that Somalia invited Turkey to drill for oil in its waters. In November 2020, Turkey offered to pay off $3.4 million of Somalia's debt to the International Monetary Fund.[23] In January 2021, the Somali government officially opened the country to foreign oil exploration.

Another Red Sea African country Erdoğan was eager to develop a strategic relationship with was Sudan. In December 2017, Erdoğan visited Khartoum. He had a kindred spirit—and a potential geostrategic ally—in Sudan's Islamist dictator, Omar al-Bashir. One of the most significant agreements he signed in 2017 with al-Bashir was a lease to Suakin Island. Located on the Red Sea across from the Saudi port of Jeddah, Suakin was a central seat of power for the Ottoman Empire. From the mid-sixteenth century to the early nineteenth century, Suakin was the capitol of the Ottoman province of Habeş and a vital link for trade between Africa and the western Arabian Peninsula. However, Erdoğan's hopes of establishing a presence in Sudan were crushed in the spring of 2019, when Sudan's dictator, Omar al-Bashir, was overthrown in a military coup.

Though the current Sudanese government maintains—and wishes to keep—good relations with Turkey, it does not want to jeopardize its relations with its two neighbors, Egypt and Saudi Arabia, who also happen to be the two most powerful Arab countries and resent Turkey's hegemonic aspirations. Therefore, Sudan's new government canceled Turkey's lease to Suakin Island.

Despite his setback with Sudan, Erdoğan uses everything at his disposal—building and development projects, diplomatic corps, educational initiatives,

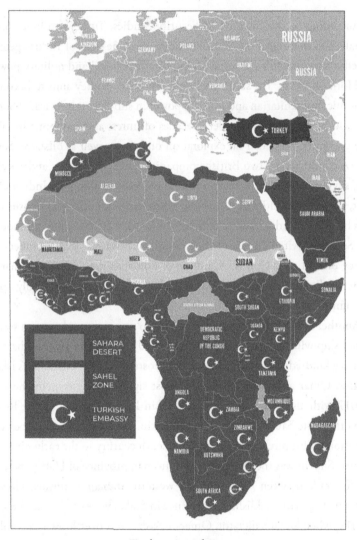

Turkey in Africa

humanitarian aid, soft power, the Turkish military and his proxies—to court players and spread Turkish influence throughout the African continent.

The Horn of Africa offers Erdoğan the perfect location to spread Turkish imperialism through a combination of soft and hard power.

And one of Erdoğan's most controversial and proactive African engagements has been inserting himself in the civil war in Libya. The war in Libya

Turkey—*Mavi Vatan* "The Blue Homeland"

(which we will explore in Chapter 4) and the war in Syria (which we will explore in Chapter 6) are prime examples of Erdoğan inserting himself into complicated wars to secure Turkey's interests, spread his power and influence, and promote his own ambitions. Eager to entrench himself in North Africa on the Mediterranean, right next door to Egypt, and at the crossroads of Africa and Europe, Erdoğan aggravates regional and global players.

A 2020 study by the Emirates Policy Center (EPC) gives an overview of the vast scale of Turkey's influence in Central and West Africa: "Turkey continues its relentless pursuit of developing its African relations, especially in the Sahel and Sahara region and the western part of the continent, with the aim of building multiple partnerships to achieve its strategic objectives that center

around finding a foothold in this strategic part of the continent and contributing to the reengineering of the regional equation in the Sahel and Sahara."[24]

On March 3, 2021, former United Nations Economic Commission for
Africa chief Carlos Lopes tweeted, "Turkey's footprint in Africa is getting
larger than most European countries in a very short period of time."[25] And
this is indeed what Erdoğan sees when he looks around.

Erdoğan views Africa as a stage where he can gain influence and power at
the expense of the leading European powers and counter some of his Middle
East rivals.

"Mavi Vatan" ("Blue Homeland") Doctrine: Turkey and the Eastern Basin of the Mediterranean Sea

Of all the areas Erdoğan is looking to control to achieve his hegemonic ambitions, he is most interested in the eastern Mediterranean, which is another
sensitive arena of regional and global importance. The eastern Mediterranean
is where Erdoğan has been the most active—and the most aggressive.

In 2006, Turkey announced a new maritime strategy called "Mavi Vatan"
"The Blue Homeland Doctrine." The plan is presented to end Turkey's near-complete dependence on foreign energy sources and convert Turkey into a net energy
exporter by controlling the surrounding waterways—the Black Sea, the Aegean
Sea, and the Mediterranean Sea. Turkey is a massive consumer of natural gas and
depends on external sources. Its two major suppliers are Russia and Iran.

However, in its essence, Mavi Vatan is an expansionist hegemonic strategy
that Turkey has developed to exert its regional and international economic,
militaristic, and political superiority to aggressively assert a claim over the
contested, potentially gas- and oil-rich regions of the Eastern Mediterranean.
In the current geopolitical vernacular, Mavi Vatan is shorthand for Turkey's
desire to control the Eastern Mediterranean.

The Eastern Mediterranean is an area of utmost importance to the states
in the region and a potential source of explosive geopolitical tensions. Over
the past decade, the Mediterranean countries and the Gulf monarchies have
become geopolitically linked. And much of this is due to Erdoğan's increasing
pursuit to upend the balance of power by looking for every opportunity to
insert himself and pursue his neo-Ottoman hyper-nationalist agenda.

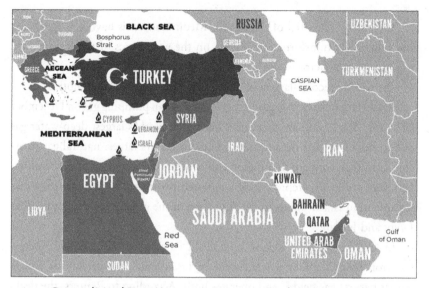

Geopolitical Tensions over Eastern Mediterranean Gas
Link the Gulf and Eastern Mediterranean Countries against Turkey

The economic, geostrategic, and militaristic significance of the Mediterranean Sea's eastern basin is underscored by the discovery of vast gas fields and the economic potential they hold for the Mediterranean countries. The natural gas reserves in the Eastern Mediterranean are in the territorial waters of Cyprus, Egypt, Greece, Israel, Lebanon, Syria, and Turkey: "Estimates of the region's hydrocarbon potential have ranged from North Sea–sized reserves to potentially holding as much as 50 billion barrels of petroleum, or BOP, and upward of 500 trillion cubic feet, or TCF, of natural gas. The latter number is roughly comparable to US continental reserves. More significantly, the geologic evidence suggests that these discoveries are just the beginning of a Mediterranean-wide hydrocarbon bonanza. It is possible that the hydrocarbon potential might exceed even the most optimistic assessment. The Mediterranean could well develop into a major supplier of natural gas to Europe to the detriment of Russia's gas exports and, to a lesser extent, America's LNG export plans."[26]

Given the magnitude of these reserves, they are a significant asset and offer economic, geopolitical, and strategic benefits to those who control them.

The energy potential of the eastern Mediterranean is having a significant and potentially transformative impact on the geopolitics of the region. And will be a pivotal factor in the geopolitical construct of the new era.

The world's second-largest oil company, Chevron, has taken notice.

Israel's largest natural gas field, Leviathan, began pumping gas on December 31, 2019. The Leviathan reservoir is one of the world's largest deep-water gas discoveries of the last decade and the Levant Basin's largest natural gas reservoir. Leviathan contains 649 billion cubic meters of natural gas and 41 million barrels of crude oil—representing a reported two-thirds of total gas resources discovered in Israeli waters so far. A portion of the gas extracted is supplied to Egypt and Jordan.

In October 2020, Chevron completed its acquisition of Noble Energy. Chevron holds a 39.66 percent stake in Leviathan, 32.5 percent of Israel's Tamar natural gas field,[27] and operates both. According to Reuters, the deal's value was about $4.2 billion, in addition to an $8 billion Noble Energy debt

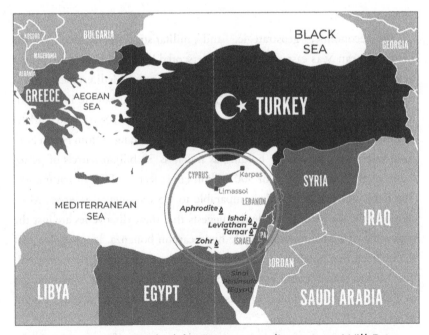

The Energy Potential of the Eastern Mediterranean Will Be a
Pivotal Factor in the Geopolitical Construct of the New Era

that Chevron will take on.[28] In August 2021, given unanticipated demand for Israel's Leviathan gas field in the first half of 2021—mainly from Egypt—Chevron moved up its plans to drill a fifth production well to boost production to early 2022.

Chevron has pivoted to the Middle East and is preparing to pitch new gas deals in Egypt, Israel, and Qatar while cutting spending on American shale exploration.[29]

Egypt's largest gas field, Zohr, opened in January 2018. Italian multinational oil and gas company ENI holds 50 percent of the shares. According to the Egyptian minister of energy, Tariq al-Mula, as of the end of 2019, Egypt had invested $11.5 billion in the field and plans to develop the field further and increase daily production.[30] Egypt is counting on the fields to help address its economic challenges and position Egypt as an oil hub. In mid-February 2020, Egypt signed agreements with Shell, Chevron, BP, Total, and ExxonMobil for deep-water exploration in the western part of Egypt's Mediterranean zone.[31]

In January 2021, Chevron reported that it would invest $235 million in building a gas pipeline from Israel to Egypt.[32] In August 2021, Egyptian petroleum minister Tarek El-Molla announced that Chevron is planning to pump new investments into Egypt's gas and oil exploration sector. Chevron is currently carrying out oil and gas exploration projects across four areas along Egypt's Mediterranean coast. El Molla said that Chevron will be the leading operator and is investing up to $360 million.[33]

Chevron is also currently bidding on additional tenders in the Eastern Mediterranean and is also a partner in the Aphrodite-Ishai gas field, a joint Israeli-Cypriot field.[34]

Whatever the future of natural gas, the fields in the Eastern Mediterranean and the subterranean infrastructure, which can carry hydrogen (a cleaner energy source), are of the highest strategic importance for countries in the East Mediterranean basin.

As I always say, everything in the Middle East is connected, and what happens in the Middle East does not stay in the Middle East. When it comes to the gas reserves in the Eastern Mediterranean, there are lots of interests.

Countries included in Southern Gas Corridor (SGC) and the
Trans-Anatolian Natural Gas Pipeline (TANAP)

The European Union wants to ensure a secure and diverse energy supply. A very ambitious 2,000-mile pipeline project that includes over a dozen energy companies called the Southern Gas Corridor (SGC) will bring natural gas from the Caspian Sea to Europe. The planned SGC pipeline will cross seven countries. It will connect Azerbaijan on the Caspian Sea, Georgia, Turkey, Greece, and Albania. Then it crosses the Mediterranean to Italy.

The part of the pipeline going through Turkey is known as the Trans-Anatolian Natural Gas Pipeline (TANAP). Turkey, Azerbaijan, the State Oil Company of the Azerbaijan Republic (SOCAR), and British Petroleum (BP) own shares in TANAP. Turkey owns 30 percent, the government of Azerbaijan and SOCAR (The State Oil Company of Azerbaijan Republic) own 58 percent, and British Petroleum (BP) owns 12 percent. TANAP is a major strategic card for Turkey. Erdoğan wants to be sure that he controls all the natural gas that flows through Turkish territory so he can maximize 'the gas card.'

In January 2019, the energy ministers of Egypt, Cyprus, Greece, Israel, Italy, Jordan, and the Palestinian Authority met in Cairo to discuss the Eastern Mediterranean Gas Forum (EMGF) establishment. Headquartered in Cairo, the EMGF is the umbrella for cooperation, dialogue, investment, and partnerships regarding the exploration, development, and export of gas resources in the region.

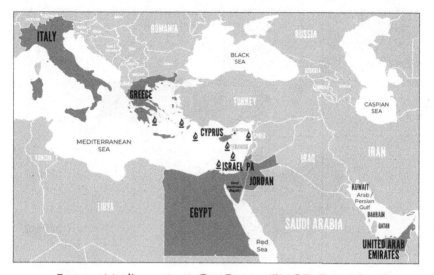

Eastern Mediterranean Gas Forum (EMGF) Countries

Erdoğan views the EMGF alliance as a threat to the "Blue Homeland" vision. Therefore, Turkey's increasingly aggressive strategy in the eastern Mediterranean has been to initiate provocations and to set facts on the water.

In July 2019, Turkey began drilling near the Karpas Peninsula in northern Cyprus. Cyprus and the EU demanded Turkey stop drilling in Cypriot waters, but Turkey refused and became more aggressive and intrusive. Reportedly, in December 2019, the Turkish Navy forced an Israeli gas research ship to leave the area of Cyprus. Turkish provocations continue, including unauthorized drilling, particularly around Cyprus.

As we said, Erdoğan, like Iran, looks for opportunities in areas that suffer from constant instability. Looking across the Mediterranean, Erdoğan saw the perfect opportunity to expand his influence and advance his Mati Vatan agenda: the Civil War in Libya. (We will delve more into the war in Libya in Chapter 4.) One of Turkey's more brazen moves among many brazen acts when it comes to his involvement in the war in Libya took place in November 2019 when Turkey signed an agreement with the Tripoli-based Libyan Government of National Accord (GNA; one of the two competing governments in Libya at the time). The deal marked the maritime borders between Turkey and Libya, and gave Turkey a naval base in Libya. And in return for Turkey arming and training

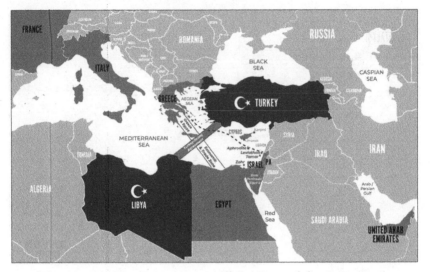

The Eastern Mediterranean Will Be One of the Epicenters
of the New Era

the GNA, Turkey would be able to invest in the Libyan oil sector. However, the competing Eastern Libyan government dismissed the agreement. It argued that the GNA had no mandate to sign such a contract.

In January 2020, Israel signed an agreement with Cyprus and Greece to build the Eastern Mediterranean (EastMed) pipeline, a project to connect the gas reserves in the Eastern Mediterranean with Greece. The deal paves the way for a 1,200-mile undersea natural gas pipeline from the Israeli Leviathan and Cypriot Aphrodite gas field, located about a hundred miles south of Limassol, Cyprus, and which borders Israel's gas fields. The EastMed pipeline would enable natural gas transport from the Mediterranean Sea's gas fields to Europe.

The EastMed pipeline further frustrated Erdoğan's goal to control the Eastern Mediterranean gas.

In May 2020, Cyprus, Egypt, France, Greece, and the UAE condemned Turkey's provocations against Cyprus, Greece, and Libya in the Mediterranean Sea. They demanded Turkey respect states' sovereignty and international maritime law.[35] They reprimanded Erdoğan's illegal attempts to drill for oil in the Cypriot Exclusive Economic Zone, Turkey's violation of the UN Convention

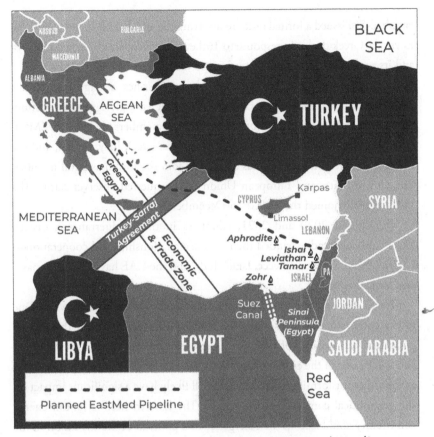

Turkey-Libya (GNA/Sarraj) Agreement, EastMed Pipeline,
Egyptian-Greek Economic and Trade Zone

on the Law of the Sea, its escalating provocations, and increasing violations of Greek air space, and a host of other violations.

In August 2020, Egyptian and Greek foreign ministers signed an agreement agreeing to a "partial demarcation of the sea boundaries between the two countries, and that the remaining demarcation would be achieved through consultations."[36] The agreement also created an exclusive trade and economic zone allowing Egypt and Greece to share oil and gas drilling rights in the demarcated area. This deal could allow both Egypt and Greece to maximize the potential oil and gas reserves they share. In October 2020, Egyptian President Abdel

Fattah al-Sisi issued a formal order re-asserting the agreement. In large part, the Egyptian-Greek deal is in response to Turkey's involvement in the war in Libya and its aggressive gas exploration in waters that do not belong to Ankara.

And Greece and Egypt are not the only ones strengthening their Mediterranean alliances in the face of Turkey's increasingly aggressive posture.

In September 2020, the forum's founding members signed the EMGF Charter. Its members are Cyprus, Egypt, Greece, Israel, Italy, Jordan, and the Palestinian Authority. France has applied to join the forum as a full member. The United States and European Union have requested observer status. The UAE officially joined the EMGF in December 2020.

Throughout 2020 and 2021, countries in the Mediterranean's eastern basin cultivated and expanded their military relationships and cooperation—Cyprus, Egypt, France, Greece, Israel, Italy, and the UAE have held joint naval and air maneuvers.

The name of this book is *Inside the Middle East | Entering A New Era*. One of the cornerstones of this era is the shifting alliances based on threats and opportunities. Because of the vast gas reserves, the eastern Mediterranean is and will be one of the epicenters of this new era. The geopolitical ramifications are already transforming alliances. And will likely have a significant impact on the geopolitical construct of the region. The Eastern Mediterranean energy community could lead to the emergence of a political-economic union in the eastern Mediterranean and beyond.

What Does the Future Hold for Turkey's Hegemonic Vision?

Erdoğan's Achievements

In his quest for domination, expanding his power, achieving regional superiority, and being a global power broker, Erdoğan looks for opportunities and rifts to become a partner and a patron.

His multipronged strategy has many routes and faces, a combination of Islamic populism, nationalism, and authoritarianism. He uses diplomacy, education, financial patronage, supporting state and non-state legal and illicit entities, including terror groups, and providing various forms of military support—from deploying Turkish troops and military hardware to sending his proxies from the Syrian theater. The troops he sends are in addition to the training and know-how he provides as a tool to gain allies and cultivate proxies. And Erdoğan's network of armed subcontractors is growing. (We will

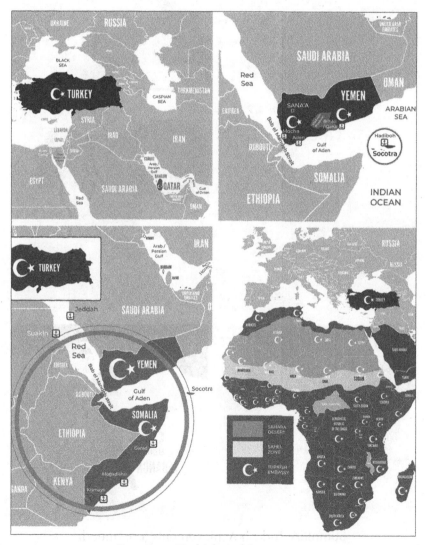

Summary Turkish Achievements

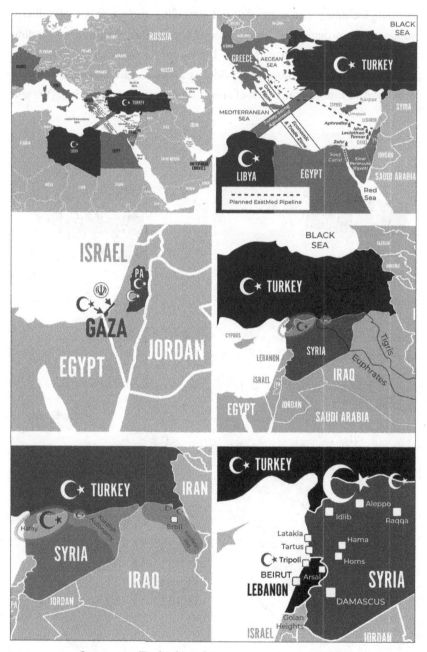

Summary Turkish Achievements (continued)

discuss the war in Syria and specifically Turkey's role in the war in depth in Chapter 6.)

And as of 2021, Erdoğan can mark several achievements.

Turkey has secured a military base in Qatar, gaining Ankara a military foothold in the Gulf in the heart of the Sunni monarchies.

And south of the Gulf, in the Gulf of Aden, Erdoğan has established a base in Qana in southern Yemen—a very strategic location.

West of the Gulf at the crossroads of the Bab el Mandeb and the Red Sea on the Horn of Africa, Turkey has its most extensive military base outside of Turkey in Somalia in East Africa.

Over the past decade, Turkey has significantly deepened its influence in Africa. It has developed commercial, diplomatic, educational, military, and religious footholds across the continent. Today Turkey's footprint in Africa is getting more extensive than most European countries.

As far as Erdoğan's gamble in Libya and across the Mediterranean in Syria (which we will explore further in Chapters 4 and 6). So far, inserting himself into these complicated wars to secure Turkey's interests, spread his power and influence, and promote his own ambitions has served Erdoğan.

Erdoğan is gradually nurturing a power base in another country on the shores of the Mediterranean Sea, Lebanon. (We will explore this further in Chapter 6.) Beyond being a trusted patron of Hamas, Erdoğan is expanding his influence in the Gaza Strip (ruled by Hamas) and the West Bank (partially governed by the Palestinian Authority) through creating and supporting aid, education, and welfare efforts. (We will discuss this in more detail in Chapters 9 and 10.)

All of these efforts combined are spreading Turkey's influence, presence, and reach and are bolstering Erdoğan's position as a regional power broker.

Challenges to Erdoğan's Hegemonic Vision

Turkey's hegemonic vision faces some severe challenges.

Turkey's hegemonic ambitions sustained a setback in two locations. One is the lease Sudan canceled to Suakin Island on the Red Sea. And the other is its failure to gain control over the Socotra Island south of Yemen.

But Erdoğan faces another broader challenge. And that is the changing landscape within political Islam. Let me explain.

Changing Landscape within Political Islam

Erdoğan is Sunni Islamist, and he wants to be the Sunni Muslim camp leader in the region. He is closely affiliated specifically with the Muslim Brotherhood. Using political Islam as a tool to gain allies and supporters and advance his agenda serves Erdoğan. It provides him with a friendly base of political Islam parties, particularly the Muslim Brotherhood—the most prominent Sunni movement. However, at the same time, it could also backfire on him. To explain why I would like to refer to a paragraph from my 2016 book:

> The Arab Awakening offered political Islam an historic opportunity to take a meaningful step in the direction of actualizing its vision. But the leaders of political Islam, especially within the Muslim Brotherhood, mismanaged the opportunity, and no amount of "belly dancing" was enough to keep them in power ... But despite its setbacks, political Islam is by no means down for the count; it is too deeply planted in the broad avenues of the Arab world ... At this stage and in the foreseeable future, the Muslim Brotherhood will continue to focus on reorganization and a political strategy that will preserve its core values and enable it to be attractive to voters who demand real solutions to the challenges of Arab societies. As a result of the need to reconcile ideology with practicalities, struggles between the pragmatic camp and the ideological camp within political Islam will continue. This power struggle is likely to result in the strengthening of the pragmatic camp within political Islam.[37]

And this is precisely what has transpired over the past four years.

The momentum and achievements of political Islam parties in Algeria, Egypt, Jordan, Libya, Morocco, and Tunisia following the 2011 Arab Spring soon became their most crushing defeat. The inability of the Muslim

Brotherhood and other political Islam parties to provide real answers to real problems quickly got them voted out of office. And that defeat resulted in the process of introspection. Should political Islam groups be dogmatic or pragmatic? In that struggle, those who believe pragmatism is the right direction for political Islam are defining the movement's direction.

How does this impact Erdoğan?

Given Erdoğan's profile, political Islam parties are a natural ally. However, as political Islam parties become more pragmatic, and in some cases also prioritize particularistic nationalism (the philosophy/concept/idea of a sovereign, independent political entity [state, autonomy, etc.] based on distinct features and characteristics—geography, language/dialect, food, tradition, culture, etc.) as a central issue on their political agenda, they may prioritize the needs of the state they are in and the political system they are a part of over the pan-Islamist agenda, and hegemonic vision of Erdoğan.

Erdoğan cannot blindly rely on political Islam parties in an environment where political Islam is going through this transformation phase from dogmatism to pragmatism. Please note, I said pragmatism—not moderation. They are not interchangeable terms, and they are not the same thing.

Here are two examples where political Islam's move toward pragmatism has compromised support for Erdoğan.

Turkey is deeply involved in the civil war in Libya. With the consent of the Turkish Parliament, in January 2020, Turkey, as a result of the November 2019 agreement Erdoğan signed, declared it was deploying troops and arms to support the Libyan Islamist Government of National Accord (GNA)—then one of the two rival Libyan governments vying to control and govern Libya. At this juncture, Turkey's direct military intervention changed the tide of the Libyan civil war and helped put the GNA on top.

The Muslim Brotherhood party leader in Tunisia—and the speaker of the Assembly of the Representatives of the People of Tunisia—Rashid al-Ghannouchi, rushed to congratulate GNA and Erdoğan. Tunisia's president, Kais Saied, who himself enjoyed the MB al-Nahda party's support during the election campaign, and other politicians and leaders in Tunisia were unhappy with al-Ghannouchi's diplomatic demonstration on behalf of Tunisia. They argued that al-Ghannouchi bypassed the president and dragged Tunisia into the Libyan conflict, thus compromising Tunisia's national security interests. Therefore, they demanded al-Ghannouchi resign. In Tunisia, the labor union went on a "warning" strike, protesting Turkey's involvement in Libya's war and criticizing al-Ghannouchi for supporting Turkey.

In July 2021, facing a continuing political crisis (we will discuss this more in Chapter 5), Saied dismissed the government and dispersed the parliament. Despite protests by al-Ghannouchi and Islamists, the Tunisian president's move was welcomed by wide circles in Tunisia. The lesson Erdoğan can take away is that he cannot automatically rely on Islamist parties to support his hegemonic policies in the region.

Another example is in Morocco.

Morocco signed a normalization agreement with Israel in December 2020. The reaction of the Islamic parties in Morocco to that agreement is an interesting example of the split in political Islam's ranks between the pragmatic camp and the dogmatic camp.

The Islamic parties that oppose the regime, such as the *Al 'Adl w'al Ihssan* "The Justice and Spirituality" party or the *Al-Tawhid w'al Islah,* "The Oneness of God and Reform" party, vehemently attacked the agreement.[38] On the other hand, the Moroccan Muslim Brotherhood *Al 'Adallah w'al Islah,* "The Justice and Reform" party, praised Morocco's outstanding achievement in signing the normalization agreement. Their response to Morocco's normalization agreement with Israel focused on the fact that the United States recognized Morocco's sovereignty in the Western Sahara. In their response, they were also sure to pay lip service to the Palestinian cause by endorsing the core Palestinian narratives, such as the right of return, Jerusalem is the Palestinian state's capitol, etc.

The reason for the al 'Adallah w'al Islah's position is that it is the majority party in the Moroccan government (General elections are scheduled for September 2021). The party gave priority to Morocco's national interests—sovereignty over the Western Sahara—even if it means that they distance themselves from their fellow Islamist and Muslim Brotherhood supporter Erdoğan, who rejected the normalization agreement.

The head of al 'Adallah w'al Islah party, Dr. (MD) Saed Eddin El-Othmani, has been Morocco's prime minister since March 2017.

In watching his political career, Dr. Othmani has shifted from dogmatism to pragmatism. In the late 1970s, he was a member of the Islamic Youth Movement. Othmani objected to the movement's violence. Therefore, he left the movement and co-founded *Al-Jamiyah al-Islamiyah,* "The Islamic Society," in 1981.

In 1991 the group changed its name to *Al-Islah w'al Tajdid,* "The Reform and Renewal" party. In 1996 the movement changed its name once again to the Al-Tawhid w'al Islah, "The Movement of Oneness of God and Reform" party. From 1999 to 2004, el-Othmani was the deputy secretary-general of the Muslim Brotherhood *al-Adalah w'alTanmiyh,* "The Justice and Development" party.[39]

Interestingly, *al-Tawhid w'al Islah* party el-Othmani co-founded in the early 1990s strongly opposed the normalization agreement that he, as the prime minister of Morocco, signed in 2021.

Given the multitude of calculations regional leaders need to balance the shifting geopolitical sands in the region, Erdoğan cannot rely on Islamist parties in the Arab world to automatically support his hegemonic vision or policies on specific issues. Their political and pragmatic calculations may dictate a policy that does not necessarily serve—let alone comply with—Erdoğan's policy and vision.

Erdoğan's Complex Relationship with the Major Arab States

There is another obstacle on Erdoğan's path to becoming the leader of the Sunni Middle East. The major Arab states—Egypt, Saudi Arabia, and the UAE—strongly oppose Turkey's hegemonic vision. They don't like his interference in countries and conflicts beyond Ankara's borders—Libya, Qatar, and Yemen are a few examples. They are also disturbed by his manipulation of the Israeli-Palestinian conflict for his own gain, whether sending humanitarian aid flotillas to Gaza, supporting Hamas in Gaza, or cultivating relationships with Islamic groups in the West Bank and Jerusalem. They resent his bullying in the Eastern Mediterranean as he tries to gobble up all the gas fields either to use as leverage or to secure Turkey as an energy broker. And they resent Erdoğan's neo-Ottoman hyper-nationalism and his attempt to crown himself as the leader of the Sunni camp in the region. They look at Erdoğan as someone who wants to challenge their leadership and unseat them as the regional leaders and powers.

Furthermore, he supports the Muslim Brotherhood and its offspring, Hamas. Whereas Egypt, Saudi Arabia, and the UAE view the Muslim Brotherhood as a threat, and they view Hamas as a destabilizing Iranian-backed agent. In 2019 and 2020, Saudi Arabia arrested Palestinians in the Kingdom and accused them of being Hamas activists.[40] On August 8, 2021, the Saudi court published the sentences of sixty-nine Hamas operatives living in Saudi Arabia and Jordan. They were sentenced to various periods of imprisonment between six months and twenty-two years; five were found innocent and released.[41]

The resentment of the major Arab countries to Erdoğan's ambitions has translated into actions.

In the summer of 2020, Egypt conducted an extensive military exercise on its border with Libya. The same summer, al-Sisi also proposed the Cairo Initiative to end the war in Libya. When Turkey and Fayez al-Sarraj (then prime minister of the Government of National Accord in Libya) rejected his efforts, he put Egyptian troops on notice to be ready to defend Egypt anywhere.

In October 2020, Chairman, Council of Saudi Chambers of Commerce and Industry, Ajlan Al Ajlan, called for an economic boycott of Turkey's goods and products, including a boycott of Turkish tourism. The trade between the two countries exceeds $6 billion a year. In an October 2, 2020, tweet, he wrote: "The boycott is on everything that is Turkish, in the field of imports, investments or tourism, the reason for this is the continued Turkish hostility to Saudi Arabia, its leadership and its citizens."[42] Al-Ajlan made this personal statement under a directive from the Saudi Royal House. The Royal House would not make an official announcement because it would be against international law to call for such a boycott. The boycott is unofficial because Saudi Arabia is concerned that Turkey will file a complaint to the World Trade Organization.[43] Following his tweet, Turkish companies complained that Saudi Arabia was making it difficult to bring Turkish goods into the Kingdom, preventing it from importing some goods or delaying other goods in the port for a long time until they were released from customs. As of the summer of 2021, Saudi's informal boycott is still in place.

In 2020 and 2021, joint military exercises between Cyprus, Greece, Egypt, Israel, Italy, the UAE in the Red Sea, and the Mediterranean were meant to send a strong signal to Ankara that the evolving Mediterranean-Gulf monarchy alliances were not happy with Erdoğan's behavior.

In August 2021, al-Sisi has been clear, in word and deed, that he views Turkey's ambitions in the eastern basin of the Mediterranean Sea, the Red Sea, the Arab Gulf, and Yemen as a severe threat to Egypt's national security and interests.

Because of his behavior, the shifting alliances from the Mediterranean have clearly sidelined Erdoğan.

In the spring of 2021, Erdoğan blinked. He began to publicly court Cairo, and since then, the relationship between Egypt and Turkey has somewhat warmed. The two countries formally expressed interest and willingness to solve the controversy over maritime borders diplomatically.

At the beginning of May 2021, a Turkish delegation led by the Turkish minister of Foreign Affairs arrived in Cairo for the first time in eight years.

I attribute Erdoğan's and al-Sisi's change of heart to several factors.

First, both Erdoğan and al-Sisi are interested in calming tensions between the two countries stemming from their conflicting interests in Libya. (We will further delve into this in the next chapter.)

Second, Erdoğan's relationship with the Biden administration did not get off to a stellar start as far as Erdoğan is concerned. President Biden did not call the Turkish president until April 2021—more than three months into his term. And it was not the call Erdoğan wanted to receive. Joe Biden told the Turkish president that he intended to recognize the 1915 massacres of Armenians in the Ottoman Empire as genocide. Moreover, given the prominence of civil and human rights on the Democratic agenda, both al-Sisi and Erdoğan have reasons to be worried. As a counterbalance, both strive to position themselves as leaders who can contribute to regional stability.[44,45]

Third, Egypt is not the only Sunni power Erdoğan is trying to mend fences with in the summer of 2021. The Turkish president is currently in different stages of discussions with Egypt and the Gulf monarchies—particularly Saudi Arabia and the UAE. The primary reason for Erdoğan's efforts is the economy. The trade between Turkey and Arab countries is estimated to be $50 billion a year.[46] Saudi investments in Turkey represent about 30 percent of the total foreign investments in Turkey. And one hundred thousand Turks work in Saudi Arabia.[47]

However, given their interests, positions, and roles, I expect the relationship between al-Sisi and Erdoğan to experience peaks and valleys.

Here is an example:

In Turkey, there are Muslim Brotherhood satellite television channels—*Al-Sharq* and *Mekameleen*. These channels are known for their harsh critics of the Egyptian regime. As part of Erdoğan's rapprochement policy, in March and April 2021, Turkey 'silenced' political commentators and programs that harshly criticized Egypt.[48]

However, in May 2021, Erdoğan allowed them to 'resume their regularly scheduled programming.' In other words, he let them be as critical of al-Sisi as they wanted. The reason for Erdoğan's change of heart—and of policy—was the war between Israel and Hamas in May 2021 (we will explore the war in Chapters 9 and 10).

Egypt, as usual, was the mediator and the country that brokered the ceasefire. Egypt views Hamas, which defines itself as the Muslim Brotherhood chapter in Gaza, as a destabilizing factor. Al-Sisi does not want violence in Gaza to ignite protests in Egypt.

But in atypical fashion, this time Cairo waited a while until they began to intervene. The delay was al-Sisi's way of letting Hamas know that Cairo was not happy that Hamas had started the war. Al-Sisi wanted Hamas to be taught a lesson. And Israeli military strikes on Hamas served that purpose. So, al-Sisi did not rush in so quickly to invest in calming the flames.

For Erdoğan, Gaza is a vital card to further his hegemonic ambitions and position himself as the Sunni camp leader. He does not intend to give up this card. By allowing the critics of al-Sisi to return to the Turkish stage, Erdoğan gained two 'points.'

First, he positioned himself as the defender of the Palestinians, while Cairo had abandoned them—at least in the beginning of the conflict.

And second, he wanted to show al-Sisi that Egypt is not the only Sunni power in the Gaza arena. As I mentioned earlier, in May 2021, the Turkish news agency published the article "Only Erdoğan can protect the innocent children of Palestine." The article accused the Arabs of forgetting Palestine and positioned the Turkish president as the only solution to the current crisis in Palestine.[49]

However, in July, Erdoğan flipped again. In parallel to pursuing warmer relations with the Gulf states, Turkey once again 'silenced' Egypt's harsh critics. Egypt's foreign minister, Sameh Shoukry, praised Erdoğan's efforts. "The decision to prevent fugitives and the Muslim Brotherhood from appearing on the media and social media is a policy that is consistent with the rules of international law. This step, if it stabilizes and continues, will lead to the normalization of relations and the continuation of contacts at various levels to set a framework for the resumption of relations."[50]

Israel and Turkey

Another regional power concerned with Erdoğan's ambitions and provocations is Israel. Turkey and Israel have a history of mutually beneficial relationships in multiple fields, including security, commerce, trade, and tourism.

Like Iran and many other Arab and Muslim leaders, Erdoğan uses al-Muqawama (the Resistance), al-Quds (Jerusalem), and his support for the Palestinians as one of the pillars of his hegemonic strategy. His support for the Palestinians, and specifically his support for the Palestinian Islamist organization Hamas, which vows to eliminate the State of Israel using violence, is a central source of tension in the Israeli-Turkish relationship. As a public demonstration of his commitment to the Palestinian cause, Erdoğan has launched humanitarian flotillas to Gaza. He hosts Hamas senior leadership in Istanbul and provides financial support for Hamas.

Erdoğan's anti-Israeli policy—primarily his support of Hamas—has damaged the diplomatic relations and military cooperation between Turkey and Israel. The relationship—excluding trade—has deteriorated over the years.

However, toward the end of 2020, Turkey signaled its interest in improving its relationship with Israel. In my analysis, Erdoğan's change of heart—similar to his rapprochement with Egypt and the Gulf—has a lot to do with the new US administration. As I said before, Erdoğan was anticipating a tense relationship with President Biden. And he was looking for ways to begin on a positive note. He believed that changing his tune toward Israel was a step to that end.

However, Israel has had bad experiences with Erdoğan. Therefore, Israel did not rush to reciprocate Turkey's flirtations. Israel's reserved and skeptical approach proved to be justified. During the May 2021 war with Hamas, Erdoğan was one of Israel's most vocal and harshest critics.

Turkey's vitriolic rhetoric was accompanied by diplomatic efforts, mainly but not exclusively, directed at leaders of Muslim countries. Turkey also took extensive action through government media aimed at the international community. Following the escalation, the Turkish foreign minister threatened that the Muslim world would send a global force to Jerusalem to prevent any recurrence of the measures taken by Israel. He tweeted in Hebrew condemning "the despicable Israeli attacks" at al-Aqsa. Statements by decision-makers in Ankara repeatedly accused Israel of being a "terrorist state."[51]

Turkey and the International Community

Internationally, Erdoğan's policies and provocations have also raised tensions with European players. His interference in Libya, his growing engagement in Africa, his threats to flood Europe with Syrian refugees, his provocative oil drilling in Cypriot waters, and his claims to the Aegean Sea fuel growing tensions with France, Germany, Greece, and Italy. In December 2020, EU leaders imposed sanctions on several Turkish officials and entities involved in gas drilling in Cypriot-claimed waters.

Erdoğan's policy has also resulted in growing tensions with the United States. The sides are at odds over a series of issues, including Armenia, Iran, the Kurds, Syria, human rights violations, etc. There is a general sense of mutual mistrust.

Aggravated by Turkey's moves, the United States in 2019 refused to deliver advanced F-35 fighter jets to Turkey, sanctioned senior Turkish officials, and raised tariffs on Turkish steel exports. And both branches of Congress passed a resolution (H. Res 296 from October 2019 and S. Res 150 from December 2019) recognizing the 1915 massacre of Armenians in the Ottoman Empire as genocide.

During the first half of 2021, President Biden's administration sent strong signals to Turkey, expressing its resentment of Turkey's policy.

In the wake of Turkey's deal to buy S-400 missiles from Russia, in March 2021, the Biden administration decided to freeze cooperation with Turkey on the F-35 aircraft. Turkey is one of the countries licensed to manufacture parts of the F-35. The Turkish Air Force is due to receive its first F-35 in November 2021. Yet, the United States has informed Turkey that it is freezing the shipment of parts Turkey needs to absorb the F-35 aircraft into the Turkish Air Force. In addition, the United States is examining the possibility of revoking the permit given to Turkey to manufacture parts of the F-35.

The United States also exhibited its displeasure with Erdoğan's regional policy on the water. In February 2021, the United States conducted naval exercises near Turkey with the Greek and Cypriot navies. This was a clear hint from the United States to Turkey to stop its provocative drilling in Greek and Cypriot territorial waters.

As I said earlier, the first call President Biden placed to President Erdoğan was in April 2021, three months after Biden's election. During the conversation, Biden updated the Turkish president on his decision to recognize the Armenian Holocaust as a genocide committed by the Ottomans. As expected, Biden's statement sparked an angry Turkish protest.

As of the summer of 2021, Turkish-US relations can be described as chilly—and even tense. Some analysts believe Turkey and the United States' relationship will become increasingly strained under the Biden administration. The Democratic administration will likely emphasize human rights. Assessments are that Erdoğan's regional provocations and brutal dictatorship at home will fuel growing tensions between DC and Ankara. However, it is essential to remember that Tukey is a major regional player and is a central member—and one of the most significant powers—in NATO. Given all of Biden's considerations, I believe that his administration will prioritize realpolitik calculations when it comes to the US relationship with Turkey at the end of the day.

So . . . Where Does All of This Leave Turkey and Specifically Erdoğan?

Domestically, Erdoğan's political power is eroding.

As of 2021, Turkey faces growing economic challenges and shrinking cash reserves, with a $33 billion budget deficit. In 2020 its economy shrunk by

10 percent. And unemployment in Turkey has reached 14 percent. There is currently no path to recovery.[52]

Resolutely dismissive of human and civil rights, Erdoğan brutally and ruthlessly crushes local opposition. And his violent tyranny fuels growing discontent and polarization inside Turkey. These trends erode Erdoğan's political power. In Turkey's 2018 general elections, Erdoğan won decisively. But a year later, his party, the Justice and Development Party (AKP), was defeated in the municipal elections of Turkey's three major cities—Ankara, Istanbul, and Izmir (including a repeat round in Istanbul). These events suggest that his reign and that of the AKP are not necessarily irreversible. The next elections for the Turkish parliament and presidency are scheduled for June 2023. At present, no leader on the horizon poses a threat to Erdoğan's rule. However, given the growing challenges in Turkey and the complex Turkish political fabric, there is a possibility that Turkey could see a change of guard in 2023.

Abroad, Recep Tayyip Erdoğan is seen by both his allies and his rivals as a thug and a provocative, destabilizing leader. His personality plays a significant role in his leadership of Turkey. He walks on the edge and is the regional provocateur.

His ultimate goal is to alter the geopolitical status quo to benefit himself.

Turkey is a regional power with global aspirations. Fueled by a Pan-Islamic ideology, Erdoğan is determined for Turkey to lead the Sunni camp in the Middle East. Aspiring to revive the glory days of the Ottoman Empire, Erdoğan wants to be a frontline leader of the Islamic world.

To achieve these goals, he focuses on advancing Turkey's primary strategic interests, including energy security, commercial trade, and expanding markets for its products—particularly its military industry.

Erdoğan unilaterally pursues military interventions and seeks to control foreign territory. He inserted himself into the war in Libya and Syria, maintains bases overseas in Somalia and Qatar, and gathers and deploys proxies from Syria to Africa. In Syria, he is demographically engineering territory to secure his control and power. And in Africa, he is striving to upset the power balance.

He ignores international law and violates the water-sharing agreements he signed with Iraq and Syria by building dams on the Euphrates and the Tigris Rivers. His unilateral actions are causing humanitarian and environmental

disasters in both of those countries. Determined to prevent a Kurdish autonomy, he ignores borders and set up military bases in Iraqi territory.

When it comes to Cyprus, Greece, and Egypt, he drills in their waters,
challenges maritime boundaries, disregards signed agreements, and violates
the sovereignty of other nations.

He launches flotillas to the Gaza Strip and inserts himself into Palestinian
affairs in the West Bank. And he threatens to flood Europe with Syrian refugees as a card to get countries to capitulate to his desires.

In July 2020, he turned the world-famous Hagia Sophia museum in
Istanbul—originally a cathedral—back into a mosque while completely ignoring the international community's discontent and criticism.

As tensions with France over Turkey's provocations in the Mediterranean
increased, Erdoğan used offensive language and behavior toward French
President Emmanuel Macron. Breaking the diplomatic protocol code,
Erdoğan publicly addressed the French president and said, "You should check
whether you are brain-dead."[53]

Erdoğan knows you cannot be—or claim to be—a regional superpower, let
alone a global power if you don't have a presence or exert influence in strategic
arenas such as the Mediterranean Sea, the Red Sea, the Indian Ocean, and
Africa. He concentrates on these arenas to achieve his grandiose ambitions.
The importance of these arenas to Turkey has grown even more given the
new geostrategic construct emerging in the Middle East. Therefore, Turkey's
regional policy will strive to ensure and increase Turkish interests in these arenas as much as Erdoğan possibly can.

However, Turkey's hegemonic vision collides with the vital interests of
key Middle East players, including the alliance of moderation, the Eastern
Mediterranean Gas Forum (EMGF), Turkey's neighbors—Cyprus, Greece,
Iraq, and Syria—and the European Union.

The extensive pushback to Erdoğan's ongoing competition for power,
aggressive and intrusive provocations in pursuit of his hyper-national, hegemonic, neo-Ottoman, pan-Islamic ambitions, combined with Turkey's profound socio-economic challenges, will likely be an obstacle to Erdoğan's
pursuit of his hegemonic dreams. We may even witness the Erdoğan era coming to an end by the middle of this decade.

CHAPTER 4

LIBYA | A STRATEGIC ARENA TO BE WATCHED CLOSELY

Libya—An Overview

Libya is an Arab state that has been engulfed in a brutal civil war for the last decade. A war that has turned the country into a stage for the conflicting interests of regional and global players.

Before discussing this very complex conflict, I would like to give you some background about Libya and the war that has engulfed the country since 2011.

Libya is the fourth-largest country land-wise in Africa, spanning over 700,000 square miles, with a population of 6.8 million people. It is a tribal and conservative society. It is composed of two major ethnic groups—*Arabs* and *Berbers* native to North Africa.

Libyan Dictator Muammar al-Gaddafi ruled Libya for forty-two years, from 1969 until he was ousted (and lynched) in October 2011. Since then, Libya has been embroiled in a civil war where various Libyan powers—mainly armed militias and tribes—have been fighting for power and control.

The violence in Libya has also provided fertile ground for militant Islamist organizations affiliated with al-Qaeda, ISIS, and the Muslim Brotherhood to grow their network, recruit more militants, and increase their activities.

Libya has two main assets that everyone is fighting to control.

One is the "Oil Crescent"—a coastal area stretching from Ras Lanuf in eastern Libya to Sirte's city in northern Libya to the district of Jufra in southern Libya. The Oil Crescent is where most of Libya's export terminals are located, and more than 60 percent of Libya's oil is produced. Libya has the largest oil reserves in Africa and has the ninth-largest oil reserves on the planet. Almost 70 percent of Libya's revenue comes from exporting oil, and oil and gas make up roughly 60 percent of Libya's GDP.

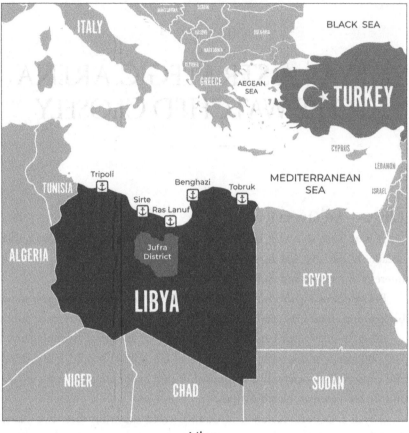

Libya

The other Libyan "asset" is the fact that Libya is the main smuggling corridor between Africa and Europe.

Following Gaddafi's ouster, Libya sank into a civil war between the tribes in eastern Libya and the tribes in western Libya.

The Civil War in Libya—Two Competing Centers of Power, the GNA, and the LNA

The civil war in Libya has resulted in the formation of two competing power centers. One is the eastern government, based in Tobruk. The other is an Islamist-affiliated western government based in Tripoli.

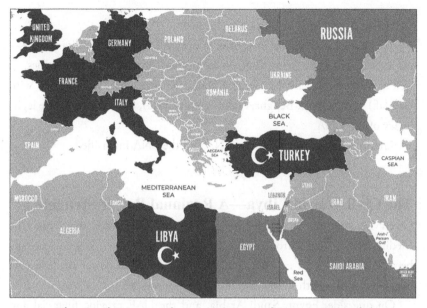

The Civil War in Libya—A Regional Power Struggle

In December 2015, in an attempt to end the civil war and resolve the dispute between the eastern and western seats of government, the United Nations brokered an agreement known as the Libyan Political Agreement (LPA) or the Skihrat Agreement (since it was signed in Skihrat, Morocco).

The LPA created a Presidency Council—a body tasked to form a unity government. The United Nations Security Council endorsed the agreement (UNSCR 2259) and called on the Presidency Council to form a Government of National Accord (GNA).

The Tripoli-based GNA was supposed to be the official government of Libya. The UNSCR also called on all member states not to support or contact any other entity outside the GNA that claims to be Libya's official representative or government.

In March 2016, the GNA was established under the leadership of Fayez al-Sarraj. The GNA has a military force comprised of tribes and Islamist militias, particularly militias affiliated with the Muslim Brotherhood. France, Germany, Italy, the United Kingdom, and the United States recognized the GNA as the official representative of Libya.

However, the crisis in Libya was not over.

The parallel government in Tobruk in eastern Libya and its military force—the Libyan National Army (LNA)—comprised of eastern Libyan tribes, as well as Salafists, and led by General Haftar Khalifa (who was affiliated with Gaddafi) and based in Benghazi (also in east Libya), did not accept the legitimacy of the GNA.

And the civil war between the GNA and the LNA intensified.

The Civil War in Libya—A Regional Power Struggle

Given its strategic location—the gateway to Africa directly across the Mediterranean from Europe—and its oil, the Libyan Civil War increasingly became a stage for an evolving and flammable regional power struggle over hegemony and wealth in the eastern Mediterranean Sea.

On one side, Egypt, Saudi Arabia, and the UAE provide financial and military support to Haftar's LNA. Reportedly, Israel is also, to a lesser extent, involved—providing the LNA with military training and the means to intercept hostile drones.[1]

Russia also provides military and financial support to the LNA, and the Russian paramilitary mercenary organization, the "Wagner Group," fights side by side with Haftar's LNA militias on the ground. For Russia, Libya is a lucrative strategic opportunity. Gas and oil deals, arms sales, and construction projects to rehabilitate Libya's infrastructure are attractive reasons Vladimir Putin wants to engage in Libya. Moreover, it helps Moscow further secure itself in the region—a process that began in 2015 when Iran asked Putin to intervene militarily in the war in Syria to save Assad's rule. (We will discuss this much more in Chapter 6.)

Since then, Putin has focused on entrenching himself in the region and re-establishing Russia as a superpower in the Middle East. Putin is in Syria and has no intention of ceding any influence there. A permanent Russian presence in Libya—including a possible naval base—would be another notch in his belt. Putin wants to build on his success in Syria to secure his place in the Middle East and the Eastern Mediterranean. To that end, Libya is perfectly positioned.

Since the United States ambassador to Libya, Christopher Stevens, and another three United States personnel were killed in Libya in September 2012, the United States has become more reluctant to broaden its engagement beyond the realm of fighting terror. The Trump administration zigzagged in the evolving power struggle between al-Sarraj's GNA and Haftar's LNA.

After a status quo in the fighting, in April 2019, General Haftar attempted to expand his control from eastern Libya into western Libya. He launched a military campaign that included trying to capture Tripoli—the seat of al-Sarraj's government. In response, US Secretary of State Mike Pompeo called for a stop in the fighting and emphasized the need for negotiations. However, shortly afterward, Donald Trump had a phone call with Haftar in which he praised the general for fighting terror.

Turkey and the War in Libya

The war in Libya has become a stage for regional and global powers fighting over influence, money, power, and resources. However, one of the most provocative and controversial players on the world stage today sees Libya as a cornerstone of his hegemonic ambitions. And that is the figure we met in the previous chapter—none other than President Recep Tayyip Erdoğan.

Erdoğan, like Iran, looks for opportunities in areas that suffer from constant instability. Taking advantage of instability in Africa, Turkey is significantly concentrating on expanding its reach through the continent from Somalia through the Sahara Belt and Central and Western Africa.

The Civil War in Libya offered Erdoğan another perfect opportunity to expand his influence, advance his Mati Vatan agenda, and further his hegemonic vision.

A foothold in Libya would position Erdoğan at the doorstep of two of Turkey's primary foreign policy objectives to win him regional hegemony. Expanding Turkey's economic, military, and political influence throughout Africa; and controlling the gas in the eastern Mediterranean.

Given Erdoğan's African ambitions, establishing a military foothold in North Africa on the southern Mediterranean doorstep of the continent offers Erdoğan a powerful platform to increase his relationships and influence throughout Africa. Ankara already has its most extensive military base

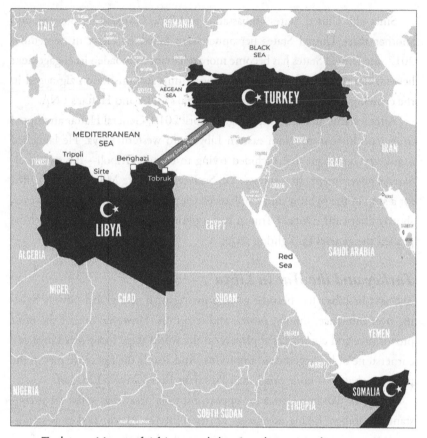

Turkey—Horn of Africa and the Southern Mediterranean

outside Turkey in Somalia in East Africa on the Arabian Sea and the Indian Ocean. Libya offers him a second military installation in Africa, this time on the Mediterranean Sea.

As we discussed in the previous chapter, one of Turkey's primary strategic interests is energy security. Having a presence in Libya puts Erdoğan on top of the largest oil reserves in Africa—a position that would also help alleviate Turkey's financial distress and energy challenges.

Securing Turkey in Libya would allow Erdoğan to create a Turkish-controlled vertical corridor stretching from Turkey to Libya, positioning Erdoğan north and south of the Mediterranean's gas fields at the entrance to the Eastern basin of the Mediterranean. This extraordinarily strategic position is a staggeringly valuable card and one of Erdoğan's most primary strategic objectives.

Adding to Libya's value is the fact that it is Europe's gateway to Africa—and Africa's gateway to Europe. For a cunning and cynical leader like Erdoğan—looking ahead, this position gives him enormous opportunities and leverage.

From an additional angle, the two Arab countries west of Libya—Tunisia, which borders Libya, and its neighbor, Algeria—are potential allies for Erdoğan. The Sunni Muslim Brotherhood parties are central players in both of those countries.

And in his fight for Sunni supremacy, a stronghold in Libya positions Turkey directly next to Egypt, its major rival.

So now that we understand the advantages Libya offers Turkey, let's look at Erdoğan's engagement in the war.

Military Support and Joined Territorial Waters

Erdoğan inserted himself into the civil war in Libya in 2014 when the al-Sarraj government asked for his help. In response, Turkey provided military support and training to the al-Sarraj GNA government and the Muslim Brotherhood militias in western Libya.

Over time, Turkey's involvement in the conflict and directly in the war deepened.

In November 2019, Turkey signed an agreement with al-Sarraj's GNA. Turkey would send troops and arm the GNA, and Erdoğan would be able to invest in the Libyan oil sector.

The most salient points of the agreement are that it gives Turkey a naval base in Libya and joins Libya's and Turkey's territorial waters. This article of the contract has some legal basis. The 1994 United Nations Convention on the Law of the Sea (UNCLOS) determined that countries can assert their sovereignty over twelve nautical miles (twenty-two kilometers) from their coasts. Beyond these "territorial waters," they also get another twelve nautical miles as a "contiguous zone" of control. And they can establish an "exclusive economic zone" for 200 nautical miles from shore. The law also includes the "continental shelf," the seabed below, and whatever oil and gas may be in it.[2]

Turkey Could Control the Entrance to the Eastern Mediterranean

Erdoğan's agreement with al-Sarraj was condemned by many Mediterranean countries, the European Union, and the United States. General Haftar, the Libyan National Army (LNA) commander, dismissed the agreement, arguing that the GNA had no mandate to sign such a contract. He denounced it as a "flagrant breach" of the country's security and sovereignty.

The Libyan parliament refused to ratify the Turkey-Sarraj agreement. On January 27, 2021, the Al Bayda Court of Appeals of Libya canceled the Turkish-GNA memorandum on maritime zones. Erdoğan, however, has continued to insist that the agreement is a valid demarcation of Turkish-controlled waters.[3]

The Turkish-Libyan GNA agreement that cuts across the Egyptian and Greek exclusive economic zones and has a legal footing is a shrewd and tactical maneuver. It is a significant step in the practical actualization of Erdoğan's Mavi Vatan ambition.

Furthermore, it could give Erdoğan the ability to create a north-south corridor—a "Turkish-Territorial Zone" across the Mediterranean from Libya to Turkey. And anyone who crosses the Mediterranean between Turkey and Libya would have to ask their permission. The likelihood of them going that far is slim. But given the escalating atmosphere in the Mediterranean, this maritime agreement at the entrance of the eastern basin of the Mediterranean Sea is disturbing.

In 2020, Turkey Turned the Tide of the War for al-Sarraj and the GNA

In mid-December 2019, following the signing of the agreement with Ankara, al-Sarraj asked Turkey for air protection, military training, and intelligence. Turkey arms the GNA with weapons and provides them with tactical intelligence. Erdoğan avoids sending Turkish troops to Libya and circumvents putting Turkish boots on the ground in Libya by sending his proxy militias from Syria. At the end of 2019, it was estimated that Erdoğan had sent hundreds (and—according to other reports—a few thousand) of Syrian and non-Syrian militants to fight in Libya.[4]

At the beginning of 2020, the military campaign Haftar began in April 2019 to expand his control from eastern Libya into Tripoli and western Libya was gaining momentum.

In January 2020, Haftar's LNA occupied the central coastal city of Sirte. Sirte is roughly halfway between Tripoli and Benghazi and was controlled by al-Sarraj's GNA.

In the same month, January 2020, in an attempt to end the war and bring the LNA and the GNA back to the negotiating table, Germany and Russia hosted a conference in Berlin. The conference's concluding statement reiterated the need to move toward an agreement based upon the December 2015 Skhirat agreement and subsequent UNSC Resolution 2259. Haftar dismissed the conference's conclusions.

In February 2020, with complete disregard for international efforts to end the conflict, an LNA spokesperson reported that Turkey had sent 6,000 Syrian militants and 1,500 al-Qaeda militants to Libya.[5]

Throughout April and May 2020, the number of Turkish proxies in Libya reportedly rose quickly and reached 10,000–12,000.[6]

On May 11, 2020, the foreign ministers of Cyprus, Egypt, France, Greece, and the UAE made a joint statement. They rebuked Turkey's increasingly belligerent behavior, proactive involvement in the war in Libya, and flagrant violations of Eastern Mediterranean countries' sovereignty and sovereign spaces. As far as the relationship between Turkey and Libya, the leaders firmly denounced Turkey's involvement in the war in Libya and Erdoğan's maritime borders agreement with al-Sarraj. They chastised him for his belligerence in the Mediterranean, violating the Libyan arms embargo, and for sending foreign fighters from Syria to Libya. The demands were precise. Stop interfering and causing instability in the Eastern Mediterranean. Their pleas fell on deaf ears.

On May 18, 2020, al-Sarraj's GNA forces, assisted by Turkish attack drones and the Turkish Navy, seized control of the Al-Watiya airbase on the southwest outskirts of Tripoli.

Late May 2020 was a turning point in the battle for Tripoli and the war in general.

Turkey and al-Sarraj's GNA gained momentum on the ground. Haftar's LNA forces retreated from the outskirts of Tripoli. And GNA forces secured their control of western Libya.

Turkey's involvement and support—and specifically Istanbul's multi-pronged efforts to neutralize the LNA's airpower capabilities—turned the tide in the war and tipped the scales in favor of al-Sarraj and the GNA.

Regional Powers Continued Consternation

In June 2020, after the GNA's military momentum, Putin sent Turkey a strong signal that Moscow was unhappy with Erdoğan. To support and strengthen Haftar, Russia supplied the LNA with eight Russian jet fighters. And LNA Air Force Commander Saqr al-Joroushi said that "all Turkish targets are legitimate targets" for their fighter jets.[7]

And if that wasn't clear enough—on June 26, 2020, Putin sent another message to the GNA. The Russian paramilitary Wagner Group entered Libya's most extensive oil field—the Sharara oil field—in eastern Libya, controlled by Haftar's forces. The militias entered and stopped work in Libya's largest oil field, which produces more than 300,000 barrels a day of crude oil, accounting for about one-third of Libya's oil production.

Egypt shares a 700-mile-long wide-open border with Libya. Instability in Libya is fertile ground for ISIS and other militant Islamic groups. They use Libya as a base to launch terror attacks on Egypt and Europe. The terror bases in Libya and the free flow of terrorists, militants, and weapons unabated from Libya crossing Egypt is a significant security threat for Egypt. Stability in Libya is of primary importance to Egypt.

In the summer of 2020, Egypt became increasingly annoyed by Turkey's growing foothold in Libya.

Over the ensuing months, Egypt conducted an extensive military exercise on its border with Libya, including firing missiles from submarines and warships.

And on June 6, 2020, Egyptian President Abdel Fattah al-Sisi proposed a peace plan called "the Cairo Initiative" to end Libya's war. It included a cease-fire, removing foreign militants from Libya, and moving forward with the 2015 agreements. The international community welcomed Egypt's initiative, including Germany, Jordan, Russia, Saudi Arabia, Russia, the United Arab Emirates, and the United States. General Haftar accepted Cairo's proposal. But al-Sarraj's GNA and Turkey rejected al-Sisi's initiative. Al-Sisi was not happy that al-Sarraj and Turkey refused the proposal.

On June 20, 2020, he made a formal statement during a visit to an Egyptian airbase near the Libyan border. In the presence of Libya's eastern tribal leaders, the Egyptian president said, "Occupying the area stretching from Sirte to Jufra is a red line that Egypt will not allow to be crossed."[8] Addressing Egyptian military personnel, al-Sisi also said, "Be prepared to carry out any mission here inside our borders." In response, the GNA announced that al-Sisi "has declared a war on Libya."[9]

Undeterred, Erdoğan continues to entrench himself in this ongoing war. According to an August 2020 report by the United States Military's Africa

Command (AFRICOM), approximately 5,000 Syrians were fighting in Libya's GNA ranks. The report states that the "Syrians fighting for the GNA are paid and supervised by 'several dozen' military trainers from a Turkish company called Sadat, which also trains GNA-aligned militias." Meanwhile, the Syrian Observatory for Human Rights puts the number higher (at 17,000). And SOHR claims that 471 Syrians have been killed in Libya.[10]

And we must not forget that Erdoğan is not only engaged in the war in Libya to ensure a foothold in Libya. This is part of his larger and multi-faceted strategy to spread his influence throughout Africa. His continuing and evolving engagement in the war in Libya has future implications in Africa beyond Erdoğan wanting to upset the geopolitical power balance and seize more control.

According to an August 2020 study by the Emirates Policy Center (EPC), 229 senior leaders of terrorist organizations from the Jabhat al-Nusrah and ISIS were sent from Turkey to Tripoli, Libya. This means that militants from these terror organizations can easily spread to other regions in Africa.[11]

So, Where Does This Leave Turkey's Involvement in Libya in the Summer of 2021?

On the one hand, Erdoğan has a lot to gain from the GNA's achievements that he has made possible. His involvement in Libya positions Erdoğan at the doorstep of two of Turkey's primary foreign policy objectives to win him regional hegemony. Expanding Turkey's economic, military, and political influence throughout Africa and controlling the gas in the Mediterranean.

These are excellent reasons for Erdoğan to entrench himself in Libya further.

On the other hand, Turkey's ambition to maintain and increase its influence in Libya faces significant obstacles.

One obstacle is that a protracted military engagement in Libya could reverse Erdoğan's achievements. General Haftar has already called on Libyans to fight against the "Turkish Imperialist Invasion mercilessly."[12]

But there is a second obstacle, perhaps more critical to Erdoğan's broader interests. Continuing to stay in Libya may exacerbate Egyptian and Russian ire. Erdoğan remembers when Putin gave Haftar the fighter jets in June 2020 and his seizure of the Sharara oil field. In the same month, when al-Sisi commanded his troops to be prepared to protect Egypt anywhere, Erdoğan understood the message. Both Egypt and Russia were signaling that it was time to get back to the negotiating table.

And Erdoğan remembers that aggravating the Russian bear is dangerous. On November 24, 2015, Turkey shot down a Russian jet, arguing it had infiltrated Turkey's territory. Putin retaliated with economic and trade sanctions, including suspending gas delivery to Turkey. Following that incident, Erdoğan had to go to Moscow to make a personal plea to Putin.

As I always say, everything in the Middle East is connected. Nothing stands alone. Regarding Turkey in Libya, it is essential to consider Erdoğan's relationship with Russia in another theater—Syria.

We will further explore Turkey's engagement in Syria in Chapter 6. But I want to explain what I just said. Because as important as Africa is to Erdoğan, Turkey's top strategic priority is preventing a Kurdish autonomy. How are the two connected?

In March 2020, following a military skirmish between Turkey and Assad regime forces in northern Syria, Turkey and Russia signed an agreement to end the fighting and restore calm in northern Syria. That agreement is critical to preserving Erdoğan's control of the Syrian-Turkish border. And controlling the Turkish-Syrian border is of utmost strategic importance to Erdoğan. That is because he wants to suffocate the Kurdish autonomous entity in that area and be sure an independent Kurdish entity does not evolve in that region. Erdoğan knows that stepping on Putin's foot in Libya would be counterproductive and dangerous. Putin could end the agreement. The resumption of fighting between Turkey and Assad on the Turkish border could jeopardize one of Erdoğan's most critical geostrategic goals—preventing Kurdish independence.

With the Formation of the GNU, Is the End of the War in Sight?

Egypt is not happy with Turkey's growing foothold in Libya or its increasing activity in the eastern Mediterranean in general. However, at the same time, Egypt is struggling with its never-ending profound economic and social challenges. And President al-Sisi is focused on addressing those domestic challenges. Adding to that, Egypt is embroiled in an escalating conflict with Ethiopia. A decade of failed negotiations about the Grand Ethiopian Renaissance Dam Project has now escalated into threats of war from both sides.

Since 2015, Saudi Arabia and the UAE have been fighting the Iranian-backed Houthi Shi'ite tribes in Yemen. Riyadh and Abu Dhabi share a common interest in fighting the Houthis to ensure Iran does not control Yemen. This ongoing war consumes considerable resources. And the end of the conflict is nowhere in sight. The war in Yemen, Iranian-generated threats and instabilities from the Red Sea to the Gulf, and unstable oil prices (the primary revenue sources for Saudi Arabia and the UAE), together with the challenges of COVID-19, exacerbate the problems of these two Sunni powers.

So, when looking at their priorities, at this point, Haftar's supporters in Egypt, Saudi Arabia, and the UAE prefer to save the money and energy they invest in Libya. And instead, focus on their most urgent domestic and regional challenges.

Egypt's shifting priorities are evidenced by Cairo cooling its relationship with Haftar. Al-Sisi continues to nurture Haftar as a local agent of influence in Libya. But what concerns Egypt most is stability in Libya. Given this goal, al-Sisi is looking to broaden his relationships in Libya to advance an arrangement to stabilize the situation. Haftar will have to be tuned to Egypt's needs.[13]

The central European Union states, namely France, Germany, and Italy, also have interests in Libya. One is Libya's oil. And the other is the fact that Libya is the African migrant's gateway to Europe.

On August 22, 2020, following intensive and wide-reaching diplomatic efforts by Germany, the United Nations, and the United States, a ceasefire was announced in Libya.

In October 2020, the UN Support Mission in Libya (UNSMIL) brokered a permanent cease-fire agreement. According to the agreement signed in Geneva, an immediate cease-fire was to go into effect, all forces were to return to their previous positions, and all foreign fighters must leave Libya.

In November 2020, the 5 + 5 Joint Military Commission (five senior military officers chosen by the GNA and five senior military officers selected by Haftar) met for the sixth time since February 2020. This time they met in Sirte (controlled by Haftar) to discuss moving forward to implement the terms of the October permanent ceasefire agreement—including all foreign forces leaving Libya within ninety days.

On November 9, 2020, UNSMIL hosted a conference in Tunisia. Seventy-five delegates of the Libyan Political Dialogue Forum (LPDF) launched a series of discussions. The LPDF delegates represent a wide range of Libyan society. They approved a roadmap drawn up by UNSMIL, which will create a new interim three-person Presidency Council (PC) and a Government of National Unity (GNU). The roadmap includes elections to be held in December 2021. In January 2021, the LPDF reached an agreement regarding the body that will monitor the election process.

In March 2021, a Libyan Government of National Unity (GNU) led by Prime Minister Abdul Hamid Dbeibeh was sworn in. For Turkey, this presented Erdoğan with opportunities to expand his influence. Yet, at the same time, it could also limit Istanbul's influence. On the one hand, the Libyan government is looking to establish and develop commercial, military, and economic relations with Turkey. On the other hand, the Libyan government has reportedly asked Turkey to evacuate its armed proxy militias so Libya can comply with UNSC resolutions.[14]

In April 2021, Prime Minister Dbeibeh, accompanied by Libya's energy and foreign affairs ministers, visited Russia to discuss future cooperation. Russia is back in the Middle East, and they are back in the Middle East to stay. And Russia doesn't provide any free meals—not in Syria and not in Libya. Putin expects to be paid back handsomely for his engagement in both arenas. During the Libyan leader's visit to Moscow, and subsequently, the Russians made it clear that they would appreciate signing energy, construction, and military contracts with Libya's government. Putin has made it clear—he intends to deepen Russia's presence and influence in Libya.

Turkey and Russia continued to be at odds throughout the spring and summer of 2021. On the other hand, it looked like the situation in Libya was stabilizing. Libya and the international community were paving the way toward elections to be held in December 2021.

During that time—a lull in the fighting—companies, and countries worldwide began vying for the reconstruction effort. After a decade of being ravaged by war, the reconstruction of Libya is currently estimated to be in the neighborhood of half a trillion dollars. Estimated costs make Libya the most expensive reconstruction project in the Middle East and North Africa. Foreign companies from many countries, including Egypt, Turkey, Tunisia, France, and Germany, are lining up to be a part of the reconstruction efforts and win much sought-after government contracts to rebuild the country.[15]

In April 2021, Prime Minister Dbeibeh announced that Egypt would reopen its Embassy and Consulates in Libya as soon as possible (as of August 2021, this has not happened). And the following month, after an eight-year hiatus, a joint Libyan-Egyptian consular committee resumed their work. In May 2021, Egyptian Prime Minister Mostafa Madbouli, accompanied by eleven Egyptian ministers, visited Libya. The prime minister was the most senior Egyptian official to visit Libya since 2010. The delegation reportedly signed multiple Memorandums of Understanding in various areas, including construction, infrastructure, military training, etc.

In July 2021, Egypt inaugurated the "July 3rd Naval Base" at the entrance of the Eastern Mediterranean Sea and very close to the Libyan border. Egypt's newest base covers more than 2,500 acres, houses numerous combat units, and scores of facilities—an operations center, joint exercise center, seven training fields, and facilities that can host large cargo and commercial ships. As we have learned, Egypt considers the developments in Libya an Egyptian national security issue. This base shows Egypt's intention to be able to intervene in Libya from the sea in a rapid time. According to Egyptian Navy Chief Vice Admiral Ahmed Khaled, the new base will host two FREMM Bergamini frigates, an Egyptian Gowind-class frigate, a 209 submarine, and fifteen different types of smaller naval assets.[16]

In May 2021, the highest-ranking US diplomat to visit the country since 2014 arrived in Tripoli. It has been reported that the administration has deployed a team there to work out the daunting logistics of reopening the embassy.[17] There have also been reports of President Biden discussing troop withdrawal with Russia and Turkey[18] as part of a roadmap to end the war. But little has come from the American administration directly that could indicate a serious focus on the issue at this point. As of August 2021, President Biden's Libya policy is unclear.

Skeptical observers don't see any actual ability to enforce the evacuation of foreign forces from Libya.[19] That skepticism is well-founded because, as of August 2021, foreign militias are still in Libya, and their evacuation does not appear to be in sight.

Given the combination of Libya's complex tribal fabric, its enormous wealth, ethnic diversity, conflicting interests, and the plethora of weapons, it is more likely Libya will continue to experience constant instability. Speaking at the Fourth Abu Dhabi Strategic Debate in November 2017, Libya's late Prime Minister Mahmoud Jibril, who was the prime minister of Libya's transitional government (March to November 2011), said this about Libya: "There are 1,600 militias in Libya, 300 million firearms, and inconceivable corruption."[20]

An already complex environment, Libya is further fueled by the escalating and flammable power struggle over hegemony and wealth in the Mediterranean Sea's central and eastern basins. As Libya becomes part and parcel of this evolving regional and global power struggle, its strategic importance will only increase.

The agreement to hold elections in December 2021 indicates that there is also an ability in a system based on tribalism and particularistic interests to establish agreed rules of the game. In the case of Libya, it is possible that these elections—assuming they take place—will be a milestone on the path to the establishment of Libya as a nation-state in a federal model.

CHAPTER 5

THE EMERGENCE OF A NEW MODEL OF STATEHOOD IN THE MIDDLE EAST?

As we discussed in Chapter 1, one of the leading causes of the constant instability and chaos in the Middle East is the weakness of the nation-state in the region. Over the last three chapters, we have begun to explore how Iran and Turkey leverage states' weakness and instability to advance their own ambitions.

In this chapter, I want to see if we are heading toward a new, healthier, more stable statehood model in the Arab world.

From the end of the thirteenth century until the beginning of the twentieth century, the vast majority of the people in the Middle East were a part of the Ottoman Empire. In addition to being subjects of the Ottoman Empire, their identity was based on things like religion, ethnicity, dialect, family, geographical location, lineage, tribe, etc.

With the decline and the eventual demise of the Ottoman Empire in the 1920s, the people of the region, most of whom were Muslim Arabs, began to take their first steps toward self-determination. And, with that, they started to grapple with the following question: "What will be the future political structure of the region?"

Roughly speaking, three competing ideologies regarding the struggle over the path, identity, and direction of the people in the region captured the intellectual, political, and cultural discussion: *Caliphate*, *Qaum*, and *Wataniya*.

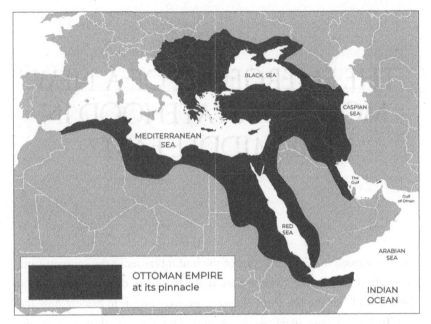

Ottoman Empire at Its Height

Caliphate. All Muslims should live in one global Islamic entity (Caliphate) ruled by sharī ʿah law.

Qaum. Otherwise known as Pan-Arabism. All Arabs should live in one united political Arab entity as one nation and with no physical borders.

Wataniya. Particularistic Nationalism, National Particularistic Statehood—the Homeland. The people of the region should live in independent states based on various particularistic denominators, including ethnicity, geographical location, religion, etc.

The Twentieth-Century Nation-State Model in the Middle East Has Failed

At the end of the nineteenth and the beginning of the twentieth century, the construct of the nation-state appeared in the Middle East. Disparate peoples, religions, and cultures were introduced to the concept of nationalism.

The problem was that the different groups did not develop a sense of "togetherness" or the idea of a "common destiny" or "mutual responsibility."

Those are essential building blocks for the establishment of a particularistic national state. The traditional components of their identity—their religion, ethnicity, geographic region, and tribe—remained the dominant part of their identity. The notion of "statehood," although it existed, was a secondary component of their individual and collective identity.

The first chapter of *Inside the Middle East: Making Sense of the Most Dangerous and Complicated Region on Earth* was called "The Distorted Compass." It is not by chance that I began with that chapter. Many Arab states in the region were run by authoritarian dictators whose wealth and power rose as the fate of their constituents withered. Instead of offering real answers to real problems, these demagogues offered hollow slogans. Instead of solutions, they encouraged people to look elsewhere for the causes of their difficulties. They instilled a distorted view of reality and created an atmosphere where conspiracy theories run rampant.

Emad El-Din Adib, the chairman of the Board of Directors of the Egyptian newspaper *Al-Alam Al-Youm*, accurately sums up the failure of the current nation-state model in the Middle East, writing: "The characteristics of the Arab world are poverty at home, corrupt governments, militias and duality of weapons, loyalty to external factors, and uprising on the street."[1]

The Arab Spring—An Indictment of the Failed Nation-State

A decade has passed since a young Tunisian man, Tarek al-Tayeb Mohamed Bouazizi, set himself on fire in a gruesome act of despair in the face of a difficult life and a hopeless future. In his death, Bouazizi set fire to the Middle East, generating a massive wave of protests that became known as the "Arab Spring." Or, as I like to call it, the "Arab Awakening." Some in the world call it the "Arab Winter."

The Arab Spring was, in its essence, an indictment of the failed nation-state. People rose up across the Middle East and Africa because their governments and rulers had failed to provide them life's most basic needs. The Arab Spring was a demand that a government must provide its constituents with real answers to real problems. The Arab Spring was a demand for clean water, education, food, healthcare, housing, jobs, sanitation, etc. It was a cry for a life of hope and dignity.

Here are two examples of the severe challenges of the Arab world.

The Food and Agriculture Organization of the United Nations (FAU) published a report in 2021 focusing on enhancing the resilience of food systems in the Arab States. The study reads, "In 2019, the number of hungry people stood at 51.4 million, or 12.2 percent of the region's population. If such trends continue, even ignoring the potential impact of Covid-19, the number of undernourished in the region will exceed 75 million people by 2030."[2]

Another severe and growing challenge is water. Two processes feed and intensify the severe water crisis in the Arab world. One is climate change, which increases the drought in areas that innately have high temperatures and little rainfall. The second is a dramatic increase in water consumption because of development and population growth—the population is growing at a rate of 2 percent per year. A 2020 report by the Arab Monetary Fund (AMF) indicates a rapid decrease in the water quotas per individual in the Arab world. The report shows that in the 1950s, there were 3,430 cubic meters of water annually available for each individual. In 2019, it fell to 800 cubic meters. By 2025, it is expected to plummet to 667 cubic meters. According to the report, the water quota for individuals in the Arab world is 10 percent of the average personal consumption in the world. The problem is exacerbated by governments allocating minimal resources for infrastructure development to improve the water economy, such as building dams, treatment plants, and desalination facilities. The budget required is estimated at $200 billion.[3]

The name of my 2009 North American lecture tour was "Smoking Volcano Fertile Ground." In the years leading up to what became known as the Arab Spring, it was clear to me that the Arab world was on the verge of an eruption. And that the explosion would be a defining moment—a turning point for the region.

Indeed, my prediction was fully materialized. During the decade that has followed, the Middle East has suffered enormous upheaval. Regimes have collapsed. Tyrants were ousted. Countries have been destroyed. Hundreds of thousands have been killed. Millions find themselves refugees. Violence and chaos continue to spread. Young Muslims growing up in the troubled Muslim world—and some growing up in Western countries—have turned into murderers who slaughter men, women, and children, Muslims, and non-Muslims alike, in the name of a distorted ideology.

However, as I argue, erupting volcanoes also produce fertile ground.

I argue that amid the chaos and destruction that prevails in parts of the region, we are again on the precipice of a defining moment—a new era. The turbulence many Arab states are experiencing today provides fertile ground for the seeds for the possible emergence of a new statehood model in the region. In 2021, ten years after the outbreak of the Arab Spring, several factors coincide in an unprecedented way. Combined, they may pave the way toward a new model of statehood.

I believe that the path toward a new statehood model will be one of the defining factors in the region's geopolitical landscape in the twenty-first century.

In this chapter and the next, we will explore the factors I argue contribute to the possible emergence of a new statehood model in the Middle East.

We will try to assess which Arab countries may take that path and which Arab countries are less likely to take that path.

Narratives and Slogans Out—Foreshadowing the Emergence of a New Statehood Model

I started this chapter by emphasizing that the idea of nationalism and statehood introduced to people of the Middle East at the end of the nineteenth and the twentieth century was an alien concept. The people's connection to each other under a "flag" was artificial to a large extent. Traditional, historic identity features such as religion, ethnicity, tribe, family, geographical origin, dialect, customs, and norms were more powerful than the vague concept of national statehood as a core identity feature of the individual and the community.

Given this reality, the independent Arab states established during the twentieth century suffered a built-in instability and weakness. And many of these states were run by dictators who used the state to consolidate their own wealth and power—paying little or no attention to their constituents and their needs. Their tactic to keep the masses quiet was to espouse slogans such as "Arab Unity" or "Arab Solidarity." Leaders would tell people that their problems were coming from "the other"—the Colonialists, the West, the Zionists, etc.

Instead of offering people real solutions like education, food, jobs, security, etc., they sedated with slogans. And they told people to look elsewhere for the causes of their challenges.

The combination of demagogue dictators and sectarianism, deep corruption, coupled with an absence of national cohesion, has had a detrimental impact on the character, course, and evolution of societies in the region.

In June 2019, Saudi journalist Abdullah bin Bakhit wrote an article titled "The Vision Louder than the Sound of Battle." Here is an excerpt:

> When I review the lists of projects that Arab media have talked about since the 1960s, you will not find among them a strategic project that addresses the everyday life needs of the individual. Instead, words like *'uzza,* "bravery," *karama,* "dignity," etc., ruled … People's daily lives have no value in front of the intelligence and police of the state that governs them, and there is nothing wrong with bribing, deceiving, and begging. These peoples' dignity is preserved by victory over Israel, defeating Zionism, confronting Western plots, and establishing a caliphate.[4]

There is a phrase in Arabic, "*Anza Walou Tarat,*" literally translated, "Even if it is flying, it is still a goat." The meaning of the phrase is "a fossilized mind does not change." And to be honest, every day I come across countless examples. Here are just a few:

On April 4, 2020, Saleh al-Qulab, a former Jordanian minister of Culture and Communication and a senior journalist, wrote an article called "Houthis Do Not Own the Decision." Here is a quote from that article. "The Arabs' swords successfully opposed and rejected Iran's attempt to take over Arab lands."[5] When we explore Lebanon, Syria, and Iraq, I believe you will agree that his opinion rarely dialogues with the reality.

The month of Ramadan in the Muslim world is famous for television series. Some shows are produced especially for this month as people spend their evenings gathered around their TV sets. During the 2020 month of Ramadan, an Egyptian fictional TV series took center stage. The name of the show was *Al-Nihaya* "The End." The series takes place in 2120. The United States has been destroyed, and Jews have been deported from Palestine (implicating that the Jews were exterminated). The series resulted in an official Israeli diplomatic protest, and it evoked a heated discussion on Arab social media platforms. The Middle East Freedom forum president, Magdi Khalil, wrote: "It is as an Arabization of a Western fictional movie ... it transfers science fiction to a distorted, sick political fiction."[6] In response, series creator 'Amr Samir 'Atef said, "Every Arab wishes for the liberation of al-Quds (Jerusalem)."[7]

Indeed, slogans, demagoguery, and narratives are powerful marketing tools for the masses. However, there is a parallel counter process that I believe will further grow. In my analysis, there is a sobriety that is inching its way into the public discourse.

In August 2018, Abdel Monem Sa'id, al-Ahram Center for Political and Strategic Studies director in Cairo, wrote an article. He called it "The New Middle East." In the piece, he writes, "The axis of Egypt-Saudi Arabia-Jordan represents a new Arab mindset, which is based upon a realistic evaluation of means and capacities, and not based on hollow slogans and demagoguery."[8] (We will further explore these evolving alliances later in the book.)

In March 2020, Lebanese analyst Khairallah Khairallah said in an article he penned, "In the absence of courage ... Lebanon is a disaster!" "... Lebanon's current catastrophic situation results from a series of wrong decisions based upon slogans and demagoguery."[9]

In June 2021, Saudi columnist Maha Mohammed al-Sherif wrote an article she called "Iran and Its Wreaking Havoc in The Arab World." She says Iran has manipulated the Arab masses with the slogans of liberating al-Quds and the Resistance. The outcome is that the Arab masses are standing in the queue (to buy commodities, fuel, etc.).[10]

These are just a few of the many examples I come across every day. I have been operating in Arab cities and communities for many years. In my research and daily interactions with Arabs from across the region, I detect a significant shift. The voices like the ones I have highlighted are growing and gaining strength.

Slogans, symbols, and narratives are deeply embedded in the region. Denial of reality has been a common feature of the Arab world. And divorcing them will not be an easy or smooth process. It will take time. But a change is underway. I believe we are witnessing the beginnings of a departure from slogans. And with that, a pivot toward the public demanding their governments provide real solutions to their very real problems.

This was the essence of the Arab Spring. The people cried for the governments to stop selling them slogans like "*Al Islam Huwa al-Hal*"—"Islam is the solution"—or "*let us go free Palestine.*" People went to the street to demand real tangible solutions and accountability from their leaders.

Today, ten years after the outbreak of the Arab Spring, people from across the spectrum—conservatives, leftists, nationalists, political Islamists, supporters of civil society, etc.—increasingly share the understanding that poverty, corruption, illiteracy, and the many other challenges Arab societies face cannot be solved with buzzwords and empty narratives that sound good but don't provide real solutions to people's real problems.

With this background, I want to explore several factors that coincide today—in the third decade of the twenty-first century—in an unprecedented way. Combined, they may pave the way toward a new model of statehood.

What Are the Factors that Could Generate the Possible Emergence of a New Nation-State Model?

There are some fundamental evolutions currently unfolding that could provide a healthier nation-state.

These evolutions are:

- In the battle between dogmatism and pragmatism in political Islam, pragmatism is gaining momentum and strengthening.
- Some political Islam parties are prioritizing particularistic nationalism as a collective identity feature over Islam on their agendas. And some are even making nationalism a central focus of their political platform.
- Civil society values are becoming more prevalent, as is their impact on society and politics.
- Governments increasingly understand that they have a responsibility and accountability to their citizens. This has resulted in rulers adapting their policies. And consequently, citizens are developing a sense of civic responsibility.

- Increasing access to information, the ubiquity of the Internet, the growing influence of social media, and expanding communication.
- The hegemonic visions of Iran and Turkey are triggering a counter-reaction manifested in the strengthening of particularistic nationalism, unity, and patriotism.

Let's look at these factors that I argue, separately and together, will define the nature and character of statehood in the Arab world in the new era in the Middle East.

Promising Evolutions—The Strengthening of the Pragmatic Camp within Political Islam, the Centralization of Particularistic Nationalism, and the Growing Presence of Civil Society

I want to begin by shortly focusing on the three trends that could generate a new statehood model in the Middle East. Two of which—the strengthening of the pragmatic camp within political Islam and the growing presence and impact of civil society values—I foresaw and discussed in my 2016 book. And the third—which is connected to the swing toward pragmatism in political Islam—is that some political Islam parties are prioritizing particularistic nationalism as a collective identity feature over Islam on the political agendas. Some are even making it a centerpiece of their platforms.

Political Islam and civil society camps are, in my view, the most significant camps that influence the current character of Arab society. And they also are the main factors that will shape the future trajectory of statehood in the Arab world in the new era we are entering. What they have in common is that they are value-driven, albeit by opposite values. That said, some of their core narratives and values are not only different—they are conflicting.

Political Islam strives for a Caliphate run by sharī 'ah law.

The civil society camp, for lack of a better term, promotes more "Western-generated" values.

Political Islam, Particularistic Nationalism, Civil Society

These three trends—the strengthening of the pragmatic camp within political Islam, the centralization of particularistic nationalism on political Islam's political agenda, and the growing presence and impact of civil society—are evolutions with positive, constructive potential.

These three phenomena combined could offer a framework that could include the various camps' different, sometimes conflicting, needs and perspectives. This inclusive political system could provide a broad platform to create a functioning government that works for everyone. And that would be a monumental step toward stability. And stability strengthens a government's ability to meet peoples' evolving and increasing needs. A rising tide lifts all boats—a government meeting its peoples' needs will improve everyone's lives, regardless of their ideological, political, or religious orientation.

Pragmatism Becoming a Major Feature of Political Islam

Let us begin by understanding why pragmatism in political Islam is essential for the emergence of a new statehood model in the Arab world.

Islam is a dedication to the complete and absolute acceptance of the idea of one God, *Allah*. Islam is what defines the identity, moral compass, societal norms, and values of most people in the Middle East.

Islam is not only a Muslim's religion, culture, heritage, etc., but it is part and parcel of their individual and collective identity. Islam does not make a separation between state and religion. Islam provides Muslims a detailed codex—the sharī'ah law. The sharī'ah defines and guides every aspect of a Muslim's life. Both as an individual and as a member of the community. Islam views sharī'ah law as the master plan given to humanity by Allah. Thus, it is flawless and perfect. Islam rejects all other constructs—communism, democracy, socialism, etc. because they are human-made.

Political Islam offers a cultural, legislative, political structure—and ultimately a society and a way of life that integrates Islamic values and lives by the sharī'ah law. The ultimate objective of political Islam is to create a global Islamic cultural, political, and religious entity—the Caliphate, governed and ruled by sharī'ah law. This combination of elements is why political Islam resonates with so many people throughout the Muslim world.

As we said earlier, the Muslim Brotherhood is the largest political Islam entity and the largest Sunni movement in the Muslim world.

Political Islam's central slogan is 'Islam is the Solution' *"Al Islam Huwa al-Hal."* Following the outbreak of the Arab Spring, as challenges deepened in the Arab world and chaos expanded, that slogan appealed more than ever to people. That is what got the Muslim Brotherhood and other political Islam parties into office. The Muslim Brotherhood gained momentum in Algeria, Jordan, Libya, and Morocco. Political Islam parties won spectacular victories in Egypt and Tunisia. However, that was a short-term achievement. People quickly realized that *Islam is the Solution* does not put bread on the table or get you a job. In other words, behind the slogans, the winning parties did not have any real, tangible solutions. People's disappointment was palpable, and the Muslim Brotherhood party's tenures were short-lived. The newly elected Muslim Brotherhood governments in Egypt and Tunisia were swiftly ejected from office.

The meteoric rise and fall of political Islam governments and political parties across the Middle East following the 2011 Arab Spring sent shock waves through political Islam.

As I wrote in 2016, "as a result of the need to reconcile ideology with practicalities, struggles between the pragmatic camp and the ideological camp within political Islam will continue. This power struggle is likely to result in the strengthening of the practical faction within political Islam."[11] And this is precisely what has transpired over the past four years. The pragmatic wing in political Islam has indeed gained momentum at the expense of the dogmatic wing.

Please note I said pragmatic. Not moderate. They are not interchangeable terms and are not the same thing. This is important to emphasize because people in the West often misinterpret pragmatism for moderation. Islamists are marathon runners. Islamists are not moderate. However, they can be pragmatic.

The rebuke political Islam suffered after the Arab Spring victories fueled an ideological and political crisis in the movement regarding the right path for political Islam organizations to take.

Frictions within the movement developed. Muslim Brotherhood chapters in Algeria, Egypt, Jordan, and Tunisia split. One of the main byproducts of this crisis and the subsequent fracturing of political Islam from within—particularly within the Muslim Brotherhood—was that the pragmatic camp in political Islam grew and got stronger.

Parallel to the strengthening of the pragmatic camp, there is another significant development within political Islam.

A growing number of political Islam political parties, movements, and organizations realize that they need to be more inclusive. To appeal to a broader audience and gain voters, some political Islam parties are pivoting. They are downplaying their parties' religious aspects and shifting their focus to more national issues. And some are even prioritizing and centralizing particularistic nationalism in their political agenda.

Particularistic Nationalism

First, I would like to define particularism and particularistic nationalism. Particularism is an exclusive attachment to one's own group, party, or nation. Particularistic nationalism is the desire for national autonomy based on national characteristics and a distinct and particular culture that evolves into the demand for political sovereignty. In particularistic nationalism, patriotism is linked to maintaining cultural integrity, which aims to secure and maintain a people's right to its own territory. A statehood model based on particularism is a state that centers on the concept of "*Watan*" "the Homeland." *Wataniya*— "particularistic nationalism"—emphasizes the state's unique characteristics (local history, traditions, societal fabric, dialect, etc.) and its independence and sovereignty.

In August 2016, the Muslim Brotherhood party in Tunisia, *Al-Nahda* "The Renaissance" party, held its tenth convention. At the meeting, the party announced it was transforming from a religious-based party to a national party that would be open to everyone.[12] This change was the prologue for growing friction within the party. The tensions grew between those who wanted to preserve the Islamic religious nature of the movement and those who wished to expand, grow, and make it a more broad-based organization. In November 2020, the party canceled the convention because of a power struggle between the young and senior leaders.[13] The younger generation wanted to be more open and inclusive and not accept people based only on their religious observance.

In 2017, the *Al-Jamma'ah al-Islamiayh* movement in Lebanon introduced the party's new political platform at the party's convention. The updated vision was called "A National Perspective." Addressing the conference's participants, Al-Jamma'ah al-Islamiayh's leader, Azzam Ayoubi, said, "The change we are making has nothing to do with the movement's core Islamic values. Islam is our noble, irreplaceable core ideology. However, it is also revisable, adjusting to reality."[14]

In June 2019, a Muslim Brotherhood splinter group in Jordan, known as the Reform Wing, published its constitution. The document emphasized that first and foremost, the organization is a Jordanian body committed to acting to strengthen Jordanian nationalism.[15]

Another example is in Morocco. In December 2020, Morocco signed a normalization agreement with Israel. The reaction of the Islamic parties to the normalization demonstrates the split between the pragmatic camp and the dogmatic camp within the ranks of Morocco's political Islam parties. And it highlights the parties' prioritization of the state's interest over their commitment to the traditional core Islamic agenda.

The Islamic parties that oppose the regime, such as Al 'Adl w'al Ihssan and Al-Tawhid w'al Islah, vehemently attacked the agreement.[16]

On the other hand, the Moroccan Muslim Brotherhood al 'Adallah w'al Tanmiyah—the party of the current Moroccan Prime Minister, Dr. (MD) Saed Eddin El-Othmani—who reminding you, was himself one of the founders of al-Tawhid w'al Islah in the early 1990s—praised Morocco's outstanding achievement of normalization. The Al 'Adallah w'al Tanmiyah statement emphasized the fact that the United States recognized Morocco's sovereignty over Western Sahara. Their reaction clearly prioritized how the agreement impacted their home country, Morocco. Morocco's Muslim Brotherhood party made the conscious decision that their Islamic agenda that prioritizes rejecting Israel and objecting to normalization with Israel was less important than their nationalist agenda.

In May 2021, the Muslim Brotherhood in Libya—the "Justice and Construction" Party, founded in 2012—announced that it would operate as an NGO moving forward. They changed their name to "Revival and Renewal." The new Muslim Brotherhood's mission statement calls on all Libyans to work to establish a pluralistic civil society and work together for the homeland. A member of the "Revival and Renewal" movement clarified that they decided to become a non-profit organization so that they do not have to be subjected to the ideology or decisions of the global Muslim Brotherhood movement. And it allows the organization to focus exclusively on Libya.[17]

Growing Impact of Civil Society Camp

Let's look at the growing role and strengthen the characteristics of what I call "Civil Society." Civil Society "includes the full range of formal and informal organizations outside the state and the state apparatus. It is a wide array of organizations, community groups, and non-governmental organizations [NGOs]."[18] Including charitable institutions, community organizations, faith-based groups, foundations, mass-based membership organizations, professional associations, social movements, volunteer organizations and communities, and citizens acting individually and collectively."[19] Civil society advances, as I said, for lack of a better term, "Western" ideals and values. That includes but is not limited to civil marriage, gender equality, inclusivity, pluralism, protecting the rights of women, children, LGBTQ, etc.

One of the most significant and fascinating changes I see in the Arab world is the integration of these values, the rise of organizations operating in this space, and the public discourse generated by individuals advocating civil society values. The pace and scale of change varies from country to country. However, the common denominator is that the process is evolving and gaining momentum. And it is irreversible.

Let us look at a couple of examples, starting with Libya. Given what we have learned about Libya, it is fascinating to see that a vibrant civil society has flourished ten years after an uprising despite a civil war. Activists and organizations like "Lawyers for Justice in Libya" are working to build an inclusive, just, and sustainable future, amplifying the voices of marginalized groups, including women, youth, and ethnic minorities. Here is an excerpt from the organization's Mission Statement:

> Our vision is of a Libya, which embodies the values and principles
> of human rights and the rule of law and is a society committed to

justice. We work on and in Libya with a growing network of lawyers, activists, and grassroots communities across and outside the country. We see ourselves not merely as observers but as active participants during Libya's transition and beyond … We seek justice in Libya through advocacy and outreach, accountability, transitional justice initiatives, and capacity building, underpinned by our own independent research.[20]

On February 1, 2021, the organization released this statement:

Ahead of voting on the candidates for the interim executive authorities that will lead Libya towards national elections on 24 December 2021, Lawyers for Justice in Libya (LFJL) is calling on the members of the Libyan Political Dialogue Forum (LPDF) to make human rights, justice, and accountability key priorities when selecting the members of the Presidency Council and the Prime Minister.[21]

In 2020, the Libyan "Together We Build It" organization prepared a list of the "20 Libyan women you should know" to highlight the successes of Libyan women who lead change.[22] The project was in celebration of the twentieth anniversary of United Nations Security Council Resolution 1325 that "reaffirms the important role of women in the prevention and resolution of conflicts, peace negotiations, peace-building, peacekeeping, humanitarian response and in post-conflict reconstruction and stresses the importance of their equal participation and full involvement in all efforts for the maintenance and promotion of peace and security … urges all actors to increase the participation of women and incorporate gender perspectives in all United Nations peace and security efforts."[23]

Here is how Together We Build It describes itself:

We are an inter-generational non-profit organization working to promote peace and security in Libya. TWBI believes in the important role of an inter-generational gender approach to formal and non-formal peace-building. TWBI continues to lead projects on women, peace, and security, including; advocating women's meaningful political participation, prevention and raising awareness on harmful gender norms and Gender-Based Violence (GBV), gender research, reporting to the international mechanism on human rights, and capacity building for Libyan groups and actors on peace-building.[24]

Saudi Arabia is another example. In recent years, in ultra-conservative Saudi Arabia, the people have increasingly called for expanded civic rights. In response to these demands, the government has offered slow, incremental moves toward reform. Over the past few years, Saudi Arabia's Crown Prince Mohammad bin Salman bin Abdulaziz Al-Saud (known as MBS) has rolled out several social reforms.

In June 2018, after many years of bitter controversy, women gained the right to drive. In 2019, they eased restrictions that forbade women from traveling abroad alone and abolished the law that forced women to wear an 'abaya (a dark cloth covering the whole body). In October 2019, Saudi Arabia authorized the drafting of women to its military forces.[25]

In February 2021, Saudi Arabia announced new judicial reforms, putting the Kingdom on a path toward a codified law. The current legal system is wholly based on sharī'ah law. Crown Prince Mohammad bin Salman bin Abdulaziz Al-Saud described the current legal system as "painful for many individuals and families, especially women, permitting some to evade their responsibilities. This will not take place again once these laws are promulgated pursuant to legislative laws and procedures." The statement did not outline further details of what specific practices and penalties would be changed. Ali Shihabi, a Saudi analyst close to the Kingdom's royal court, described the news as "an important step in legal reform and one that recognizes that the Saudi legal system has a way to go to reach international standards and that the leadership appreciates the urgency and importance of such reform."[26] He also announced more reforms would be laid out over the course of 2021.

Throughout 2021, there are economic and social reforms, including adult women being allowed to live independently without first having to get permission from their father or another male relative. In July 2021, the hajj ministry officially permitted women of all ages to make the *hajj* pilgrimage to Mecca without a male relative on the condition that they go in a group. And for the first time, Saudi women soldiers were allowed to work in Islam's holiest sites Mecca and Medina. And in the summer of 2021, they helped secure the annual hajj pilgrimage.

Women play a significant role in championing civic space. In Lebanon, women have been at the forefront of the popular uprising. In Iraq, thousands of women have participated in the popular protest movement. In Algeria, women participated in demonstrations against then-President Abdelaziz Bouteflika. They used the historical moment as an opportunity to shed light on the challenges they faced.

There has also been a concerted effort to mandate women's involvement in organized politics. Since the 1990s, women's representation in parliaments across the Middle East has more than quadrupled. There has been a continued movement to secure and expand women's rights and equality. For example, political parties must have equal representation.

Today women represent, on average, about 18 percent of parliamentary members. Across the Arab world today, it is more common to see female entrepreneurs and women in senior political, financial, security, academic, and media positions. In 2018 Souad Abderrahim was elected as the mayor of Tunis, the capitol of Tunisia. Also in Tunisia, Abir Moussi is the leader of the Tunisian Parti Destourien Libre (PDL) Constitution Free Party. In 2019, Egypt amended its constitution. Included in the changes was a mandate that 25 percent of the Egyptian Parliament's members must be women. In 2019 Princess Reema bint Bandar bin Sultan bin Abdulaziz Al Saud was nominated as and became the Saudi ambassador to the United States.

With the expansion of women's rights and their role in society, politics, sports, etc., sensitive issues related to women and essential to women have also improved.

An example of such a change is the issue of sexual assault and rape. Until recently, legislation like Article 308 in Jordan's Penal Code and Articles 505, 522 of the Lebanese Penal Code offered sex offenders and rapists a way to escape punishment. They could escape prosecution if they married the victim. Following intense public campaigns led by organizations advocating for civil and women's rights in those countries, in August 2017, Jordan and Lebanon simultaneously abolished those articles.

In December 2020, Lebanon passed the "Law to Criminalize Sexual Harassment and [for] Rehabilitation of Its Victims." The law is a step forward by making sexual harassment a crime and outlining whistleblower protections. However, Human Rights Watch argues the law falls short of international standards because it addresses sexual harassment solely as a crime. It neglects efforts at prevention, reforms in labor laws, monitoring efforts, and civil remedies.[27]

In August 2021, President Abdel Fattah al-Sisi ratified a law amending some articles of the Egyptian Penal Law to confront sexual harassment. The amendments increase penalties against people who harass others either in public or private places by making sexual insinuations—gestures, words, or actions. Under the newly introduced amendments, repeat offenders will face a double punishment.[28]

In Egypt, the National Council for Women (NCW), in cooperation with Egypt National Railways (ENR) and the European Bank for Reconstruction and Development (EBRD), are working together to make Egypt's railway network safer for female passengers. They are also working on an awareness campaign against sexual harassment on public transport in particular and violence against women in general.[29]

In most Muslim countries, the LGBTQ community faces significant challenges. NGOs and public and private individuals and organizations are trying to change legislation in Egypt, Jordan, Kuwait, Lebanon, Tunisia, and other countries, but change will be gradual. There has been progress on the societal level, but not been much progress on the constitutional or judicial level. For example, Article 534 of the Lebanese Penal Code prohibits "sexual relations that are against nature" and sanctions imprisonment from one to twelve months plus a fine. Indeed, Lebanon was the only state that refused to sign the concluding statement of the Second International Conference on Freedom of Speech and Media (November 2020). The refusal is attributed to an article in the statement that ensured LGBTQ people's freedom of expression.[30]

Helem, the Arab world's first LGBTQ+ civil society organization, was formed in Lebanon at the turn of the century. Still, legally it is in limbo because Lebanese authorities have ignored its application for registration.[31]

Organizations have received official recognition in Tunisia, but homosexuals face draconian punishments, including flogging, stoning, and execution.[32] However, in March 2020, in a first for Tunisia and the Arab world, Shams, an association founded in early 2015 to defend LGBTQ rights, was granted legal protection. The March 2020 decision upheld the decisions of previous courts and rejected the government's longstanding bid to shut down Shams.

An LGBTQ initiative to establish an organization in Kuwait evoked public outcry. Reportedly, the Commercial Control and Consumer Protection Sector have issued a warning against one of the shops in Kuwait for displaying the "LGBT+ logo."[33]

Equaldex is a "collaborative knowledge base for the LGBT+ (lesbian, gay, bisexual, transgender) movement." Equaldex's mission is to track LGBTQ+ rights and legislation around the world. The initiative's mission is "to crowdsource every law related to LGBT rights and to provide a comprehensive and global view of the LGBT rights movement." Its "visual knowledgebase" measures specific criteria, including legal status, legal protection, discrimination, same-sex marriage, etc. Looking at the Arab world, the picture is quite bleak. In most Arab countries, LGBTQ+ individuals are discriminated against and deprived of rights.[34]

Another common phenomenon in the Arab world is underage marriage. Advertising campaigns in Egypt and Tunisia led to the government outlawing this practice. There is hope that similar campaigns in Algeria, Jordan, and Lebanon will also result in similar legislation.

In September 2020, Kuwait passed a new family protection law. This law is a significant step forward for a country that suffers from high levels of hidden domestic abuse. Over 53 percent of women report men abuse them.[35] But the real challenge in Kuwait will be ensuring the law is translated to practical action.

In November 2020, the United Arab Emirates announced a substantial overhaul of its Islamic personal laws. The amendments allow unmarried couples to cohabitate, loosen alcohol restrictions, and criminalize so-called honor killings. But to be clear, this groundbreaking move by the UAE is quite exceptional.

Across the region, countries have instituted laws against domestic violence and abuse. Unfortunately, like in many other countries, COVID-19 has led to increased domestic abuse in the Middle East—testing the new laws and frameworks put into place to address the problem.

I deliberately presented a mixed picture—and of course, this only scratches the surface. Do not get me wrong. Arab societies have a long way to go regarding civil rights, equality, protections, etc. However, the changes we see and the issues the countries and the communities are beginning to grapple with and discuss openly prove that changes in conservative societies are possible.

Government Accountability and Civic Responsibility— Pact Building

The fourth evolution currently unfolding that could provide a healthier nation-state is that governments increasingly understand that they have a responsibility and accountability to their citizens. This recognition has resulted in rulers adapting their policies. And consequently, citizens are developing a sense of civic responsibility.

This shift is one of the most profound impacts of the Arab Spring. It changed the nature of the relationship—the pact, so to speak—between rulers and citizens.

Before the Arab Spring events, rulers' endurance and their citizens' well-being were detached issues, both in the public discourse and the rulers' mindset. Following the Arab Spring, rulers and governments know failing to show they are really working toward their citizens' well-being will cost them dearly.

A decade after the outbreak of the Arab Awakening, we are witnessing a process of pact building in Arab countries.

In August 2019, King Mohammed VI of Morocco presented the idea of a "new pact." In honor of Morocco's sixty-second Independence Day, he addressed Morocco's citizens. He emphasized the following: "Morocco must address serious challenges through increasing progress ... The wellbeing of the individual citizen is at the heart of reforms and political action ... The reforms are required to strengthen the middle class ... Through the new reforms, we strive to create a new solid foundation for a new pact, including all country sectors."[36] In April 2021, the king launched an ambitious plan to regulate health insurance and secure pension rights for thirty million

Moroccans. The cost of implementing the program by 2025 is estimated at $ 5.7 billion a year.

Let us look at another Arab monarchy—Jordan. I believe events in Jordan are significant when it comes to the pact between government and citizens.

Since 2016 the hardships in Jordan have deepened—high unemployment, low growth, and rising debt. The Kingdom's financial burden has been exacerbated by decades of shouldering the responsibility of absorbing refugees from Iraq and Syria. COVID-19 added an unexpected and devastating blow to an already struggling economy.

World Bank Report 2020 examined the effects of the epidemic on the economy of Jordan and described the following situation:

> Jordan's economy has been hit hard by the COVID-19 pandemic amid already low growth, high unemployment, and growing debt. The World Bank estimated the Jordanian economy to have contracted by 1.6% in 2020 (the first contraction in three decades), with unemployment rising to 24.7% in the fourth quarter of 2020 (as compared to 19.0 percent recorded in the same period last year) and youth unemployment rates reaching an unprecedented fifty percent. The economic shock of COVID-19 has exacerbated both existing structural weaknesses in the economy and unresolved social challenges, putting pressure on the country's fragile macroeconomic stance. This is the first contraction of the economy in three decades. While historic for Jordan, it is among the lowest economic contraction in the world in 2020. Part of this reduced impact can be attributed to the government's large fiscal and monetary stimulus packages and targeted cash support to poor and vulnerable households, totaling about 10.5% of GDP.[37]

The lockdowns and slumps in demand have had a substantial impact on the private sector. The pandemic has increased extreme poverty and led to a rise in income inequality in Jordan. Going forward, Jordan's economy is expected to recover gradually from the COVID-19 crisis. Real GDP in 2021 is projected to grow by 1.4 percent. The World Bank says that the real question for Jordan is how to grow and get back on the path to recovery. A sustained and inclusive recovery growth path requires significant adjustments in policymaking. Reforms are needed to support strong recovery given that Jordan was experiencing weakening economic growth and stagnating productivity before the COVID crisis.[38]

The deepening social hardships in Jordan are fueling growing unrest and public criticism. Critics target the political and professional system, but there is also increasing criticism of the monarchy. It is also worth noting that the Bedouin tribes in Jordan—which have always been the backbone of the Kingdom—are increasingly critical and dissatisfied.

In the summer of 2021, the Hashemite Kingdom of Jordan marked one hundred years since its founding. And with ironic timing, there were two events in Jordan that rattled and deeply shocked King Abdullah II and the royal house.

In April 2021, there was an open rift in the Hashemite family. By order of the king, Abdullah II, Prince Hamza bin Hussein, the King's half-brother, was placed under house arrest. Hamza is the fourth son of King Hussein's fourth wife, Queen Noor. Abdullah is the first son of Princess Muna, King Hussein's second wife.

Prince Hamza (born in 1980) is a retired brigadier general of the Jordanian army. King Abdullah II also appointed him as the crown prince, a role he served in between 1999 and 2004.

Given the increasing distress in Jordan, Hamza openly and increasingly criticizes the palace, and he particularly accuses the monarchy of corruption.

The spark for the April rift was the March 2021 tragedy in which seven patients died in a Jordanian hospital due to a lack of oxygen. The incident stirred public opinion in Jordan. The king hurried to the hospital to be there in person. Upon arrival, he ordered the hospital director to be fired immediately. When the head of the King's Chamber came to visit the hospital, he was ejected. On the other hand, when Prince Hamza arrived, he was received with applause.

Commentators claim that Hamza was arrested in April because he was involved in a coup attempt. The Jordanian Royal House resolutely denied the allegations. Prince Hassan, the uncle of King Abdullah II and Hamza, intervened, and the house's peace was restored. But the visible fissure in the Hashemite family illustrates the growing unrest in the Kingdom.

The second incident took place in June 2021. A Jordanian member of Parliament, Osama al-'Ajarmeh, known for his extreme positions and belligerent rhetoric, addressed his supporters while waving a sword. His remarks implied that he was calling for rebellion in the royal house. And there were even those who interpreted his remarks as a direct threat to assassinate the king.

In response, 108 out of 119 members of the Jordanian parliament voted to remove al-'Arjameh. As a result, riots broke out in Na'ura, a few miles south of the capitol Amman and a stronghold of the Al-'Ajarmeh tribe. During the riots, there were armed clashes between security forces and armed members of the tribe, and four police officers were injured. The Jordanian public supported the Parliament's decision to dismiss al-'Ajarmeh. There was a broad consensus that he crossed a red line both in his behavior and in his rhetoric.

Despite the Jordanians' hardship and the criticism, the Hashemite monarchy stands at the heart of the consensus of the Jordanians, who see it as a central and primary symbol of their identity.

However, the events of the summer of 2021 in Jordan sound the alarm bells in the palace. Deep emotional identification and consensus can be eroded. As difficulties and hardships grow, there is an acute need for the royal house to meet the people's real and concrete plight and needs.

An article by the Qatari-owned Arab Center for Research and Policy Studies (ACRPS) analyzed the events that took place in Jordan in the summer of 2021. They assess that though the crisis has largely passed, King Abdullah II must allow for political reforms that will enable broader sectors to participate in the Kingdom's decision-making and steering processes.[39]

In my 2016 book, I pointed out the profound challenges Jordan was facing economically, socially, and politically at the beginning of the twenty-first century. I projected that the stability of the Hashemite dynasty would be maintained. At the same time, I reasoned there would be a gradual process in which the weight of power increasingly shifts to the representative and executive system of government at the expense of the monarchy.[40]

In August 2021, Palestinian journalist Daoud Kuttab reported that the Jordanian Royal Commission is conducting secret discussions regarding a three-phase process that will result in a constitutional monarchy similar to the United Kingdom or Sweden within the decade.[41]

An essential step in creating a new, more successful statehood model in the Middle East is defining and implementing a new pact among the different political entities and between the citizens and their governments. A successful contract between citizens and government is when the government's goal is to work for its citizens' welfare and future, and the citizens have the power to hold the government accountable. Such a pact is an essential component for the evolution of a new individual and a healthy functioning state. Furthermore, it is a vital building block for a collective identity in which the sentiment of 'national statehood' acts as a uniting factor for people from different ethnicities, religions, and walks of life.

Previously absent in many Arab states, these processes could lead to a new, healthier, and more stable statehood.

On the Road to a New Model of Statehood?

The traditional elements of identity that shape the political system in the Arab world are religion (mainly Sunni/Shi'ite Islam), ethnicity (mostly Arab), tribal identity, and geographic identity. They will not disappear.

On the other hand, the integration of modern civil society values—intensified by the fifth evolution that could lead to a healthier nation-state model—the diversification of communication, the rise of social media, and unfiltered access to the outside world empowers individuals and therefore increases their ability to generate a change. This process is a one-way street. It cannot be reversed. And its impact on the people and, ultimately, the Middle East societies will only grow stronger. The ability to generate a change—mainly if that ability develops over time—is the foundation upon which a new nation-state model in the Arab world could emerge.

I began to formulate my thesis that a new model of statehood may very well be emerging based on accumulated information I have collected, closely observing day-to-day developments in the region and my personal and professional interactions across the region.

However, my observations were not supported by verifiable data until 2020, when I came across a 2016/2017 study conducted by the University of Leipzig in Germany and the Friedrich-Ebert-Stiftung Foundation. This was the first time I had seen an in-depth survey that provided empirical, data-based support to my observation.

Throughout 2016 and 2017, the University of Leipzig and the Friedrich-Ebert-Stiftung foundation surveyed 9,000 sixteen-to-thirty-year-olds from Bahrain, Egypt, Jordan, Lebanon, Morocco, Palestine, Syria, Tunisia, and Yemen. Given the breadth of the research, it is the most comprehensive, in-depth study of young people in the MENA region to date. The study was published as a book in 2018, and it is called *Coping with Uncertainty: Youth in the Middle East and North Africa*.[42] I was unaware of the study until 2020.

The study identifies three common needs: security, quality of life, and a respectable source of income. The study presents several key findings in the following fields: Religion and Identity; Gender and Family; Society and Economy; Communication; and Civil Society.

Religion and Identity. Most of the respondents described themselves as "very religious" or "to some extent religious." However, the researchers noticed that the Arab youth do not view religion as a political identity. Instead, they look at religion as "individual, spiritual self-expression." The researchers attribute that trend to the need to search for an anchor in challenging times. Jordanian anthropologist Khawla Tomaleh refers to that characteristic and uses the month of Ramadan as an example. She reasons that many young Arabs associate the month of Ramadan with a spiritual ritual, something that, to quote her, is "no different from yoga."[43]

Gender and Family. Arab societies are still overwhelmingly patriarchal and male-dominated. This is one of the major features of Arab culture. The family continues to be the most critical societal framework, and many prefer to continue living with their family. There is a desire to get married and leave the house; however, it is difficult to get married in the current reality. The economic challenges have a clear impact on the institution of marriage and the family.

Society and Economy. The middle class has been decimated because of the violent upheavals in the Arab world. Young people are clearly concerned about personal security and economic security. Young Arabs are inclined to engage in occupations that are seen as more global such as tourism, real estate, and energy. Young Arabs who hold academic degrees are less inclined to pursue governmental positions or careers in public service.

When asked about their future, 10 percent want to leave where they are and go somewhere else. However, the migration of young people is a relatively limited phenomenon. The exception is Syrian refugees who wish to try and rebuild their lives away from Syria for obvious reasons. Most of the survey participants hold the state responsible for their lack of personal security and economic challenges. However, some attribute this to foreign involvement.

Communication and Information. Social media networks play a central role in young Arabs' lives. The young generation does not view established media and government sources as reliable sources of information.

Civil Society. Social media networks empower the young generation to engage with others in society and make a difference. Because of increased communication and social media, more young people are becoming involved with activities that emphasize service and/or have a social aspect. A third of the respondents said they are involved in one type of social service activity—environmental initiatives, helping the needy, group study programs, etc. They prefer activities offered by non-profits, charity organizations, and associations instead of activities provided by political institutions or organizations.

Although the survey was conducted six years ago, it is still considered a preeminent survey. This distinct study supports my core arguments and my underlying thesis regarding the possible emergence of a new statehood model. As a political ideology, Islam is less attractive for young people. Young people believe the government is responsible for the well-being of the citizens. Social media empowers the young generation. And the presence of civil society initiatives engages and empowers people—it drives them to make an impact and influences their values.

Egypt, Algeria, Sudan, and Tunisia—On the Path?

In July 2020, Dr. Amal Moussa, a sociology professor at the University of Tunisia, wrote, "It is the Second Nation-State." She describes her vision of the future of the nation-state in the Middle East: "Today, after the winds of reform and revolutions blew, the civil society is growing stronger to defend freedom … after the change of the Arab and Muslim people, the rise in the level of protest and the diversity of its forms and practices … the nation-state will have to adjust to the changes we are going through."[44]

In April 2021, another Tunisian columnist, Mohamed Hnid, wrote an article, "Tunisia—the Struggle of Depth and Revolution." Here is a quote. "The victory of the revolution and the consolidation of the democratic path with all its mistakes will form the nucleus of an Arab salvation that will be cut off once and for all from the possibility of renewing the conditions of tyranny. Just as Tunisia was the cradle of the spring, it will inevitably be the cradle of the Arab democratic experiment, even if it will take a long time."[45]

In my opinion, both observations are fundamentally correct. However, we need to look at the reality in some Arab countries as of 2021. And then, we will be able to assess the relevance of their observations and determine the likelihood of their predictions coming true. Does reality in the Middle East in 2021 support their statements? Is the nation-state in the Arab world "adjusting to a new reality and reflecting the change its people are going through?"

To answer that question, let's look at the situation as of 2021 in some Arab countries—Algeria, Egypt, Sudan, and Tunisia. What we will see is a complex, dynamic, and multifaceted picture.

Let's begin with Egypt.

Egypt

Egypt is the most populous Arab state—with over one hundred million people, over 90 percent of whom are Sunni. Egypt—the Arab world's traditional leader—is the most important country in the Arab world.

Within one decade—between 2010 and 2020—the Egyptians, who were ruled by powerful dictators for decades, ousted two presidents. President Abdel-Fatah al-Sisi is the third leader Egypt has had since 2011.

In February 2011, President Hosni Mubarak (1928–2020) resigned after almost thirty years in power.

In June 2012, Mohammed Morsi, a senior member of the Muslim Brotherhood, won the presidential election. Though he ran as an independent candidate and not as the Muslim Brotherhood candidate, Morsi's political and popular base was Islamist.

A year later, in July 2013, following mass protests against Morsi's Egyptian government and growing anarchy, Egypt's minister of defense, Abdel Fattah al-Sisi, ousted President Morsi. Morsi then faced an extended trial in Egypt. He died in Cairo in June 2019 during a court hearing.

We have discussed the fact that the Muslim Brotherhood's historically epic win turned out to be their biggest failure. In Egypt, specifically, this was because, during Morsi's short time in office, the Islamists failed to prove to Egyptians that they had a strategy to address the challenges practically.

I want to focus on this point because this episode relates to two of the factors that I believe can set the stage for a healthier nation-state: The increasing presence and impact of civil society values and institutions and the emergence of mutual accountability and responsibility between a government and its citizens.

In June 2014, Abdel Fattah al-Sisi was elected the sixth president of Egypt.

In 2018, al-Sisi was re-elected. Many argue that even though there was another candidate—Musa Mustafa Musa—it was a "fixed game." Egypt's Elections Committee formally announced that al-Sisi won 97.08 percent of the votes.[46] That figure can certainly support the argument that it was a "fixed game." In April 2019, a public referendum in Egypt approved amendments to the Egyptian constitution, including extending al-Sisi's term as president until 2024 with an option to extend until 2030. According to the elections committee, twenty-seven million Egyptians (out of sixty-one million people eligible to vote) voted in the referendum.[47]

As president, he pledged to focus his agenda primarily on Egypt's economic and social challenges. Although his policies have made considerable strides in reducing unemployment, improving infrastructure, expanding and diversifying the country's income sources, and implementing economic and administrative reforms to encourage foreign investment, it is clear to all Egyptians that Egypt will continue to face enormous challenges that may even grow over time.

One example is Egypt's most pressing—and perennial need—housing solutions. In 1985 Egypt's population was 49 million. In 2021, its population doubled and now exceeds 100 million.

According to a June 2020 government report, hundreds of thousands of housing units have been built under al-Sisi's rule, and hundreds of thousands are under construction. The housing projects offer different types of housing units according to income. The lion's share of the housing units being built are meant to be solutions for low-income buyers and young couples. The report also addresses other issues such as water and roads. According to the report, the government has implemented as many as 295 water projects and is currently working on sixty-two more. Also, 2,345 kilometers of roads have been developed, and 150 kilometers of roads are being constructed.[48]

Al-Sisi praises the role of civil society organizations and their contribution to Egypt. He makes genuine and considerable efforts to address the needs of young Egyptians. In one of his speeches, he said, "The Egyptian state needs the role of the civil society organizations and their work; we are happy with that role; we appreciate it and support it." According to al-Sisi, more than 45,000 civil society organizations are currently working in Egypt to support the state. He added that it is essential to let Egyptian citizens know what is happening in all sectors.

Al-Sisi also added that the Egyptian state was working to provide job opportunities—including building fifteen new industrial zones. He stated that there should be a balance between the owners' and tenants' needs when it comes to housing.[49]

In response to al-Sisi's August 2021 amendments to sexual harassment laws, the United Nations resident coordinator in Egypt, Elena Panova, thanked President al-Sisi. "With the approval of amendments to Law 141 2021 by President al-Sisi, Egypt is embarking on a new era of ending different forms of violence against women and addressing the crime of sexual harassment." She congratulated Egypt's National Council for Women and its president Maya Morsy for "the great achievement."[50]

Civil society groups and organizations in Egypt are gradually impacting Egyptian society and the Egyptian political system. And while they can mark some achievements and progress, the path ahead is long, winding, and challenging.

Al-Sisi's government is, in a way, schizophrenic. On the one hand, al-Sisi meets one of the significant conditions for the emergence of a new statehood model. And that is governmental responsibility for its citizens' well-being. He is seriously addressing the social and economic challenges the Egyptian people face. As president, he emphasizes women's critical roles and the young generation's centrality in Egypt and Egypt's future. And he invests in efforts to address and engage these groups. Al-Sisi continually emphasizes the need to set a higher bar of goals for Egypt. Al-Sisi—rightly so—stresses time and time again that he has no magic solutions to Egypt's problems and that the road toward a better future will be long and hard. In terms of governmental responsibility, al-Sisi presents a positive role model as a leader and a president.

On the other hand, al-Sisi also suppresses freedom of speech and political activity. He systematically represses and imprisons political opponents, activists, and critics. Journalists are imprisoned for their opinions. His government designates the Muslim Brotherhood as a terror organization. The movement's activists and leaders are arrested and put in prison. In June 2020, the Supreme Court ordered the dissolution of the political party of the *Al-Jama'ah al-Islamiyah*, "The Islamist Group."

When it comes to Egypt, it is essential to emphasize that though there are enormous challenges, the regime can be mercilessly oppressive and repressive. However, it is an open society. People are allowed to argue, debate, disagree and share. The public discourse in Egypt is a very active and vibrant space. Whether it be on social media, in more institutional communication frameworks, in the parliament, or on the streets where public protests are commonplace. These official and informal frameworks offer Egyptians a broad and open platform to share their varying opinions, vent their frustrations, influence public opinion, and influence legislation.

Protests—which, as I said, are common in Egypt—sometimes escalate violently. We saw this as recently as the fall of 2019 when a wave of protests swept the Arab world. In Egypt, the demonstrations escalated and were violent, but not to the point of undermining the stability of the regime. A major reason that the protests do not boil over is that the Egyptian people understand there are no magic solutions. And no less important; they appreciate al-Sisi's efforts to address issues that affect people's everyday lives and impact their future. This understanding is manifested in the fact that demonstrations protesting al-Sisi's policies have not gained momentum, unlike his predecessors Mubarak and Morsi.

Over the past decade—and specifically, in the al-Sisi era—Egypt is a clear example of how governmental responsibility is gaining momentum even if it is uneven and not always pretty.

The demonstration of government responsibility and accountability is leading Egypt to a different place than it was under al-Sisi's predecessors. Al-Sisi says to the Egyptians, 'I do not have magic solutions, but I am committed to work for you.' And the Egyptians appreciate that. And the public has responded by showing—for the most part—that they will support a government and rulers that are devoted to addressing their challenges. Public trust is essential for stability and helps to address challenges more effectively. Given this, in my estimation, Egypt and its government will be stable for the foreseeable future.

Algeria

Located in North Africa, bordering to the east Libya and Tunisia, and Morocco to the west, Algeria is, land-wise, the largest state in Africa and the largest Arab State. Algeria became independent in 1962. The president of Algeria, President Abdelaziz Bouteflika, was first elected in 1999. In 2019—elderly and in bad health—he was preparing to run for a fifth term.

His announcement sparked mass protests in Algeria called the *Hirak* "the Movement," which began on February 22, 2019. The millions of protesters deemed Bouteflika unfit to rule. They demanded he not run, that his government resign, and for a complete overhaul of Algeria's entrenched corrupt political system. The protesters represented a cross-section of Algerian society—left-wing, right-wing, conservative, progressive, Islamist, secular—and came from all walks of life, ages, and persuasions. People took to the streets showing their feelings, marching for recognition and dignity, and indicting an entire political system. And their slogan was simply *"Irhal"* "Go Away." Enough is enough!

And the non-violent protests worked. On April 3, 2019, the frail, eighty-two-year-old Bouteflika resigned and announced that he would not seek another term.

In December 2019, the former prime minister of Algeria, Abdelmadjid Tebboune, was elected Algeria's eighth president. The election was widely boycotted—voter turnout was less than 40 percent. Because the protesters saw the candidates—all of whom served under Bouteflika—as representing the same corrupt regime they were trying to replace. Seventy-five-year-old Tebboune's health is in question. It is very possible he will not stay in power for much longer.

Throughout 2020, tensions in Algeria deepened. In an attempt to demonstrate 'democracy' and that the new government listened to the protesters, the parliament proposed a host of seventy-three amendments to the Algerian constitution. However, the suggested changes basically consolidated governmental power. And a very controversial Article 29 expanded the authority of the army beyond Algeria's borders. This article raised concerns among Algerians as to how the army's powers would evolve. A referendum on the constitutional changes was held in early November 2020. The referendum passed by over 65 percent. But it was the lowest turnout for a referendum in Algeria. Barely 24 percent of the people (five million out of twenty-three million) eligible to vote went to the polls. With the voter turnout being so low, the public did not accept the demonstration of democracy the government was hoping they would.

COVID-19 tempered Algeria's demonstrations. But it was clear that they would be back. And they would not hesitate to demand reforms the constitutional amendments ignore for change, freedom, and dignity.

And that is precisely what happened. In February 2021, two years after their protests that led to Bouteflika's resignation, Hirak led the people back to the streets. This time under the slogan *Yitnahawga3*, "they all have to go!" And they are not the only protesters in Algeria. Throughout the country, there are sporadic yet ongoing demonstrations of the unemployed and underserved. And professionals have also joined the ranks. Doctors, firefighters, teachers, etc., have staged strikes. Algerians are rising up against a regime that is trying unsuccessfully to govern with a strategy combining goodwill gestures side by side with continued repression of activists, journalists, and demonstrators.

In Algeria—as in other Arab countries—we see a political map dominated by the two camps we have been discussing in this chapter.

One whose core agenda is the nation-state and the values of civil society. And the second, whose core agenda is Islamist.

However, in Algeria and across the region, neither of the camps—neither the nationalist nor the Islamist—are made of one ideology, opinion, voice, or vision. Within each camp, there are different individuals, movements, parties, organizations, etc., that emphasize and prioritize varying elements of the agenda. And the balance of ideology and political priorities differs from one to the other.

The outcome of the latest parliamentary elections held in Algeria in June 2021 demonstrates the fractured nature of these two camps.

The Algerian parliament, the People's National Assembly, has a total of 407 seats. Following the elections, the two major parties in the Parliament are FLN—the National Liberation Front (ninety-eight Deputies)—and the Independent Movement (eighty-four Deputies). Both parties represent the national-civic camp. The third-largest party is the Movement of the Society for Peace (MSP). MSP is the largest Islamic party in Algeria, and it has sixty-five Deputies in the current parliament.

MSP and other Islamic parties did join the government.[51] However, Hirak, the national-civic movement, which had organized a mass boycott of national elections, refused to join the National Liberation Front and the Independent Movement. They did not want to be a part of the established government. They preferred to be in opposition.

In July 2021, President Tebboune announced he was forming a new government under Prime Minister Ayman Bin Abd al-Rahman, finance minister in the previous government. Although there is currently a government, the turnout for the elections barely surpassed 30 percent.[52]

Growing unrest and the fluid situation lead to several question marks regarding Algeria's path. The challenge is manifested, among other things, by the fact that Algeria has held two elections in a row with a record low turnout. Will the government be able to create and maintain a stable political system that can effectively and constructively fulfill its obligations to its citizens? Will it be able to legislate at all?

To the protesters, the effort the government made to amend the Constitution was seen as a sham meant to "look like Democracy." And the June 2021 elections reflected the public's same malaise. On the other hand, Algerians have no intention of capitulating and accepting the status quo.

Algeria's path will continue to be fraught with serious bumps and difficulties. However, in my observation, two aspects of the Algerian political and public system lay the groundwork for cautious optimism.

The first encouraging sign is that the Islamic and national civic camps demonstrated that they could build a political partnership centered around one common denominator. They both decided to prioritize the nation-state. And even though they have different ideologies, they have chosen to work together to strengthen and stabilize the state of Algeria.

The second encouraging factor is that despite the vigorous, sometimes aggressive public debate and political struggle, Algerians are managing to avoid sliding down a dangerous slope that could lead to disintegration.

The next steps are dangerous for Algeria and Algerians. It is difficult to estimate the outcomes of the Algerians' struggle to define their path and create a state that represents and works for the benefit of all Algerians. Like other Arab states, Algeria's course to define a new nation-state model is long and fraught with difficulties and risks.

But the 2019 and 2021 protests sent a clear message that a new era is dawning. Algerians are standing up, holding their government accountable, and not accepting cosmetic changes. The message is clear. The past must be put in the past. We want to shape our own future.[53] One week after Algeria's President Abdelaziz Bouteflika stepped down in East Africa, another national uprising ended the three-decade regime of a dictator. And this time, it was in Sudan or, as it is called in Arabic, *Bilad al-Sudan,* "Land of Blacks."

Sudan

Located on the Red Sea, south of Egypt, Sudan—which borders six countries—has never been a homogeneous political or ethnic unit. Like Libya and Yemen, the tribal alignment and affiliations, the geographical distribution of the tribes, and religious and ethnic identities (predominantly either Arab or African) shape Sudan's history more than anything else.

Sudan became an independent state in 1965. The history of Sudan, again like Libya and Yemen, is rife with constant violence. Tribal wars, military coups, destroyed infrastructure, and lack of services have made Sudan a failed state.

Since independence, southern Sudan has been plagued with violence. The primary reasons for this are a combination of the fact that Sudan's oil fields are in the south. And that, while most Sudanese are Muslims, southern Sudan is primarily Christian.

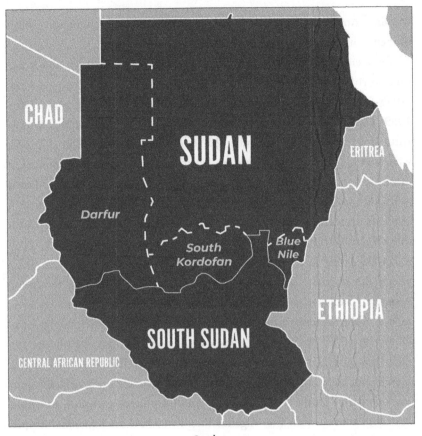

Sudan

In 2003, rebels in Darfur (a predominantly Muslim region in western Sudan) launched an insurrection against the Sudanese government for oppressing Darfur's non-Arab population. The government responded by using Arab militias—later named *Janjaweed*—to carry out genocide and ethnic cleansing. It is estimated that as many as five hundred thousand people—mainly African Muslims—were killed by the government-supported militias. Millions of Sudanese have become destitute refugees. The war in Darfur has been the most violent and ongoing conflict that plagues Sudan until today.

In 2011, the government held a referendum. Sudan split into two states: Sudan with a population of about thirty-four million—the vast majority,

Muslims. And South Sudan, with a population of about eleven million—most of them Christians.

Between 1990 and 2019, three figures—sometimes as partners and sometimes as rivals—simultaneously shaped Sudan's path. One was Sadiq al-Mahdi (1935–2020). He was prime minister of Sudan from 1966–1967 and 1986 – 1989. He headed the country's largest political party, the National Umma Party, until his death in November 2020. The second was Hassan al-Turabi, who died in 2016. Al-Turabi was an Islamic politician who led a process of the Islamization of Sudan and its government. The third is General Omar al-Bashir, the seventh president of Sudan, an Islamist, who came to power in 1989 after launching a military coup against al-Mahdi's government. Al-Bashir ruled Sudan for thirty years until he himself was ousted in March 2019.

In December 2018, protests began in Sudan. Sparked by a rise in bread prices, the disparate protests quickly evolved into a wholesale revolution against the Sudanese government. And particularly Omar al-Bashir. The average age of the Sudanese is nineteen years old. And this overwhelmingly peaceful revolution led by the young middle and upper class took their future and their lives into their own hands. They were resolute. They were done with a corrupt and inept regime that brought the country to the brink of bankruptcy and offered no future. Their relatively peaceful protests prevailed. On April 11, 2019, about a week after Algeria's President Abdelaziz Bouteflika stepped down, the Sudanese military overthrew al-Bashir.

After al-Bashir was ousted, a Transitional Military Council (TMC) was set up in Sudan. In early July 2019, the TMC reached an agreement with the Forces for Freedom and Change (FFC) coalition. The FFC is a movement of civil society and rebel groups that led the uprising resulting in al-Bashir's ouster.

In August 2019, the TMC and the FFC came to a power-sharing deal. A political map and a Constitutional Declaration outlined Sudan's three-year transition from a military dictatorship to a democracy. The sides agreed that three governing bodies will rule the country: the Sovereign Council, a Council of Ministers, and a Legislative Council (Parliament).

According to the agreement, the Sovereign Council—made up of eleven members—is the most powerful and will lead the government through the three-year transition phase. The Sovereign Council will approve the prime minister and the cabinet, oversee the judiciary system, represent Sudan on the international stage, and hold other extensive powers. The council's eleven members will be divided accordingly: five civilians appointed by the FFC; five military personnel designated by the TMC; and one "national figure" who will be a "neutral" member and act as an arbitrator when there are disagreements among the council members. According to the agreement, a military figure will head the Sovereign Council for a year and nine months. A civilian will head the Sovereign Council for the remaining transitional period of a year and three months.

General Abdel Fattah Abdelrahman al-Burhan was appointed to chair the Sovereign Council. Al-Burhan was born in Sudan. He is the former commander of the Sudanese ground forces and the Sudanese army's third most high-ranking general. In 2015, Saudi Arabia and the UAE recruited Sudan in their fight against the Iranian-backed Yemenite Houthis. Al-Burhan was in charge of the Sudanese troops in the Arab Coalition. He has a good relationship with Saudi Arabia and the United Arab Emirates. Al-Bashir appointed him as inspector general of the national army a few months before he was overthrown.

The Sovereign Council appointed Abdalla Hamdok as prime minister. He is a respected economist with a BS from the University of Khartoum. He has a PhD from the University of Manchester. He was a senior official in Sudan's Ministry of Finance and Economic Planning and has held leadership roles in the African Development Bank, the International Labour Organization, the United Nations Economic Commission for Africa, etc. Hamdok has over thirty years of experience as an economist and senior policy analyst specializing in economic development across Africa. As prime minister, he created an eighteen-member cabinet (a transitional government) to manage the country's day-to-day operations during the three-year transition period. His cabinet includes four women, including the country's first-ever female Foreign Affairs minister, Asma Mohamed Abdalla.

Regarding the Legislative Council (Parliament), the August 2019 Constitutional Declaration states that the FFC will appoint two-thirds of the Legislative Council members. The rest will be determined by the other organizations that participated in the protests.

By the end of 2020, less than two years after Omar al-Bashir's overthrow and the agreement between the TMC and the FFC to rule Sudan, four dramatic developments have occurred in Sudan.

First, the country re-evaluated its traditional relationship with Iran, Qatar, and Turkey. It has pivoted now more toward Egypt, Saudi Arabia, and the United Arab Emirates.

Second, on October 3, 2020, a peace agreement known as the Juba Peace Agreement was signed between the transitional government of Sudan and the "Sudan Revolutionary Front"—a coalition of militias operating in the provinces of Darfur, Blue Nile, and South Kordofan. These agreements are supposed to be the first step on the path to restoring peace in the Blue Nile, Darfur, and South Kordofan after many years of deadly conflicts. However, it should be noted that some of the militias in West and North Sudan did not join the agreement.

A few weeks after the signing of the Juba Peace Agreement, another dramatic event happened in Sudan. And that is the official declaration of a US-mediated Sudan-Israel Normalization Agreement, announced by Donald Trump on October 23, 2020. In an official joint statement, Sudan and Israel agreed to normalize relations and "end the state of belligerence between their nations."[54] Israel and Sudan also agreed to establish commercial and economic ties, emphasize agriculture, and open negotiations for cooperation in aviation, trade, Sudanese fleeing to Israel, etc. Sudan follows the UAE and Bahrain, who signed the Abraham Accords (the Peace Agreement between the UAE and Israel and the launching of peace talks between Israel and Bahrain, signed on September 15, 2020).

In December 2020, Sudan was removed from the American State Sponsor of Terrorism list. The United States put Sudan on the list in 1993. The US said Sudan supported terrorist groups, sheltered Osama Bin Laden, and assisted in the 1998 bombings of the United States embassies in Kenya and Tanzania in 1998 and the bombing of the USS *Cole* in 2000. Former President Donald Trump removed Sudan from the list after the government agreed to pay $335 million for victims of terror attacks.

In July 2021, the International Monetary Fund (IMF) and World Bank, following policy implementations and other actions from the Sudanese transitional government, officially declared Sudan eligible for over $50 billion in debt relief. The country will continue to benefit if they continue implementing reforms over the next three years. This relief will help Sudan's government invest more money into improving citizens' lives and make more resources available to address poverty and other social conditions.

According to a July 2021 report published by the Organization for World Peace, debt relief from the IMF and World Bank will be essential for Sudan reintegrating into the international community and continuing to improve poverty and social conditions. However, there are concerns about how the debt relief provided by the IMF and World Bank will affect Sudan's poorer citizens. Historically, the World Bank has backed many projects in various countries to end poverty and increase income levels for the poorest people. However, many poor people end up being displaced with no livelihood and very little government support after the projects are created. With the IMF and World Bank's debt relief and the $2 billion grants for projects targeting poverty, people's displacement will continue. There is also concern about foreign investment and how influential foreign investors could be in the country. Some critics point to the possibility of neo-colonial policies being implemented. Such concerns reflect the history of Western involvement in Africa and Sudan and test Sudan's transitional—and eventually permanent—government. But as of now, the debt relief should help ease economic tensions and allow for further progress toward ending poverty, improving people's social conditions, and reintegrating Sudan into the international community.[55]

The joint military-civilian government ruling Sudan since 2019 has made strides to balance its books, rejoin the international community, and create a responsible and functioning government—though clearly not a government that serves all Sudanese.

That said, it is essential to clarify that—like Algeria—the road to a stable, functioning political system and government in Sudan is long and dangerous.

On the ground, developments during the first half of 2021 indicate the fragility of the situation in Sudan.

Protests, tensions, unrest, and violence in Sudan continue. Amid ongoing violence, hundreds of people in the Darfur region have been killed, and thousands have been displaced. In June 2021, fighting between tribal militias in

South Kordofan re-erupted. Sudan's eastern district (the Red Sea district) is also a stage for a constant unrest and protest. Those local frictions and unrest are likely to continue.

In February 2021, the leader of the Islamic Movement in Sudan called for a non-violent civil outcry in protest of the difficult economic and social situation in the country.

The young people that led the revolution seem to be disappointed, disillusioned, disenfranchised, and deflated. The enthusiasm and zeal that brought about the revolution have dissipated. The antagonism toward al-Bashir's regime, which unified the young people during the revolution, unraveled after his downfall. Another source for instability is the fragile partnership of the Transitional Military Council (TMC) and the Forces for Freedom and Change (FFC). The existence of two power centers—one military and other civilian sharing power is not an ideal formula. Frictions between the two camps are very likely to take place, resulting instability.

So, where is Sudan heading?

In my assessment, Sudan's new state model—if it develops—will eventually have to reflect Sudan's tribal, geographical, and ethnic features. The Juba Peace Agreement offers some insight into what that might look like. The Juba agreement differentiates between specific provinces—Darfur, the Blue Nile, central Sudan, East Sudan, north Sudan, and South Kordofan—and relates to each individually. The agreement suggests a structure of a federal government with autonomous governments in the provinces. This model, on the one hand, could bring stability to the country. But on the other hand, there is a risk that the power struggle between TMC and FFC, together with ongoing friction between the central government and the provinces will create a constant state of instability. Again, the key will be the central government's ability to address the provinces' economic and societal challenges effectively.

Tunisia

Almost a decade has passed since the twenty-six-year-old Tunisian peddler Mohamed Bouazizi set himself on fire. Bouazizi's cart remained abandoned in the warehouse at his parents' home.[56] But Bouazizi made it into the history books. Because his final act of desperation on December 10, 2011, ignited a fire in the Arab world. A fire that, little did he know, would become known as the "Arab Spring." A wave of protests that rocked the Arab world ousted regimes and enormously impacted the Middle East.

In the decade that has passed, Tunisia, the cradle of the Arab Spring, has experienced internal political unrest and growing economic and social challenges. As of now, in the summer of 2021, Tunisia finds itself in a dangerous and precarious situation.

Looking at Tunisian domestic politics over the last decade, we see many parties and an endless sea of political rivals. Often with conflicting ideologies and interests. And all trying to push and pull Tunisians in different directions.

The military has always been a—if not *the*—principal power broker in Tunisia. However, over the past decade, two power centers have emerged in Tunisian politics.

One is *Al-Nahda* (also spelled *Ennahda*), "The Renaissance." Al-Nahda is an Islamic Muslim Brotherhood party. And it is the largest party in Tunisia.

The opposing camp is an array of nationalist (some with a tinge of socialism) organizations and parties. The leading nationalist camp parties are the Heart of Tunisia, the People's Movement, the Popular Front, and *Nidaa Tounes,* "Call of Tunisia." Former Tunisian President Beji Caid Essebsi, who died in July 2019, founded Nidaa Tounes. Once a powerful party, Nidaa Tounes was resolutely crushed in the 2019 elections.

On the one hand, Tunisia has made impressive achievements since 2011. Tunisia has had three democratic elections (2011, 2014, and 2019) and seven governments. In 2014, despite challenges and political crises, Tunisia succeeded in passing a new constitution. The constitution laid the foundations for a democratic regime, defined the separation of powers, and emphasized the state's commitment to human rights.

On the other hand, since 2011, political instability in Tunisia has deepened because of three main factors: the difficulty of forming a stable coalition in a multi-party system in which small parties can bargain and have leverage that outweighs their actual size; growing economic and social challenges; and deep crises within the two main parties—Nidaa Tounes and Al-Nahdah.

Nidaa Tounes was founded in 2012 by Beji Caid Essebsi. Essebsi played a pivotal role in Tunisia's history and is considered the father of Tunisian independence and Tunisia's transformation into a democracy. He was elected president of Tunisia in 2014—the first democratically elected president in Tunisian history. He served as president until his death in July 2019 at the age of ninety-two. In the 2014 elections and winning the presidency, his party, Nidaa Tounes, won eighty-six seats out of 217 in the Tunisian parliament and became the biggest party. But, within five years, the party had completely imploded. In September 2018, the Nidaa Tounes party split. This friction was the precursor to its total collapse in the 2019 elections.

In the 2019 elections, the party secured only three seats in the parliament. The reason Nidaa self-destructed was succession. Some of the party leaders wanted Hafez Caïd Essebsi, the son of Beji Caid Essebsi, to succeed his father as party leader. Others in the party virulently opposed the younger Essebsi taking the helm.

Al Nahda, an Islamist Muslim Brotherhood party, was founded in the 1970s. President Zine el-Abidine Ben Ali, the second president of Tunisia from 1987 until 2011, banned the party after it did unexpectedly well in the 1989 elections. Zine el-Abidine Ben Ali was the first casualty of the Arab Spring. The autocratic ruler and his family fled to Saudi Arabia in January 2011.

In October 2011, Tunisia's first democratic elections—al-Nahda received about 40 percent of the votes, which was more than any other party. One of the reasons for al-Nahda's success was the return to Tunisia of one of al-Nahda's founders, the exiled Rached al-Ghannouchi, who returned to Tunisia after the fall of Ben Ali. Under al-Ghannouchi's leadership, al-Nahda won the majority in the parliament and became the leading political power in Tunisia.

Like many other Muslim Brotherhood parties which rose to power on the heels of the Arab Spring events, for al-Nahda, the 2014 elections told a different story. The public opposed the party's attempt to "Islamize" Tunisia. Furthermore, Tunisians suspected the party was behind assassinations of political opponents. In 2014, the short-lived rule of the Al-Nahda government came to an end.

In the 2019 parliamentary elections, the al-Nahda party won fifty-four seats. For the second time since 2011, al-Nahda was again the biggest party.

Tunisia's next presidential elections were in September 2019. This election was the second direct vote for the presidency since the 2011 revolution.

In October 2019, an independent candidate named Mr. Kais Saied—an expert in Constitutional Law—was elected the fifth president in the third free elections in Tunisia. He is the second president to be democratically elected in Tunisia. It is widely believed that he won due to his image as a clean-handed man, not tainted by corrupt politics.

In January, President Saied appointed Elyes Fakhfakh to serve as prime minister. The Assembly approved his government on February 27, 2020.

In July 2020, Elyes Fakhfakh and his government resigned. Fakhfakh resigned because of a corruption scandal. Saied then appointed Interior Minister Hichem Mechichi as prime minister and handed him the new government mandate. As Mechichi was trying to create his government, the economic and social crisis in the country was growing, fueled to no small degree by the COVID-19 pandemic.

In November 2020, the prime minister declared that Tunisia was experiencing an unprecedented economic crisis. He added that the costs of the pandemic on the Tunisian economy amounted to almost $3 billion. One of the hardest-hit sectors that completely collapsed was the tourism industry, which is the source of livelihood for millions of Tunisians.

Meanwhile, in November 2020, the crisis deepened within the ranks of the Muslim Brotherhood al-Nahda party. The eleventh convention of the party was canceled due to ideological and political power struggles within the party. One of the core reasons for the power struggle was, and is, the tension between the dogmatists and pragmatists.[57]

In parallel, al-Nahda's relationship with Tunisian president Saied took an unexpected shift.

Saied is a conservative. For example, he spoke out against the LGBT movement and foreign civil society organizations operating in Tunisia. He also expressed opposition to the bill for equality of inheritance rights between the two sexes. Saied is also known for his anti-Israel stance and strongly opposes normalization with Israel. Given these positions, Saied won the support of the al-Nahda party in the presidential election.

However, the alliance between Saied and the al-Nahda party has cracked. Al-Nahda's leader, Rached al-Ghannouchi, who also serves as chairman of the Tunisian parliament, has tried to coerce Saied into pursuing a regional foreign policy in line with al-Nahda's Islamic agenda.

An example of al-Ghannouchi trying to have Tunisia pursue an Islamic agenda was when he officially expressed support for Erdoğan's involvement in the war in Libya. Saied reprimanded al-Ghannouchi for his statements. Yes, a conservative, but Saied is not an Islamist and does not want Tunisia to be Islamist. The leader of al-Nahda also sharply and openly criticized President Saied for his thunderous silence in response to the Abraham Accords. Al-Ghannouchi's and al-Nahda's positions have caused growing tensions in his relationship with the Tunisian president.

In January 2021, violent riots broke out across Tunisia. As the economic crisis intensified, the political system found itself paralyzed. Caught in a multi-front power struggle between the various Tunisian political parties and between the president and the al-Nahda party. The government's wheels came to a screeching halt.

That was the situation in Tunisia at the beginning of 2021. A paralyzed and impotent government, a public demanding its leaders work for fundamental change to improve the situation, and deepening unrest.

In April 2021, a series of incidents illustrated the complete rift between the president and the al-Nahda party. During that month, President Saied thwarted an attempt by the al-Nahda party to pass a Constitutional Amendment that would change the rules of the Assembly of Representatives (the Legislative Branch) of the Tunisian government. According to the law, a vote of 145 Representatives (out of 217) is needed to pass a law. Al-Nahda proposed a law that would reduce the number to 131. One of the reasons Saied rejected the proposed law was that he was concerned that the al-Nahda would evoke article 88 in the Tunisian Constitution to impeach him.

On April 9, President Saied paid a three-day official visit to Egypt. The al-Nahda party sharply criticized the visit because Egypt officially classifies the Muslim Brotherhood as a terror group.

Later that month, Saied delivered a speech. He emphasized that in addition to his powers as commander-in-chief of the military forces, he is also the commander-in-chief of the internal security forces. That statement evoked the ire of the al-Nahda party. They saw it as a veiled threat. Al-Nahda responded with a scathing statement condemning the president for exceeding his authority.

The rift reached a climax when Kais Saied gave an official speech addressing the problem of corruption. In the speech, he alluded to the fact that al-Ghannouchi's son is involved in bribery and corruption cases.

Two main factors fuel the rift between Saied and the Muslim Brotherhood, al-Nahda party.

First, the Islamist camp mistakenly thought that the president's conservative views meant that his political agenda was Islamic. Saied's positions as president illustrate that his agenda is dictated by calculations and considerations that are not necessarily in line with the Islamic agenda of the al-Nahda Party.

A second factor is that while al-Nahda—for political and ideological reasons—supports a centralized government, President Kais supports a decentralized system of government. Saied is a proponent of giving a significant amount of power and responsibility to the middle levels of the government structure, especially municipalities and rural councils.

On July 25, 2021, President Saied took a dramatic step. In a speech to the nation, which he broadcasted on state television, he announced he was activating Article 80 of the Tunisian constitution:

Article 80   Imminent danger, necessary measures

In the event of imminent danger threatening the nation's institutions or the security or independence of the country, and hampering the normal functioning of the state, the President of the Republic may take any measures necessitated by the exceptional circumstances, after consultation with the Head of Government and the Speaker of the Assembly of the Representatives of the People and informing the President of the Constitutional Court. The President shall announce the measures in a statement to the people.

The measures shall guarantee, as soon as possible, a return to the normal functioning of state institutions and services. The Assembly of the Representatives of the People shall be deemed to be in a state of continuous session throughout such a period. In this situation, the President of the Republic cannot dissolve the Assembly of the Representatives of the People and a motion of censure against the government cannot be presented.

Thirty days after the entry into force of these measures, and at any time thereafter, the Speaker of the Assembly of the Representatives of the People or thirty of the members thereof shall be entitled to apply to the Constitutional Court with a view to verifying whether or not the circumstances remain exceptional. The Court shall rule upon and publicly issue its decision within a period not exceeding fifteen days. These measures cease to be in force as soon as the circumstances justifying their implementation no longer apply. The President of the Republic shall address a message to the people to this effect.[58]

Shortly after his announcement, his office issued a presidential order that included the following: He dismissed Prime Minister Hichem Mechichi; suspended the parliament for thirty days; he rescinded lawmakers' and parliament members' immunity from investigation and prosecution; and he dismissed key ministers.

Saied's supporters went out to the street celebrating Saied's move. They believe it was a step toward governmental accountability and responsibility.

On the other hand, the Islamist camp criticized Saied's act, arguing it was a coup against democracy. Islamists went to the street protesting. They believe it is an attempt to sideline and defeat the Muslim Brotherhood and smother the Islamist voices in Tunisia.

Sporadic demonstrations and limited clashes between the camps took place in front of the Parliament building. Eighty-year-old al-Ghannouchi, the head of the al-Nahda party, tried to enter the Parliament building, but the army blocked his entrance. Islamist supporters described Saied's move as a "coup." Some even urged the people to "resist by all means."[59]

However, after the first wave of protests, it seems as if Saied has the public's support. A few days after his announcement, Saied took a walk along Tunisia's capitol's main street, and he was received with applause.

At the time this book is being submitted to the publisher, in August 2021, Tunisia is at a critical juncture.

Will it contain the crisis and continue its journey toward a vibrant, pluralistic democratic society as it has successfully done over the past decade? Or will the weight of economic, political, and social crises overwhelm the Tunisians, and will Tunisia be embroiled in ongoing violence?

Tunisian political analyst Amin Bin Masoud believes that the Islamist camp will refrain from a reaction that might escalate the situation. He instead evaluates that the Islamic camp will wait for Saied and his allies in the nationalist camp to fail to address Tunisia's economic and social challenges. And then the Islamists will try to monetize the nationalists' failures to get back in power.

It seems as if the first part of his evaluation is—as of August 2021—accurate. Al-Nahda has apparently accepted the reality. In August 2021, al-Ghannouchi wrote the following on the party's official website: "We have received the signal from the people....We will reflect on our mistakes, and we are willing to sacrifice. The only way to move forward is through dialogue. Whoever thinks that Democracy in Tunisia can be spared is delusional."[60]

It would appear that Tunisia's turbulent journey toward a new statehood model marches on.

Accountability, Responsibility, and Civil Society— It's a Start...

I would like to remind you what Dr. Amal Moussa, a sociology professor at the University of Tunisia, wrote in her 2020 article, "It is the Second Nation-State": "Today, after the winds of reform and revolutions blew, the civil society is growing stronger to defend freedom ... after the change of the Arab and Muslim people, the rise in the level of protest and the diversity of its forms and practices ... the nation-state will have to adjust to the changes we are going through."[61]

I believe the trajectory of events in Egypt, Algeria, Sudan, and Tunisia supports the observation made by Dr. Moussa and myself. Both rulers and citizens are changing and adjusting. And this will design the new era of the Middle East.

I think that evaluation is supported by the fact that in each of these countries, one can detect the following features:

- On varying levels, governments have internalized that they need to be accountable.
- This understanding is leading to an evolving two-way pact where, on one side, citizens demand that their government take responsibility and be held accountable. On the other side, governments understand that they need to address the people's needs if they want to stay in power.
- Civil society values and institutions are growing—as is their power and impact.

That said, I think it is essential to address the relationship between democracy and a potential new statehood model in the Middle East.

In January 2021, Moroccan poet and writer Mohammed Bennis's wrote an article, "The Arab Spring and the Rule of Societies." Here is an excerpt: "as of 2019, it seems as if the Arab Spring has reached a point of maturity and was able to overcome divisiveness caused by sectorial, ethnical, racial, and tribal schisms. However, future leaders that emerge from possible next waves of the Arab Spring will have not only to stay away from the dividing factors; they will also have to establish a new political culture that serves the process of a shift towards modern democracy."[62]

Bennis's observation offers a significant insight that Western policymakers need to understand and consider in the new era.

The emergence of a new statehood model in the Middle East does not necessarily mean that it will look like a twentieth- or twenty-first-century Western-style democracy. It would be a mistake to assume a-priory that Arab societies are looking to adopt Western-style democracy. I posit that the possible new statehood model in the Arab world will undoubtedly have some democratic characteristics. However, Western-style democracy will not be the core of a new statehood model in the Arab world.

CHAPTER 6

FIGHTING FOR THEIR INDEPENDENCE | SYRIA, LEBANON, AND IRAQ

Occupation, Protectorates, Freedom, and Independence

Some Arab countries are taking their first steps toward a possible new statehood model. One that perhaps will be more successful than the twentieth-century nation-state model in the Arab world.

At the same time, as of 2021, for five Arab countries, the road toward a possible new statehood model is even more challenging. Wars and violence continue to ravage Libya and Yemen. Lebanon and Iraq are fighting for their independence. Syria is ruined following ten years of war. Their struggles, which we will explore in this chapter, and, of course, the outcomes will write the next chapter in these countries. What happens in Syria, Lebanon, and Iraq will have significant ramifications on the Middle East, the societies, and the people.

As we have learned, the weakness of the nation-state is one of the leading causes of the constant instability and chaos in the Middle East.

In Chapters 2 and 3, we began to explore how Iran and Turkey leverage states' weakness and instability to advance their own hegemonic ambitions.

Let's zoom out to see what this looks like 'from space.'

Iran controls Lebanon. Hezbollah, Iran's most powerful army of terror, rules Lebanon. Iran physically occupies parts of Syria. Turkey and its proxies occupy parts of northern Syria. Turkey has created a Turkish protectorate from the Mediterranean Sea eastward along the Turkish-Syrian border. Turkey has a military presence in northern Iraq.

Turkey and Iran—Military Presence in Syria and Iraq

Turkey has created over thirty-seven Turkish military bases in northern Iraq. Iran through its militias and political allies has excessive influence in Iraq.

Throughout the following three sections, we will explore the complex and precarious geopolitical environment of Syria, Lebanon, and Iraq at the beginning of the third decade of the twenty-first century.

Syria: The Shattered Dreams of Freedom

Let us start with Syria. A country that, in the twenty-first century, to quote UN High Commissioner for Human Rights Zeid Ra'ad Al Hussein in 2017, became "the stage of the worse manmade disaster the world has seen since World War II."[1] The Syrian people's battle for freedom and independence ended in catastrophe.

I want to begin by correcting a term you might have heard in the media or the public discourse. And that term is the "civil war" in Syria.

The war in Syria indeed began as a domestic event. In March 2011, Syrians took to the streets peacefully, calling for the brutal and violent dictator, President Bashar al-Assad, to conduct political reforms and address the

Syria: Iran's Most Critical Asset in the Corridor, the Crescent, the
Axis of Resistance, and Iran's Quest for Hegemony

country's growing hardships. The mass protests and demonstrations continued through the spring of 2011. Al-Assad—determined to crush the demonstrations—killed an increasing number of civilian protesters in cold blood.

In June 2011, due to escalating violence, the events in Syria turned into a
civil war. And by the end of 2011, the civil war in Syria evolved into a stage
for an epic regional and global power struggle.

For over a decade, the war in Syria has been a Sunni-Shi'ite Arab-
Persian (Iranian) war. Sunni and Shi'ite militias and individual Sunnis and
Shi'ites streamed into Syria to join the battle. Iran, Russia, and Turkey are
all actively involved. And as the central power brokers in the war, Ankara,

Moscow, and Tehran all want to gain power in Syria for their own hegemonic ambitions.

Syria: Iran's Most Critical Asset in the Corridor, the Crescent, the Axis of Resistance, and Iran's Quest for Hegemony

As we discussed in Chapter 2, Syria is Iran's most important asset. To achieve
its objectives and become the regional superpower, Tehran must control Syria.
Syria is the key to the axis of resistance, the Shi'ite crescent, and the Iranian
land corridor—all cornerstones of Iran's foreign policy.

- Syria is overwhelmingly Sunni and is ruled by a minority dictatorship—the
  Alawites, representing about 10 percent of Syria's population. The Alawites
  are a distant branch of the Shi'ites even though the Alawites have different
  values, norms, and cultural and societal codes than the Iranian Shi'ites.
- IRG, officers, commanders of the al-Quds Force, Iranian agents, militias, and proxies all meet in Damascus.

Syria Offers Iran Access to the Mediterranean Sea

- Iran has built a military industry in Syria that manufactures missiles and rockets to send to Hezbollah in Lebanon.
- Tehran has created a sophisticated supply route through Syria that it uses to transfer militants, military hardware, and ammunition to Hezbollah.
- Syria offers Iran access to the Mediterranean Sea.
- Syria borders Israel and is in a state of war with Israel. It is a vital part of the "noose"—the mullah-created platform from which Iran or its proxies can launch attacks on Israel.

For Tehran, Syria is the lynchpin of its regional and global strategy.

Imagine the axis of resistance as a tent—Syria is literally the pole holding up the tent. If Iran loses control over Syria, the entire axis, corridor, and crescent infrastructure will fall.

If al-Assad lost the war in Syria, it would have been a massive blow to Iran and its hegemonic vision. That is why Iran has been directly and massively involved in the war in Syria since 2011—practically since the beginning. Iran arms al-Assad and provides him with—among other things—weapons, fuel,

Iran Has Built a Military Infrastructure in Syria and Syria Completes the Noose Around Israel

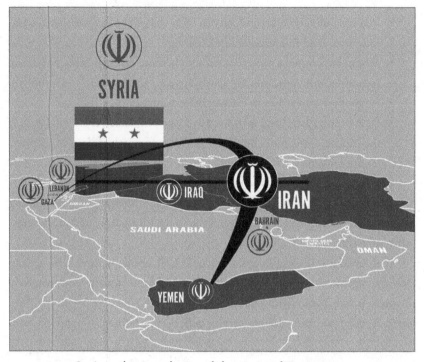

Syria—the Lynchpin of the Axis of Resistance

militants, and money. Most significantly, Iran has sent its militias to save the al-Assad regime and ensure Iranian control of Syria.

Russia: Iran Opened the Door for Putin to Come Back to the Middle East, and He Is Here to Stay

In the fall of 2015, when it seemed the Iran-Syria axis was on the verge of defeat, Tehran was extremely alarmed and concerned. Desperate, the mullah regime turned to Russia. The Iranians asked Putin to intervene militarily to save the al-Assad rule. Putin agreed. Russian aerial bombings destroyed cities and villages in Syria and caused the death of tens of thousands of people. Russia's direct military intervention in the war in Syria turned the war around and has kept Assad in power. Putin saved Assad—and the Iranians—from being defeated by the Syrian rebels.

The al-Assad-Iran-Russia axis is an alliance of convenience. To stay in power, the Assad regime needs Iran and Russia's military support. Al-Assad justifies Iranian and Russian presence in Syria by maintaining that they are helping Syria fight terror. Bashar al-Assad markets the war in Syria as a war on terror. He argues he is protecting the Syrian homeland. His marketing strategy is to present the Syrian people who revolted against his brutal, oppressive regime as al-Qaeda or ISIS.

For Putin, he sees his engagement in Syria as a way for him to reinsert himself in the Middle East. However, he does not want Russian boots on the ground, so he uses airpower.

And the on-the-ground day-to-day combat to ensure Iran and al-Assad retain control of Syria is carried out by al-Assad's forces—the Arab Syrian Army, and Iran and its proxies, including Afghan Shi'ite militias, Iraqi Shi'ite militias, Lebanese Shi'ite Hezbollah, and Pakistani Shi'ite militias.

Summer of 2021: A Decade Long War—A Snapshot

In the summer of 2021, after ten years of war and incomprehensible devastation, the al-Assad-Iran-Russia axis has succeeded in crushing the Syrian rebels.

However, and quite ironically, despite its military accomplishments on the ground, the al-Assad regime has significant challenges ahead:

There are three major reasons for my evaluation:

1. Tensions within the al-Assad-Iran-Russia axis.
2. The Arab world's refusal to accept al-Assad back into the fold.
3. The United States' June 2020 Caesar Syria Civilian Protection Act.

Tensions Surface within Syria-Iran-Russia Axis: And Then There's Turkey...

The military achievements have increased the tensions and conflicts of interest within the al-Assad-Iran-Russia axis, especially between Iran and Russia. Why?

Iran and Russia have conflicting interests in Syria. Iran wants to irreversibly secure its military presence in Syria. Russia, on the other hand, does not want to share control of Syria.

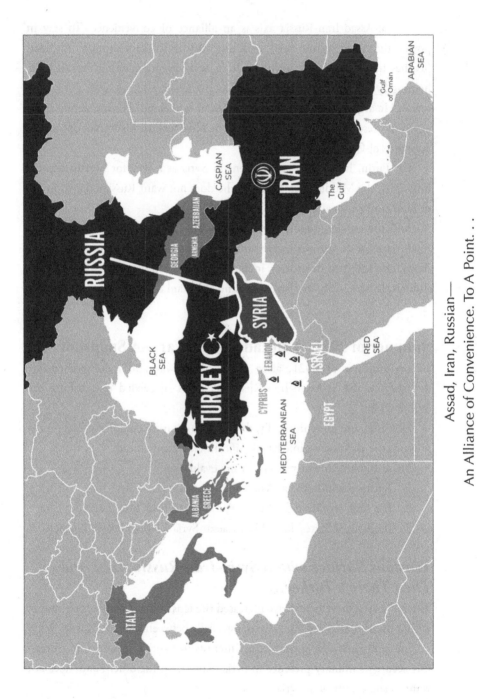

Assad, Iran, Russian—
An Alliance of Convenience. To A Point. . .

To that end, they have both invested heavily in Syria. In 2019, Ankara-based political analyst and researcher Ali Bakir estimated that since the outbreak of the Syrian revolution in March 2011, Iran had spent around $15 billion annually to keep al-Assad in power.[2]

As for Putin, accumulating information suggests that Russia has spent about $1 billion a year in Syria since he joined the war militarily in 2015 at Iran's request to save al-Assad.[3]

Both Iran and Russia want to "harvest the dividends" for their investments in preserving the Assad regime. Financially, they both expect to profit from Syria's civilian and military reconstruction by winning the bids to rebuild the country. In addition to expecting a return on their investment, both want to entrench themselves in Syria; both want a Mediterranean port; both want access to the Eastern Mediterranean's gas reserves; and both want to be on the central axis of the gas and oil supply route from Central Asia to Europe.

Another point of contention between Iran and Russia is that Russia accepts Israel's attacks on Iran's military assets and its militias in Syria. Russia's tacit permission does not sit well with al-Assad and Iran.

And speaking of not sitting well with al-Assad or Iran, Putin took advantage of his power in Syria to create his own proxy. Division 5 of Assad's army—the Arab Syrian Army includes many former Syrian rebels. Division 5 is primarily concentrated in southern Syria, in the districts of Dara'a and Quneitra, both of which border the Israeli Golan Heights. Division 5 is a part of al-Assad's military. However, practically, they are controlled by Russia.

One of Division 5's neighbors is another one of al-Assad's forces, Division 4 of the Arab Syrian Army. Division 4 includes Islamic Revolutionary Guard officers and Iranian specialists. Accumulating information shows that the power struggle in the Dara'a region between Russia and Iran escalated throughout 2020. Hundreds of people, mostly Syrians and an unclear number of Iranian officers and Iranian-backed Shi'ite militants, were killed in a series of assassinations and battles.[4]

In the summer of 2021, Russia has extended its military presence toward eastern Syria and into the Syrian Desert. Some three hundred soldiers of Division 5 are deployed in eastern Syria along major east-west routes crossing the Syrian desert.[5,6] The Russian move is strategically significant. By

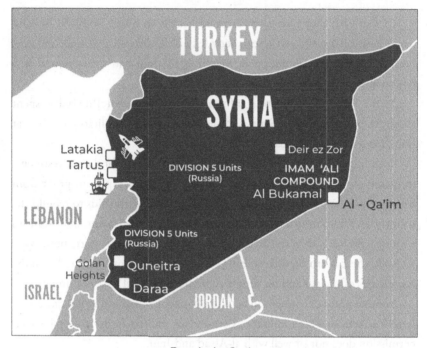

Russia in Syria

positioning Division 5 units in eastern Syria along the east-west route, Putin can block Iran's land corridor at a critical point—the Syrian-Iraq border crossing.

So far, Putin has made out very well in Syria. By helping Iran keep al-Assad in power, Putin has already gained two permanent military bases—an air force base in the Latakia Province in western Syria and a naval base in Tartus on the Mediterranean Sea. Thousands of Russian military personnel remain in the country, conducting daily operations and flying sorties. And in addition to military bases on the Mediterranean, Russia has a civilian and commercial foothold on the sea as well. Russia now controls and runs the Tartus commercial port. Moscow is in Syria, and Putin plans to expand his military and civilian presence in Syria.

For Iran and Russia, Syria is a zero-sum game. If Iran gains control of Syria, it will be at the expense of Russia. If Russia gains control of Syria, it will be at the cost of Iran. And neither side is willing to give up anything for the other.

Both Russia and Iran have one common denominator in Syria. They look after their interests, not the interests or welfare of Syria or the Syrian people.

Northern Syria—Turkish Protectorate

As I foresaw in my 2016 book, Turkey has created a Turkish Protectorate in northern Syria.[7] Turkey's entrenchment in northern Syria further complicates the power struggle between the al-Assad regime, Iran, Russia, and Turkey.

What Do I Mean by a Turkish Protectorate?

Turkey created a Turkish jurisdiction running parallel to the Turkish-Syrian border and spanning eastward and westward of the Euphrates River. Turkey now controls a 5,500-square-mile piece of Syrian territory along the Syrian-Turkish border.

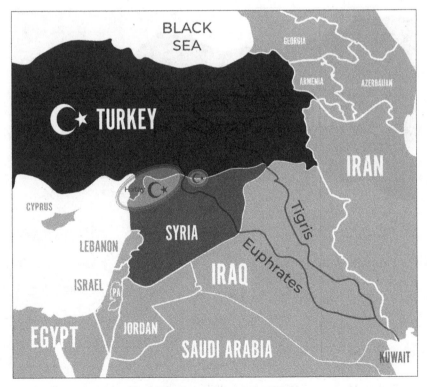

Turkish Protectorate in Syria

To secure the protectorate, Erdoğan has placed Turkish troops and Turkish proxy militias on the Syrian side of the Turkish-Syrian border. And in addition to a military presence, Turkey has created an administrative, civil, financial, and social service system for the Syrian residents under its control. This includes:

- The Turkish governor of the Hatay District in southern Turkey is now the Turkish protectorate governor in northern Syria.
- Turkish offices and officials control all administrative and governmental services for the Syrians in northern Syria, such as electricity, licenses, mail, permits, transportation, water, etc.
- Branches of the government ministries in northern Syria that used to be Syrian now operate under the Turkish flag.

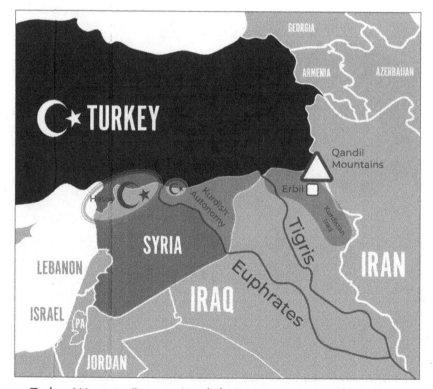

Turkey Wants to Prevent Kurdish Autonomy in Northern Syria

- In northern Syria, economic and commercial transactions are primarily in Turkish lira—the Turkish currency. And financial transactions in the region are processed by the Turkish banking system.
- The schools in northern Syria are controlled and managed by Turkey. The Syrian students in the Turkish-controlled areas must now learn Turkish as a mandatory subject.

Why Did Turkey Take Over Northern Syria?

One of Turkey's foremost policy objectives is to prevent a Kurdish autonomy in northeast Syria.

There are 30 million Kurds, and the vast majority are in the Middle East. The majority of Kurds are Muslims, and most of them are Sunni. They are primarily in Turkey (16 million, mainly in southeastern Turkey), northwestern Iran (8 million), northern Iraq (5.5 million), and northeastern Syria (before the war, 4 million and currently about 2 million).

The Kurds are undoubtedly a nation. Geographically concentrated, they have a shared history, language, culture, etc. But there is no independent Kurdish state. In northern Iraq (also called Kurdistan Iraq), there is a Kurdish regional government (KRG). The KRG is part of the Iraqi federal government.

The Turkish Kurds hold considerable power in the Turkish political system, primarily via the Kurdish Democratic Party (DBP) and the People's Democratic Party (HDP).

However, among the Kurds in Turkey, some want to create an independent entity in Turkey. This desire has created increasing friction between the Turkish government and the Kurds. The tensions rose at the beginning of the 1980s. The conflict evolved into a war between Turkey and the Kurdish Workers' Party (PKK). The PKK was established in 1978. The militant organization's goal is to gain greater cultural and political rights for Kurds. Its ultimate goal is to create an independent Kurdish state. From the 1980s until today, the PKK has waged a violent struggle against Turkey for a separate, independent Kurdish entity in Turkey.

During the war in Syria, the Kurds did create an autonomous, independent entity in northeastern Syria. The autonomy includes a military force—the People's Protection Units (YPG)—which includes a female military unit, the

Women's Protection Units (YPJ). That evolution alarms Turkey because they fear it will encourage independence sentiments among the 16 million Kurds who live in Turkey. Furthermore, Turkey argues that the primary Syrian Kurdish political entity in northern Syria—the Democratic Unionist Party (PYD, *Partiya Yekita Democrat*) and its military force, the YPG—are branches of the PKK.

Turkey is determined to eradicate the Kurdish autonomy in northeastern Syria or prevent it from becoming a semi-state entity. In 2014, an estimated 4 million Kurds were living in Syria—predominately in northeast Syria. In 2020, following a decade of war in Syria, it is estimated that there are now between 1

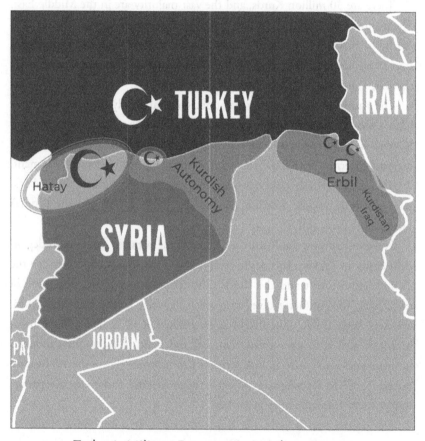

Turkey's Military Presence in Northern Iraq to
Pressure the PKK

and 2.5 million Kurds left in Syria. It is challenging to get accurate numbers. But what is clear is that the war in Syria has caused many Kurds to go elsewhere.

As we learned in Chapter 3, as an outcome of the war in Syria, Erdoğan commands a network of armed proxies and jihadist militias in north and northeastern Syria. Turkish-backed proxies are a tool Erdoğan uses to threaten and attack the Kurdish autonomous entity. There have been clashes between Turkish-backed proxies and the YPG more than once. And future skirmishes are likely.

As part of its plan, Turkey is also trying to create a new demographic reality in northern Syria. To this end, one of Erdoğan's strategies has been to resettle Syrian Arab refugees in northern Syria. The purpose of this policy is clear. It is to dilute the Kurdish majority in north Syria. And by doing that, destroy any chance the Kurds have of securing an independent entity.

As I said above, there are about 5.5 million Kurds in northern Iraq. Turkey is trying to eradicate PKK forces in the Qandil Mountains on the Iraq-Iran-Turkey border triangle. Turkish military forces are shelling and bombarding the PKK positions in northern Iraq. Moreover, Turkey has also occupied parts of northern Iraq (Kurdistan Iraq) to secure its strategic interests.

Turkish Protectorate and (non-contiguous) Presence Parallel to Iranian Corridor

A map published in July 2020 by the Turkish Presidential Directorate shows that Erdoğan has established thirty-seven Turkish military bases in northern Iraq, infiltrating as much as thirty-five miles into Iraqi territory.[8]

As should be expected, Baghdad demands Turkey end its military presence in Iraqi territory. As of the summer of 2021, Turkey shows no intention to comply with Iraq's demand.

In looking at the map of the Turkish Protectorate in Syria and the parts of Iraq Turkey has now occupied, Turkey has created its own semi-corridor that runs from the Iranian-Turkish-Iraqi border westward along the Turkish-Syria border to the Mediterranean Sea, parallel to the Iranian corridor. The Turkish semi-corridor is not a contiguous territory.

Through establishing a Turkish protectorate in northern Syria and placing the Turkish military in northeastern Iraq, Erdoğan is trying to achieve one of his most important objectives. Restraining the Kurdish semi-autonomy and thereby preventing it from evolving into a fully independent Kurdish autonomy. The emergence of a Kurdish independent entity, should it take place, presents a serious threat to Turkey. Because it could fuel and increase the independence sentiments and aspirations of the Kurds in Turkey.

How Did Turkey Gain Control of the Syrian-Turkish Border and Create the Protectorate?

Turkey has taken over and occupied northern Syria through a series of military operations that began in 2016. Operation "Defender of the Euphrates" (August 2016–March 2017); Operation "Olive Branch" (January–March 2018); Operation "Spring of Peace" (October 2019); and Operation "Spring Shield" (February 2020).

In addition to the Turkish army, as we discussed in Chapter 3, Turkey fortifies its control of this area by creating, nurturing, and controlling a network of military proxies in north Syria. Most of Turkey's proxies are controlled and commanded by the Turkish military.[9] Other proxies like Hayat Tahrir al-sham (HTS) operate independently, but Turkey partially or entirely funds their operations.

A significant step toward the Turkish protectorate and a turning point in Erdoğan's quest to gain legitimacy as a power in Syria was in September

Area of Idlib and Latakia, Syria

2018. Putin invited Erdoğan to a meeting in Sochi, Russia. Russia—which had already become a key power broker in the war in Syria—wanted Turkey's help in creating a demilitarized zone to stabilize the situation in northern Syria. The two agreed that Turkey would establish a six- to eight-square-mile demilitarized zone in Idlib.

The Idlib Province is in northwestern Syria, on the Turkish-Syrian border. The capitol of the province is the city of Idlib, which is about thirty-five miles south of the Turkish border. Idlib sits between two significant Syrian areas. East of Idlib is Aleppo, the largest city in northern Syria with an estimated 4.6 million people. Southwest of Idlib is the district of Latakia and the major cities along the Syrian coast, predominately populated by Alawites.

The district of Idlib became an enclave of the Syrian rebels and the focal stage for intense fighting between rebels and al-Assad forces in northern Syria. (As a side note, there are also enclaves of Syrian rebels in southern Syria.)

According to the agreement, Turkey would disarm all the rebel groups in the region and remove all heavy weapons, rocket launchers, rifles, and mortar shells from the area. Turkey would monitor the demilitarized zone with Turkish mobile patrol groups and Russian military police units.

However, the Sochi Agreement fell apart and was never implemented to any significant degree.

In early December 2019, al-Assad, Iran, and Russia became determined to crush the Syrian rebels' last stronghold concentrated in northwestern Syria. To that end, the axis launched a widespread military offensive against a rebel outpost in Idlib and the surrounding area—which included rebel strongholds in the Turkish protectorate in northern Syria.

The al-Assad-Iranian-Russian attacks at the end of 2019 killed many civilians and created another wave of Syrian refugees. As a result of the fighting in and around Idlib, an estimated one million Syrians headed toward the Turkish border.

On February 27, 2020, alarmed with the streaming of more Syrian refugees into Turkey—a country that already hosts some three million Syrian refugees—Turkey launched "Operation: Spring Shield."

In "Operation: Spring Shield," Erdoğan sent military forces to the Syrian-Turkish border to stop Syrian refugees from coming into Turkey. This Turkish offensive led to fighting between Turkish armed forces and their proxies against the al-Assad-Iran-Russia axis forces, including Hezbollah. Dozens of Turkish soldiers were killed in the fighting.

On March 3, 2020, Turkish Defense Minister Hulusi Akar said Turkey had "neutralized" (meaning killed) 2,212 members of the Syrian forces.[10]

The widening military confrontation between the sides led to a new Turkish-Russian cease-fire agreement signed on March 5, 2020. The deal forbids the deployment of Turkish, Syrian, or Syrian-affiliated military forces in the six- to eight-square-mile demilitarized zone in Idlib. It creates a safe zone for civilians on both sides of the major highway connecting the city of Idlib with the Syrian coastline.

The fragile cease-fire was maintained for about a year.

But in the summer of 2021, Russia renewed its aerial attacks on the Turkish-backed rebel groups in Idlib. A wide-scale collision is once again around the corner.

Iran and the Turkish Protectorate in Northern Syria

Iran—the other power in the al-Assad-Russia-Iranian triangle—expresses a dichotomous position concerning the Turkish invasion of northern Syria. On the one hand, official Iranian spokesmen said they "understand Turkey's security concerns."[11] But in the same breath, they call on Turkey to immediately withdraw from Syria.

For Iran, the situation in northern Syria is complicated.

Turkey supports Iran in the face of US sanctions and supports the regime diplomatically in the international arena. Therefore, Iran does not want to attack Turkey directly and overtly.

On the other hand, as we discussed earlier in the chapter, Iran expects to be paid back for its investment in Syria. And one of the ways it wants to be paid back is by getting its hands on the revenue from the oil fields in northern Syria. If Turkey rules north Syria, Iran won't be able to control those assets.

Furthermore, Turkish control in north Syria will be secured primarily by Sunni-Syrian military forces. Such forces—under a Turkish military umbrella—could turn against the Iranian-backed Shi'ite militias in Syria.

And far away from the Syrian arena, Iran must consider a domestic consideration regarding how Tehran reacts to the Turkish assault on the Kurds in northern Syria. Iran has a complicated but generally good relationship with the Kurds in Iraq and Syria. On the other hand, the Kurdish underground in Iran attacks Iranian targets in northwestern Iran. A growing Kurdish death toll in northern Syria as a result of the Turkish invasion could trigger a chain of Kurdish protests that could, among other things, lead to intensifying attacks by the Kurdish underground in Iran.

The Arab World and the War in Syria

In September 2011, the Arab League froze Syria's membership in the organization. In early 2012, the Gulf States recalled their ambassadors from Syria. These were among the starkest expressions of the Arab world's anger with the al-Assad regime for its brutality against the Syrian people.

The Arab world and the international community have demanded that the al-Assad regime implement the 2015 UNSC Resolution 2254 and the

Geneva One Accord. These agreements outline three conditions for a political settlement in Syria:

1. The return of Syrian refugees to their homes while ensuring their security and civil rights.
2. Hold free elections that will give authentic expression to the wishes of the Syrian people.
3. All foreign forces leave Syria.

The Arab public opinion is—for now—unready and unwilling to forgive al-Assad for the devastation he has inflicted on Syria. But this is not a reason to shut the door permanently in his face. After all, history teaches us that violent, tyrannical, brutal leaders like Saddam Hussein in Iraq, Moammar Ghaddafi in Libya, and Ali Abdullah Saleh in Yemen—though condemned in the Arab world for slaughtering their people—were legitimized in official Arab political forums for decades before they were finally ousted.

Since the end of 2018, there have been some cracks in the Arab world regarding their relationship with Bashar al-Assad.

In late 2018, Bahrain announced it was re-opening its embassy in Damascus. The same month, the head of Egypt's intelligence services met with the chief of the Syrian intelligence services in Cairo.

Throughout 2019, voices across the Arab world began advocating—openly or implicitly—for the Arab world to "forgive" the al-Assad regime. Some justify it by saying that it is the duty of the Arabs to provide their Syrian Arab brothers with humanitarian aid. Others argue that it is the only way to end the Iranian occupation of Syria.[12]

Jordan has gradually resumed its trade and commercial relations with Syria, including holding an official meeting in Damascus between the Syrian and Jordanian ministers of commerce in March 2020. In the same month, the crown prince of Abu Dhabi, Mohammed Bin Zayed, called President al-Assad to express solidarity with the Syrians facing the coronavirus's challenge. In October 2020, Oman reinstated its ambassador to Syria.[13]

In March 2021, Egypt called for Syria's return to the Arab League. However, Egypt's Foreign Minister Sameh Shoukry stressed the need for "Syria to pragmatically demonstrate a will to move towards a political solution based on the UN Security Council resolutions." He added, "Accommodating the [Syrian] national opposition would reduce the intensity of the conflict and pave the way for Syria to emerge from the furnace of this ongoing war to safety."[14] As of August 2021, Syria has not been readmitted into the Arab League. In fact, the motion has not even been formally submitted to the League for deliberation.

According to reports evaluated to be reliable, in early May 2021, a delegation of high-level Saudi security officials met with the head of the Syrian intelligence services (and perhaps al-Assad) in Damascus. Reportedly, one of the meeting goals was to prepare the groundwork for a gradual resumption of relations between Saudi Arabia and Syria.[15]

On May 26, 2021, Syria held "general elections." Not surprisingly, al-Assad "won" a majority of the votes. As expected, the international community and vast circles in the Arab world rightly dismiss the "elections" as a farce.

However, following the elections on May 30, 2021, UAE political analyst Dr. Salem al-Ketbi wrote an article called "Syrian Elections and Exiting the Tunnel." He said, "For pragmatic reasons, the endurance of al-Assad's rule is necessary for the recovery of Syria." Some Arab commentators express a similar view.[16] This may indicate some more small baby steps of Arab rapprochement toward al-Assad that have taken place for some time.

As of 2021, Arab public opinion is overwhelmingly not ready or willing to forgive al-Assad. Arab leaders are aware of that. In June 2021, Saudi and Qatari senior officials made it clear that talks about the Saudis or Qatar rehabilitating the al-Assad regime were baseless. They emphasized that the al-Assad government must meet some critical conditions before talking about rehabilitation.[17]

Will the Arab world accept al-Assad back into the family? The bottom line is—yes. It will, however, be a gradual process in which leaders and opinion influencers will likely emphasize the need to help the Syrian people. Therefore, I estimate we will witness more Arab gestures toward al-Assad.

However, even though the door has been slightly opened for his possible return to the Arab world, as of the summer of 2021, I think it is premature to talk about the complete restoration of the al-Assad regime into the Arab world. The next episode demonstrates that very well.

In late August 2021, Iraq hosted a regional summit, including its neighbors and international delegations. Before the conference, there were rumors that Syria was going to be invited as well. It did not happen. Iraqi Foreign Minister Fouad Hussein explained that Syria was not invited because "It is a matter that has regional and global moral aspects. And our Syrian brothers understand that we could not invite them because we want to stay away from controversies."[18]

There is a crucial aspect of Syria and its relationship with the Arab world. It is difficult to see how the Arab world will rehabilitate—let alone support—al-Assad and help him rebuild his power and country while Iran is occupying Syria. In that context, it is important to note two things.

First, in October 2019, the Arab League strongly condemned the Turkish presence in Syria. They described it as a "rude violation of UN decisions and particularly UNSC decision 2254, which emphasizes the need to secure the integrity and independence of Syria … Turkey's invasion of Syria is also a threat to Arabs security as well as to the region and the world."[19] If the Arab world, which is predominately Sunni, condemns Turkey, which is also predominately Sunni, for invading Syria, how could the Arab world accept Shi'ite Iran occupying Syria?

Second, the threat Iran poses is one reason for the formation of the alliance of moderation, which includes leading Arab states like Egypt, Jordan, Oman, Saudi Arabia, the UAE, and Israel. That alliance wants all pro-Iranian militias to leave Syria. (We will explore the Alliance of Moderation in Chapter 8.) But Iran has other plans.

Iran Seeks to Tighten Its Grip in Syria

Both the international community and the Arab world demand Iran get out of Syria. Is that going to happen?

Iran has a dual strategy to ensure its control over Syria and secure the most critical element of the Iranian corridor.

One is to continue to militarize and increase its military hold over Syria. As we know, Iran has been involved in the war in Syria from the beginning. But as we can also see from Iran's modus operandi, they rarely put Iranian lives at risk. Iran's strategy is to use—and sacrifice—proxy militias, such as Lebanese

Hezbollah, Iraqi Shi'ite militias, Afghani (Liwa Fatemiyoun), and Pakistani (Liwa Zainebiyoun) militias on the altar of Iran's hegemonic ambitions. In contrast, the mullah regime sits safely in Tehran. The war in Syria has been a quintessential example of this strategy.

As far as actual Iranian 'boots on the ground,' Tehran has stationed an estimated several hundred Iranian officers and military instructors from the Islamic Revolutionary Guards in Syria.

The mullah regime has no intention of leaving Syria. And therefore, it needs to be assured it has an unending supply of militants—armies of terror— to ensure its control. To that end, accumulating information indicates that, in addition to foreign militias Iran has placed in Syria, Tehran continues to create local proxy militias for the Syrian theater. Their recruitment efforts primarily focus on recruiting militants from Arab tribes in eastern Syria.[20] The Syrian Observatory for Human Rights (SOHR) estimated that, in March 2021, Iran had 25,000 militants in Syria. According to the report, that number includes foreign proxies and locally recruited militants.[21]

To ensure its military occupation of Syria and to work toward its total appropriation of Syria, Iran is also taking an additional route to ensure that Tehran's investment secures Syria as an Iranian stronghold.

Before the war in Syria, Sunnis made up three-quarters of the population. A distant branch of the Shi'ites, Alawites are about 10 percent (about two million people) out of twenty-two million Syrians.

To keep and strengthen its hold on Syria, Iran is trying to "*Iranize*" and "*Shi'atize*" Syria. According to the SOHR, "Iran continues its efforts to strengthen its presence in Syria through attracting the Syrian men, women, youth, and children, by instilling its ideology in the Syrian society."[22]

Tehran has established institutions and organizations like the Iranian Cultural Center, the People's Committee for Syrian-Iranian Friendship, and the Office of the Iranian Cultural Adviser in Damascus.

The Iranian government is increasingly creating Iranian cultural institutes that conduct plays and cultural events. It is building schools and promoting formal and informal educational opportunities to learn Persian and spread Shi'ism. To attract people to these institutions, Iran is positioning itself as the benevolent benefactor—handing out cash to needy Syrians, food baskets, and free health care. Tehran builds parks where Shi'ite militants organize games focused on Shi'ite legends and showing how Iran fights Israel and the West. The Iranian government renovates Shi'ite shrines and offers trips to tourist spots to encourage conversion.

Tehran uses Shi'ite sectarianism to strengthen and unify the Shi'ite community and foster Shi'ite allegiance to the mullah regime. But Tehran's goal is to appeal to the Shi'ites in Syria as well as the Sunnis. When it comes to the Sunnis, at a minimum, Iran wants to soften the antagonism toward the Persian Shi'ite regime.

A lot of Tehran's efforts focus on the youth. The mullah regime provides scholarships, stipends, and very generous rewards to people—especially young people and children—who come to study at religious seminaries, schools in Syria, or universities in Iran.

And then there are the youth movements. There are at least two Iranian-backed Shi'ite scout movements in Syria. "*Al-Wilayah* (the one that subscribes to the order of Iran's Supreme Leader) *Scouts*" movement and the "*Imam al-Mahdi Scouts*" movement. The Imam Mahdi Scout movement was established with Iranian assistance in Lebanon in 1985. It is Hezbollah's youth movement. The initiative, now being replicated in Iraq and Syria, is intended to create a new generation of operatives inculcated with Khomeini's ideology, to join Hezbollah's civilian and military ranks, participate in the violent struggle against Israel, and help build the Shi'ite community. Like in Lebanon and Iraq, the Imam Mahdi Scouts in Syria undergo physical training, weapons training, and ideological indoctrination. Shi'ite religious leaders teach them the principles of Shi'ism. The scouts march in military parades waving Iranian flags and carrying images of Khomeini and Khamenei and other Iranian and Shi'ite symbols.[23] This strategy is not only creating more Shi'ites and Iranian loyalists, but it is also ensuring a steady supply of militants for the Iranian-backed militias.[24]

And if you join a militia and convert to Shi'ism, not only is your family going to be protected and safe. But you also get perks and a lot of money in your pocket to afford whatever you need.[25]

For disenfranchised Syrians who are suffering and ignored by their own government, these are very effective and powerful tools to foster supporters and create loyalty to the Persian Shi'ite mullah regime.

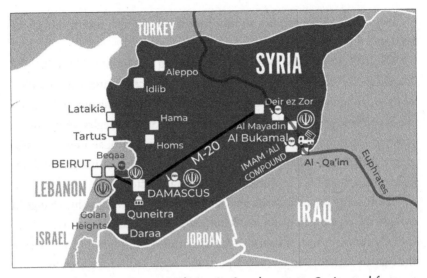

IRG and Iranian Proxy Militias in Southeastern Syria and from Damascus to Beqaa in Lebanon

And Iran is not only trying to cultivate Shi'ites and woo Sunnis. Tehran is attempting to change and rearrange the population. In cooperation with al-Assad, the Shi'ite regime is actively working to re-engineer Syria's cultural and religious fabric.

It is reported that Iran is offering Syrian citizenship to Shi'ites from outside of Syria. Iran is encouraging Iraqi Shi'ite families, the families of IRG fighters, and the families of the various Shi'ite militias to move to Syria. Tehran is resettling Iranian-backed militias and their families from Iraq and Lebanon to live in Syria. They live in either homes that Syrians abandoned during the war or were confiscated by the militias. Iran finances the purchases and renovations.[26]

In a strategic move, Iran uses its militias to create a Shi'ite populated corridor in two areas in Syria.

One is an eighty-five-mile- long corridor (a two-and-a-half-hour drive) running northwest from the Al-Qa'im/Al Bukamal Iraq-Syria border crossing, through the Imam 'Ali Compound, along the Euphrates River, through the city of Al Mayadin, to Deir ez-Zor. The Euphrates flows from Syria, through the Syria-Iraq border, crossing through Iraq to the Gulf.

Iran's Iraqi Shi'ite militias already partially secure the eastern side of the border.

The IRG controls the road from the Iran-Iraq border to Al Mayadin—the Iranian forces' center in eastern Syria. Iran has placed a large concentration of its proxy militias, including the Afghan Shi'ite al-Fatemiyoun militias, on the Syrian side of the border. This area of eastern Syria struggles from extreme poverty. The militias here are engaged in welfare, outreach, and religious programs. Already controlling Al Maydin, this combination of military and soft power has turned Deir ez-Zor into an Iranian protectorate.[27]

The strategy is part of Iran's plans to implement a demographic change in Syria so the regime can play a much more significant role and increase its hold over the country. And, of course, it is also a critical part of their plan to secure the Iranian corridor. Arab media reports that some locals have been forced to flee due to their properties changing hands.[28]

Solidifying Iran's hold on Deir ez-Zor gives Tehran a direct route to the main highway, the M20, which leads to Damascus.

And that brings us to the second area Iran is trying to "Shi'atize." And that is the area that connects Damascus with the Beqaa region of Lebanon. Iran is settling Lebanese and Syrian Shi'ites in this area.[29] Hezbollah controls the Beqaa region of Lebanon.

For Iran, having complete control of the Iraq-Syria crossing, north through Deir ez-Zor, to Damascus, to Lebanon, not only goes a long way to securing the Iranian corridor. It also ensures that Iran has a direct supply overland line to its most vital proxy Hezbollah. And that Hezbollah has a direct undisturbed link to Tehran.

In addition to attempting to change the demographics from the Iraqi-Syrian border through Damascus to Lebanon (an area controlled by Iranian militias) and in addition to taking over property that is either abandoned or inhabited, it now seems that Iranian businessmen who are either part of or associated with the Iranian Islamic Revolutionary Guards are purchasing real estate in Syria's capitol, Damascus.[30]

Tehran provides convenient loans to individuals who want to buy real estate in Syria. Therefore, in recent years Iranian contractors, businessmen, and militia members have become real estate moguls in strategic locations in the Syrian capitol. Iran is also building a twelve-story trade center in

Damascus, which is supposed to host twenty-four Iranian companies.[31] And the *"Shi'azation"* of Damascus is not limited to the commercial sector. Iran is creating Shi'ite neighborhoods in Damascus. In southern Beirut, there is a neighborhood called Al-Dahiye—it is Hezbollah's stronghold in Lebanon's capitol. Iran seems to be trying to replicate the model by creating Shi'ite areas populated by the IRG in Damascus.

And in an attempt to rewrite history and highlight the (almost non-existent) Shi'ite history in Syria, Iran is renaming streets in these neighborhoods and near a Shi'ite religious compound, known as the Sayyidah Zaynab Mosque in southern Damascus. According to Shi'ite tradition, this is the location of the grave of Zaynab, one of the daughters of 'Ali Bin Abi Talib and Fatimah, the daughter of the Prophet Muhammad.[32] And to increase the effect, there are pictures of Iranian-backed militants killed in the war in Syria and Shi'ite slogans surrounding the shrine.[33] The Iranian-backed al-Wilayah Scouts are primarily responsible for guarding Zaynab's Tomb.

In addition to all of the above, Iranian businessmen and institutions, including banks affiliated with the IRG and IRG enterprises and corporations, have won tenders in key and strategic Syrian sectors. Iran currently controls Syrian agriculture, its phosphate mines, its harbors, and more. In August 2021, Iran's formal news agency *Fars* reported that Iranian experts have started building a power plant in Latakia province in Western Syria.[34]

And finally—to be sure to flood Syria with Iranian goods and increase the revenue to Iran's coffers—Iran is exempt from customs tax when it exports goods to Syria. This move significantly increased Iranian exports to Syria.[35]

Navvar Saban, a conflict expert at the Omran Center for Strategic Studies who specializes in Syria-Iran relations, said Iran had slowly but steadily cultivated ties with Syrians of all backgrounds. They weaved a spider's web in Syria and have their people everywhere, in the army, in the government, even among Sunni and Christian businessmen.[36]

Iran Does Face Obstacles in Syria

However, Iran's deepening presence in Syria does face obstacles. We have discussed some of them, including the Arab and international community's demand that Iran withdraws its proxies, forces, and militias from Syria;

Russia's military presence and ambitions in Syria; and the constant Israeli military activity against the Iranian military infrastructure in Syria.

To these obstacles, we should remember that, for the Syrian people, Iran is an occupying power. There are currently about seventeen million people living in Syria, the vast majority of whom are Sunni Arabs. The Syrian people are broken and crushed in the wake of the war. But the fire of rebellion and resistance continues to burn beneath the surface, and it emerges again and again.

In July 2021, heavy fighting broke out again between Syrian rebels and the Assad regime forces in the Dara'a region in southwestern Syria. And in the wake of the Iranian occupation of Syria, Shi'ite settlers, cultural and religious structures, and economic and commercial assets are becoming the targets of attacks.

There is another interesting and lesser-known obstacle to the Iranian establishment project in Syria. The backbone of the Syrian regime is the Alawite minority, also known as *Nusayris*. As we have said before, the Alawites are a branch (albeit distant) of the Shi'ites. However, as we also mentioned, the Alawites are different from the ultra-conservative Iranian mullah regime. Furthermore, the Syrian government is officially part of the *Ba'ath* "Renaissance" pan-Arab socialist ideology. Pan-Arab Ba'athism is the polar opposite of a Persian Shi'ite Islamic theocracy.

Bashar al-Assad is aligned with the mullah regime so he—and the Alawites—can survive and stay in power. However, they are not ideological or religious kindred spirits.

Why does that matter?

Because the relationship between al-Assad and the Iranian regime in 2021 is different than it was between 2011 and 2020.

Without Iran—and more significantly without Russia's airpower—al-Assad would have lost the war, and the regime and the Alawites would have been crushed. Iran's military presence in Syria has helped al-Assad and kept him in power.

As of 2021, the al-Assad regime has crushed the revolt. Though pockets of resistance to his rule remain, it is unlikely that the rebellion will reignite with the same intensity as it was at the peak of the war. So, at this point, for al-Assad, the Iranian military presence in Syria is primarily a bargaining chip.

Al-Assad could theoretically give away that chip in return for the Arab world rebuilding Syria and taking him back into the fold.

Kuwaiti-born Hasan Ismaik, the chairman of the Board of the Strategiecs Think Tank and business entrepreneur, wrote in his December 2020 article "'The West and the Syrian-Iranian Alliance: A Card that Should be Played," the following:

> Today, Syria is experiencing a serious impasse. The country is living in a state of 'no war, no peace' ... Contrary to what many believe, the Syrian-Iranian alliance is not unbreakable. It has no solid foundations and only came about due to a *fait accompli* created by the dynamics of events in the Middle East. Syria has always portrayed itself as an Arab-nationalist state, while Iranian politicians spare no opportunities to indicate that Iran is a Persian state ... In this context, the prevailing misconception that Iran is welcome in Syria needs to be corrected. In fact, Syrians are not satisfied that their country is described as "the 35th province of Iran ... The "Syrian-Iranian alliance" [is] a burden on Damascus, which is aware of the risks and dangers of its relationship with Iran at political, military, and cultural levels. This makes reaching a deal possible and even something to be expected.[37]

In July 2021, a senior Israeli security source observed that al-Assad was redeploying the Syrian army and limiting Iran's activities in Syria to prevent friction between the Iranians, their militias, Shi'ite settlers, and the Syrian population.[38]

The Iranian regime has repeatedly stressed that its military presence in Syria is at the request of the al-Assad regime with the aim of "fighting terrorism." The same way he invited Iran into Syria, al-Assad can ask the Iranians to end their military presence in Syria.

Yet, some Arab analysts are skeptical that that is a realistic scenario. In a June 2021 article called "Cherry on the Iranian Cake," Lebanese commentator Sam Mansi writes, "Assad became an Iranian lackey after he enabled them to infiltrate deep into the Syrian regime militarily and economically ... Whoever thinks that Syria will deport Iran in return for the rehabilitation of Assad's rule is naïve."[39]

In his July 2021 article "Which Syria Should Be Saved?" Lebanese commentator Khairallah Khairallah writes, "Iran did not enter Syria, nor did it invest billions of dollars in it, and it did not make a demographic change just to leave the next day."[40]

However, should al-Assad ask Iran to leave, this could have significant consequences.

First, it would be the first step in the reconstruction of Syria.

Second, it would loosen Iran's suffocating grip on two Arab states that border Syria, Iraq to the east and Lebanon to the west. Both of which are critical links in the crescent and the corridor, both of whom are fighting to break free from Iran's shackles.

Third, it could trigger a process of negotiations between the al-Assad regime and Israel regarding the Golan Heights. Syria demands Israel withdraw entirely from the Golan Heights that Israel captured in the 1967 War. Israel annexed the Golan in 1981. In March 2019, President Trump officially recognized Israel's sovereignty in the Golan Heights. As of the summer of 2021, the Biden administration has not revoked Trump's decision. The Golan Heights is a consensus issue in Israel. Israelis believe Israel controlling the Golan Heights is critical to Israel's security. Therefore, do not expect any Israeli concession regarding Israel's sovereignty in the Golan Heights.

Given that reality, what would Damascus and Jerusalem have to negotiate?

Well, there is another dramatic development in the region that happened in 2020 and might provide an answer. The 2020 Abraham Accords. The peace treaty between Israel and the UAE, the beginning of peace talks between Israel and Bahrain, and the normalization agreements between Israel and Sudan and Israel and Morocco.

Iran and Turkey and their allies and proxies, and some circles in the Arab world, including Algeria, the Palestinians, and Tunisia, have criticized Bahrain, Morocco, Sudan, and the United Arab Emirates for signing the agreements with Israel. In response, the accused said that each country's foreign policy— including signing a peace treaty with Israel—is a solely sovereign decision. It is not a pan-Arab or pan-Islamic affair. The days when Arab countries' decision-making—especially regarding Israel—is subject to pan-Arab or pan-Islamic consensus are gone.

This argument could offer the al-Assad regime some flexibility regarding future talks with Israel about the Golan Heights. Al-Assad could justify accepting the continuation of Israeli sovereignty over the Golan Heights by saying that Syria has the right to make an independent decision in that matter. The UAE and other Arab countries decided unilaterally to sign peace normalization agreements with Israel. Accordingly, al-Assad could argue that the Golan Heights is also not subject to pan-Arab consensus and that it is legitimate for Syria to make an independent decision.

In my analysis, as of 2021, an Israeli-Syrian formal arrangement on the Golan Heights is impossible. However, the combination of al-Assad's desire to stay in power; the conditions set by the international community and the Arab world to end the war in Syria; the evolving Iranian-Russia power struggle in Syria; and the Abraham Accords could create the circumstances and set the groundwork for an interesting informal Syrian-Israeli arrangement.

The deal could look like this. Al-Assad asks Iran to withdraw all Iranian military presence—including proxy militias—from Syria. Al-Assad silently agrees to accept permanent de-facto Israeli rule on the Golan Heights—a situation that in any event is the reality on the ground since 1967. And in return—or in advance—the Arab world will open the door to al-Assad and accept him back into the family. This arrangement would be a win-win for al-Assad, Israel, Russia, and the United States. Some Arab commentators think that scenario is a real possibility.[41]

Syrian commentator Ghazi Duhman writes in his January 2021 article, "Normalization is Assad's Bridge to Stay in Power": "Assad does not even need to have a peace agreement with Israel ... All he needs to do is adopt the Sudan-Israel normalization model and drive Iran out of Syria. If he does that, Assad will regain legitimacy in the Arab world in a heartbeat.[42]

Palestinian commentator Adly Sadiq writes in his May 2021 article, "Indications of the Israeli Bombing of Targets in Western Syria": "One should expect a surprise regarding the Syrian-Israeli relations. In return for making some symbolic cosmetics reforms, and by adopting normalization with Israel through minimizing the controversial issues with Israel, Assad will restore his legitimacy in the Arab world."[43]

In that context, in early 2021, Arab media platforms affiliated with Turkey that oppose al-Assad's rule reported that meetings brokered by Russia took place between former Israeli senior security figures and senior Syrian intelligence and military officers. Reportedly, the purpose of the meetings was to explore a peace agreement between Israel and Syria. The reports outlined that the talks centered on the following guidelines: Al-Assad will tell the Iranians to leave Syria. And in return, Israel will leverage its influence in the United States and its connections with the Arab world to pave the way for al-Assad's return and rehabilitate al-Assad's image. Following that phase, the Golan Heights will be "internationalized," and Russia will guarantee Israel's security needs.[44] The fact that the sources for the reports are affiliated with Turkey and are clearly hostile to al-Assad does not necessarily mean the information about the meetings is false.

Exiled Syrian poet and commentator Ibrahim Al-Jabeen hints at that scenario. In his July 2021 article "Damascus and the Upcoming Deal of the Century," he writes, "The Arab world no longer buys the slogan of resistance; the Palestinian cause has plummeted on the Arab world's political agenda following the Oslo agreement [a series of accords signed between Israel and the Palestinians in the 1990s]... Therefore, the center of the next deal of the century is in Damascus, not Jerusalem."[45]

Al-Assad has another incentive to consider ending the Iranian military presence in Syria. And that is the growing US sanctions on al-Assad and his inner circle.

The US Caesar Syria Civilian Protection Act

On June 17, 2020, the United States activated the 2019 Caesar Syria Civilian Protection Act.[46] "Caesar" is the nickname of the Syrian photographer who shared thousands of photographs documenting torture in al-Assad's prisons with the world.

The Caesar Act sanctions thirty-nine individuals associated with the al-Assad regime—including al-Assad and his wife Asma—and companies and entities cooperating with the Syrian regime. The next day Syrian currency—the Syrian Pound (SYP) (in Arabic, the Lira)—collapsed. The exchange rate skyrocketed. 3,000 Syrian Lira equaled $1. To compare, in 2011, fifty Lira equaled $1. In August 2021, 1,257 Syrian Lira equal $1.

Syria is already destroyed, and its economy is shattered. And al-Assad's allies Russia and Iran cannot rescue the collapsing Syrian economy. One of the conditions for lifting the sanctions is that all foreign forces leave Syria.

China and Syria

Al-Assad understands that Iran and Russia cannot rebuild Syria's economy and physical infrastructure destroyed in the war. Therefore, he is very keen to enlist China's help. But the Chinese are in no hurry and are unlikely to rush in to invest in Syria.

The Chinese have provided some funding to the Syrian regime. But the scope of China's investment is negligible, amounting to a few tens of millions of dollars, primarily for humanitarian and medical purposes.

In July 2021, the Chinese foreign minister did visit Syria as part of a tour of the Middle East and suggested that Syria join the Chinese Belt and Road Initiative (BRI), a global infrastructure connecting China with different areas of the globe. On the surface, the Chinese offer sounded tempting. China talked about building roads, hotels, communication systems, etc.

But it is highly unlikely any of this will come to fruition.

First, in China's view, Syria has no unique advantage to justify Chinese investment. Syria leased the Mediterranean port of Tartus to Russia for forty-nine years. Iran and Russia are both entrenching themselves in the Latakia port. And China already has contracts with Egypt, Israel, Greece, and Turkey to operate ports on the Mediterranean Sea.

Second, China has overland routes to Europe via Iran or Turkey that are shorter and safer than the Syrian overland route.

Third, considering the complex geopolitical reality in Syria, a significant investment in Syria is too risky. Investing in railways, roads, or energy infrastructure in such a hostile and unstable environment that al-Assad, Iran, Russia, Turkey, and their militias are all fighting over, which are also frequently attacked by Israel and the United States, does not seem to be currently a sound investment.

Fourth, the Gulf States are of great strategic and economic importance to China. The financial and investment card is the most significant pressure card the Arab world has to incentivize al-Assad to show Iran the door. Chinese investment in Syria would undermine that leverage.

Finally, for Chinese companies, investing in Syria risks US sanctions.

For all these calculations, Syria is simply not worth the risk. Therefore, in the foreseeable future, I do not expect significant Chinese economic involvement in Syria.[47]

Syria: The Summer of 2021

In my 2016 book, I end the chapter about the war in Syria with a quote from a Shi'ite journalist, 'Ali al-Amin: "The Syrian revolution is an orphan. Yet, its will is invincible ... and the Syrian revolution will win ... Assad cut off their fingers. Yet, the blood from their cut fingers will give birth to a new Syria. A free Syria."[48]

A March 2020 report by the Syrian Network for Human Rights (SNHR) found that the number of conflict-related deaths had reached 690,000, including 570,000 directly killed due to the war. Thirteen million had been displaced and were refugees from their homes.[49]

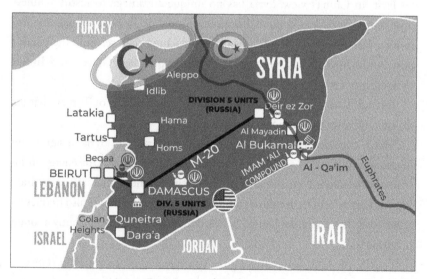

Iran, Russia, and Turkey in Syria

The report provides the following figures regarding the death toll in Syria. More than 226,247 civilians, including 29,257 children and 16,021 women (adult female), have been killed since March 2011. Syrian-Russian alliance forces killed 91.36 percent. A disproportionately high percentage of those killed, 18 percent, were women and children. That statistic is another indicator that the Syrian-Russian alliance forces deliberately target civilians. The report further notes that as of March 2020, at least 129,989 individuals were still being detained or have forcibly disappeared in the Syrian regime's official and unofficial detention centers.[50]

According to a May 2020 SNHR report, the total economic losses in Syria since the war began amounted to $530 billion. In addition, 40 percent of the infrastructure has been damaged.

According to an April 2019 report by the UN Secretary-General's Office on Humanitarian Affairs, Syrian refugees outside Syria were estimated to be six million.[51] A 2021 United Nations Children's Emergency Fund (UNICEF) report highlights that "The Syrian refugee crisis remains the largest displacement crisis globally, with almost 25 million people in need, of which thirty-two percent are children."[52]

A May 2020 report by the Syrian Center for Policy Research (SCPR) says, "The average number of years of schooling has dropped significantly since the start of the conflict. The estimated lost years of primary schooling in 2019 was 1.47 million years. The overall loss in basic education during 2011–2019 reached 25.5 million schooling years compared to the counterfactual scenario (had the conflict not occurred). The overall loss in the years of schooling for all educational levels reached about 46 million years between 2011 and 2019, and the estimated cost of this loss is estimated at USD 34.6 billion. The Syrian population continues to lose millions of years of schooling. In 2019 2.4 million children (5-17) were not in school—24 million years of teaching Syrians have been lost, and this complicates the chances of advancement in the future."[53]

A detailed 2020 study by the independent Turkey-based Jusoor For Studies institute reports that 60 percent of the workforce is unemployed. And it emphasized that prices have risen at least ten times since the beginning of the war. In 2020, the average salary was 60,000 SYP (barely more than

$25) a month, while a family's needs were estimated to be at least ten times that number. An average salary is only enough to sustain a family for three days—a week if two breadwinners are in the same family. More than 90 percent of Syrians are in deep poverty, living on less than $1.9 a day. The report expects the situation to continue along the same lines and further deteriorate in 2021.[54]

As of 2021, the al-Assad regime has almost completely crushed the insurgency, excluding pockets of occasional unrest and skirmishes in the district of Dara'a in southern Syria and the Idlib Province area in northern Syria. These two pockets are the last major strongholds of the Syrian rebels and the non-Syrian Sunni militias.

As of 2021, Bashar al-Assad is still the president. But his homeland, Syria, is destroyed.

As of 2021, the Syrian people find themselves in a destroyed country while Iran, Russia, and Turkey compete to divide the spoils.

As of 2021, journalist al-Amin's hope for a new and free Syria remains a sad wish. The Syrian people that stood up to fight for freedom and independence were brutally crushed. He was clearly right about one thing: the Syrian revolution was an orphan. The aforementioned May 2020 SPCR report said, "The global governance system failed to protect civilians in Syria and to activate humanitarian international law and/or effectively enhance the prospect of a just and sustainable settlement."[55]

The Syrian people's 2011 uprising began as a call for political reforms. They wanted their government to address their grievances. It turned into a war to rid themselves of a brutal dictator. The regime brutally crushed all the Syrian people's efforts. The ensuing civil war evolved into an all-out Sunni-Shi'ite Arab-Iranian-Turkish-Russian war that has ripped the country apart. And each power wants the pieces to further their own agenda.

What Is Next for Syria?

From the outset, I have argued that the war in Syria is not a civil war. It's an epic fateful regional power struggle. The reality today that I have just described validates my analysis.

Syria has become a regional and global wrestling ring, involving regional players like Iran, Israel, Saudi Arabia, and Turkey, and international players like China, Russia, and the United States. In 2021, Syria is hostage to this multi-player struggle. In the middle of 2021, ten years after the beginning of the war in Syria, Syria and the new nation-state model exist in two separate worlds. It is a morbid statement to talk about governmental accountability in a country whose government murdered hundreds of thousands of citizens and destroyed cities and towns just to stay in power. It is a macabre statement to discuss civic responsibility and national solidarity in a country where an ocean of blood and hatred separates ethnic groups. As of 2021, the Syrian people's dreams of freedom and hope are shattered. Crushed and devastated, the majority of Syrians are just struggling to survive the day.

It is critical to remember that there are seventeen million Syrians in Syria—in addition to the six million who have fled. And most of them hate the al-Assad regime and the Iranians who have conquered and destroyed their homeland. Al-Assad, the Russians, and the Iranians destroyed Syria's cities and villages but failed to completely suppress the fire of resistance and revolt, which occasionally bursts to the surface. History teaches us that occupation and oppression result in intensifying counter-reactions. Thus, in 2021, we are looking at a chapter—not the end of the story—in the Syrian people's struggle for independence.

Western leaders failed to help the Syrian people. Abandoned and ignored, the Syrians were left to their own fate. This is something the Syrian people will not forget. There is a "lost generation" of Syrians in Syria and around the world who are angry. Their anger, disappointment, and frustration make them easy prey for radical movements and preachers.

What happens in the Middle East does not stay in the Middle East. The repercussions of the war in Syria will echo around the world for a very long time.

Lebanon and Iraq: The Fight for Independence

During the fall of 2019 and into 2020 and 2021, ongoing public unrest evolved into mass protests in Lebanon and Iraq. The fact that the protests broke out in these countries individually and almost simultaneously is not accidental. The public revolts in Lebanon and Iraq have three main common denominators:

1. Outrage against deeply embedded and systemic political corruption.
2. Despair in the face of deepening economic and social hardships.
3. Rejection of the Iranian mullah regime that aggressively dictates the lives of the Lebanese and Iraqi people through networks of militias and corrupt politicians.

These factors combined both create and define their struggle for independence.

But will they gain their independence? Are they on the path toward a new statehood model? Let's explore the current situation in Lebanon and Iraq to find out.

Lebanon: The Bleak Fate of the Paris of the Middle East

2019–2021 Protests in Lebanon—Corruption Out! Iran Out! We are Lebanese!

In October 2019, protests began in Lebanon. In its early stage, the demonstrations were calm. There was no violence—it was almost one big Lebanese love festival. The atmosphere was optimistic and colorful. But the demands were clear. Twenty-four-seven, around the clock, hundreds of thousands of people protested the corruption, the country's increasingly imploding economy, and the lack of essential services like education, employment, infrastructure, security, etc. They demanded profound and substantial changes and governmental accountability. They made it clear they would not settle for cosmetic repairs and political games that made no real, significant, and sustainable changes.

One of the unique characteristics of the protests, and one that is very important when it comes to the struggle over the path, identity, and direction in Lebanon, is the fact that the protests included all Lebanese—Christians, Druze, Shi'ites, Sunnis, etc. Across the board, the Lebanese people demanded redesigning the current political system and replacing it with one that does not favor one ethnic group over another.

This display of Lebanese nationalism did not make Hezbollah and the Iranian-affiliated 'Amal Lebanese Shi'ite party happy. For decades, Hezbollah and its ally, the 'Amal party, have manipulated the Lebanese system to increase their power and Iran's hold over Lebanon.

As we have discussed before, when it comes to Lebanon, it is crucial to remember that as of 2021, Lebanon, to no small extent, is a shell. A facade. When we look at Lebanon, we see a flag, a government, a parliament, ministers, officials, etc. But let there be no mistake. The real boss in Lebanon is Iran and its proxy Hezbollah.

In the 1980s, Iran created Hezbollah. Hezbollah is now Iran's most powerful and important proxy. Iran massively arms Hezbollah. And Hezbollah uses its Iranian-provided military might to threaten and terrorize the Lebanese people so Hezbollah can impose Iran's interests and will upon Lebanon.

Iran used Hezbollah to kidnap Lebanon from within, so Lebanon could serve Iran's interests. Not the Lebanese interests. Hezbollah, a party in the Lebanese government since 2005, has turned Lebanon into an Iranian satellite. The terror organization assassinates opponents, political rivals and suffocates voices that object to Hezbollah. In 2008, for example, when the Lebanese government took steps to curtail Hezbollah's private telecommunications network, Hezbollah took over Beirut, killing dozens of people.

In June 2019, Lebanon's President Michel 'Aoun said, "Lebanon is like the Titanic heading for disaster."[56] He is right, though very conveniently, he failed to note that since October 2016, he has been the captain of that ship. Lebanon has been teetering on the brink of disaster. But in his statement, 'Aoun preferred not to mention his personal responsibility for Lebanon's tragedy. 'Aoun sits in the Presidential Palace in Beirut thanks to the spears of his political ally, Hezbollah, the kidnapper of Lebanon.

'Aoun founded the Free Patriotic Movement, the largest political party in Lebanon. 'Aoun is Christian, and his power base is Lebanese Christians. According to the Lebanese Constitution, the president must be a Maronite Christian. In October 2016, 'Aoun was sworn in as the president of Lebanon.

Hezbollah was one of the main parties that supported his candidacy. As soon as he took office, he established a political alliance with Hezbollah. 'Aoun himself helped Hezbollah further deepen its hold on Lebanon. And he continues to be Hezbollah's advocate and defender.

Hezbollah argues that its weapons—the same weapons with which it kidnapped and terrorizes Lebanon—are necessary to shield Lebanon from Israel. In an interview in February 2017, 'Aoun supported Hezbollah's argument by claiming that "the Lebanese army is too weak to defend the country against Israeli plots."[57]

A few months later, in November 2017, 'Aoun justified Hezbollah's involvement in the war in Syria by saying that Hezbollah would return to Lebanon after "eradicating terrorism in Syria is completed."[58] In May 2013, four years before 'Aoun's declaration, former Lebanese Prime Minister, Sa'ad al-Din al-Hariri said, "By Iran's order, Hezbollah has burnt Lebanon to save the Assad rule in Syria ... Iran and Hezbollah present a threat to the security of Lebanon and the region."[59]

Understanding that Iran and Hezbollah are the real bosses in Lebanon is essential. Because side-by-side, protesting the state's failings and demanding government accountability to all its citizens, the Lebanese people insisted that the Lebanese government stop allowing Iran, via Hezbollah, to control and dictate Lebanon's domestic and foreign policy.

Determined to define their own identity, carve their own path, chart their own course, and take their destiny into their own hands, Lebanese of all religions and sects cry out, *"we are Lebanese, and Lebanon is our homeland."*

In light of the unrest, Sa'ad al-Din al-Hariri, who served as prime minister of Lebanon from 2009 to 2011 and again from 2016, resigned from the premiership at the end of October 2019.

The Lebanese parliament elected Hassan Diab to succeed al-Hariri. He took office as prime minister of Lebanon in January 2020. Although his government was portrayed as being an apolitical government whose purpose was to save the disintegrating Lebanese economy, the Lebanese public did not trust the new administration. One of the main reasons for their suspicion was the widely held view among many circles that Diab's government, again, was a Hezbollah—meaning an Iranian—puppet.

With the outbreak of COVID-19 in March 2020, the protests stopped. But they resumed with a vengeance toward the end of April 2020.

When the demonstrations re-erupted at the end of April, the face of the protests had changed.

Protesters burned banks in Beirut, Sidon, Tripoli, and Tyre down to the ground and blocked roads throughout the country. The Lebanese army used tear gas to restore order. Dozens of civilians and soldiers were reportedly injured, and one person was killed.

Every day the Lebanese people's despair continues to deepen. And accordingly, the intensity of the protests.[60]

In 2021, Lebanese are screaming in the streets, "*We are starving!*" In January 2021, there were riots in Tripoli, Lebanon's second-largest city. The Lebanese army dispersed the riots using live ammunition. Hundreds of the protesters were wounded. Reportedly, the protesters also used live ammunition and hand grenades.

One thing that remained the same—the protesters protested under the banner of "Lebanon." They disassociated themselves from any ethnic identity to show national solidarity.

On the other hand, Hezbollah and 'Amal supporters gathered in the streets. They tried to instigate violence by screaming, "*Shiah, Shiah!*" Their goal was to break the Lebanese people's unity by emphasizing that the Lebanese are not "one people"—and that sectarian and religious identity come before Lebanese nationality.

That brings me to another significant difference between the fall of 2019 and the spring of 2020. In the fall of 2019, there was "veiled" criticism of Hezbollah and Iran. It was not overt. Since the demonstrations have resurged, more and more Lebanese are openly demanding Hezbollah disarm. Yet, Hezbollah will not disarm itself out of its own volition.

In March 2020, Lebanese Shi'ite journalist 'Ali al-Amin wrote an article, "Be part of the Resistance Camp and Loot as Much as You Wish." Here is a quote from the article: "Lebanon destroyed by corrupt politicians and kidnapped by Hezbollah … is at crossroads facing the biggest challenge ever to its identity and future."[61] I wholly join his assessment.

Beirut Harbor Mega Explosion and the Verdict of the Special Tribunal for Lebanon (STL)

In the summer of 2020, COVID-19 was taking its toll. The economy was continuing to implode, and the protesters were losing patience. Two events in August 2020 further confirmed al-Amin's assessment, exacerbated the crisis in Lebanon, and pushed the country one step closer toward the abyss.

Beirut Harbor Mega Explosion

On August 4, 2020, a massive explosion took place in the port of Beirut, the capitol of Lebanon. According to official Lebanese reports, the blast occurred in a warehouse located on the 12th Wharf of the Port of Beirut where 2,750 tons of ammonium nitrate—a dangerous substance that can be used both for fertilizer and to create explosives—were stored. Apparently, the chain of events that led to the explosion began with a fire in an adjacent warehouse that reportedly contained fireworks.

The explosion killed more than two hundred people and injured more than 6,000. The blast caused enormous damage for miles in each direction. Among other things, residential buildings, offices, shops, streets, vehicles, etc., were severely damaged. The financial damage is estimated to be in the billions of dollars. Reportedly, a quarter of a million Lebanese lost their homes because of the explosion.[62] The Lebanese army's November 2020 data states that the blast destroyed 62,087 residential units, 14,848 shops, and 5,251 offices. Hotels, restaurants, coffeehouses, etc., were also damaged.[63]

Official Lebanese spokespeople admit that the materials had been stored on Wharf 12 since 2013. And although various Lebanese law enforcement agencies issued at least six alerts that the location was a ticking time bomb, Lebanese authorities did nothing to address the threat. It is a shocking and deadly failure.

The Lebanese see this disaster as yet another failure in an endless chain of incompetence and failures of the authorities to address Lebanon's acute problems, including transportation, garbage removal, drainage and sewage, electricity, public health services, and more. The overwhelming majority of Lebanese believed the bomb-making materials that Hezbollah stored in the Beirut Port caused the explosion. They also believe Hezbollah prevented the chemicals from being evacuated from the pier. Many think that Hezbollah kept rockets and missiles in the port and that those rockets and missiles also exploded in the blast.

Furious and desperate, the Lebanese erected gallows in the streets of Beirut. They symbolically executed Lebanese President Michel 'Aoun, the Amal Shi'ite party leader and Chairman of the Lebanese Parliament Nabih Berri, and Hezbollah's leader, Hassan Nasrallah.[64] In response to the Lebanese people's anger, President 'Aoun hurried to protect Hezbollah and clear it of all responsibility.[65]

It is not only the Lebanese that accuse Hezbollah of being responsible for the port disaster. Many in the Arab world openly state or hint that the thousands of tons of ammonium nitrate stored in the port belonged to Hezbollah.

Lebanese journalist and political analyst Huda al-Husseini wrote this about Hezbollah and the port explosion. "Lebanon will not remain as long as there are illegal weapons on its land. Sovereignty will not return to Lebanon as long as the entire political system partners with the owners of illegal weapons. Every honorable Lebanese prays for all of you to sleep every night and see yourselves drowning in the blood of the innocents you killed. The day will come when you suffocate with this pure blood. We pray that it will be soon!"[66]

Iraqi writer Dawood Al-Farhan wrote this in his article he called "The Great Catastrophe of Beirut."

> Before we get into the details, Lebanon is the only country in the world that allocates a warehouse in its main seaport to a religious and sectarian political party, "Hezbollah."
>
> The sectarian religious and political parties loyal to Iran in Iraq learned from the "master" Hassan Nasrallah. They [Iraqi militias] surpassed him by controlling the docks in Iraq's ports in the Arabian Gulf. And their warehouses, like the sheds of the port of Beirut, are in densely populated areas. Some may think that these truncated sectors are run by specialists, technicians, engineers, and experts in maritime and air transport, but this is not the case, gentlemen. The semi-illiterate militias in the two countries control the air, sea, and

land ports on the borders. The militias have been and are still taking the revenues from these activities without any accountability from the specialized state agencies...

Preliminary investigations revealed that ammonium nitrate had been stored in Wharf 12 since 2014. More than that, the Lebanese media figure, Fatima Othman, revealed that Hezbollah owns "a gate called (Fatima's Gate) where goods enter and exit unchecked in Beirut port."

Hezbollah claims that Wharf 12 is for the "resistance"! And no one says a word.

Why do the innocent residents of Beirut and its suburbs pay the price for Hezbollah's recklessness, arrogance, and barbarism, which led to the destruction of the most beautiful Arab capital? [67]

A report published by *Al Arabiya* says that after the US and the EU imposed sanctions on Syria, Assad had to find alternative ways to ensure the flow of oil, weapons, and explosive materials. To this end, the regime developed a network of fake companies that developed relationships with Azerbaijan, Georgia, and Russia. The shipments would arrive destined for either these fake companies or Hezbollah front companies. They would be stored in the port of Beirut before being transferred to Syria. The *Al-Arabiya* report outlines a complex multi-national network, an extensive, complex network of Lebanese and Syrian businessmen working for the Assad regime, circumventing US sanctions through front companies to finance the purchase of ammonium nitrate, explosives, and weapons for the Assad regime.[68]

These writers are likely correct.

First, Hezbollah controls all entry points into Lebanon. By controlling the ports and airports, Hezbollah secures an air and sea communication and transportation network. Its bases extend from Yemen to Latin and North America, passing through the Levant and the Middle East, from northern Europe to West Africa, and from far Asia to Australia . . . Iranians enter Lebanon, Iraq, and Syria, often without their passports being stamped. Hezbollah runs areas that are 'off limits' at the airport. Hezbollah determines where Iranian planes land. Hezbollah unloads and loads the shipments. The organization forbids civil or military authorities to object to anyone coming in or coming out who is connected to the "Quds Force." In one sentence: Beirut's airport and port have been in the hands of Hezbollah for years.[69]

Second, storing ammunition, weapons, artillery, etc., 'in plain sight' is characteristic of the organization. Hezbollah already has a stockpile of about 120,000 to 150,000 missiles and rockets. If launched on Israeli cities and infrastructure, it would cause tremendous destruction. Hezbollah deliberately holds its massive rocket and missile arsenal inside and underneath densely populated towns, picturesque rural villages, and giant urban centers throughout Lebanon.

Following the port explosion, the local municipal councils of Ba'abdeh and Al-Luweiza, two Beirut suburbs, appealed to Interior Ministry and the Lebanese Army. They voiced concern that Hezbollah stores missiles and explosives in and under their neighborhood. And they were especially concerned about such storage facilities near the St. Charles Hospital in Beirut.[70] In response, the Lebanese army questioned the council members about their claims. After interviewing them, the military concluded that their concerns were unfounded and announced that the information regarding stored missiles and explosives in the area was baseless.[71] That announcement did not convince the council members. Eleven out of the fifteen collectively resigned from the council. Their act was a protest expressing a justified distrust in the Lebanese army for how they handled the investigation. Instead of exploring their severe and life-threatening claims of missiles and rockets stored in their neighborhood and near a hospital, the military, either as a tool of Hezbollah or afraid of Hezbollah—or both—decided to deem their claims unfounded.

The massive explosion and the vast destruction caused by the blast provide a clear picture of the severe threat Iran and its proxies—particularly Hezbollah in Lebanon—pose to Israel.

In a speech in February 2021, Israeli Chief of General Staff Lieutenant General Aviv Kochavi emphasized the following. Hezbollah, he said, spreads its missiles, rockets, and warehouses across urban and other civilian areas in a way that blatantly ignores international humanitarian law. Hezbollah does this, he said, to limit Israel's operational freedom since any attack in such areas would, by its nature, result in civilian casualties. However, he clearly stated that as far as Israel is concerned, civilian infrastructures such as power stations and buildings that are also used for military purposes are legitimate military targets. Every fifth building in Lebanon stores either missiles or rockets or is a military warehouse. Soberingly, he clarified that whatever the IDF does, the next war will result in massive barrages of missiles and rockets raining down in Israel. Given this reality, it is incumbent upon the IDF to strike anywhere weapons are being stored to minimize the price Israel will have to pay. [72]

History has a sense of irony. In a speech Hezbollah leader Hassan Nasrallah delivered in February 2016, he threatened to fire missiles at an ammonia reservoir in Haifa Bay, Israel's largest port city. Looking amused, Nasrallah stated in his speech that such an attack was equivalent to a nuclear weapon and would kill hundreds of thousands of Israelis. After the Beirut harbor's explosion, a video mocking Nasrallah went viral on Arab social media networks. The post quoted Nasrallah's 2016 speech and ended with footage of the blast. The headline in Arabic read: "We [i.e., the Lebanese—not Israel] were the ones hit in the head."[73]

I would like to share a quote from an article published on August 5, 2020, a day after the explosion. The writer is Ibrahim al-Amin, the editor-in-chief of the Lebanese *Al-Akhbar* "The News" called "The Great Collapse":

> Whether it is an accident, or deliberate sabotage, or any other reason, the event reveals Lebanon's great collapse. A collapse of an entire system resulting from a way of thinking and behaving cannot deal with crises. It is also a moral collapse that has undermined the whole set of values that are essential to create solidarity and social and human mutual responsibility. It is a collapse of catastrophic proportions.
>
> Yet, it will not prevent certain elements and individuals from exploiting this collapse to advance their despicable interests. It's a collapse of a state where no one has any more faith in the individual, the system, or the institution. In a few hours, the collapse revealed to us that a disastrous catastrophe awaits us behind the door.[74]

Why did I choose this specific quote? Because the writer is a supporter of Hezbollah and published his piece on a pro-Hezbollah news platform. And so, while he mentions general—and accurate reasons—for the collapse of

Lebanon, he fails to say even one word about a—if not the—primary reason for Lebanon's dismal reality. And that is Hezbollah. Al-Amin, like most Lebanese, knows that fact very well. And like many, he prefers to ignore it.

As of August 2021, Lebanese authorities object to an international investigation into the Beirut explosion. The Lebanese claim they are conducting their own investigation. The council members' complaint gives us a glimpse into how effective a Lebanese investigation will be. In addition to that episode, a former Lebanese Customs Authority senior official and a Lebanese photographer were assassinated shortly after the blast. Reportedly, they both had vital information and documentation about the materials stored in Beirut's harbor that caused the explosion.[75]

As of August 2021, one year after the blast, the Lebanese government has done nothing to investigate the catastrophic and massive explosion. Frustrated Lebanese demanding justice for their loved ones killed in the explosion once again went to the streets. Their scream, once again, fell on deaf ears. And accordingly their anger grows.

The Verdict of the Special Tribunal for Lebanon (STL)

Political assassinations, and coverup of assassinations, are an integral part of Lebanese past and present. One of Lebanon's most significant episodes proves this to be true.

On February 14, 2005, former Lebanese Prime Minister Rafik al-Hariri was assassinated in Beirut. The United Nations Security Council created a special team and launched an investigation to determine who killed al-Hariri. Based on their findings, on May 30, 2007, the UNSC adopted Resolution 1757. UNSCR 1757 authorized the formation of an international tribunal to investigate the assassination.[76] The body was called the Special Tribunal for Lebanon (STL).[77] Its mandate was to investigate people only. It did not have the authority to bring organizations or governments to trial. The tribunal was empowered to act under Chapter 7 of the UN Charter. Chapter 7 allows the use of force and sanctions against countries that do not cooperate with the STL's orders and demands.[78]

The STL investigation identified five Lebanese suspects in the murder of al-Hariri. All were linked to the Lebanese Hezbollah. Throughout its investigation, the tribunal repeatedly requested the Lebanese government bring the suspects to the tribunal for questioning. Time and again, the government said it did not know the suspects' whereabouts. Hassan Nasrallah, the leader of Hezbollah, said the STL was an Israeli-American conspiracy. He, therefore, announced that he did not recognize the tribunal's authority. Referring to the STL's request to bring the suspects for interrogation, Nasrallah said, "the suspects will not be arrested within thirty days, nor sixty days, nor within 300 years."[79]

On August 18, 2020, exactly two weeks after the explosion in the Beirut Port, the STL presented its final verdict. The tribunal found a Lebanese citizen named Salim Jamil Ayyash guilty in absentia of al-Hariri's assassination. The STL identified Ayyash as a senior member of Hezbollah. Three other Lebanese suspects—also determined by the STL as Hezbollah members or supporters—were acquitted due to lack of conclusive evidence. The case of another Lebanese suspected of being involved in the assassination—Mustafa Badr al-Din (spelled "Badreddine" in the document)—who was the commander of Hezbollah's forces in Syria was not concluded. That is because he was killed in Syria in May 2016. Accumulative information alleges Hezbollah leader Hassan Nasrallah and Iranian al-Quds Force commander General Qasem Soleimani ordered Badr al-Din's bodyguards to assassinate him.[80]

Captain Wissam Eid of the Lebanese Security Forces, who specialized in technology, provided the STL with a detailed picture of a sophisticated telephone system used by the assassins. The center of the network was located in the area of Dahiyeh—Hezbollah's stronghold in the southern district of Beirut. On January 25, 2008, Captain Eid, like al-Hariri, was assassinated when a bomb obliterated his armored vehicle as it traveled through Beirut's streets. His bodyguard and three civilians were also killed in the blast.

Brigadier General Wissam al-Hassan, of the Lebanese Internal Security Forces (ISF) and the head of its Intelligence Information branch, provided essential and extensive evidence. He provided the type of explosives used in the attack and recordings of the four suspects' telephone conversations from the attack scene. He was also eliminated in a car bomb blast in Beirut in 2012.

The STL's verdict fills more than 2,600 pages and covers many aspects of the plot. The report includes the background and the lead-up to the crime, a detailed rendering of the murder scene, and the specific explosives used in the murder. When it comes to the suspects—among other details—it traces their movements leading up to February 14, 2005. The report provides the location of the suspects at the time of the assassination. It outlines the mobile telephone network they created to support their activity and carry out the attack. It is a fascinating and impressive legal and investigative document that is worth reading.

Here is the STL's summary of events:

Just before 13:00 on Monday 14 February 2005, the former prime minister of Lebanon, Mr Rafik Hariri, was traveling in his convoy in Beirut between the Lebanese Parliament and his home, Quraitem Palace.

As the convoy approached the St Georges Hotel, near the coast, a massive explosion was detonated. Mr Hariri was killed in the blast. Twenty-one others, including eight members of Mr Hariri's convoy, and innocent bystanders, also died. Three of the victims died after the explosion, two on the following day, and the third, the Lebanese MP, Mr Bassel Fuleihan, succumbed after lying in a coma for two months.

At least another 226 people were injured, some very seriously. People passing in the street and working in nearby buildings sustained terrible injuries. Many buildings were badly damaged.

The explosion was triggered by a suicide bomber in a Mitsubishi Canter—a light tarpaulin-covered truck, loaded with more than two tonnes of RDX high-grade explosives that detonated as Mr Hariri's heavily protected six-vehicle convoy passed the St Georges Hotel. The explosives had the equivalent of 2,500 to 3,000 kilograms of TNT. The explosion left a crater in the road over ten meters wide and almost two meters deep.[81]

Here is a summary of the verdict:

Among other things, the Trial Chamber unanimously found Mr. Ayyash "guilty beyond a reasonable doubt" of co-perpetrating a conspiracy to commit an act of terrorism and to intentionally assassinate Mr. Hariri with the premeditated use of explosives.

In reading the verdict, the judges noted that "there is no evidence that the Hezbollah leadership had any involvement in Mr. Hariri's murder and there is no direct evidence of Syrian involvement," adding, however, that "the trial chamber is of the view that Syria and Hezbollah may have had motives to eliminate Mr. Hariri and his political allies."[82]

Below are some sample quotes from the official verdict published by the STL.[83]

The Identity of the Suspects

762. The Trial Chamber can safely conclude that Mr. Badreddine, Mr. Ayyash, Mr. Oneissi, and Mr. Sabra were Hezbollah supporters. It has insufficient evidence to make this finding in Mr. Merhi's case. Still, it notes that a member of his immediate family certainly fell into that category. Mr. Badreddine was undoubtedly a valued senior Hezbollah military commander.

Direct Involvement of the Hezbollah Leader (Hassan Nasrallah) and the al-Assad regime in the Assassination

765. The Trial Chamber received no positive evidence that either any specific Hezbollah member or its leadership, and in particular, Mr. Nasrallah, had any motive to kill Mr. Hariri.

769. The Accused's actions alone demonstrated their participation in the conspiracy and their criminal responsibility. However, the Trial Chamber does not need to find that the Accused were acting on behalf of or at the behest of any organization for a conviction. Links between the Accused and Hezbollah demonstrate the Accused's common interests and explain the political context in which the attack occurred.

787. The Trial Chamber is satisfied from the evidence that: Syria and Hezbollah may have had motives to eliminate Mr. Hariri and some of his political allies.

Conviction

6807. Accordingly, the Trial Chamber also finds that Mr. Ayyash's actions directly contributed to the execution of the crime of intentional homicide of Mr. Rafik Hariri through his central and leading role in the execution of the attack.

6831. The Trial Chamber, therefore, finds Mr. Ayyash guilty, as a co-perpetrator, of the intentional homicide of 21 persons, in addition to Mr. Rafik Hariri.

6839. Accordingly, the Trial Chamber finds Mr. Ayyash guilty, as a co-perpetrator, of the attempted intentional homicide of the 226 people.

6841. For all the reasons outlined above, the Trial Chamber is satisfied beyond reasonable doubt that the Prosecution has proved the guilt of Salim Jamil Ayyash on all counts charged in the amended consolidated indictment.

6903. In these circumstances, the Trial Chamber's decision to acquit Mr. Merhi, Mr. Oneissi, and Mr. Sabra.

The Killers Attempt to Mislead the World: The Case of Ahmad Abu 'Adass

On the afternoon of Monday, February 14, 2005, some hours after the assassination, international media outlets reported that a man named Ahmad Abu 'Adass claimed responsibility for the attack. Reports claimed 'Adass had killed al-Hariri on behalf of an unknown fundamentalist group called *El-Nusrah w'al-Jihadi fi-Bilad-El-Sham*. Ahmad Abu 'Adass was a Palestinian born in Saudi Arabia in 1982. He came to Lebanon at the age of nine.

As part of the plot, Abu 'Adass was used as a scapegoat by the killers.

I would like to expand on this case because there are—and there will be—those who, out of an overt or hidden agenda, will echo this story.

Here is one example. In August 2019, the Lebanese daily newspaper, *Al-Akhbar*, published an article titled "Why is the Tribunal hiding information about Ahmad Abu 'Adass?"[84] From the title of the article, the theme is clear. In the report, Omar Nashabe accused the STL of preventing—even perhaps sabotaging—a thorough investigation of the case against Abu 'Adass. Nashabe clearly tries to discredit the STL's professionalism and objectivity. One should ask, why does Nashabe perpetuate this narrative? One possible answer might have to do with Nashabe himself being a consultant to the team defending one of the suspects before the STL. When considering his piece, one might also think about who might be interested in echoing Nashabe's claim. From that perspective, it is vital to consider that Nashabe's article was published in *Al-Akhbar*, a pro-Hezbollah Lebanese news platform.

The STL investigation revealed the truth. Abu 'Adass's claim of responsibility was staged. It was fake.

Here are the STL's significant findings on the matter of Abu 'Adass:

5769. (Finally) The Trial Chamber agrees with the Prosecution and the Sabra Defense that Mr. Abu 'Adass was an ideal scapegoat.

5770. After carefully considering all the circumstances outlined above, the Trial Chamber is of the view that it can be satisfied beyond reasonable doubt that the claim of responsibility for the attack, as shown in the video, letter, and telephone calls to Reuters and Al-Jazeera, was a false claim. The most likely explanation is that those responsible for Mr. Hariri's assassination attempted to turn attention away from themselves by diverting it to someone claiming a hatred of Mr. Hariri based upon his connections with Saudi Arabia, ostensibly to avenge the deaths of those who Saudi security forces had killed.

5772. The Trial Chamber also cannot make any explicit finding about Mr. Abu 'Adass' fate; he is most likely deceased, and most probably, it would appear, from soon after his disappearance. There is no evidence on the record from which the Trial Chamber can make a definite finding about what happened to him, or when.

5773. The Trial Chamber finds that Mr. Abu 'Adass was not the suicide bomber, and his disappearance is consistent with him being used to set up a false claim of responsibility for the attack by those who perpetrated it. The evidence also suggests that the group El-Nusrah w'al-Jihadi fi-Bilad-El-Sham was fictitious, meaning that both aspects of the false claim were indeed false.

The STL's final verdict clearly proves that Abu 'Adass was innocent and that Nashabe's argument was baseless. Through a thorough, in-depth investigation, the STL proved beyond a doubt that Ahmad Abu 'Adass did not perpetrate the attack and that he did not assassinate al-Hariri. The real killers likely murdered Abu 'Adass.

Reactions in Lebanon to the STL Ruling

Following the STL's verdict, leading Lebanese politicians, including President 'Aoun and Amal leader and Parliamentary Speaker Nabih Berri, issued general statements glorifying the memory of Rafik al-Hariri and calling for national unity. They avoided any mention of the fact that a senior member of their political partner, Hezbollah, was convicted of the murder.[85]

Many Lebanese blame Hezbollah but will not say it openly because they fear Hezbollah will harm them or their families.

Former Lebanese prime minister and son of Rafik-al-Hariri, Saad el-Din al-Hariri, stated that "his family, the family of all victims, and the Lebanese people accept the court's ruling. The assassination squad belonged to Hezbollah, and Hezbollah must pay the price. The days when it is possible to murder on political grounds without being punished are over."[86] This was the first time, to the best of my knowledge, al-Hariri explicitly accused Hezbollah of killing his father.

On August 18, 2020, the day of the verdict, the Lebanese daily paper, the *Beirut Observer*, published an editorial. Here is an excerpt: "Although the STL did not find evidence linking Hezbollah's leadership to the assassination, most Lebanese believe that Hezbollah assassinated al-Hariri."[87] I share this diagnosis.

There were Lebanese who openly blamed Hezbollah, even before the ruling.

On July 2, 2020, Lebanese Shi'ite journalist Nadim Koteich declared on an independent media station, *MTV Lebanon*, that Hezbollah had assassinated al-Hariri. His statement received resounding applause from the studio audience.

Hassan Nasrallah, the leader of Hezbollah, has not commented on the verdict. However, Hezbollah supporters use the fact that the STL ruled there is no conclusive evidence linking Nasrallah to the murder as a complete acquittal of the organization.

In the streets of the Beirut suburb of Dahiyeh—Hezbollah's main stronghold, they fired into the air as a sign of joy and handed out sweets in response to the verdict. In the village of Haruf, the birthplace of Salim Ayyash, who was the only person convicted by the STL as the murderer, a poster was hung expressing the village's solidarity and pride.[88]

This is not the first time Hezbollah has provoked the Lebanese over the killing of Rafik al-Hariri. In September 2018, Hezbollah named one of Dahiyeh's streets after Mustafa Badr al-Din—the military commander killed in Syria in

May 2016. You may remember that Mustafa Badr al-Din was one of the STL's suspects believed to have killed al-Hariri. The assumption is Nasrallah and Qasem Soleimani ordered his bodyguards to kill him.

The STL in the Summer of 2021

The United Nations created the Special Tribunal for Lebanon in 2007. In 2009 the STL began its work to investigate the assassination of Prime Minister Rafik Hariri.

Over a decade since its investigation began, in August 2020, the STL issued its first verdict. The Tribunal found Hezbollah member Salim Ayyash guilty for the bombing that killed Prime Minister Rafik Hariri and twenty-one others.

The tribunal's budget was $67 million in 2020.[89] An exclusive report by Reuters in May 2021 revealed that the STL, which is funded 51 percent by voluntary contributions and 49 percent by the Lebanese government, had run out of money.[90]

In June 2021, the tribunal was supposed to begin a second trial about the assassination of prominent Lebanese politicians George Hawi (2005), who was also openly critical of Syria's interference in Lebanon, and the attempted murders of Marwan Hamadeh in 2004 and Elias Murr in 2005.

But in June 2021, Lebanese caretaker government prime minister Hassan Diab informed the United Nations Secretary-General Antonio Guterres that "due to the country's deep economic crisis,"[91] they were not going to be able to pay their share and that they were going to default on their payments.

Indeed, in June 2021, according to Wajed Ramadan, the tribunal's public affairs officer, "The STL is threatened by imminent closure unless it receives contributions before the end of the month. Without resources, the tribunal will be unable to continue its work beyond July."[92]

After the August port explosion in Beirut, the Lebanese government resigned and became a transitional government. On top of that, the government is Hezbollah's puppet. Therefore, it is doubtful that Lebanon will comply with the STL's verdict and extradite Ayyash. Given that the STL was created under Article 7 of the UN Charter, some hope that the UN Security Council will enforce Article 7 and force the Lebanese government to sentence

Ayyash for the murder. However, given the catastrophic situation Lebanon finds itself in, it is doubtful that any single international entity will support the implementation of Article 7—whether in the form of economic or military sanctions—against Lebanon.

Following the 2005 assassination of Rafik Hariri, a billboard demanding "the truth" was erected in downtown Beirut. It came with a digital counter tracking the number of days since the murder. As the tally approached 1,000 days, the three-digit counter was set to run out of room. In late 2007, the sign was expanded to include an extra digit. In 2009, after the establishment of the STL tasked to investigate and prosecute Hariri's killers, the billboard's tagline was changed to "Time of Justice," and the counter reset to zero.[93]

Closing the tribunal would dash the hopes of families of victims in the al-Hariri murder and other attacks. But beyond that, the dreams of those demanding that a UN tribunal bring to justice those responsible for the August 2020 Beirut port blast that killed 200 and injured 6,500 will, no pun intended, go up in smoke.

On the Verge of Civil War?

Practically speaking, as of the summer of 2021, Lebanon is at the point of complete bankruptcy.

Its economy has imploded. The Lebanese currency is worthless. As of late August, $1 equals 1,512.38 Lebanese Lira. And added to all of this, the catastrophe caused by Beirut's port explosion will cost Lebanon billions of dollars to rebuild. And that is on top of Lebanon's national debt, which is estimated to exceed $100 billion.

The protests continue, and the country has enormous and widening economic, social, and environmental challenges. Throughout 2021, the disintegration of Lebanon has accelerated. The Lebanese are fighting in supermarkets over essential food items like bread, eggs, and milk. The lines at gas stations for fuel are miles long. Electricity is available for a scant few hours a day. The Lebanese currency has completely collapsed.

Under those circumstances, the ghost of civil war is back.

Lebanon has suffered two civil wars (1958 and 1975–1990). In Lebanon, every household has a weapon. Over the past decade, tensions between Sunnis and Shi'ites in Lebanon have resulted in sporadic violence in major cities like Beirut, Sidon, Tripoli, and Tyre.

A US-based veteran journalist of Lebanese origin and founder and executive chair of the Beirut Institute, Raghida Dergham, described Lebanon's plight well. In an August 16, 2020, article "Lebanon's Lebanon in the Claws of Israel's and Iran's Lebanon," she wrote, "Beirut the capital is finally assassinated. Now, Lebanon's assassination has begun. The Lebanese may be left with only one of two choices, bear the cost of capitulation and assassination, or take the costly path to reconquer life."[94] The expensive path to "reconquer life" she refers to is a civil war.

On August 26 and 27, 2020, the Lebanese got a little reminder. On August 26, 2020, Hezbollah members hung a sign in the predominantly Sunni town of Khalde, located some seven miles south of Beirut. The banner marked the upcoming Shi'ite holy Day of 'Ashura. 'Ashura is a holiday commemorating the death in 680 CE of Hussein Bin 'Ali Bin Abi Talib in the battle at Karbala. The exact sequence of events is unclear, but the results were: hours of fighting between the Sunni Clan and Hezbollah militants using heavy machine guns, anti-tank rockets, etc., left two people dead, cars were torched, and a commercial center was burned to the ground.

The only thing that has prevented Lebanon from sliding into another civil war so far has been fear. The Lebanese know that this time, the boat will sink into the abyss with everyone on board. However, Lebanon may have reached a point where the despair is so deep and absolute that the fear of a civil war may be gone.

In her October 2019 article "Why Didn't Nasrallah Take the Streets?" Saudi commentator Amal Abdulaziz Al-Hazani wrote, "The fear of Nasrallah's weapon is a barrier that the Lebanese demonstrators broke. . . If the Lebanese will not internalize that they have their rights and those citizens are more important than any political leader, their losses will double, and their future will be frightening."[95]

Lebanese intellectual and writer, Dr. Mona Fayad expressed this in her August 16, 2020, article titled "Nasrallah – Enough is Enough!" when she said, "A drowning person has nothing to lose."[96]

But it might be too late for the Lebanese.

For the last three decades, Lebanon has been slowly, steadily, and according to a very organized and calculated plan, been kidnapped by the Iranian regime and its proxy in Lebanon, Hezbollah.

Hezbollah uses brute force to impose its will upon the country of Lebanon and the people of Lebanon. They kill political opponents, including the former Lebanese Prime Minister Rafik al-Hariri. They use their weapons to impose their demands on the Lebanese. And due to a generous allowance of $800 million a year from Iran plus the money they earn from drugs and smuggling, they have created an economy that functions parallel to the Lebanese economy. And Hezbollah's economy is stronger than that of the state of Lebanon. That is how Hezbollah took over Lebanon.

A major milestone in the Iranian takeover of Lebanon was the appointment of Michel 'Aoun as the president of Lebanon. 'Aoun was chosen by the Lebanese parliament after reaching an agreement with Hezbollah that grants Hezbollah a veto bloc in the Lebanese government. Meaning, Hezbollah can oppose anything that they, meaning Tehran, does not endorse. 'Aoun, a Maronite Christian, has sealed the deal. Selling Lebanon to the Iranians to keep his throne.

Looking at 'Aoun's biography, one should not be surprised. 'Aoun, a cynical politician, has changed his skin more than once. In the past, he was a bitter opponent of Hafez al-Assad, who ruled Syria from 1970 to 2000. At one point, 'Aoun had to flee Lebanon to France, fearing al-Assad would eliminate him. In the last decade, during the presidency of Hafez's son and successor, Bashar al-Assad, 'Aoun has become a valuable servant in the service of the al-Assad-Iran-Hezbollah axis.

Since October 2019, when al-Sa'ad al-Din al Hariri resigned in the shadow of the protests, all attempts to form a professional government of reliable officials to stop the deterioration and put Lebanon back on the track toward reconstruction have failed.

In March 2020, president 'Aoun asked al-Hariri to form a government. In July 2021, after many months of fruitless attempts, Prime Minister-designate Saad al-Din al-Hariri gave up his attempts to assemble a government. The reason for his failure was no other than 'Aoun himself. Under Hezbollah's orders,

'Aoun refused to authorize al-Hariri's suggested government because an account-able, professional, and reliable government would repeal Hezbollah's veto power.

In the eyes of Hezbollah and its masters in Iran, it is time to end the mission and finally, take over Lebanon. The plan is simple and cynical. Bring the Lebanese to the abyss of despair until they are ready to do anything to try and save themselves.

The Lebanese know Iran is taking over their country. The Lebanese across the board—including Shi'ite Lebanese—oppose Iran's intervention and influence. However, when you worry about putting bread on the table and getting medicine for your children, your priorities change accordingly. Hezbollah leader Hassan Nasrallah has already assured the Lebanese that Iranian oil will be the source of their salvation. Indeed in August 2021, Nasrallah announced that the first of many Iranian ships loaded with diesel would head toward Lebanon. Describing the ship as "Lebanese soil," he warned Israel and the US not to intercept the shipment.

The Iranian plan has a delicate equilibrium. On the one hand, the Iranians and Hezbollah want the Lebanese to be so desperate that they will accept the Iranian takeover. On the other hand, the Iranians do not want the Lebanese despair to be so great that it will lead to a total explosion in Lebanon.

In April 2021, talks between Western powers and Iran about re-entering the Iran Deal began in Vienna. But, Tehran "paused the negotiations" on June 20, a mere two days after Iran's new president, Ebrahim Raisi, was elected. At the time this book is being submitted to the publisher, in August 2021, Iran has yet to return to the negotiating table.

The pause in the talks reflects that the negotiations are all about 'who will blink first?' The Iranians are gambling. And the mullah regime, like the mullah regime, makes others pay the price for its bet. For example, Lebanon. The mullah regime hopes that just moments before the final explosion in Lebanon, the Biden administration will blink and remove the heavy sanctions on Iran.

If the US removes sanctions, Iran will be able to immediately rush funds to "save" Lebanon. And, therefore, actually, deepen its grip.

However, as the crisis in Lebanon deepens, there is a genuine possibility that massive violence will erupt in Lebanon, and the country will just be dragged to complete havoc. The fear of this scenario is palpable. And this is something that all elements in Lebanon—including Hezbollah—want to avoid.

As of August 2021, Lebanon is in a race against the clock.

Can ...Will Anyone Save Lebanon?

In an August 2020 article titled "Oh Lebanon, change your System to Rest!" renowned Lebanese journalist and political analyst Huda Al-Husseini succinctly summed up how most Lebanese view their reality. She wrote, "Lebanon is ruled by a corrupt sectoral system that protects terrorists (i.e., Hezbollah) who, in its turn, protects the corrupt Lebanese system."[97]

Desperate, some Lebanese pray that other countries—namely the Gulf States, France, Turkey, and the United States—will save Lebanon from itself. However, I doubt their prayers will be answered.

Will the Gulf Monarchies Save Lebanon?

The Gulf States were, directly and indirectly, the backbone of the Lebanese economy. In Lebanon's heyday, when Beirut was known as "the Paris of the Middle East," the wealthy tourists who flocked to Lebanon from the Gulf contributed to its economic prosperity. Gulf countries were the primary investors in Lebanon's commercial, construction, and financial system, infrastructure and real estate projects, and the trade and tourism industries. Furthermore, the Gulf States employ hundreds of thousands of Lebanese who send their salaries back home to support their families in Lebanon.

Ironically, while the Gulf monarchies kept Lebanon afloat, Hezbollah dragged Lebanon into the abyss in the service of Iran. Beirut's pro-Iranian position aggravates the Gulf States and has increasingly pitted Lebanon against Saudi Arabia and the UAE.

Thus, it is difficult to see the Gulf states lending a hand to a country that asks for their money yet sides with their bitter enemy—the mullah regime. Disgruntled with Lebanon's alliance with Iran and facing their own economic challenges, they will not rush to give Lebanon billions of dollars that will either end up in the pockets of corrupt Lebanese politicians and/or finance Hezbollah and Iran's control over Lebanon.

Indeed, in August 2021, a statement issued by Saudi Arabia said the Kingdom affirms its "solidarity with the Lebanese people...But any assistance provided to the current or future government depends on it carrying out serious and tangible reforms while ensuring that aid reaches its beneficiaries and avoiding mechanisms that enable the corrupt to control the fate of Lebanon."[98]

Riyadh has made it clear. For Saudi Arabia to resume its support of Lebanon, Lebanon must curb Iran and Hezbollah's influence in Lebanon.

Qatar, which is always pursuing opportunities to position itself as a power broker, is trying to further take advantage of the crisis and deepen its influence in Lebanon.

In July 2021, Qatar announced it would provide the Lebanese army with seventy tons of food a month. This is not the first time Qatar has stepped into say it will save Lebanon. With little results. For example, in June 2019, a senior Qatari official announced that Qatar would buy Lebanese bonds as part of Qatar's plan to invest half a billion dollars in Lebanon. To date, no such investment has taken place.

Qatar's offer to help the Lebanese army is mostly a marketing pitch to show that it is a regional player as well. But we should not expect any significant Qatari efforts or investments to save Lebanon.

Will France Save Lebanon?

The Lebanese hope France will help them.

In April 2018, France hosted the CEDRE Conference (Conférence économique pour le développement, par les réformes et avec les entreprises) for international donors and investors to support Lebanon's economy. The Paris conference convened fifty countries and international organizations, including Qatar, Russia, Saudi Arabia, and the United States. The meeting pledged $11 billion in financial support for Lebanon. However, the money was conditional on Lebanese government reforms in energy production, waste management, taxation, fighting corruption, and more. The conference attendees tracked Lebanon's progress toward the required reforms. The problem was that the Lebanese system is so corrupt, none of the political players were willing to make the changes necessary to receive the support.

Therefore, the financial support the CEDRE Conference pledged remained on paper.

French President Emanuel Macron visited Lebanon immediately after the Beirut explosion. And he came again on August 31, 2020. During both of Macron's visits, he urged the Lebanese to assemble a government as soon as possible. As he did at the CEDRE Conference in 2018, he also emphasized that if France were going to support—or advocate for support of—Lebanon, there would need to be fundamental reforms of the Lebanese political and administrative systems. During his official visit, Macron continued to argue that Hezbollah was a legitimate political factor in Lebanon. He did not once mention the need to disarm Hezbollah.

It was not long before Macron experienced the bitter taste of Lebanese politics. On August 10, 2020, less than a week after the explosion, and with a public seething with anger, Prime Minister Hassan Diab, who took office in January 2020, resigned.

On September 1, 2020, President 'Aoun nominated the former Lebanese ambassador to Germany, Doctor Mustapha Adib, to succeed Diab. But Adib failed to assemble a government, and on September 26, 2020, he also resigned. The prime minister-designate failed because Lebanese politicians—even when Lebanon is on the verge of total collapse—failed to agree on the process to form the cabinet and who would get which portfolio.

Following this fiasco, very undiplomatically, Macron announced that the Lebanese politicians were "betraying" Lebanon. He also changed his tune about Hezbollah. Addressing Hezbollah directly, Macron said, "you (Hezbollah) cannot be a Lebanese political party, a militia fighting in Syria, and an army threatening Israel."[99] Regrettably, Macron fails to recognize—or deliberately ignores—the simple truth. Even if it represents voters, a political party is not a legitimate political player if it has an independent militia and uses the militia's weapons to enforce its political goals, whatever those goals are. Would Macron argue that a political party in France with its own militia that uses its militia and guns to enforce its political will upon the French people is a "legitimate political party"?

In a way, Macron's first meeting on his second visit to Lebanon at the end of August sums up Lebanon's tragic story. The French president met with a

Lebanese Christian woman named Nouhad Wadie' Haddad. Macron awarded her the Order of the French Legion—the highest decoration in France. The meeting was defined as "private," and no information about the meeting's content was provided to the press.

Nouhad Wadie' Haddad is a singer better known by her stage name, Fairuz, which means gemstone. Fans add the title *"Jarat Al-Kamar,"* which means "gem of the moon." Born in Lebanon in 1934, Fairuz is a legendary cultural icon in Lebanon and the Arab world. A Christian, synonymous with Arab identity and culture, her career has spanned decades. She has recorded over eight hundred songs. Her voice—called the *Voice of Lebanon*—her striking looks and emotive singing are famous throughout the Arab world. Fairuz is "certainly one of the greatest Arab singers of the 20th century," Virginia Danielson, an expert in Middle Eastern music, told the *New York Times* in 1999."[100]

In recent years, Fairuz has remained silent about what was happening in her homeland. Her silence fuels constant speculations among the Lebanese public. In December 2013, Fairuz—against her will or choice—was at the heart of a media, political, and emotional storm in the Arab world. In an interview, Fairuz's son, Ziad al-Rahbani, said that his mother "loves Hezbollah leader Hassan Nasrallah." [101] This statement shocked and angered many of Fairuz's fans.

Fairuz's daughter, Rima, immediately Tweeted that her brother's assertion was "baseless and that her mother, who has always been known for not expressing her political views in public, had kept silent on the matter as well."[102] Of the two children, Rima is the one closest to Fairuz. She is also her business manager. Rima, not Ziad, attended the meeting with the French President. I assess that Ziad's statement about his mother "loving Hezbollah leader Hassan Nasrallah" is very far from the truth.

And that brings us back to the Fairuz-Macron meeting. A reporter asked Macron what they discussed. The French president replied that "Fairuz is the one who will decide whether she wants to provide information on this matter."[103]

Fairuz may one day break her silence. One can only imagine what she said to Macron. I am quite confident—and this is an understatement—that Fairuz does not belong to the camp of Hezbollah supporters. I assume that Fairuz's thoughts about Hezbollah and its responsibility for Lebanon's situation came up in the conversation. According to unverified information, the meeting was recorded. It would be interesting to see if this video exists. Following the Macron-Fairuz meeting, the former Libyan Minister of Foreign Affairs, Abdel Rahman Shalgam, wrote an article titled "Macron Between Nasrallah and Fairuz," He said the following: "Fairuz and Nasrallah cannot dwell under the same flag."[104]

I would like to bring a personal angle, which for me, is very out of character.

I am a Jew and an Israeli. However, Fairuz and her songs are also part of my cultural landscape. I grew up in Jerusalem. Israeli television began broadcasting in the mid-1960s. I remember we would all gather around to watch the miracle called TV. There were only three channels: the Israel channel, the Jordanian channel, and the Lebanese channel. And Fairuz was on every evening. That is how I first got to know Fairuz. As an adult, I spent a lot of time in Arabic-speaking environments. Time and again, I met Fairuz on radio stations and on TV screens. I remember an extraordinary experience. Once during a dinner with several Arab dignitaries, they began to sing one of Fairuz's songs. I can attest to the fact that more than one man at the table did not hide his tears.

Will Turkey Save Lebanon?

Accumulating information indicates that Turkey's interest in Lebanon is growing. Erdoğan is using his humanitarian hat to expand his network and supporters in Lebanon.

Ankara provides financial support for Sunni organizations and associations in Lebanon, especially in northern Lebanon and particularly in Tripoli. And to a lesser extent, Erdoğan is trying to expand Turkey's influence in southern Lebanon, which is predominantly Shi'ite.[105]

Following the massive explosion in Beirut's port on August 4, 2020, Turkey expressed a willingness to reconstruct Beirut's port. And the Turkish foreign minister Mevlüt Çavuşoğlu visited Lebanon and stated that "We will grant Turkish citizenship to our brothers who say, 'I am Turkish, I am Turkmen,' and express their desire to become a citizen."[106] That gesture captured my attention.

Why?

Erdoğan often uses the issue of Turkmen Turks communities in the Middle East as a pawn to advance Turkey's interests in the region.

One example is Libya. In December 2019, Turkey justified its involvement in Libya's war by saying, "there are a million Libyans of Turkmen origin in Libya."[107]

Another example of Erdoğan's interest in the Turkmens is in Iraq. There are about 400,000 Turkmen Turks in Iraq. They are concentrated primarily in the oil-rich Kirkuk area in north Iraq—also known as Kurdistan Iraq. In October 2017, following a burst of violence between Turkmens and Kurds in north Iraq, Erdoğan hosted a large delegation of Iraqi Turkmen Turks. After the meeting, the Turkish Presidential Palace released an official statement repeatedly

Turkmen Mostly Live in Southwestern Central Asia

emphasizing that "Iraqi Turkmen are of great importance to Turkey."[108] Since then, as we learned in the section on the war in Syria, Erdoğan has created bases and occupies a significant portion of northern Iraq.

Before we go on, let me define Turkmen. Turkmen are Turkic people living throughout Eurasia and Central Asia. Turkmen belong to the West Oghuz branch of the Turkic language family. There are an estimated 8 million Turkmens worldwide. Most live in southwestern Central Asia—Afghanistan, Kazakhstan, Iran, Pakistan, Russia, Uzbekistan, Ukraine, and around the Caspian Sea.[109]

In Lebanon, there are an estimated 40,000 Turkmen—in addition to Syrian Turkmen. Since the outbreak of the war in Syria, the Turkish-Lebanese

Turkmen in Lebanon and Syria and Turkey in Tripoli

population has increased significantly with the arrival of Syrian Turkmen refugees.

Most Syrian Turkmen live near the Syrian-Turkish border, which runs from the northwestern governorates of Idlib, Aleppo, to Raqqa. Others live in the Turkmen Mountain near Latakia, the city of Homs, and its vicinity to Hama, Damascus, and the southwestern governorates of Dara'a, and Quneitra. During the war, many Syrian Turkmen were involved in military actions against the al-Assad regime and looked to Turkey and the Turkish Army for support and protection. In 2015, there were approximately 120,000–150,000 Syrian Turkmen refugees in Lebanon.[110] About 90,000 Syrian Turkmen are living in Arsal, a war-ravaged Lebanese town on the Syrian border.[111] By 2018, the number of Syrian Turkmen refugees throughout Lebanon had increased to approximately 200,000.[112]

Erdoğan sees this combination of circumstances as an opportunity to use soft power to cultivate relationships and foster Turkmen pride, which can help widen his circle of loyalists, and ultimately grow his influence and power in Lebanon.

To that end, Turkey provides cultural, educational, social activities, and Turkish language and culture classes. Ankara builds Turkish cultural centers, renovates Ottoman structures, provides scholarships. Granting citizenship has also become a major Turkish endeavor. Thousands of Lebanese, many of whom are Turkmen or claim Turkish origins, have received Turkish nationality.[113]

As I said earlier, Erdoğan has particularly focused on increasing his presence and influence in Tripoli, Lebanon's second-largest city.

The population of Tripoli is about 730,000—the vast majority of whom are Sunni Muslims.

Erdoğan is working on restoring Ottoman archeological sites, monuments, and buildings in Tripoli. Including a large clock tower in the Al-Tal square that was a gift from Sultan Abdul-Hamid II, the thirty-fourth Sultan who ruled the Ottoman Empire from 1876–1909. And the Tripoli train station of the famous Hejaz railway that from 1908 to 1920 traveled from Damascus, Syria, to Medina, Saudi Arabia.

It is also reported that Turkey arms Sunnis in Tripoli. So beyond building a broad base of support and positioning Erdoğan as the patron of the Sunnis in

Lebanon, it appears Turkey is also trying to create an armed proxy in Tripoli. The coastal city of Tripoli would be a significant and strategic military and a political stronghold for Erdoğan.[114]

Tripoli is also home to Lebanon's second-largest harbor. The sailing time from Tripoli's port westward to Turkey's eastern port of Taşucu is about fifteen hours. For those reasons, compounded by the fact that most of the population is Sunni, when Erdoğan looks at Lebanon, Tripoli clearly is the perfect candidate to offer Turkey a very friendly base to build a stronghold in Lebanon. And in the eastern basin of the Mediterranean.

It is clear, Erdoğan sees an opportunity to deepen a stronghold in Tripoli, increase his power base, and influence among the Sunnis in Lebanon. And

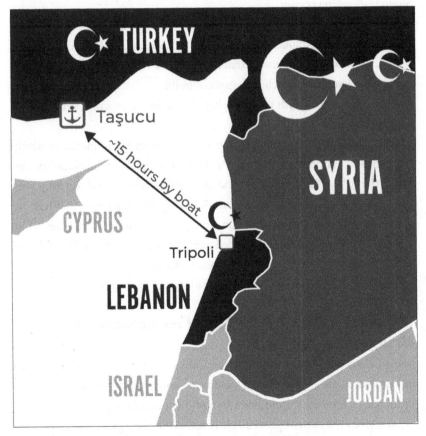

Turkey in Tripoli across from Taşucu

there is no doubt in my mind he will continue to work through multiple channels and varied efforts to expand his patronage, power, and presence in Lebanon.

In January 2021, Turkey's president hosted former Lebanese Prime Minister Saad al-Din al-Hariri in Ankara. At that time, al-Hariri was attempting unsuccessfully to form a Lebanese government.

I believe this was a sign from Erdoğan that he supports Lebanon and the stability of Lebanon. There was likely a second level to Erdoğan's invitation. The increasing influence of Iran and Hezbollah in Lebanon has made Beirut's traditional Sunni Gulf allies and supporters—as we saw above in the case of Saudi Arabia—distance themselves from Lebanon. This situation leaves a Sunni leadership vacuum.

We must remember that at the end of the day, Hezbollah and Iran are Turkey's rivals. The Iranian grip on Lebanon concerns Erdoğan. And Erdoğan is proactively working to ensure that Ankara has a stable base of influence and power in Lebanon on which Erdoğan can build.

But will Erdoğan rush to save Lebanon, a country in a dire situation and perhaps on the verge of a civil war?

Erdoğan will continue cultivating and increasing his influence in northern Lebanon via domestic factors. Particularly through Lebanese politicians, Sunni clergy, and Sunni militias. And through developing and fostering popular support through his various educational and development initiatives.

Erdoğan will not, however, pour money into Lebanon. Like other Sunni powers, he knows that funds intended to help Lebanon will quickly find their way to the pockets of the 'Aoun-Hezbollah alliance.

So, the Lebanese should not expect Erdoğan to save them.

Will the West Step Up and Help Free Lebanon from Hezbollah's Grip?

Many Lebanese see the Beirut blast, the STL's verdict, and the deepening crisis in Lebanon as an unprecedented window of opportunity for the Lebanese to break free of Hezbollah's and Iran's iron grip once and for all.

Yet, given the current geostrategic construct of the region, as Iran expands its influence and aggression, one must doubt how realistic that wish is. . .

On August 21, 2020, Lebanese Professor Dr. Ridwan al-Sayyid wrote: "Before and after the International Tribunal." In the article, he correctly indicates the necessary conditions for a genuine and healthy change in Lebanon. "Some argue Lebanon post-Beirut blast or post-STL is not the same Lebanon. Wrong. Nothing will change unless the Lebanese fight to end the rule of corruption and fight to disarm Hezbollah."[115] I wholly share his outlook.

The Lebanese cannot disarm Hezbollah. Will the West?

There are some United Nations Security Council resolutions regarding Lebanon.

2004 UNSC Resolution 1559 calls for:

- Free and fair presidential elections in Lebanon are to be conducted according to the Lebanese constitutional rules, without foreign interference or influence.
- Disbanding and disarming all Lebanese and non-Lebanese militias.
- All foreign forces to withdraw from Lebanon.
- All parties must cooperate fully and urgently with the Security Council to fully implement all its resolutions concerning restoring Lebanon's territorial integrity, full sovereignty, and political independence.[116]

2006 UNSC Resolution 1701 calls for:

- Full cessation of hostilities in the month-long war between Israel and Hezbollah, mapping out a formula for the phased withdrawal of the Israel Defence Forces from southern Lebanon.
- 15,000 United Nations peacekeepers will help Lebanese troops take control of the area.
- Immediate cessation by Hezbollah of all attacks.
- The immediate cessation by Israel of all offensive military operations in Lebanon.
- A buffer zone free of "any armed personnel"—both Hezbollah militants and Israeli troops—between the United Nations-drawn Blue Line in southern Lebanon and the Litani River (12 miles from the Israeli border).
- Both Israel and Lebanon are to support a permanent ceasefire and comprehensive solution to the crisis.
- No foreign forces in Lebanon without the consent of its government.

- No sales or supply of arms and related material to Lebanon except as authorized by its government.
- All remaining maps of landmines in Lebanon in Israel's possession are to be handed over to the UN.
- The government of Lebanon to extend its control over all Lebanese territory according to UNSC resolutions 1559 (2004) and 1680 (2006).
- The Lebanese government to secure its borders and other entry points to prevent the entry, without its consent, of arms or related material.
- All States shall take the necessary measures to prevent, "by their nationals or from their territories or using their flag vessels or aircraft" the sale or supply of arms and related material of all types to any entity or individual in Lebanon.[117]

In addition, one should remember that the STL operates according to Article 7 of the United Nations Security Council. Given that designation, sanctions are permitted—including military sanctions—for governments who fail to obey the STL orders and verdict.

Enforcing these sanctions would strengthen Lebanon and Lebanon's sovereignty—and could go a long way toward stabilizing the region.

But Will the International Community—and Particularly the Western Powers—Enforce UNSC Resolutions?

The answer is not encouraging.

To date, President Biden's administration's policy regarding Iran is somewhere between the policy of the Obama administration and the Trump administration.

Indeed, the Biden administration acknowledges Iran's aggression as a serious challenge that must be addressed. However, with the growing weight of the progressive wing of the Democratic party—which seems increasingly empathetic and supportive of the mullah regime—the Biden administration will find it difficult to continue its hard line against Tehran. Moreover, given the possibility that Lebanon's acute crisis may evolve into a humanitarian crisis, it will be challenging for the US to maximize sanctions against Hezbollah.

France seems to have accepted Iran's influence on Lebanon as a *fait accompli*. French policy has been to defend Iran. Macron did not support the August 2020 US initiative to extend the UNSC Iranian arms embargo. The embargo expired in October 2020. And France, Germany, and the United Kingdom signed a letter opposing the United States' demand to activate the JCPOA Snapback Clause that would resume Iranian sanctions.

In January 2021, France said that "the United States under new President Joe Biden needs to adopt a more realistic attitude towards the Iranian-backed Hezbollah to help break Lebanon's political and economic impasse."[118] That was the worse message most Lebanese wanted to hear. Recognizing and accepting Iran's proxy, Hezbollah, as a legitimate political entity in Lebanon secures Hezbollah. It dooms the future of Lebanon and the Lebanese people.

The historical irony is uncanny. In 1979, after years of exile living comfortably in a French mansion, Ruhollah Ayatollah Khomeini, the founder of the Islamic Revolution and the founder and leader of the Islamic Republic of Iran, until he died in 1989, returned to Iran on a French plane.

Since his return to Iran, the murderous, extremist regime Khomeini created has taken over, through terror and violence, Lebanon—whose cultural, intellectual, and political history is deeply intertwined with France. The current president of France, in the name of France's deep historical connection to Lebanon, is with one hand trying to save Lebanon. And with the other hand, he is trying to secure and strengthen Iran. A regime that is strangling Lebanon and has dragged the country into an abyss of despair, destruction, and death.

Major Western leaders continue to shield the mullah regime. They seem to ignore the basic fact that protecting the current Iranian government perpetuates and deepens Hezbollah's grip on Lebanon, destabilizes the region, and threatens the lives of millions of people in Israel, in Lebanon, and throughout the area.

Thus, I am skeptical that the international community will take advantage of the unprecedented window of opportunity to thwart Iran's control over Lebanon and save Lebanon.

Unfortunately, UNSC resolutions 1559 and 1701 or the STL order are words on paper. And it will probably stay that way.

Will Syria Regain Its Influence in Lebanon?

Lebanon became an independent country in 1943. However, Syria has always considered Lebanon a part of Syria. From its independence until 2005, Syria was the key player in Lebanon. Everyone, including Hezbollah, was attentive to Damascus.

In response to widespread protests in Lebanon and under international pressure, Syria withdrew from Lebanon in 2005. That said, Syria has never given up its position that Lebanon is part of Syria.

Al-Assad's dependence on Iran and Hezbollah during the war in Syria has flipped the tables in the relationship. Since 2011, Damascus is attentive to Tehran and Hezbollah. But tomorrow, the picture could be reversed again.

Should al-Assad ask Iran to evacuate its proxy militias from Syria, he could rebuild Syria with Gulf resources, restore his image, and regain his position as a central Arab leader. A rehabilitated al-Assad could use the crisis in Lebanon to renew Syria's influence there.

Al-Assad knows that the Arab world and most Lebanese will be happy to see Hezbollah weakened.

And al-Assad can make it happen.

Tehran transports weapons and ammunition through Syria to Hezbollah. And the mullah regime has built a military infrastructure in Syria that also manufactures weapons for Hezbollah. In short, Iran uses Syria to arm, supply, and support Hezbollah. Al-Assad could block the flow of weapons to Hezbollah. Blocking Iran's ability to use Syria as an Iranian-Hezbollah highway would weaken Hezbollah. Undermining Iran and Hezbollah would provide al-Assad the silent consent of the Arab world to reassert his influence in Lebanon.

As of 2021, that scenario seems like a shot in the dark. However, that scenario is in a direct correlation with the process of rehabilitation of al-Assad in the Arab world. In my view, the more the process evolves, the likelihood of that scenario grows.

Summer of 2021—Where Is Lebanon Going?

In November 2020, Lebanon marked its seventy-seventh year of independence. Once a vibrant, cultural, financial, and touristic center, Lebanon's capitol Beirut used to be known as the "Paris of the Middle East." But as of 2021, no matter how you look at it, the country is destroyed.

In 2021, it is literally sinking in garbage because of a corrupt culture and a gang mentality. Its once beautiful coastline is a trash heap. And the legendary "Paris of the Middle East" does not even have enough electricity to keep the lights on. Gas stations run out of fuel. Pharmacies and hospitals are out of medicine. The Lebanese people are fighting each other in stores over the most basic food commodities.

As of the summer of 2021, Lebanon is very close to total disintegration. And if it falls apart, it is very possible it will be a bloody and extremely violent process.

Lebanon, like many other Arab states, is struggling to define its path and its identity. But unlike most Arab states, which are taking steps down the path toward a possible new statehood model, Lebanon—occupied from within by Hezbollah in the service of Iran—must also fight for its independence as a sovereign state. And as terrible as it is, it may be that the Lebanese only hope will be to destroy what is left of Lebanon and rebuild their homeland from the ruins.

Lebanese Shi'ite journalist Nadim Koteich expresses that sad understanding in his December 2019 article. In "The Price of Hezbollah's Autumn," he said, "Lebanon may—or might not—skip the model of the Iraqi or Iranian blood bath. One thing is clear: Ending Hezbollah's guardianship over Lebanon involves a heavy price."[119]

Lebanon's bleak reality is the outcome of the combination of its built-in illnesses: sectarianism, corrupt politicians, narrow-minded politics guided by ethnic, religious, or geographic identity, and a gang-land mindset demonstrated by the fact that every household has weapons. And on top of all of this, Iran's proxy Hezbollah holds the country hostage with its weapons.

That said, as of 2021, when it comes to inner-Lebanese trends, some bright spots in Lebanon could provide a ray of hope.

The disaster Hezbollah and Iran have brought upon the Lebanese has created a counterreaction. In a country plagued by sectarianism, they have found their patriotism.

The ongoing protests show that the Lebanese demands for government accountability will not disappear. And on the other side of that coin, there is a growing sense of civic responsibility. People are becoming more aware of the environment and gaining respect for their surroundings through initiatives like cleaning the beaches and reducing litter. Civil society values are beginning to hold as organizations fighting for children's rights, women's rights, gender equality, etc., grow in Lebanon. But it might be too little, too late.

It is shocking to see how Lebanese politicians and leaders fail to compromise and take responsibility even when the country is on the verge of the abyss. They refuse to sacrifice their narrow interests or join hands to save the sinking boat they are both a part of—and responsible for. It is a suicidal strategy.

Iran and Hezbollah will not loosen their tight grip in Lebanon voluntarily. The West rightly demands deep political, administrative, legislative, and political reform in Lebanon as a condition for saving Lebanon. Pouring billions into Lebanon while Hezbollah rules the country will only perpetuate and deepen Hezbollah's and Iran's control over Lebanon—with Western money. Arab Gulf monarchies will not pour billions into Lebanon if Hezbollah and Iran dictate Lebanese regional policy to attack the Arab Gulf monarchies. And Erdoğan's increasing fingerprint is yet another bad omen for instability, violence, and chaos.

Taking all of this into account and examining Lebanon's reality as of 2021 brings me to the sad conclusion that the chances of the Lebanese gaining their independence and having the opportunity to build a new and healthier model of statehood are in the foreseeable future slim.

Lebanon is caught in a vicious circle. Lebanon is first and foremost a victim of itself. The Lebanese have been burying their heads in the sand—out of fear, hypocrisy, or narrow sectarian political interests.

Asked during a September 2020 press conference in Arabic what the future holds for Lebanon if it fails to address its challenges, Lebanese President Michel 'Aoun answered, "We are going to Hell. No doubt."[120]

Iraq: A Duel in the Land of Two Rivers

Iran views Iraq as its jurisdiction. And Iraq is the key to the mullah regime's land corridor and its hegemonic vision. Without Iraq, there is no Iranian land corridor. Iran is determined to maintain and secure its control over Iraq. And accordingly, Iran is determined to expand its influence and power and crush the uprising in Iraq.

Parallel to Lebanon, in early October 2019, widespread demonstrations and riots also broke out in Iraq. Iraq is primarily a Shi'ite country. About 65 percent of Iraqis are Shi'ite. And the epicenter of the protests, which have continued on and off into and throughout 2021, is in southern Iraq—mainly populated by Shi'ites—including in the major cities like Basra, Baghdad, Karbala, and Najaf.

Like in Lebanon, the uprising in Iraq focused on corruption, the country's shattered economy, lack of services, and the people's demand to end Iran's control of Iraq's domestic and foreign policy.

However, even though both uprisings revolve around similar issues, there are some differences between the protests in Iraq and Lebanon.

The protesters in Lebanon represent the width and breadth of Lebanese society. In Iraq, the protesters are primarily Shi'ite Iraqis. However, to be clear, this does not mean that Iraq's other two major groups, the Sunni Arabs (who make up about 30 percent of Iraq's population) and the Kurds (who are about 20 percent of Iraq's population), welcome Iran's involvement in Iraq.

In addition to the protesters' homogeneous identity, another difference was that, different from Lebanon—hundreds of Iraqi protesters were killed in the 2019 protests in Iraq. Iranian-supported Iraqi Shi'ite militias targeted protesters—killing them in cold blood and executing people in the streets. The Iraqi government and the Iraqi army stood on the sidelines and did nothing to protect the civilian protesters.

According to the Human Rights Office of the United Nations Assistance Mission for Iraq (UNAMI), 545 Iraqis—mostly civilians—were killed. More than twenty-four thousand were injured, and hundreds were arrested or disappeared in the protests that took place in Iraq at the end of 2019 and the beginning of 2020.[121]

In the demonstrations held in Iraq during late 2020, we saw a different picture. The pro-Iranian Iraqi militias that killed the protesters in the 2019 and early 2020 demonstrations had disappeared from the streets, and the army and security forces took command.

That said, between the Fall of 2019 until July 2021, seventy political activists have been murdered, and dozens have been abducted and disappeared.[122] In most cases, these activists are people who oppose Iranian intervention in Iraq and support Iraqi sovereignty.

Iraq: Independent Arab Country or an Iranian Satellite?

In a March 2020 article, Iraqi analyst Dr. Majid al-Samarrai wrote, "Iraq experiences a struggle between Nationalist Iraqi Shi'ites and Non-Nationalist Iraqi Shi'ites."[123]

Earlier in the book, we shortly discussed Iraqi nationalists and non-nationalists, but I want to repeat it here.

The overwhelming majority of Iraqis are Arabs—either Sunni or Shi'ite or Christians. (Kurds are the second-largest ethnic group in Iraq.) Most Iraqi Arab nationalists, therefore, argue that Iraq is an integral part of the Arab world.

Iraqi non-nationalists argue that Iraq's core identity is religious—Shi'ite (as we said above, about 65 percent of Iraqis are Shi'ites), not ethnic—Arab /Kurd. Therefore, in their view, Iraq should not be a part of the Arab world. Instead, it should be part of Shi'ite Iran and be under Iran's umbrella.

An additional and increasingly explosive and pivotal layer to this complex struggle is the conflict between the Iraqi nationalists who want Iran to stop interfering in Iraq and Iraqi affairs and the Iraqi Shi'ites who side with Iran and support Iranian intervention in Iraq.

Iraqi commentator Bahirah al-Sheikhli expressed a similar evaluation in her March 2020 article "The Division Within Shi'ite Camp Might Result in Fighting in Iraq."[124] Let us take a more in-depth look to understand why this could happen.

First, the Shi'ite tribes in southern Iraq—who have been leading the protests and demonstrations—are politically powerful and massively armed. And they have made it clear that they will not tolerate the continued slaughter of the protesters—most of whom are their sons, by other Shi'ites—in the service of Iran.

Another indicator of an impending Shi'ite crisis is brewing within the Popular Mobilization Units Al-Hashd al-Sha'abi, the PMU.

I have discussed the PMU earlier, but now I would like to take the opportunity to take an in-depth look at the PMU because it is a significant factor in Iraq. Understanding the PMU's role, how they were established, and by whom will provide essential insight into Iraq. Furthermore, it is one of the keys to understanding the current geopolitical climate of the Middle East.

So, let me take this opportunity to provide some background on the evolution of the PMU and why it is so significant today.

Al-Hashd al-Sha'abi, The Popular Mobilization Units, PMU

On June 10, 2014, the militant Sunni Islam group ISIS defeated the Iraqi army in Mosul, the second-largest city in Iraq. In response, Iraqi-based Grand Ayatollah Sayyid Ali Hosseini al-Sistani, viewed by many as the most powerful and influential Shi'ite Cleric in Iraq, issued a *fard al-kifāya jihad fatwah.*

A *fatwah* is a religious ordinance.

Jihad, we translated earlier as an ultimate spiritual effort, is a word that has become associated with more violent actions over time.

A *fard al-kifāya* is a duty imposed on the whole community of believers (known as the *ummah* in Arabic). When a fard al-kifāya is issued, the individual is not obligated to follow the directive, provided a sufficient number of community members follow the directive.

Al-Sistani's fard al-kifāya jihad fatwah called on every Iraqi male capable of fighting to take up arms to defeat ISIS forces in Iraq.

In response to al-Sistani's 2014 fard al-kifāya jihad fatwah, the Shi'ite *al-'Ataba* established four military units to fight ISIS.

Al-'Ataba are Shi'ite religious centers. There are five in Iraq, all located near the burial sites of key Shi'ite historical figures. The centers offer religious studies and are a destination for Shi'ite pilgrims. The al-'Ataba are also hubs for commercial and political activities. In response to al-Sistani's fatwa, al-'Ataba centers throughout Iraq invited Shi'ites to come and join militias. The collective name of the Shi'ite militias al-'Ataba initiated is *al-'Atabat-al-Hashd al-Sha'abi.* And they are entirely loyal to al-Sistani.

However, other major Shi'ite militias also fighting ISIS in Iraq were not part of the al-'Atabat-al-Hashd al-Sha'abi. They were commanded and trained by the Islamic Revolutionary Guards. Some existed before, and some evolved as a result of al-Sistani's request.

The military infrastructure that evolved due to al-Sistani's fard al-kifāya laid the foundation for establishing what would—about two and a half years later—become the PMU.

In July 2016, Iraq Prime Minister (2014–2018) Haidar al-Abadi, a Shi'ite close with Iran, issued an executive order. By his command, he incorporated these Iraqi Shi'ite militias—some of whom, reminding you, were supported and guided by the Islamic Revolutionary Guards—into Iraq's armed forces. Moreover, he incorporated these militias into the Iraqi armed forces as an independent military entity.

Four months after al-Abadi's decree, in November 2016, the Iraqi parliament passed an official law establishing these militias as a new military force. By doing so, the Iraqi government created an additional official Iraqi military enterprise that works in parallel but is separate from the Iraqi armed forces. They called this new framework al-Hashd al-Sha'abi (the Popular Mobilization Units—the PMU).

In July 2019, 'Adel Abd al-Mahdi (the Shi'ite prime minister of Iraq from October 2018 until May 2020) took a further step in creating this parallel Iraqi military establishment. He issued a decree ordering the merging of all PMU units into the official Iraqi security establishment. The legislation also mandated that all PMU units have standard military titles and numbers (Brigade, Division, etc.) and that all its members have ranks like in the armed forces.

The PMU is funded and armed by the Iraqi government and functions parallel to but independent and separate from the Iraqi armed forces.

As of August 2021, the PMU is made up of eighty-three Iraqi-Shi'ite militias. However, despite the fact all those militias are funded by the Iraqi government and are part of the Iraqi security establishment, forty of the eighty-three are commanded by Iran's Islamic Revolutionary Guards. The Iranian-controlled Iraqi Shi'ite militias in the PMU are known as "*al-Wilaiyah*," meaning "the one that subscribes to the order of Iran's Supreme Leader." The PMU *al-Wilaiyah* are militias made up of Iraqi citizens who live in Iraq and want Iran to increase its hold over Iraq.

In April 2021, the two largest pro-Iranian parties in the Iraqi parliament, the *al-Fath* "The Triumph" coalition and the pro-Iranian Iraqi *Dawlat al-Kanoun* party "The State of Law" who combined held seventy-four out of 329 seats, pressured the Iraqi parliament to pass a law instructing the Iraqi government to allow an additional thirty thousand people—affiliated with pro-Iranian al-Wilaiyah militias—to be absorbed into the PMU. Some have fought in Syria in the service of Iran to save al-Assad and ensure Iran's continued power in—and over—Syria.

Once these thirty thousand people are added to the PMU, the total number of people on the PMU payroll—including administration, logistics, management, etc.—will be 160,000 people. The average salary of a PMU militant is $800 a month. The administrative structure and the massive number of people on the payroll leave an enormous space for corruption.

There are suspicions that the numbers quoted by the PMU leaders are fictitious and that the thirty thousand people are only names on paper. One Iraqi commentator explains how it works. The money goes directly to the militias' commanders, and they are the ones who distribute the salaries. The commanders inflate the number of the alleged salary receivers, and they keep the money in their own pockets. An Iraqi researcher claims that the actual number of PMU combatants is only about forty-three thousand.[125] Another place for widespread corruption within the PMU is compensations for families of fallen PMU fighters. Reportedly, a budget of $68 million has been allocated to purchase land for fallen PMU fighters' families. Yet, since 2014 only 3,500 lots have been purchased—that is way less than the total budget allocated for the families of fallen soldiers.[126]

As we can see, al-Sistani's 2014 fatwah played into Iran's hands because the PMU became a significant instrument Iran uses to deepen its influence and presence in Iraq.

That development is ironic for two reasons.

First, Grand Ayatollah Sayyid Ali Hosseini al-Sistani, viewed by many as the most powerful and influential Shi'ite cleric in Iraq, is a bitter ideological opponent of Iran's mullah regime. More than that, he fundamentally disagrees with their theocratic model and one of the fundamental principles *Wilayat al-Faqih* "The Governance of the Jurist." Wilayat al-Faqih means that Iran's supreme leader (since 1989, Ali Khamenei) has full authority to make all decisions. His rule and judgments cannot be questioned or challenged. Although under certain circumstances, he can be removed from office by the "Council of Experts."

Furthermore, the Iraqi government pays pro-Iran Iraqi Shi'ite al-Wilaiyah militias to violently force Iraq and Iraqis to succumb to Iran's will. So, the Iraqi government is paying militias loyal to another country—in this case, Iran—to take over Iraq. This takes kidnapping from within to a whole other level.

The increasing Iranian intervention in Iraq has escalated the tension between Iraqi Shi'ites who oppose Iran's influence in Iraq and Iraqi Shi'ites who support Iran's deepening influence in Iraq.

Tensions between Iraqi Shi'ite Nationalists and Iraqi Shi'ite Supporters of Iran and Deepening Friction and Tensions within the PMU

The tension between the two camps is inevitably reflected in the two major power centers in Iraq. One is the PMU, and the other is the Iraqi political system.

A dramatic event revealed the tensions between the Iraqi Shi'ite nationalists and the Iraqi Shi'ite non-nationalist camps within the PMU itself.

On January 3, 2020, a US strike killed Iranian al-Quds Commander Qasem Soleimani and the deputy chief of the PMU, Abu Mahdi al-Muhandis. Apparently, four other Iranian officers were also killed in the strike.[127]

The Iranian-backed PMU al-Wilaiyah militias wanted a pro-Iranian figure to replace al-Muhandis.

In February 2020, in a swift move without even getting the official approval of Prime Minister Mahdi, who formally is their supreme commander, the PMU pro-Iran al-wilaiyah militias appointed a pro-Iranian Iraqi official, Abdul 'Aziz al-Mohammadawi, to replace al-Muhandis as deputy chief of the PMU. Al-Mohammadawi's nomination deepened the rift within the PMU between the Iranian-backed Iraqi Shi'ite al-Wilaiyah PMU militias and the Iraqi Shi'ite al-'Atabat PMU militias loyal to al-Sistani who—as we know—is against Iran's intervention in Iraq and opposes the mullah regime's core ideology.

Al-'Atabat al-Hashd al-Sha'abi (also known as the 'Atabat PMU) objected to the appointment of al-Mohammadawi, maintaining it was illegal and illegitimate. However, al-Mohammadawi did replace al-Muhandis as the deputy leader of the PMU, and he remains in the position until today.

Reportedly, the Iranian-backed al-Wilaiyah militias have also established a military forum within the PMU called *Majlis Shura al-Hashd*, "the Legislative Council of the PMU."[128]

In December 2020, al-'Atabat-al-Hashd al-Sha'abi published an official statement expressing allegiance to the Iraqi constitution and vowing to stay out of the political arena. The al-'Atabat-al-Hashd al-Sha'abi is estimated to be twenty thousand strong. It intends to be a counterforce to the Iranian-backed Iraqi Shi'ite al-Wilaiyah PMU militias.[129] In response, the leader of 'Asaib Ahl al-Haq, one of Iran's most important proxies in Iraq, defined al-'Atabat-al-Hashd al-Sha'abi as an Israeli and American agent.[130]

Deepening Friction and Tensions within Iraqi Political System

In November 2019, as the protests raged in Iraq, Shi'ite Prime Minister 'Adel Abd al-Mahdi resigned, and the sitting government became a transitional government.

In March 2020, Iraqi President Barham Salih, who is Kurdish and Sunni, appointed an Iraqi Shi'ite nationalist politician, Adnan al-Zurfi, to replace 'Adel Abd al-Mahdi as prime minister. I'll bet that by now, you can guess this did not go smoothly.

The Shi'ite parties were split. The bloc in the government that opposes Iranian involvement and influence in Iraq and supports Iraqi sovereignty supported al-Zurfi's nomination. On the other hand, the Iranian-affiliated Iraqi Shi'ite political parties and politicians opposed al-Zurfi's nomination.

Let's dig a little deeper to look at the construct of the 329-seat Iraqi parliament as of the summer of 2021.

The largest—primarily Shi'ite—coalition is called *Saeroun* "Marching On." They have fifty-five seats. Muqtada al-Sadr (who we will discuss later in this chapter) leads the Saeroun coalition. In addition to leading the largest alliance in parliament, Muqtada al-Sadr—like some other Iraqi politicians—is also the head of *Saraya al-Salam,* "The Peace Companies," a powerful militia that is not a part of the PMU or the Iraqi armed forces.

The second—primarily Shi'ite pro-Iranian—coalition is the al-Fath coalition (the same one who urged the parliament to pass the law in 2021 to absorb the thirty thousand people into the PMU). They have forty-eight seats. Hadi al-Amiri leads the al-Fath coalition. In addition to being the second-largest coalition in the Iraqi parliament, al-Fath is also the largest pro-Iranian political party in Iraq. Like al-Sadr, al-Amiri is also the leader of a powerful Shi'ite Iranian-backed al-Wilaiyah militia called the *al-Badr* militia.

In early April 2020, eight Iranian-affiliated Iraqi Shi'ite al-Wilaiyah militias announced they officially rejected al-Zurfi's candidacy, describing him as an "American and Israeli agent." Among the parties rejecting al-Zurfi was the pro-Iranian Iraqi Dawlat al-Kanoun party (that along with al-Fath urged the parliament to pass the law in 2021 to absorb thirty thousand people into the PMU) led by former Iraqi Shi'ite Prime Minister (2006–2014) Nouri al-Maliki (who was close with Iran), and which has twenty-six seats.

On April 9, 2020, al-Zurfi announced he was dropping out.

Iraqi President Salih then appointed Iraqi National Intelligence Service Director Mustafa al-Kadhimi as prime minister and transferred him the mandate to assemble a government. Al-Kadhimi's appointment as prime minister of Iraq was welcomed by the United States and Iran, although Tehran was not very enthusiastic.

Iran's reaction offers a glimpse into the complex labyrinth of Iraqi politics. And it illustrates the deep Iranian intervention in Iraqi politics.

In March 2020, a spokesperson for the Iranian-backed Iraqi Shi'ite militia, Kataib Hezbollah, wrote: "Al-Kadhimi is one of the people accused of helping the American enemy carry out the crime (in January 2020) of assassinating Haj Soleimani, the commander of the IRG al-Quds force [Haj (m) or Hajah (f) is the title given to a person who conducted the religious imperative of pilgrimage to Mecca] and Abu Mahdi al-Muhandis (the PMU's second in command)."[131] However, in April 2020, they changed their tune, and Tehran directed the Iranian-backed Iraqi political parties and militias to support al-Kadhimi for prime minister of Iraq.

Al-Kadhimi was clearly not Iran's first choice. So, why then did the Iranians change their mind and support him?

Facing many challenges at home and across the region, the mullah regime decided to lose the battle to win the war.

In the spring of 2020, the soaring COVID-19 death toll in Iran fueled increasing public anger and unrest. In early April 2020, the economy continued to spiral downward as the number of cases soared upward. Concerned with the possibility that mass demonstrations in Iraq would percolate into

Iran and fuel unrest inside Iran, Tehran wanted to calm the situation in Iraq. Therefore, Iran decided to make a temporary concession in Iraq and accept an Iraqi Shi'ite nationalist candidate in return for hopefully getting one challenge (i.e., the protests in Iraq) off Iran's plate.

On May 7, 2020, al-Kadhimi was sworn in as Iraq's forty-third prime minister. In his first speech as the prime minister, Mustafa al-Kadhimi emphasized the need to keep the state's sovereignty and integrity. He declared that his government would serve the needs and interests of the Iraqi people. He stressed that all weapons must be held only by Iraqi armed forces. He also pledged to keep and protect the freedom of expression and protest. And he promised he would bring those responsible for the killing of Iraqi protesters to justice.

Who Holds the Power in Iraq?

It is essential to understand that the power is only partially in the prime minister's hands when it comes to Iraq. Some people and institutions wield more power and influence on the future of the Shi'ites in Iraq and on the future of Iraq, period.

One such figure is a man we just discussed: Grand Ayatollah Sayyid Ali Hosseini al-Sistani. The other is a religious body known as Marja'iyat Najaf.

Who is al-Sistani? And what is the Marja'iyat Najaf?

Before we discuss either, we need to begin by understanding a little more about the Shi'ites.

As we discussed in Chapter 2, the largest denomination in Shia Islam is the Twelver branch, also known in Arabic as the *Imamiyyah*. About 85 percent of Shi'ites are Twelvers. Twelvers believe that twelve divinely ordained imams succeeded the Prophet Muhammad. The first imam was the fourth Caliph 'Ali Bin Abi Talib. According to the Twelvers, the last imam, Mohammed bin Hasan al-Askari (born in 870), is the *Imam al-Mahdi*, *"The Redeemer."* Shi'ites believe he is waiting "outside of time" to come back as the *Mahdi*, "the rightly guided one." In the Shia narrative he is described as "the Master of Time." When he returns, this messianic figure will save humanity through a process in which most people in the world will perish. Then humankind will live in endless justice and prosperity.

When we talked about the Iranian government's structure in Chapter 2, we said the Shi'ite clerical order is hierarchical. The most senior cleric in the Twelvish Shi'ite clergy is ayatollah 'uzma—the Grand Ayatollah. There are four ayatollah 'uzma in Iraq. Only one of the four was born in Iraq—eighty-six-year-old Mohammed Sayyid al-Hakim. Grand Ayatollah Sayyid Ali Hosseini al-Sistani is ninety years old and was born in Iran. As mentioned before, a great and wise learned spiritual leader, al-Sistani is the most powerful and influential Iraqi Shi'ite cleric in Iraq.

The four ayatollah 'uzma in Iraq are known as the *Marja'iyaht Najaf*. The word *Marja'iyah* means the "source of spiritual, theological jurisdiction." Najaf is a city in southern Iraq. The holiest Shi'ite religious and pilgrimage sites are in Najaf and Karbala in Iraq and Qom and Mashhad in Iran. These cities are also home to the leading Shi'ite theological educational centers. Marja'iyaht Najaf is literally translated "the Najaf source for theological guidance."

Although they are not directly involved in Iraqi politics, the Marja'iyaht Najaf wield massive influence over Iraqi politics and the Iraqi street. No less significant, the Marja'iyaht Najaf is viewed by many Shi'ites as the highest Shi'ite spiritual and theological authoritative source.

Grand Ayatollah 'Ali al-Sistani and the Marja'iyaht Najaf are two very powerful Iraqi Shi'ite power brokers that could impact the trajectory of the evolving struggle among the Iraqi Shi'ites. They could also profoundly influence the future of Iraq.

In March 2021, Pope Francis visited Iraq. During his three-day historic visit, the pope held a closed-door meeting with al-Sistani. Following the meeting, al-Sistani's office published a statement describing the content of the meeting. Though diplomatically phrased, the statement hinted that one of the issues discussed was the need to thwart Iran's intervention in Iraq.[132]

Now, we know that al-Sistani—who is "the first among equals" of the Marja'iyaht Najaf—objects to Iranian intervention in Iraq. But even more than that, as we previously mentioned, he opposes the entire premise of the mullah regime. He argues that Islam should not mix politics and religion. Moreover, as we have also discussed, al-Sistani rejects the core religious ideology and the mullah regime's fundamental premise—wilayat al-faqih, "the governance of the jurist."

As an institution, the Marja'iyaht Najaf, led by al-Sistani, strongly objects to Iranian intervention in Iraq as well. It emphasizes that Iraqi independence and sovereignty must be preserved. Given their positions, prestige, and influence, the Marja'iyaht Najaf presents a significant challenge to the mullah regime and its Iraqi Shi'ite al-Wilaiyah proxies.

The current senior members of Marja'iyat Najaf are old. It is expected that, in the incoming Marja'iyah, one possible new member could be al-Sistani's eldest son, Ayatollah Mohammed Rida (born in 1962). He will continue his father's position of opposing Iran's intervention in Iraq.

Iran is concerned that the Marja'iyaht Najaf may compromise Iran's presence and influence in Iraq. Therefore, Tehran is trying to establish a competing power base. To that end, the mullah regime is thus nurturing new cohorts of Marja'iyah in the Shi'ite holiest cities. Iran is building Shi'ite theological centers in Najaf itself, as well as in Karbala in Iraq. Iran's goal is to develop a new Marja'iyah in Iraq that will be friendlier to Iran.

When we talked about the Iraqi parliament's construct earlier in this chapter, I introduced a man named Muqtada al-Sadr. He is another Shi'ite figure that impacts the trajectory of the inner-Shi'ite power struggle in Iraq.

Born in 1974, Muqtada al-Sadr is another very influential Shi'ite leader. In addition to being a religious figure, as we said, he is the leader of the Saeroun, the largest political coalition in Iraq. He is also the commander of the Saraya al-Salam militia, a powerful Shi'ite militia in Iraq.

Al-Sadr is a classic "Machiavellian"-style leader.

Throughout the 2000s, al-Sadr was Iran's most valuable subcontractor in Iraq. Under Iranian orders, his militia, which was then called *Jaish al-Mahdi* "the Messiah's Army," spearheaded attacks on US forces in Iraq.

But in 2018, al-Sadr changed his stripes. In Iraq's 2018 elections, al-Sadr's campaign focused on limiting Iran's intervention in Iraq, fighting corruption, and disarming Iraqi militias—even though he himself commands a militia.

When the protests broke out in Iraq in October 2019, al-Sadr first placed himself on the side of the Iraqi protesters who demanded to end Iran's intervention in Iraq.

But, in January 2020, al-Sadr yet again changed his colors. He took Iran's side and ordered his supporters to crush the Iraqi protests. Some observers attribute al-Sadr's change of heart to an Iranian promise that he will be the leader of the alternative Marja'iyah that Iran is trying to establish in Iraq.

In January 2021, he once again played the card of Iraqi nationalism, sovereignty, and unity. Iran provides Iraq with gas and electricity. Al-Sadr said Iraqis should find themselves an alternative source of gas.[133]

On July 15, 2021, al-Sadr announced that he would boycott Iraq's parliamentary elections scheduled for October 2021. His threat sent a shockwave through the Iraqi political establishment. Iraqi political observers attributed his move to his current weakened position stemming from the fact that he set himself on a collision course with both the Iranian-backed camp as well as the protesters camp. By now, you will not be surprised to know that al-Sadr once again changed his stripes at the end of August. In August 2021, he announced that he would participate in the October elections.

Al-Sadr is a critical player in Iraqi politics. One must then wonder how al-Sadr's next political zig-zag will impact the trajectory of the inner Iraqi Shi'ite tensions as well as the future of Iraq's struggle to free itself of the Iranian grip?

Iraq—A Platform for US-Iranian Conflict

As we first discussed in Chapter 2, Iran turned Iraq into a platform to attack the United States.

Iran unleashed its Iraqi proxies to attack US military bases, US civilians, and US infrastructure in Iraq.

Toward the end of 2019 and throughout 2020 and 2021, Iranian-backed Iraqi militias accelerated their rocket attacks on US bases, the US Embassy, and civil infrastructure and projects in Iraq.

On December 27, 2019, Kataib Hezbollah launched rockets on a military base near Kirkuk, killing one US civilian and injuring four US service members and two Iraqis.

On December 29, 2019, the United States attacked a Kataib Hezbollah base killing dozens of militants, apparently including several IRG officers.

On December 31, 2019, Iranian-backed Iraqi militants, dressed in civilian clothes, stormed the US Embassy in Baghdad and blockaded it for several days.

Throughout 2020, the friction between Iran and the United States in Iraq intensified.

On January 3, 2020, in Baghdad, the United States eliminated Major General Qasem Soleimani, the Iranian al-Quds force commander and the man tasked to plan and execute Iran's goal to be the regional superpower, and Abu Mahdi al-Muhandis, the second in command of the PMU.

On January 8, 2020, the Iranians retaliated by shooting missiles from inside Iran, targeting US military personnel in the Al-Harir and Ayn al-Assad military bases in Iraq. The Iranian retaliation did not cause any fatalities, but it did injure dozens of US military personnel—some seriously.

On March 11 and March 14, 2020, Kataib Hezbollah launched a rocket attack on the Camp Taji military base, located about fifteen miles north of Baghdad. Three soldiers, two Americans and one British, were killed. Dozens were injured. In response, the United States attacked the Imam 'Ali military compound and struck five weapon storage facilities belonging to Kataib Hezbollah. The continuing military attacks have reportedly resulted in the US

Iraq—Platform for Iranian-backed al-Wilaiyah Shi'ite Militias to Attack US and International Assets

plans to eliminate the Iranian-backed Iraqi militia, Kataib Hezbollah.[134] As we said in Chapter 2, as of August 2021, that has not happened.

Throughout 2021 the attacks on US troops escalated. Here is a partial list.

On February 25, 2021, a rocket attack at a US-led military base in Kurdish northern Iraq killed a civilian contractor and wounded five other people, including a US service member.

On March 3, 2021, a barrage of rockets was fired at the Ayn al-Assad air-base housing US troops in Iraq's western Al-Anbar province.

On April 14, 2021, a drone dropped explosives near US forces stationed in Erbil in northern Iraq.

On May 24, 2021, a missile targeted a base housing American forces in Anbar province.

On June 28, 2021, US troops came under fire in the Al-Omar oil fields in Deir ez-Zor, in eastern Syria.

On Monday, July 5, 2021, three rockets were fired at Ayn al-Assad airbase, and then a drone was shot down near the US Embassy in Baghdad.

Then on Tuesday, July 6, 2021, an explosive-laden drone attacked US troops at Erbil airbase in northern Iraq.

On July 7, 2021, three attacks targeted troops in Iraq and Syria: at least fourteen rockets hit Ayn al-Assad, injuring two US service members; two missiles were fired at the US Embassy in Baghdad's Green Zone; and a drone attacked the Al-Omar oilfield in eastern Syria, where US troops were hit with multiple rockets on June 28.[135] The Al-Omar oilfield is near the Maydin area, which Iran controls.

On July 24, 2021—two days before Iraqi Prime Minister al-Kadhimi was scheduled to meet President Joe Biden at the White House to discuss US troop withdrawal from Iraq—a military base hosting US troops near the Al-Harir base, forty-five miles northeast of Erbil, the capitol of Iraq's semi-autonomous Kurdish region, was attacked. The attacks of the Iranian-backed Shi'ite militias against US targets and assets—including the US Embassy in Baghdad—intensified in the second half of 2020 and continue in 2021.

One of the results of this escalation is growing tensions between the Iraqi government and the Iranian-backed Shi'ite militias. The Iraqi government needs to make a decision. Are they going to preserve the sovereignty of Iraq or surrender to the Iranian-backed militias?

The Battle for Iraqi Sovereignty

Will Iranian influence, interference, and intervention in Iraq be irreversible to the point Iraq's domestic and regional policies will be determined in Tehran? Or will Iraq balk Iranian efforts and regain its independence and sovereignty?

Like in Lebanon, if the Iranian-backed PMU Iraqi militias continue to use their weapons—which are provided to them by none other than the Iraqi government—to subdue Iraq's domestic and regional policy to Iran's interests, Iraq will neither be independent nor sovereign.

Just as in Lebanon, disarming those militias in Iraq is an extraordinarily challenging task. In a June 2020 article called "Al-Kadhimi and Iranian Armed Militias," Jordanian commentator Dr. Fateen al-Baddad wrote, "Iranian-backed armed militias are defying and challenging Iraq and the Iraqi people ... There are two options. One is that those militias armed by Iran to their teeth will be incorporated into the Iraqi armed forces. The other option is that they continue to impose and dictate Iran's will on the poor Iraqis."[136]

In June 2020, Iraqi SWAT teams stormed the Iranian-backed Iraqi Kataib Hezbollah militia base in Baghdad. The operation reportedly intercepted rocket attacks Kataib Hezbollah was getting ready to launch against the US Embassy in Baghdad. Iraqi forces arrested thirteen militants, including, according to one report, an Iranian rocket expert.[137] Leaders of the Iranian-backed Iraqi militias widely condemned this operation. In response, Qais al-Khazali, the leader of the Iranian-backed Iraqi militia, 'Asaib Ahl al-Haq, made a speech. He directly addressed Iraqi Prime Minister Mustafa al-Kadhimi. He urged him to continue the policy of his predecessor, 'Adel Abd al-Mahdi, and tolerate attacks on US targets in Iraq. A few days later, the arrested militants were released.

On July 6, 2020, an Iraqi analyst and a former advisor on counterterror affairs for the Iraqi government, Hisham al-Hashimi, was assassinated in Baghdad. Al-Hashimi was an expert on militant Islamist groups and was known for his robust opposition to Iran's Iraq intervention.

In July 2020, al-Kadhimi announced that the Iraqi government had decided to confiscate the weapons of the Iraqi southern Shi'ite tribes and their political parties. Observers doubt that this Iraqi government—or any Iraqi government—will be able to do that. The chief of police of Basra's Iraqi southern city said that the number of weapons held by non-governmental entities in Basra alone is equal to two fully armed divisions.[138] As of 2021, al-Kadhimi's statement about confiscating the weapons remains on paper.

In 2021, al-Kadhimi's "nationalist" government has the support of the prominent Shi'ite, Sunni, and Kurdish parties. However, to keep that support, it needs to act quickly and simultaneously on two fronts.

First, al-Kadhimi has to address the domestic challenges. His government needs to prove to Iraqis that his administration can improve their everyday lives. If it fails to speedily—and effectively—address Iraq's challenges, the government will face increasing demonstrations of public unrest.

Two, in the face of Iran's intervention, al-Kadhimi's government needs to restore Iraq's sovereignty. In May 2021, al-Kadhimi ordered the removal of billboards showing pictures of Qasem Soleimani, the commander of the Iranian elite al-Quds force that the United States eliminated in January 2020; Ayatollah Ruhollah Khomeini, the founder of the Islamic Revolution who established the Islamic Republic of Iran by overthrowing the Shah of Iran in 1979 and who was the supreme leader of Iran until he died in 1989; Ali Khamenei, the supreme leader of Iran since 1989; and Abu Mahdi al-Muhandis, the Iraqi commander of the Popular Mobilization units who was killed with Qasem Soleimani. The billboards were provocatively posted in a predominately Sunni neighborhood in Baghdad.

The billboard incident in May 2021 was the beginning of a direct power struggle between the Iraqi government and the Iranian-backed PMU al-Wilaiyah militias.

On May 26, the Iraqi government arrested a senior PMU military official named Qasem al-Musleh, who is close to the Iranian Revolutionary Guards. He was suspected of being involved in the assassination of political activists affiliated with the Iraqi nationalist camp. Following the arrest, Iranian-backed PMU militias descended on Baghdad. They surrounded and lay siege to the capitol city's high-security area called the Green Zone, where foreign embassies, diplomatic missions, and the government's top headquarters are located.

After several days of negotiations and mediation, al-Musleh was released. The Iraqi government stated that the reason for the release was that they found no conclusive evidence for the allegations.

The episode resulted in mixed—and conflicting—reactions in Iraq and the Arab world. The Iraqi government presented the arrest of al-Musleh as an expression of sovereignty. Both Iraqi Prime Minister al-Kadhimi and the Iraqi minister of defense, Juma And, maintained that the government's decision does not reflect weakness but is a wise and responsible decision to prevent bloodshed. On the other hand, others argue the episode demonstrates the weakness of the Iraqi government, the lack of Iraqi sovereignty, and the strengthening grip of Iran in Iraq.[139]

The one thing most commentators agree on is that the incident deepened the friction between the Iraqi nationalists and the Iranian-backed militias. Some argue that the incident also heightened the tensions within the Iranian-backed PMU al-Wilaiyah militias.[140] Being an Iraqi citizen in an Iranian-backed Iraqi militia that supports Iranian intervention in Iraq creates friction with friends, family, and the greater Iraqi society. This tension inevitably percolates into al-Wilaiyah militias. .

I argue that this story clearly demonstrates that the Iraqi government is not the sole sovereign of Iraq and that the road to Iraq's sovereignty is long and turbulent.

On the Road to Independence and a New State?

In 2021, Iraqis—like the Lebanese—may find solace in the fact that they are aware of the need for governmental accountability and civic responsibility as a fundamental condition for the possible formation of a new nation-state model. Young Iraqis are willing to die—and are doing so—to get that message across. And the Iraqi government is getting the message.

When demonstrations erupted in October 2019, the Iraqi government abandoned the protesters and left them to their fate. Pro-Iranian Iraqi Shi'ite militias suppressed the protesters (mostly Shi'ites) by deliberately firing live ammunition and executing them in the streets in cold blood. About six hundred protesters were killed in the demonstrations, and thousands were injured during the October 2019 and early 2020 demonstrations in Iraq. The 2019 protests secured a place in the hall of fame of Iraq's national narrative. The protests were popularly known as the "tuk-tuk protests." A tuk-tuk is a small, motorized rickshaw that they use in Iraq for taxis. Lacking any official government response, the tuk-tuk drivers risked their own lives to rescue the wounded and the dead from the streets and took them under fire to hospitals.

One year later, in October 2020, thousands of Iraqis marked the anniversary of the protests. This time the scene was entirely different. Iraqi security forces were deployed in the streets to secure order and to protect the protesters. There were isolated cases of violence. But it was evident government forces were making every effort to avoid harming the protesters.

Iraqi researcher Dr. Bahira al-Sheikhly wrote an article in October 2020, "The ethnic-based political parties in Iraq change their skin." She argues that the younger generation's growing weight has not gone unnoticed by the Iraqi political parties. The politicians are trying to gain the support of young people by blurring or disguising their ethnic agenda and creating 'ghost parties' that will compete in the elections. However, she argues, this camouflage and fraud does not fool the young generation. She sums up by saying, "the young Iraqi generation continues to make its way through the jungle of militias and Iraqi politics."[141]

I cannot think of a better way to describe present-day Iraq.

Like the Lebanese, Iraqis face tremendous challenges in building a functional society and a healthier nation-state. Iraq is a chaotic, violent, and dangerous country. In an unstable and volatile environment—plagued with endless wars, unrelenting violence, deep corruption, staggering poverty, and unemployment—Iraqis have had to learn to fend for themselves in a failed state with a completely dysfunctional government. In such an environment, where you have learned to rely only on yourself, it is challenging to instill a sense of civic duty and social responsibility. Furthermore, in an environment where the most prevalent way to solve problems between the various groups and sects is through violence and weapons, creating mechanisms to bridge differences and solve conflicts through fruitful dialogue will not be easy.

In January 2021, the Iraqi government announced that general elections, which had been scheduled to take place in June 2021, had been postponed to October 2021. The elections—should they take place—will find Iraq at a critical juncture.

Iraq's destiny as a country will be defined first and foremost by the outcome of the power struggle between Iraqi Shi'ite nationalists and Iranian-backed Iraqi Shi'ite militias and politicians. That power struggle is currently playing out in two major power centers in Iraq—the PMU and the Iraqi political system. And as of 2021, the tension between the two camps is overt and escalating.

If Iraq wants to take the path toward building a possible new statehood model, it must demonstrate its sovereignty decisively. And to that end, Iraq must end, one way or another, the Iranian-backed Iraqi Shi'ite militias' ability to dictate Iran's will on Iraq. This move may involve a violent collision between the camps.

I opened this section quoting Iraqi analyst Dr. Majid al-Samarrai who, in March 2020, wrote that the struggle is between "Nationalist Iraqi Shi'ites and Non-Nationalist Iraqi Shi'ites."[142] I hope this section has explained that quote and given you more insight into Iraqi society's increasing fragmentation.

The Arab Energy Network Project: A Strategic Project to Loosen Iran's Grip on Iraq, Lebanon, and Syria?

In his struggle to restore Iraq's sovereignty and thwart Iran's intervention, al-Kadhimi turns to his natural hub—the Arab world.

In October 2020, Prime Minister Mostafa Kamal Madbouly of Egypt, accompanied by several Egyptian ministers, visited Iraq. In Baghdad, al-Kadhimi and his Egyptian counterpart, who also co-chair the Egyptian-Iraqi High Commission for Cooperation of the two countries, signed fifteen MOUs (Memoranda of Understandings) and cooperation protocols. During his official visit, the Egyptian prime minister declared that Iraq and Egypt will advance cooperation in Iraq based on the principle of "oil in exchange for development."[143]

In November 2020, a high-level Saudi delegation visited Baghdad. The two countries signed agreements in the fields of agriculture, defense, trade, etc. The joint concluding statement implicitly references Saudi Arabia and

Iraq's shared interest in curbing Iranian aggression. As part of the Saudi-Iraqi rapprochement, the Ar'ar border crossing between Iraq and Saudi Arabia was opened in December 2020 after having been closed for decades.

In June 2021, al-Kadhimi hosted a small summit with the president of Egypt, Abd al-Fatah al-Sisi, and King Abdullah II of Jordan. It was the first time in thirty years that an Egyptian president had visited Iraq. The summit's final statement, issued on June 27, confirmed the expansion of tripartite cooperation and trilateral collaboration.

> The final statement of the Trilateral Leaders' Summit (Iraq, Jordan, Egypt) emphasizes and reaffirms the keenness to strengthen the partnership and relationship between the Republic of Iraq, the Hashemite Kingdom of Jordan, and the Arab Republic of Egypt within the framework of a tripartite cooperation mechanism, and based on the sincere desire of the three brotherly countries to enhance paths of cooperation and increase coordination mechanisms within the political, economic, commercial, industrial, security and other fields. With the aim of continuing to establish the factors of prosperity and the elements of development, and to promote joint efforts in pursuit of

OPEC Members

Algeria
Angola
Equatorial Guinea Gabon
Iran
Iraq
Kuwait
Libya
Nigeria
Republic of the Congo
Saudi Arabia
United Arab Emirates
Venezuela

OPEC (Organization of the Petroleum Exporting Countries) Members strategic integration, cooperation, coordination and strategic integration between the three sister countries, Iraq, Jordan, and Egypt.[144]

One of the central focal points of regional cooperation and friction is in the field of energy.

Iraq, Lebanon, Syria, and Iran are struggling to keep the lights on—literally. None of these countries have enough electricity. Not surprisingly, this acute energy crisis has geopolitical ramifications. Electricity and oil are part and parcel of the power struggle for control of the land corridor that connects Iran, Iraq, Syria, and Lebanon.

GCC (The Cooperation Council for the Arab States of the Gulf) Members

Iraq is OPEC's (Organization of the Petroleum Exporting Countries) second-largest oil producer. Despite this, Iraq's electrical grid is insufficient. It is not able to create enough electricity for Iraq. Therefore, Baghdad relies on Tehran for about 40 percent of Iraq's electricity. Iran providing electricity to Iraq is ironic because Iran doesn't have enough electricity to run its own country or provide its own citizens.

Here is the situation in Iran in July 2021: "regular blackouts spread chaos and confusion on the streets of the capitol, Tehran, and other cities, knocking out traffic lights, shutting factories, disrupting telecommunications, and affecting metro systems. Repeaters—devices around cities that enhance mobile phone signals—have failed, along with electronic cash registers. Towns in Iran's north reported limited access to water because the power cuts affected the piped supply."[145]

Iran's electricity infrastructure is falling apart. But that did not stop Iran from signing an agreement with Iraq in 2020 to supply Iraq with electricity for a minimum of two years.[146] By continuing to keep Iraq dependent on Iran for electricity, Iran deepens its hold on Iraq. Providing electricity to Iraq, Syria, and Lebanon is one of Iran's tools to build and keep its grip on the land corridor.

Iraq is looking to diversify its electricity providers and perhaps also to loosen Iran's grip. Over the past few years, Iraq has signed several energy agreements with regional partners aside from Iran. Between 2019 and 2021, Iraq and Saudi Arabia signed multiple MOUs in various fields—including Saudi Arabia supplying energy to Iraq. The deals with Saudi Arabia are in addition to agreements Iraq signed with the GCC for a transmissions line from Kuwait[147] and solar and renewable energy projects with the UAE.[148] And Iraq is not only looking to solidify energy agreements with the Arab Gulf. In September 2020, Iraq and Jordan signed agreements that Jordan would supply Iraq with electricity by connecting Iraq to Jordan's electrical grids.[149] There are also plans to connect Egypt as well to the same grid.

And beyond the region, in August 2020, Iraqi Prime Minister Mustafa al-Kadhimi went to the United States. To boost Iraq's energy independence from Iran, the Iraqi government signed over $8 billion of energy agreements with five major US energy companies during his visit. [150]

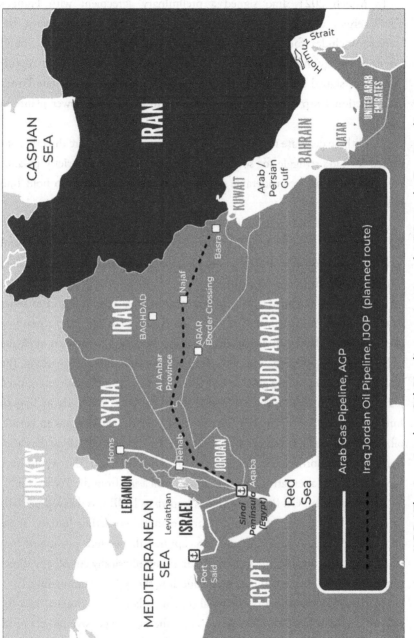

IJOP (The Iraq Jordan Oil Pipeline project) and AGP (Arab Gas Pipeline)

In March 2021, Iraq signed a preliminary agreement with France's TotalEnergies, a French multinational integrated oil and gas company. The contract includes four projects to develop oil fields, produce gas, build extensive energy infrastructure, and generate solar energy.[151] And in August 2021, Iraq signed a deal with the Chinese state-owned conglomerate Power Construction Corp of China (Power China) to build solar power plants in Iraq.[152]

All of these deals are not only about electricity. The efforts are directly connected to Iraq's struggle for sovereignty. Iraq reducing its electricity reliance on Iran would be a considerable step in reducing Iran's ability to hold Iraq hostage to Iran's will.

Iraq's regional and global outreach and alliances might explain the fact that throughout the summer of 2021, unknown factors continue to attack and sabotage Iraq's electricity infrastructure. It is very likely these attacks are linked to the struggle for Iraqi sovereignty.[153]

In parallel to Baghdad's plans to connect the Iraqi electrical grid to other Arab countries, in the summer of 2021, Iraq and Jordan agreed to reexamine the feasibility of laying an oil pipeline from southern Iraq to the port of Aqaba in Jordan. Currently, Jordan imports nearly 97 percent of its energy needs. The plan they are reexamining goes back to 2013 when Iraq and Jordan announced plans to build a dual-purpose pipeline from the Basra oil fields in Iraq to Jordan's Red Sea port of Aqaba. The proposed pipeline, carrying gas and crude oil, would stretch from southeastern Iraq, near the city of Najaf, along the Saudi borders, to the northernmost point of the Red Sea. For Iraq, this would have provided Iraq an alternative route to export its oil aside from the Persian Gulf.

The Iraq Jordan Oil Pipeline project, known as IJOP, was delayed in 2014 when Iraq lost control of the al-Anbar province—bordering Jordan, Syria, and Saudi Arabia—to ISIS. When ISIS captured the western portion of Iraq (the Al-Anbar province), the militant Islam group physically cut off any direct route to Jordan. That, of course, made building the pipeline impossible.

In 2017, Iraq canceled the original pipeline plan. The estimated cost for the original plan was $18 billion, making it the most expensive project of its kind in the world. Instead, Iraq decided to build only a crude oil pipeline, with an estimated price tag of $5 to $7 billion.[154]

In July 2019, the Iraqi Cabinet approved the Iraq Jordan Oil Pipeline. According to a statement by the nation's oil ministry, the IJOP would increase Iraq's export capacity by one million barrels per day.[155] Iraqi Prime Minister 'Adel Abd al-Mahdi announced that the Council of Ministers approved the Iraqi Jordanian Oil Pipeline project. He stressed that any impediment to exporting oil through the Strait of Hormuz would affect the Iraqi economy, which depends on oil exports. The official statement emphasized that the Iraqi government was considering alternatives to find diverse routes to ensure the continuation of swift Iraqi oil exports.[156] The portion of the planned pipeline linking Najaf to Aqaba will provide between 150,000 to 200,000 BPD to Jordan. At the same time, the rest would be transported to Egypt and the international market. Because the pipeline ends in Jordan's port in Aqaba, it has been reported that Jordan would receive up to $3 billion a year.[157]

Is an Arab Energy Network Project Feasible? Is the IJOP a Solution?

Some assess that connecting Iraq and Egypt to the Jordanian power grid will decrease Iran's grip on Iraq.

However, others argue the opposite, saying that it will increase Iran's influence because it will make Jordan and Egypt dependent on cheap Iraqi oil.[158] According to that outlook, Iran will benefit because the revenues Iraq will gain from the oil deal with Jordan and Egypt will be allocated to fund al-Hashd al-Sha'abi. Including the Iranian-backed al-Wilaiyah Iraqi militias. In other words, Iraqi oil will fund Iran's takeover of Iraq. That is the perfect deal for Iran.

However, the feasibility of IJOP is questionable. As attractive as cheap Iraqi oil is to Egypt and Jordan, both will be reluctant to rely on a more-than-a-thousand-mile-long oil pipeline that could be an easy target for attack for terrorists. Militant Islam groups frequently attack the Egyptian gas and oil infrastructure in the Sinai Peninsula. So, their concern is warranted, and the danger is very acute.

Second, Jordan has historically relied primarily on natural gas coming from Egypt's Arab Gas Pipeline (AGP). The AGP is a trans-regional gas export pipeline built to carry natural gas from Egypt to Jordan, Syria, and Lebanon. Jordan's other current gas source is the Israel-Jordan 65-kilometer pipeline that supplies natural gas to Jordan from Israel's largest offshore natural gas field Leviathan. Currently, these are Jordan's leading energy suppliers.

Third, Egypt and Jordan both have access to immediate and secured oil supply from Saudi Arabia.

Connecting Lebanon to the Jordanian Electricity Grid and the AGP through Syria?

In August 2021, an interesting episode occurred that illustrates the importance of the energy issue (in this case, electricity) in the context of the regional power struggle over the land corridor.

As Lebanon continued to spiral and crumble, on August 20, 2021, the United States informed Lebanon that it had decided to help the country get electricity from Jordan through Syria. This is the route. Egypt would supply more natural gas to Jordan through the AGP. Jordan would then use the natural gas to generate additional electricity. The extra electricity would then flow through Syria to Lebanon. The deal would also help facilitate the transfer of natural gas to Lebanon through the AGP.[159]

According to United States Ambassador Dorothy Shea, "Negotiations are ongoing with the World Bank to secure funding for the Egyptian gas and repair, reinforce, and maintain power lines and gas pipelines. The World Bank is willing to provide help with funding such a project under the condition that Lebanese officials agree to strict measures of transparency and the implementation of the World Bank's model."[160,161]

It is important to note that Ambassador Shea's comments came on the heels of Hezbollah's Secretary-General Hassan Nasrallah's August 19, 2021, announcement. On that day, he announced that Hezbollah had organized a shipment of Iranian fuel oil that would be setting sail for Lebanon. Nasrallah warned the US and Israel that the ship would be considered Lebanese soil as soon as it set sail. He went on to say that other ships would follow to help the Lebanese people who are enduring crippling fuel shortages because of the country's two-year-long financial meltdown.[162]

Reportedly, the United States had been working on this deal for months.[163] But the timing of the US announcements underscores the need to free Lebanon of Hezbollah and Iran's control.

This project, if implemented, has many benefits for the al-Assad regime. The electricity that will pass through Syria will help provide more energy to Syria, whose infrastructure has been decimated. In addition, the al-Assad government will be able to tax Lebanon for the gas that will flow through Syria to Lebanon. And of course, it would be an important step toward rehabilitating the regime and facilitating the path to remove sanctions on the government.

However, using the AGP infrastructure has several obstacles. First, there are hundreds of kilometers of electricity and gas lines, most of which pass through Syrian territory and are therefore vulnerable to attacks and sabotage. Second, implementing such a project would require a very complex set of commercial, economic, and legal agreements between the four relevant countries—Egypt, Jordan, Lebanon, and Syria—regarding responsibilities, financial investments, profit sharing, etc. Third, the Biden administration will have to get the United States Congress's approval to remove the sanctions over the al-Assad regime.

As of August 2021, in my estimation, the most important aspect of this project is that it could potentially expedite a process to end Iran's military presence in Syria. Why? The project is very tempting to al-Assad. The benefits to the regime are clear. Yet, the price is also clear. In exchange for implementing the project, al-Assad will have to comply with the international community, and Arab countries demand to carry out fundamental political reforms in Syria. Especially, he is expected to put an end to the Iranian military presence in Syria.

Iraq, Syria, and Lebanon: The Tragic Loop of Destruction—A Summary

This chapter looked at three Arab countries—Syria, Lebanon, and Iraq—as of 2021. The picture is bleak. And in the case of Syria, catastrophic.

Two common denominators have brought these countries to their bleak circumstances.

One is the failure of the modern nation-state. This failure is the bitter fruit of the fact that in these three countries (like other Arab states such as Libya, Somalia, Sudan, and Yemen), ethnicity, religion, tribalism, and narrow

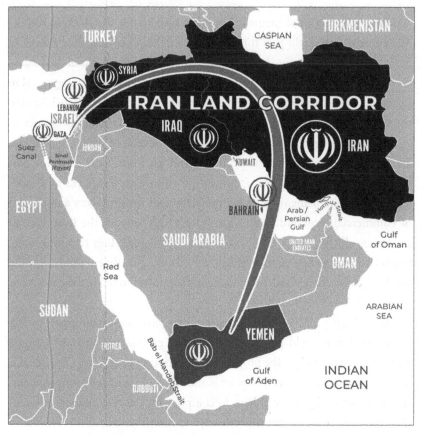

Iranian Corridor and Shi'ite Crescent

particularistic interest politics have been more powerful than the core values which are critical to the existence of a functioning nation-state: civic responsibility, governmental accountability, and the rule of law.

The other thing that Iraq, Lebanon, and Syria have in common is the fact that they have fallen prey to the hegemonic vision of the Iranian regime. Pay attention to the map. These three countries make up the land corridor, a critical component of the Iranian regime's hegemonic strategy that we have discussed at length in this book.

The failure of these countries as nation-states played into the hands of the Iranian regime. The mullah regime exploited the weakness of these states to take them over by armed force and with great sophistication.

The combination of failed states and Iran's hegemonic aspirations are how Iraq, Lebanon, and Syria were subjected to a cruel loop of destruction, disintegration, and death.

The area stretching from the Mediterranean shores of Lebanon, through Syria and Iraq to Iran, is one of the most volatile areas of the Middle East. The developments in this arena will have enormous significance on the geostrategic construct and characteristics of the Middle East as we move into the new era. The ramifications of the developments in that arena will exceed the region.

The Possible Emergence of a New Statehood Model in the Middle East: A Short Summary and Looking Ahead

The twentieth-century models of the nation-state in the Middle East face severe challenges and, in some cases, have failed. Traditional affiliations and identities—denomination, ethnicity, geographical region, religion, tribal structure, etc.—were more powerful than the concept of statehood.

Although it existed, the idea of statehood, particularistic nationalism as a source of solidarity that binds different sectors, was a secondary component of people's individual and collective identity.

The state's failure is one of the leading causes of constant instability and chaos in the Middle East.

The traditional elements of identity that shape the political system and social fabric in the Arab world will not disappear.

However, as of 2021, I maintain that some Arab countries have begun to walk the path toward building a new pact between citizens and states. And this could be the foundation for the building of a new statehood model.

This process is primarily the outcome of a combination of three main trends in the Arab/Muslim world:

- Increasing pragmatism and the growing weight of particularistic nationalism on political Islam's agenda.
- The rising presence, impact, and political power of civil society, which are supported and intensified by the ease of communication, the Internet, and social media.

- The assimilation of concepts of government accountability as well as civic responsibility.

Given these trends, despite all the severe inner challenges Arab countries across the Middle East struggle with—and they are many—the current environment offers the region's peoples an opportunity to foster the emergence of a new, more successful statehood model. The pace and scale of change varies from country to country. And the road is long, complex, and turbulent. However, to the best of my evaluation, that process is evolving and gaining momentum in Algeria, Egypt, the Gulf Arab monarchies, Jordan, Morocco, Sudan, and Tunisia.

When looking at Iraq, Lebanon, Libya, Syria, and Yemen, the picture is totally different.

Realistically, in 2021, it is very difficult to imagine the emergence of a more successful national model in Libya, Syria, or Yemen.

At the time I am writing this book, I do not detect a particularistic national consciousness or any kind of national-patriotic unity that can bring the people of those countries to a place where they can be 'one people under one flag.'

Libya instead seems to be on the path toward a national federal structure—a confederation of entities reflecting its geography and tribal political power centers.

Yemen has practically disintegrated.

Syria is formally under the sovereign rule of the al-Assad regime. However, in practice, a quarter of its inhabitants have fled, and another quarter have become refugees in their own land. Furthermore, Syria is controlled by various regional and international forces—namely Iran, Russia, and Turkey. They are more focused on gaining the spoils of war than they are on the welfare and fate of the Syrians.

I struggle at this point of time to see Libyans, Syrians, and Yemenites coming around one flag willingly.

In the case of Iraq and Lebanon, it is possible to imagine most Lebanese and Iraqis volunteering to unite under one flag. And one of the reasons for that is that the growing Iranian intervention has generated a counter-reaction—a strengthening of particularistic nationalist consciousness in both Iraq and Lebanon that was previously largely absent. In the face of their homeland being occupied, commandeered, and appropriated for Iran's dangerous, violent, and deadly hegemonic ambitions, Iraqis and Lebanese from across the ideological and political spectrum have found their patriotism. They don't want to see their heritage, history, and homeland sacrificed on the altar of the Shi'ite mullah regime's apocalyptic vision.

However, as of August 2021, the only thing that can be said for sure about Iraq and Lebanon is that they have failed to address the two primary reasons for their grim reality successfully. Namely their corrupt political systems, their ethnic sectarianism, and Iran's suffocating hold over their countries.

It will take a highly complex operation and set of conditions to end Iran's occupation of Iraq, Lebanon, and Syria. And it will require regional and international intervention and support. One of the critical, if not the key, questions is how determined are the Iraqis, Lebanese, and Syrians to rid themselves of Iranian control? Will they be resilient enough to regain their sovereignty and independence at all costs? Ultimately, the degree of their determination will determine their fate. The question is, will the terrible price the Syrians have paid in their—as of now—failed struggle for independence deter or incentivize the Iraqis and Lebanese? The answer is in their hands.

CHAPTER 7

COVID-19 AND A NEW MODEL OF NATIONAL STATEHOOD IN THE MIDDLE EAST

A Brief Look at COVID-19 in the Middle East

Unexpected events have a way of accelerating and condensing long-term processes into a short timeline. The COVID-19 pandemic that is gripping the world in 2020 and 2021 has the potential to be such an event.

The COVID-19 pandemic caught the Middle East at a particularly critical and delicate juncture. The region is facing complex and intensifying challenges. The early seeds of possible new models of national statehood are beginning to sprout. And Iraqis, Lebanese, and Syrians are in the throes of fighting for their independence and survival. What impact will the pandemic—and its ramifications—have on the evolution and trajectory of these processes?

For all countries globally, COVID-19 presents two significant severe threats: the collapse of medical systems and the collapse of the economy. Both threats separately, let alone combined, can endanger the fabric of society and public order. Failing to address these challenges will likely fuel the current unrest and increase turbulence and instability.

The COVID-19 pandemic did not skip the Middle East. Here are the officially reported fatality figures as of August 2021: Turkey (pop. 84 million people—52,565 deaths); Tunisia (pop. 11.5 million—21,220 deaths); Iraq (pop. 38 .5 million—19,402 deaths); Egypt (pop. 100 million—16,597 deaths); Jordan (pop. almost 10 million, including hundreds of thousands of Syrian refugees in northern Jordan—10,158 deaths); Morocco (pop. 36 million—10,607 deaths); Saudi Arabia (pop. 33.7 million—8,311 deaths);

Lebanon (pop. 6.8 million—7,958); Israel (pop. 9.5 million people—6,587 deaths); Algeria (pop. 42 million—4654 deaths); Oman (pop. 4.8 million—3,968 deaths); West Bank & Gaza Strip (pop. 3.6 million—3,601 deaths); Libya (pop. 6.6 million—3,811 deaths); Sudan (pop. 41.8 million people—2,776 deaths); Kuwait (pop. 4.1 million—2,378 deaths); United Arab Emirates (pop. 9.6 million—1,988 deaths); Syria (pop. 17 million people—1,927 deaths); Bahrain (1.5 million—1,384 deaths); Yemen (pop. 28.5 million—1,392 deaths); and Qatar (pop. 2.7 million—601 deaths).[1]

I do want to caution that we have to take the statistics with a grain of salt. The data's reliability is questionable and may not have been accurately reported due to political calculations or an inefficient or dysfunctional health system, particularly in Iraq, Lebanon, Libya, Syria, and Yemen.

That said, these figures suggest that in August 2021, the Middle East's death toll is within—perhaps even below—global statistics of the COVID-19 death toll. That is puzzling, given that countries in the region have large populations and dense communities. What increased the concern was that the medical and sanitation services and hygienic infrastructure in many countries in the area are limited and insufficient—and sometimes extremely minimal, like in Syria, Iraq, and Yemen.

Some of the suggested explanations for the low death toll in the region have been: the majority of the populations in the Middle East are young people; compared to Europe, the volume of foreigners visiting is small, and therefore, the spread of the disease is smaller; and the region's warm climate is a less optimal environment for the virus. One of the most interesting theories was a preliminary study published by the Society of Genetic Engineers in Jordan (JSGE) claiming that people of Middle Eastern origin might have a genetic variation, making them less likely to contract the disease. They have a specific DNA element, "SNPS" (a polymorphism in single-nucleotide polymorphism), differing them from East Asia and Europe. And that genetic variation may make their lungs more resistant to the virus. According to the study, the immunity comes from the difference in the number of pulmonary receptors, such as ACE-2, the coronavirus receptor, to enter human cells, between those of Middle Eastern origin and those from East Asia and Europe.[2]

But I must emphasize that as COVID-19 began to spread in the region, most Middle East governments made a concerted effort to stem the disease's spread. They enacted and enforced strict measures to prevent the spread of the pandemic. They launched public service campaigns, implemented curfews, isolated cities, imposed travel restrictions, shut down stores, prohibited gatherings, closed mosques, and asked people to pray at home.

There were governments in the region—like Jordan, Saudi Arabia, and the UAE—who, from the beginning of the crisis and at critical points in the spread of the disease, developed a reliable and healthy dialogue with their citizens and took concrete action to confront the disease. The UAE built the world's second-largest laboratory to process dozens of thousands of tests per day. In April 2020, Egyptian President Abd al-Fatah al-Sisi announced that the Egyptian army built six hospitals with 1,200 beds.

Even if the regional statistics are less than stellar, Iran is unquestionably at the epicenter of the COVID-19 pandemic in the Middle East.

According to the Johns Hopkins University (JHU) Coronavirus Resource Center, in mid-July 2021, the death toll in Iran was more than 89,479 people.[3] However, the Iranian opposition group, the People's Mojahedin Organization of Iran (PMOI/MEK), continually argues that the death toll is much higher. In January 2021, the organization claimed that more than 203,000 people[4] had lost their lives across Iran due to COVID-19.[5] In August 2021, the opposition group argued that over 357,200 people have died of the novel coronavirus in 547 cities across all of Iran's thirty-one provinces. The official death toll declared by the regime stands at 95,647, around a fourth of the actual figure.[6]

There are good reasons to assume that Iran's death toll is higher than the Iranian government's official data. I base my assessment on the following information.

On April 15, 2020, a report attributed to the Research Center of the Iranian Parliament reported the death toll in Iran from COVID-19 was 8,600.[7] On the same day, Iranian Deputy Health Minister Ali Rida Raisi admitted that the actual number of infected in Iran is "significantly much bigger than the figures provided by the government."[8] And then, on April 21, 2020, a spokesperson for the Iranian Ministry of Health announced that the death toll was 5,297.[9]

Another piece of information also supports the assumption that the death toll is higher than the government reported. According to opposition sources, a classified study conducted by the Pandemic Task Force in the Iranian Ministry of Health was submitted to the government by the Research Center of the Iranian Parliament in April 2020. This report anticipated a second deadly wave that would result in the death of more than thirty thousand people. Mohammed Qasemi, the director of the Research Center of the Iranian Parliament, denied that information, claiming it was "false."[10]

There is no question—whatever the exact number—that Iran is the epicenter of the COVID-19 outbreak in the Middle East. The main reason for this is that the regime simply hid the fact that the virus was spreading in Iran for a long time. Information I evaluate as reliable presents a fascinating chronology of the outbreak and spread of COVID-19 in Iran. The Iranian regime reportedly had information about the virus very early—as early as late December 2019/early January 2020. Moreover, they worked in lockstep with China from the early stages of the crisis.[11] The Iranian government concealed the information from the Iranians and increased the spread of the epidemic in Iran.

On February 3, 2020, a privately owned Iranian-UK news network reported that a Chinese person from Wuhan working in Iran was hospitalized in Iran.[12] In late March, the regime indirectly confirmed that information when an official spokesperson acknowledged that the coronavirus was already spreading in Iran in mid to late January 2020.[13] Until February 19, 2020, the government continued to deny any reports of coronavirus infections in Iran. However, it published guidelines on how to protect oneself from the virus, including limiting the size of gatherings and practicing personal hygiene—but it denied the virus was present in Iran. On February 21, 2020—at least a month after Iranian leaders knew the coronavirus was in Iran—the government held parliamentary elections, which brought millions to gather at the voting stations. Mass pilgrimages of Iranians and non-Iranians to the holy Shi'ite religious sites in cities like Mashhad and Qom continued unabated. Public transportation, commercial activity, and markets operated as usual. It was not until the last week in March that the government announced the application of hygiene practices, social distancing guidelines, closed businesses, and offices, and quarantines and travel restrictions. To add fuel to the fire, on April 21, 2020, 'Ali Rida Marandi, the head of the medical task force advising Iran's supreme leader, sent a letter to President Hasan Rouhani urging him to order mosques to reopen.[14] Indeed, reportedly the authorities ordered all mosques in mid-May to reopen.[15]

Iran's authorities did not bother addressing the challenge of COVID-19. If there was any doubt, President Rouhani's announcement in July 2020 that the Iranian Ministry of Health evaluated that a staggering 25 million Iranians were infected[16] proved the government did practically nothing to protect the people.

The mullah regime deliberately kept its citizens in the dark. Authorities provided misleading announcements, confused and inconsistent policies and statements. They followed a continuous and deliberate effort to conceal accumulating and life-threatening—or life-saving—information from the public. Given that, one can understand why Iran is one of the epicenters of the pandemic.

The coronavirus death toll in Iran should particularly concern countries like Iraq, Lebanon, and Syria. Iranian traffic into these countries is unmonitored, and the Iranian presence in those states is unsupervised. In the spring of 2020, Iranian officials announced they would resume Shi'ite pilgrimages from Iran to Iraq and Syria. On March 8, the Iraqi authorities shut five commercial crossing points with Iran in an effort to contain the spread of coronavirus in Iraq. The Iraqi government announced that its borders with Iran would remain closed.[17] However, over the summer of 2020, three border passages between the two countries—two in south Iraq and one in central Iraq—were open, and they remain open today.[18]

Managing COVID-19 and the New Statehood Model— Preliminary Reflections

Looking retrospectively, as of mid-2021, almost one and a half years after the outbreak of COVID-19, I believe that the factors that I posit could generate the possible emergence of a new nation-state model, namely: growing pragmatism and the prioritization of particularistic nationalism in political Islam, the growing power of civil society entities and values, and the assimilation of government accountability and civic responsibility were present during the COVID crisis.

Let's look closer to see how those components exhibited themselves throughout the crisis.

During COVID, political Islam parties demonstrated pragmatism—prioritizing particularistic nationalism over religion was a top priority. The Muslim establishment worked closely with governments to reduce the infection rates. They closed mosques and banned pilgrimages to Islamic sites, including the most important Muslim religious observance and ritual—the annual *al-Haj* and *Umrah* pilgrimage to Mecca. And when the ban on pilgrimages lifted, meticulous means to reduce infection were applied.

Another interesting example has to do with the COVID-19 vaccine. Muslim scholars in Malaysia and Indonesia expressed concern with using the vaccine because it contains gelatin extracted from hogs—an animal Islam views as impure.[19] On the other hand, the Egyptian Authority for Islamic Ordinance, *Dar al-Ifta Al-Misriyyah*, issued a fatwah permitting the use of the vaccine. Their ruling argued that the gel's nature changes when it is extracted from hog to make the vaccine. Therefore, from an Islamic law perspective, it is permissible to get vaccinated.[20]

When it comes to governmental accountability, it was clear that many governments did take proactive measures to make up-to-date information accessible. Whether online or through public service advertising campaigns, most governments tried to communicate and provide instructions for the public. Most governments took preventive measures such as inspecting public facilities, airports, etc. And some took more extreme steps like lockdowns, curfews, closing schools, shops, and businesses, limiting or stopping public transportation.

As of August 2021, the threat of collapsing medical systems because of COVID-19 has not happened in the region. The economies of Arab countries (excluding Lebanon, Syria, and Yemen, whose economy is destroyed for other reasons) did not collapse.

It would be too extreme to say that the fact that medical facilities and economies in Arab countries did not collapse under the strain of the COVID-19 crisis indicates that a new statehood model is here.

However, I believe the fact that economies and medical systems did not collapse because of the crisis can be partially attributed to the preventive and proactive measures governments employed and the generally responsible public cooperation.

I think it would be fair to argue that COVID-19 offered the opportunity to strengthen governmental accountability, civic responsibility, and mutual responsibility. Successfully addressing the challenge of COVID-19 can be a catalyst to enhance the relationship between citizens and their governments. If, as an outcome of governmental policy and/or mass vaccination, COVID-19 continues to be under control in Arab countries—in the sense that medical services and economies do not collapse—I believe it will augment the state's sovereignty as a social and political system and bolster its position as a unifying factor and a component of personal and collective identity.

CHAPTER 8

MIHWAR AL-E'ITIDAL—THE ALLIANCE OF MODERATION AND THE ABRAHAM ACCORDS

The Changing Geopolitical Landscape

In this book, we have dedicated a lot of time discussing Iran's and Turkey's multifaceted policies that are designed to spread their reach and influence. We have learned how Iran and Turkey benefit from and encourage instability. We have explored the impact of the Iranian and Turkish hegemonic ambitions and how the pursuit of their goals impacts and shapes the Middle East's geopolitical and geostrategic landscape. We have seen that countries across the Arab world are engaged in an ongoing struggle to define their path, identity, and direction. And some are fighting for their own survival.

There is also a linked and significant parallel process.

Arab countries working to address their economic and social challenges are looking to strengthen and diversify their economies by expanding their traditional income sources and creating a skilled workforce. They are particularly interested in leveraging technology in critical areas, including agriculture, communications, food security, health care and medicine, and water. In addition to allocating tremendous financial investments and resources, obtaining those objectives requires alliances, cooperation, and stability.

The Arab world's desire to position itself and strengthen its position in the twenty-first-century economy, hand in hand with their need to counter Turkey and Iran's hegemonic ambitions, is at heart a regional alliance that I

first introduced in this book in the chapter on Iran. This informal confederation is known as *Mihwar al E'itidal*—the "Alliance of Moderation."

The formation of this alliance was something I predicted in my 2016
book.[1]

Mihwar al E'itidal — The Alliance of Moderation—
Plus External Circle of Sudan

The members of the alliance of moderation (in alphabetical order) are Bahrain, Egypt, Jordan, Kuwait, Morocco, Oman, Saudi Arabia, and the United Arab Emirates. On the perimeter of this coalition, we can also add Arab countries like Sudan, and Tunisia, who, for the most part, advocate for and support policies that are aligned with the alliance's interests.

In its essence, the paramount goal for the alliance of moderation is stability. Stability within their own individual countries—and stability throughout the region.

There is another silent yet significant member of this coalition. And that is Israel. Israel is a regional power, and Israel is also directly threatened by the Iranian and Turkish hegemonic aspirations. The Arab members of the alliance see Israel as a stable, valuable, and strong strategic partner. Israel's role within

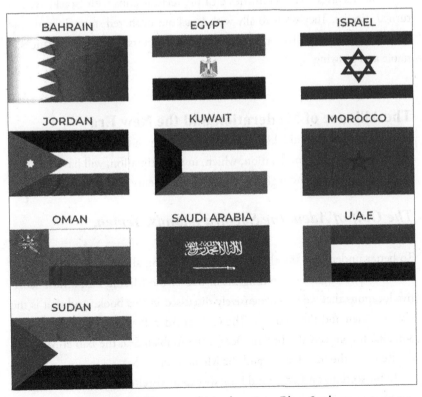

Flags of Alliance of Moderation Plus Sudan

the framework of the alliance of moderation is a very well-known secret. The relationship between Israel and the Arab Gulf monarchies has evolved and deepened. The security cooperation between Israel and Egypt as well as between Israel and Jordan has grown and expanded. One can assume Israel has a strong and strengthening intelligence and security cooperation with other members of the alliance—even with those with which Israel has no formal relations.

Many people ask me about the future of the burgeoning relationships between Israel and the Arab world in general and the Gulf countries in particular. They ask if I think they are stable and will last. In that regard, I must emphasize two things.

First, the changing Middle East has laid the foundation for the partnership between Israel and the Arab Gulf states. And second, these alliances are not based on "feelings"—the countries creating relationships with Israel have not turned Zionist. They want to ally with Israel out of shared strategic goals and long-term interests. Given this combination of factors, I see these alliances as stable and growing.

The Alliance of Moderation and the New Era

In this chapter, I would like to begin to deepen our understanding of the emerging alliance of moderation, which, in my estimation, will have a significant role in shaping the region's new era in the twenty-first century.

The Gulf of Aden, the Socotra Islands, Yemen, and the Red Sea

To better understand the threats and the emerging alliance of moderation, I would like to begin by zooming in on one of the Middle East's most sensitive locations that we have extensively discussed in this book. And that is the Gulf of Aden and the Red Sea. The Gulf of Aden flows between Yemen and Somalia. It connects the Indian Ocean, the Arabian Sea, the Bab el-Mandeb, the Red Sea, the Suez Canal, and the Mediterranean Sea.

In the sections on Turkey and Iran, we explored Tehran and Ankara's aggressive regional policy behavior in this area in depth. Iran and Turkey threaten the

Arab Gulf monarchies, Egypt, Jordan, and Israel, in this arena. Furthermore, taking advantage of the chaotic conditions in the Sinai Peninsula, Somalia, and Yemen, militant Islam groups like al-Qaeda, al-Shabab, ISIS, and others are also expanding their activities throughout the Middle East and Africa. This process increases their ability to threaten maritime traffic.

One of the most critical strategic priorities for the alliance of moderation is securing the shipping lanes connecting the Indian Ocean, the Arabian Sea, the Red Sea, and the Mediterranean.

And that, of course, brings us back to Yemen. As I have said many times, but I cannot emphasize enough, Yemen is one of the world's most strategic locations. Whoever controls Yemen and the surrounding waterways has enormous power. It is not only a regional issue—it is global.

And south of Yemen, and under Yemen's sovereignty, is the Socotra archipelago at the entrance to the Gulf of Aden. As we discussed in Chapter 3, Socotra sits on one of the world's busiest shipping lanes and the gateway to the Bab el-Mandeb and the Suez Canal—the world's most vital maritime transport routes.

This whole corridor is the fastest route between the East and the West. And right in the middle of this most sensitive passage is Socotra.

In the waterways around Yemen, Iran's most significant stronghold is the port of Al-Hodeidah, in western Yemen on the Red Sea. The Houthis, one of Iran's most essential proxies, controls Al-Hodeidah, the fourth largest city in Yemen, located about a hundred miles north of the Bab el-Mandeb Strait and Yemen's primary Red Sea port. But beyond the water, it is essential to remember that Iran has a significant influence in Yemen because it supports the Houthis. With Iran's backing, its Houthi proxy launched a coup in 2014 and occupied Yemen's capitol Sana'a until today. Thwarting Iran's takeover of Yemen is a strategic interest of the alliance. And it should be a strategic interest of the international community.

Erdoğan has also tried to gain a foothold near Yemen and Socotra. His attempt to control Socotra itself has not been successful. However, it is essential to remember that he is cultivating a proxy in southern Yemen—a militia called al-Tajamm'u al-Yamani Lil-Islah or the Yemenite Reform Coalition. And he seems to be successful in securing footholds in Qana at the entrance

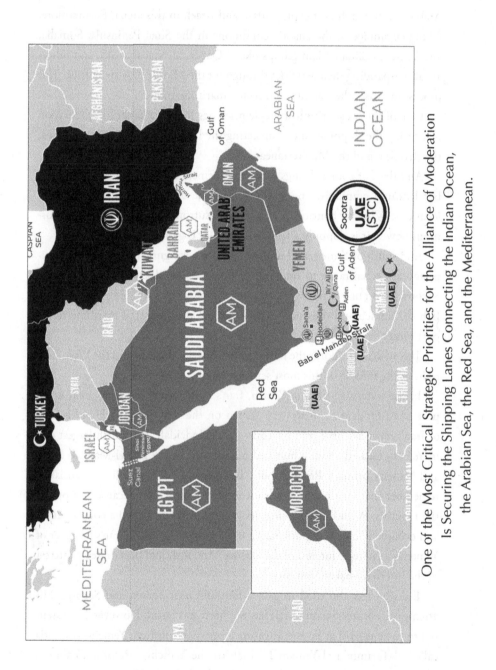

One of the Most Critical Strategic Priorities for the Alliance of Moderation
Is Securing the Shipping Lanes Connecting the Indian Ocean,
the Arabian Sea, the Red Sea, and the Mediterranean.

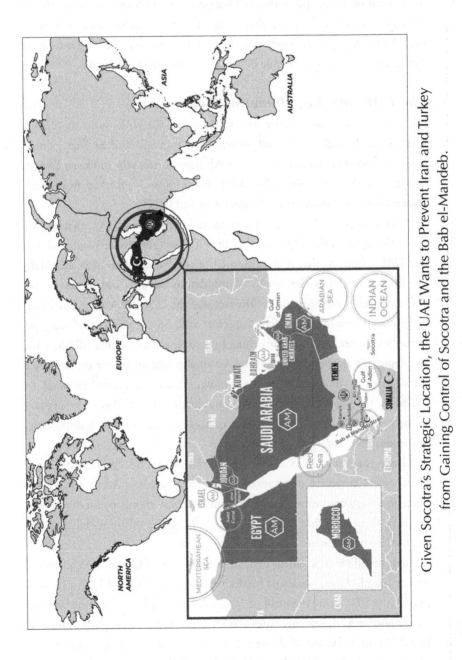

Given Socotra's Strategic Location, the UAE Wants to Prevent Iran and Turkey from Gaining Control of Socotra and the Bab el-Mandeb.

to the Gulf of Aden, and in the Red Sea port city of Mocha, at the northern-most point of the Bab el-Mandeb Strait,[2] about fifty miles south of Yemen's main Red Sea port of Al-Hodeidah. And west of Socotra, Turkey has its most significant military base outside of Turkey, in Mogadishu, Somalia.

The UAE and the Alliance of Moderation

Given Socotra's extraordinarily strategic location, the UAE wants to secure a foothold in the archipelago and prevent both Iran and Turkey from gaining control of Socotra. To that end, the UAE uses its proxy in southern Yemen, a UAE-backed militia—including Salafi-jihadi militias—of tribes from south Yemen called the Southern Transitional Council (STC).

I want to pause here for a moment and explain why I emphasize that the UAE supports the STC and that the STC includes Salafi-jihadi militias. The UAE maintains that it is committed to combating terrorism. The Salafi-jihadist movement is the womb of murderous terrorist organizations like al-Qaeda and its offspring, ISIS. The fact that the UAE can, on the one hand, be genuinely committed to fighting terror and, on the other hand, support terror groups demonstrates something I try to emphasize. In the Middle East, an enemy can also, at the same time, be an ally, and an enemy can also be a useful pawn. It all depends on the context, circumstances, and interests. In this sense, the United Arab Emirates is no different from other regional players such as Iran, Qatar, Saudi Arabia, or Turkey. They all have a duplicitous relationship with Islamist terror groups.

Getting back to the STC. After the Houthis 2014 coup, President Mansour Hadi's exiled Yemenite government moved from Sana'a to Aden. The STC is a Yemenite separatist movement that wants to create an independent entity in southern Yemen. To that end, in 2017, the STC broke off from Hadi's exiled, Aden-based government.

In June 2020, in a bid to control Socotra, the STC launched an attack on the Island. After a series of battles between the STC and Islah (Turkey's proxy), the STC gained control of Hadiboh—the capitol of Socotra, located on the northern edge of the island and its largest town. Throughout June and July 2020, the STC wrestled control of the Socotra archipelago from Hadi's government. In July 2020, the UAE-backed STC gained control of Socotra, taking over all Yemenite government and military institutions and hoisting the flag of the People's Democratic Republic of Yemen, a country that existed from 1967 to 1990.

Information estimated to be reliable indicates that Israel assisted the UAE and the STC in this endeavor. It appears Israel provided intelligence and military training to the STC. As part of Israel's assistance, Israeli intelligence personnel, senior members of the STC, and senior UAE officials reportedly met in the United Arab Emirates—and possibly also in Israel.[3] The STC vice-chairman, Hani Bin Briek, overtly hinted about Israel's security and military cooperation and the United Arab Emirates. In a June 2020 tweet, he said, "Israel has good very good relations with Qatar. Why is what is legitimate for Qatar forbidden to us?"[4]

As for Israel, senior Israeli Middle East expert Ehud Ya'ari wrote that Israel is "satisfied with the fact that the UAE took over Socotra."[5]

West of Socotra, the UAE has also established a military foothold on the Horn of Africa in Eritrea and Somalia. Abu Dhabi has both army and naval

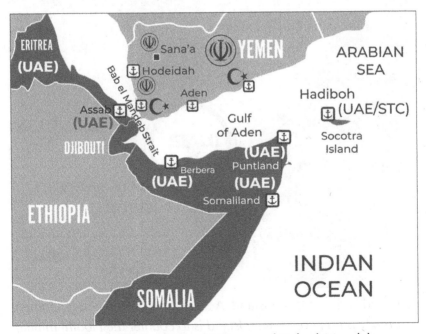

UAE in Socotra, Horn of Africa, and Bab el-Mandeb

bases in Somaliland and Puntland; both semi-independent Somalian entities formed during the 1991–2012 civil war. Somaliland and Puntland are in northern Somalia, directly across the Gulf of Aden from Yemen. In addition, the UAE has a twenty-five-year lease on the Berbera Port in Somaliland, immediately south of the Bab el-Mandeb Strait. And directly north of the Bab el-Mandeb, in Eritrea, the UAE has a thirty-year lease on the port of Assab.

Reportedly, the UAE is also building a runway and a military base on the strategic island of Perim, also known in Arabic as Mayun. Located at the narrowest point of the Bab el-Mandeb, Perim is a small island (five square miles) in Yemen's territory located five miles from the mainland of Yemen.[6] The Island was captured by the Saudi-led coalition in 2015.

In May 2021, the Saudi state news agency, SPA, cited an unnamed official in the Saudi-led coalition, saying, "All equipment currently present on Mayun Island is under control of the Coalition Command and is situated

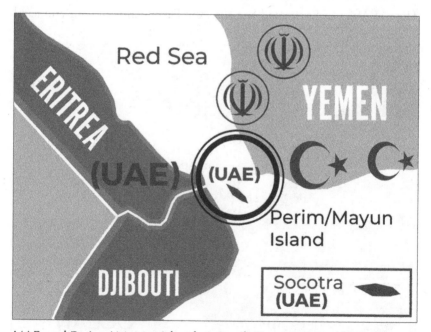

UAE and Perim / Mayun Island. A Saudi Source says, *All equipment currently present on Mayun Island is to counter the Houthi militia, secure maritime navigation, and support the alliance forces.*

there to … counter the Houthi militia, secure maritime navigation, and support the alliance forces."[7]

In addition to the Saudis and the Emiratis, all the core members of the alliance of moderation—Bahrain, Egypt, Jordan, Kuwait, Oman, Saudi Arabia, and the United Arab Emirates—have common goals in this arena. They want to secure maritime freedom, protect themselves from Iran and Turkey, and stabilize the vital area for their country's security and income.

Both Israel and Jordan have Red Sea ports. For Israel, the Israeli Red Sea port of Eilat is vital for Israel's security and its trade with Africa and Asia. And the Red Sea port of Aqaba is Jordan's only access to the sea.

More than 10 percent of the world's trade flows through the Suez Canal. Egyptian President al-Sisi has made it clear that free maritime traffic in the Red Sea is a national security priority for Egypt. Backing up his statements,

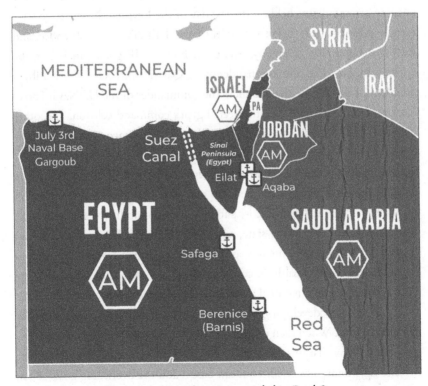

Alliance of Moderation and the Red Sea

Cairo is massively expanding its military, particularly its naval capacities and maritime presence. Egypt has one of the largest military fleets in the world and is the largest in Africa and the Middle East.

In January 2017, al-Sisi inaugurated the headquarters of Egypt's southern naval fleet at the Red Sea port of Safaga—Egypt's central naval base. On January 15, 2020, al-Sisi inaugurated Cairo's second Red Sea naval base and one of the largest military bases in the Middle East—the Berenice (Barnis) base. Berenice is a 150,000-acre installation and includes air and naval bases. Located south of Safaga, Berenice sits on the Red Sea about five hundred miles south of the Suez Canal and about 150 miles north of the Egypt-Sudan border. Berenice is one of three identical naval installations Egypt is currently building.

In July 2021, as we discussed in Chapters 3 and 4, Egypt inaugurated the "July 3rd Naval Base" on the Mediterranean Sea in the Gargoub area, on the Egyptian northwestern Mediterranean coast near the border with Libya. The opening ceremony was held on the last day of the Egyptian Navy's large-scale exercise, Qader-2021. Egypt's President, Abdel Fattah al-Sisi, attended and led the inauguration ceremony. The event hosted VIP guests, including the crown prince of UAE, the commander of the Qatari Emiri Naval Force, Libya's president of the Presidential Council, the commander of the US Naval Forces Central Command and US 5th Fleet, Egypt's command echelon, and other high-level officials. The naval forces, the advanced equipment—including helicopter carriers, modern frigates, missile boats, submarines—and the base itself are designed to secure the country's northern and western border and shipping lines. This is how al-Sisi described the new base in an official inauguration document: "[The July 3rd Base is] part of our responsibility to strengthen the comprehensive power of the state, and to maximize the Egyptian capabilities in all fields and sectors; foremost of which is the armed forces whose role is to protect the State's wealth, in continuation of the process of supporting the pillars of the Egyptian national security on all strategic directions."[8]

In addition to developing new ports, Egypt is presently expanding four existing harbors. When each project is completed, Egypt will have seven maritime military installations divided between the Red Sea and the Mediterranean.

The Egyptians' new Mediterranean base—and the overriding goals al-Sisi presents, to preserve the country's national economic wealth, secure shipping lines, maintain maritime security, and support Egypt's national security in all directions—clearly demonstrates the region's new geopolitical reality.

Countries in the region are looking to diversify and build military capabilities and secure their strategic interests—in sea, land, and air. And that calls for looking for strategic partners and building alliances with players that can be useful.

Council of the Arab and African Countries of the Red Sea and the Gulf of Aden

One example of the desire to build coalitions and the importance of the Gulf of Aden and the Red Sea was emphasized in early January 2020.

On January 6, 2020, in Riyadh, Saudi Arabia, eight Arab countries signed a treaty to establish a new organization called the "Council of the Arab and African countries of the Red Sea and the Gulf of Aden." The eight members are Djibouti, Egypt, Eritrea, Jordan, Saudi Arabia, Somalia, Sudan, and Yemen.

Saudi Arabia's Foreign Minister Faisal bin Farhan stressed the following. The new entity, which Saudi Arabia initiated in 2018, will prioritize efforts to address "the threats and challenges facing our region, and safeguard the security of the Red Sea and Gulf of Aden."[9] The threats he referred to are, first and foremost, Iran's and Turkey's ambitions to establish strongholds in the Red Sea.

The council provides a framework for broad cooperation. For example, the Dubai Port Company manages the Egyptian port of Ain al-Soukhna in the Red Sea. Ain al-Soukhna is Egypt's southernmost port and Egypt's largest commercial gateway.[10]

And one of the exceptional features of the council is that it links the Arab and African sides of the Red Sea that have closely intertwined interests. For example, throughout 2020, the Sudanese government reportedly conducted secret negotiations with one of the Gulf States (according to sources, probably the United Arab Emirates) about the possibility of selling or leasing the main Port of Sudan. The Port of Sudan is on the Red Sea and is located midway between Eritrea and Egypt. Sudanese officials have denied these reports.[11]

The Council of the Arab and African countries of the Red Sea and the Gulf of Aden is an example of an alliance created out of joint long-term strategic interests.

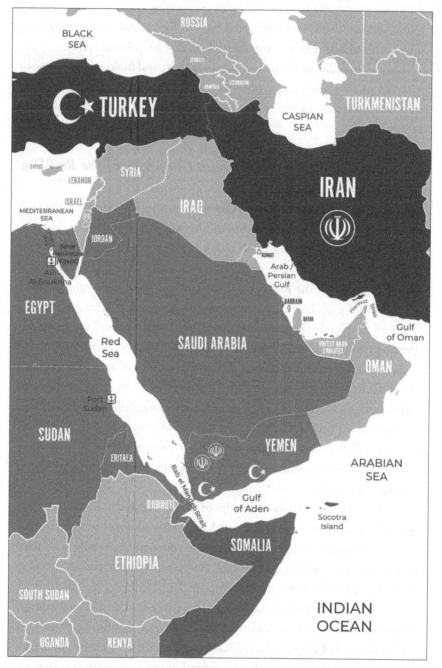

Council of the Arab and African countries of the Red Sea
and the Gulf of Aden

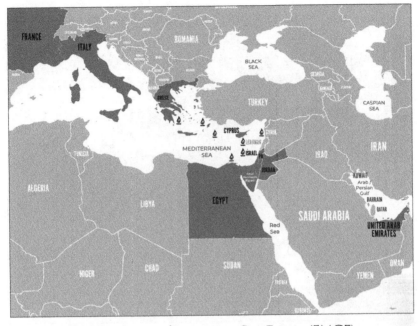

The Eastern Mediterranean Gas Forum (EMGF)

In Chapter 3, we discussed another key partnership that began in 2019. The Cairo-based Eastern Mediterranean Gas Forum (EMGF). The members are Cyprus, Egypt, France, Greece, Israel, Italy, Jordan, the Palestinian Authority, and the UAE. The EMGF seeks to bring together the energy-rich countries of the Eastern Mediterranean to pursue common interests.

And at the end of 2020, we witnessed another historic moment borne out of the same conjunction of interests. The UAE and Israel signed a peace agreement known as the Abraham Accords. We will delve into the Abraham Accords later in this chapter. At this juncture, I want to focus on one element of the treaty that could benefit the alliance of moderation in the Red Sea area.

The Abraham Accords, Israel, the Gulf, and Oil

The UAE-Israel agreement states the intention to cooperate in the following fields: agriculture, environment, innovation, and technology. One clause reads, "the parties will promote and develop collaborations in projects in the

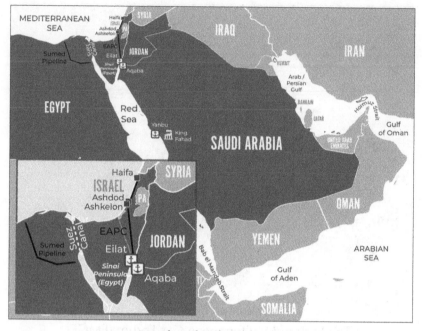

Israel and Oil Transport

field of energy, including regional transmission systems to increase energy security."[12]

That article deserves added attention, so let me explain. Today, most oil exports from the Gulf head east to countries like China and India. But the western route to Europe and North America is still a significant trading channel. Today there are two paths to export oil from the Arabian Peninsula to the West. One option is from the Red Sea through the Suez Canal to the Mediterranean. The other is the two-hundred-mile-long Sumed pipeline that bypasses the Suez Canal and connects oil from the Red Sea to the Mediterranean Sea. The Sumed pipeline can transfer 2.5 million barrels a day.

Saudi Arabia is one of the leading oil exporters in the world. About 70 percent of the world's proven petroleum reserves are in Saudi Arabia. The oil and gas sector accounts for about 50 percent of Saudi Arabia's gross domestic product and 70 percent of its export earnings.[13]

The northernmost point of the Gulf oil transport system is the Saudi Red Sea port of Yanbu, home to the King Fahad Industrial Port—the largest port for loading crude oil, refined products, and petrochemicals in the Red Sea. Yanbu port is located about 541 nautical miles (equals about six hundred 'land' miles) south of the Suez Canal. It is the closest Saudi port to Europe and North America. And it is also about 438 nautical miles (492 'land' miles) south of the Israeli port city of Eilat. Eilat is located at the northernmost end of the Gulf of Aqaba and the northeast branch of the Red Sea.

As I said, there is an article in the Abraham Accords that specifically outlines the following. "The parties will promote and develop collaborations in projects in the field of energy, including regional transmission systems to increase energy security." This sentence paves the way for cooperation between Israel and the Gulf States in the field of oil transportation.

As we have learned, the sea route is a long and dangerous track that Iran threatens in the Persian Gulf, the Straits of Hormuz, the Arabian Sea, and Yemen's waterways. No less significant are the pirate attacks from Somalia that plague the entrance to the Red Sea.

Cooperation with Israel in oil transportation offers three opportunities: One possibility is an underwater pipeline directly connecting the port cities of Yanbu and Eilat. The second is a land pipeline connecting Yanbu to the Jordanian port city of Aqaba, Eilat's next-door neighbor. Then from Aqaba, the oil could cross to Eilat. A land pipeline of this nature would allow the Arab Gulf producers to reduce their use of sea routes to export oil to the West. The third opportunity Israel offers is that supertankers—which are too big to cross the Suez Canal—could anchor in the port of Eilat, which can accommodate large vessels. In all of these scenarios, the oil could then travel overland to the Mediterranean Sea.

But why is Israel relevant for the transportation of oil? The answer is that Israel already has an oil transport infrastructure. In 1968, Israel and Iran established a company called the Eilat Ashkelon Pipeline Corporation. The joint project created an infrastructure, including a pipeline and storage facilities, to transport crude oil from the Persian Gulf oil-producing countries to Europe. When the pipeline was in use, Tehran would ship some of its Europe-bound oil to Eilat and then pipe it to Ashkelon on the Mediterranean. After the 1979 Iranian Revolution, the relationship between Iran and Israel changed from friends to enemies. The Eilat Ashkelon Pipeline Corporation was purchased by the Europe Asia Pipeline Company Ltd. (EAPC), a partnership between a private Israeli company and the Israeli government. Three pipelines link Eilat and the Mediterranean Sea. The largest goes to Ashkelon's oil facilities. And the two additional pipelines supply the refineries in Haifa and Ashdod. The company also operates an oil port and an oil terminal in Eilat and Ashkelon, with a storage capacity of 3.7 million cubic meters for crude oil and petroleum products. It has a total capacity of 600,000 barrels a day and almost 23 million barrels of storage space.

Creating a joint infrastructure to connect with the EAPC and enhancing cooperation between Israel and Arab Gulf oil producers in oil transportation is a win-win for everyone involved.

For Israel, cooperation in oil transport could generate hundreds of millions of dollars a year in revenue. And it further bolsters its strategic significance.

For the Gulf States, the project offers a strategic advantage. Israel provides the Gulf States a third path for oil transport that has two significant benefits.

One advantage is financial. The oil supertankers cannot cross the Suez Canal because it is too shallow. Using the Suez Canal forces oil suppliers to divide their petroleum into small tankers. Each vessel pays between $300,000 and $400,000 to use the Canal. Supertankers can dock at Eilat's deep-water harbor and save significant passage fees.

The second advantage is security. Land pipelines are attacked continuously by terror groups operating in the Sinai Peninsula and other areas in Egypt. Shipments through the Suez Canal are also at risk for terror attacks. The existing Israeli land pipeline connecting the Israeli ports of Eilat and Ashkelon is more secure.

The United Arab Emirates saw the advantage for them in partnering with Israel on oil transport. Following the signing of the Abraham Accords in September 2020, the UAE signed an agreement with Israel that follows that exact route. Gulf oil would be brought to the Red Sea port of Eilat by tanker. And then it would be moved by pipeline through mainland Israel to the Mediterranean port of Ashkelon, from where it would be shipped to Europe.

However, as of August 2021, it is unclear if this will go through as planned. The proposed project has angered environmentalists concerned with the damage it can do to Israel's coral reefs and beaches in Eilat and the Negev Dessert.

Citing the environmental concerns, Israel's Environmental Protection Ministry said it was delaying implementing the proposed oil transport deal with the UAE. Israel's Environmental Protection Minister Tamar Zandberg said that the government must conduct a strategic survey regarding the value of the project. According to her current understanding, the agreement with the UAE will not contribute anything to the Israeli economy. But it will threaten the coral reefs of the Gulf Eilat and the resort town's tourism.[14]

As I previously said, Israel's role within the framework of the alliance of moderation is a very well-known secret. The relationship between Israel and the Arab Gulf monarchies has evolved and deepened. The security cooperation between Israel and Egypt as well as between Israel and Jordan has grown and expanded.

The emerging alliances we have discussed in this book are one of the critical features of the new era.

The Alliance of Moderation—Arenas of Focus

The alliance of moderation is an informal partnership with the following common goals:

- Geopolitically, the coalition is currently focused on three main geographical arenas:
  o The Eastern Mediterranean.
  o The Iranian Land Corridor from Iran to Lebanon (and the Mediterranean).
  o The waterways from the Gulf to the Horn of Africa, the Red Sea, and the Mediterranean.
- The alliance wants to block Iran and Turkey from controlling these arenas and stabilize these critical areas for regional and global security.

Normalization Agreements and the Abraham Accords

The evolution and creation of the alliance of moderation are one of two crucial parallel processes that have led to a dramatic historical development.

I am referring to the development of the Abraham Accords—the peace agreement between Israel and the UAE. And the normalization agreements signed between Israel and Bahrain, Israel and Sudan, and Israel and Morocco.

We already understand an essential component that led to the agreements—and that is the changing needs and priorities of the Arab world and the evolving Middle East geopolitical landscape.

I want to explore the agreements and the regional reactions to the deals. But before we do that, I want to shortly discuss the term "normalization"—tatbi'e in Arabic—in the Arab public and intellectual discourse.

Normalization—Tatbi'e

I emphasize *Tatbi'e* because the UAE signed a peace agreement with Israel, Bahrain, Morocco, and Sudan signed normalization agreements. So, I want to be sure the terms are all clear.

One translation of the term tatbi'e is "making things natural"—or in short, "normalization." One might then think that the fact that Arabs use this term to describe Israel's recognition and acceptance means that the word "normalization" has a positive connotation.

But Arabic is a complex, rich, and nuanced language. Tatbi'e can also be translated as "to create something artificial." Another translation of the word is "to stain." You probably can see that these translations have a negative connotation.

The use of the term tatbi'e in the Arab public discourse is primarily negative. Having a relationship with Israel was, and is, frowned upon within wide circles of large parts of the Arab world. Tatbi'e implies that many in the Arab world actually reject the idea of recognizing and accepting Israel.

When it comes to the issue of tatbi'e—normalization—there are roughly three camps in the Arab world.

Unequivocally Reject Normalization

Political Islam and militant Islam categorically and unwaveringly reject any and all normalization with Israel.

Their position is rooted in the Muslim-Sunni and Muslim-Shi'ite theology. Most Sunni and Shi'ite Muslim theologians refuse to recognize Jews as a "nation." Islam recognizes both Judaism and Christianity as monotheistic religions. However, in the eyes of Muslim scholars, Islam existed in heaven prior to Judaism and Christianity, and is the final and flawless monotheistic religion

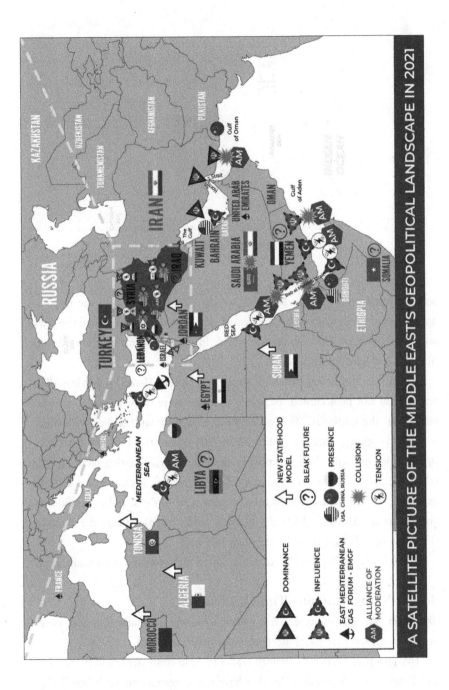

Countries of the Abraham Accords

sent to humanity by Allah. Islam argues that the Jews betrayed the mission
appointed to them to spread Allah's word. Therefore, Allah punished the Jews
and scattered them throughout the world, forever to be cursed. In addition,
Shi'ites view Jews as "impure."

Given this, the establishment of a state for the Jews (Israel) is defying Allah
and should not be accepted. Islamists view the State of Israel as an artificial
entity that the Christian West established on Islamic land (Palestine), which
is Allah's property. Thus, according to the Islamist outlook, Israel is occupying Islamic land, and the land must be liberated by eliminating Israel. In the
Islamist eyes, Israel has no right to exist. This outlook is clearly and directly
expressed by various Islamic factors—Sunnis and Shi'ites, political Islamists
and militant Islamists, al-Qaeda, Hamas, ISIS, Islamic Jihad, the Muslim
Brotherhood (all Sunni), and Hezbollah (Shi'ite).

With this first camp, there is, of course, no room to talk about normalization.

Accept Normalization—With Conditions

The second camp is the one that is willing to accept normalization with Israel
on the condition that Israel meets all Palestinian demands.

This group includes non-Islamist circles in Arab countries (including Jordan
and Egypt—two Arab countries that have peace agreements with Israel) that

oppose normalization. Organizations against recognition of, and relationships with, Israel include organized bodies of academics, engineers, students, and associations of architects, engineers, farmers, intellectuals, lawyers, trade unions, etc. They repeatedly call for Egypt and Jordan to cancel their peace agreements with Israel and demand to cancel all normalization agreements.

The conditions this camp presents makes normalization, practically speaking, unachievable. A primary Palestinian demand is to allow millions of people the Palestinians define as refugees to return to Israel. The vast majority of Israelis reject this demand entirely because it would mean the end of the State of Israel.

Accepts Normalization

The third camp in the Arab world is a camp that claims that normalization with Israel is in the Arabs' interest.

In their view, normalization with Israel should not be predicated on resolving the Israeli-Palestinian conflict. According to this school of thought, it is possible and necessary to pursue both tracks—normalization and conflict resolution simultaneously.

The Difference between Normalization Agreements and Peace Agreements

The primary differences between normalization agreements and peace agreements are official diplomatic representation, the scale and scope of areas of cooperation, and some legal aspects related to international pacts, treaties, etc.

The Abraham Accords: Peace between Israel and the United Emirates and Normalization with Bahrain, Sudan, and Morocco

Peace with the United Emirates and Normalization with Bahrain

On the White House lawn on September 15, 2020, Israel and the UAE signed a peace treaty known as the Abraham Accords. During that ceremony, Israel and Bahrain signed an agreement to officially launch peace talks. The agreement specifies many areas of cooperation between the countries, including tourism, trade, technology, energy, investments, and more.

Here is the declaration signed by the Minister of Foreign Affairs of Bahrain Dr. Abdullatif bin Rashid Al-Zayani; Israeli Prime Minister Benjamin Netanyahu; Minister of Foreign Affairs for the United Arab Emirates Abdullah bin Zayed Al-Nahyan; and US President Donald J. Trump:

> The Abraham Accords Declaration: We, the undersigned, recognize the importance of maintaining and strengthening peace in the Middle East and around the world based on mutual understanding and coexistence, as well as respect for human dignity and freedom, including religious freedom. We encourage efforts to promote interfaith and intercultural dialogue to advance a culture of peace among the three Abrahamic religions and all humanity. We believe that the best way to address challenges is through cooperation and dialogue and that developing friendly relations among States advances the interests of lasting peace in the Middle East and around the world. We seek tolerance and respect for every person in order to make this world a place where all can enjoy a life of dignity and hope, no matter their race, faith or ethnicity. We support science, art, medicine, and commerce to inspire humankind, maximize human potential and bring nations closer together. We seek to end radicalization and conflict to provide all children a better future. We pursue a vision of peace, security, and prosperity in the Middle East and around the world. In this spirit, we warmly welcome and are encouraged by the progress already made in establishing diplomatic relations between Israel and its neighbors in the region under the Abraham Accords' principles. We are encouraged by the ongoing efforts to consolidate and expand such friendly relations based on shared interests and a shared commitment to a better future.[15]

The Israel-UAE document says both nations will establish "full normalization of bilateral ties," embassies with resident ambassadors, and cooperation in various areas, from investment to tourism to agriculture. It also calls for both parties to "foster mutual understanding, respect, co-existence, and a culture of peace between their societies in the spirit of their common ancestor, Abraham."[16]

The Israel-Bahrain document signed in September said that they would negotiate specific agreements in the coming weeks. On October 18, 2020, Bahrain and Israel signed an official Normalization Agreement.

Israel-Sudan Normalization Agreement

A little more than a month later, on October 23, 2020, Israel, Sudan, and the United States issued a joint statement. Here is an excerpt:

> The leaders agreed to normalize relations between Sudan and Israel and end the belligerence between their nations. In addition, the leaders agreed to begin economic and trade relations, with an initial focus on agriculture. The leaders also agreed that delegations will meet in the coming weeks to negotiate agreements of cooperation in those areas as well as in agriculture technology, aviation, migration issues and other areas for the benefit of the two peoples. The leaders also resolved to work together to build a better future and advance the cause of peace in the region. This move will improve regional security and unlock new opportunities for the people of Sudan, Israel, the Middle East, and Africa.[17]

Sudan joined the Abraham Accords in January 2021. When it comes to Sudan, it is important to emphasize that the parliament must ratify the agreement. And as of August 2021, the Sudanese government has not officially approved the accord.

However, while in the UAE, the agreement with Israel has been warmly welcomed, the picture is different in Sudan. There are critical players in Sudan who reject the deal, like Sudan's former Prime Minister Sadiq al-Mahdi (1935–2020), who led the country's largest political party until his death in November 2020.

Furthermore, while the UAE and Bahrain have many interests in building a long-term, multifaceted, strategic, and mutually beneficial relationship with

Israel, Sudan's primary motivation for signing the agreement was due primarily to an immediate and pressing need. The United States defined Sudan as a sponsor of terrorism and added Sudan to the American State Sponsor of Terrorism list in 1993, accusing it of aiding terrorist groups. The US sanctions on Sudan had increased Sudan's severe financial distress—exacerbated and intensified by severe floods Sudan suffered in 2020 that caused catastrophic damage. Sudan desperately needed economic oxygen. The normalization agreement with Israel paved the way toward the lifting of US sanctions. Furthermore, it would open the door for desperately needed international aid to flow to Sudan.

Indeed, the United States formally rescinded Sudan's status as a state-sponsor of terrorism in December 2020. In July 2021, the International Monetary Fund (IMF) and World Bank officially declared Sudan eligible for over $50 billion in debt relief, following policy implementations and other actions from the Sudanese transitional government.

The Abraham Accords is a dramatic development. The joining of Sudan has an additional dramatic dimension. Unlike the UAE and Bahrain, Sudan had historically played a proactive role in the camp that strives to eliminate Israel.

Sudan's capitol, Khartoum, is where the Arab League met in 1967 after the Six-Day War. It was at that conference that the Arab League issued the famous "*Three No's*"—*No Peace, No Recognition, No Negotiations.*" The Arab League categorically rejected any engagement with Israel whatsoever and supported the continued state of war.

As we discussed in Chapter 3, when Omar al-Bashir was President of Sudan (1993–2019), Sudan had intimate ties with Iran, Turkey, the Muslim Brotherhood, Hamas, Islamic Jihad in Palestine, and other terror organizations dedicated to Israel's destruction. And not only did Sudan have relationships with these entities, but Sudan was also a vital part of the supply route for these organizations and others who used the country to smuggle weapons from Iran to the Gaza Strip. Over the past two decades, it was reported that Israel attacked convoys of weapons in Sudan and weapons depots in Sudan on numerous occasions.

Although Sudan has not officially ratified the normalization agreement, and the character of the normalization agreement is different than it is with

Bahrain, Morocco, and the United Arab Emirates, the following event manifests the dramatic change in the relationship between Israel and Sudan. In January 2021, the Israeli minister of intelligence affairs and Israeli intelligence and security officials formally visited Sudan. The delegation met with senior Sudanese officials to discuss issues of common interests. While the delegation was in Khartoum, they signed several memorandums of understanding in the fields of intelligence, security, and more.

Israel-Morocco Normalization Agreement

On December 10, 2020, the White House announced a normalization agreement between Israel and Morocco. On December 22, 2020, the two countries signed a normalization agreement. Here is an excerpt:

> Morocco and Israel agreed to make peace, normalize their relations, and resume full diplomatic relations in the coming weeks. The agreement will allow the two to work to promote increased economic cooperation, reopen the liaison offices in Rabat and Tel Aviv, and discuss other areas of cooperation.[18]

Morocco became the sixth Arab nation to establish formal relations with Israel. Egypt and Israel signed a peace treaty in 1979. Israel and Jordan signed a peace treaty in 1994. The UAE and Israel signed a peace treaty in 2020. And Bahrain, Sudan, and Morocco signed normalization agreements in 2020.

The Abraham Accords—The Beginning of Dynamic and Diverse Relationships

On August 13, 2020, former Prime Minister Benjamin Netanyahu said:

Today we usher in a new era of peace between Israel and the Arab world.

I just came from a historic virtual conference between President Donald Trump and Crown Prince Mohammed bin Zayed Al-Nahyan of the United Arab Emirates. Together we announced the establishment of a full and formal peace between Israel and the UAE, which includes the mutual opening of embassies, direct flights, and many other bilateral agreements...Today, I am honored to announce formal peace with the United Arab Emirates under

President Khalifa bin Zayed and Crown Prince Mohammed bin Zayed. I believe we will soon see more Arab countries join this expanding circle of peace.[19]

Since that historic announcement, Israel, as we have discussed, has signed normalization agreements with Bahrain, Morocco, and Sudan.

But how has this translated on the ground? I would like to briefly summarize the events since and how these events are defining the new era.

Diplomatically, in February 2021, the United Arab Emirates appointed Mohamed Al Khaja, the former chief of staff to the Minister of Foreign Affairs and International Cooperation, to be the first Gulf ambassador to Israel. In March 2021, Bahrain appointed Khaled Yousef Al-Jalahma, the former director of Operations of the Bahraini Foreign Office and deputy ambassador of Bahrain to the United States, to be Bahrain's first ambassador to Israel. In June 2021, Israel's Foreign Minister Yair Lapid made history—the first official visit by an Israeli foreign minister to the UAE. On that state visit, he inaugurated the new Israeli embassy in Abu Dhabi. In July 2021, the UAE officially opened its embassy, becoming the first Gulf state to open an embassy in Israel. In the same month, Israel appointed Amir Hayek, the president of the Israel Hotel Association, to be Israel's first official Gulf ambassador. Mr. Hayek replaced Eitan Naeh, who held the position until Israel appointed a permanent ambassador. A seasoned Israeli diplomat, Mr. Hayek was previously Israel's Ambassador to Turkey and Deputy Head of Mission in London. In August 2021, Yair Lapid was the first Israeli foreign minister to visit the Kingdom of Morocco since the Abraham Accords were signed. During his visit, he reopened the Israeli Liaison Office in Rabat. Morocco and Israel had liaison offices in the 1990s before closing them during the second *intifada*. (Intifada is the word for the Palestinian uprisings against Israel between 1987 - 1993 and between 2000 - 2007. I will elaborate on that matter in Chapter 9.) And on August 31, 2021, Khaled Yousef al-Jalahmah, Bahrain's ambassador to Israel, landed at Ben Gurion International Airport. "The opportunity to fulfill His Majesty King Hamad bin Isa Al Khalifa's vision of peaceful coexistence with all nations is a privilege that I will hold in high regard," al-Jalahmah posted to Twitter in Arabic and Hebrew before touching down in Israel.[20] These high-level appointments and official visits are in addition to other military and diplomatic exchanges—including at least two Israeli delegations to Sudan.

Militarily, in April 2021, the Israeli and UAE Air Force conducted a joint military drill in Greece. Reportedly Israel and the UAE have participated in joint military drills in the past. But this is the first time the UAE was willing to openly share that it was participating in a military exercise with Israel. The maneuvers took place in Greece and included air forces from Canada, Cyprus, Spain, and Slovakia. In August 2021, Bahraini Undersecretary for Political Affairs Dr. Shaikh Abdulla bin Ahmed Al Khalifa, the deputy secretary-general of the Supreme Defense Council, met with the head of the Israel Defense Forces (IDF) Strategic Planning and Cooperation Directorate, Major General Tal Kelman. This meeting was the first open and public encounter between Bahrain and an Israeli military official. In an August interview with the *Jerusalem Post*, the undersecretary said: "We do have collaboration on the security front," he said. "It's very important." He explained that Bahrain prefers to be transparent about its partnerships with Israel: "It's nothing to shy away from. The relationship is based on trust and mutual interests. We are contributing to security and saving the lives of innocent civilians ... Regional stability [and] security require collaboration, and there are continuous efforts to work collectively to address common challenges."[21] These official exchanges and encounters are parallel to ongoing discussions of individual and regional security and defense pacts.

Economically, trade between Israel and the UAE has exceeded $600 million and is expected to double this year. Trade between the two may reach $1 billion for the whole of 2021 and could exceed $3 billion within three years.[22] Israel's goods exports to Morocco in the first half of 2021 amounted to $13.2 million, compared with $8.1 million in the first half of 2020. Imports of goods from Morocco amounted to $6 million in the first half of 2021, up from a total of $9.8 million in 2019.[23]

The details of each normalization deal vary. Some include tax and trade treaties and cooperation in key sectors such as advanced technologies, agritech, communication, cybersecurity, food tech, entertainment, energy, health, logistics, media, pharmaceuticals, renewable energy, security, sports, water, and more. Educational institutions, hospitals, media organizations, think tanks, and non-governmental and non-profit organizations have also partnered to advance collaborative efforts, learning, and research.

And these are not agreements on paper alone. One of the earliest public results was in the early stages of the COVID-19 pandemic when the UAE and Israel developed technology to monitor and combat the coronavirus.[24]

A host of frameworks and organizations have sprouted to support this emerging and diversified cooperative environment spanning government and private institutions, an array of investors and venture capital firms, non-profits, and corporate joint ventures. The growing list includes the Abrahamic Business Circle, Abu Dhabi-Israel Business Hub, the Gulf-Israel Green Ventures, the Gulf-Israel Women's Forum, Israeli Emirati Forum, the UAE-Israel Business Council, the UAE Israel Innovation Office, UAE-IL Tech Zone, and chambers of commerce from Israel to the Gulf to Morocco are engaged in efforts to boost and support a vast array of initiatives and engagements.

And the Abraham Accords have not skipped the public sector.

Including Sharaka, who describes their mission as "To build bonds between young Israeli and Gulf leaders to strengthen peace, trust, and cooperation between our societies. We believe that this will lead to a brighter future for our nations and all the peoples of the region."[25]

Another innovative NGO, called Israel-Is, says:

> We bring people from all around the region together through different initiatives. We created this partnership from old dreams. We always believed in living in prosperity and peace. The recent Abraham Accords were a catalyst for us to discover each other. From old neighbors with no relations, we became friends. We have the power to lead our people to a better future. We are the leaders of tomorrow. We seek a future of genuine friendships between our nations. Each country has a different story; a different "is" that shares their heritage and history. We aspire to bring young people from all across the globe together to make a better world. We are here to inspire and get inspired.[26]

And speaking of delegations, tourism—though hampered by COVID-19—still thrived. In October 2020, Israel and Jordan signed an aviation agreement allowing flights to cross both countries' airspace. That move will shorten flight times and potentially unlock new routes. Commercial airlines will now be able to fly through the Israel-Jordan corridor, which will "significantly shorten flight times" from the Gulf States and Asia to destinations in Europe and North America.[27] The official announcement stated that the move "will lead to substantial savings in fuel, will reduce polluting emissions, and contribute to the quality of the environment."[28]

In January 2021, the UAE and Israel signed a visa waiver agreement, so Israelis and Emiratis can travel back and forth without a visa. But it was suspended due to COVID. Nonetheless, nearly 230,000 Israelis have traveled to the UAE since commercial flights from Israel to Dubai began in August 2020. Emirati air carriers began flying the Dubai-Tel Aviv route in October 2020. In April 2021, Israel and Bahrain established the world's first bilateral agreement for COVID-19 vaccine passports. In July 2021, Israel and Morocco launched nonstop commercial flights to Marrakesh from Tel Aviv.

These normalization and peace agreements signed between Israel and Bahrain, Morocco, Sudan, and the United Arab Emirates build on the other peace treaties Israel has signed with Egypt and Jordan.

The agreements offer a platform for an unprecedented level of travel, collaboration, communication, partnerships, and people-to-people experiences.

The Abraham Accords are reflecting and building the new era of the Middle East.

The Abraham Accords: Regional Reactions

I would now like to focus on the regional reactions to the Abraham Accords and these dramatic agreements. The different regional players' responses, to a large extent, reflect the structure of alliances and interests of the various actors in the region.

The Opposing Camp

Iran and Iran's agents and proxies—such as the Lebanese Hezbollah, the pro-Iranian al-Fath Coalition in Iraq, the Houthis in Yemen, etc.—the Palestinians and Turkey all virulently oppose the agreement. In addition to the statements repeatedly coming out of this camp accusing the countries signing the agreements of betraying the Palestinians and making a severe strategic mistake, they also accuse them (and specifically the UAE) of "*abandoning al-Quds*" and "*betraying al-Aqsa.*"

Before we explore the reactions, let's understand better these terms and why they are so significant.

Al-Quds and Al-Aqsa

In Hebrew, the name for Jerusalem is *Yerushalayim.* Yerushalayim is the most sacred place for Jews. In biblical times, Jerusalem was the capitol of the ancient Jewish kingdom in Judea and Samaria. Today, Judea and Samaria are geographically identified as the "West Bank." Also referred to as the "Palestinian territories" or the "occupied territories." Throughout history, Yerushalayim has been the religious and spiritual center of Jews living in the land of Israel and the diaspora.

In Arabic, the name for Jerusalem is *al-Quds.* Al-Quds is literally translated as "the Holy." The phrase al-Quds is taken from the Hebrew word for holy, which is *kadosh.* Al-Quds is the third-most-sacred place for Sunni Muslims after Mecca and Medina, which are located in the Arabian Peninsula. Islam describes al-Quds as "the first direction of prayer and the third in religious sanctity." Let me briefly explain the phrase "First Direction of Prayer." During the first years of Islam, Muslims prayed toward Jerusalem because the Prophet Muhammad—the founder of Islam—wanted to win the support of the Jewish tribes of the Arabian Peninsula. But the Jews rejected Muhammad's offer. Following the Jews' rejection, when Muslims pray, they face Mecca, the birthplace of the Prophet Muhammad.

In the heart of the Old City of Jerusalem is the Temple Mount Compound. In Hebrew, it is called *Har Ha-Bayit,* "the mountain of the two Jewish Temples"— that is the etymology of the term the Temple Mount. Foreign powers destroyed both Jewish temples. The Babylonians destroyed the First Jewish Temple in 586 BCE. And the Romans destroyed the Second Jewish Temple in 70 CE.

In Arabic, the Temple Mount Compound is called *al-Haram al-Sharif,* "The Noble Sacred Compound." On al-Haram al-Sharif, two important symbols of Islam were built during the Islamic conquests of the late seventh and early eighth centuries. One is the Dome of the Rock, and the other is the Al-Aqsa Mosque.

The word *al-Aqsa* in Arabic is literally translated as "the Far Edge." It appears in the first verse of Chapter 17 of the *Qur'an* (the Islamic Bible). Chapter 17 describes Muhammad's miraculous night journey to a place called "al-Aqsa." For a long time, Islamist theologians identified "al-Aqsa" with heaven. Over the years, popular traditions and political circumstances caused Islamist theologians to change their interpretations. Since the late Middle Ages, the term "al-Aqsa" in Islam has been identified with al-Quds (Jerusalem).

Jordan ruled al-Haram al-Sharif / Har ha-Bayit / the Temple Mount between 1948 and 1967. Before that, Jerusalem and the Temple Mount were part of the British Mandate for the Land of Israel / Palestine (1922–1948). Before that, Jerusalem and the Temple Mount were under the rule of the Ottoman Empire (1299–1920).

After the 1967 War between Israel and Arab states in the Jewish-Israeli-Zionist terminology, Israel liberated Yerushalayim and Har ha-Bayit. In the Arab-Muslim terminology, Israel occupied al-Quds and al-Haram-al-Sharif.

In the Muslim world in general and the Arab world in particular, the call to "*Liberate al-Aqsa*" is a compelling and powerful concept—culturally, emotionally, politically, and religiously. "Liberating al-Aqsa" is an authentic and genuine narrative that appeals to Muslims' emotions worldwide. However, Muslim rulers and governments often use it as a useful propaganda narrative to distract people from their domestic, economic, and social challenges. And, as we have explored, regimes like Iran and Turkey rally the masses to "Liberate al-Aqsa" in order to advance their geopolitical goals.

Speaking of al-Aqsa, I would like to share a story with you that is a quintessential reflective of the current geopolitical environment.

Over the past few years, some in the Arab world—Egyptian, Saudi, and Syrian scholars and theologians—have presented a new theory about al-Aqsa. They argue that the al-Aqsa mosque is not in Jerusalem at all. According to this theory, the al-Aqsa mosque is a mosque called al-Ja'arneh, located some twenty miles north of Mecca in the Arabian Peninsula.[29] Those advocating the theory that al-Aqsa is in the Arab Peninsula base their arguments on Islamic scripture and early Islamic traditions.

As expected, that narrative evokes stormy reactions in the Arab and Muslim world.[30]

Al-Ja'arneh Mosque

For example, in November 2020, Kuwaiti scholar Issa Sawfan Kadoumi, the editor of *al-Quds Magazine*, wrote, "'Where is Al-Aqsa Mosque?' What made these people write and say such things that even Hebrew newspapers do not dare to say??"[31]

This whole episode is a fascinating story. A few years ago, even mentioning the idea that Al-Aqsa is not in al-Quds would have been considered heresy. The reason this story has recently emerged is because of the current political climate in the region.

First, there were the Abraham Accords. Palestinian columnist Daoud Kuttab argues that the Israel-UAE peace agreement downgrades the sanctity of al-Aqsa and al-Haram al-Sharif. Why? First, he cites the clause in the accords that refers to praying in the Al-Aqsa Mosque—but not in other parts of the compound. He argues that this cause disconnects—in terms of holiness—the mosque from al-Haram al-Sharif. A second element of the agreement that dilutes the Islamic sanctity of al-Aqsa, he argues, is that according to the agreement, people of all religions can pray on the al-Haram al-Sharif. [32]

Another reason people are willing to openly discuss the idea that al-Aqsa might be in the Arabian Peninsula and not Jerusalem has to do with the Iranian-Arab power struggle. It is important to note that those echoing and endorsing this theory are often from the Arab Peninsula. It is difficult to believe that the Saudi monarchy and the influential Saudi theological establishment would tolerate such a theory unless they were comfortable with the concept. Their silent consent may reflect a Saudi attempt to prevent the Iranians from continuing to use "liberating al-Aqsa" to further their own hegemonic ambitions.

Iran Monetizes the Slogan of "Liberating Al-Aqsa"

Every year, on the last Friday of the Muslim month of Ramadan, worshippers around the world mark *Al-Quds Day*. In 2020, as part of Al-Quds Day, the Iranian regime published posters highlighting the narrative of "Praying in Al-Quds and Al-Aqsa." This poster is an excellent example of the Iranian government using the "Liberating al-Aqsa" narrative to position itself as the uniter of the Arab Muslim world and the leader that is defending al-Quds, al-Haram-al-Sharif, and al-Aqsa.

The poster shows senior leaders of the Iranian-backed Axis of Resistance like Hassan Nasrallah, the Lebanese Hezbollah leader; Ismail Haniyeh, the chairman of Hamas's political bureau; Ziyad al-Nakhalah, the leader of Islamic Jihad in Palestine; and others. In addition, the poster shows General Qasem Soleimani, the commander of the al-Quds force, who the United States killed in January 2020. Soleimani appears in the poster in the shape of a cloud, overlooking the al-Haram al-Sharif compound.

Let's get acquainted with some of the poster figures (the numerical order is arbitrary).

1 **Hassan Nasrallah**: The leader of the Lebanese Shi'ite Hezbollah. An organization Iran created in Lebanon in the 1980s.

2 **Ismail Haniyeh**: The leader of the Palestinian Sunni Islamist movement Hamas. Hamas has governed Gaza since 2007, and Hamas is the strongest militant organization in Gaza.

3 A **Sunni** Cleric: The figure resembles **Ahmad Badreddin Hassoun**, the grand mufti of Syria. The grand mufti is the highest clerical position in Sunni Islam.

4 **Ziad Al-Nakhalah**: The leader of the Islamic Jihad in Palestine (IJIP). IJIP is Sunni and is the second-largest Palestinian military power in the Gaza Strip.

5 **Issa Ahmad Qasem**: The ayatollah 'uzma (the grand ayatollah) and head of the leading Shi'ite political party in Bahrain. The grand ayatollah is the highest rank in the Shi'ite religious order. Few Shi'ite religious scholars hold this rank. (By the way—most of the people in Bahrain are Shi'ite Arabs, but a Sunni minority rules Bahrain).

6 **Bashar al-Assad**: The president of Syria.

7 Major General **Ismail Qa'ani**: The commander of the al-Quds Force of the Islamic Revolutionary Guards. Qa'ani replaced Major General Qasem Soleimani.

8 **Abdel-Malek al-Houthi**: The leader of the coalition of Houthi Shi'ite tribes in Yemen. And the leader of the Iranian-backed Houthi militia, *Ansar Allah*.

9 I believe (though I am not 100 percent certain) that this is **Falih al-Fayyadh**: Iraq's former national security advisor and leader of the Popular Mobilization Units (PMU—Al-Hashd Al-Shabi).

10 Major General **Qasem Soleimani**: The former, eliminated leader of the al-Quds Force.

11 **Ibrahim El Zakzaky**: A Shi'ite Islamic leader in Nigeria and head of Nigeria's Islamic movement. He has been in prison since December 2015 because of initiating acts of violence against the government.

Iran Al-Quds Day Poster

A well-known and outspoken opponent of the Iranian regime, Ayatollah Abdol-Hamid Masoumi-Tehrani, makes a very forthcoming statement about the poster. In a January 2021 interview, he said, "The Israeli-Palestinian conflict is a political issue. The Iranian regime tries to make it a religious issue because it serves their interests." In the past, Tehrani's criticism of the regime has landed him in jail. As punishment, he was also forbidden to wear the clothes of a mullah, and his title of ayatollah was taken away from him.[33]

Turkey Monetizes the Slogan of "Liberating al-Aqsa"

Turkey also monetizes the issue of al-Quds. Speaking at the Al-Quds Forum in Istanbul in 2017, Erdoğan called on Turks to visit the al-Aqsa Mosque often to protect the Holy place's Muslim identity. He said, "Turkey places the utmost importance on the Palestinians' justified resistance. And Turkey will not let Israeli attempts to change the status quo at the Al-Aqsa mosque succeed. As a Muslim community, we need to visit the Al-Aqsa Mosque often. Every day Jerusalem is under occupation is an insult to us."[34]

In July 2020, Turkey's president resurrected the Hagia Sophia church as a mosque. In his speech, he said, "The resurrection of Hagia Sophia heralds the liberation of the Al-Aqsa mosque."[35]

In June 2021, Ali Arbash, head of the Religious Affairs of the Republic of Turkey, announced that "Turkey will continue to carry the flag of the Palestinian cause in all international forums and emphasize the centrality of al-Quds for every Muslim."[36]

Iran and Turkey—Fanning the Flames of the Israeli-Palestinian Conflict

Both Erdoğan and the mullah regime have skillfully and successfully positioned themselves as defenders of the Palestinians. They have appropriated the Israeli-Palestinian conflict to achieve their own hegemonic aspirations. And therefore, it is in their interest for it to continue. If they themselves can fan the flames, even better.

In an official statement, the Turkish Foreign Ministry described the agreement between Israel and the United Arab Emirates as "a betrayal of the Palestinian cause and that the Emirates sacrificed the Palestinians on the altar of their political interests."[37]

The Iranian Foreign Ministry defined the agreement as "a dangerous and illegal move which does not help the axis of resistance." Moreover, Iran has sent an implicit threat to the Gulf States that they will "bear the consequences of Israel's foothold in the Gulf region."[38]

The Palestinians and the Abraham Accords

Of course, the Palestinian Authority (PA) and Hamas—the two central Palestinian powers—have harshly criticized and entirely rejected the agreement.

On a practical level, the Palestinian Authority announced that it would immediately return the Palestinian ambassador from the UAE.

On September 3, 2020, leaders of fourteen Palestinian organizations held a virtual summit. Mahmoud Abbas, the chairman of the Palestinian Authority, called on the United Nations to have a 'peace summit' and announced that the Palestinians would not accept the United States as the sole mediator in the Israeli-Palestinian dispute.

Ismail Haniyeh, the head of Hamas's Political Bureau, vowed to free Palestinians in Israeli prisons.

At the same time, Ziyad al- Nakhalah, the Islamic Jihad leader in Palestine (IJIP), called for abolishing the Oslo Accords (a pair of agreements signed between Israel and the Palestinian Liberation Organization in 1993 and 1995) and called on the Palestinian Authority to refuse to accept Israel's right to exist.[39]

Mu'in Hamed, the leader of a minor Syrian-backed Palestinian organization Al-Sai'qa said, "Since its establishment, the UAE has been afraid of the 400,000 Palestinians there, who can entirely change UAE society. Why shouldn't they play a role [in confronting the agreement]? Why shouldn't the [Palestinian] factions be in contact with [the Palestinians in the UAE], so that they can play an active role in dissuading any country from following the UAE [and signing an agreement with Israel]?"[40] His statement was viewed by many in the Arab world as a call to violence and a message to the Palestinians to provoke instability in the UAE. Accordingly, his statement caused resentments and was widely and virulently condemned across the Arab world—including among Palestinians living and working in the Arab Gulf monarchies.[41]

The Supporting Camp

Egypt and Oman expressed immediate support for the agreement.

It is worth noting that as of August 2021, Saudi Arabia has not made an official announcement regarding the agreements. However, there should be no misunderstanding. The agreements between Israel, the UAE, and Bahrain would not have happened without Saudi Arabia's blessing.

In response to the criticism—primarily the Iranian and Turkish rhetoric—supporters of the agreement present two main arguments.

One argument directly attacks Iran and Turkey. This argument emphasizes that Iran and Turkey have caused more destruction and damage in the Arab world than any other entity. For example, on August 14, 2020, Saudi journalist Mashari Althaydy wrote an article titled: "The UAE-Israel Agreement… Breakthrough to the barrier of Illusion."[42] Here is a quote: "Let us remember that Turkey and Iran caused the Arab world damage and destruction—Turkey in Libya, Iran in Lebanon, Iraq, Syria, and Yemen."[43]

Another argument is that the peace agreement between Israel and the UAE secured a core Palestinian interest because it halted Israel's annexation of the West Bank. On August 13, 2020, UAE crown-prince Sheikh Mohammed bin Zayed Al Nahyan, the United Arab Emirates ruler, tweeted the following: "During a call with President Trump and Prime Minister Netanyahu, an agreement was reached to stop further Israeli annexation of Palestinian territories. The UAE and Israel also agreed to cooperate and to set a roadmap towards establishing a bilateral relationship."[44] This refrain has been echoed by the crown prince in subsequent interviews, messages, etc. And many in the Arab world, who support the agreement, highlight this exact aspect.[45]

An interesting note is that on August 15, 2020, Palestinian writer Suha Al-Jundi published an article, "Emirates and Peace with Israel,"[46] in which she reluctantly supports the agreement with the following: "This agreement could expose the Arab world to a (young and Left-leaning) Israeli public, who are interested in living in peace with the Palestinians. And this could promote peace between Israelis and Palestinians."[47]

Other Significant Responses

Some interesting responses in the Arab world to the Abraham Accords provide insights into different regional players' complex calculations. Their response is also an excellent example of one of my core arguments—the Middle East is a chain of links, and what happens in one place impacts what happens in another. Let us look at some of the responses.

Jordan

The Jordanian response is reserved. The official Jordanian statement regarding the agreement emphasizes that the ultimate test for the advancement of peace is an Israeli commitment to a two-state solution in which an independent Palestinian state—with Jerusalem as its capitol—will be established alongside Israel.[48]

Jordan's response is puzzling for three reasons: Jordan has had a peace agreement with Israel since 1994. The United Arab Emirates provides economic support to Jordan. The peace agreement between Israel and the United Arab Emirates could cool the voices in Jordan, pressuring King Abdullah II to cancel the peace agreement between Israel and Jordan.

So why the tepid response? Jordan's reaction does not reflect a lack of support for the accords. Instead, it reflects that Jordan—of all the Arab states—has a highly complex relationship with the Palestinian issue. Why? It is important to take into account that Jordan ruled the West Bank for nearly twenty years (1948–1967). Most of Jordan's population is Palestinian. An estimated four million Palestinians live in Jordan, most of whom are Jordanian citizens. Most Palestinians in Jordan are from the West Bank. However, there are also hundreds of thousands of Palestinians in Jordan who are from the Gaza Strip. Most of them live in Palestinian refugee camps in Jordan, and most do not have Jordanian citizenship. King Abdullah II's biggest fear is that the Palestinians' demand for an independent state will morph into a request to include Jordan as part of the Palestinian State. Therefore, Jordan emphasizes that resolving the Israeli-Palestinian conflict requires establishing an independent Palestinian state alongside the State of Israel and Jordan. Not in Jordan.

Jordan's reserved reaction to the Abraham Accords must be viewed side by side with President Trump's "Peace to Prosperity" plan introduced in January

2020. (We will look more into the plan in Chapter 9.) Jordan is concerned that the proposed peace plan and the Abraham Accords are pushing the Palestinians to the wall. They feel their dream of a state is fading. This situation could result in a Palestinian counteraction that could evoke a wave of violence that could spread to Jordan.

Though Jordan is committed to the establishment of an independent Palestinian state with East Jerusalem as its capitol, Jordan views itself—and not the Palestinians—as the only legitimate Muslim factor to rule the Haram-al-Sharif. Indeed, Article 9 of the 1994 Israeli Jordanian Peace Treaty emphasizes that Jordan is the counterpart for discussion regarding the Islamic sacred sites in Jerusalem—as well as, of course, the most important place, al-Haram al-Sharif. As you can imagine, that article is a source of constant tension between Jordan and the Palestinians.

Qatar

Qatar has refrained from an official response. Qatar's silence is not accidental.

Qatar aspires to be a regional power like Iran and Turkey. It is always looking for opportunities to amass power and gain leverage. This is one reason Qatar has positioned itself as the primary funder of the Hamas government in the Gaza Strip.

Given Qatar's policies—especially supporting the Muslim Brotherhood and militant Islam organizations, aligning itself with Turkey, and having a friendly policy toward Iran—one would have expected Qatar to be formally a part of the "opposing camp."

But that is not the case. Qatar approached the subject of the agreements differently.

First, Qatar was silent for a long time. In January 2021, when referring to the issue of possible normalization agreements between Qatar and Israel, Qatar's Foreign Minister Mohammad Bin Abdel al Rahman al-Thani said, "It is an issue for each country to decide for itself." He added that "Qatari-Israeli normalization is conditioned upon Israel fully accepting the Arab peace initiative." He refers to the late Saudi King Saud Abdulaziz bin 'Abd-al-Rahman Al-Saud's 2002 Saudi Initiative (we will discuss this more in Chapter 9). He added, "It would also be conditioned on complete Israeli withdrawal from the Golan Heights and areas Israel occupies in south Lebanon."[49]

Qatar's position reflects its desire to dance at both weddings. On the one hand, Qatar did not openly condemn or criticize the Abraham Accords because Qatar did not want to risk tension with the Trump administration. On the other hand, Qatar wants to signal its partners—Turkey and Iran—that the monarchy shares its rejection of the agreement.

Tunisia

Islamists are influential in Tunisia. Not surprisingly, the Islamists vocally oppose the Israel-UAE agreement and the Abraham Accords. The intriguing thing is the position of Tunisia's president, Kais Saied. He is a vocal opponent of Israel and a supporter of the Palestinian Islamist movement, Hamas. He is known for his robust rejection of any normalization with Israel.

Given that profile, we could expect that Saied would oppose the agreement. But that is not the case. Saied refrained from criticizing the agreements and justified his position, announcing that it was a UAE internal affair. The Tunisian president wants to clarify that he is not necessarily in "Turkey's pocket." He wants Turkey and the UAE to know that he is interested in maintaining good relations with the UAE.

Saied's position rewarded him. During the political crisis in Tunisia in July 2021, which we discussed in Chapter 5, the foreign minister of Bahrain and the senior political advisor of the ruler of the UAE both came to Tunisia to express solidarity and support for Saied.

Yemen

In response to the Israel-UAE agreement and the Abraham Accords, the ousted Yemenite government led by Abd Rabbu Mansour Hadi officially announced that it "adheres to its support for the Palestinian cause and Palestinian demands." A senior advisor of Hadi, al-Malek al-Khalafi, tweeted the following: "Normalization with the enemy (Israel) is not acceptable to the Arab people and is contrary to the Arab solidarity and Arab interests. It harms the Palestinian cause and serves the Zionist project and other projects that harm the Arab nation."[50]

Al-Khalafi's 'chilly' response is interesting because the UAE is one of Hadi's prominent supporters and wants to regain his ousted government's rule. So, why was Hadi's response so cold—some would even say thankless?

To understand it, we need to remember the construct of the war in Yemen and its evolution.

While the UAE supports Hadi's government in its fight with the Houthis and Iran to restore Hadi's control over Yemen, there is also the conflict between Hadi and the UAE in southern Yemen.

We need to remember that the STC, a secessionist militia—backed by the UAE—broke off from Hadi's exiled Aden-based government. And in the summer of 2020, the STC took over the Socotra Island and raised South Yemen's flag—the entity they want to create.

The UAE supports the STC because Abu Dhabi wants to be sure it controls the Socotra archipelago and the path to the Bab el-Mandeb and the Red Sea. So, when al-Khalafi mentioned "the other projects that harm the Arab nation," he referred to the UAE's takeover of Socotra.

Formalizing the Relationship Between Israel and the Arab Gulf Monarchies?

Since September 2020, one of the most popular questions I have been asked in every briefing, class, course, or seminar I have taught is, "Will Saudi Arabia join the train of normalization?"

I would like to reiterate an important point. Bahrain and the UAE would not have entered the agreement with Israel without the approval of Saudi Arabia.

Saudi Arabia and Israel share long-term strategic interests. One should assume they maintain various communication channels and cooperation areas, particularly in the security and intelligence fields. However, as of the summer of 2021, formally joining the train of normalization holds no particular benefit for the Saudis. I asses that transfer of the royal scepter to MBS may lead to a change in Saudi Arabia's position.

Though they have not joined the Abraham Accords, two other Arab gulf monarchies—Oman and Qatar—have a relationship with Israel. Former Israeli Prime Minister Benjamin Netanyahu made an official visit to Oman in October 2018 and met with the late Omani ruler, Sultan Qaboos bin Said. Qatar and Israel also have ongoing communication and cooperation. Some of the connection and coordination have to do with Gaza. For example, coordinating Qatar's money transfers to the Gaza Strip. Qatari delegations that visit Gaza also enter Gaza from Israel. But the relationship between Jerusalem and Doha goes beyond purely administrative and logistic issues.

However, like Saudi Arabia, formally joining the train of normalization holds no particular benefit to Oman or Qatar. The two will, therefore, in the immediate future, likely maintain the current nature of their relationships with Israel.

In Kuwait, Islamist circles vocally oppose any normalization with Israel. Though in the December 2020 elections in Kuwait, Islamists lost power, normalization between Israel and Kuwait is unlikely in the foreseeable future.

However, I do believe that Saudi Arabia will formalize its relationship with Israel in this decade. Following that, I believe other Arab Gulf monarchies will also establish official relationships with the State of Israel.

I opened this chapter explaining that the Abraham Accords is the outcome of two critical processes that reflect the Middle East's changing geopolitical landscape. One process is the formation of the alliance of moderation.

The other process that led to the Abraham Accords is that the Palestinian cause—or as it is known in Arabic, *Al Qadiyah al-Filastiniyah*—has plummeted on the Arab political agenda. We will explore that development in the next chapter.

CHAPTER 9

THE CHANGING MIDDLE EAST | AND ITS IMPACT ON THE TRAJECTORY OF THE ISRAELI-PALESTINIAN CONFLICT

Challenging Western Narratives

A common refrain in the West is that the Israeli-Palestinian conflict shapes the Middle East. Anyone familiar with my work knows that I argue the exact opposite. It is events and developments in the Middle East that shape the trajectory of the Israeli-Palestinian conflict.

This chapter will connect the dots between events in the region. The trajectory of the Israeli-Palestinian conflict, the Abraham Accords, the normalization agreements, and the Peace to Prosperity plan that former US President Donald Trump presented in January 2020.

Six Phases of the Israeli-Palestinian Conflict

Since the early phases of the conflict between the Zionist movement and the Arabs in the area then known as Palestine / *Eretz Yisrael,* "the Land of Israel," the Palestinian cause has had a central place in the intellectual and political discourse in the Arab world. When surveying the position of the Palestinian cause on the political agenda of the Arab world, there are six distinct phases.

Phase 1. The first phase was from the late nineteenth to the early twentieth century until the end of World War I (1914–1918). At that time, the conflict was primarily confined to agricultural and domestic disputes—land use and water rights, whose cattle could graze where, and so forth.

Phase 2. The second phase was post-World War I (1918) until 1948. It was during this period that the conflict took on a nationalistic tone. The Jewish Zionists on one side and the Arab Palestinians on the other side. The main difference between the Jews and the Arabs in Eretz Yisrael/the Land of Palestine at this juncture was that the Zionists undoubtedly had a sense of nationalism—they were building the Jewish state. In contrast, a sense of Palestinian particularistic nationalism was yet in its early phase.

As the conflict between the Jews and Palestinians escalated on the ground, the Arab world became increasingly involved in the growing conflict.

The war of 1948 transformed the local domestic conflict into a war between the State of Israel and Arab armies, particularly Egypt, Iraq, Jordan, and Syria.

Phase 3. The third phase was from 1948 to 1967. After the 1948 war, the Arab world took upon itself to "Liberate Palestine" from the "Zionist invasion." Arab leaders vowed to eliminate the state of Israel using military force.

This desire—spearheaded particularly by Egyptian President (1956–1970) Gamal Abdel Nasser—is what led to the 1967 War between Israel and Arab armies from mainly Egypt, Jordan, and Syria.

Israel defeated the Arab armies and occupied the Sinai Peninsula, the West Bank (including the part of Jerusalem that Jordan ruled between 1948 and 1967), the Gaza Strip, and the Golan Heights.

Phase 4. The fourth phase was between 1967 and 1987. A milestone in that phase was the 1973 war between Israel and Egypt, and Syria. The 1973 war was the last military confrontation between Israel and Egypt.

Another milestone in that phase—influenced by Egyptian President (1970–1981) Muhammad Anwar al-Sadat's realization that Israel could not be defeated militarily—was in 1979 when Sadat signed a peace treaty with Israel.

Phase 5. The fifth phase was between 1987 and 2005. In 1987, the first Palestinian popular uprising—the Intifada—began. The word *intifada* in

Arabic means "to shake off a bad disease." The first intifada was when the Israeli-Palestinian conflict severely escalated. Over one thousand Palestinians and almost one hundred Israelis were killed during the intifada.

The intifada generated a political and diplomatic process that led to the signing of the Oslo Accords between Israel and the Palestinian Liberation Organization (PLO).

On September 13, 1993, Israeli Prime Minister Yitzhak Rabin and Palestine Liberation Organization (PLO) Negotiator Mahmoud Abbas signed a Declaration of Principles on Interim Self-Government Arrangements, commonly referred to as the "Oslo Accord," at the White House. Israel accepted the PLO as the representative of the Palestinians, and the PLO renounced terrorism and recognized Israel's right to exist in peace. Both sides agreed that a Palestinian Authority (PA) would be established and assume governing responsibilities in the West Bank and Gaza Strip over five years. Then, permanent status talks on the issues of borders, refugees, and Jerusalem would be held.[1]

The Oslo Accords raised hopes for a peaceful solution of the conflict. But the high hopes crashed into the ground of reality.

During the second part of the 1990s, the Palestinian Islamic organizations Hamas and Islamic Jihad in Palestine perpetrated terror attacks targeting Israeli civilians and Israeli cities—including suicide bombers.

The Palestinians blamed Israel for the escalation, arguing Israel was continuing to build settlements in the West Bank and Gaza. The Israelis blamed the Palestinians for the escalation because of the violence and the deaths they caused. The sides got caught in an endless loop of blaming each other.

In an attempt to reverse the deterioration that evolved on the ground since signing the Oslo Accords in 1993, the United States hosted the Camp David Summit in July 2000. The summit failed.

And in October 2000, a volcano of massive violence erupted between the Israelis and Palestinians. The events between 2000 and 2006 are generally called "the Second Intifada." The Arabs call it the "Al-Quds Intifada."

Between 1989 and 2007, there were over 150 Palestinian suicide bombing attacks. Most of the attackers came from the areas the Palestinian Authority governed in the West Bank. Most of the victims were Israeli civilians.

Between 2000 and 2006, more than five thousand Palestinians (roughly half were civilians) and one thousand Israelis (mostly civilians) were killed. Tens of thousands of Palestinians and Israelis were injured.

The lethal outcomes of the violence during the al-Quds intifada prompted Israel to launch a military campaign in 2002. In Operation Defensive Shield, the IDF (Israeli Defense Forces) restored Israeli control over most of the areas controlled by the Palestinian Authority. During the operation, Israel dismantled Hamas and Islamic Jihad in Palestine's infrastructure in the West Bank responsible for planning and executing the suicide bomber attacks. Operation Defensive Shield succeeded in significantly reducing the volume of attacks.

During this time, the Arab world was committed to stand by the Palestinians. The leading Arab states—Egypt and Saudi Arabia—engaged in diplomatic efforts to advance a process to resolve the conflict through negotiations and compromises. Saudi Arabian Crown Prince (and later the king) Abdullah bin Abdulaziz Al-Saud promoted a peace initiative called "the Arab Peace Initiative" or "the Saudi Initiative." The Arab League adopted his proposal in 2002. During that period, the prominent Arab leaders continued to stand by the Palestinians and their cause and tried to promote a diplomatic effort to resolve the conflict.

Phase 6. The sixth phase takes place from 2005 until today. In 2005, Israel unilaterally withdrew from Gaza and handed governance of the Gaza Strip to the Palestinian Authority.

The PA rule over Gaza did not last long. In 2007 Hamas launched a coup, violently overthrowing the Palestinian Authority.

Since the 2007 coup, there has been a split between Hamas and the Palestinian Authority. And the competing governments—Hamas in the Gaza Strip and the Palestinian Authority in the West Bank—since 2007 have been unable to reconcile.

Arab leaders—specifically Egypt and Saudi Arabia—have tried to resolve the split. All efforts failed because neither Hamas nor the Palestinian Authority honored the numerous Arab-brokered reconciliation agreements they signed. Their behavior insulted the most important leaders of the Arab world. And finally, in addition to refusing to reconcile their own inner-differences, the Arab world increasingly saw that the Palestinians did not want to compromise with the Israelis either.

To summarize the evolution of the relationship between the Arab world and the Palestinians: Over time, the trajectory has shifted. Until the 1967 war, the Arab world viewed the Palestinian cause as an Arab task that the Arabs must solve by force. Following the 1967 war, the Arab narrative changed and emphasized the need to achieve a diplomatic solution to the conflict. Thus, the Arab world took the responsibility to support a diplomatic solution. However, it is first and foremost the Palestinians' responsibility.

Since 2007, the Changing Geopolitical Environment Has Caused the Palestinian Issue to Plummet on the Arab World's Political Agenda

Since 2007, although Arab rhetoric continues to emphasize Arab solidarity with the Palestinians, the Palestinian cause has become less of a priority on the political agenda of the Arab world and its leadership. The central Arab leaders do not consider themselves obligated to automatically support the Palestinians—let alone solve their problems.

This process has occurred in parallel—and not by chance—with three developments discussed in this book: Iran's hegemonic ambitions, Turkey's hegemonic aspirations, and the struggle over path, identity, and direction in Arab societies.

Parallel to the Arab world becoming more frustrated with Palestinian stubbornness, the Arab world's problems were also mounting at the beginning of the twenty-first century. Domestically, socio-economic and political challenges were literally ripping countries apart.

The Arab world, engulfed with its own mounting challenges, now expects the Palestinians to adjust their expectations and narratives to the region's new geopolitical map.

Moreover, the fact that Hamas and IJIP side with Iran and Turkey—two rivals of the Arab world—further fuels Arab anger and frustration with the Palestinians.

The Palestinians have alienated their brothers, the major Arab countries, who genuinely care for the Palestinians and want to help them and their cause.

We saw the overt indicators of this shift when the United States moved its embassy to Jerusalem in May 2018. Voices in the West and the Western media forecasted a violent uproar. They were wrong. The reaction in the Arab world was minimal. The streets in the Arab countries remained quiet. There was no overwhelming public outcry. And Arab governments' responses were mostly limited to diplomatic statements rejecting the move.

As the geopolitical features of the Middle East change, the Palestinian cause and the Palestinian people find themselves—domestically, regionally, and internationally—at an all-time low.

The Palestinians are angry and disappointed with the Arab world's increasingly shifting policy. And they are aware that their cause has plummeted on the Arab world's list of priorities. Dr. Nasser al-Laham, the chief-editor of the official Palestinian Authority news agency Ma'an, reflects this in a January 28, 2020, article called "A Syrian Style Reply." In his piece, he writes: "…We (Palestinians) know that (Arab) missiles will not rain down on Tel Aviv. We know that Arab countries will not sever ties with the US. We know that Arab armies are not going to gather next to Israel's borders. We know that Arab leaders will kiss Trump's hand in the back room. Yet, Trump's plan will result in another one hundred years of suffering and misery."[2]

On the same day that article was published, thousands of miles away from the region, a significant milestone occurred in the Israeli-Palestinian conflict.

US President Donald Trump's "Peace to Prosperity" Plan

On Tuesday, January 28, 2020, former US President Donald Trump presented his plan to end the Israeli-Palestinian conflict. A plan he called "Peace to Prosperity: A Vision to Improve the Lives of the Palestinian and Israeli People" was introduced in a ceremony at the White House. Attendees included Israeli Prime Minister Benjamin Netanyahu, senior US government officials, and the Bahrain, Oman, and United Arab Emirates ambassadors.

The plan's central points were the following:

Establishing a Palestinian State:

- A demilitarized Palestinian State will be established in 70 percent of the West Bank.
- Ninety-seven percent of the Palestinians in the West Bank will live in the Palestinian state.
- That state will be physically connected to the Gaza Strip.
- The Palestinian state will be offered additional lands in the Western part of the Negev in southern Israel to compensate for the West Bank lands, where Israeli settlements already exist.
- The Palestinian State will have security forces to enforce the law and public order and prevent the launching of terror attacks from the Palestinian State on Israel, Jordan, and Egypt.

Establishing the Palestinian State will be done gradually and subject to conditions including:
- Restoring the Palestinian Authority as the governing body in the Gaza Strip.
- Disarming Hamas, Islamic Jihad, and all other Palestinian militias.
- Demilitarizing the Gaza Strip.
- Hamas can be part of the Palestinian government, provided it will accept Israel's right to exist, stop terror, and comply with previous agreements signed between Israel and the Palestinians.
- Recognizing Israel as the homeland of the Jewish people.
- Ending incitement and fighting terror.

Security Arrangements:
- Israel alone will secure its borders.
- Israel's eastern border is the Jordan River.
- Israel will maintain control over the air space west of the Jordan River.
- Israel will have at least one early warning system within the Palestinian territory.

Settlements:
- Settlements will not be dismantled, and they will become part of Israel.

- Isolated settlements will stay as Israeli enclaves.
- Israel will freeze building in the West Bank during the four years of the negotiation phase.

The Status of Jerusalem:

- Jerusalem will remain united and undivided under Israel's sovereignty.
- Freedom of worship for all religions in Jerusalem will be secured.
- The security fence Israel built in Jerusalem will remain and will be a physical border.
- The Palestinian capitol will be located in Arab neighborhoods that are east and north of the current security fence.
- The United States will open an Embassy in the Palestinian capitol.

Palestinian Refugees:

- Palestinian refugees cannot live in Israel.
- Palestinian refugees can choose to live in the Palestinian State or, subject to the hosting state's consent, to be incorporated where they are currently living. For ten years, fifty thousand refugees will be offered the option to settle in Muslim countries (subject to the country's consent).

Economy:

- Establishing an international fund that will allocate tens of billions of dollars to build the Palestinian State's economy, infrastructure, trade, tourism, education, etc.
- The Palestinian State can use designated piers at Israeli and Jordanian ports. A Palestinian harbor and an airport will be subject to fulfilling the conditions of the agreement.
- The United States will sign a Free Trade Agreement with the Palestinian government.

Prisoners:

- Palestinians convicted of murder or terror plots to commit murder will not be released.
- The rest of the prisoners will be released in two phases:

o Phase 1: Women, people over fifty years old, minors, prisoners who are currently ill, those who already served more than two-thirds of their sentence.

o Phase 2: Israel will determine the numbers of prisoners to be released, as well as their profile at a later (undetermined) date.

The Responses in the Middle East to the Proposal
Israel
In Israel, the Israeli public opinion generally welcomed the plan. Israeli Arabs, the Israeli left, and the Israeli far-right opposed.

The Palestinians
The Palestinians rejected the plan.

The Region
The same camp that today opposes the Abraham Accords opposed Trump's plan. That includes the al-Assad regime in Syria, Hezbollah, Iran, the Palestinians, Tunisia, and Turkey.

At the Palestinian President Mahmoud Abbas's request, foreign ministers of Arab League members met in Cairo on February 1, 2020. There was a unanimous agreement and a formal statement issued by the Arab League rejecting Trump's plan after the meeting.

The announcement emphasized that the plan should be based on the Arab Peace Initiative offered by the late Saudi King Abdullah bin Abdulaziz Al-Saud, which was officially adopted in Beirut's Arab Summit in March 2002. The Arab League reaffirmed the initiative in a March 2007 Summit in Saudi Arabia. This initiative outlines the following terms for Israeli-Arab peace:

- The establishment of a Palestinian state.
- The establishment of a Palestinian State within the 1967 borders with its capitol in East Jerusalem.
- The agreement must comply with United Nations Security Council Resolutions.
- Settling the Palestinian refugee issue.
- Israeli withdrawal from the Golan Heights.

Arab leaders—including Saudi King Salman bin Abdul Aziz Al Saud and Egyptian President Abd al-Fatah al-Sisi—said they would support any decision the Palestinians make.

The subtext of that statement was that Arab major leaders expect the Palestinians to adopt a pragmatic approach toward the Israeli-Palestinian conflict.

The Importance of Trump's Plan

Critics of President Trump's plan correctly argued that the proposal is very close to Israel's position and that the Palestinians will never accept it. The critics, therefore, concluded that the framework is of no importance. I think that outlook calls for closer inspection.

Indeed, it should be clear that Trump's outline was not even the beginning of the beginning. The construct proposed by the Trump administration was, at most, perhaps the starting point of an awfully long journey that has no certainty of being fulfilled. The path to practical, sustainable arrangements—let alone "peace"—is long. I would say the same for any plan.

However, I argue that Trump's plan is significant for three reasons.

First, though the Quorum of Arab League foreign ministers officially rejected the plan, it is important to note that at the same time, another message to the Palestinians is echoed in the Arab public discourse. The message is, "things have changed, the world has changed, the region has changed. And you (the Palestinians) need to consider taking what you have been offered." Here are some examples.

Lebanese senior columnist Elias Harfoush accurately addresses this matter in his January 31, 2020, article titled "This Deal is the Result of the Region's Conditions." He wrote, "We should admit that this deal reflects the balance of power between the Israelis and the Palestinians and between Israel and the Arabs as well. It also reflects the reality of Arabs' priority and the place of the Palestinian cause among those priorities."[3]

On February 5, 2020, senior Egyptian journalist Abdelmonem Saeid wrote an article, "The 'Deal of the Century' is Back!" in which he said, "the Arabs do not reject President Trump's initiative but see it as the basis for negotiations."[4]

On February 24, 2020, Egyptian writer Khaled al-Berry wrote, "If I Were Palestinian." In the article, he says, "Palestinians must recognize the reality and adopt a practical approach that will enable them to build a future of dignity and hope. They should reject slogans like 'the armed resistance.'"[5]

The second reason Trump's plan is significant is that it marked the end of the paradigm that has dominated previous Western diplomatic efforts to end the conflict.

The proposal raised three points that the West never presented as elements of a settlement.

- Jerusalem will not be divided and remains under Israeli sovereignty.
- Hamas, Islamic Jihad in Palestine, and all other Palestinian militias must disarm as a condition for establishing a Palestinian state.
- Once and for all, Palestinians must relinquish their demand that Palestinian refugees and their descendants be resettled in Israel, a Palestinian concept known as "the Right of Return"—*Haq al-'Awda* in Arabic.

And finally, the framework is significant because it will set the tone for future frameworks. On that matter, Lebanese columnist Hussam Itani wrote an article published on January 30, 2020, titled "Trump's Plan: Imposing the *Fait Accompli* on the Palestinians." He said, "Trump's successor may not agree with Trump on anything other than the need to adopt Trump's approach toward the Israeli-Palestinian issue."[6]

The fact that the forty-sixth president of the United States, Joe Biden, is a Democrat and will likely be much friendlier to the Palestinians than the Trump administration does not contradict my observation about the importance of Trump's Middle East legacy, including his Peace to Prosperity plan. In fact, it strengthens it. To a certain extent, Trump's approach will help President Biden. Trump's Middle East policy successfully challenged Western policy assumptions about the conflict. For example, the narrative that moving the US Embassy to Jerusalem or the United States recognizing Israeli sovereignty in the Golan Heights would cause a diplomatic Arab tsunami and ignite widespread violence. In both cases, neither happened.

Trump also proved that the assumption that peace between Israel and other Arab states was unachievable without a solution or at least a breakthrough in the Israeli-Palestinian conflict was wrong. The Abraham Accords and the normalization agreements between Israel, the UAE, Bahrain, Sudan, and Morocco are the proof. Trump, to say it figuratively, paved the road for a different approach.

Former President Trump's plan and the Abraham Accords can potentially positively impact the Israeli-Palestinian conflict trajectory. In that regard, in April 2021, Palestinian scholar Dr. Nagi Sadeq Sharab wrote an article "Biden, Palestine and the Palestinian State." Biden has better odds than his predecessors to succeed on the Israeli-Palestinian case because the political atmosphere is more receptive to an Israeli-Palestinian solution. One reason for that is the legacy of the Trump administration that created some facts on the ground— like in Jerusalem, the settlements, the Palestinian State, and other issues.[7]

The Impact of Trump's Plan and the Abraham Accords on the Trajectory of the Israeli-Palestinian Conflict

I opened this chapter by highlighting that the common narrative is that the Israeli-Palestinian conflict is what impacts the geopolitical environment of the Middle East. I want to emphasize that it is the other way around. The changing geopolitical landscape of the Middle East provided the conditions and ground for Trump's Peace to Prosperity plan and the Abraham Accords.

Those developments in 2020, the Abraham Accords and Trump's approach to the Israeli-Palestinian conflict, divorced themselves from narratives and concepts that did not dialogue with or reflect the reality on the ground.

Peace to Prosperity and the Abraham Accords offered the Israelis and the Palestinians a new path that had the potential to be a constructive framework. Unfortunately, once again, the sides failed to seize the opportunity.

The War between Israel and Hamas, May 10 - 21, 2021

The Palestinian Elections Fiasco and Its Ramifications

The Palestinians were angry, concerned, and frustrated with both Trump's peace plan and the Abraham Accords. The Palestinians needed to stop what they viewed as an avalanche.

In January 2021, exactly one year after the publication of the Trump plan, Palestinian President Mahmoud Abbas signed a Presidential Decree to hold elections for the Palestinian Parliament, the Presidency, and the National Palestinian Council. The Palestinian Authority elections were to take place in three phases—May, July, and August 2021, respectively.

However, as we will see, that path ended up in a dead-end. Above all, the cul-de-sac reflects the fact that the Palestinians are caught in the loop of their own divide. And once again, the results were tragic for both Palestinians and Israelis.

The first elections for the Palestinian Parliament and the position of chairman of the Palestinian Authority (PA) took place in 1996. The Palestinian Authority, created by the Oslo Accords, rules parts of the West Bank and governs the majority of the Palestinians in the West Bank. In 1996, the *Fath* movement won the majority of the seats. And Yasser Arafat, the chairman of the Fath party until he died in 2004, was elected as the chairman of the Palestinian Authority.

The second election for the Palestinian parliament took place in 2006. Hamas won the majority of the seats.

Mahmoud Abbas (Abu Mazen), who succeeded Yasser Arafat as the chairman of Fath, was elected in 2005 to be the Palestinian Authority's chairman. His position is commonly described as "president"—both by Palestinian as well as international circles. Therefore, I will use the term president. In 2009, the Central Council of the PLO extended his term as president of the Palestinian Authority indefinitely.

What Motivated Mahmoud Abbas to Hold Elections?

Some European Union members had been pressuring Abbas to hold elections. However, at the same time, the Biden administration hinted it did not think it was the right time for elections. Therefore, in my estimation, it is unlikely that Abbas's decision stemmed from international pressure.

To understand Abbas's objectives in announcing the elections, I would like to share what I believe were Abbas's underlying assumptions.

First, Hamas was at a crossroads. In the 2006 elections, Hamas won seventy-four out of 132 seats of the Palestinian parliament. It was unlikely Hamas would win as many seats in 2021 as it did in 2006. Since 2006, Hamas has been broadly and increasingly criticized both by Palestinians and the Arab world for its violent takeover of Gaza, the despair and destruction Hamas's rule has inflicted on Gaza, and Hamas's support for Iran. In the international arena, the United States and the European Union define Hamas as a terrorist organization. Hamas defines itself as the branch of the Muslim Brotherhood in Palestine. In addition to all the challenges it faces as the government in Gaza, Hamas, like political Islam chapters across the Middle East, faces inner tensions between dogmatism and pragmatism. Hamas's growing challenges are increasing the divide within Hamas regarding its path ahead.

Second, Abbas structured the elections in a way that Hamas could not secure a majority in the Palestinian parliament. Therefore, Abbas was confident that Fath could form a coalition to secure a majority in the parliament.

Third, Hamas reportedly said it would not run a candidate for the presidential election. Therefore, the next president would continue to be a member of Fath.

Abbas apparently thought that holding elections was his opportunity to secure Fath's control in the main power centers: the parliament and the presidency.

I believe Abbas had two goals when he decided to hold elections.

As we have discussed, the Palestinian cause—or as it is known in Arabic, al Qadiyah al-Filastiniyah—has plummeted on the Arab political agenda. President Abbas wanted to stop the erosion. A significant obstacle on that path is the justified critics that argue since Abbas and PA were not democratically re-elected once their term expired in 2009, they have no legitimacy. Furthermore, the Palestinian Parliament has not convened since the last elections in 2006—meaning, they have not convened at all. He believed securing Fath and the PA's governance through elections would provide them the legitimacy they needed to both regain their central place on the political agenda of the Arab states and bolster the status of the Palestinian Authority in the regional and international arena.

Another goal was connected to his own legacy. Palestinian President Mahmoud Abbas is eighty-five years old, and his health is declining. Since the beginning of the Palestinian national movement, he has been one of its central leaders. He represents the generation who founded Fath. It is the twilight of his tenure and the sunset of Fath's founding leadership. Fath is not only facing a leadership change—it is facing a generational shift. Securing Fath and the PA's rule through elections would mark a triumph of Fath over its major rival—Hamas. A victory that would decisively prove that Fath's path, which includes negotiations and public diplomacy, as opposed to Hamas's path of violence, is the right path for the Palestinians to pursue.

But Abbas's January 2021 announcement was received with mixed feelings in the Palestinian and Arab streets. Some hoped the elections would pave the way to Palestinian reconciliation between Hamas and the Palestinian Authority. Some even speculated that Hamas and Fath would create a joint list and run together.

However, the dominant sentiment on the Palestinian street was one of skepticism. Many Palestinians doubted the elections would end the Palestinian split. Many Palestinians doubted the elections would take place at all. And if they did, given their history, people wondered if Hamas and Fath would respect and accept the results. Hamas violently overthrew the Palestinian Authority in Gaza in 2007. And since then, both have subsequently ignored all reconciliation agreements they signed since the 2007 coup.

These doubts and skepticism were fully justified. Less than five months later, Abbas canceled the elections.

Why Did President Abbas Cancel the Elections?

On April 29, 2021, President Abbas canceled the Palestinian elections on the grounds that Israel had refused to allow Jerusalemite Palestinians to vote in the elections.

Jerusalemite Palestinians

I would like to explain the term *Jerusalemite Palestinian*. Jerusalem is the capitol of Israel. The city's population is about 940,000 people. About 563,000 are Jews, and 360,000 are Arabs, of whom 345,000 are Muslims.[8]

Most of the Arabs in the city are also known as Jerusalemite Palestinians. Most of the Jerusalemite Palestinians are permanent residents of the State of Israel.

Permanent residents in Israel are not Israeli citizens. They do not hold an Israeli passport. On the other hand, permanent residents have official Israeli Identity Cards (*Teudat Zehut*). They can live and work anywhere in Israel. They are entitled to receive all the benefits and social services an Israeli citizen receives—education, health insurance, medical services, social security, pension, unemployment benefits, etc. A permanent resident in Israel, including a Jerusalem Palestinian, has the full right to become an Israeli citizen and receive all the benefits of an Israeli citizen. And indeed, many of the Jerusalemite Palestinians have chosen to exercise this right.

A permanent resident cannot participate in Israeli general elections (neither as a voter nor a candidate).

However, Jerusalemite Palestinians are able to run and vote in the Jerusalem Municipal elections. According to the Oslo Accords, Jerusalemite Palestinians who are permanent residents can vote in the Palestinian Authority elections. Indeed, in the 2006 Palestinian Authority elections, about six thousand Jerusalemite Palestinians voted. However, according to the Oslo Accords, Jerusalemite Palestinians cannot run for elected office in the Palestinian Authority. This time, in 2021, the Palestinian Authority demanded Israel allow Jerusalemite Palestinians to run for elected office in the Palestinian Authority. Israel refused their demand. That refusal provided Abbas the excuse to cancel the elections.

But the issue of participation of Jerusalemite Palestinians in the elections was an excuse. What were the real reasons Abbas decided to cancel the elections?

To answer that question, I would like to zoom out. Let's expand our perspective and explore Palestinian politics. Particularly the two major Palestinian powers: the Palestinian National Authority (PA) and its Fath movement, the major party in the PA, and the Islamist movement Hamas.

The Palestinian National Authority (PA) and Fath

The word Fath is commonly spelled and pronounced in English as 'Fatah.' But the correct spelling is Fath—pronounced 'Fateh.' Fath is a reverse acronym in Arabic of *Harakat Tahrir Filastin,* or "the Palestinian Liberation Movement." There are two reasons for reversing the name. First, *hatf* in Arabic means "sudden death." Second, one of the meanings of the word *fath* is "conquering"—a term that associates the movement with the times Islam spread throughout the region by waging military campaigns in the seventh century.

Fath was established in Kuwait in 1959. In 1964, Egypt created the Palestinian Liberation Organization (PLO), a network of various Palestinian organizations to counter the power of Fath. However, by 1969 Fath had taken over the PLO. Yasser Arafat, one of the founders of Fath, became the chairman of the PLO. And Fath became the major Palestinian organization in the PLO.

The Oslo Accords created the Palestinian National Authority (PNA or PA) as a semi-state entity. According to Oslo, the PA is the Palestinians' interim governing body in the West Bank and Gaza until a final agreement is signed between Israel and the Palestinians. Formally, the Palestinian Authority is not recognized as a state. However, in practice, it has functioned as a state since it was established in 1994, and it governs parts of the West Bank. The Palestinian Authority rules the overwhelming majority of Palestinians in the West Bank. The Palestinian Authority includes other PLO groups, but Fath is the largest party and is the PA's backbone.

In October 2005, Israel completed its unilateral evacuation of all settlers and settlements from the Gaza Strip. Upon leaving Gaza, Israel handed control of the Gaza Strip to the Palestinian Authority. Yet, the PA's rule over Gaza did not last long.

In June 2007, Hamas violently overthrew the Palestinian Authority's government in Gaza. Since then, Hamas has ruled the Gaza Strip.

Hamas

The other major Palestinian power is Hamas. Hamas has two meanings. The English translation is "zeal." But Hamas is also the acronym for *Harakat Al-Muqawama Al-Islamia,* or "the Islamic Resistance Movement."

Established in the Gaza Strip in 1987, Hamas defines itself as the branch of the Muslim Brotherhood in Palestine. Some in the West erroneously think that Hamas's final objective is to create a Palestinian state. However, Hamas is a part of the Muslim Brotherhood and therefore adheres to political Islam. Therefore, ideologically, Hamas objects to the concept of a particularistic nationalism, including Palestinian nationalism. As adherents of political Islam, Hamas's goal is the creation of a global caliphate.

However, like all political Islam organizations (as we have discussed earlier in the book), Hamas can be pragmatic (not moderate). So, for the time being, on the road to the caliphate, Hamas is willing to accept the existence of a Palestinian State.

Hamas's founding charter (1987) vows to eliminate Israel through violence (jihad). Hamas rejects any compromise. Hamas does not accept Israel's right to exist. Hamas's charter also expresses extreme anti-Jewish and anti-Western rhetoric. Hamas is a member of the Iranian-backed axis of resistance.

Since 2007 Hamas has ruled the Gaza Strip while the PA rules parts of the West Bank.

Let Us Now Go Back and Explore Why Abbas Canceled the Elections...

As the election day neared, it became more apparent that Fath and Abbas would use the Jerusalemite Palestinians exit card. And, as we just discussed, they did. There were a few reasons they decided to cancel.

One reason was that as election day was approaching, Hamas was demonstrating one united political front. Fath, on the other hand, was clearly and publicly experiencing an inner-political split. In that context, I would like to draw your attention to a specific political factor within Fath—Mohammed Dahlan.

Born in Gaza in 1961, Dahlan was a senior Fath official and was the head of the Palestinian Authority's security forces in Gaza from 1990 until the Hamas coup in June 2007. Given his position, Dahlan was blamed for the collapse of the Palestinian Authority's rule in Gaza and Hamas taking over Gaza. Following Hamas's coup, a bitter rivalry ensued between Dahlan and senior Fath members, particularly Palestinian President Mahmoud Abbas.

In 2011, Fath (Abbas) kicked Dahlan out of the party. He was later convicted in absentia by a Palestinian court of embezzling $1.6 million in funds given to the Palestinian Authority.

For the last decade, Dahlan has been based in the United Arab Emirates. He reportedly serves as an adviser with a security-focused portfolio for Abu Dhabi prince Mohammad Bin Zayed. He has also been described as a middleman for funneling weapons to UAE-backed militias in Libya.[9] Dahlan is also considered to be close with Egyptian President Abdel Fattah al-Sisi. Reportedly, he has led Egyptian diplomatic missions, including negotiations for a dam project—the Grand Ethiopian Renaissance Dam—on the Nile River with Ethiopia and Sudan.

With the UAE and Egypt's support, Dahlan has built a power base in the West Bank—particularly in the major Palestinian refugee camps in the West Bank. Though he holds no formal position in the Democratic Reform Bloc of Fath, Dahlan is considered its leader.

Some Arab observers argue that President Abbas decided to call for Palestinian elections because Abbas and other prominent Fath figures wanted to block Dahlan's growing political power. The rationale of that thesis is that they could ban Dahlan's participation in the elections, arguing that he was kicked out of Fath and was therefore not eligible to run. To me, that seems like weak reasoning. As I mentioned, Dahlan has no formal position in the Democratic Reform Bloc. Therefore, Abbas and Fath could not ban the list from running in the elections.

On the other hand, it was reported that Egypt and Jordan urged Abbas to reconcile with Dahlan and take him back into the Fath party. They argued this would prevent an inner split within Fath. It was clear to everyone that an internal division within Fath would serve Hamas. One way or another, it seemed as if Dahlan, to quote a Palestinian commentator, was to become the "kingmaker" if the Palestinian elections were to take place.

The second reason Abbas canceled the elections was the growing concern among the alliance of moderation powers that Hamas would win and take over the West Bank. Reportedly, Egypt, Israel, Jordan, Saudi Arabia, and the UAE sent messages to Abbas expressing their deep concern about the elections. They all urged Abbas to reconcile with Dahlan and prevent a power struggle within Fath that would serve Hamas.

If Hamas won the elections, it would have served Iran and Turkey—both supporters of Hamas and rivals of the alliance of moderation. Iran and Turkey would have likely done whatever they could to help Hamas get elected. Both Iran and Turkey knew that Hamas would be re-elected in Gaza. And both hoped that Hamas would get stronger in the West Bank. In that regard, Palestinian analyst Dr. Ahmad Rafiq 'Awad evaluated that most Palestinians would not vote for Hamas. But he did expect Hamas would get a total of one-third of the votes. [10]

Iran and Turkey in the West Bank

As we know, Iran and Turkey are heavily engaged in Gaza.

Thus far, Israel and the PA security services have intercepted Iran's attempts to extend its influence into the West Bank.

On the other hand, Turkey has a significant presence in the West Bank and the areas controlled by the PA. Turkey funds religious and cultural non-profit organizations in the West Bank—areas that the Palestinian Authority controls. Turkey funds religious and cultural non-profit organizations in

Turkey and Iran's Presence in the Palestinian Territories

East Jerusalem and has purchased properties in the Old City of Jerusalem, both under Israeli sovereignty.

We have already discussed Erdoğan's support of Hamas. Both ideologically, because they are both adherents of political Islam and the Muslim Brotherhood ideology, and politically, to gain and secure public support in the Arab and Muslim world. Besides supporting Hamas, Erdoğan hosts Hamas's senior leaders, including military leaders, in Turkey.

Turkey, therefore, has an open channel with both of the major Palestinian players—Hamas and Fath. And Erdoğan, as usual, is dancing at both weddings.

For example, in July 2021, Mahmoud Abbas went to Turkey after the May 2021 war between Israel and Hamas (that we will explore shortly). While he was there, he reportedly asked the Turkish president to pressure Hamas to stop its incitement against Fath and the PA.[11] One can assume that Hamas also uses the funds Turkey provides Hamas with to incite against Fath and the Palestinian Authority.

And speaking of Turkey and Palestinian politics here is another intriguing aspect: the nature of Turkey's relationship with Dahlan.

As mentioned above, both Egypt and the UAE support Dahlan. Given the tense relationships between Egypt, the UAE, and Turkey, Dahlan echoes the UAE and Egypt's anti-Turkish rhetoric very loudly. This criticism has set him on a collision course with Turkey. So, in 2020, Erdoğan asked Interpol to issue an arrest warrant for Dahlan. The request was rejected.

Given Dahlan's behavior and Erdoğan's response, one would expect that Turkey would seek to support Dahlan's rivals. However, that may not necessarily be the case. Why?

As I always say, everything in the Middle East is connected. You need to know where to look to connect the dots.

Toward the end of 2020, Turkey changed its tune and signaled interest in improving its diplomatic relations with Israel. The standard explanation for Turkey changing its tune was that Erdoğan wanted to create a positive relationship with the new US administration under President Joe Biden. It was commonly agreed that the Biden administration would pursue a two-state solution. And therefore, it would likely support Palestinian leaders who have the power to play a positive role toward that end. The UAE and Egypt overtly support Dahlan, and he has the Saudis' silent approval. So, Dahlan had the support of all the most significant Arab powers and the members of the alliance of moderation. Given all of this, Erdoğan could not ignore the possibility that Dahlan would become a figure that the Biden administration may view as someone with whom you can negotiate. Looking to have a positive relationship with the Biden administration, Erdoğan may change his tune toward Dahlan. Yesterday's enemy may tomorrow be my best friend.

As Michael Corleone (played by Al Pacino) says to his older brother Sonny *"Santino"* (played by James Caan) in *The Godfather,* "It's not personal Sonny, it's strictly business."[12]

The third reason Abbas canceled the elections was that according to several sources, the Biden administration was transparent that it thought that the time was not suitable for such elections. The messages ranged from alarm to concern and understanding. Dr. Mohsen Mohamed Saleh, professor of Palestinian Studies and president and director general of Al-Zaytouna Center for Studies and Consultations, refers to that in his April 2021 article "A Road Map to Palestinian Legislative Council Elections."

> All signs indicate that the multiple divisions within Fath and the quasi-tribal conflict between the various factions of Fath will reduce its ability to mobilize the Palestinians to enable them to defeat Hamas. The rise of Palestinian forces rejecting the two-state solution, rejecting abandoning violence, refusing to stop the anti-Israel and US rhetoric, and refusing to abandon incitement to the decision-making position will complicate or even completely dispel prospects for the two-state solution.... Certainly, the United States supports and encourages free, fair, transparent, and periodic elections everywhere if possible. But it was also aware of various challenges faced by the Palestinians ... the Biden administration will look with understanding at the possibility of postponing the elections for some time.[13]

It is likely that the Biden administration—like the alliance of moderation—was concerned that Hamas would win its political power or, at a minimum, increase its power.

Those were the reasons Abbas decided to cancel the elections. That decision had immediate and dramatic ramifications on the ground.

Immediate Ratifications of the Palestinian Election Fiasco—Israel-Gaza War, May 10–21, 2021

Monday, May 10, 2021, was "Jerusalem Day." Jerusalem Day is a day when most Israeli Jews celebrate the "unification" (in the Zionist-Israeli narrative) of the city of Jerusalem when Israel won the 1967 War.

On May 10, 2021, at 6:00 p.m., Hamas attacked Jerusalem with rockets. Hamas's attack ignited an eleven-day war, May 10–21, 2021, between Israel and Palestinian Islamists powers in Gaza, namely Hamas and Islamic Jihad in Palestine (IJIP).

During the war, the Palestinians shot around 4,500 rockets and thousands of mortar shells at Israeli cities and communities—including the metropolitan area of Gush Dan and the city of Tel Aviv.

The Israeli air force conducted about 1,500 raids, mainly using high precision weapons targeting Hamas and IJIP tunnels—the METRO, headquarters, training bases, missiles, rocket launchers, and more.

According to a May 24, 2021, Palestinian Ministry of Health report, 256 Palestinians were killed, and 1,948 were injured during the war. On May 30, 2021, the Palestinian National Authority press agency, *Wafa*, reported 257 Palestinians were killed in the war. The Meir Amit Intelligence and Information Center based in Israel documented 260 Palestinians that were killed in the war. According to the Meir Amit Center's report, 153 were men, forty-one were women, and sixty-two were children (under the age of seventeen). At least twenty-one of the civilians that died were killed by failed rocket launches that landed in Gaza. According to the report, upon researching the victims' names, at least 112 of the Palestinians killed in the war (47.8 percent) were active in terrorist organizations. Most of them were militants of Hamas and the Islamic Jihad in Palestine.[14] Significant damage was caused to properties and infrastructure.

On the Israeli side, fourteen people were killed, including one soldier. Hundreds of Israeli civilians were injured, and damage was caused to properties and infrastructure.

At this juncture, I would like to challenge an alarmingly disturbing narrative echoed by some Western media and political circles. And that is the issue of the Israeli Iron Dome missile defense system co-developed by Israel and the United States. The technology assesses and intercepts a variety of short-range rockets. The critics claim that the fact Israel has the Iron Dome is not fair because the Palestinians do not have a missile defense system. Media personality John Oliver described it as an "imbalance."[15] Oliver's view is disturbingly distorted.

But more important is the fact that the Iron Dome does not just protect Israeli lives. Iron Dome saves Palestinian lives. Without the Iron Dome, the thousands of rockets launched from the Gaza Strip would have killed an untold number of Israeli civilians. In that scenario, the Israeli Defense Forces would have no choice but to do whatever it takes to eliminate that threat. The devastation to Gaza would be unthinkable. Iron Dome saves lives—Israeli lives and Palestinian lives.

What Led to the War? The Surface and Underlying Reasons

On the surface, a conjunction of a chain of events in Jerusalem triggered the war.

In 2021, the holy month of *Ramadan* was in May. During Ramadan, Muslims fast during the day. During Ramadan, many more Muslims—and particularly young Muslims—come to the Temple Mount Compound (al-Haram al-Sharif/Har ha-Bayit) than on other days during the year. This year, as Ramadan was approaching, tensions were growing in the city of Jerusalem. The issue was a property dispute in an Arab neighborhood in East Jerusalem called Sheikh Jarrah. The issue, which, as of August 2021, is being appealed in the Israeli Supreme Court, is between Arabs who live in the houses in Sheikh Jarrah and Jews that have the deeds to the property. The tensions in the neighborhood fueled growing frictions between Palestinians and the Israeli police in Jerusalem—and particularly in the Old City and the al-Haram al-Sharif.

However, I must be clear that the chain of events described above was the surface trigger for the war. The real catalyst for the war lies on a deeper level.

The actual reason for the war lies in the inner-Palestinian arena.

The reason for the May 2021 war between Israel and Gaza was the four central political issues the Palestinian political leadership is struggling with, and they are:

- The Palestinian inner split.
- The power struggle between Hamas and Fath.
- The canceling of the elections.
- The continuing erosion of the Palestinian cause on the political agenda of the Arab world.

The violence in Jerusalem in the days preceding the outbreak of the war was intentionally encouraged and generated by both Fath and Hamas. Why?

Let's begin with the Palestinian Authority. For Fath, fanning the flames in Jerusalem against Israel helped mitigate the mounting criticism within the Palestinian community over the fact that Abbas canceled the elections. Furthermore, instigating anger diverts people's attention and energies. Taking out their exasperation on Israel allows the Palestinians—and especially the younger generation—to vent their anger and frustration about their economic, political, and social challenges.

As for Hamas, the organization is widely criticized both by Palestinians and Arabs for the death, devastation, and destruction its militant ideology has wrought on Gaza and the people of Gaza. By positioning itself as the "defender of Jerusalem on behalf of the Palestinians and Muslims around the world," Hamas was trying to soften the criticism. Furthermore, by fanning the flames in Jerusalem, Hamas had hoped that it could prove that its way—the way *al-muqawama al-Masullah* "the Armed Resistance"—is the right path for the Palestinians to pursue. So, Hamas also hoped to score points in its political and ideological struggle with Fath. Hamas thus decided to take advantage of the flare-up in Jerusalem to create a new equation in the balance of power with Israel.

On Monday, May 10, 2021, Hamas gave Israel an ultimatum. Hamas said that Israel must evacuate all Israeli police from the Temple Mount Compound and evacuate all Jewish settlers from the neighborhood of Sheikh Jarrah by 6:00 p.m. that day, or Hamas would attack Jerusalem. Hamas went through with its ultimatum and shot six rockets toward Jerusalem.

I estimate that Hamas's decision to attack Israel was based on two assumptions.

One was that Hamas believed that an Israeli retaliation—even a severe one—would not overshadow Hamas's achievements of shooting rockets at Jerusalem.

The second assumption was that Israel's response would be confined to a short period of time. The reason for that assumption was that the month of Ramadan was going to end in three days on Thursday, May 13, 2021. And the month of Ramadan is immediately followed by the Muslim holiday of *Id al-Fitr*. Hamas apparently estimated that Israel would not conduct a military operation over the holiday.

Both assumptions proved wrong.

What Were the Outcomes of the War?

The Israeli military campaign was intense and powerful. Thirty-six hours into the war, under Israel's mounting strikes, Hamas requested an immediate cease-fire. Israel refused and continued to strike Hamas and IJIP targets in Gaza.

An Egyptian-brokered ceasefire did not happen until May 21, 2021.

As in previous military rounds, Hamas rushed to announce a "triumph." And like in previous rounds, the Arab world by and large did not buy Hamas's triumphant proclamations.

As in previous rounds, many Arab commentators highlight Hamas's responsibility for the disastrous situation in Gaza. In each round, the Arab voices criticizing Hamas become more prevalent and are louder and harsher.

The core arguments of Hamas's critics are that Hamas's militant agenda:

- Has dragged Gaza to more despair and destruction.
- Sacrifices Gaza and the people of Gaza to advance Iran's hegemonic aspirations.
- Perpetuates the Palestinian split, and therefore blocks the path toward any future of hope.
- Damages Palestinian arguments and the Palestinian's image in the world.

Here are just a few examples of the Arab criticism of Hamas.

When writing about the May 2021 war, former Jordanian minister Salih al-Quleib wrote, "Hamas has attacked Israel by Iran's order. This war was an Iranian attack on Israel."[16]

Palestinian columnist Majed Kayali wrote, "The concept of the armed struggle is irrelevant. While Palestinians are echoing hollow slogans, Israel is getting stronger. Hamas rules Gaza. But what is its strategy? Is it planning just to continue and bother Israel, or will Hamas offer Gaza a constructive path?"[17]

Iraqi columnist Muthni Abdullah writes, "Hamas hugs Iran that occupies Arab countries and butchers Arabs. Hamas gains Iran's missiles and rockets, but it has lost the support of the Arabs."[18]

Lebanese commentator Khairallah Khairallah writes, "Hamas' Islamic Emirate inflicted destruction upon Gaza."[19]

In his June 2021 article "Investing in the Gaza War," Emirati commentator Mohammed Khalfan al-Sawafi writes, "Hamas sticks to its delusional triumph announcements. Yet, the international community is sick and tired of militias disguised as movements."[20]

These are only a few samples of the broad and growing criticism in the Arab world vis a vis Hamas.[21]

Given the calculations of Fath and Hamas, what was the Palestinian public opinion following the war?

The Palestinian Center for Policy and Survey Research based in Ramallah, the power center of the Palestinian Authority, conducted a survey immediately after the war. According to the study published in cooperation with the Konrad Adenauer Stiftung Foundation, Palestinians agree that Hamas won, and Hamas appears to be the correct factor to lead the Palestinians. The survey also indicated that Hamas would win a landslide victory if elections were held after the war.

The survey's editors emphasize that the survey's findings are identical to the results of the polls conducted following previous rounds of fighting between Israel and Hamas. Therefore, the poll's editors conclude that the poll's findings should be understood as an emotional response and not necessarily a political position.[22]

I share their observation. It is essential to understand what fuels that "emotional response" because it provides a better understanding of the Palestinian mindset.

The Palestinian narrative has three core elements. One is "Victimhood," the second is "David vs. Goliath," and the third is the "Armed Struggle." When

Hamas fights Israel, they address these three core Palestinian narratives. They frame the struggle in a way that resonates with people's emotional psyche. And this provides the Palestinians with emotional satisfaction. Yet, the pleasure is short-lived. Once the dust settles and the smoke disappears, the devastating outcomes are exposed. And no less important, once again, Palestinians realize that nothing was really achieved other than short-term emotional satisfaction. In fact, their situation is worse.

At this point, rational thinking takes over. Once the reality sinks in, the Palestinians weigh their reality according to a simple calculation of gains and losses, benefits, and disadvantages. And it is at this point, the short-term sense of emotional satisfaction is dimmed, and the Palestinians' criticism of Hamas rises. Hence, the response was emotional and did not necessarily reflect a political position.[23]

In June 2021, following the war, Kifah Mahmoud Karim, an Iraqi-Kurdish columnist, wrote an article he aptly called "The Festivals of Defeats!" Here is a quote: "Thus, since the tragedy of 1948, and at the end of every war with Israel, the political generals and the pulpits announce a brilliant victory over the Zionist enemy by holding festivals and announcing the enemy's losses that shook its entity and shook the earth under its feet."[24]

The Palestinian poll following the latest war certainly illustrates his argument.

Notes for Western Leaders

There are two critical things for decision-makers and public opinion leaders in the West to understand in the context of Israel and Gaza.

The first thing is that Hamas and Islamic Jihad are the two major and military powers in Gaza. They also strive to expand their military infrastructure in the Palestinian territories ruled by the Palestinian Authority. Thus far, those attempts have been intercepted by both Israel and the PA security forces.

Hamas and Islamic Jihad are resolutely and unequivocally, ideologically and politically, committed to an extreme agenda of death and destruction. They do not want a compromise with Israel and will not agree to a settlement with Israel. Therefore, it is necessary to deter both organizations resolutely. It is in the interest of moderate and pragmatic Jews and Arabs,

Israelis and Palestinians, and anyone who rejects violence and seeks constructive and productive solutions to deter Hamas and Islamic Jihad.

Decisively deterring Hamas and Islamic Jihad is not just in Israel's interest. Decisively deterring Hamas and Islamic Jihad is in the Palestinians' interest. It is in the interest of the region's key Arab states. And it is in the interest of the international community.

The second thing to know is that Iran supports both Hamas and Islamic Jihad. Iran supports them financially. Iran trains them and provides them with weapons and comprehensive and sophisticated military know-how to produce their own missiles and rockets. Indeed, following the May war, Hamas's leader Ismail Haniyeh expressed gratitude to Iran for arming Hamas with missiles and rockets and for financing Hamas.[25] Hamas's representative in Iran, Dr. Khaled al-Qaddumi, echoed Haniyeh's statement.[26]

On August 6, 2021, only two days after his inauguration, Iran's new president Ebrahim Raisi met in Tehran with Hamas leader Ismail Haniyeh (who lives in Qatar). In the meeting, Raisi committed to further support Hamas and the "resistance."[27] In other words, one of the first things Raisi did as president of Iran was to promise to further fuel the flames of the Israeli-Palestinian conflict.

For Iran, Hamas and Islamic Jihad are effective and vital proxies that serve and further the Iranian regime's hegemonic vision. Therefore, it is in Iran's interest to perpetuate and escalate the Israeli-Palestinian conflict. The mullah regime is steadfast in its efforts to perpetuate the conflict and works tirelessly to ensure the flames of the conflict escalate. Internalizing that, one can now understand why, in his first speech as Iran's president, Ebrahim Raisi emphasized that "Iran will continue to defend Palestine and support the Palestinians."[28]

If the Iranian regime continues to deepen its grip and influence in the region, the odds of any positive progress in the Israeli-Palestinian conflict (which is very low in any case) further diminish exponentially.

Summer 2021: The Palestinians Are at a Crossroads

The Peace to Prosperity Plan and the Abraham Accords reflect the new era of the Middle East. They also clearly manifest how the changing landscape of the Middle East shapes the trajectory of the Israeli-Palestinian conflict.

Some may argue that Trump's plan and the Abraham Accords are the reasons for the 2021 war between Israel and Gaza. But looking closely at the underlying issues that led to the war, which I presented in this chapter, proves that to be a wrong conclusion.

Trump's plan and the Abraham Accords offered the Palestinians a launchpad to shape a better future for themselves. No one expected the Palestinians to adopt Trump's plan blindly. They could have started a negotiation process and gained the support of their brothers, the Arabs.

Yet, the Palestinians failed to seize the opportunity. Unfortunately, the Palestinians have once again chosen to let their split and their narratives dictate their path. The canceling of the elections and the May 2021 war are sad manifestations of that decision. As of the summer of 2021, the tragic impasse the Palestinians are locked in still shapes their future.

Ghassan Kanfani, a former advisor to Palestinian leader Yasser Arafat, writes in his January 2020 article "The Deep Hibernation Season of the Palestinian Cause."

> Today, a Palestinian slumber, chosen by the two largest Palestinian factions, Fatah and Hamas, prevails.
>
> Wrapped in the claim that is imposed on them; a justification that no one is convinced of; dreams of continuing control and leadership; and sharing what remains of the Palestinian people's land. We [the Palestinians] await the death blow to what was called Palestine.
>
> Today, we are a people who do not have leaders with goals and plans that lead to a better future.
>
> The Palestinian people live out their days and do not see a future for their descendants.
>
> The goals of our 'national resistance' are death and not life.
>
> And the Arabs active support during the years of our people's political struggle is now at its best being discussed at a meeting of permanent Arab delegates in the Arab League.[29]

The Palestinians face two paths.

One is to stick to their narratives that do not dialogue with the changing environment.

The other is to revisit their narratives and adjust their path to the changing climate.

In their essence, the Peace to Prosperity plan and the Abraham Accords send a clear message to the Palestinians. The region is changing. The world is changing. It is time for you to adopt a pragmatic approach. You might not get everything you want, but adopting a practical approach will better serve your cause.

The ball is now in the Palestinians' court.

Palestinian scholar Dr. Amjad Ahmed Jabril writes in his July 2021 article, "The Role of Egypt and Hamas' Relations with the Region":

> Five factors dictate Hamas's regional and domestic policy:
>
> The internal Palestinian split;
>
> The weakness of the "Arab framework" (i.e., The Arab League);
>
> The absence of the Palestinian cause as an integral component of pan-Arab security and the pan-Arab agenda;
>
> The polarization between the axis of resistance (Iran, Hezbollah) of which Hamas is part of and the axis of Arab stability (Saudi Arabia, Egypt, UAE);
>
> And the fact that major Western countries label Hamas as a terror organization…
>
> Hamas must revise its way and the statements of its leaders. At the end of the day, Hamas's policy serves an unrealistic ideology that hurts the Palestinian people in the long run.
>
> Hamas must implement a cohesive, comprehensive policy.[30]

Indeed, the Palestinians need to decide between pragmatism and dogmatism. Do they want to pursue the path of al-muqawama al-Masullah, the armed resistance? Do they want to sacrifice their life and future for the sake of Iran's hegemonic aspirations? Or do they want to pursue the path of negotiations and compromises? Will they continue to allow the narrative of victimhood to dictate their path perpetually? Or will they take responsibility for their failures?

The Trajectory of the Israeli-Palestinian Conflict in the Third Decade of the Twenty-First Century

As I have been consistently and accurately claiming, an Israeli-Palestinian peace agreement is not feasible in the foreseeable future. However, I do see the potential for a positive breakthrough in the trajectory of the conflict in the coming decade.

As I have alluded to above, the inner-Palestinian debate has increasingly become centered around the issue of pragmatism vs. dogmatism. This process is inevitable because of the changing geopolitical landscape of the Middle East. In this inner-Palestinian struggle, I believe that the conflict between Iran and the alliance of moderation, combined with the possible emergence of a new statehood model in the region, will strengthen the pragmatic Palestinian camp.

Therefore, I predict the emergence of a new political player in the Palestinian arena. In my estimation, this new entity will include current members of the two major Palestinian factions, Fath and Hamas, plus independent political activists, particularly from the civil society camp.

Given the current climate, such an actor could be a significant player on the Palestinian political map. It could profoundly, and possibly positively, accelerate the move toward pragmatism in the Palestinian political and public realm. Should this happen, it will have a significant impact on the Palestinians and on the trajectory of the Israeli-Palestinian conflict.

In my 2016 book, I emphasized that the Arab world must be an integral part of an agreement between Israel and the Palestinians. Here is a quote:

> Israelis and Palestinians have a long road to take on the path toward reconciliation. But the Arab Awakening has brought hope of changes throughout the region. The key to progress in the Israeli-Palestinian arena is the proactive involvement of Arab states—and this is in their interest too. The evolution of an Israeli-Arab axis might incentivize

an Israeli-Arab discussion regarding a possible arrangement between Israel and the Palestinians. Such an arrangement would be motivated by the assumption that an Israeli-Palestinian agreement would contribute to regional stability—a primary goal of the axis. The Israeli-Arab axis, together with the proactive involvement of Arab states in the Israeli-Palestinian arena, could develop a creative out-of-the-box strategy and apparatus to tackle the Israeli-Palestinian issue and achieve tangible results that enable all sides to move down a path of stability toward an eventual agreement.[31]

Today, six years later, the geopolitical construct of the Middle East, namely the alliance of moderation, the Abraham Accords, and the normalization agreements, provides the framework for such arrangements. So, while peace is not possible between Israelis and Palestinians in the foreseeable future, agreements can be achieved. The current geostrategic environment provides the environment and the platform to advance this framework.

In the emerging multidimensional geopolitical construct of the Middle East, I believe we will see an interim Israeli-Palestinian arrangement in the coming decade. The initiative will be led and negotiated by the alliance of moderation in cooperation with regional players and supported by global powers. A key factor that is essential for the success of such an initiative is the revisiting of Western narratives and assumptions. That is the topic I will discuss in the next chapter.

CHAPTER 10

CONSTRUCTIVELY ADDRESSING THE ISRAELI-PALESTINIAN CONFLICT

Western Policy Makers Need to Revisit Assumptions

If Western activists, influencers, policymakers, and thought leaders want to advance a constructive and productive path for Israelis and Palestinians, they must re-evaluate their underlying assumptions and narratives about the conflict. And that is the subject of this chapter.

In the previous chapter, I challenged a major Western narrative that the Israeli-Palestinian conflict shapes the Middle East. I have demonstrated that the reality is the other way around. It is the Middle East that shapes the trajectory of the Israeli-Palestinian conflict.

In this chapter, I would like to further challenge some other Western narratives.

I would like to begin by addressing one of the most widely-discussed narratives when it comes to the Israeli-Palestinian conflict, the "Two State Solution."

Achieving a "Two State Solution" has been the cornerstone of Western policy to resolve the Israeli-Palestinian conflict. But objectively looking at the conflict's trajectory leads to the inevitable conclusion that mantra was—and is—totally irrelevant.

Here is the reality. The first Palestinian uprising, known as the intifada, was in 1987. The first intifada that lasted from 1987–1993 was also known as the "Stones Uprising." It was characterized mainly by mass protests and riots, stone-throwing, Molotov cocktails, stabbings, and shootings. I remember this time well because of my professional position in those years, which put me square in the middle of the intifada.

A generation has passed since the Stones Uprising. The Israeli-Palestinian conflict has evolved into a battlefield of drones, homicide bombers, infantry, missiles, rockets, tanks, missile interception systems—"The Arrow," "The Iron Dome," "David's Sling"—mortars, missiles—short-range, mid-range, long-range—intrusive tunnels, smuggling tunnels, terror tunnels, above ground and below ground barriers, fences, walls, incendiary balloons, and fire kites. Tens of thousands of Palestinians have been killed. Thousands of Israelis have been killed. A generation of Israelis and Palestinians deeply suffers from PTSD. And the list goes on.

Peace—along the lines of the Western narrative—between Palestinians and Israelis is impossible in the foreseeable future, and the end of the Israeli-Palestinian conflict is nowhere in sight. I will repeat the same thing I have been saying for decades. This is not a political statement, nor does it reflect my desires or my ideology, nor is it a game of blame. I find both Israelis and Palestinians responsible for their dismal reality. The fact that I say that peace is not a realistic goal is simply a statement that truly reflects the reality on the ground.

So, why do Western policymakers fail to see the reality? Why do Western policymakers insist on a policy that is clearly irrelevant and doomed to fail?

The Harmful Impact of False Narratives

A central tenet over the last generation was the concept of the "validity of all narratives" and the mantra of "agree to disagree respectfully." This orientation allegedly expanded perspectives, led to fruitful and productive discussions, and encouraged positive values such as tolerance and pluralism. Unfortunately, though this might contribute to an environment where everyone feels 'good,' 'safe,' 'validated,' etc., I maintain that this environment harms the public discourse and society. And inevitably, policy.

When all narratives are valid, it devalues the pursuit of knowledge comprised of facts, context, the sequence of events, cause and effect, actions, and reactions. When the database of knowledge narrows, history and the present become subdued to buzzwords, concepts, narratives, and theories. When critical thinking and media literacy are diminished, conveyors of knowledge are exempt from accountability for the accuracy of their theories and opinions.

The combination of facile narratives, disregard for data, and a dearth of critical thinking and media literacy has led to an environment in which a complicated multi-layered Middle East is flattened into a two-dimensional Westernized soundbite and discussions about the Middle East scarcely reflect the complex reality on the ground.

Policy failures do not stem from a lack of resources, capacity, or dedicated and committed professionals. They stem from a systemic flaw that prevents an accurate interpretation of the Middle East reality and compromises the ability to navigate an increasingly complex global reality.

The systemic flaw is the direct result of the combination of two factors.

Western mediators of knowledge—guided by a Western mindset and Western codes of thinking—developed concepts, narratives, and theories regarding the Middle East. Viewing the Middle East's complex reality through Western concepts, lenses, and narratives thwarts their ability to understand and thus analyze and present unfolding events accurately.

Additionally, most Western influencers of public opinion and policy regarding the Middle East do not speak the languages of the Middle East. Lacking the language skills, they are dependent upon mediated, translated, and sometimes deliberately manipulated information. This prevents them from having their finger on the pulse of events and compromises their ability to critically analyze the information they are provided.

The above has led to an environment in which a complicated multi-layered Middle East is flattened into a two-dimensional Westernized soundbite. Discussions about the Middle East scarcely reflect the complex reality on the ground. Critical thinking and media literacy are not encouraged, and conveyors of knowledge are exempted from professional accountability for the validity of their theories and analyses.

The outcome of this process is a 'looping echo chamber' in which *Concepts* became "*Facts.*" *Narratives* became "*Reality.*" *Theories* became "*Truth.*" And based upon these almost non-controversial *Facts, Realities,* and *Truths*—Western Middle East policy was created.

The challenge is that the concepts and narratives were based upon a false reading of reality. The reality on the ground was quite different. Therefore, inevitably, the policies failed.

Here are some examples of narratives that have harmfully impacted Western policy regarding the Israeli-Palestinian conflict.

In 2016, John Kerry, then the US secretary of state, made the following statement at the Saban Forum very determinedly:

> There will be no separate peace between Israel and the Arab world. I want to make that very clear to all of you. I have heard several prominent politicians in Israel sometimes saying, "well, the Arab world is in a different place now; we just have to reach out to them, and we can work something with the Arab world, and we'll deal with the Palestinians." No! No, No, and No! ... There will be no advance and separate peace with the Arab world without the Palestinian process and Palestinian peace. Everybody needs to understand that. That is a hard reality. [1]

The Abraham Accords and the normalization agreements prove Kerry's reading of reality was inaccurate.

I do not have access to the intelligence or the diplomatic resources and capacities Kerry enjoyed. However, in 2015 I was able to identify the formation of Israeli-Arab alliances and the changing orientation of major Arab countries toward Israel. Why was Secretary of State Kerry unable to see what I saw? Did intelligence and diplomatic agencies fail to present him with the reality? Or did they explain the reality accurately, and did a top US policymaker choose to subdue the reality to narratives? Whatever the reason, the result was a disturbingly flawed evaluation—and flawed policy followed.

Here is an example of another harmful narrative: Israel is responsible for the situation in the Gaza Strip.

Here is the reality.

Israel unilaterally withdrew from the Gaza Strip in 2005 and handed over control to the Palestinian Authority. In June 2007, Hamas launched a violent and bloody coup overthrowing the Palestinian Authority and expelling the PA from Gaza. Since then, Hamas has governed Gaza.

Hamas employs thousands of officials, civil servants, teachers, preachers, etc. Hamas has a police force, security agencies, and an army. Hamas administers schools and creates curriculum. Hamas makes laws and has courts to enforce legislation. Hamas exacts payments and collects taxes. Hamas has dip-lomatic representation in some Arab countries and in Turkey, Russia, and Iran.

According to every parameter, Hamas is a government.

Understanding that reality should make Western policymakers hold Hamas accountable for its actions, the same way that any other government should be held responsible for its actions.

However, the narrative is more powerful than the reality.

Guided by the narrative that "Israel is responsible for the Gaza Strip," some political and intellectual circles in the West exempt Hamas from any respon-sibility—either as a government or as an agent of instability.

Exempting Hamas from responsibility does a disservice to both Israelis and Palestinians. It dooms both to misery, fear, death, and destruction. It blocks the path toward any positive breakthrough of the conflict.

In this book, I have highlighted Arab voices that also hold Hamas—not only Israel—accountable for the disaster in Gaza. If Western activists, policy-makers, and influencers want to improve Palestinians' and Israelis' lives, they should hold the Israeli government *and* the Hamas government accountable for their actions.

And furthermore, they should support Palestinians and other Arab leaders and influencers who openly hold Hamas responsible. This policy approach would empower Palestinians and be the most constructive and productive path to a sustainable and productive arrangement for Israelis, Palestinians, and the region.

Another false narrative that needs to be replaced and looked at with new lenses is that solving the Israeli-Palestinian conflict will bring peace to the Middle East. I hope this book proves that the reality is totally different. The enormous turbulence in the region has nothing to do with the Israeli-Palestinian conflict.

Narratives are part of what makes us human. I—like anyone else—have narratives. Narratives enrich our life. But when narratives replace or under-mine or ignore facts, context, the chronology of events, causes, and outcomes, the results are destructive.

Clearly, a change of approach to ensure a more effective policy is required. And it starts with changing the lenses.

Change the Lenses

Change the Language

To effectively address the Israeli-Palestinian conflict, the West must change lenses to clearly decipher the reality and divorce itself from the entrenched narratives and paradigms that have not worked thus far and will not work in the future. Changing the lenses and the language is essential for any progress.

Instead of repeating the Western mantra about achieving "Peace between Israel and Palestinians," the West should adopt the mindset and language of the Middle East.

You will notice that at the end of the previous chapter, I used the word "arrangement." That was not a random word I chose. Arab and Islamic culture does not use the absolute language of war and peace. Instead, it focuses on "arrangements" to achieve a short-term truce that can be revised and renewed when necessary. During the truce period, the dissenting parties negotiate a long-term agreement to address future conflicts effectively.

Though "Peace between Israel and Palestinians" is not feasible in the foreseeable future, as I laid out at the end of Chapter 9, arrangements that can lead to sustainable agreements are currently possible.

But to achieve arrangements, it is essential to identify the key players and understand the links in the chain.

Identifying the Key Players and the Links of the Chain

I mentioned this in passing before, but I want to repeat it here. The Middle East is a chain of links. Nothing stands alone. What happens in one place impacts what happens in another.

Knowing who drives, leverages, and derives dividends from the conflict—and their motivations to do so—is critical to decipher events accurately and then estimate their trajectory.

Unfortunately, Western policymakers have repeatedly failed to identify the key players and how they are connected. Or, if they have identified them, they have refused to move to act to quell their destructive behavior.

The best example is Iran and Turkey. As we have discussed at length in this book, both powers are interested in fueling the flames of the conflict because it serves their hegemonic aspirations.

Ahmad Zeidabadi was born in Iran in 1966. He is a political analyst and writer who spent many years of his life in the Iranian mullah regime's prison for his opinions. He was awarded the UNESCO Guillermo World Press Freedom Prize in 2011. At the time, he was serving five years in prison for his participation in the Green Revolution (the 2009 protests in Iran). In May 2020, he wrote the following about the relationship between the Iranian government and the Palestinians: "I, of course, strongly oppose the Zionist project. However, I believe supporting the Palestinian cause has to do with the balance of power inside Iran more than it does with the objective reality of the region or the suffering of the Palestinians."[2]

Saudi columnist Mishari al-Thaidy summed it up perfectly in his January 29, 2020 article, "The Deal of the Century and the Bidding Festival." "The Iranian axis and the Muslim Brotherhood supporters will likely use Trump's plan to further enhance their interests at the expense of the deprived Palestinian people ... Unfortunately, this year, we will see a massive market for trading again on the Palestinian issue, without any sense of 'realism' or responsibility towards this afflicted people."[3]

As Iranians increased their aggression in the region—mainly at the expense of the Arab countries—Arabs started to realize that the Iranian regime had cynically manipulated them. They began to see that the combination of 'al-Muqawama and "Liberating Palestine" was no more than a card the mullah regime uses to destroy the Arab world from within. I have stopped counting the number of articles published by Arab commentators, echoing that understanding. Here are just a few examples.

In February 2020, Iraqi commentator Ibrahim al- Zubaidi wrote, "Death to Israel and America, Victory to Iran." Here is a quote: "All the human disasters inflicted by the Revolutionary Guards on the peoples of Iran, Iraq, Syria, Lebanon, Yemen, and Palestine, for forty years, were not for the sake of Palestine."[4]

In an April 14, 2020 article, "Syrians View on Israel's Image Shifts," exiled Syrian journalist Ra'fat Al-Ghanem, wrote the following: "From its early days, the Syrian Ba'ath regime used the card of 'liberating Palestine' to disguise the crimes it commits against the Syrian people as well as against its neighbors ... There are Palestinians and Arabs who think that the outcry of the Syrian people massacred by the Assad regime diminishes the narrative of Palestinian victimhood. Therefore they argue that the Syrian cries should be suffocated."[5]

In his December 2020 article called "Captagon Party: for Entrepreneurship, Trade, Abuse and Promotion of all Kind of Drugs," senior Syrian journalist Faisal al-Qassem wrote the following: "Hezbollah's deceiving slogans drugged us (the Arabs) … The drummer of al-Muqawama [Meaning Hasan Nasrallah, the leader of Hezbollah] drugged us all with fake al-Muqawama slogans."[6]

In June 2021, Saudi commentator Khalid al-Matrifi wrote an article he called "The Cartoon Resistance Axis." "During the war between Israel and Hamas," he writes, "the axis of resistance that waves the flag of liberating al-Quds did nothing to support the Palestinians. Instead, the axis was busy at that time, deepening its aggression in Syria, Yemen, and Iraq."[7]

In her June 2021 article "Iran and its Wreaking Havoc in the Arab World," Saudi commentator Maha Mohammed al-Sharif wrote, "Cleverly monetizing the slogans of Liberating al-Quds and the Resistance, Iran took over the Arab world. And the result is that everywhere Iran took over, the Arab people stand in the queue (to buy basic commodities—fuel, medicines, etc.)."[8]

I emphasize these voices because these are perspectives from the region that, unfortunately, people in the West are not exposed to. Anyone who wants to bring stability to the region must be aware that these expanding and growing opinions are part of the current geopolitical reality of the new era in the Middle East.

If Western policymakers fail to understand that regional players use the Israeli-Palestinian conflict as a pawn to advance their own goals, Western policies will not bear positive results, the situation in the region will continue to deteriorate, and violence and bloodshed throughout the Middle East will escalate.

But that is only half of the equation. There are not only actors who benefit from the conflict.

There are also actors whose interests can be leveraged to help advance solutions on the ground that reduce conflict potential between Israelis and Palestinians.

Understanding this is the only way to achieve a sustainable arrangement.

It is critical to identify the direct and indirect players involved in the conflict, their goals, interests, and priorities. To impact reality, one must understand the reality.

The 2021 Israel-Gaza war provides an excellent example of how Iran and Turkey attempt to derive benefit from the conflict. At the same time, the war provides an example of how other regional players contribute to stability.

In the case of the Gaza Strip, the most significant regional player is Egypt.

Egypt—A Key Player in the Gaza Challenge

Egypt shares an eight-mile-long border with Gaza. Egypt ruled Gaza from 1948 to 1967. When Egypt governed the Gaza Strip, it did not annex Gaza. Nor did it grant Gazans Egyptian citizenship. And though Egypt has no desire to control the Gaza Strip—in many aspects, Gaza is an inseparable part of Egypt.

Gaza's southern border with Egypt is the Rafah Crossing. The crossing is Gaza's primary gateway to the world. Before Hamas took over Gaza in 2007, hundreds of thousands of Palestinians from Gaza crossed through the Rafah Crossing—going in and out of Egypt for school or work, seeing family or visiting friends, etc. When Hamas overthrew the Palestinian Authority and took control of Gaza in 2007, one of its first acts was to burn the Rafah Crossing down to the ground. Egypt closed the passage. Since 2007 Egypt has never opened the crossing permanently. They open it from time to time.

The Rafah Crossing is a card Egypt uses to pressure Hamas to maintain calm and stability in Gaza.

Egypt is concerned that the military rounds between Israel and Hamas might ignite the Egyptian streets. We need to remember that Hamas defines itself as "the branch of the Muslim Brotherhood in Palestine." The Muslim Brotherhood was born in Egypt in 1928. It is the most prominent Sunni movement in the world. It is deeply rooted in the hearts and minds of Egypt's Sunni population. Al-Sisi's administration oppresses the Muslim Brotherhood movement and sees it as a threat to the regime. The combination of a war in Gaza, the oppression of the Muslim Brotherhood in Egypt, and Egypt's economic challenges could potentially ignite the Egyptian street.

Since restoring the Palestinian Authority's rule over Gaza is not on the horizon, Egypt prefers Hamas to continue to be the ruling power in Gaza. Don't get me wrong. Egypt does not like Hamas. However, Egypt is concerned that a war with Israel could weaken or bring down Hamas. That would create a power vacuum that would play into the hands of Salafi-jihadi militant organizations in Gaza, like ISIS. Egypt has been conducting an ongoing campaign—with limited success—trying to eliminate militant Islam groups, particularly in the northern area of the Sinai Peninsula.

Gaza is geographically part of northern Sinai. Many Gazans are connected to people that live in northern Sinai. They are friends, have worked together, are relatives, either directly or by marriage, etc. The Palestinian refugee camps in southern Gaza, bordering north Sinai, are a vibrant hub for Salafi-jihadi ideology and the recruitment of militants.

Hamas, like Egypt, views these groups as a threat to its rule and accordingly oppresses their activists and leaders in Gaza.

Following the Taliban takeover of Afghanistan in the summer of 2021, Hamas rushed to congratulate the Afghan people for being free of American occupation. However, Hamas did not congratulate the Taliban.

Hamas is concerned that the revived Afghan Islamist hub, and the current momentum the renewal of Taliban rule provides Salafi-jihadi groups (though the Taliban does not embrace Salafi-Jihadi ideology), will empower Gaza-based Salafi groups to challenge Hamas's rule.

In the war of May 2021—like in all previous military rounds between Israel and Gaza—Egypt brokered the cease-fire. However, unlike in previous rounds, in the war of 2021, Egypt's role was much more significant.

Immediately following the war, Egypt began reconstruction work in Gaza, including laying the cornerstone for a residential project in southern Gaza. Egypt's active role following the war stemmed from another Egyptian interest. And that is Egyptian-US relations. As we have discussed before in the context of Saudi Arabia and Turkey, the Biden administration's prioritizing of human and civil rights could potentially fuel tensions with Egypt. Therefore, al-Sisi is looking to minimize the friction and gain credibility with the Biden administration. Al-Sisi's major card to that end is his role as a stabilizing factor.

Indeed, as of the summer of 2021, the Biden administration has clearly acknowledged and officially praised Egypt's efforts in playing a stabilizing role. In early August 2021, Dana Stroul, the deputy assistant secretary of defense for the Middle East at the US Department of Defense, stressed Egypt's importance to the United States. In a statement to the US Senate Foreign Relations

Committee, Stroll said: "Egypt is important to us in many files, such as ensuring the safety of navigation in the Red Sea and the Suez Canal." She added that Egypt also plays a constructive role in the security of Libya's borders and stabilizing the situation in Gaza. She added that "foreign military funding" from the US Department of Defense remains an important tool to ensure that Egypt has defense equipment of US-origin geared toward common security threats."[9]

The May 2021 war between Israel and Gaza provided al-Sisi yet another opportunity to gain further credibility as a stabilizing factor. And he seized the opportunity.

The last component required to generate a more effective policy is to think out of the box.

Constructively Addressing the Israeli-Palestinian Conflict: Thinking Out of the Box

The Middle East has entered a new era. We have seen this reality play out right before our eyes over the first two decades of the twenty-first century.

The combination of domestic challenges; power struggles over the characteristics of nation-states; the fight for independence and freedom; and Iran's and Turkey's hegemonic visions all coincide and are creating—and will continue to affect—substantial changes on the political agendas, priorities, and public discourse in the Arab world. And this is what will define the geopolitical construct of the region. Any plan or proposal that does not understand the 'neighborhood' (the Middle East) and does not consider—and address—the 'links in the chain' will fail.

In my 2016 book, I urged leaders to apply an out-of-the-box approach. The events since then revalidate my plea.

As I have said, I believe the alliance of moderation is a long-term alliance. The coalition can, and should, play a central role in designing and implementing an Israeli-Palestinian arrangement based on a long-term, multi-phase road map.

The first step should be establishing a council representing the alliance of moderation, Israel, and the Palestinians.

It is my recommendation that the council be a hybrid of an advisory and executive body. Similar to the model of the United Nations and the United Nations Security Council. The decisions made by that council will be binding. And the members of the executive body will have veto power. That council will have a term of twenty-five years with an extension option.

This council should pursue practical arrangements on issues that are immediately critical to both sides. Priority should be given to matters relating to well-being and security. The list of topics to address is long and complex. To name a few: economic development projects in Gaza and the West Bank; addressing the challenge of energy supply and water sources in the West Bank and Gaza Strip; restoring the PA's control over Gaza; agreeing on the oversight of the Islamic sites in Jerusalem; determining the status of Israeli settlements in the West Bank.

It is neither practical nor required to address each issue comprehensively from the beginning. However, the council could create a long-term, multi-phase framework detailing each topic, the exact measures, steps, oversight, etc. The committees must also define an arbitrator mechanism to mediate controversies between Israelis and Palestinians.

What I have presented is a very preliminary suggestion and framework. But I want to emphasize and underscore that that there are two critical elements to making constructive, productive, and sustainable progress on the Israeli-Palestinian issue.

One, any arrangement must involve the regional Arab powers. The shifting geopolitical map, and specifically the Abraham Accords, provides a more "official," and I believe, a sustainable framework to advance arrangements with leaders who have the ability and interest to support these agreements.

The second thing I want to emphasize is that the key to making real progress that will enhance the lives of Israelis, Palestinians, and the region is to focus on arrangements on very tangible issues, such as the ones I presented. A framework that will provide immediate answers to some of the sides' most pressing issues and build trust among all the parties involved is the only way to begin building a safe and secure future for Israelis and Palestinians. It is time to stop repeating the same phrases that have led to more death, instability, and violence. It is time to adopt a new mindset and think out of the box. The new era allows it, and the new era demands it.

CHAPTER 11

LAST MINUTE UPDATE | THE TALIBAN RECLAIMS AFGHANISTAN

A Short Overview—The Rise of the Taliban and the US Departure from Afghanistan

Just as this book is being submitted to my publisher (in late August 2021), a dramatic event is taking place in Central Asia. The Taliban has retaken Afghanistan.

Unfortunately, given the timing of this event, just days before I submit the final manuscript, I cannot provide a comprehensive description of their rise to power. Nor can I provide a full in-depth analysis of what I believe this means for Afghanistan and the region.

However, I would like to offer a few preliminary thoughts and observations regarding what I see as the immediate and possible ramifications—at least in the short-term—of the US withdrawal from Afghanistan and the Taliban regaining control of the country.

Afghanistan's population is estimated to be thirty-nine million. Eighty percent of Afghans are Sunni Muslims, and about 19 percent are Shi'ites. Afghanistan is a tribal society, and its largest ethnic group—over 40 percent— are Pashtuns. The second-largest ethnic group—about 27 percent—are Tajiki, and the third—about 10 percent, are Hazara. The Pashtuns and Tajiki are Sunni, and the Hazara are Shi'ite.

As a brief background, the ultra-conservative Taliban evolved in Afghanistan through the 1980s and 1990s. The *Taliban* (a word meaning "students") was formed by young Afghan *mujahedeen*—"Muslims who fight (jihad) on behalf of the faith or the Muslim community (ummah)." The Taliban gained their education in Pakistani *Madaris*—Islamic schools. And the Taliban was nurtured by the Pakistani intelligence services.

The mujahedeen were the spearhead of the Afghan war to end the Russian invasion of Afghanistan in 1979. During the war (1979–1989), Afghanistan quickly became a hub for Sunni militants, many of whom were from various Arab and Muslim countries. The mujahedeen inspired many Muslims around the world. One of them was Osama bin Laden, the son of a self-made billionaire, Muhammad bin Laden.

Toward the late 1980s, Osama bin Laden settled in Pakistan. In 1988, bin Laden, Ayman al-Zawahiri, the leader of Egyptian Islamic Jihad, and Abdullah Yusuf Azzam, a Salafi-jihadi theologist and military commander of Palestinian origin, established al-Qaeda in Afghanistan.

Following the Russian withdrawal from Afghanistan, the Taliban expanded their control over Afghanistan through a series of military campaigns. And in

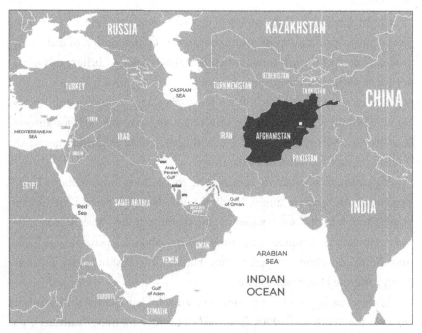

Afghanistan

1996, they took over the capitol, Kabul. Bin Laden, who was deported from Sudan in the same year, moved to Afghanistan.

Over the next few years, the Taliban took over Afghanistan. They ran and ruled the country according to an extreme and radical interpretation of sharī'ah law.

Following the September 11, 2001, terror attack by the Sunni terrorist organization al-Qaeda on the United States, President George W. Bush, the forty-third president of the United States, launched "Operation Enduring Freedom," targeting the Taliban and al-Qaeda. Less than a month later, in October 2001, the United States invaded Afghanistan. In November 2001, the US-backed Northern Alliance—a coalition of anti-Taliban militias—overthrew the Taliban regime. In December 2001, Afghan politician Hamid Karzai was named interim president and was then formally elected president, a position he held until 2014. In the 2014 elections, Ashraf Ghani was elected president and served until August 15, 2021, when the Taliban reclaimed the embattled country.

In February 2020, after almost twenty years of fighting the Taliban in Afghanistan, the United States and the Taliban signed a peace agreement in Qatar.

The four US commitments to the Taliban include:

- Within 135 days of signing the agreement, the United States would reduce the number of US troops from 12,000 to 14,000 to 8,600.
- By March 10, 2020, a prisoner exchange would be complete. The United States would release 5,000 Taliban prisoners in exchange for 1,000 prisoners from "the other side."
- By May 29, 2020, the United Nations would remove all UN sanctions against the Taliban.
- By August 27, 2020, the United States would remove all US sanctions against the Taliban.
- By late April 2021, the United States would completely withdraw all US military from Afghanistan.
- The United States pledged not to threaten the Afghans with force, violate the sovereignty of Afghanistan, or intervene in Afghanistan's domestic affairs.

The Taliban, in return, made two commitments to the United States:

- The Taliban would act to prevent threats to the security of the US and its allies, including, but not limited to al-Qaeda. That included Afghan groups or groups that have Afghan support.
- Beginning March 10, 2020, the Taliban would engage in intra-Afghan negotiations to reach a settlement between domestic stakeholders to end the conflict and outline the configuration of a new, unified system of governance.

Immediate Repercussions of the US Withdrawal and Taliban Takeover

In July and August 2021, the United States began a hasty withdrawal process from Afghanistan. During the retreat, the Taliban swiftly regained control of the country.

In the immediate to short-term, the US withdrawal from Afghanistan gives momentum to Islamists—Sunni and Shi'ite alike—who see the West, its culture, and its values as a weak and morally corrupt system that is doomed to disappear from the annals of history.

In that context, Tunisian columnist Al-Habib al-Aswad wrote an article on August 17, 2021, that he called "What is US Defeat in Afghanistan?"—the US defeat, he says, is not only military. It is the defeat of power that represents democracy, pluralism, and human rights.[1]

The momentum that militant Islam is currently experiencing could translate into increased terrorist attacks across the region and worldwide.

In that context, it is worth noting that Western intelligence services estimate there is a significant concentration of dormant Muslim terror cells in Europe. There is an additional concern that the current radical Islamist momentum will translate into an increase of the "lone-wolf" terror attack phenomenon in which an individual who lives 'under the radar' of the intelligence services perpetrates a terror attack.

That being said, extremism does not need incentives. Whoever kills in the name of an extremist ideology does not need special incentives to be an extremist or to act in an extremist manner.

The backwind that militant Islam is currently experiencing because of the Taliban victory could have another interesting consequence in Afghanistan itself.

In Afghanistan—a Collision between the Taliban and ISIS

The Taliban Islamic Emirate that was born in Afghanistan and ruled Afghanistan from 1996 until the US invasion in 2001 was an economic, ideological, logistical, military, physical, and spiritual hub for Sunni militant Islam.

Sunni Islam has four orthodox legal schools of thought (*Hanafi, Hanbali, Maliki, and Shafi'i*).

The origins of the Taliban philosophy come from the Hanafi school.

Hanafi is named after an eighth-century scholar, Abu Hanifa bin Nu'man Ibn Thabit. The Hanafi school is considered the oldest and most liberal school of Islamic jurisprudence. And it is the largest. Of the four schools, Hanafi is the most flexible and adjustable in its interpretation of Islam and its application of sharī'ah law.

The Taliban has other interesting ideological roots. And that is the Deobandi Sufi order that emerged in India. *Sufism* is rooted in early Islam. It can be generally described as the mystical practice of Islam. The word *suf* means "wool" or a "cloth." Practitioners of Sufism are called *Sufis*. Historically, Sufis have often belonged to different *tariqa* or *turuq* (in plural) "orders." The "orders" are congregations formed around a grand master referred to as a *wali*.

In a seemingly antithetical posture, inspired by Muslim Indian and Pakistani theologians, the Taliban integrated elements from the most dogmatic Sunni school of thought, the Hanbali jurisprudence.

The Hanbali school of thought is named after a very influential Islamic theologist named Ahmad Ibn Hanbal, who lived between 780 and 855. That period was also known as "the Golden Age of Islam." Hanbali orthodoxy is the smallest and most dogmatic stream of Sunni orthodoxy. It demands Muslims live only according to the Quran and the *Sunnah* (the teachings of the Prophet Muhammad) as they were interpreted during the first three generations of Islam. The Hanbali reject any reform, translation, and adjustment of Islamic law and practice that occurred after "the Golden Age of Islam."

In 2021, the Taliban returned to power in a world different than twenty years ago when they last ruled Afghanistan.

One change is the evolution of an ideological and violent power struggle between two leading forces of Sunni militant Islam—al-Qaeda and its own offspring, ISIS. ISIS began as al-Qaeda's branch in Iraq. But in 2014,

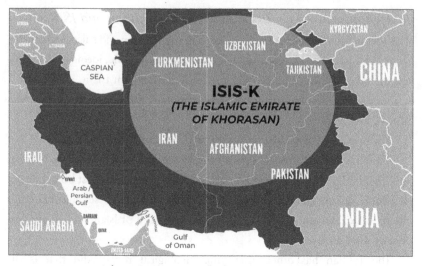

Islamic Emirate of Khorasan / ISIS-K

it broke off and established itself as a separate and independent entity. Since then, al-Qaeda and ISIS have competed for power and territory—as well as hearts and minds. Over the past few years, the power struggle between the two Sunni militant radical Islamic organizations has expanded and escalated. It has evolved to an intercontinental power struggle that stretches from Africa through the Middle East, to Central and Southeast Asia.

One of the most substantial ISIS branches globally is the "Islamic Emirate of Khorasan," also known as *ISIS-K*. Khorasan is a vast geographical area in Central Asia. The area includes northeast Iran, northwest Afghanistan, Tajikistan, Turkmenistan, and Uzbekistan. The militants of the Islamic Emirate of Khorasan are Afghans, Arabs, Kurds (from Iran), and recruits from Central Asian countries that border Afghanistan—Tajikistan, Turkmenistan, and Uzbekistan.

It is possible that the US withdrawal from Afghanistan will strengthen ISIS-K and further fuel the growing power struggle in Afghanistan between the Taliban and al-Qaeda on one side and ISIS-K on the other side.

On August 26, amid the US withdrawal, ISIS-K conducted a suicide bombing attack at the gates of the Kabul airport. The suicide bomber killed almost two hundred people, including thirteen US military personnel, US citizens, Taliban militants, and Afghan civilians.

This event could foreshadow a Taliban-ISIS-K collision course.

On the other hand, the Taliban could also decide that it will tolerate ISIS's base in Afghanistan and prevent it from using Afghanistan as a base to launch attacks, provided it does not challenge Taliban rule or intervene in Afghan internal politics.[2]

The Taliban Rule and Regional Players—China, Iran, and Russia

The Taliban's takeover of Afghanistan adds another variable to the already tangled Middle East power equilibrium.

In June 2021, Abdulrahman al-Rashed, the chairman of *Al Arabiya's* Editorial Board, wrote, "Will it End or Start a New Afghan War?"—"Afghanistan will be the scene of a power struggle between the United States, China, Russia, Iran, Turkey, Pakistan, and India. The Afghan arena will have a significant impact on the region."[3]

The unfolding developments in Afghanistan reveal a multifaceted fabric of both conflicting as well as intersecting interests. For each of the major world players, Afghanistan potentially presents both opportunities as well as threats.

Let us start with one aspect. And that is the fact that the United States is leaving Afghanistan.

China, Iran, and Russia—all US rivals—had a dichotomous position toward the US presence in Afghanistan. On the one hand, the US military presence in Afghanistan was a source of concern for these countries. On the other hand, the US presence in Afghanistan served China, Iran, and Russia for over twenty years, primarily for two reasons.

One reason was the human and financial toll the US paid for invading Afghanistan, called "the United States' longest war." A detailed report, the Human and Budgetary Costs to Date of the US War in Afghanistan—2001–2021, published by the Watson Institute of International and Public Affairs at Brown University—said that as of April 2021, the war in Afghanistan had cost the United States $2.261 trillion. According to the same report, a total of 6,294 American citizens died in the war—2,442 US military personnel, six Department of Defense civilians, and 3,846 United States contractors.[4]

Afghan Borders

The death toll and the vast military and financial resources that the United States invested in Afghanistan exhausted the United States, which serves China, Russia, and Iran.

The second reason the US military presence in Afghanistan served China, Russia, and Iran was because the US presence prevented the growth of militant Sunni Islam in Afghanistan. Sunni militant Islam is not only a threat to the West. China and Russia are all concerned about the rise of Sunni militant Islam. For all three, it is a domestic threat as well as a threat to their global aspirations.

Iran borders Afghanistan from the west, and China is Afghanistan's eastern neighbor. And although Russia itself does not border Afghanistan, Tajikistan, Turkmenistan, and Uzbekistan—all of which are affiliated with Russia— make up Afghanistan's border and provide a 'buffer' between Afghanistan and Russia. The growth of Sunni militant Islam in Afghanistan is a security challenge to all three countries.

Now that the United States is leaving Afghanistan, China, Iran, and Russia have the opportunity to deepen their influence in Afghanistan and Central Asia. But at the same time, they are all concerned with the possibility that with Afghanistan being under Taliban rule, Sunni militant Islam will become an increasing threat domestically and regionally.

A closer look at the nature of relations between the Taliban and China, Iran, and Russia, reveals a complex picture.

One major common denominator is the fact that ideologically, the Taliban considers them all enemies. No less than the Taliban views the United States and the West as enemies. Shi'ites and Iran are two of the Sunni Taliban's enemies. And the Taliban completely rejects and abhors atheism—China and Russia. The Taliban's innate hostility to these countries is further fueled by the fact that Sunni Muslim communities in China, Iran, and Russia are repressed cruelly.

Iran and the Taliban

Iran shares a 560-mile-long border with Afghanistan. Geographically and otherwise, Iran and Afghanistan are very intertwined, including a vibrant commercial and trade relationship. However, Iran and the Taliban have a very complicated and thorny relationship punctuated with spheres of high-tension fueled by some major conflictual issues.

One is the ideological hostility between the Sunni Taliban and Shi'ite Iran. Three significant factors further exacerbate that hostility.

First, Iran's hegemonic vision in the Middle East. An ambition that, by virtue of its goal, is at the expense of the Arabs, who are primarily Sunni.

Second, the fact that Iran oppresses and discriminates against the Sunni minority in Iran. Sunni Arabs comprise about 10 percent of Iran's population—about eight million people, based primarily in two Iranian provinces. One is the oil-rich Khuzestan Province in southwestern Iran on the Gulf nestled between Kuwait, Iraq, and Iran—its capitol is a city called Ahvaz. The people that live there are Ahwazi Arabs. The area is undeveloped, and the population is discriminated against. They are deprived of services and suffer severe unemployment and poverty. Facing acute drought and lack of water, during the summer of 2021, the regime provided water sporadically and

Afghanistan and Iran

intermittently to the province. This situation has ignited major riots and protests across the area. These riots are brutally oppressed by the Iranian regime.
The second predominantly Sunni province is farther down the Gulf on the
other side of the Hormuz Strait. The Sistan and Baluchistan Province is Iran's
southeastern border with Afghanistan and Pakistan. The Sunni minorities
in both of these provinces are systematically discriminated against. And like
Khuzestan, the Sistan and Baluchistan Province is also a stage for constant
resistance against the Iranian regime.

The third major focus of contention between Afghanistan and Iran is the
tense relationship between the Taliban and the Hazara Shi'ites in Afghanistan
that, from time to time, erupts into a military confrontation. The Hazaras
are the third-largest ethnic group in Afghanistan. They are primarily concentrated in the mountainous area of central Afghanistan in the Hazara Province,
known as Hazaristan—or the land of the Hazara. Iran has strong ties with the
Hazara. Iran has long supported the Hazaras, a historically oppressed ethnic
minority who make up about 15 and 20 percent of Afghanistan's population. Most Hazaras, like most Iranians, are Shi'ite. They also speak a dialect of
Persian. After the 1979 invasion of Afghanistan, Iran aided the Hazara mujahedeen, who fought the Soviets. Iran cultivates influence among the Hazaras

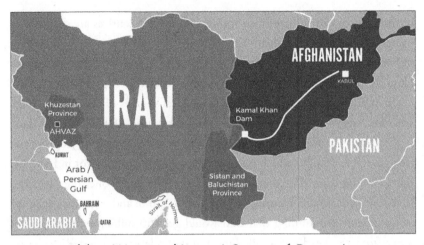

Afghan Water and Iran—A Source of Contention

by funding cultural and religious activities as well as the local media. The IRG reportedly provides the Hazara in Afghanistan with financial and military support.[5] However, Iranian support for the Hazara is not only because of solidarity. The IRG sees Afghanistan as an optimal location to grow its next powerful regional proxy to secure Iranian interests.[6] The Hazara have become a manpower source for Iran's axis of proxies.

Earlier in the book, we discussed the Iranian-backed Afghan Fatemiyoun Brigade Iran uses in Syria to fight to secure the Assad regime—and, of course, Iran's control in Syria. The Fatemiyoun Brigade joined the war around 2012 and subsequently became one of the largest Iranian-backed militias in Syria. The Fatemiyoun militia, estimated at ten to twenty thousand Afghans, is comprised of Hazara Shi'ites and Afghan Shi'ite refugees who live in Iran.[7]

Most of the approximately three million Afghan refugees in Iran live a precarious existence, pressed by extreme economic hardship on the one hand, and harsh xenophobic discrimination on the other. To entice the Afghan Shi'ite refugees in Iran to join the Fatemiyoun, Iran broadens their rights in Iran, meaning they can move around more freely in Iran. They get paid a salary—each fighter receives about $400 to $500 per month and other benefits like education, healthcare, etc. And the families of fallen fighters also receive ongoing benefits. Individuals joining the brigade are also required to attend ideological courses and embrace Shi'ism. All these incentives are designed to increase their status in Iranian society.[8] Over the past few years, Fatemiyoun militants have also been deployed to Yemen to support the Iranian-backed Houthis. Some returned to Iran, and many relocated to Afghanistan.[9]

In addition to these three major ideological sources of contention, there are other issues that fuel friction and tensions between Afghanistan and Iran.

One that we should follow very closely is water. Iran is drying up and facing a severe drought which is destroying the agricultural sector in Iran. The rivers flowing from Afghanistan, particularly the longest one, the Helmand River, are critical water sources for Iran. In 1973, Iran and Afghanistan signed an agreement determining that Iran would get 850 million cubic meters of water from the nearly 800-mile-long transboundary Helmand River basin. But the deals were never ratified or fully implemented because of political developments in both countries. Including a coup in Afghanistan, the Iranian revolution, the Soviet occupation in the 1980s, and the rise of the Taliban.[10]

Afghanistan does provide Iran water, and both argue the other takes more than its share. In March 2021, Afghanistan completed the building of the Kamal Khan Dam, a hydroelectric and irrigation project on the Helmand River. Upon completing the project, Afghan president Ashraf Ghani (who fled Afghanistan for the UAE as the Taliban were taking over) announced that Iran would need to provide Afghanistan with free oil in exchange for the water Iran takes that exceeds its quotas.[11]

Another sensitive issue between the two countries is drugs. Afghanistan dominates the worldwide opium market and is the world's largest producer of opium. Opium poppy plants can be refined to form the basis for several highly addictive drugs, including heroin. Afghanistan's opium harvest accounts for more than 80 percent of the world's supply. In 2018, the United Nations Office on Drugs and Crime (UNODC) estimated that opium production contributed up to 11 percent of the country's economy.[12]

And above the traditional poppy trade, the fastest-growing illicit drug in Afghanistan is methamphetamine. Around the world, most meth is made from synthetic ephedrine. In 2015, Afghanistan's producers began experimenting with extracting ephedrine from the ephedra plant. This plant has grown wild and abundantly across Afghanistan's mountainous central highlands for centuries. Today, the plant is behind the dramatic growth in the methamphetamine industry in Afghanistan. Data from UNODC suggests that Afghanistan has become a producer and supplier of relatively large quantities of low-cost ephedrine and methamphetamine in a short period. The unregulated output has the potential to rival the value of the country's infamous levels of poppy-derived opiates.[13]

Opium has been one of Afghanistan's leading cash-generating economic activities. In 2017 UNODC estimated the gross value of the Afghan opiate economy—including cultivation of poppy, processing into heroin, and trafficking up to Afghan borders—to be between US$4.1 billion and US$6.6 billion in 2017 and, due to drought and lower prices, between US$1.2 billion and US$2.2 billion in 2018. UNODC then estimated that the opiate economy is worth between 6 and 11 percent of Afghanistan's GDP. According to the Afghanistan opium survey of 2019, the overall income generated by domestic consumption, production, and exports of opiates in Afghanistan was estimated at between $1.2 billion and $2.1 billion in 2019.

But when one takes into account economic spillovers, with drugs underpinning much of the other legal, economic activity (such as construction and the purchases of both durables and non-durables), drugs easily constitute a much more significant portion of the Afghan economy.[14] The gross income from opiates exceeded the value of the country's officially recorded licit exports in 2019.[15]

Iran is the most critical trans-shipment point for Afghan opiates to Europe, the Gulf, and Africa. And the illicit drug trade is one of the most important illicit economies in Iran. It is a multibillion-dollar industry. An October 2020 report published by the Global Initiative Against Transnational Organized Crime reported that there had been rapid changes in the drug economy over the past eighteen months. Iran has quickly evolved into a transshipment point for Afghan-produced methamphetamine. It is a crucial transit point for two of the most significant global drug routes emanating from Afghanistan. The Balkan route supplies Western and Central Europe through the Islamic Republic of Iran and Turkey via South-Eastern Europe. And the southern route, through Pakistan and the Islamic Republic of Iran to the Gulf region, Africa, South Asia, and, to a lesser extent, South-East Asia, Oceania, and North America.

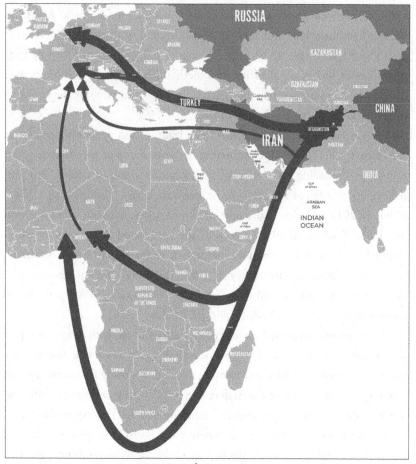

International Drug Routes—
The Balkan Route and the Southern Route

But this situation, inevitably, has a price tag and severe ramifications.

According to an October 2021 report "Drugs, security, and counternarcotics policies in Afghanistan" by Vanda Felbab-Brown, Brookings Scholar of Crime, Conflict, & Nontraditional Security Threats:

> Although time series, baselines, and reliable data are lacking; there is a widespread sense that opiate use and opioid use disorder has been on a dangerous rise in Afghanistan. In 2010, the US government

highlighted the alarming prevalence of drug use among adult men and women, adolescents, and children. In 2012, the Afghan Ministry of Counternarcotics posited that 2.7 percent of the adult population in Afghanistan are regular opiate users and that there had been substantial increases in the use of both opium and heroin in the last few years. The US Department of State assessed that in 2012, 3.5 percent of Afghan adults used some form of opioids. In 2015, the United Nations (UN) estimated that there were as many as 1.6 million drug users in Afghan cities and perhaps another 3 million in the rural areas. There is no reason to believe that both the absolute numbers and the drug use trends have changed significantly. A confluence of dangerous conditions spurs on drug abuse: a highly traumatized population dealing with economic deprivation, insecurity, and war; the availability of cheap drugs; and a regional setting of extensive drug use in Pakistan, Iran, Central Asia, and Russia.[16]

The Iranian Drug Control Headquarters (DCHQ) reported that in 2019, an estimated 2.8 million Iranians (5.4 percent of the adult population aged fifteen to sixty-five) were living with substance use disorders. This included an estimated 225,000 regular methamphetamine users. Since mid-2019, Iranian public officials have reported that methamphetamine use has been increasing. This is, of course, due to the influx of cheap Afghan methamphetamine and a simultaneous rise in the prices of other drugs.[17] The *Fars* news agency reports Iran has about five million drug users—one of the world's highest rates of opiate addiction. But experts believe the actual figure is higher.[18]

In addition to an increase in drug addiction in both countries, such significant levels of drug use go hand-in-hand with crime. A joint report submitted in June 2020 by the Abdorrahman Boroumand Center for Human Rights in Iran and Harm Reduction International quotes an Iranian Parliament report that 60 percent of the criminal cases in Iran involve drugs.[19]

For Iran, the stream of narcotics from Afghanistan to Iran is a double-edged sword. On the one hand, it is a significant form of income given Iran's location on global trade routes. On the other hand, the toll of drug addiction is increasingly weighing on Iranian society.

Another tangled issue in the relationship between Iran and Afghanistan is the Afghan refugees.

There are almost one million registered Afghan refugees in Iran and between 2.1 to 2.5 million undocumented Afghan refugees who overwhelmingly live in urban areas.[20] In recent years, Iran has increased the allocation and renewal of refugee identity cards. The card grants registered refugees conditional freedom of movement, temporary work permits, and access to the national education and healthcare systems. Undocumented Afghans, on the other hand, live under extreme restrictions. They have limited work options, limited access to education and healthcare, and live under Iranian authorities' constant threat of deportation. In 2020, 856,793 undocumented Afghans returned to their country of origin, of which 324,779 were deported.[21]

Iran and the Taliban have very open channels of ongoing communication. However, as Foad Izadi, a professor at the Faculty of World Studies at the University of Tehran, accurately indicates, "Iran realized some time ago that the Taliban were

Afghanistan and Russia

gaining strength ... It is because of this that Iran has developed a working relationship with the Taliban. It's not because Iran particularly likes them."[22]

Given the labyrinthine relationship, it is not surprising that some Arab analysts evaluate that Iran is looking for a proxy power to secure its border with Afghanistan. The Hazara Shi'ites in Afghanistan[23] and the Afghan Fatemiyoun militia operating in Syria,[24] as I said earlier, would be the natural address for Iran to create a new proxy to secure its border with Afghanistan.

Russia and the Taliban

Russia does not border Afghanistan. But Russia also has a long history of complex relations with the large Muslim population that lives within the boundaries of the Soviet Union—Uzbekistan, Turkmenistan, and Tajikistan—all three of which border Afghanistan and were once part of the Soviet Union. Russia views these countries as its backyard and areas of strategic importance to Russia.

Militant Sunni Islam is a challenge Russia deals with constantly. One possible scenario which concerns Russia is that Sunni militants disguised as Afghan refugees will set up Taliban bases in Uzbekistan, Turkmenistan, and Tajikistan.

It is no wonder that President Putin rushed to announce that the Taliban takeover has immediate ramifications on Russia's security.[25] And addressing an online summit of the Collective Security Treaty Organization (CSTO), he told Central Asian leaders that it is vital to avoid any spillover of "radical Islam" into the region from Afghanistan and said it was important to keep "Islamist extremists" at bay following the Taliban's takeover of power.[26]

China and the Taliban

China shares a short border with Afghanistan—less than sixty miles in length. However, the Chinese side of the border is the province of Xinjiang. That fact is significant for two primary reasons.

One is that the Xinjiang province is predominately populated by some ten million Uighurs—Muslims of Turkish origin. Two is that China brutally oppresses the Uighurs.

China is concerned with the possibility that under the Taliban's rule Afghanistan will become a hub for Uighur militants who will fuel growing violence in the Xinjiang province. What increases the Chinese concern is the

Afghanistan and China

possibility that Sunni Uighur militants that are fighting in Syria will move to Afghanistan, bringing with them combat experience and military know-how. Having Sunni Uighur militias on both sides of the Chinese-Afghanistan border concerns China.

On that note, it has been reported that Beijing is working to enact a Land Borders Law that would permit the use of weapons against people who cross the border illegally and commit violent acts and allow for border areas to be locked down in emergencies. Beijing has bolstered its military presence at the Afghan border.[27]

And then there is Pakistan. The Chinese are concerned with the relationship between Afghanistan and Pakistan. The two countries share a 1,660-mile-long border known as the Durand Line—and each one lays claims to the area.

Pakistan viewed the Afghan-Russian War (1979–1989) as an opportunity to advance its goals and establish a Pashtun-friendly government in Afghanistan. To that end, Pakistan helped and supported the Afghan mujahedeen in their war against the Soviets. But over time, the relationship between the Taliban and Pakistan took a dramatic shift.

The Pashtun are native to the land comprising southern Afghanistan and northwestern Pakistan.

In Afghanistan, the Pashtun are the largest ethnic group—comprising almost half of the population of Afghanistan; they live mainly in the south and the east of the country.

In Pakistan, the Pashtun are the second-largest ethnic group—about 16 percent of its total population. The western and northwestern Pakistan area—the Federally Administered Tribal Area (FATA)—is populated by tribes, principally the Pashtun. FATA is inhabited by five and a half million people suffering from acute and persistent institutional neglect, poverty, ignorance, and Pakistan's most severe economic underdevelopment. The tribal areas in Pakistan are fertile ground for radical Islam.

Parallel to establishing its rule over Afghanistan in the 1990s, the Afghan Taliban also established a power base in the tribal areas in Pakistan, which had fallen out of the Pakistani government's control at the time.

Over time, the Pakistani Taliban spread outside the tribal strip into the northwestern province, also called the Northwestern Frontier Province (NWFP) in northwest Pakistan on the Afghan-Pakistani border and in and around the Swat Valley directly east of Kabul on the Pakistani side. This area—dominated by Salafi-jihadi Taliban ideology, ruled by local tribal warlords, and housing a narcotic traffic corridor—presents a growing challenge to the Pakistani government. Hence, it makes the region very unstable and volatile.

Pakistan is a critical component of the Chinese Belt and Road Initiative (BRI). China has invested considerable resources in Pakistan to firm up that portion of the route. Instability in Pakistan caused by the growing power of the Taliban on both sides of the Afghan-Pakistan border could compromise a cornerstone of Chinese policy.

The Trajectory of Relations between the Taliban and Iran, China, and Russia in the Foreseeable Future

China, Russia, and Iran maintain communication channels with the Taliban. We saw how Iran and Afghanistan are, to a large extent, intertwined. China and Russia have currently stepped up and offered to be political and financial partners to help rebuild Afghanistan. That said, to ensure their engagement—and investment—both rising regional superpowers will need stability.

China, Iran, and Russia will keep a close eye on developments in Afghanistan.

However, I estimate that the inherent frictions will not be a significant source of tension in the foreseeable future. All players have communication channels with the Taliban. It is unlikely that creating conflict with these big players will be at the forefront of the Taliban's priorities in the foreseeable future.

The Taliban and the Arab World

The Taliban and the al-Qaeda camp are in a power struggle with ISIS.

Al-Qaeda and ISIS ideologies are rooted mainly in Hanbali orthodoxy (the most dogmatic stream) and the extremist Salafi-jihadi ideology. Both believe that the rulers and governments of Muslim countries are not governing according to the principles of pure Islam. Therefore, they share the parallel goal that these rulers and governments should be overthrown.

That objective stems from a school of thought that has evolved within Salafi-jihadi militant Islam ideology called *takfir*.

The term takfir is connected to a fundamental concept in Islam known as *kufr billah* "heresy." As we discussed initially in Chapter 3, the word *Islam* means the total emotional, intellectual, physical, and spiritual willingness of a person to subdue themselves to the concept of monotheism to the one god, Allah. A *Muslim* then is a person who submits willingly and consciously to Allah's rule. All those who do not entirely subject themselves to that concept are not Muslims; therefore, they are *Kafirun* or *Kuffar* "infidels."

Takfir ideology argues that there are Muslims who do not fulfill the commandments of Islam in "the true and correct" manner. Therefore, they should not be considered Muslims. Instead, they should be viewed as enemies of Islam whose danger is even greater than those of the non-Muslim infidels.

Why? Because—according to takfir ideology—the Muslim "infidels" are "corrupting" and "contaminating" Islam and its values from within. And as long as Islam is not pure from within, the ultimate vision of establishing Allah's dominion on earth cannot be realized. Therefore, takfir ideology believes that Islam must be "purified" of "Muslim impersonators."

In a twist of irony, the Saudi monarchy is on the top of takfir adherents' list to bring down. That is ironic because the ultra-conservative *Wahabi* Sunni orthodoxy that originated in Saudi Arabia drew some of its core principles from the Hanbali orthodoxy. And elements of the Wahabi school of thought have also percolated to the Hanafi-based Taliban school of thought.

Salafi-jihadi groups such as ISIS and al-Qaeda target Saudi Arabia because the Saudi monarchy is the custodian of Islam's two (out of three—the third is al-Aqsa) sacred sites—Mecca and Medina. And in the eyes of al-Qaeda and ISIS, the cradle of Islam—the Arabian Peninsula and its Muslim holy sites—are ruled by a fake Muslim government.

There are different opinions regarding the threat posed by Salafi-jihadi groups, specifically al-Qaeda and ISIS, following the Taliban takeover to the Arab world in general and the Arab monarchies specifically.

Abdel Monem Said, the director of al-Ahram Center for Political and Strategic Studies in Cairo, estimates that the threat will increase. He cites three main reasons for his theory.

One reason is that because of the concept of takfir, the desire to overthrow these regimes is high on the ideological priority list of militant Islam, whether it is al-Qaeda, ISIS/the Islamic State, the Taliban, etc.

A second reason is that within the ranks of al-Qaeda and the Islamic State, there are many Arabs—Algerians, Iraqis, Jordanians, Libyans, Saudis, Syrians, etc. This fact helps militant Islam organizations expand their activities throughout the Arab world.

A third reason is the instability and upheaval in the Arab world. Chaos is the strategic ally of militant Islam—the more that chaos and turmoil prosper, the more powerful militant Islam becomes. Militant Islam exploits the growing chaos in the Middle East and the power vacuum it creates to grow, build momentum, and deepen its hold through initiating violence and terror that creates and feeds chaos and brings anarchy, which creates more violence and terror. It is a vicious cycle that serves militant Islam well.[28]

On the other hand, there are those who believe that in a scenario of a power struggle in Afghanistan between the al-Qaeda-Taliban camps on the one hand and ISIS on the other, the threat of militant Islam may instead be diverted from the Middle East into Central and Southeast Asia.[29]

In my 2016 book, I posited that the need to confront the growing threat of militant Islam is one of the factors that offers a common ground for cooperation between Israel, Egypt, and the major Arab monarchies.[30] Both the Abraham Accords and the alliance of moderation that I have presented in this book prove my prediction to have been correct.

The Taliban regaining control of Afghanistan is the wind beneath the wings of militant Islam groups. This development has the potential to further destabilize the region.

Therefore, I predict that the momentum militant Islam will experience in the immediate future will further strengthen the foundations of the Abraham Accords and the alliance of moderation. I say that because the partners in these coalitions have the desire—and need—for stability.

Impact of Taliban Rule and the US-Iran Power Balance

Many eyes followed the hasty US withdrawal from Afghanistan. Both enemies and allies of the United States in the region view the hurried US withdrawal as an expression of US weakness and confusion.

While the United States was scrambling to get out of Afghanistan, Hezbollah leader Hassan Nasrallah declared that the first of many Iranian ships loaded with diesel would make its way to Lebanon. Describing the ship as "Lebanese soil," he warned Israel and the United States not to harm the ship. Nasrallah openly and provocatively defies US sanctions on Iranian oil exports. His move and the timing were not coincidental. It reflects the assessment of US enemies in the region that the United States is confused, indecisive, and weak.

Not surprisingly, some commentators argue that the hasty US withdrawal will result in Iran hardening its position in its negotiations with the West. Furthermore, they believe it will encourage Iranian-backed Iraqi Shi'ite militias whose goal is to drive the United States out of Iraq to increase their attacks against US forces in Iraq.[31]

There is, however, an opposite outlook. For example, former executive director of the International Institute for Strategic Studies (IISS-Americas),

Mark Fitzpatrick, argues that Biden cannot appear to be giving in to Iran's hard-liners. Therefore, he estimates that to compensate, the United States may be inclined to take the opposite tack and apply more pressure on Iran.[32]

Any attempt to evaluate the long-term ramifications of the Taliban's renewed rule over Afghanistan on the region will be mere speculation and a shot in the dark.

But three things are evident in this phase.

One, militant Islam gains momentum. That is a concern on both a regional as well as a global level.

Two, the hasty US withdrawal from Afghanistan emboldens US enemies while increasing US allies' apprehension and consternation.

Three, it is yet another manifestation of the end of Western hegemony in the Middle East—as we will discuss in the next chapter.

CHAPTER 12

THE END OF WESTERN HEGEMONY IN THE MIDDLE EAST

Western Hegemony in the Middle East Ends in the Twenty-First Century

In the twenty-first century, Western hegemony in the Middle East will come to an end.

A significant reason for the setting sun of Western hegemony is the West's accumulative failure to create and implement effective policy in the region. When I say "failure of effective policy," I am referring to two aspects. One is the declining ability to effect policy that serves Western interests. And the second is the failure to bring stability to the volatile Middle East geopolitical ecosystem.

One factor that has compromised Western policy in the Middle East is the increasing tension between *idealpolitik* and *realpolitik* policies.

Increasing Tension between Value-Driven Idealpolitik and Realpolitik Policy

Western civilization has played a significant role in the shaping of the Middle East. For centuries, European powers like France, Italy, Germany, Russia, and the United Kingdom have been engaged in this region. The United States is a relatively new player but has had a tremendous impact and influence.

A significant component that helped the West become the superpower in the Middle East was a focused, often aggressive policy, driven by a realpolitik worldview designed to secure Western powers' economic, commercial, and security interests. The political and ideological power struggle between the West and the Soviet Union also motivated the West to want to achieve and secure its superiority in the region.

Here are some examples of Western realpolitik-driven policy in the Middle East.

The 1956 joint Anglo-Israeli military operation in the Sinai Peninsula secured free shipping in the Suez Canal and the Red Sea. The US military intervened in Lebanon's first Civil War in 1958 to intercept the leftist nationalist's take-over. In 1991, the United States led the international coalition—including Arab forces from Bahrain, Egypt, Morocco, Oman, Qatar, and Saudi Arabia—during the first Gulf War to push Saddam Hussein out of Kuwait and secure the West's oil supply. In 2003, in "Operation Iraqi Freedom" (also known as the Second Gulf War), US and UK military forces—without the support of Arab forces this time—occupied Iraq. Based on intelligence that later turned out to be flawed, the impetus for the war was that Iraqi Dictator Saddam Hussein possessed weapons of mass destruction.

After the collapse of the Soviet Union and toward the end of the twentieth century, there was a shift in the Western cultural, political, and intellectual discourse, which impacted Western powers' domestic and foreign policy.

Following the end of the Cold War and toward the end of the twentieth century, realpolitik as the norm in foreign policy began to sunset, and a new day dawned. Ronald Reagan wanted to preserve freedom as well as peace by fostering the infrastructure of democracy. Western leaders like British Prime Minister Tony Blair and US President Bill Clinton charted a new centrist path—the Third Way, a blend of conservatism and social democracy.

The pursuit of national interests has always been the bedrock from which foreign policy was formulated. The changing drivers of Western domestic and foreign policy generated growing tensions and gaps between realpolitik policy—one that is based on practical rather than moral or ideological considerations. And idealpolitik policy—believing that Western ideals and values such as community, equality, identity, inclusiveness, human rights, multilateralism, responsibility, etc., can and should be at the core of domestic and foreign policy.

For the West, trying to create an effective foreign policy in the volatile Middle East while holding the stick on both ends, keeping realpolitik policy in line with higher principles and purposes, gave way to an incoherent, scattered Western policy with competing, often incompatible goals. And questionable, if not counterproductive, results.

Western countries face a challenge. They want to advance their interests, adhere to their values, and at the same time maintain good relationships. A sensitive dance inevitably ensues. One in which the West uses primarily informal channels, including NGOs and backtrack diplomacy, to promote its idealpolitk agenda. This approach allows the West to express its commitment to its core values and promote its ideals without risking diplomatic incidents or damaging relationships. Sometimes things go awry, and the conflict escalates. More than once, what begins with an attempt to achieve a "win-win" ends up in a "lose-lose."

Here are two examples.

On August 3, 2018, the Canadian government tweeted the following: "Canada is gravely concerned about additional arrests of civil society and women's rights activists in #SaudiArabia, including Samar Badawi. We urge the Saudi authorities to immediately release them and all other peaceful #humanrights activists."[1] Saudi Arabia responded by expelling Canadian ambassador Dennis Horak and recalling its ambassador from Canada. Furthermore, the Saudis brought back fifteen thousand Saudi students studying at universities and colleges in Canada. The Kingdom also froze all investments and commercial trade with Canada. The Canadian government followed suit by placing an embargo on exporting weapons to Saudi Arabia.

Two years later, in April 2020, Canada lifted the embargo. The reason for the policy change was a $14 billion deal signed by the Canadian division of General Dynamics and Saudi Arabia. The corporation was to supply almost one thousand armed personnel carriers to the Saudis.[2]

Subsequently, Canada has made some effort to repair the relationship. But the road will be long, challenging, and uncertain, and those who championed Canada's principled stance may denounce their efforts. Meanwhile, the students have not returned. Canada is no longer a part of a flagship Saudi teacher training program, which was one of their cornerstone initiatives and very important to Canada. Canada sacrificed its ability to improve human rights in Saudi Arabia from within, which had been one of Ottawa's goals in its relationship with the Kingdom. To quote Ambassador Horak, "Canada's determination to stand its ground and absorb the costs won it plaudits from human rights constituencies at home and abroad. But it was a pyrrhic victory. Canada's ability to actually have an impact and genuinely advance its values or human rights agenda in Saudi Arabia suffered."[3]

The second example of an idealpolitik strategy gone awry is the United States' policy vis-à-vis the war in Yemen. This US policy, in my analysis, is a quintessential example of the push and pull of idealpolitik vs. realpolitik.

In October 2018, Saudi journalist Jamal Khashoggi entered the Saudi Arabian Consulate in Turkey. That was the last time he was seen alive. It is commonly assumed he was murdered in the Saudi Consulate by Saudi agents.

In December 2018, the United States Senate approved two resolutions. One resolution blamed Saudi Crown Prince Mohammad bin Salman bin Abdulaziz Al-Saud for the murder and insisted that Saudi Arabia hold any-one responsible for his death accountable. The second resolution was to end US military support for Saudi Arabia in the war in Yemen. President Trump vetoed the Senate's resolutions.

The Biden administration revoked one of the Trump administration's final acts—designating the Houthis and three of its leaders (Abdul Malik al-Houthi, Abd al-Khaliq Badr al-Din al-Houthi, and Abdullah Yahya al-Hakim) as for-eign terrorists. Biden's rapprochement toward the Houthis stemmed from the administration's intention to foster a political solution that would end the war in Yemen and end the humanitarian crisis.

In parallel, pressured by the idealpolitik camp over the Khashoggi case, President Joe Biden also decided to ban the sale of offensive weapons to Saudi Arabia.[4]

Making the Khashoggi case, a factor that guided and shaped US policy in Yemen, has doubly backfired on the United States. First, Biden's decision to ban the sale of offensive weapons to Saudi Arabia boosted Houthi and Iranian aggression. Therefore, the war—and accordingly the humanitarian crisis—have both escalated. Second, the tensions between the United States and its allies Saudi Arabia, UAE, and Israel have grown.

President Biden could have taken another path to end the war in Yemen and alleviate the escalating humanitarian crisis. The 2018 UNSC 2451 demands that all foreign forces withdraw from the city and port of Al-Hodeidah and that the area surrounding Al-Hodeidah is demilitarized. Forcing the Houthis to adhere to existing international legislative demands would be a much more constructive and effective US policy to end the war between Yemen and Saudi Arabia and alleviate the humanitarian crisis. Furthermore, enforcing UNSC 2451 would also contribute to stability in the Red Sea, the Bab el-Mandeb, and the Middle East as a whole.

In the twenty-first century, the Middle East's turbulent reality presents Western policymakers with a dilemma. Prioritizing a value-driven policy over a real-politic policy could endanger Western core interests. And prioritizing real-politics over a value-driven policy could result in an intellectual, political, and social crisis because of the West's need to compromise its core agenda values for realpolitik calculations.

Moral and Legal Confusion and a Lack of Clarity

In Chapter 10, I argued that a combination of looking at the Middle East through Western lenses, a lack of linguistic proficiency in the region's languages, and an environment in which soundbites, buzzwords, and shallow narratives have replaced the pursuit of knowledge and critical thinking, prevents an accurate interpretation of the Middle East reality and compromises the ability to navigate an increasingly complex global reality.

Flattening a complex reality into a simplistic discussion has created a situation that clouds and compromises Western policymakers' ability to develop and implement a coherent policy in the turbulent Middle East. A major manifestation of that is the confusion regarding the legal and moral aspects of using military might.

And a core concept related to that issue is the concept of a "*threat.*" Defining and identifying a "threat" can cause a fierce debate and discussion in Western cultural, intellectual, legal, and political circles. Determining a threat results in legislation and official policy to address the threat.

But another term plays a significant role in determining the legal and moral parameters of using military might. Unlike "threat," this term does not translate into a legal definition that provides a basis for legislation. Nor does it result in a specific official policy.

The term I am referring to is "evil."

In the following section, I argue that these two terms—threat and evil—have created confusion in the cultural and intellectual discussion in the West. The core of that confusion is the inability to understand that *"evil"* is not necessarily the most significant "threat." A threat that is not identified as "evil" can be much more severe than a threat that is identified as "evil."

I argue that this confusion impairs the West's ability to identify a threat that is more dangerous than "evil." The lack of clarity prevents the West from acting decisively and firmly to intercept that threat. And it fogs the West's ability to identify the legal and moral justification for using its might—even if the situation justifies it.

I will give two examples to support my argument. Both are in the context of Iran.

One is the elimination of Major General Qasem Soleimani, the commander of the al-Quds force. The second example is the JCPOA.

Elimination of Major-General Qasem Soleimani, the Commander of the Al-Quds Force

On January 3, 2020, the United States eliminated the Iranian al-Quds Force commander, Major-General Qasem Soleimani. A fierce debate ensued in the West regarding the legality of such an act. For example, on July 7, 2020, a UN Human Rights investigator said, "The January US drone strike in Iraq that killed top Iranian general Qasem Soleimani and nine other people represented a violation of international law."[5]

As we said in Chapter 2, the al-Quds force's specific mission is to spearhead Iran's goal of regional hegemony strategically and tactically. Its task is to develop, command, nurture, and manage a network of Iranian proxies, agents, and terror cells in the region and around the world to achieve this goal. Afghan militias, Hamas, and Islamic Jihad in the Gaza Strip, Iraqi Shi'ite militias, Hezbollah in Lebanon, Pakistani militias, Yemeni Houthi forces, the list goes on. Major-General Qasem Soleimani was the strategic mastermind.

Soleimani's responsibility was to spread and entrench Iranian power and influence and build and manage Iran's platforms to execute its destructive and deadly regional policy.

As commander of the al-Quds force, Soleimani spearheaded Iran's dangerous and deadly hegemonic policy. He bears direct and personal responsibility for carnage and destruction across the Middle East. The orders Soleimani gave to the militias under his command resulted in the deaths of tens of thousands of people—most of whom were civilians—throughout the region. His victims include Americans, Israelis, Iraqis, Palestinians, Lebanese, Syrians, Yemenites, Christians, Jews, Muslims, Alawites, Sunnis, Shi'ites, etc. He ordered the militias to carry out Iranian foreign policy that destroyed Syria and dragged Lebanon and Iraq into a whirlpool of violence and disintegration.

As I mentioned in Chapter 2, Tehran was shaken by the elimination of Soleimani. The act caught the regime, the IRG, and the al-Quds force off guard and took them out of balance. Tehran's confusion was evident from its reaction and retaliation to the assassination.

The regime fired missiles from Iran toward the area of two Iraqi bases hosting US forces. Iranian state television rushed to show videos of the missile launches and reported that at least eighty US soldiers had been killed in the attack. It added that the attack had caused severe damage to American helicopters and military equipment.[6] That was false information. Or in the modern vernacular, 'fake news.' No American soldiers were killed, though several soldiers were wounded, some seriously.

Two aspects of this story indicate the regime's concern in the face of the attack on Soleimani. First, the fact that Tehran lied about the attack's impact indicated that it wanted to preserve its image and maintain its deterrence posture. The second is the nature of the attack. If Iran had actually wanted the United States to pay a heavy price for eliminating Soleimani, it certainly has the ability to exact a heavy toll. The verbal bluster and 'mild' results of the Iranian retaliation made it clear that Tehran wanted to avoid further escalation. The regime did not want to test Trump. Because after America killed Soleimani, Tehran was not able to confidently assess what the US retaliation would be for killing United States soldiers.

Accumulating information suggests that killing Soleimani harmed and disrupted the activities of the Iranian-backed militias.[7] In an interview, Dr.

Nima Mina, professor of Iranian Studies at the School of Oriental and African
Studies in London, said the following:

> As head of the Quds Force, the Islamic Revolutionary Guards Corps
> (IRGC) expeditionary arm, Soleimani and his unit built a reputation
> for brutality in foreign theaters from Aleppo to Sana'a. The Quds'
> network of proxies assassinated foreign politicians, laid siege to cities
> and fomented chaos across the Middle East. In pursuit of the so-called
> Islamic Revolution, it seemed that Soleimani would stop at nothing.
>
> But after six months without its infamous commander, evidence
> is mounting that the Quds Force's power and corrosive influence
> may be in decline. Six months since his death, "Iran's strategy in the
> region hasn't changed, but they are in a much weaker position to
> achieve their strategic goals.[8]

Eliminating Major-General Qasem Soleimani, commander of the IRG
al-Quds force serves the United States' interest and the need for stability.

When the United States killed the founder and leader of al-Qaeda, Osama
Bin Laden, in Pakistan in 2011, and when US forces eliminated the leader of
ISIS, Abu Bakr al Baghdadi, in Syria in 2019, there was no debate about the
legality of the act. There were no accusations of violating international law.
They were labeled as *evil*.

Soleimani presented a much greater threat to the West and its interests
than Bin Ladin or al-Baghdadi. Yet, some in the West argue killing Soleimani
was not legitimate because he was a military officer. Soleimani was not labeled
evil. Does the fact that Soleimani had a military rank and wore an Iranian
uniform, as opposed to hiding in a cave and wearing a *galabiya*, make him any
less of a mega-terrorist that presented a continuing and severe threat to the
region, to the West, and to Western interests?

The Joint Comprehensive Plan of Action (JCPOA)

Iran came to the negotiating table in 2015 because they were desperate and
knew they had a very weak hand. However, it was clear that the West was eager
to close a deal at any cost.

On July 23, 2015, a week after the JCPOA was signed, influential *New York Times* columnist Thomas Friedman said in an interview with Charlie Rose:

> If they (Iran) want a bomb, they will get it. The idea that we can permanently prevent them from getting the nuclear fuel cycle with or without sanctions is an illusion. They are going to get that capability. The question is, will they have the intention. We need to be signaling through Congress much more forcefully now authorizing the President and future Presidents very clearly the right to destroy an Iranian nuclear weapon if they develop one. We need to use all means necessary—and ALL in caps. This Iranian regime acquiring a bomb crosses a red line for us, for America. It will be bad for the world.[9]

Friedman is not a policymaker. However, his voice reflects the intellectual and political atmosphere that dominated and shaped Western negotiators' mindset and approach. That is why I would like to challenge his observation.

I think the critical observation Friedman provides is, "The idea that we can permanently prevent them from getting the nuclear fuel cycle with or without sanctions is an 'illusion'." I emphasize the word "illusion" because it is the vital component.

If preventing Iran from getting nuclear fuel cycle is an illusion, then what is the use of UNSC resolutions? Why should you have IAEA inspections?

If the idea of preventing Iran from achieving a nuclear fuel cycle is an illusion, is destroying the Iranian bomb once Iran has a nuclear weapon really something the West will do?

The West used all its means—particularly its military power—to eliminate the Islamic State in Iraq and Syria. Because there was a consensus in the West that ISIS was *evil*. And the West realized that the only way to defeat evil was with lethal military force. Therefore, the West concluded that eradicating ISIS in Iraq and Syria was legally and morally legitimate. No one in the West argued that destroying the Islamic State in Iraq and Syria was an "illusion," illegal, or immoral.

So, why does the West not act proactively to prevent or intercept Iran's activities when "an Iranian nuclear bomb crosses red lines and is bad for the world"?

The answer lies in the word "illusion." It is the keyword because it signifies Western confusion.

Today, Iran—without nuclear weapons—presents a much more severe and tangible threat to the West than ISIS. Friedman wonders "if they will have the intention?" but his question is totally irrelevant because once it has a nuclear weapon, Iran's extortion capacity will be practically boundless. The mullah regime in Iran, by far, poses a much more severe threat than the evil of ISIS.

However, the mullah regime is not identified as *evil.*

The essence—and the danger—of the Western confusion is that it fails to understand that *evil* is not necessarily the most significant threat. A threat that *is not* identified as "evil" can present a much more severe danger than a threat that *is* identified as "evil." That confusion impedes the West's ability to identify a threat that is more dangerous than evil. It compromises the West's ability to identify the legal and moral justification for acting decisively and firmly to intercept that threat. Including the use of military might (as a last resort) even if the situation justifies military action. Even when, to quote Freidman, it "crosses red lines and is bad news for the world." A nuclear weapon in the hands of a brutal and violent regime motivated by apocalyptic narratives and visions of hegemony is indeed bad for the world.

A common question people often ask me is, "Is the Middle East on the verge of a nuclear arms race?" And the answer is always: No, not yet, but we are close. It is likely that once the mullah regime has an atomic bomb, others in the region will have one in very rapid order. In November 2020, we had proof. The Saudi minister of state for Foreign Affairs, Adel al-Jubeir, said, "If Iran's path towards a bomb is not blocked, then Saudi Arabia reserves itself the right to have a nuclear weapon. And other nations in the region may do the same as well."[10]

An analysis published at the beginning of 2021 by the Israeli Institute for National Security Studies (INSS) estimates that once Iran decides to spring toward making its first nuclear bomb, it will take anywhere between a couple of months—in the pessimistic scenario—to two years—in the optimistic scenario.[11] At the same time, Israel Defense Forces chief-of-staff, Lieutenant-General Aviv Kochavi, has reportedly ordered the IDF to prepare operational plans to confront Iran's possible sprint toward a nuclear bomb.[12]

Anne Applebaum, a staff writer at *The Atlantic*, a fellow at the SNF Agora Institute at Johns Hopkins University, and the author of *Twilight Democracy: The Seductive Lure of Authoritarianism* writes in her August 2021 article "Liberal Democracy is Worth a Fight,": "In the real world, the battle to defend liberal democracy is sometimes a real battle, a military battle, not merely an ideological battle. It cannot always be fought with language, arguments, conferences, or diplomacy, or by deploying human-rights organizations, UN declarations, and fierce EU statements of concern. Or rather, you can try to fight it that way, but you will lose."[13]

Effective policy requires being able to identify when there is legal and moral legitimacy to pursue an aggressive option. And sometimes, that ability is the most crucial element in designing the right policy.

In my view, that ability has been compromised due to tension between policies based on practical considerations and policies based on ideal moral and ethical considerations. And the harmful age of ignorance compounds the challenge.

The Age of Ignorance

In the chapter about the Israeli-Palestinian conflict, I addressed the harmful impact of false narratives. That phenomenon is one of the sources feeding the age of ignorance.

This disturbing development has been exacerbated by the dominance of social media that glorifies flat, easy-to-digest narratives and slogans. Our news and social media feeds are chock full of shallow discourse, narratives, theories, and concepts that sound good. But catchphrases and soundbites—no matter how good they sound—do not lead to further understanding or bring us closer to a sustainable solution. We are steeped in sloppy, populist, often intolerant 'communication'—if that term can be used at all in that context—of 280 characters or less. Social media elevates sensationalism and shallowness over real depth and discourse. Increasingly, the only relevant parameter is the number of "likes" and "followers."

I want to share with you an example of the harmful impact of the age of ignorance.

In the fall of 2019, I attended a conference in Washington, DC. One of the panels I listened to explored what a progressive US policy in the Middle East would look like. Before leaving for the conference, I was getting caught up on the latest Middle East updates, as is my standard daily practice. The headlines of that day included: mass protests in Lebanon; hundreds of Iraqi protesters were executed point-blank in the streets; killing and destruction in Syria and Yemen continued unabated, etc.

I listened in amazement to the five speakers on the stage. Not one of them said a single word about the bloody events in Iraq, Lebanon, Syria, or Yemen. In fact, not one of them said a single thing about what was happening in the Middle East. A dais of academics, journalists, thought leaders, and heads of think tanks all echoed the narrative that the United States is the source of the Middle East's problems. They spoke enthusiastically about a progressive US policy in the Middle East that should focus on "building coalitions and providing rewards." They did not discuss what challenges they would address in the region. Nor did they outline with whom to build coalitions or to what end. They didn't explain the similarities and differences between the United States and the Middle East or what unites and divides the regional actors. They didn't present any policy goals, what US interests they want to ensure, what is acceptable and what is not, and what they would do if US interests were jeopardized.

I am sorry to say that panel was a profoundly disturbing expression of ignorance, guided by Western narratives and soundbites that rarely—if at all—dialogue with the Middle East's complex reality. To me, this experience was a sad and quintessential example of Western thought leaders, guided by shallow thinking, presenting narratives, theories, and concepts that sound good to the Western ear but do not lead to further understanding, nor bring us closer to a constructive, effective, and sustainable policy. The odds that the approach the panel suggested will bring stability and hope to the people of the Middle East and effectively serve core Western interests is highly questionable. Unless the interest of this policy is to nullify any Western interests.

In an increasingly complex world in the age of 'fake news' and 'deep fake news,' people don't need more provocative and divisive stories that sound good but don't further understanding or bring us closer to a constructive, productive, realistic, and sustainable solution.

People need to be equipped to understand a complex reality. People need to reestablish the feeling they can effectively navigate a world in which they are overwhelmed by a flood of information—both factual and fake.

The West Has Failed to Address Core Regional Conflicts Effectively

The tension between the realpolitik and idealpolitik, the rise of the age of ignorance, and the growing difficulty in identifying when the West has a legal right and moral imperative to act have eroded the effectiveness of Western policy in the Middle East.

Faced with the turbulent and violent course and outcomes of the Arab Spring; the war in Libya; the war in Syria; the war in Yemen; the crumbling of Lebanon and Iraq; increasing Iranian aggression; escalating Turkish intrusions; repeated and escalating rounds of military confrontations between Israel and Gaza; and the violation of civil, human, LGBTQ, and women's rights across the region, the West has failed time and again to formulate and implement policies that serve the area and serve Western interests.

Failing to understand the region's dynamic, dramatically changing landscape, Western policymakers and shapers of public opinion often continue to fixate on their comfortable yet often misguided narratives and perspectives.

In place of leading and producing informed, constructive, and practical policy in the face of a complex and violent Middle East reality, Western foreign policy has become chiefly a hybrid construct in which value considerations coexist uncomfortably with the stark realities of interest-driven realpolitik. As a result, Western policy has increasingly inched toward a niche of toothless resolutions, mantras, and rhetoric whose effectiveness is limited, if effective at all.

Hollow and inconsequential rhetoric has become the policy of the West.

Two former foreign policy advisors in President Obama's administration published an article in May 2020 titled "America's Opportunity in the Middle East—Diplomacy Could Succeed Where Military Force Has Failed." Referring to the Iranian-Saudi tensions, the authors say that "not interfering in each other's affairs is significant progress."[14] That does not seem to be an overly ambitious or inspiring objective for the world's leading superpower.

On October 11, 2020, an article, "For Trump, Defying Mideast Truisms Produced Breakthroughs and Backfires," was published in the *New York Times*. Here is an excerpt:

> Again, and again, in the Middle East, where volatility has burnished or battered previous presidential legacies, President Trump has run roughshod over conventional thinking, advancing key policy aims or fulfilling campaign promises in ways that experts warned could set off a conflagration or blow up in his face. Not only did the predicted disasters not materialize, but in many cases, his policies produced demonstrable achievements.[15]

In other words, the co-authors accurately observe that Trump's Middle East policy bore some fruit because it departed from conventional narratives and assumptions which have ruled the Western discourse and dictated United States policy. And his achievements—namely, the Abraham Accords and the normalization agreements Israel has signed—are significant and will impact the Middle East's geopolitical construct in the twenty-first century.

What Will Characterize Western Middle East Policy in the Twenty-first Century?

Martin Indyk, who served as the US special envoy for the Israeli-Palestinian negotiations from July 2013 to June 2014, published an article in January 2020 titled "The Middle East Isn't Worth It Anymore." He wrote:

> Previously, presidents of both parties shared a broad understanding of US interests in the region, including a consensus that those interests were vital to the country—worth putting American lives and resources on the line to forge peace and, when necessary, wage war. Today, however, with US troops still in harm's way in Iraq and Afghanistan and tensions high over Iran, Americans remain

war-weary. Yet, we seem incapable of mustering a consensus or pursuing a consistent policy in the Middle East.[16]

Indyk's comments are not occurring in a vacuum. Current economic, political, demographic, societal, and cultural developments shape a new geopolitical landscape in Europe and the United States.

In the United States, there is an increased tendency toward isolationism and detachment from the Middle East. President Obama's refrain of "leading from behind" and President Trump's slogan "America first" in many ways are two sides of the same coin.

President Joe Biden portrays ambitious foreign policy objectives, emphasizing an idealpolitik agenda and blocking China. But with an alarmingly bifurcated American public and with COVID-19 continuing to spin out of control—of which the economic ramifications are yet unclear—it is to yet to be seen how much time he will have to focus on overseas affairs. Moreover, as of August 2021, Biden appears to be continuing in the footsteps of Obama and Trump, both of whom, for different reasons, pursued an increasing isolationist posture. Biden has scaled back US military presence in the Gulf. He has exited Afghanistan. And has spoken about decreasing US troops in Iraq by the end of 2021.

In Europe, a new political agenda is underway that centers around the reemergence of particularistic nationalism and a preference to focus on domestic social and economic challenges, such as unemployment, migration policy, an aging population, COVID-19, etc. Increasing voices are calling for limiting—if not ending—Europe's engagement in the region. The Middle East will likely be less of a priority on the emerging European political agenda.

What are the Middle East's reactions to the change of power in the United States following the 2020 elections? And what do I expect of the Biden administration's Middle East policy? We will address those questions in the next chapter.

CHAPTER 13

THE BIDEN ADMINISTRATION AND THE MIDDLE EAST, NOVEMBER 2020 THROUGH AUGUST 2021 | A VIEW FROM THE REGION

From Cautious Optimism to Concern and Criticism

On January 20, 2021, Joe Biden was sworn in as the forty-sixth president of the United States of America. After four years of President Donald Trump, the Democrats have returned to the White House. The Democrats held onto the House and now have an incredibly narrow majority in the Senate.

Naturally, leading up to his presidency—and since his tenure began—there has been a lot of conversation in the Middle East, both in official and informal forums, about Biden's victory and the Biden presidency.

Of course, on the official and diplomatic level, most of the region's leaders were quick to congratulate Biden on his victory. It is worth noting that Israel, the Saudi Royal House, and Turkey waited almost a day until they sent their good wishes.

There are two distinct phases when looking at the unofficial commentary and reactions in the Arab world to President Biden. Specifically, articles published in the Arab press and conversations on Arab social media and other media outlets until August 2021.

November 2020–February 2021: A Mixture of Suspicion and Cautious Optimism

The Arab world, the Israeli government, and the Israeli right-wing were suspiciously looking over Biden's shoulder. The Arab world—and Israel—were concerned that behind Biden was the shadow of the forty-fourth president of the United States, Barack Obama.

This is because, across the board, the consensus in the Arab world is that President Obama bears significant responsibility for chaos in the Middle East because of his outreach to Iran and the Muslim Brotherhood.

In official circles, Arab governments and Arab leaders were primarily concerned because President Biden was vice president under President Obama. As such, he had a significant role in the Obama administration's Middle East policy.

Iraqi British journalist Mina Al-Oraibi expressed the Arab concern. In her November 11, 2020, article called "The Incoming Biden Administration and the Arab World," she wrote:

> The Libyan, Syrian, and Palestinian files are all awaiting the moves of the new president. But the most prominent, of course, will be the Iranian file and the Iranian expansion in Iraq, Lebanon, Syria, and Yemen. The Democrats have made it clear that they want to conclude an agreement with Iran. But the question is what this agreement will look like and how it will impact the Arab world? The answer depends on the policies that will be implemented in the Arab countries suffering from Iranian interference. For example, Biden assumed oversight over the Iraq file during Obama's presidency and played a pivotal role in the US decision to support Nuri al-Maliki to take over as prime minister after the 2010 elections. Despite Iyad Allawi's victory in Parliament. That historic decision changed the course of Iraq. [*Author's Note for Context:* Al-Maliki is very close with the Iranian regime, and choosing al-Maliki as the Iranian prime minister basically made Iran in charge of Iraq.] Biden was also against the intervention in Syria; As the developments in it after 2011 were seen as a "sectarian struggle" and not a popular revolution.[1]

Another source of concern for Arab governments is the weight of the centrist-progressive fault line within the Democratic Party. A US Middle East policy that is shaped by issues of human rights, civil rights, gender equality, individual liberties, relationships with authoritarian regimes, etc., will likely increase the potential for friction between the United States and these governments.

In contrast to Arab rulers' concerns, civil society activists in Arab countries expected and hoped that the Biden administration would pursue a human rights-driven foreign policy and promote civil, individual, and human rights issues.

In an article, he called "US Elections are an Egyptian Affair," Egyptian anthropologist and social activist Dr. Essam Shaaban wrote, "Current Arab regimes fear that inspired by the legacy of Obama, the Biden administration will focus on defending the 'Arab Revolutions.'" Shaaban went on to say, "these regimes fear that pressure exerted by the Biden administration on human rights issues will jeopardize the current political system in their countries."[2]

The term 'Arab Revolutions' is the code word for the different camps in the Arab world that oppose the current regimes and rulers. It is important to note that this term is used by both Islamists and civil society activists, even though the two camps stand for different, sometimes opposing, goals, ideals, ideologies, and politics.

However, many Arab commentators presented arguments to calm the Arab concern that the Biden administration would be a replay of the Obama administration.

The chief editor of the Egyptian newspaper *Al-Shourouk*, Emad El-Din Hussein, in November 2020, wrote an article called "What Shall We Do With Biden?" In it, he said, "It's likely that a human rights-based agenda will be a high priority for the upcoming administration. But that does not necessarily mean it will bring the United States into conflict with Egypt. Biden will be busy with many other domestic issues. The concern is that the people around him may come from the mindset of Obama."[3]

Egyptian scholar Dr. Mamoun Fandy, director of the London Global Strategy Institute, in his November 9, 2020, article, asked, "Will Biden Be an Extension of Obama?" He anticipated that Biden would focus on the Iranian nuclear issue and use it to revive American leadership alliances and reposition the United States as a global power. On the progressive agenda, he says:

> We must expect that the file of democracy and human rights will be a priority in Biden's view of the Middle East and will push towards it with a force that we did not know before. Although Biden appears calm with his age, he is very enthusiastic about what he thinks is right. He does not leave anything but finishes it. In addition to democracy and human rights, we will find Biden also very enthusiastic about women's empowerment issues, primarily through his deputy, [Kamala] Harris, who cares about minority issues.... But he sees himself in the ranks of leaders like President Franklin Roosevelt, a leader who wants to change America's face internally and around the world ... more like George Bush than Obama.

Fandy ends his article decisively by saying that "Biden is not an extension of Obama, he is an entirely different man."[4]

Another argument was that the world, including the United States, has completely changed since the time of the Obama administration.

For example, Ghassan Charbel, editor-in-chief of the influential Saudi daily *Al-Sharq al-Awsat*, wrote an article on November 9, 2020, titled "Biden's US in a World That Has Changed." He wrote:

> When Biden opens the world map at the White House, he will discover that he is the president of an America that has changed in a world of change ... Trump's passage in American politics and the White House was not a fleeting one. And the votes he won against Biden indicate that ... America has changed, the world has changed ... How will he deal with the Middle East, destabilization policies, nuclear dreams, and mercenaries' excursions between near and far fires? The Middle East has changed too. The Iranian penetrations do not carry a prescription for stability but rather confrontation. The Turkish role is greater than the ability of the region and its neighborhood to bear. The Arab-Israeli scene has witnessed fundamental changes in the

recent period. And the GCC countries have learned lessons from their past experiences with policies and administrations.[5]

And another argument was that Biden has extensive knowledge in foreign policy. He has many years of political and experience under his belt and was aware of the Middle East reality and the dramatic changes the region is experiencing. For example, on November 9, 2020, in an interview with *Sky News Arabia*, the former head of Saudi intelligence and the King Faisal Center for Studies head, Prince Turki bin Faisal Al-Saud, said, "Biden is well aware of the American interest in the Middle East." He also emphasized that Saudi Arabia is the United States' largest strategic partner in the Middle East and that there is close cooperation—specifically in the fields of security—between the two countries regardless of a Democratic or Republican administration.[6]

However, in the first three-quarters of 2021, the atmosphere has changed. The mixture of suspicion and cautious optimism has been replaced by growing concern.

Throughout 2021: Growing Arab Concern and Criticism

As 2021 unfolds, so does the Arab world's criticism of Biden.

The Arab world began changing its tune because they sensed that under pressure from the progressive wing of the Democratic Party, Biden was pursuing a hesitant and weak policy that fails to address the concerns of Arab governments. And particularly fails to address the Iranian aggression.

February 2021 was a significant milestone in the Arab world's perception of President Biden. The main criticism focused on Biden's policy in Yemen, the administration's tense relationship with Saudi Arabia, and the fact that the United States seemed to be deliberately determined to avoid confronting—diplomatically, militarily, or otherwise—Iran about its growing aggression in the region in general, and in the Gulf in particular.

On February 16, 2021, Saudi columnist Haila al-Mushawah wrote an article called "Who Will Stand Up to Iran?":

If the world's policeman [America], since President Joe Biden has taken charge, has started with evasive statements about Iran and its

nuclear program and its tampering in the region, and is more interested in vetoing everything Trump did ... then we are facing imminent Iranian danger. With a soft American administration, who will
confront Iran's dangerous military threat? We are facing Iranian danger for the next four years unless an event deters this perilous absur-
dity. Syria is devastated, Hezbollah dominates a collapsed Lebanon,
Iraq is under the arms and militias of Iranian terrorism, and the
Houthis and al-Qaeda are tampering with a broken and afflicted
Yemen ... So, what next? Who will tackle the head of the snake?[7]

On February 17, 2021, former Saudi editor-in-chief of the *Al-Sharq
al-Awsat* newspaper and former general manager of *Al-Arabiya* channel, Abdul
Rahman Al-Rashed, wrote an article he called "Tehran Sees Biden as Weak":

Since taking office, Iran has repeatedly tested Joe Biden's resolve
by launching attacks on several fronts in less than eight weeks.
Thousands of Houthi militants, Iranian proxies, rushed towards the
Yemeni city of Marib. Dozens of missiles and rockets were fired by
Iranian militias in Basra and Baghdad, and more recently, in Erbil
and Iraqi Kurdistan, killing and wounding an American. In Beirut,
Luqman Salim, the most critical opponent and strong voice against
Iran, was killed, and his body was thrown on the side of the road.
Tehran and the Revolutionary Guards believe that the new president is weak and does not resemble former President Donald Trump,
and these operations are tests of his administration. So far, he has
issued only verbal condemnation. Trump's sanctions are the best gift
to Biden. He could have increased them, forcing Tehran to negotiate
or risk the collapse of their regime.[8]

On March 6, 2021, Emirati political scientist Salem Al-Ketbi penned his
article, "Biden and the 'Carrot' Policy Without the Stick":

Biden knew before his election that one of the most severe challenges
facing security and stability in the Middle East stems from the spread

of sectarian and terrorist militias ... Eradicating the roots of these militias is supposed to be one of the most critical priorities of the new US administration—or at least supporting regional countries that seek to confront these militias and prevent their danger. But in Yemen, immediately after assuming power, the US administration gave a lot to the Houthis without getting a single thing in return ... At a time when US officials were negotiating with the Houthis, the Houthis continued to bombard Saudi cities and strategic sites to strengthen their negotiating position and to obtain the concessions they want—from the Saudis or the Americans. It is certain that allowing these practices to continue is not in the interest of security and stability because it undermines international law and conventions and provides free lessons that can be reproduced by the rest of the rogue terrorist organizations and militias. Without harmonizing and carefully balancing the "stick" and "carrot" in the American dealings, not only with the militias but with their well-known financiers and sponsors who use the militias to achieve their own strategic objectives, the hesitant or cautious stick will have a completely opposite effect—the continuation of chaos and instability.[9]

On March 7, Abdulah Bin Bijad Al- Otaibi, a Saudi Islamic specialist, wrote an article with an interesting name, "The Western Coddling of Iran":

Within a month and a half of Biden coming into office, the Iranian terrorists escalated their hostile operations. The West responded with an unwillingness to confront the regime and a desperation to revive the failed nuclear agreement with Iran. America's allies in the region cannot ignore all these Western signals—the daily conversations about easing sanctions, statements of friendliness, leniency, and tolerance. Especially when we know that several of the new officials have a nice history with the Iranian regime. It raises doubts about the seriousness that is required when dealing with Iran. Western countries' perception of the Iranian threat is very different from the countries in the region. While the Western official finds nothing wrong when he is mistaken in his calculations towards Iran. The issue for the countries of the region is one of existence and non-existence. The Iranian regime has learned from its negotiating experience. They drag out the discussions forever. And in parallel, they continue to expand, impose their hegemony and revitalize the Persian Empire—while Western officials admire their history. This is how the regime wins. Maximum sanctions almost brought Iran to its senses, while the strategy of coddling and indulging made Iran more ferocious.[10]

Naturally, Arab commentators from the Gulf criticize the Biden administration, especially regarding the administration's policies regarding the Iranian threat. But non-Gulf commentators also express similar criticism—and sometimes even more bluntly.

As a response to President Biden's presentation of his "Interim National Security Strategy," on March 3, 2021, US-based Lebanese commentator, and founder and executive chair of the Beirut Institute, Raghida Dergham wrote an article "Twinning Democracy and Diplomacy is Biden's Security Strategy":

> The Islamic Republic of Iran slipped from the rank of a US national security threat. Now [according to the new administration], Iran is less of a threat than China and has moved to the "deterrence" category. Democracy and diplomacy are twins in Biden's national security strategy. But his document is devoid of tools of tangible influence …
> If the Biden administration is so concerned with human rights, how about starting with the Lebanese people's right to an international investigation of [Hezbollah and Iran] who committed crimes against humanity by storing explosive nitrates in civilian locations and demanding those involved in the horrific bombing of the Port of Beirut do not get away with murder … This is not a question of regime change in Lebanon. It is a matter of flagrant violations of people's rights to escape from the domination of the ruling authority that is determined to carry out its violations because the so-called international community refuses to hold it accountable and allows it to go unpunished…

Biden's document does not talk about assigning negotiating tasks to European countries as part of the US national security strategy. Still, in practice, it does exactly that by letting them [the EU] mediate the negotiations between Washington and the Islamic Republic of Iran. Tehran will not back down. It is convinced that the Biden administration has to deal with Iran, not the other way around. There is overwhelming confidence among the pillars of the regime in Iran, self-confidence, and confidence in the Europeans' submission to the Iranian strategy, and confidence that twinning diplomacy and democracy in the Biden administration's national security strategy is entirely in the Iranian interest.

Neither Iran nor China nor Russia nor North Korea shivered in fear when the US president presented his "interim national security strategy" document either. The twinning strategy of democracy and diplomacy in confronting those countries is laughable.[11]

Also, in March 2021, UK-based Iraqi commentator Haitham El-Zobaidi wrote, "Russia is Coming to the Gulf: The West Left the Gulf, Not the Other Way Around": "Taking advantage of the weak and vague US policy, Russia has deepened and will continue to deepen and broaden its engagement and influence throughout the region. More than ever, Russia is back in the Middle East. And it is here to stay."[12]

In a June 2021 article, Lebanese commentator Sam Mansi sums up the growing Arab criticism toward Biden's policy very well in his essay, "Cherry on the Iranian Cake." Biden's policy towards Iran, he maintains, provides Iran and its proxies momentum. To back up his argument, Mr. Mansi gives examples, including: the Houthis intensifying their attacks in Yemen and on Saudi Arabia; the Iraqi Shi'ite militias escalating their attacks on US assets in Iraq; the fact that Hassan Nasrallah, the leader of Hezbollah, vetoes the establishment of a new government in Lebanon; and the war Hamas initiated against Israel in May 2021. "The Houthis escalate tensions in Yemen and use drones against American bases despite the American openness to the Houthis and the Omani mediation. And Iran sits in Tehran, distancing itself from the events and holding Saudi Arabia and the Houthis responsible. This is the heart and soul of Iran's strategy from Lebanon to Iraq, Syria, and the Palestinian arena. The mullah regime controls and commands its proxies while claiming Tehran has no responsibility for the actions of its agents and proxies. Agents and proxies the regime uses for its own purposes and to advance its own agenda and goals."[13]

As of August 2021, Mansi's outlook is becoming more and more prevalent in the Arab discourse. Biden's failed policy in Yemen—the administration's first foreign policy move in the Middle East—coupled with its stance toward Iran is empowering Iran and the Houthis, the Iranian-backed Shi'ite militias in Iraq, and providing momentum to Iran's agents and proxies throughout the region. And these counterproductive policies are leaving the countries in the region that suffer the aggression, oppression, and violence of Iran and its proxy armies to fend for themselves to defend their country and their citizens.[14]

The tension is not only heard. As 2021 unfolded, it was clear that US-Saudi relations were becoming increasingly strained.

In July 2021, Saudi Defense Minister Prince Khaled bin Salman (brother of Crown Prince Mohammad bin Salman bin Abdulaziz Al-Saud and son of the current Saudi King Salman bin Abdulaziz Al-Saud) visited Washington, DC. Prince Khaled was the highest-ranking Saudi official to visit the United States since President Joe Biden took office and since the release of the US intelligence report that found Crown Prince Mohammad bin Salman bin Abdulaziz Al-Saud responsible for approving the killing of journalist Jamal Khashoggi.

While in Washington, Prince Khaled's meetings included United States Defense Secretary Lloyd Austin, Secretary of State Anthony Blinken, Under Secretary of Defense for Policy Colin Kahl, Chairman of the Joint Chiefs of Staff Mark Milley, Under Secretary of State for Political Affairs Victoria Nuland, and United States National Security Adviser Jake Sullivan.

To mark the defense minister's visit, Her Royal Highness Princess Reema bint Bandar bin Sultan bin Abd al Aziz Al-Saud was scheduled to host a dinner at the ambassador's residence in Washington, DC. The Saudis canceled the official dinner, whose guests included President Biden and other top US officials, just a few hours before the dinner was scheduled to begin.

Reportedly, the reason for the cancellation was the uncomfortable discussions between Prince Khaled and Secretary of State Anthony Blinken, who, according to the reports, "joined the group for part of the meeting to discuss efforts to achieve a comprehensive ceasefire and transition to a political process in Yemen, the need for economic reform and humanitarian relief for the Lebanese people, and other key bilateral issues, including human rights." While there is no confirmation from the State Department, the National Security Council, or Saudi officials that the Khashoggi case was discussed, there is pressure on the US administration to urge the Saudis to bring Saud al-Qahtani, a close advisor to the crown prince, to justice for his involvement in the murder of Khashoggi.[15]

Iran and the Biden Administration

When Joe Biden was elected, the official Iranian response was that it doesn't matter to them who is in office or which party they represent.

On November 3, 2020, the Iranian Supreme Leader Ali Khamenei tweeted, "The election results will not change Iran's US policy. What is clear is that the American regime is suffering from severe political, moral, and civil degradation, no matter who is elected."[16]

In his November 11, 2020 article "Did Iran Bet On A Trump Win?" Lebanese political commentator and social activist Mustafa Fahs suggested a unique perspective to explain the Iranians' seemingly indifferent and cold reaction to Biden's win. Fahs argued that, in fact, Iran hoped Trump would win because the Iranians believed that in a second term, Trump would seek an agreement with Iran. In his analysis, Iran's hope was based on the Iranians' experience with President George W. Bush and President Obama, who, in the second term of their presidencies, were more generous to the Iranian regime. President Bush accepted Iran's grip on Iraq as a fact, and President Obama accepted Iran's grip on Syria and legitimized the Iranian nuclear program by signing the JCPOA. Fahs further argued that it would be impossible for Joe Biden's team to return to the previous nuclear agreement. The new administration, he reasoned, will likely start from the point the previous administration ended. As for Tehran, Fahs said, it will go to negotiations under the weight of harsh sanctions, more of which are likely to be imposed by the Trump administration in its final weeks. Moreover, he argued, after the killing of Qasem Soleimani, Tehran suffers from a political and security vacuum that affects its negotiating ability.[17]

As of August 2021, the Vienna rounds of six conversations between the West and Iran that began in early April 2021 and ended in late June have come to a halt. Talks ended on June 20, 2021, two days after ultraconservative Ebrahim Raisi was elected as president of Iran.

The Iranian regime refuses to return to the JCPOA before all sanctions are lifted. The Biden administration rejects that demand. The sides are walking on the edge. And the question is—who will blink first?

As a way of exerting pressure on the West, Iran boosted its uranium enrichment throughout 2021. One of Iran's underlying assumptions is that enriching uranium will create a sense of urgency within the European Union who will thus pressure Biden to accept Iran's demands. Yet, on the other hand, one should note that unlike the period of the Trump administration, Biden and the EU are in agreement on the Iran issue, and therefore, present a solid Western front.

Tehran's gamble may prove to be successful—or a mistake.

In July 2021, US Secretary of State Anthony Blinken said, "Negotiations with Iran cannot go on indefinitely." He stressed that "Our patience is not endless," adding that "at some point, the gains achieved by the JCPOA cannot be fully recovered by a return to the JCPOA if Iran continues the activities that it's undertaken regarding its nuclear program."[18]

On August 18, 2021, *Politico* reported that Robert Malley, the United States special envoy for Iran, was preparing options for President Biden if an agreement cannot be reached in the coming months.[19]

The next day, on August 19, 2021, the EU3—France, Germany, and the United Kingdom—issued the following joint statement:

> We, the governments of France, Germany, and the United Kingdom, note with grave concern the latest reports by the IAEA confirming that Iran has produced uranium metal-enriched up to 20% for the first time, and has significantly increased its production capacity of uranium enriched up to 60%.
>
> We reiterate that these are serious violations of Iran's commitments under the Joint Comprehensive Plan of Action (JCPoA). Both are key steps in the development of a nuclear weapon, and Iran has no credible civilian need for either measure. Our concerns are

deepened by the fact that Iran has significantly limited IAEA access through withdrawing from JCPoA-agreed monitoring arrangements and ceasing application of the Additional Protocol.

Iran's activities are all the more troubling given the fact talks in Vienna have been interrupted upon Tehran's request for two months now and that Iran has not yet committed to a date for their resumption. While refusing to negotiate, Iran is instead establishing facts on the ground, which make a return to the JCPoA more complicated.

Iran must halt all activities in violation of the JCPOA without delay. We urge Iran to return to the negotiations in Vienna as soon as possible with a view to bringing them to a swift, successful conclusion. We have repeatedly stressed that time is on no one's side.[20]

They reiterated the same request on September 1, 2021.[21]

As for Iran, on September 1, 2021, in a televised interview on Iran state-run television, Foreign Minister Hossein Amir-Abdollahian said, the Vienna talks are "one of the questions on the foreign policy and government agenda."[22]

Israel and the Biden Administration

The relationship between the United States and Israel in the second decade of the twenty-first century has fluctuated from one extreme to another.

During this period, Benjamin Netanyahu was the prime minister of Israel. Like other major Arab players—Egypt, Saudi Arabia, and the UAE—Israel was very disturbed with the Obama administration's Iran policy and its outreach to the Muslim Brotherhood. The JCPOA was the tipping point in the relationship between Netanyahu and Obama. A deal Netanyahu continuously claimed was a "historic mistake." Almost immediately after the agreement was signed in 2015, the undercurrent of discontent burst on the world stage.

On March 3, 2015, Prime Minister Netanyahu took the rostrum in the historic chamber of the House of Representatives. He told a joint meeting of Congress that instead of stopping Iran from obtaining nuclear weapons, Mr. Obama's diplomatic initiative "would all but guarantee" that it does, in turn setting off a regional arms race. "This deal won't be a farewell to arms," Mr. Netanyahu told the lawmakers, who responded to him with a succession of standing ovations. "It would be a farewell to arms control. And the Middle East would soon be crisscrossed by nuclear tripwires. A region where small skirmishes can trigger big wars would turn into a nuclear tinderbox."[23]

Netanyahu was relentless and unwavering in his criticism of the JCPOA.

In January 2017, the relationship between Netanyahu and the US administration changed practically overnight.

The Trump-Netanyahu period saw an almost unprecedented level of agreement in the history of the relations between the two countries. The Trump administration's policy vis a vis the main issues that concern Israel—especially regarding the Iranian threat—were almost identical to the Israeli policy under the Netanyahu administration. During former President Trump's tenure, Israel saw unprecedented political achievements such as the relocation of the United States Embassy to Jerusalem, United States official recognition of the Golan Heights as part of Israel, Trump's Peace to Prosperity Plan, and the Abraham Accords.

In November 2020, the election of Biden and the growing weight of the progressive camp in the Democratic Party once again raised concerns among Israel's right-wing. It was clear that the Biden administration was not going to be the Trump administration.

In the first months of Biden's tenure, the Israeli prime minister was still Benjamin Netanyahu. Estimates were that the relationship would be tense and that the friction between Israel and the United States would increase again. That assessment was further fueled by the fact that Netanyahu had made the tension between himself and President Obama public. Biden, as Obama's vice president, saw Netanyahu's behavior as problematic. The first major test in the relationship between Netanyahu's government and the Biden administration was the May 2021 war between Israel and Hamas. The bottom line was the Biden administration supported Israel in the war.

As of August 2021, it seems that the potential for friction between Israel and the Biden administration has subsided to some extent.

One reason for the reduced friction is the change of government in Israel. In June 2021, a new government was formed in Israel under the leadership of Naftali Bennett. This ended the more than a decade-long reign of Benjamin Netanyahu, who served continuously as prime minister from 2009 to 2021.

Prime Minister Bennet's goal is to engage in dialogue with the United States without making the difference of opinions and disagreements between the two countries public.

A second reason for easing potential tensions between the two is that as of August 2021, the Israeli-Palestinian issue is not a high priority on the Biden administration's agenda.

A third reason is that there is an understanding between Israel and the United States that they need to jointly formulate a new policy to deal with the Iranian challenge.

In August 2021, amid the United States' withdrawal from Afghanistan, Prime Minister Bennett met with President Biden. Both sides agreed the meeting was most positive and friendly—reflecting the easing of potential tensions between the two countries.

The Palestinians and the Biden Administration

On the surface, the Palestinians did not hide their joy over Trump's defeat. In the Palestinian view, the Trump administration was the most pro-Israel administration and, accordingly, the most anti-Palestinian. Objectively the Palestinians are right. However, once the celebratory voices of the Palestinians faded, they were concerned.

First and foremost, most Palestinians believe that any American administration—Democratic or Republican—automatically sides with Israel.

Second, they know that in the Arab world, the Palestinian issue has plummeted. And to make things worse, as their cause has descended, the rapprochement between major Arab states and Israel has increased at a historically unprecedented clip. The Abraham Accords, the normalization agreements, and the alliance of moderation all exhibit that profound change.

Third, they know that the Biden administration supports a two-state solution. And this means that at the end of the day, Biden will expect the Palestinians to make concessions and compromises. And the Palestinians are simply not able to do that. Why? Because of the split between Hamas and the Palestinian Authority. Indeed, the chief of Hamas's political bureau, Ismail Haniyeh, announced that the "Palestinians should have no illusions and should not fall in the trap of negotiations."[24]

Nabil Shaath, an advisor to Palestinian President Mahmoud Abbas, expressed that internal Palestinian challenge by writing: "The election results should not be linked to the issue of Palestinian reconciliation. Biden's election raises our (Palestinian) fear that there will be a significant setback in the issue of internal Palestinian reconciliation."[25] Shaath's deliberately vague statement's subtext is that the Biden administration will demand that the Palestinians compromise—and that demand will only sharpen the internal Palestinian rift.

Nonetheless, Fath and the Palestinian Authority should be grateful for the Biden administration's position vis a vis the announced and canceled Palestinian elections.

The Biden administration's decision to let the PA know that the time was not right to hold elections, in a sense, played into the hands of the Palestinian Authority and Fath. Biden might have very well saved the PA from losing to Hamas.

Had the Biden administration taken a different position, Abbas, Fath, and the PA could have found themselves at a dead end. In that context, it is worth noting that the Palestinians draw encouragement from the growing weight of the progressive camp who almost blindly supports the Palestinian narratives. Understandably, the Palestinians hope that the weight of the progressive wing will grow stronger.

Fortunately for Abbas and the Palestinian Authority, the Biden administration was content to give lip service when it came to the elections, expressing its regret that the elections were canceled. Biden's position allowed Abbas to cross the election cancellation safely.

Turkey and the Biden Administration

Like Saudi Arabia, Turkish president Erdoğan was in no hurry to congratulate Biden on his victory. As for Biden—he waited more than three months to make his first call to Erdoğan. And the conversation was undoubtedly not what Erdoğan had hoped. Biden's first official conversation with Erdoğan included notifying the Turkish president that the United States would recognize the Ottoman slaughter of the Armenians in 1915 as genocide.

With Biden in the Oval Office, the odds of a Turkish-US standoff considerably increase. The course of the relationship of these two NATO powers since Biden first took office is proof the odds are correct.

First of all, like other regimes, Turkey's president is concerned that the progressive wing will have a large bearing on Biden's Middle East policy. A US foreign policy linked to civil and human rights would not bode well for Erdoğan, who gets a failing grade on both counts.

Another issue that concerns Turkey is Biden's policy regarding the Kurds. On the one hand, Biden has shown that he is tuned to Erdoğan's concerns about the Kurdish autonomy in northeastern Syria. For example, he has supported Turkey's demand that the Kurdish Syrian armed forces stay east of the Euphrates River[26] and not cross west of the river. This is currently the area of the Turkish protectorate Erdoğan has secured in northern Syria. That said, Biden will likely veto any attempt Turkey makes to use military force against the Kurdish autonomy in northeastern Syria. And he will likely object to Turkey bombing Kurdish militants strongholds in northern Iraq. Speaking of which, Turkey's military presence in north Iraq further fuels the tension between the two. When it comes to the issue of the Kurds, the common assessment is that Biden will be friendlier toward the Kurds in Syria and Iraq and less supportive of Erdoğan.[27]

One issue of agreement between the United States and the alliance of moderation is that Erdoğan's aggressive activities to expand Ankara's control of territory and resources in the Eastern Mediterranean, the Gulf, and the Yemen arena must be curtailed.

During the first half of 2021, President Biden's administration sent strong signals to Turkey, expressing its discontent with Turkish policy. Biden began his relationship with Erdoğan by waiting three months to call the Turkish president. And since then, Biden has continued to express his resentment of his fellow NATO power's policy. From recognizing the Ottoman 1915 slaughter of Armenians as genocide; to freezing cooperation on the F-35 and for all intents and purposes preventing Ankara from absorbing the aircraft into its military; to conducting joint naval exercises with Cyprus and Greece; and pressuring Erdoğan to withdraw troops from Libya.

As of August 2021, Turkish-US relations can be described as chilly—and even tense.

Assessments of the Biden Administration's Middle East Policy

The Joe Biden presidency, in my view, will provide an interesting case study in the tension between realpolitik and idealpolitik in Western foreign policy. It is reasonable to assume that the tension between realpolitik and idealpolitik that was dormant during the Trump administration will return to the forefront in the Biden administration. It is also likely that Biden will give greater weight to issues such as civil liberties, human rights, etc. As we have said, this may lead to tense relations with key countries in the Middle East such as Egypt, Israel, Saudi Arabia, and Turkey. However, in my opinion, he will generally give priority to realpolitik considerations. Thus, in my evaluation, the parties will likely succeed in containing these tensions and avoid reaching a state of overt and acute conflict.

The Biden administration is facing a new era in the Middle East. As I complete this book in the summer of 2021, two aspects of the Biden administration's policy toward Iran concern US allies in the region.

One aspect that is difficult to ignore is the impression that the progressive wing's empathy for the mullah regime also appeals to Democrats who are not progressive.

Saudi columnist Abdullah Bin Bijad al-Otaibi wrote an article in June 2021 he called "The Iranian Elections and the 'Appearance Theory'": "The Iranian regime realized that the tougher it will be with the leftist liberals in the West, the more they will subscribe to the regime's demands."[28]

I find it hard to believe that the very forgiving and protective attitude of the progressive camp and some Democratic circles toward the mullah regime stems from a lack of knowledge or ignorance regarding the regime's brutality. I must admit that I cannot ignore the thought that forgiving the Iranian regime lies in a contorted progressive narrative that somehow labels the Iranian regime as the "victim."

A second aspect that concerns US allies in the region is the return of the original JCPOA team, including Robert Malley and Wendy Sherman. Both of them had a central role in crafting the JCPOA. This book has demonstrated how the JCPOA agreement fueled Iranian aggression and increased instability in the region. Even the most enthusiastic JCPOA supporters admit it has significant flaws and weaknesses—like the sunset clause. Iraqi commentator 'Ali al-Sarraf writes in his May 2021 article "Welcome Robert Malley:: "You (Malley) know well how murderous and vicious the mullah regime is, yet you prefer to turn a blind eye."[29]

I foresee the built-in tension between realpolitik and idealpolitik—something we did not see in the Trump administration—to be more pronounced in the Biden administration. And this will strain some of the relationships between the United States and its Middle East allies. I do not believe it will jeopardize the US alliances in the region. But I do expect it to generate tense episodes.

The United States and Europe will continue to play a central role in shaping the Middle East. However, it will be a different ball game. The era of the West's unchallenged influence in the Middle East has come to an end.

In parallel, we witness Russia's return to the Middle East. And the most significant change is the appearance of China as a new and powerful player in the arena.

CHAPTER 14

CHINA & INDIA | THE EASTERN GIANTS

China—and down the road, India—will play a central role in the new power balance in the Middle East.

Let me begin with India.

With a population of 1.3 billion people, India is the fifth-largest economy globally and the second-most-populous country in the world. India is a very significant hub of advanced technology. Similar to China, India is one of the largest manufacturers in the world. In 2020, the World Intellectual Property Organization (WIPO) ranked India forty-eighth out of 131 countries on the WIPO global innovation index.

Similar to China, energy security is a vital interest for India. Its energy consumption will increase significantly over the next few decades. India, therefore, maintains close relations with the Gulf countries. Dependence on energy suppliers from the Gulf region will continue to be a central factor in India's policies. Hand in hand with reliance on the Gulf region, India invests tremendous resources in the Gulf. New Delhi is particularly invested in the fields of biotechnology, petrochemicals, telecommunications, and tourism. And the Gulf and India are economically and physically intertwined. An estimated 3.5 million Indian nationals are currently working in the Gulf region. These workers send home remittances of close to $25 billion every year.[1]

India also has a growing and widening relationship with Israel. India and Israel established diplomatic relations in 1992. In 1992 the bilateral trade was $200 million a year. Today it tops $5 billion[2].

China—A New Sheriff in Town

As I said, India, as a central regional power, is on the horizon. But the new and rapidly rising power in the Middle East is China.

China's approach to foreign policy is the antithesis of the West's. Realpolitiks drive China's policies. Idealpolitik values are non-existent and play no role in policy considerations, foreign or otherwise. While the West praises multi-culturalism, China views its culture as superior. While the West's policy is decentralized and scattered, China's policy is centralized and laser-focused.

US-based journalist of Lebanese origin, and founder and executive chair of the Beirut Institute, Raghida Dergham writes the following in her March 2021 article "Twinning Diplomacy and Democracy is Biden's Security Strategy":

> Neither Iran, China, Russia, nor North Korea shivered in fear when the US president announced his "interim national security strategy." The idea of twinning democracy and diplomacy in confronting these countries is laughable. These regimes want above all else to survive. Their strategies may be ideological, but they are pragmatic par excellence. None of these countries will hate the United States of America because of Biden's interim document. Because each one believes that the United States of America is not run by a four-year elected administration. They believe the United States is by the ruling institution or what they call the "deep state." In these countries' opinion, the document's naivety aims to cover up malign American policies.[3]

China's flagship foreign policy initiative is the Belt and Road Initiative (BRI), also known as the "New Silk Road" or "One Belt One Road." It is a massive infrastructure project stretching from East Asia to Europe. The plan has two pillars: the overland Silk Road and the Maritime Silk Road Economic, Commercial, and Trade Belt. The BRI is a vast network of railways, energy pipelines, highways, harbors, etc., connecting China with different areas of the globe. To date, more than sixty countries—accounting for two-thirds of the world's population—have signed on to projects or indicated an interest in taking part in the initiative.

As voices in the West—including policymakers—contemplate departing the region, China deepens its presence in the Middle East.

In their August 2020 detailed analysis "China's Emerging Middle Eastern Kingdom," Michael Doran and Peter Rough, both senior fellows at the Hudson Institute in Washington, DC, cite the following figures:

> Since the launch of the Belt and Road Initiative in 2013, Beijing has invested more than $123 billion in the Middle East and North Africa. If these numbers suggest that the region is a top strategic priority, the relative trend lines are even more expressive. China is now the Middle East's largest source of foreign investment. While China's global investments decreased by $100 billion in 2018, its investments in the Middle East and North Africa actually grew that year by over $28 billion.[4]

China's Engagement from Iran to Israel

The Chinese are focused on key players like Egypt, Israel, Iran, Iraq, Saudi Arabia, Turkey, and the UAE.

China is the largest trading partner, oil importer, and investor in Iran. And at the same time, China is the largest trading partner of the GCC countries, including Kuwait, Oman, Saudi Arabia, and the United Arab Emirates. About 40 percent of the nine million barrels of oil China imports daily comes from the Middle East. Nearly one million Chinese citizens live and work in the Middle East and North Africa—300,000 Chinese people work in the United Arab Emirates alone.

By this point in the book, it probably won't surprise you that China has chosen to position itself on the critical maritime trade routes we have discussed in the book: the Gulf, the Bab el-Mandeb in the Red Sea, and the eastern basin of the Mediterranean Sea.

The deepest port in the world is in Gwadar, Pakistan. The Gwadar Seaport lies in the Indian Ocean, east of the Straits of Hormuz, at the entrance to the Gulf of Oman, midway between Hormuz and India. China financed a majority of the port's upgrade. And Beijing has managed the port since 2013 when

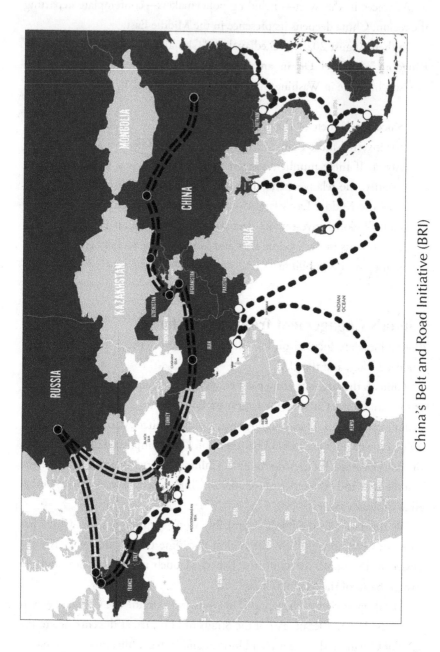

China's Belt and Road Initiative (BRI)

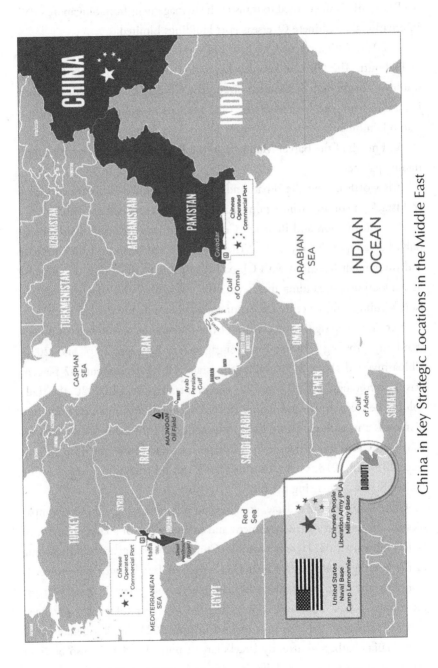

China in Key Strategic Locations in the Middle East

the Pakistani Cabinet voted to transfer the management from Singapore's PSA International to Chinese Overseas Port Holdings Limited.

In 2017, China opened its first and only naval base outside its borders in Djibouti. The Chinese People's Liberation Army (PLA) Support Base is southwest of the Bab el-Mandeb Strait. The Chinese built the base less than five miles from the United States' only permanent military base in Africa, Camp Lemonier.

And north of the Bab el-Mandeb, on the Red Sea, China is Egypt's largest trading partner.

It is worth noting the broad and expanding connection between China and Israel—a country whose population is less than one percent of China's.

The Information and Research Center of the Israeli Knesset [Parliament] published a report in July 2021, "The Economic and Strategic Issues in Trade and Investment Relations with China." According to the report, the volume of transactions—including direct Chinese investment and construction—in Israel's public infrastructure has exponentially expanded in the last decade.

Here are some significant statistics from the report that can help us understand the growing Chinese-Israel engagement. Between 2007 and 2020, China invested about $19.4 billion in Israel. Of its investment, 47 percent was in technology, and 30.4 percent was in infrastructure. In 2020, the trade volume between Israel and China (including goods and services, excluding diamonds and without Hong Kong) was about $11.9 billion. Trade between Israel and China has increased by 1,276 percent since 2000 and 45.6 percent since 2011. In 2018, China became Israel's second trading partner after the United States—bypassing the EU.[5]

China's investment in Israel goes beyond pure financing. Chinese companies are involved in the management and maintenance of a large segment of Israel's infrastructure. Here is a sample. Chinese companies are building some of the new light rail in the Gush Dan region of Israel. Once the project is complete, the same companies will help operate the system in Israel's largest metropolis. China built and is operating the new technologically advanced port in Haifa Bay. The new port opened in June 2021. It will operate parallel to Haifa's harbor—currently Israel's largest port. And China also built an extensive tunnel system in Haifa, Israel's northernmost metropolitan area. In the south, Chinese firms are building a port in Israel's second-largest harbor located in the city of Ashdod.

Throughout the Middle East, from the Gulf to the coast of the Mediterranean Sea, China is investing, increasing its foothold, grip—and influence in the region. The Chinese giant will not look favorably upon its investments and interests being harmed. This reality is significant in the case of Israel and the regional threats it faces—specifically from Hezbollah in the north and Hamas and IJIP in the south.

Beijing's Influence on the Emerging Nation-State

Another interesting aspect to consider is the impact of the intensifying Chinese influence on the emergence of a new nation-state model in the Middle East.

Realpolitiks drive the Chinese foreign policy. However, as we have discussed, civil society principles are gaining momentum in the Middle East. And these ideals and values will play an important role in the emergence of a new model of statehood in the region.

These two facts foreshadow the tension we can anticipate between the Chinese, who will continue to pursue an agenda driven by realpolitiks, and countries who are in the midst of a struggle to define their path, identity, direction, and future.

In the context of that struggle, we already see an interesting and significant test case emerging in Iraq.

China and Iraq: A Test Case for the Possible Impact of China on Iraq's Sovereignty

In October 2019, the Middle East Institute published a series of articles exploring China's activities in different areas. I found an article written by John Calabrese called "China-Iraq Relations: Poised for a Quantum-Leap?" Particularly interesting. Dr. Calabrese's piece provides a close look at the nature of the relations between China and Iraq.

According to his report, bilateral trade between China and Iraq topped $30 billion in 2018. That year, China displaced India, Iraq's traditional trading partner.

Furthermore, China is massively invested in Iraqi oil fields. And Iraq has become China's third-largest source of imported oil. More than half of the oil Iraq produces is exported to China.[6]

In February 2020, China and Iraq signed a trade deal. Baghdad will supply China with 130,000 barrels of oil a day with an option of tripling the amount.

As part of the growing cooperation between the two countries, in exchange for increased access to the Iraqi oil supply, China reportedly will upgrade the Majnoon oil field in southern Iraq—one of the world's largest oil fields—with an estimated capacity of up to thirty-eight billion barrels. Reportedly, Iraq has offered China a very generous deal. In return for developing the Majnoon field, China will receive a twenty-five-year term contract to buy Iraqi oil at a reduced price. And the twenty-five-year arrangement would begin two years after the contract is signed. In return, China will build medical facilities and develop housing, transportation, and infrastructure projects in Iraq.

As an oil supplier, Iraq is of utmost importance to China. Therefore, stability in Iraq is crucial for China. As we saw, Iraq's aspirations to break free from the Iranian grip creates turbulence in Iraq. Iran will not give up its control and influence in Iraq. Therefore, tensions in Iraq between Iraqi nationalists and pro-Iranian Iraqi interventionists will escalate, resulting in growing instability in Iraq. That trajectory could lead to tension between Iran and China.

The way China navigates its relations with Iran and Iraq will have a crucial impact on Iraq's future.

However, Iraqi commentator Diyari Salih is skeptical that China will significantly strengthen Iraq's independence and sovereignty. In his article, "Great Power Competition Comes to the Middle East: Iraq and the China-Iran Agreement," he writes:

> As Iraqis, we must mention that there is a grand illusion that some sides are now trying to market to the public—one that portrays China as Iraq's savior. Some parties forget that China never took any tangible steps to pressure Saddam Hussein's regime to amend its internal policies, especially towards the Shi'ites. They also deny that if China had been able to choose, it would not have hesitated to keep

the [Iraqi] Ba'ath regime in power so long as that brutal regime gave Chinese companies oil.[7]

China and the Trajectory of the Israeli-Palestinian Conflict and Israel's Geostrategic Posture

In my estimation, China's foreign policy and increasing engagement in the region could also have an interesting impact on the Israeli-Palestinian conflict.

Earlier in the book, I argued that China will curb Iran's aggression. I believe this will radiate onto the Israeli-Palestinian conflict.

China has a history of long and good relations with the Palestinians and particularly the PLO. Traditionally, China has taken a sympathetic approach toward the Palestinian arguments. However, at the same time, China also expresses an understanding of Israel's vital interests and needs. Given China's dual loyalty, Beijing shares the desire to peacefully resolve the conflict along the line of a "two-state solution."

As I have discussed in length, Iran fuels the flames of the conflict because it serves its hegemonic aspirations. I have also laid out the Iranian blueprint to use its proxies to exhaust Israel through military rounds, targeting Israeli cities and infrastructure.

But as China deepens its involvement and investment in the region—and particularly in Israel—the Iranian masterplan collides with China's interests. The massive and deepening Chinese investment in Israel that I described earlier in this chapter is not an act of charity. A detailed report by the RAND Institute, "The Evolving Israel-China Relationship," discusses the growing relationship and the opportunities and challenges it poses for Israel:

> Israel and the People's Republic of China (PRC) have expanded and transformed the nature of their relationship in recent years. Both have much to gain. China seeks Israeli advanced technology and would like to learn from Israel's success in innovation, among other interests. Israel, on the other hand, can benefit from diversifying its relationships and expanding its diplomatic and economic ties with the world's fastest-growing major economy.[8]

A section of the 2019 study outlines why China views Israel as a significant and valuable long-term strategic ally:

> First, and most important, Chinese analysts and officials tend to view Israel as a country that can help China spur indigenous innovation and R&D as the country continues its economic and military modernization.
>
> Second, China looks to Israeli policies, experience, and technology in defense, security, cyber, and CT as a means of promoting China's own needs in military and domestic security capabilities.
>
> Third, China views Israel as an important player in China's overall Middle East policy and seeks to balance its historically close relations with other countries in the region with increasing ties with Israel. Within this geostrategic context might lie an effort on the part of China to make inroads with a key U.S. ally in the region with the intent to undermine global U.S. alliance and partner networks.
>
> Finally, China sees Israel as an important component of the BRI.[9]

The RAND report raises concerns both for Israel's security and its relationship with the United States, which objects to Israel's growing relationship with China. I support these concerns.

Galia Lavi, an Israeli expert on China and a senior researcher at the Israeli Institute for National Security Studies (INSS), brings another valuable perspective regarding the nature of the triangle of relations between the United States, China, and Israel. In her August 2021 article "China and the Middle East: The Israeli-Palestinian Conflict on the Agenda," she writes:

> But as the rivalry between China and the US grows, Beijing is expected to step up its efforts to cast Washington as a two-faced and irresponsible power while brushing away any criticisms relating to human rights. In this sense, the Israeli-Palestinian conflict is very useful, and China's position has broad international support even among some US allies. China's support for Iran, its increasing assertiveness in international organizations, and its use of the Israeli-Palestinian

dispute to taunt the United States could create problems for relations between Jerusalem and Beijing, and even lead Israel to re-examine its relations with China.[10]

One of the growing challenges, not only for the United States—but for all regional players—is the decisions you make when none of your choices are optimal.

I do believe Chinese investment in Israel can have a positive impact on Israel's geostrategic posture and on the Israeli-Palestinian conflict.

Iran and its proxies like Hezbollah in Lebanon and Hamas and Islamic Jihad in Gaza Strip threaten to attack Israel's infrastructure and cities with rockets, attack drones, and missiles.

Massive Chinese investment in Israel's infrastructure may lead Iran and its proxies to reconsider their plans. Jeopardizing China's strategic assets, interests, investments, personnel, and property in Israel is a bad idea.

Therefore, I believe that China's needs and interests will restrict Iran's ability to continue and fuel the flames of the Israeli-Palestinian conflict. This result of China's engagement would be a positive development. It could lower the tensions, reduce the violence, and provide growing space for the pragmatic camp on both sides.

Pivot from the West to the East

As China deepens its presence and involvement in the region, Beijing will play an increasingly leading role in shaping the Middle East's geopolitical environment. Looking ahead, I anticipate a move toward Sinocentrism (the concept of China as the leading power in the region as opposed to the traditional Western powers) in the Middle East.

Countries will increasingly be concerned with China's interests in the Middle East. And to ensure its top interests—energy security and food security—China will want stability above anything else. Tensions and threats in the Arabian Gulf, the Red Sea, and the Eastern Mediterranean basin threaten China's oil supplies, maritime trade routes, and increasing large-scale investments in the region. These are all critical components of China's vision of domination. And no country in the Middle East will ignore China's need for stability.

CHAPTER 15

2021 | THE MIDDLE EAST IS ENTERING A NEW ERA

The Middle East Is a Multi-Dimensional Game of Chess

As I said in the introduction, and as the book title emphasizes, the Middle East is entering a new era. The new era we are entering is fraught with challenges and full of opportunities. Is it a new dawn? Or is it a setting sun?

One thing is certain. A complex, multifaceted, and intricate pluri-dimensional equilibrium will write the next chapter of this region. Ancient and modern, domestic, regional, and international factors, forces, and underlying currents join together in an unprecedented manner. These forces are reshaping the labyrinthine geostrategic contours of this ancient landscape and are redesigning the geopolitical map.

To understand regional events or design and implement constructive, effective, and sustainable policy, it is crucial to know that all these components make up the Middle East's geopolitical system. It is vital to understand that they are all interrelated. And even more importantly, it is essential to connect the dots to see the links in the chain. Knowing how all these elements interact with one another and how they impact and affect each other will help you build a multi-dimensional picture of reality. To positively and productively *impact* reality, we must *understand* reality.

In this book, we have discussed each one of those components at length. In this closing chapter, I would like to provide you with a "satellite perspective" of the geopolitical features of the region.

But before that, let me reiterate my major predictions briefly.

Recapping My Predictions

In the Preface, I emphasized my commitment to predictions. As I emphasized, as an intelligence analyst, I can only assess if my analysis is accurate by putting my neck on the line and making predictions. I also promised to include forecasts in the book, which I did. As we come to the end of our journey, I would like to reiterate here some of the most salient predictions which I believe will design the new era of the Middle East.

The Mullah Regime's Hegemonic Aspirations

Since coming to power in 1979, the Islamic Republic of Iran has pursued a focused and multi-pronged foreign policy designed to export the Islamic Revolution and secure Iran's position as the hegemon.

Gains and Losses in the Crescent and the Corridor

The regime has made some significant strides toward its goals.

Iran has significantly deepened and expanded its influence in the Middle East. Iran is the dominant power in the Arab/Persian Gulf. At the beginning of the third decade of the century, the mullah regime continues to resolutely persevere in fomenting and capitalizing on the chaos in Iraq, the war in Syria, the disintegration of Lebanon, and the Hamas takeover of the Gaza Strip, to secure the Shi'ite Iranian crescent and expand its influence from Iran to the Mediterranean Sea.

On the other hand, the mullah's hegemonic aspirations face several significant obstacles.

In response to Iran's destructive policies to advance and protect its own interests, there has been a counteraction in each of these three countries. A heretofore practically absent nationalism and patriotism have emerged in Iraq, Syria, and Lebanon. This evolution challenges Iran's grip on these three countries.

An additional counter-reaction to Iran's aggressive foreign policy is the regional counter alliances that have formed to thwart Iran's dangerous hegemonic ambitions. The most significant of these confederations is the alliance of moderation. An informal regional coalition including Egypt, Israel, Saudi Arabia, and the United Arab Emirates. This alliance will spearhead the effort to counter Iran's influence and power in the maritime arenas from the Arab/Persian Gulf to the Mediterranean Sea.

The three most essential pillars of Tehran's expansionist policy are its nuclear program, ballistic missile program, and its armed agents, proxies, and Arab political allies. All three of these pillars work together, and each one is designed to protect the other. I call it a 'mutual insurance policy.'

This is Iran's strategy. The mullah regime's missiles, drones, and terror armies deter an attack on Iran's nuclear program and prevent a military retaliation in response to Iran attacking targets in the Gulf and elsewhere in the region. And vice versa. Iran's nuclear program prevents attacks on Iran's terror armies.

The lynchpin of this Iranian ecosystem is Iran's agents and proxies. They are also the Achilles' heel of the mullah's hegemonic endeavor. However, in addition to being an Iranian subcontractor, each agent, proxy, and ally is part and parcel of its own cultural, economic, political, and social environment. They do not operate in a vacuum. Iran's proxies and political Arab allies do not solely subdue their calculations and behavior to Iranian interests. This reality is true in the case of Hamas in Gaza, Hezbollah in Lebanon, the Iranian-backed al-Wilaiyah Shi'ite militias in Iraq, and the Houthis in Yemen. Their ability to impose their will and interests and advance Iran's agenda through force is significant. But not unlimited.

The most vital link in Iran's Shi'ite crescent is Syria. Syria is the cornerstone of the axis of resistance. Iran is using soft and hard power—including trying to 'Iranize' and 'Shi'atize' the overwhelmingly Sunni country of Syria. If Iran loses control of Syria, the mullah's land corridor and the Shi'ite crescent will collapse. And Iran faces some severe challenges in Syria. It is on a collision course with Russia that wants to minimize Iranian influence in Syria. Israel's attacks on Iran's military apparatus in Syria also make it difficult for the mullah regime to cement its grip on the ground.

Another challenge for Iran in Syria is its strategic partner in Syria—Bashar al-Assad. In a bid to rehabilitate his image and once again become a part of the Arab world, in exchange for the removal of US sanctions, and a promise from the Gulf monarchies to fund the rebuilding of Syria, the Syrian president might ask Iran to evacuate its militias from Syria. That will put an end to the mullah dream of a Shi'ite crescent.

If Iran's control over Syria wanes, it would also loosen the mullah's grip on Lebanon and strengthen Syrian President Bashar al-Assad. Why?

Lebanon became an independent country in 1943. However, Syria has always considered Lebanon a part of Syria. From its independence until 2005, Syria was the key player in Lebanon. Everyone, including Hezbollah, was attentive to Damascus.

In response to widespread protests in Lebanon and under international pressure, Syria withdrew from Lebanon in 2005. That said, Syria has never given up its position that Lebanon is part of Syria.

Al-Assad's dependence on Iran and Hezbollah during the war in Syria has flipped the tables in the relationship. Since 2011, Damascus has been attentive to Tehran and Hezbollah because al-Assad needs them to survive. But tomorrow, the picture could be reversed again. Should al-Assad ask Iran to evacuate its proxy militias from Syria, he could rebuild Syria with Gulf resources, restore his image, and regain his position as a central Arab leader. And the impact of this would exceed Syria.

A rehabilitated al-Assad could use the crisis in Lebanon to renew Syria's influence in Lebanon. How?

Iran uses Syria to arm, supply, and support Hezbollah. Iran transports weapons and ammunition through Syria to Hezbollah. And the mullah regime has built a military infrastructure in Syria that also manufactures weapons for Hezbollah. Syria is Hezbollah's lifeline. Al-Assad could monitor—and if needed also block—the flow of weapons to Hezbollah. Al-Assad knows that the Arab world and most Lebanese would be happy to see Hezbollah weakened. Blocking Iran's ability to use Syria as an Iranian-Hezbollah highway would weaken Hezbollah. Using that pressure card would provide al-Assad the silent consent of the Arab world to reassert his influence in Lebanon.

Iran's Nuclear Program

As we know, the three most essential pillars of Tehran's expansionist policy are its nuclear program, ballistic missile program, and its armed agents, proxies, as well as Arab political allies.

Regarding its military nuclear program, Iran has the industrial, scientific, and technical capabilities and capacity to make a nuclear weapon.

However, in my opinion, for the foreseeable future, Tehran will stay where they are and will not cross that threshold.

One reason is that a nuclear bomb is not critical for Iran to achieve hegemony. Iran's armed proxies are the perfect tool to achieve that goal. The agents and proxies cause chaos, death, and destruction while the mullah regime sits safely in Tehran. The mullah regime unleashes its dogs of war without repercussions. In contrast, an Iranian attempt to break into producing a nuclear weapon could expose the Iranian government to severe sanctions. And it might even face military action.

A second reason Iran will not cross the threshold of having a nuclear weapon in the foreseeable future is that China does not want Iran to have a nuclear weapon.

One of the hallmarks of the new era in the Middle East will be the competition between stabilizers and destabilizers.

China is the rising power in the Middle East. Iranian aggression is causing instability in areas that are critical for China's primary goals – energy and food security. China seeks stability. And therefore, if Iran's actions threaten China's strategic interests, Iran will have no choice but to curb its aggressive policies.

I must caution and be very clear. Iranian-backed armies of terror armed by Tehran's extensive and expansive conventional arsenal, under a nuclear umbrella makes Iran untouchable and Iran's power to extort will be boundless. The world will be held hostage to the mullah regime.

Opposition at Home

A major challenge to the mullah's hegemonic aspirations is at home, in Iran. The mullah's vision for the future is not necessarily how the Iranian people envision their future.

The enormous and increasing economic, environmental, and societal challenges fuel Iranians' resentment of the mullah government. The brutal repression the regime uses to crush protests and trample human and civil rights further increases anger and bitterness. The growing discontent of the Iranian people is percolating into the pillars of the regime's power bases, including the emerging generation of clergy, the middle class, and the military.

Mohsen Qalibar, a professor of Islamic Studies at Duke University, says, "I have analyzed the situation, and I assure you that more than 65 percent of Iranians are against Khamenei's management of affairs, and those who support him do not exceed 37 percent. I do not think that the regime will be able to continue this policy. The majority of Iranians are young people. I believe in the end that the future of Iran will not be the Islamic Republic."[1]

Dr. Qalibar's prediction may play out over time. However, in my opinion, given the regime's steadfast and unwavering commitment to preserving the revolutionary regime, the mullah government will maintain its iron grip on the Iranian people for the foreseeable future.

Iran's Influence Varies in Different Arenas

In conclusion, Iran is a regional power. However, the mullah's hegemonic aspirations have obstacles. Accordingly, its influence varies.

Iran is the dominant power in the Arab/Persian Gulf. However, regional forces including Egypt, Israel, Saudi Arabia, and the UAE are committed and proactively working to counter Iran's influence and power in the maritime arenas from the Gulf to the Mediterranean Sea. The alliance of moderation wants to ensure they and not Iran are the powerbrokers in this arena.

Securing a land corridor fully controlled by Iran connecting Iran to the Mediterranean Sea is an essential part of the Shi'ite crescent and a cornerstone of its hegemonic ambitions. "Fully controlled" means that the corridor will be de-facto Iranian external territory. Iran will control the land corridor in the host countries (i.e., Lebanon, Syria, and Iraq). The host country's sovereignty over the land corridor in its territory will be subdued to Iran.

Thus far, the only place Iran has successfully created such an external Iranian territory that is not subdued to the host country's sovereignty is Lebanon. Hezbollah controls each and every gateway in and out of Lebanon. Hezbollah has created an Iranian-controlled air and sea corridor between Iran and Lebanon. Iranians enter Lebanon freely—bypassing any kind of passport inspection—or any scrutiny whatsoever. Containers and shipments of commodities, fuel, goods, medicine, money, weapons, etc., from Iran, enter Lebanon by sea, air, or over land (from Syria) without any inspection.

Thus far, Iran has been able to partially duplicate the Lebanese model in Iraq and Syria. And Iran will continue to do whatever it can to increase its control, influence, and power in Syria and Iraq.

However, Iran's hegemonic dreams do face obstacles from growing resentment inside and outside of its borders. I estimate that the Iraqi nationalist camp which rejects Iranian intervention in Iraq will strengthen. I also believe that Iran will not succeed in establishing an irreversible military presence in Syria. Therefore, I do not foresee Iran succeeding in occupying and securing a fully controlled Iranian land corridor from Iran to the Mediterranean Sea.

Turkey's Hegemonic Vision

Turkey is a regional power that has gone through a profound change over the past two decades.

Recep Tayyip Erdoğan is Turkey's fourteenth president. He has been in office since 2014. Turkey's constitution states Turkey is to be a secular and democratic republic. Since taking office, Erdoğan has transformed Turkey from a democracy that enshrined secularism in its constitution to an autocracy that emphasizes religion, Islam, as the core component of its national identity.

Fueled by a pan-Islamic ideology, aspiring to revive the glory days of the Ottoman Empire, and be a frontline leader of the Islamic world, Erdoğan is determined for Turkey to be the leader of the Sunni camp in the Middle East.

To achieve his ambitious goals, he proactively pursues a multipronged, often aggressive regional policy combining military power and soft power.

Through cultivating proxies and fostering alliances, Turkey has a military presence in the Arabian Sea, the Gulf of Aden, southern Yemen, the Horn of Africa, the Bab el-Mandeb, and the Red Sea. And Somalia, the gateway to Africa, is now home to Turkey's most extensive foreign military base.

Erdoğan inserted himself into the war in Libya and Syria, maintains bases overseas in Somalia and Qatar, and gathers and deploys proxies from Syria to Africa.

He has secured a Turkish protectorate and is demographically engineering territory in north Syria to ensure his control and power to suffocate the

Kurdish semi-autonomy. With the same goal, he has violated Iraqi sovereignty by placing Turkish army bases in northeastern Iraq.

I do want to bring your attention to an issue we have not covered in depth in the book but will be a significant issue in the Iraqi-Turkish-Syrian relationship. When it comes to the dynamic of these three countries, an issue to keep your eye on is water.

Turkey has unilaterally built a set of dams that store most of the water from the Euphrates and Tigris Rivers. The dams have dramatically reduced the amount of water flowing into Iraq and Syria. The consequences of Turkey's aggressive and unilateral actions, which violate previous agreements Turkey has signed with Iraq and Syria on that matter, are severe. The agriculture sector in Iraq and Syria is collapsing, resulting in a massive migration to the cities. This phenomenon increases unemployment and creates a significant burden on the Iraqi and Syrian economies and their social service delivery systems that are already crumbling—if not nearly absent. Water will be the focus of intensifying tension between Iraq, Syria, and Turkey.

And in Africa, Erdoğan is striving to upset the power balance by expanding Turkey's influence and reach. Turkey's footprint in Africa is getting larger than most European countries in a very short period of time.

Erdoğan knows you cannot be—or claim to be—a regional superpower, let alone a global power, if you don't have a presence or exert influence in strategic arenas such as the Mediterranean Sea, the Red Sea, the Indian Ocean, and Africa. He concentrates on these arenas to achieve his grandiose ambitions. The importance of these arenas to Turkey has grown even more given the new geostrategic construct emerging in the Middle East. Therefore, Turkey's regional policy will strive to ensure and increase Turkish interests and presence in these arenas as much as Erdoğan possibly can.

The cornerstone of Erdoğan's foreign policy is his maritime "Mavi Vatan" "The Blue Homeland Doctrine." The plan is presented to end Turkey's near-complete dependence on foreign energy sources and convert Turkey into a net energy exporter by controlling the surrounding waterways—the Black Sea, the Aegean Sea, and the Mediterranean Sea. In the current geopolitical vernacular, Mavi Vatan is shorthand for Turkey's desire to control the Eastern Mediterranean.

Of all the areas Erdoğan is looking to control to achieve his hegemonic ambitions, he is most interested in the eastern Mediterranean. From Lebanon, where he is trying to build a base of support. In his quest to be the energy broker throughout the Mediterranean, he ignores borders by drilling in other countries' waters. To Libya, where he signed a deal ignoring international treaties.

However, like Iran, Turkey's hegemonic vision collides with the vital interests of key Middle East players. And like Iran, Erdoğan's aggression has resulted in the formation of counter alliances—including the alliance of moderation. Ankara's aggression in the eastern Mediterranean has also resulted in other counter alliances. One example is the Eastern Mediterranean Gas Forum (EMGF), consisting of Turkey's neighbors—Cyprus, Greece, Iraq, and Syria—and the European Union.

In addition to coming into conflict with emerging regional alliances that are designed to thwart Turkey's ambitions, the other challenge facing Erdoğan is within his natural base. The trend towards pragmatism in political Islam, specifically within the Muslim Brotherhood, and political Islam parties prioritizing the concept of national statehood on their political agendas, means that Erdogan cannot automatically assume Islamists will support his regional endeavors. Moreover, it is possible that political Islam parties will prioritize their own national state interests choosing over Erdogan's aspiration and interests.

As of August 2021, Erdoğan's challenges have led him to pursue a rapprochement policy with some of the leading Sunni powers, including Egypt, Saudi Arabia, and the UAE. But I do not foresee Erdoğan compromising his own dreams of hegemony. This reality will inevitably lead to ebbs and flows of cooperation and competition as long as Erdoğan is in power.

The extensive push back to Erdoğan's ongoing competition for power, aggressive and intrusive provocations in pursuit of his hyper-national, hegemonic, neo-Ottoman, pan-Islamic ambitions, combined with Turkey's profound socio-economic challenges, will likely be an obstacle to Erdoğan's pursuit of his hegemonic dreams.

Resolutely dismissive of human and civil rights, Erdoğan brutally and ruthlessly crushes local opposition. And his violent tyranny fuels growing discontent and polarization inside Turkey. These trends—coupled with Turkey's growing economic challenges—erode Erdoğan's political power. The next elections for the Turkish parliament and presidency are scheduled for June 2023. At present, no leader on the horizon poses a threat to Erdoğan's rule. However, given the growing challenges in Turkey and the complex Turkish political fabric, there is a possibility that Turkey could see a change of guard in 2023.

Toward a New Model of Statehood in the Arab World

I believe Algeria, Egypt, Jordan, Morocco, Sudan, and Tunisia, are undergoing a transition that has the potential to provide a broader platform for dialogue and a widening foundation for consensus.

This long-term and evolving process results from a combination of factors: political Islam's move away from dogmatism and move toward pragmatism; the centralization of particularistic nationalism on the agenda of political Islam; the increasing strength and political power of civil society; and the growing awareness of mutual accountability and responsibility between citizens and state. These intertwined factors dialogue with each other. And the result is an attempt to build a new model of statehood that will stand on three pillars: governmental accountability, civic responsibility, and nationalism as the focal point of collective and personal identity.

The changes these countries are experiencing inevitably produce friction and unrest, primarily non-violent, of varying intensities from place to place and from time to time. This turbulence will continue. But at the same time, it is a positive evolution. Broad consensus that evolves through constructive—even conflictual—process is necessary for the emergence of a new, more stable, and more successful nation-state model than that of the twentieth century.

Kuwaiti poet and commentator Saadia Mufarreh writes in her January 2021 article, "Some people think that the Arab Spring has failed and led to an Arab winter. But it is essential to remember and remind ourselves that only ten years have passed since the Arab Spring broke out, which is a blink of an eye in terms of nations and revolutions ... The Arab Spring flowers have not yet opened."[2]

I agree with her observation.

But, as of 2021, the picture is bleak for five other Arab countries—Iraq, Lebanon, Libya, Syria, and Yemen.

All of these are failed states. Their disintegration stems from built-in ill-nesses. I often say Lebanon has a 'gangland mentality.' The country is plagued by corruption, egocentric politics, ethnic divides, sectarianism, tribalism, and steeped in embedded violence. That observation is just as valid when it comes to the other four countries.

In Iraq, Lebanon, Syria, and Yemen, the already built-in dire situation is further exacerbated because Iran has directly or remotely taken over, or significantly influences, the power centers in these countries.

Libya has been bleeding for nearly a decade in a civil war. The war in Libya has also turned into a proxy war between regional and global players, including Egypt, Russia, Saudi Arabia, Turkey, and the UAE. And Libya has also become a flashpoint for friction between Turkey and European countries like Italy and France.

Iraqis, Lebanese, Libyans, Syrians, and Yemenites are paying the price for their failed states with blood, death, and destruction.

In Iraq and Lebanon, there is a process of strengthening nationalist senti-ment, both as a response to the Iranian takeover and an attempt to create an internal consensus. Yet, the path to the liberation of Iraq and Lebanon from the Iranian grip is long and bloody. Moreover, there is no guarantee it will be successful. The devastation caused to Syria and the Syrian people by the Iran-al-Assad-Russia axis is a present and terrifying reminder of the catastrophic and devastating price.

It is difficult to see Libya becoming one united country. The core elements of Libya's fabric—tribal identity, ethnic-based politics, and power struggles over its oil-rich areas—are a constant source of fuel for frictions and violence. I anticipate Libya will become a federation-like structure based on its natural geographic, ethnic, and tribal boundaries.

Yemen, a country with a modern history of separatism into northern and southern entities, has disintegrated for all intents and purposes. Like Libya, Yemen's core elements are a fabric of tribal identity, geography, and ethnic-based politics. It is challenging to see Yemen reuniting under one flag. Yemen's political future will likely mirror its current fragmentation. Yemen is de-facto divided into two separate political entities. The Houthis, which took over Yemen's capi-tol Sana'a and occupy it until today, control part of central and northern Yemen.

And the ousted government of Abdrabbuh Mansur Hadi, who fled to the southern port city of Aden, controls southern Yemen.

As I write this book, the future of all five of these Arab countries is bleak. By many parameters, these are failing countries. So, though they are all to one degree or another struggling to survive and carve a path to the future, I cannot yet see their path to a new, healthier, or more stable nation-state.

The Alliance of Moderation

Given the Middle East's evolving geopolitical environment and the competition between stabilizers and destabilizers, I estimate that the foundations of the alliance of moderation will strengthen, and the cooperation between its members will deepen. The broad and growing cooperation will range from food to water, healthcare to intelligence, investments to security, technology to tourism, etc.

Although this informal alliance has been evolving over time, the collaboration has been somewhat under the radar. The struggle between destabilizing actors and pursuers of stability made the cooperation between the members evident and overt.

This alliance will be one of the central features of the new geostrategic environment. And the trajectory of the struggle between stabilizers and destabilizers will have a tremendous impact on the new era.

The 2020 Abraham Accords are an epic and historic milestone. The normalization and peace agreements will provide one of the formal frameworks to support the stabilizer alliances.

According to a 2021 RAND article, "Abraham Accords Offer Historic Opportunity to Spur Mideast Growth," by Daniel Egel, Shira Efron, andLinda Robinson:

> While these accords represent a major political breakthrough, they also represent a possible new chapter in the region's development: away from conflict and toward a shared economic vision of prosperity. If these new relations evolve into deeper economic integration, we estimate that the economic benefits for Israel's partners in this endeavor could be particularly significant, creating about 150,000

new jobs for just the four current signatories. And this number could grow to more than 4 million new jobs and more than $1 trillion in new economic activity over a decade.[3]

Israel's position as a frontline regional power and an attractive partner will increase.

I foresee that Oman, Qatar, and Saudi Arabia will officially normalize their relations with Israel in this decade. They will either join the Abraham Accords or create independent or joint agreements. Of all the Arab Gulf monarchies, Kuwait is the most vocally opposed to the idea of normalization. And therefore, in my evaluation, Kuwait will not establish formal relations with Israel in the foreseeable future. I also anticipate that in the same time period, two other Arab countries—Djibouti (in West Africa) and Comoros (in East Africa)—will formalize relations with Israel.

An Arab country that is an intriguing candidate for establishing relations with Israel is Iraq. I do not expect any major developments toward a formal relationship in the foreseeable future. Primarily because of Iranian influence in Iraq. However, there are a number of factors that could, in due course, drive a process of establishing a connection between Baghdad and Jerusalem.

One factor is Iraqi Jewry. Jews in Iraq have played a key role in Iraqi culture, economy, and society for generations. By the 1950s, following massacres and suffering persecution by the Iraqis, the Jews left Iraq. Many of them moved to Israel. Many in Iraq express sorrow and remorse for Iraq's responsibility in the deportation of Iraqi Jewry.

A second factor is the Kurdish autonomy of northern Iraq, under the leadership of Masoud Barzani, president of the Kurdistan Democratic Party and former president of the Kurdistan Region of Iraq.

There is a historical and multifaceted connection between Israel and the Kurds—and especially with Barzani's camp. Among other things, the connection is based on the fact that the Kurds and the Jews have a clear sense of nationality and independent national aspirations. In the case of the Jews, this feeling translated into the establishment of a Jewish state—Israel. The fact that both Jews and Kurds are a minority in an Arab space, as well as the fact that Israel has a large population of Kurdish Jews, adds another layer of connectivity.

If Iraqi nationalism continues to strengthen, and Iraq chooses to assert its sovereignty and free itself from Iran's shackles and pursue its current path of being part of the Arab world, this could also be a milestone toward official Iraq-Israel relations.

Whereas I do see this as a future possibility, I must be clear, that I do not anticipate the institutionalization of relations between Iraq and Israel in the foreseeable future.

As for the Arab members of the alliance, I evaluate that the governments of Egypt, the rulers of the Gulf monarchies, and Jordan are currently stable and will be for the foreseeable future.

Jordan is one step closer to transitioning toward a British-style constitutional monarchy. This evolution could happen in the coming decade.

As far as the Gulf, it is worth noting that Saudi Arabia is on the verge of a generational change of power. King Salman bin Abdulaziz Al-Saud (1935–) has been king since 2015. The end of his reign in a significant milestone for Saudi Arabia. King Salman's brother and the youngest surviving direct male descendent of the founder of Saudi Arabia, King Abdullah bin Abdulaziz Al-Saud (1876–1953) is Prince Muqrin bin Abdulaziz Al-Saud (born 1945). Yet, he is not expected to be the next king.

For the first time in Saudi history, the next king of Saudi Arabia will be from the generation of the grandsons of Abdulaziz bin 'Abd-al-Rahman Al-Saud. The leading candidate to be the next king is Crown Prince Mohammed bin Salman bin Abdulaziz Al-Saud (1985–) also known as MBS. He does have opponents in the Saudi monarchy. His primary rival is another one of the founder's grandsons, Prince Muhammad bin Nayef. In 2015, King Salman announced Muhammad bin Nayef would be the crown prince. He was the crown prince but was ousted by King Salman in 2017. Over the last years, Crown Prince Mohammad bin Salman bin Abdulaziz Al-Saud (MBS) has fortified his position through arresting, persecuting, and targeting his opponents.

The Saudi Bedouin codes are stringent. After the death of every king, the Saudis immediately summon the tribes to swear an oath of allegiance, *bay'a*. This ceremony aims to ensure that the transition of power will be as short and as smooth as possible. I thus estimate that Crown Prince Mohammad bin Salman bin Abdulaziz Al-Saud will succeed his father as king of the Saudi monarchy.

In the Arab monarchies of the Gulf, a gradual and controlled process of political, social, and economic change is taking place. And the change centers around two primary issues.

One is the growing political power of a young and highly educated generation. In the December 2020 Kuwait parliamentary elections, for example, thirty-one of the fifty elected members of parliament were under the age of forty-five.

The second change emanates from the reality that the monarchies must diversify their sources of income beyond oil and gas. This is a significant change for the monarchies and requires reimagining and redesigning multiple sectors. The core of this extensive pivot is integrating advanced technology. And this requires an overhaul of their educational system to ensure that they have a professional workforce that can meet and overcome the challenges and take advantage of the opportunities of the twenty-first century.

In my 2016 book, I predicted that the events of the Arab Spring would not create instability in the Arab monarchies. I reasoned that the social fabric and the cultural codes, together with a balance in the distribution of political power between the tribes, produce a flexible and strong structure. Indeed, my prediction was correct. The monarchies did survive the fierce storm of the Arab Spring.

In 2020, we saw another manifestation of the stability of the monarchies.

In January 2020, the ruler of the Sultanate of Oman, Sultan Qaboos, who ruled the country since 1970 and was the Arab world's longest-serving ruler, passed away at the age of seventy-nine. He was succeeded, according to Qaboos' will, by his nephew Haitham Bin Tarik. In September 2020, the Emir of Kuwait, Sheikh Sabah al-Ahmad al-Jaber al-Sabah, who ruled Kuwait since 2006, also passed away at the age of ninety-one. His Son, Nawaf Bin Sabah al-Ahmad al-Jaber al-Sabah (who has been ruler de-facto due to his father's prolonged medical illnesses), succeeded him. In both Oman and Kuwait, the transition of power was smooth.

This does not mean that the challenges of change skip the Gulf monarchies. There are tensions of varying intensity that ebb and flow within the monarchies. But generally, the fluctuation does not pose a threat to the stability of the monarchy.

In 2021 there were demonstrations and riots in Oman. The protests were sparked by an economic crisis caused by low oil prices and the impact of COVID-19 on Oman's two other primary income sources—ports and tourism. In the wake of the crisis in Oman, Saudi Arabia provided economic aid to Oman and established a joint committee to address Oman's financial challenges.

What the monarchies, in broad strokes, have in common is a clear individual and collective identity based on shared cultural codes and social values, historical heritage, and a sense of common and shared destiny. This traditional 'glue,' combined with rulers focusing on diversifying income sources, the growing influence of the younger generation across sectors and in all power centers, and a sense of shared responsibility, provide another anchor of stability for the monarchies of the Gulf. Therefore, I estimate that the Arab monarchies in the Gulf will be stable for the foreseeable future.

The Trajectory of the Israeli-Palestinian Conflict

We are also approaching an extremely significant milestone in the Israeli-Palestinian arena. We are approaching the end of the Abbas era.

This impending change creates a power struggle within Fath. The inner-Palestinian conflict and rivalries will possibly include episodes of violence in some areas of the Palestinian territories.

Parallel to the power struggle within Fath, both Fath and Hamas will continue to resolutely battle to position themselves as the unequivocal leaders of the Palestinian people.

It is important to remember that this internal strife, both within Fath and between Fath and Hamas, is not detached from what is happening in the regional arena. And it is particularly connected to the power struggle between Iran—that fuels the flames of the conflict, and the alliance of moderation, that seeks stability.

Therefore, I predict the emergence of a new political player in the Palestinian arena. In my estimation, this new factor will include current members of the two major Palestinian players, Fath and Hamas, plus independent political activists, particularly from the civil society camp.

If a new Palestinian political entity emerges that presents a platform which offers Palestinians a horizon of hope, a vision for the future, and governmental transparency, such a new actor could be a significant player on the Palestinian political map. This evolution could profoundly, and possibly positively, accelerate the move toward pragmatism in the Palestinian political and public realm. Should a new party enter the picture, it could significantly impact the Palestinians and the trajectory of the Israeli-Palestinian conflict.

In my opinion, due to the emerging multi-dimensional geopolitical system of the Middle East, there is a chance of an interim Israeli-Palestinian arrangement. I estimate that the agreement, both in terms of planning its articles and implementing it on the ground, will be led by and include regional powers seeking stability, namely Egypt, Jordan, Saudi Arabia, and UAE. This regionally managed framework will be backed by major international players—China, the European Union, Russia, and the United States. In my analysis, this could materialize in this decade.

Militant Islam

Militant Islam continues and will remain to present a significant challenge.

The return of the Taliban's rule in Afghanistan in August 2021 provides momentum to militant Islam and its violent ideology. However, it is also important to remember that extremists do not need 'wins' to be extremists.

On the practical level, militant Islam groups are increasingly successfully harnessing technological and scientific advances and incorporating them into their terrorist activities. And their actions are not limited to 'traditional' terrorist methods of bombings and killing. They are increasingly launching sophisticated and potentially perilous cyber-attacks. Intelligence agencies estimate that a biological terrorist attack is only a matter of time. In that regard, COVID-19 has shown terror groups the potential devastation of a pandemic, its impact on everyday life, the chaos it can cause governments, and the social and public disorder it can create.

I would like to share a quote with you from the "Militant Islam: Bin Laden is Both Dead and Alive" chapter of *Inside The Middle East: Making Sense of the Most Dangerous and Complicated Region on Earth*.

> Militant Islam exploits chaos to grow, build momentum, and deepen its hold on its followers. It does this through violence and terror that brings anarchy, which in turn creates more violence and terror. It is a vicious cycle that serves militant Islam well. Because it allows militant Islamist groups to establish themselves and accumulate power in parts of the Arab world that have been neglected, communities with illiteracy, poverty, and violence. Militant Islam is the bitter fruit of the despair caused by deep corruption, neglect, violence, poverty, and oppression. These challenges will continue to accompany the Muslim world deep into the twenty-first century. When it comes to the path, identity, and direction of the Middle East – there is no doubt that militant Islam will continue to be a threat to the region and the world.[4]

That observation is as accurate today as it was five years ago.

The Sun Sets in the West and Rises in the East: The Sunset of the Western Influence in the Middle East and the Rise of the Eastern Giants—China and India

In the twenty-first century, Western hegemony in the Middle East is coming to an end.

That development is the result of a combination of factors:

- The growing tension between idealpolitiks and realpolitiks in Western policy makes it increasingly difficult for Western policymakers to formulate a coherent approach to address the turbulent region.
- The evolving debate regarding the heavy price the West has paid –in human lives and financially – for being the global policeman and positioning itself as the carrier of the torch of democracy and the beacon of freedom in the world. This debate is compounded by the fact that there is a growing recognition that Western policy in the Middle East has failed.

- The need for the West to focus on acute and complex domestic challenges facing Western societies.
- Moral and legal aspects involved in the use of military might evoke growing difficulty to design a cohesive policy.
- The growing difficulty of Western influencers, leaders, and policymakers to accurately assess and decipher what is happening in the Middle East.

This compounding and exhausting difficulty has resulted in a desire to disengage from the area.

It is time for the big giants from the east—China and India—to step in and take the reins of leadership in the Middle East.

Driven by their own needs and vision for the future, China and India will increase their engagement in the Middle East. Both of these ascending superpowers share the same top priority vital interests: energy security and food security.

Chinese policy is laser-focused, driven by a clearly prioritized agenda, and guided by practical interests. China will increase, deepen, and intensify its involvement and influence in all the region's central arenas. And at the core of China's policy is the need for stability. Security and stability along the One Belt One Road maritime and land route are critical for the Chinese to meet their food and energy security needs.

The combination of waning Western influence and the rise of China and India will result in the passing of the torch. The keys to maintaining the pluri-dimensional Middle East geopolitical ecosystem will gradually pass to the heavyweights from the East.

Beijing and New Delhi will both play a central role in the new and emerging power balance.

The West has failed to curb Iran's aggression. It has been unsuccessful in securing its core interests—securing the region's energy resources—oil and gas and securing free and safe maritime traffic on the most vital waterways of the planet.

China is a shrewd and calculated player. Their engagement in the region has many facets. The Chinese hug can hurt, but it can also stabilize the Middle East's volatile geopolitical ecosystem.

A Satellite Picture of the Middle East's Geopolitical Landscape in 2021

In order to understand reality, it is crucial to zoom in and zoom out. This helps connect the dots to give us a multi-dimensional picture. Now that we have zoomed in on some specific predictions, let's zoom out to see the big picture.

These Combined Elements Shape and Impact the Labyrinthine Middle East Geopolitical Ecosystem

- A triangular and complex equilibrium between Iran, Turkey, and the alliance of moderation. This power struggle is spread across four maritime arenas—the Gulf, the Arabian Sea, the Red Sea, the Mediterranean Sea, and a land belt stretching from Iraq through Syria and Lebanon.
- The economic, environmental, and social challenges of the people of the region.
- The political struggle over the path, identity, and direction in the Arab world. What course do we as individuals, a society, country, or movement want to take, and what do we want our future to look like?
- The evolving attempt of rulers and citizens to define the characteristics of a new nation-state model and healthy statehood in the Arab world.
- The battle for independence and to restore—or not—the state's sovereignty in three countries—Iraq, Lebanon, and Syria.
- The more lethal and increasingly sophisticated threat of militant Islamic groups.
- The sunset of Western hegemony in the Middle East. And the growing role of the giants from the East, China and India.

The Epicenter of Instability in Three Arenas

The first is a maritime arena. The Arab/Persian Gulf, the Hormuz Strait, the Arabian Sea, the Gulf of Aden, the Bab el-Mandeb Strait, the Red Sea, the Suez Canal, and the Eastern basin of the Mediterranean Sea are regional waterways. But they are a lynchpin of international trade, a cornerstone of global security, and the center of some of the world's most important natural resources. These major naval, shipping, and trade routes that cross through the region are increasingly a platform for friction, hostility, and violence fueled by the hegemonic ambitions of Iran and a lesser extent—in the Mediterranean—Turkey.

The second arena is a land corridor stretching from Iran through Iraq, Syria, and Lebanon. The Lebanese, Syrians, and Iraqis are fighting for independence and struggling for sovereignty. Their battle is the outcome of two intertwined factors that are common to all three countries. The failure of the statehood model and Iran's growing control and influence.

The third and related arena of instability is the escalating friction between two regional powers, Iran and Israel. The frictions between the two far exceed Iran and Israel's borders. One of the subcomponents of the growing battle between the two is the Israeli-Palestinian conflict. Iran fuels the flames of the conflict in the service of its hegemonic aspirations.

None of this is new. Everything I have described has been going on for at least a decade. And in some instances—decades.

So, why do I argue that the region is entering a new era?

Two Major and Unprecedented Developments with Substantial Long-Term Ramifications

The central thesis of this book is that in the third decade of the twenty-first century there is a convergence of factors:

- The economic, social, political, and environmental challenges of societies across the region.
- The hegemonic ambitions of Iran and Turkey.
- The sunset of Western hegemony in the Middle East.

Combined these factors result in two significant and unprecedented developments that will have a substantial and long-term impact on the region.

One development is happening *within* individual Arab states. Some states are reconfiguring and redesigning the original political structure upon which the state was established. The restructuring is focusing on *two combined core elements*. One is *redefining the pact between citizens and their governments* in terms of both governmental accountability and civic responsibility. The second is a *new discussion regarding the concept of national statehood.*

Because of this evolution, in the third decade of the twenty-first century—a combination of redefining the pact between citizens and their governments combined with the rise of the concept of nationalism and patriotism—we are witnessing the early seeds of a possible new statehood model in the region.

In *Inside The Middle East: Making Sense of the Most Dangerous and Complicated Region on Earth*, I wrote about the formation of "a quiet Israeli-Arab axis that includes Israel, Egypt, Jordan, and the Arab Gulf monarchies, which is based upon long term strategic interests."[5] The formation of that *quiet Israeli-Arab axis* is what—less than six years later—evolved into the alliance of moderation and the Abraham Accords.

This is the second development that will have long-term ramifications on the fabric of the region. The *conjunction of the long-term strategic interests* of major Arab players, including Egypt, Saudi Arabia, the United Arab Emirates—and Israel. These long-term strategic interests are:

- Countering Iran and Turkey's aggressive, expansionist foreign policies and hegemonic ambitions.
- Protecting oil and gas infrastructure, production, and transportation, and securing maritime trade routes from Iranian aggression, proxies, and other terror groups.
- Positioning the members for the twenty-first century, including creating, diversifying, and expanding revenue sources.
- Increasing food security through integrating technological solutions in agriculture, infrastructure, water, etc.
- Developing and integrating technology into education, healthcare, medicine, transportation, etc.

My Recommendations for Western Policymakers

The West Cannot Disengage from the Middle East

Despite the growing Western trend toward isolationism and the desire to disengage from the Middle East, the West cannot disengage from this region.

The maritime trade routes from the Arab/Persian Gulf, through the Hormuz, the Gulf of Aden, the Bab el-Mandeb, the Red Sea, and the Suez Canal to the Mediterranean Sea are vital for the global economy.

The Hormuz, the Bab el-Mandeb, and the Suez Canal are three of the most vital passages in the world. According to the Chatham House, the Royal Institute of International Affairs, the disruption of just one of these chokepoints could have devastating effects on the global food security and put millions of people at risk. Over half of the total internationally traded maize, wheat, rice, and soybean—which together account for over 60 percent of the food energy intake and protein feed supply worldwide—are shipped through at least one of these corridors. A separate study by the US Energy Information Administration (EIA) warned that blocking any one of those chokepoints, even temporarily, can lead to substantial increases in total energy costs and world energy prices.[6]

The security and stability of those waterways are critical to Western economies.

In addition to food and trade, a third of the world's oil is produced in the Middle East. Saudi Arabia, Iran, Iraq, the United Arab Emirates, Kuwait, and Qatar belong to the world's top fossil fuel suppliers. In 1940, the prominent oil executive and petroleum exploration geophysicist Everette Lee DeGolyer said, "No such galaxy of fields of the first magnitude over such a wide area has been developed in the history of the oil industry."[7] And that does not take into account the eastern Mediterranean gas. Estimates of the region's hydrocarbon potential have ranged from North Sea-sized reserves to potentially holding as much as 50 billion barrels of petroleum, or BOP, and upward of 500 trillion cubic feet, or TCF, of natural gas. More significantly, the geologic evidence suggests that these discoveries are just the beginning of a Mediterranean-wide hydrocarbon bonanza. It is possible that the hydrocarbon potential might exceed even the most optimistic assessment.[8]

Oil and gas supply from the region is still critical for the world, including the West. I do not accept the argument that US energy independence decreases the importance of the Middle East. The United States will continue to import oil from the region. Oil and gas from the region will continue to play a significant role in the global economy and markets for decades to come.

Beyond energy and security, globalization is making the world smaller and more interdependent.

The Middle East is a region of 400 million people—most of whom are young. It is a region that holds tremendous economic and trade potential. Western companies are massively invested in the Middle East—from direct investment to infrastructure, communication, and environmental projects. International corporate engagement with the Middle East is extraordinarily diversified. Ranging from energy and technology to security and the environment, tourism, and more. The Abraham Accords and the reconfigured geopolitical map open an entirely new horizon of creative, groundbreaking, and lucrative opportunities unimaginable a decade ago. Another, perhaps less considered subject in discussing Western Middle East policy is the issue of refugees. The chaos in Muslim countries in Asia and Africa has led to endless streams of millions of refugees seeking refuge and a future in Western countries.

The Keys to Formulating a Constructive and Sustainable Policy

The West completely disengaging and 'opting out' of the Middle East is neither practical nor feasible. Western policymakers will have no choice but to continue trying to formulate a coherent and effective policy that serves the interests of their countries, economies, and the interests of the region. This endeavor will be increasingly difficult as leaders and decision-makers will have to navigate a dynamic environment with ever-growing and ever-complicated challenges.

The task of formulating coherent and effective policies that serve Western and regional interests will be more complex for two reasons.

One is that the causes for the end of Western hegemony mentioned above, including: the growing tension between idealpolitik and realpolitik; the debate whether the price the West pays is worth it; the escalating domestic challenges; the adversity to using military power; and the lack of accurate understanding of the Middle East will all likely escalate.

The second reason is the formidable opponents that threaten Western interests—China, Iran, and Russia—have a different approach. Their actions and policies are very different from those of the West. If not the opposite.

I would like to offer two pieces of practical advice to Western policymakers.

Change the Lenses to See a Pluridimensional Reality

One condition for a coherent, effective, and sustainable policy is a true understanding of the reality. There are no shortcuts.

Western policy in the Middle East has failed. Which is one reason leading the West to contemplate the path of disengagement. One of the primary reasons for the failure is that Western mediators of knowledge—guided by a Western mindset and Western codes of thinking, who often do not speak the languages of the region—developed concepts, narratives, and theories regarding the Middle East. A 'looping echo chamber' ensued in which *Concepts* became *"Facts." Narratives* became *"Reality." Theories* became *"Truth."* And based upon these almost non-controversial *Facts, Realities,* and *Truths*—which sound good to the Western ear but do not accurately reflect the on-the-ground reality—Western Middle East policy was created. I cannot emphasize this enough: viewing the Middle East's complex reality through Western concepts, lenses, and narratives make it impossible to understand unfolding events accurately. Without pinpoint understanding, it is impossible to create constructive, effective, productive, and sustainable policies.

The above, combined with an environment that glorifies slogans and soundbites over fundamental education and in-depth understanding, has led to an environment in which a complicated multi-layered Middle East is flattened into a two-dimensional Westernized soundbite. Discussions about the Middle East scarcely reflect the complex reality on the ground. Critical thinking and media literacy are not encouraged, and conveyors of knowledge are exempted from professional accountability for the validity of their theories and analyses.

Creating an effective Middle East policy requires a multifaceted multidisciplined praxis. The knowledge, skills, and tools that are the building blocks are: Mastering the languages of the region. The constant and unrelenting pursuit of gathering knowledge and information in the languages of the region. And then broadening that knowledge. Processing the information using professional intelligence methodology and tools—primarily critical thinking and media literacy. And finally, combining the gathered and processed information into a coherent analysis that is as close to reality as possible. But that is just the first step. The most critical step in the analysis is to compare the analysis and predictions with the reality. Does the assessment of reality stand up to the test of reality?

Deterrence and Power Projection

Another mandatory condition for a coherent and effective policy is the ability and willingness to project power and deterrence. Western powers must make it resolutely clear that they will use might—including military might—as a last resort, to achieve their goals or protect the interests they define as essential. Deterrence and power projection are vital components in a coherent policy because they restrain your opponent.

In the triangle between projecting might, using power, and achieving vital interests, there is a clear connection. The more you radiate power and deterrence, you increase the chance of achieving your goals or preserving your interests, and you reduce the need to use your power. And the opposite is true. Failing to project might and deterrence impairs your ability to achieve or preserve your vital interests and increases the need to use your power to try and achieve your goals and preserve your interests.

Western policy to curb Iranian aggression against US and international assets in Iraq and maritime arenas critical to Western economies and global security has failed. It has failed because the West has failed to project power and hold a deterrence posture. That failure has manifested itself time and again.

In October 2011, the United States announced it had intercepted an Iranian plot to assassinate the Saudi Arabian Ambassador to the United States. After signing the JCPOA, Iranian proxies in Iraq fire missiles and rockets and launch attack drones at Western embassies and troops in Iraq. Iran arrests and humiliates US sailors. Iran provokes US ships in the Gulf. Iran operates terror cells in Europe and the United States. In February 2021, a Belgian court sentenced an Iranian diplomat to twenty years in prison after he was convicted of mastering a terror plot in Belgium and France.

These provocations take place because the West fails to project deterrence.

Iran and its subcontractors do not fire rockets at the Chinese embassy in Iraq or anywhere else. Iranians do not burn Chinese flags. Iran does not arrest and humiliate Chinese sailors. Iran does not attack ships bearing the Chinese flag. Iran does not operate terror squads in China. Because China projects deterrence. China radiates might. And therefore, it does not have to use military power.

Can the West Stabilize the Volatile Middle East?

As of 2021, the West has an opportunity to recover its deterrence power. The opportunity is the renegotiation of the JCPOA.

The West must be sure that any deal with Iran—unlike the 2015 JCPOA—resolutely addresses two of the three central pillars of Iran's hegemonic vision: its nuclear program and its armed militant proxies. And the deal should clearly state that severe sanctions will be immediately implemented if Iran violates its commitment or fails to comply with the inspections' terms. And the West must make it unequivocally clear that it is resolutely committed to acting if Iran violates the agreement.

On the nuclear issue: As I mentioned earlier, one of the severe shortfalls of the JCPOA was the "sunset clause." When it comes to Iran's nuclear program, the next deal should not have a "sunset clause" at all. Full stop. Through a strict and precise set of conditions, the agreement must ensure that Iran will not have the ability to develop or own a nuclear weapon. The agreement must clearly define inspection and monitoring mechanisms. And finally, it should clearly state that severe sanctions will be immediately implemented if Iran violates its commitment or fails to comply with the inspections' terms.

And then there are Iran's armed proxies. Iran must be held accountable for the actions of its proxies. Lifting sanctions on Iran must be linked to Tehran and its proxies abiding by decades of UNSC resolutions regarding Lebanon, Syria, and Yemen. These UNSC resolutions demand the following: the disarming of Hezbollah (at a minimum, the West must require Hezbollah to eliminate its missile stockpile); the evacuation of all foreign militias from Syria; and the demilitarization of the al-Hodeida port in Yemen.

If the West implements existing UNSC resolutions, it would be a tremendous step toward restoring the West's deterrence and power posture and stabilizing the region.

A New Era—A New Reality

In her April 2021 article, "The End Of The Middle East As We Know It," Dalia Ziada, the founding director of the Cairo-based Liberal Democracy Institute (LDI), writes:

> In short, this may be the end of the Middle East as we know it. But it will be the start of a stronger, more stable, and robust region. The current shifts in the region's traditional political alliances, built on pragmatic rather than emotional foundations, may be the beginning of establishing peace and achieving long-term stability in a region that has long suffered from endless conflicts. This is particularly possible in light of the recent steps taken by the United States and its allies to gradually withdraw from the Middle East. Let us not be afraid of change, then! Change usually produces positive results, especially when it occurs voluntarily rather than under pressure from outside forces.[9]

Indeed, right before our eyes, the changing priorities and goals of the region's peoples and societies are redesigning the geopolitical map. Dramatic and historic changes are transforming the region as we speak. These changes will define the Middle East's new era.

CLOSING NOTES

The Responsibility of Whoever Has the Honor of Being an Educator

We live in an age where many people—perhaps most of humanity—have unlimited access to vast amounts of information every second. We live in an age where technology dictates the transfer of knowledge and affects the information's content. And more than that, technology is increasingly capable of manipulating verbal, visual, and auditory content—and information of any kind.

Equipping people with the knowledge, skills, and tools to navigate a complex reality is critical now more than ever. Championing in-depth study, broadening horizons, encouraging constant exploration, and supporting critical vision will help people regain control of information and their lives, navigate an increasingly complicated world, and provide a platform for civil discourse. This is important now more than ever. The core of that educational praxis is developing and nurturing a critical thinking, media literate mindset based upon professional intelligence tools and analytical methodologies subject to professional evaluation standards.

I am honored for every platform I am offered to enhance people's understanding of the complex and dynamic Middle East geopolitical ecosystem. I do my best to counter what I see as a dangerous process, in which buzzwords, clichés, narratives, and theories about the Middle East go unchallenged. The bitter fruits of that process are clear and significant. And if we continue down this path, it is bad news for the region and terrible news for the world.

Since I have left my official intelligence and public service positions, I have dedicated myself to education. The most recent evolution is an educational praxis I have designed and use as a basis for all my educational activities. It is called "Inside the Middle East: Intelligence Perspectives (ITME)."

I provide an apolitical, non-partisan education about the Middle East and use intelligence methodology to teach critical thinking and media literacy through this proprietary praxis. Using this distinct curriculum, I have expanded my educational activities—and hopefully, my impact. I have had the honor of teaching high school and college students, community business leaders, media members, legislators, and diplomats. As education shifts, I look forward to being able to expand my activities to a broader audience.

My bio says I am a strategic intelligence analyst and a Middle East expert. But it is important to me that you know that, as I said in the prologue, in my heart of hearts, I am an educator.

My mission to teach, offer insights, and broaden horizons is inherently complex and demanding. Trying to accurately decipher a complex reality—let alone attempting to predict the future—requires the endless work of gathering information, critical thinking, self-discipline, and self-criticism. It is a demanding task—physically, mentally, and intellectually—and that is how it should be. Equally important, I must compare my knowledge, assessments, and predictions with the reality on the ground. That is the only way to maintain my professional integrity and ensure that my work is accurate, relevant, and contributing to greater understanding. And I practice what I preach. I would rather compare my diagnoses, insights, and determinations with reality at the risk of being wrong rather than find shelter behind statements or arguments that are exempt from the test of reality.

I believe that this principle should guide everyone who has the privilege—and the responsibility—to be an educator.

According to the Jewish *Kabbalah*, a person's name hints at their mission or purpose. You may be interested to know that the meaning of my last name *Melamed* is "teacher or educator."

To contact me, please email avi@avimelamed.com. To learn more, please visit: https://www.avimelamed.com/.

LEXICON

Abaya
A dark cloth covering the whole body.

Abd al-Malik al-Houthi (1979–)
Leader of the Yemenite Houthi Shi'ite tribes

Abdallah Hamdok (1956–)
Prime Minister of Sudan (2019–)

Abdelaziz Bouteflika (1937–2021)
President of Algeria from 1999–2019 when he resigned.

Abdel Fattah al-Sisi (1954–)
General and President of Egypt (2013–). Former Director of Military Intelligence, Former Minister of Defense.

Abdel Fattah Abdelrahman al-Burhan (1960–)
Appointed Chairman of the Sovereignty Council of Sudan in 2019 and head of the Transitional Military Council (TMC), which has ruled Sudan since April 2019.

Abdullah II Bin Hussein bin Talal (1962–)
The King of Jordan since February 7, 1999. He is a member of the Hashemite dynasty, the royal family of Jordan, since 1921. He is a 41st-generation direct

descendant of Muhammad. He is the first child of King Hussein and his second wife, British-born Princess Muna. He succeeded his father. King Hussein bin Talal was King of Jordan from August 1952 until his death on February 7, 1999.

King Abdullah bin Abdulaziz Al-Saud (1924–2015)
The sixth king of Saudi Arabia (2005–2015). His brother (from a different mother), King Salman bin Abdulaziz al Saud, is the current king of Saudi Arabia.

Abd Rabbuh Mansur Hadi (1945–)
Yemenite Sunni politician. President of Yemen (2012–). He was Vice President (1994–2012) under Shi'ite, Ali Abdullah Saleh.

The Abraham Accords
The agreements signed by Bahrain, Israel, the United Arab Emirates, and the United States on September 15, 2020. The UAE signed a Peace Treaty, including instating full diplomatic relations and normalization. Bahrain signed a Peace Declaration launching peace talks. Morocco joined the Abraham Accords in December 2020. And Sudan formally joined in January 2021.

Abdelmadjid Tebboune (1945–)
President of Algeria (2019–). Former Prime Minister of Algeria (May-August 2017).

Dr. Abdullatif bin Rashid Al-Zayani (1954–)
Minister of Foreign Affairs of Bahrain. He signed the Abraham Accords on behalf of Bahrain in September 2020.

Abdullah bin Zayed (1972–)
Minister of Foreign Affairs for the United Arab Emirates. He signed the Abraham Accords on behalf of the UAE in September 2020.

Abdul 'Aziz al-Mohammadawi (1968–)
Also known as Abu Fadak al-Mohammadawi, Deputy Commander (2020–)
of the Iraqi Shi'ite, al-Hashd al-Sha'abi (Popular Mobilization Units (PMU)).
He replaced Abu Mahdi al-Muhandis, who was killed in a US airstrike on
January 3, 2020. He is the former Secretary-General of the Iranian-backed
Iraqi Shi'ite militia, Kataib Hezbollah.

Abu Bakr al Baghdadi (1972–2019)
Ibrahim Awad Ibrahim Ali al-Badri al-Samarrai. The leader of the Islamic
State of Iraq and the Levant (2014–2019). Killed by the US in 2019.

Abdul Hamid Dbeibeh (1959–)
Prime Minister of Libya (2021–)

Abu Hanifa bin Nu'man Ibn Thabit (699–767)
Sunni Islam has four orthodox legal schools of thought (Hanafi, Hanbali,
Maliki, and Shafi'i). Hanafi is named after an eighth-century scholar, Abu
Hanifa bin Nu'man Ibn Thabit. The Hanafi school is considered the oldest
and largest school of Islamic jurisprudence. Of the four schools, Hanafi is the
most flexible and adjustable in its interpretation of Islam and its application
of sharī 'ah law. The origins of the Taliban philosophy come from the Hanafi
school.

Abu Mahdi al-Muhandis (1954–2020)
Jamal Abu Ja'far al-Ibrahimi. Deputy Commander (2014–2020) of the Iraqi
Shi'ite, al-Hashd al-Sha'abi (Popular Mobilization Units (PMU)). Founder of
the Iranian-backed Iraqi Shi'ite militia, Kataib Hezbollah. He was killed in
a US airstrike (along with General Qasem Soleimani) in Baghdad, Iraq, on
January 3, 2020.

Sheikh Abdullah Yusuf Azzam (1941–1989)
Palestinian Sunni Islamic scholar and Salafi-jihadi theologian. To help the
Afghan Mujahideen (militias that fought the Soviet Union when they invaded

Afghanistan in 1979) fight against the Soviets, he encouraged Muslims to commit defensive and offensive jihad. Azzam was a teacher and mentor of Osama bin Laden, and together they created al-Qaeda. Azzam was killed with his two sons in a car explosion. Hamas's Military Academy in the Gaza Strip is named after Azzam.

'Adel Abd al-Mahdi (1942–)
Shi'ite prime minister of Iraq (2018–2020)

Adnan al-Zurfi (1966–)
Prime Minister of Iraq (March–April 2020)

Ahmad Badreddin Hassoun (1949–)
The Grand Mufti of Syria

Ahmad Ibn Hanbal (780–885)
Sunni Islam has four orthodox legal schools of thought (Hanafi, Hanbali, Maliki, and Shafi'i). The Hanbali school of thought is named after a very influential Islamic theologist named Ahmad Ibn Hanbal, who lived between 780 and 855.

Sheikh Ahmad Yassin (1937–2004)
Founder of Hamas. He called for the elimination of Israel through violence and called for establishing a Palestinian Islamist entity. He was killed by Israel.

Ahwazi Arabs
Sunni and Shi'ite Arabs that live in the southern Iranian city of Ahvaz.

AKP
Recep Tayyip Erdoğan's party—the Justice and Development Party.

Al 'Adallah w'al Islah
"The Justice and Reform" party. A Moroccan Muslim Brotherhood party.

Al' Adl w'al Ihssan

"Justice and Development" Islamist party in Morocco.

Al-Aqsa

Literally translated as "The Far Edge" in Arabic. Over time the term has become synonymous with Jerusalem.

Al-Aqsa Mosque

The third holiest site in Islam, after Mecca and Al-Medina. The mosque is located in the Old City of Jerusalem on the Temple Mount Compound / Har Ha Bayit / Al-Haram al-Sharif. The original structure was built in 705 but has been rebuilt several times.

Al-'Ataba

Shi'ite religious centers. There are five in Iraq, all located near the burial sites of key Shi'ite historical figures. The center offers religious studies, and it is a destination for Shi'ite pilgrims. It is also a hub for commercial and political activities. In response to al-Sistani's fatwa, al-'Ataba invited Shi'ites to come and join militias.

Al-'Atabat-al-Hashd al-Sha'abi

The collective name of these Shi'ite militias al-'Ataba initiated. They are entirely loyal to al-Sistani.

Al Badr Corp / Militia

A Pro-Iranian Iraqi Shi'ite political party and militia headed by Hadi al-Amiri.

Al Bukamal

A Syrian town next to the Syria-Iraq border crossing. The passage on the Syrian side is called Al Bukamal. On the Iraqi side, the crossing is named al-Qaim. Iran has built on the Syrian side next to the border crossing a military infrastructure called the Ali Imam Compound. The compound is one of the most critical links in the Iranian corridor.

Al Da'wah

Literally translated as 'The Preaching.' It is one of the core ideals and principles of the Muslim Brotherhood. Al Da'wah mainly promotes educational activities in various frameworks (mosques, summer camps, schools, conferences, etc.) whose purpose is to educate according to Islam's values and strengthen the movement's support and infrastructure.

Al-Fath Coalition

An Iraqi political coalition in Iraq formed during the 2018 general elections. Hadi al-Amiri leads it. Its principal members are Iranian-affiliated Iraqi militias that are a part of the Iraqi Shi'ite al-Hashd al-Sha'abi (Popular Mobilization Units (PMU)). The coalition supports Iranian intervention in Iraq.

Al-Haj

The pilgrimage to Mecca that Muslims are required to make. It happens once a year.

Al-Hashd Al-Sha'abi

"The Popular Resistance Committees" or "PMU." A state-sponsored umbrella organization made up of Iraqi militias (most of whom are Shi'ite). The origin of the PMU was a group of militias that fought from 2014 to 2017 alongside the Iraqi army to defeat ISIS in Iraq. In July 2016, the Iraqi parliament passed a law making these militias an official Iraqi military apparatus that operates in parallel to the Iraqi military. The main PMU militias are close to Iran, and some of those militias are practically under the command of the Iranian Revolutionary Guards (IRG).

Al-Hirak

Literally means "The Movement." The name of protests that began in Algeria on February 22, 2019. The millions of protesters demanded President Abdelaziz Bouteflika not run for office again, his government resign, and a complete overhaul of Algeria's entrenched corrupt political system. The protesters represented a cross-section of Algerian society—left-wing, right-wing, conservative, progressive, Islamist, secular—and came from all walks of life, ages, and persuasions. People took to the streets showing their feelings, marching for recognition and dignity, and indicting an entire political system. And their slogan was simple "Irhal" (Go Away). Enough is enough!

Al-Hodeidah
A Yemenite town and port on the Red Sea currently controlled by the Houthis and Iran's major pipeline to supply the Houthis.

Al Hodeidah Agreement / The Stockholm Agreement
A December 2018 UN-backed ceasefire agreement between the Yemenite Government and the Houthis outlining the terms of troop withdrawal.

Al Islam Huwa al-Hal
"Islam is the Solution"—a central slogan of the Muslim Brotherhood.

Al-Ja'arneh Mosque
A mosque located some twenty miles north of Mecca in the Arabian Peninsula. Some Arab scholars and theologians say that this mosque is the Al-Aqsa mosque.

Al-Jamma'ah al-Islamiayh
Islamist movement in Lebanon.

Al-Medina
City in Saudi Arabia, burial place of Prophet Muhammad.

Al-muqawama al-Masullah
The Armed Resistance

Al-Muqawama w'al Muman'aah
"The Resistance and Defiance." It is an idea and a concept that spread within the Muslim world's intellectual, political, and cultural discourse following World War II. Initially, it was primarily in the context of the North African struggle to end Western control. The original idea was that the way Arabs

and Muslims—as communities and as individuals—can enhance their lives is through the creation of a cultural and political life that emphasizes the enlightened moral values of Islam, the noble tradition of Arab culture, combined with the modern concepts of emancipation and statehood. In the last generation, al-Muqawama has become 'the code word' for the rejection of Western power, the destruction of the State of Israel, and liberating Palestine. Under this concept, Iran embraces and finances a set of execution agents such as Hezbollah, Hamas, Islamic Jihad, and other proxies in the region.

Al-Nahda (Ennahda)

"The Renaissance." Founded by Rashid al-Ghannouchi. It is an Islamic political party in Tunisia and one of Tunisia's most active and largest Islamist movements.

Al-Qaeda

"The Base" or "The Foundation." Al-Qaeda is a Salafi-jihadi organization formed by Osama Bin Laden and Sheikh Abdullah Yusuf Azzam in the late 1980s.

Al-Qa'im

An Iraqi town next to the Iraq-Syria border crossing. The passage on the Syrian side is called Al Bukamal. On the Iraqi side, the crossing is named al-Qaim.

Al-Quds

The name in Arabic for Jerusalem. The word is taken from the Hebrew word for holy, which is *kadosh*.

Al-Quds Force

Created in the 1990s, an elite unit and the spearhead of the Islamic Revolutionary Guards Corps (the IRGC). The IRG reports directly to Iran's Supreme Leader. The al-Quds force is responsible for external operations outside of Iran. Their mission is to export the Islamic Revolution, spread the Twelver Shi'ite orthodoxy, and ensure Iran is the region's leading superpower. Their primary task is to design and spearhead a strategy to achieve that mission, the cornerstone of which is constructing and operating a network of armed proxies and agents in various parts of the Middle East and beyond. As Iran's primary arm to support and guide Iran's nonstate partners, the al-Quds force arms, equips, funds, and trains the regime's armies of terror. Since the US killed Major General Qasem Soleimani, the Al-Quds Force has been under the command of Major General Ismail Qa'ani. The al-Quds force is designated a supporter of terror by the US government.

Al-Tajamm'u Al-Yamani Lil-Islah

"The Yemenite Reform Coalition Party." A Yemenite Islamist organization, known informally as "Islah." It is reportedly affiliated with the Muslim Brotherhood. It is increasingly becoming a Yemenite proxy for Turkey.

Al-Tawhid w'al Islah

"The unification or oneness of Allah." A cornerstone of Salafi-jihadi ideology and the name of an Islamist political party in Morocco. It opposes the Abraham Accords and the normalization agreements.

Al-Ula Declaration

In January 2021, the Gulf Cooperation Council ended its boycott of Qatar. The emir of Qatar, Sheikh Tamim bin Hamad al-Thani, attended the forty-first Gulf Cooperation Council (GCC) Summit held in the Saudi city of Al-Ula. On January 5, 2021, the GCC members—Bahrain, Kuwait, Oman, Qatar, Saudi Arabia, and the UAE—signed the "Al-Ula Declaration," expressing unity and the start of a new chapter in their relationship. Egypt (not a member of the GCC) also signed the declaration.

Al-Wilaiyah

"The one that subscribes to the order of Iran's Supreme Leader." The name of the Iranian-controlled Iraqi Shi'ite militias in the PMU. The PMU al-Wilaiyah are militias made up of Iraqi citizens who live in Iraq and want Iran to increase its hold over Iraq. Also, the name of the Iranian-backed Scout movement in Syria that is responsible for guarding Zaynab's Tomb in Damascus.

The Alawites

The al-Assad family in Syria is Alawite; the Alawites, who are a minority in Syria, are a distant branch of the Shi'ites. However, they have different norms and customs in comparison to mainstream Iranian Shi'ites.

Ali al Akhbar Wilayati (1945–)

A senior adviser to Iran's supreme leader, former Minister of Foreign Affairs.

Ali Abdullah Saleh (1942–2017)

A Yemenite Shi'ite politician, President of Yemen (1990–2012). President of Yemen Arab Republic (1978–1990). Following mass protests in the Yemeni Revolution in 2011 and 2012 protesting corruption, a broken economy, unemployment, and calling for Saleh to step down, he resigned and agreed not to pass the rule to his son. He allied with the Houthis following their 2014 coup. However, tensions between Saleh and Houthi increased, and the Houthis killed him in 2017.

'Ali Bin Abi Talib (600–661)

The fourth Caliph in Islam. A cousin and son-in-law of the Prophet Muhammad, the founder of Islam. Ali was married to 9 women and had 21 children. His first wife was Fatimah, the daughter of Muhammad. And together, they had four children—two daughters—Zaineb and Um Kulthum. They also had two sons—Hassan and Hussein. 'Ali bin Abi Talib was murdered. Hassan briefly took his father's place and ruled the Caliphate. He stepped down. And then his brother, Hussein (Al Hussein bin 'Ali bin Abi Talib), took the throne.

'Ali Hosseini al-Sistani (1930–)

Iraqi Shi'ite cleric of Iranian origin. The Shi'ite clerical order is hierarchical. The most senior cleric in the Twelvish Shi'ite clergy is Ayatollah 'Uzma—the Grand Ayatollah. Al-Sistani holds this rank. There are four Ayatollah 'Uzma in Iraq. Only one of the four was born in Iraq—eighty-six-year-old Mohammed Sayyid al-Hakim. A great and wise learned spiritual leader, al-Sistani is the most powerful and influential Iraqi Shi'ite cleric in Iraq. Al-Sistani rejects Iranian intervention in Iraq. He also opposes the model of the Iranian mullah regime.

Ali Khamenei (1939–)
Iran's Supreme Leader since 1998. He succeeded Ruhollah Khomeini, the founder of the Islamic Republic of Iran.

Allah
The One God

Alliance of Moderation
"Mihwar al E'itidal," an informal alliance of central Arab states—Egypt, members of the Gulf Cooperation Council (GCC)—Bahrain, Kuwait, Oman, Saudi Arabia, UAE—Jordan, and Israel. The alliance reflects its members' joint strategic interests—blocking the Iranian and Turkish threats and fostering economic and technological cooperation to address current and expected needs.

Al-Qadiyah al-Filastiniyah
The Palestinian Cause

Amal Party
Iranian-affiliated Lebanese Shi'ite political party in Lebanon.

Amir Ayek (1964–)
Israel's first permanent ambassador to the United Arab Emirates (2021–).

Amr Kamal Eddin al-Sherbiny
Cairo withdrew its ambassador from Qatar on June 5, 2017. On June 23, 2021, Egyptian President Abdel-Fattah al-Sisi, for the first time since 2014, appointed Egyptian diplomat ambassador extraordinary and plenipotentiary to the government of Qatar.

Ansar Allah
The military force of the Shi'ite Houthi tribes in Yemen. An Iranian agent.

Arab Civilization
The Arab civilization gave birth to Islam. Arabs come from the Arabian Peninsula. The first Muslims were culturally and ethnically Arabs. Most Arabs are Sunnis. However, most Muslims are not Arabs.

Arab/Persian Gulf
A 615-mile-long extension of the Indian Ocean between Iran and the Arabian Peninsula.

Arab Spring/Arab Awakening
A wave of protests in the Arab world that began in Tunisia in 2010 and spread quickly to many Arab countries—including Algeria, Egypt, Jordan, Libya, Morocco, and Syria. At the core of the protest were demands for real answers to the profound economic and social challenges and demands for political reforms, enhancement of individual and political rights, etc.

Arab Syrian Army
The official military of Syria

Aramco
Saudi Arabian Oil Company (formerly Arabian-American Oil Company) is a Saudi Arabian public petroleum and natural gas company. As of 2020, it is one of the largest companies in the world.

'Asaib Ahl al-Haq
"The League of the Righteous." It is an Iraqi Shi'ite militia. Also known as AAH. It is one of Iran's most important Shi'ite militias.

Ash-Sham
For centuries, the Arabic name referred to a geographic area consisting of today's Israel, Jordan, Lebanon, and Syria.

Ashak and Arak

"Tears and sweat." The mullah regime sees itself as a revolutionary power that sees its role to lead the world to redemption through a process called in Farsi Ashak and Arak—in which most of humankind will die. And those that survive will be redeemed by Allah.

Ashraf Gani (1949–)

President of Afghanistan from 2014–August 2021.

Ashura

The tenth day of the month of Muharram, the first month in the Islamic calendar. For Shi'ite Muslims, it marks the day that Hussein Bin Ali Bin Abi Talib, the grandson of the prophet Muhammad was martyred in the battle of Karbala in 680. This is one of the cornerstones of the Shi'ite narrative and an intense day of mourning and exhibiting martyrdom through self-flagellation. The Sunnis also celebrate Ashura. For them, it marks the day that Moses and the Israelites were saved from Pharaoh by God, creating a path in the Sea of Reeds. Sunnis fast and ask for repentance.

'Atabat PMU

A coalition of four Shi'ite Iraq militias that split from the PMU in 2020. The alliance is affiliated with Grand Ayatollah Ali al Sistani, who rejects Iran's Iraq intervention and urges to keep Iraq independent. They seek to form an alternative to the PMU and have only nationalist militias.

Lieutenant General Aviv Kochavi (1964–)

The twenty-second Chief of Staff (2019–) of the Israel Defense Forces (IDF).

Ayman al-Zawahiri (1951–)

Leader of Egyptian Islamic Jihad. He, Osama bin Laden, and Abdullah Yusuf Azzam, a Salafi-jihadi theologist and military commander of Palestinian origin, established al-Qaeda in Afghanistan.

Aymen Benabderrahmane (1962–)
President of Algeria (2021–)

Aziz Akhannouch (1961–)
Prime Minister of Morocco (2021–)

The Axis of Resistance and Defiance

"Mihwar al Muqawama." Under the banner of Al-Muqawama w(al) Mumanna'ah (the Resistance and Defiance), Iran cultivates and finances a powerful network of allies, agents, and proxies such as Hezbollah in Lebanon, Hamas and Islamic Jihad in the Gaza Strip, Iraqi Shi'ite militias, Afghan Shi'ite militias, Pakistani Shi'ite militia, the Houthi tribes in Yemen and other proxies in the region. Their role—among other things—is to help Iran in its aspiration to become the dominant superpower.

Ayatollah

Two words in Arabic that mean "Sign of God." It is pronounced as one word; however, it is made of two words, aya (sign, flag, verse) and Allah (The God). A senior cleric status within Shi'ite theological order.

Ayatollah' Uzma

"The Grand Sign of God." The title for the most senior cleric within the Shi'ite theological order.

Bab El Mandeb Strait

"The Gate of Lamentation (or) Tears." The southern entrance to the Red Sea. Eighteen miles wide at its narrowest point, it is located on Yemen's southwestern tip, flanked from the east by Yemen and from the west by Djibouti and Eritrea. The connection between the Gulf of Aden and the Red Sea, the link between the Indian Ocean and the Mediterranean Sea, and the chokepoint between the Horn of Africa and the Middle East. The shortest route between the Mediterranean, the Indian Ocean, and East Asia—the Bab el Mandeb Strait physically connects the east and the west.

Barack H. Obama (1961–)
President of the United States (2009–2017)

Bashar Hafez al-Assad (1965–)
President of Syria and Commander-in-Chief of the Syrian military since 2000. He succeeded his father, President (1971–2000) Hafez al-Assad (1930 – 2000).

Dr. Barham Ahmed Salih Qassim (1960–)
President of Iraq (2018–). He was the Deputy Prime Minister for Economic Affairs (2005–2009), the Minister of Planning (2005) in the Iraqi transitional government (2005), and Deputy Prime Minister (2004) in Iraq's interim government. He was Prime Minister (2009–2011) of the Iraqi Kurdistan Region and was the Prime Minister (2001–2004) of the Kurdish Regional Government in Sulaymaniyah.

Bay'a
After the death of every king, the Saudis immediately summon the tribes to swear an oath of allegiance, *bay'a*. This ceremony aims to ensure that the transition of power will be as short and as smooth as possible.

Beji Caid Essebsi (1926–2019)
Considered the father of Tunisian independence and Tunisia's transformation into a democracy. He was elected president of Tunisia in 2014—the first democratically elected president in Tunisian history. He served as president until his death in July 2019 at the age of ninety-two. He founded the party, Nidaa Tounes, "Call of Tunisia."

Benjamin Netanyahu (1949–)
The prime minister of Israel from 1996–1999 and 2009–2021. He is currently the head of the opposition.

Basij Forces

"The Organization for Mobilization of the Oppressed." Created in April 1980, it is a paramilitary volunteer militia. It is an intimidating and far-reaching organization primarily charged to maintain order, suppress dissent, and protect the regime.

Boko Haram

"West is Forbidden." A jihadist terrorist organization based in northeastern Nigeria, also active in Chad, Niger, and northern Cameroon.

Caesar Syrian Protection Act

Round of US sanctions announced against the Syrian regime in June 2020.

Caliph

Caliph is part of the Arabic term "Caliphat Rasul Allah"—"the replacer of Allah's Messenger (Prophet Muhammad)." The first four Caliphs in Islam are known as the Four Rightly Guided Caliphs—who were either nominated by their predecessor or elected by a religious council.

Caliphate

A global Islamic cultural, political, and religious entity run by shariah law in which no other independent or sovereign state exists.

Caliphat Rasul Allah

Translated as "the replacer of Allah's "God's" messenger (Prophet Muhammad)." The first four caliphs in Islam are known as the Four Rightly Guided Caliphs— who were either nominated by their predecessor or elected by a religious advisory council. The fourth caliph was 'Ali Bin Abi Talib. He was a cousin and the son-in-law of the Prophet Muhammad. He ruled from 656 until he was assassinated in 661.

China's Belt and Road Initiative (BRI)

Also known as the "One Road, One Belt Project" or the New Silk Road. It is a massive infrastructure project that would stretch from East Asia to Europe. The plan has two pillars: the overland Silk Road and the Maritime Silk Road Economic, Commercial, and Trade Belt, designed to create a vast network of railways, energy pipelines, highways, harbors, etc., connecting China with different areas globally.

Council of the Arab and African countries of the Red Sea and the Gulf of Aden

A framework of eight countries bordering the Red Sea and the Gulf of Aden. The countries are Saudi Arabia, Sudan, Djibouti, Somalia, Eritrea, Egypt, Yemen, and Jordan.

Dar al-Iftah al-Misriyyah

The highest Sunni theological authority (based in Egypt).

Dawlat al-Kanoun

An Iraqi political party led by Nouri al-Maliki, former Iraqi Prime Minister. The party is known for its affiliation with Iran.

Deobandi Order

A Sufi order in India

Donald J. Trump (1946–)

President of the United States (2017–2021)

East Jerusalem

East Jerusalem currently governed by Israel, that was part of the Jordanian District of Jerusalem that Jordan ruled from 1948 to 1967.

EastMed Pipeline

A 1,2000-mile planned pipeline to transport natural gas from the Mediterranean Sea's gas fields to Europe.

Eastern Mediterranean Gas Forum

Headquartered in Cairo, the EMGF is the umbrella for cooperation, dialogue, investment, and partnerships regarding the exploration, development, and export of gas resources in the Eastern Mediterranean. Cyprus, Egypt, Greece, Israel, Italy, Jordan, and the Palestinian Authority are its current members.

Ebrahim Raisi (1960–)

President of Iran (2021–). He is associated with the ultra-extremist current in Iran. He chaired the Judiciary Authority in Iran from March 2019 until he was elected president. He was also a member of a notorious four-member committee known as "The Death Committee"—an entity that sent thousands of Iranians to their deaths on subversion charges against the regime.

Eitan Naeh (1963–)

First Israeli Ambassador to Bahrain (2021–). He was previously Israel's Ambassador to Turkey and Deputy Head of Mission in London. He was also the temporary ambassador to the UAE before Amir Hayek was appointed.

Emmanuel Macron (1977–)

President of France (2017–)

Exporting the Islamic Revolution

A strategy aimed to position the Islamic Republic of Iran as the hegemonic power in the Middle East and pave the way for the Mahdi's return (the Messiah in Shi'ite Islam).

Fairuz—Nouhad Wadie' Haddad (1950–)

A Lebanese Christian singer and icon in the Arab world.

Faleh al-Fayyad (1956–)

Iraq's former National Security Adviser. Chief of Staff of the Al-Hashd Al-Sha'abi (Popular Mobilization Units).

Fard al-kifaya

A collective or communal duty that Muslim society needs enough of its citizens to undertake.

Farḍ al-kifāya jihad fatwah

A duty imposed on the whole community of believers (known as the Ummah in Arabic). When a farḍ al-kifāya is issued, the individual is not obligated to follow the directive, as long as a sufficient number of community members do.

FATA (Federally Administered Tribal Area)

The western and northwestern Pakistan area—the Federally Administered Tribal Area (FATA)—is populated by tribes, principally the Pashtun.

Fath

The Palestine Liberation Movement. Established in 1957 in Kuwait by Yasser Arafat. Fath in Arabic means "a triumph." The word Fath is also the reverse order of Harakat Tharir Filastin's initials (The Movement for the Liberation of Palestine). They chose the word Fath instead of the initials HTF because HTF resembles the word HATF in Arabic, which means "a sudden death." Fath is the backbone of the PLO and the P.A.

Fatwah

An Islamic religious ordinance issued by an authorized Islamic cleric.

Fayez al-Sarraj (1960–)

Head of the Presidential Council of Libya and the Prime Minister of the Government of National Accord (GNA) (2015–2021).

Forces for Freedom and Change (FFC)

The FFC is a movement of civil society and rebel groups that led the uprising resulting in al-Bashir's ouster.

Free Syrian Army (FSA)

The FSA was the primary Syrian rebel body in the first years of the war in Syria. Turkey has trained and equipped the FSA since 2016. In 2019, it renamed itself the Syrian National Army (SNA). The SNA has 22,000–35,000 fighters.

G-7

The Group of Seven (G7) is an inter-governmental political forum consisting of Canada, France, Germany, Italy, Japan, the United Kingdom and the United States.

G-20

The G20 is the international forum that brings together the world's major economies. Its members account for more than 80 perecnt of world GDP, 75 percent of global trade and 60 percent of the population of the planet. The forum has met every year since 1999.

Galabiya

Loose-fitting traditional Arab garment.

The Gaza Barrier

A forty-mile-long land obstacle (wall) that circles the Gaza Strip. Israel is building the barrier to confront the terror tunnels' challenge that Hamas and Islamic Jihad dig from Gaza into Israel. The wall is also known as the ICW—an acronym for the "Indicative Concrete Wall." It is six meters above the ground and tens of meters below the ground. It has advanced technological detectors and sensors—both above and under the ground that can detect if a tunnel is being dug. The wall is in Israeli territory, east of the perimeter fence around the Gaza Strip, and is in addition to the existing border fence between Israel and Gaza. When completed, the barrier will completely encircle the entire Gaza Strip on its border with Israel. On the Gaza Strip's northern border with Israel, the barrier will extend into the sea.

Gaza Strip

An eight-by-twenty-mile strip located on the Mediterranean Sea between Israel and Egypt, Gaza's population is about 1.9 million people. Gaza was under Egyptian military rule until 1967 and under Israel's military governance from 1967–2005. In 2005 Israel withdrew from Gaza and handed control to the Palestinian National Authority. In 2007 Gaza-born Hamas Islamic organization violently terminated the rule of the P.A. in Gaza in a bloody coup. Since 2007 Hamas rules Gaza.

Gholamhossein Gheybparvar
Deputy IRG Commander and former Bassij Commander

Goreh-Jask Pipeline
A one thousand km crude oil pipeline to carry oil produced at the Goreh facilities on Iran's southwestern shore of the Gulf to the port of Jask in southeastern Iran. This allows Tehran to bypass the Strait of Hormuz.

Government of National Accord (GNA) (2015–2021)
The civil war in Libya has resulted in the formation of two competing power centers. One is the Eastern Parliament, based in Tobruk. The other, an Islamist-affiliated government based in Tripoli. Government of National Accord is an interim government for Libya that was formed under the terms of the Libyan Political Agreement (LPA), a UN–led initiative, signed on December 17, 2015.

Grand Mufti
The highest official of religious law in a Sunni or Muslim country. He issues legal opinions and edicts (fatwahs).

Gulf Cooperation Council (GCC)
A regional intergovernmental political and economic union—members are all Arab Monarchies of the Persian (Arab) Gulf—Bahrain, Kuwait, Oman, Qatar, Saudi Arabia, and the United Arab Emirates.

Hadi al-Amiri (1954–)
Hadi al-Amiri leads the Al-Fath Coalition. He is close to the Mullah regime in Iran. The Al-Fath is also the largest pro-Iranian political force in Iraq. He is also the leader of a powerful Shi'ite militia called the Al-Badr militia, part of al-Hashd al-Shabi.

Haidar al-Abadi (1952–)

The prime minister of Iraq (2014–2018). A Shi'ite close with Iran.

Haitham bin Tariq Al Said (1955–)

Sultan of Oman (2020–)

Hamad bin Isa Al Khalifa (1950–)

King of Bahrain (2002–)

Hamid Karzi (1957–)

President of Afghanistan from 2001 to 2014.

Hamas

Harakat Al-Muqawama Al-Islamia—the Islamic Resistance Movement. Hamas also is literally translated as a 'religious enthusiasm.' It is a Palestinian Islamist militant and political organization founded in the Gaza Strip in 1987. Hamas defines itself as a subsidiary of the Muslim Brotherhood movement and the branch of the Muslim Brotherhood in Palestine. Hamas's vision is to eliminate the State of Israel in a violent struggle and establish a caliphate ruled by Islamic law in all areas of Israel. Hamas has controlled the Gaza Strip since 2007 after they launched a coup against the Palestinian Authority in Gaza. Hamas is defined as a terrorist organization by many countries. Hamas is an example of an Iranian agent.

Hanafi Orthodoxy

Sunni Islam has four orthodox legal schools of thought (Hanafi, Hanbali, Maliki, and Shafi'i). Hanafi is named after an eighth-century scholar, Abu Hanifa bin Nu'man Ibn Thabit. The Hanafi school is considered the oldest and most liberal school of Islamic jurisprudence. And it is the largest. Of the four schools, Hanafi is the most flexible and adjustable in its interpretation of Islam and its application of sharī 'ah law. The origins of the Taliban philosophy come from the Hanafi school.

Hanbali Orthodoxy

Sunni Islam has four orthodox legal schools of thought (Hanafi, Hanbali, Maliki, and Shafi'i). The Hanbali school of thought is named after a very influential Islamic theologist named Ahmad Ibn Hanbal, who lived between 780 and 855. That period was also known as 'the Golden Age of Islam.' Hanbali orthodoxy is the smallest and most dogmatic stream of Sunni orthodoxy. It demands Muslims live only according to the Quran and the Sunnah (the teachings of the Prophet Muhammad) as they were interpreted during the first three generations of Islam. The Hanbali reject any reform, translation, and adjustment of Islamic law and practice that occurred after "the Golden Age of Islam." Inspired by Muslim Indian and Pakistani theologians, the Taliban has integrated elements from the Hanbali jurisprudence.

Hani Bin Briek

Vice-chairman of the UAE-backed Yemenite Southern Transitional Council (STC).

Harakat al-Shabaab al-Mujahideen (HSM)

A Salafi-jihadi group based in Somalia known as Al-Shabab (The Youth).

Harakat as-Sabreen Nasran li-Filastin

A splinter group that broke off from the Islamic Jihad in Palestine organization in Gaza Strip. Backed by Iran.

Hassan al-Bana (1906–1949)

An Egyptian educator. He founded the Muslim Brotherhood movement in the late 1920s. Al-Bana was murdered—apparently under the Egyptian Government's orders after the assassination of Egyptian Prime Minister Mahmoud Fahmi Nukrashi by a terrorist assassin (December 1948).

Hassan al-Turabi (1932–2016)

A Sudanese Islamist politician and leader of the National Islamic Front (NIF).

Hassan Nasrallah (1960–)
Secretary-General (1992–) of Lebanese Hezbollah.

Hassan Rouhani (1948–)
Seventh President of Iran (2013–2021).

Hay'at Tahrir al-Sham (HTS)
The "Organization for the Liberation of the Levant" or "Levant Liberation Committee." A coalition of Salafi-Jihadi militias in Syria.

Hazara
The Hazaras are the third largest ethnic group in Afghanistan. They are primarily concentrated in the mountainous area of central Afghanistan known as 'Hazaristan'—or the land of the Hazara. Iran has strong ties with the Hazara. Iran has long supported the Hazaras, a historically oppressed ethnic minority who make up between 10 and 20 percent of Afghanistan's population. Most Hazaras, like most Iranians, are Shi'ite. They also speak a dialect of Persian. After the 1979 invasion of Afghanistan, Iran aided the Hazara mujahedeen, who fought the Soviets. Iran cultivates influence among the Hazaras by funding cultural and religious activities as well as the local media. The IRG reportedly provides the Hazara in Afghanistan with financial and military support. However, Iranian support for the Hazara is not only because of solidarity. The IRG sees Afghanistan as an optimal location to grow its next powerful regional proxy to secure Iranian interests. The Hazara have become a manpower source for Iran's axis of proxies.

Hezbollah (Lebanese)
Two words that mean "Party of God." An armed military organization and political party in Lebanon. The Islamic Revolutionary Guards Corps (IRGC) created Hezbollah in 1983. Hezbollah's main political base is Lebanese Shi'ites. Hezbollah is Iran's most vital and powerful proxy. Hezbollah has three ministers in the Lebanese Government and 13 members of parliament. Hezbollah is defined as a terrorist organization by many countries.

Hisham al-Hashimi (1973–2020)
An Iraqi historian and researcher whose specialty was security and strategic affairs and extremist groups. He was assassinated in 2020.

Hormuz Strait
A strait between the Persian Gulf and the Gulf of Oman. It provides the only sea passage from the Persian (Arab) Gulf to the open ocean. It is one of the world's most strategically important choke points.

Hosni Mubarak (1928–2020)
The fourth president of Egypt from (1981–2011). He resigned following Arab Spring mass protests in February 2011.

Hossein Salami (1960–)
Major General. Commander of the Islamic Revolutionary Guard Corps

Houthis
A framework of Shi'ite tribes in northern Yemen, they make up about thirty-five percent of Yemen's population. The Houthis are Zaidiyyah Shi'ites—the oldest branch of Shi'ism and the second largest group after the Twelvers. The Houthi movement was created in 1992 by Hussein Badr al-Din al-Houthi, a Shi'a scholar. The Houthis have a historical relationship with Iran. In September 2014, the Iranian-backed Houthi militias ousted the Yemenite Government and expanded their control to other parts of Yemen. Following the failure to solve the crisis peacefully, a Saudi-led military coalition forces fights against the Houthis since March 2015 to restore the ousted Yemeni government.

Hussein Arnous (1953–)
Prime Minster of Syria (2020–)

Hussein bin 'Ali bin Abi Talib (600–661)
The youngest son of Ali Ben Abi Talib (the fourth Caliph) and Fatimah, the Prophet Muhammad's daughter. Hussein was Muhammad's last grandson

through direct bloodline. Caliph Yazid of Ma'awiya killed Hussein along with his supporters in Karbala (Iraq of our times) in 680. They were killed on the 10th day of the month of Muharram, the first month on the Islamic (lunar) calendar. Ashurah means ten in Arabic. And every year, Shi'ites commemorate the event known as the Day of Ashurah by performing grief and mourning rituals. The Shi'ite narrative says that "Every day is Ashurah and every place is Karbala." The killing of Hussein is the cornerstone of the Shi'ite story.

IAEA
International Atomic Energy Agency

Ibrahim El Zakzaky (1953–)
The founder and leader of the Shi'ite Islamic Movement of Nigeria (IMN). He has been in government custody since 2015.

Id Al Fitr
A three-day celebration that takes place at the end of the Holy month of Ramadan.

IDF
The Israel Defense Forces, the official name of Israel's military.

IHH
The Foundation for Human Rights and Freedoms and Humanitarian Relief (IHH) is a front charity accused of smuggling arms to al-Qaeda-affiliated jihadists in Syria. The IHH was also used to transport wounded ISIS and al-Qaeda fighters by ambulance from Syria to Turkey. Erdoğan used the IHH to organize provocative flotillas to Israel under the guise of humanitarian activity. And the IHH is reportedly expanding its activities into south Yemen.

Imam
An Islamic leadership position. It is most commonly used as the title of a worship leader of a mosque and Muslim community among Sunni Muslims.

In Shia orthodoxy, Imam is the title of the spiritual and political successors to the Prophet Muhammad.

Imamiyyah

The largest branch of Shia Islam is the Twelver—in Arabic Imamiyyah. Twelver refers to its followers' belief in twelve divinely ordained spiritual and political successors (Imams) to the Prophet Muhammad. They are known as the Twelve Imams.

Imam al Mahdi

The Twelver Shi'ites believe there were twelve divinely ordained successors to Prophet Muhammad. They believe that the last Imam was Muhammad Bin Hasan al-Askari, born in 870 and that he disappeared as a small child. The Shi'ites believe he is waiting outside of time and history to the time he will reappear to redeem humanity. He is the messianic figure in Shi'a Islam.

Imam al Mahid Scouts

Hezbollah's youth movement. Began in Lebanon in 1985 and is now being replicated in Iraq and Syria.

Imam 'Ali Brigades

Iranian-backed Iraqi Shi'ite militia.

Imam 'Ali military Compound

A complex military installation Iran has built in Syria near the Iraqi-Syrian border. It is a vital component of the Iranian land corridor. The Imam 'Ali Compound serves as the border crossing and a transition depot for Iranian-backed Iraqi militias heading to Syria. The passage's name on the Syrian side is Al-Bukamal, and the name of the crossing on the Iraqi side is Al-Qa'im. In addition to the sprawling warehouses it has built, reports are that Iran has built tunnels and bunkers in the compound that store missiles and rockets. The Imam 'Ali Compound is a keystone of the corridor. That is why it has been attacked several times by the United States. Also, reportedly Israel has attacked the installation. Israel has never claimed responsibility for those attacks.

Intifada

Literally translated as "recovering from an illness." The name of the Palestinian uprisings of 1987 to 1993 and 2000 to 2007. The first intifada occurred in 1987-1993, characterized by mass protests by Palestinians (demonstrations, strikes, riots, etc.) in the West Bank, Gaza Strip and East Jerusalem, and terrorist attacks such as Molotov Cocktails and stabbing attacks. The second uprising occurred during 2000-2007 and was characterized mainly by lethal terrorist activities, including suicide bombings attacks. Both waves of violence changed the lives of thousands of Palestinians and Israelis.

Iranian-backed Shi'ite Militia Proxies

Examples: Afghani Al-Fatemiyoun, the Iraqi 'Asaib Ahl al-Haq, Harakat al-Nujaba, Kataib Hezbollah, Imam' Ali brigades, the Lebanese Hezbollah; Pakistani Liwa Zainebiyoun; and the Palestinian Harakat as-Sabireen Nasran li-Filastin in the Gaza Strip.

Iranian Land Corridor

A land bridge that begins in Iran and travels west: it crosses through Iraq, Syria, and Lebanon and ends in the Mediterranean Sea. The corridor is critical for Iran's hegemonic vision.

Islamic Fundamentalism and Militant Islam

Islamic fundamentalism shares the same ultimate vision of political Islam. Muslim fundamentalists want to create a Caliphate ruled by the strictest interpretation of the sharī'ah. Islamic fundamentalists entirely reject Western values and call for returning to the early years of Islam's pure ideals and laws. Islamic fundamentalists that want to implement sharī'ah law according to the most puritan dogmatic interpretation are known as Salafists. The ideology they ascribe to is known as Salafi. The word salaf means "what has been previously." Salafism's core ideology is that Islam will thrive and flourish again once Muslims return to the roots, to the origin of Islam, and adopt and apply the Islamic codes, law, norms, and values as they were in the time of the Prophet Muhammad and his first four successors. Contemporary Islamic fundamentalism (called in Arabic Usuliyah, which means "going back to the origin or the roots") has two branches. One branch is the non-militant Salafi Islamist fundamentalist camp. Non-militant Salafi Islamists are called Usuliyun. Usuliyun follow a strict interpretation of sharī'ah law. But they do not try to impose it on others forcefully. Instead, they use preaching, education, and political actions to try to gain followers, grow the movement, and fulfill their religious objectives. Some choose to isolate themselves and minimize their interaction with the surrounding society, state authorities, and institutions. The other branch of contemporary Islamic fundamentalism is the militant camp—Militant Islam. Fundamental militant Islam adheres to the Salafi-Jihadi ideology. Militant Islamists are often called Usuliyun Mutashaddidun or al-Mutashaddidun al-Islamiyyun. As we said earlier, the word usilyun or usuliyah means "the origin or the roots." The word Mutashaddidun means "extremist." Militant Islamists are what is often referred to in Western media as "extreme fundamentalists" or "extreme Islamic fundamentalists" or "radical fundamentalists." The West is most familiar with the following militant Islam Salafi-jihadi ideology groups Al-Qaeda, Al-Shabab "The Youth" in Somalia, African-based Boko Haram "Western Values are Forbidden," Global Jihad, ISIS, Islamic Jihad, and the Taliban. A core value of all Salafi-jihadists is the concept of Talb a-Shahada—"the quest for martyrdom for the glory of Islam and Allah's rule." To summarize their value system: It is good, necessary, and noble to kill and be killed for the sake of Allah. For militant Islamist groups, violence is an essential tool that they must use to bring about the caliphate.

Islamic Revolutionary Guards Corps (IRG or IRGC)

The IRGC was founded in 1979. Supreme Leader Khomeini created the IRG immediately after the Islamic Revolution and the creation of the Islamic Republic of Iran. An Iranian military force whose broad mission is to defend the Iranian Revolution from foreign or domestic threats. Their primary role is to protect the Islamic Republic and the Islamic Revolution against internal and external threats. It is under the command of Iran's Supreme Leader, who, since 1989, is Ali Khamenei. The commander of the IRGC is Major General Hossein Salami. The IRG has air, ground, and naval forces. It also has aerospace, unconventional warfare, and cyber divisions. It is designated as a foreign terrorist organization by the United States. The IRG has evolved to be the wealthiest and most powerful entity in Iran and essentially controls Iran's economy and foreign policy and wields significant influence over Iran's domestic policy.

Iranian Agents

Examples of Iranian agents are the Palestinian Sunni Islamist groups, Hamas and Islamic Jihad in Palestine (IJIP) in the Gaza Strip (though both are Sunni, not Shi'ite), and Ansar Allah, the military force of the Shi'ite Houthi tribes in Yemen.

Iranian Proxies

Examples of Iranian proxy Shi'ite militias Iran has created are the Afghani Al-Fatemiyoun, the Iraqi 'Asaib Ahl al-Haq, Harakat al-Nujaba, Kataib Hezbollah, Imam' Ali brigades, the Lebanese Hezbollah; Pakistani Liwa Zainebiyoun; and the Palestinian Harakat as-Sabireen Nasran li-Filastin in the Gaza Strip.

ISIS/ISIL/The Islamic State

ISIS began in 2006 as a militant Islamic militia of Sunni tribes in central Iraq. ISIS is an acronym for the "Islamic State of Iraq and Syria" or the "Islamic State of Iraq and ash-Sham." For centuries, Ash-Sham is the Arabic name that referred to a geographic area of Mesopotamia—consisting of what is today Israel, Jordan, Lebanon, Syria, and Iraq. In Arabic, ISIS is called Da'esh. The term "Da'esh" is made of the initials "Al-Dawla al-Islamiya fi(l) Iraq wal-Sham" (the Islamic State in Iraq and ash-Sham). In April 2013, ISIS became the branch of Al-Qaeda in Iraq. They called themselves "Al-Qaeda in the Two River Countries." The rivers are the Tigris and the Euphrates—a region historically known as Mesopotamia. In June 2014, ISIS declared its "Caliphate"—the Islamic State (I.S.). At its height, the Islamic State encompassed 30 percent of Syria and 40 percent of Iraq. In July 2014, the leader of ISIS—Ibrahim 'Awad Ibrahim 'Ali al-Badri al-Sameraai a.k.a. Abu Bakr al-Baghdadi—announced himself the Caliph Ibrahim. In the second half of 2017, the military pressure of the international coalition forces that joined together to fight the Islamic

State began to reverse some of ISIS's gains. Throughout 2017, 2018, and 2019 ISIS suffered mounting casualties and lost strongholds. The Islamic State came to an end in 2019. The United States killed Abu Bakr al-Baghdadi in October 2019. One of the most substantial ISIS branches globally is the "Islamic Emirate of Khorasan," also known as

ISIS- K
ISIS' branch in Central Asia.

Islam
A dedication to the complete and absolute acceptance of the idea of one god—Allah.

Islamic Jihad
Salafi Jihadi global organization.

Islamic Jihad in Palestine (IJIP, also known as PIJ)
IJIP, in Arabic, Harakat al-Jihād al-Islāmi fi Filastīn is a Palestinian Islamist militant organization. Established in the 1980s and supported by Iran. Considered as the second-largest military power in Gaza Strip (after Hamas). IJIP calls for the destruction of Israel in a violent struggle. IJIP military force called Saraya al-Quds—"The Jerusalem Companies." IJIP is an example of an Iranian agent.

Islamic Revolution
In a series of events called the Islamic Revolution, Ayatollah Ruhollah Khomeini, and his followers seized power from Shah Mohammad Reza Pahlavi, who had ruled Iran since 1941. The Pahlavi dynasty had ruled Iran since 1925.

Islamist
A Muslim that is committed to proactively spreading and implementing Islam through political, cultural, or militant action. It can be different versions of Islam, according to their orthodoxy and ideology.

Ismail Haniyeh (1962–)
Born in Gaza. The Chairman of Hamas's Political Wing / Bureau, Former Hamas Prime Minister of the Gaza Strip.

Major General Ismail Qa'ani (1958–)
Commander of the IRGC al-Quds force. He replaced Major General Qasem Soleimani, who was killed in January 2020 by the United States.

Issa Ahmad Qasem (1937–)
Grand Ayatollah Sheikh Isa Ahmed Qassim is Bahrain's leading Shi'ite cleric and a politician. He is the spiritual leader of Al Wefaq, Bahrain's biggest opposition society.

Izz ad-Din al-Qassam Brigades
Hamas's military wing. It is named after an Islamic preacher of Syrian origin killed in the 1930s during the Arab revolt against the British Mandate in Palestine/Land of Israel.

Jabhat al Nusrah (li) Ahl as-Sham/Jabhat Fatah al-Sham
Front of the Supporters of the People of Syria/the Levant. Originally Al-Qaeda's branch in Syria. In 2015 rebranded as Jabhat Fatah al-Sham ("Front for the Conquest of the Levant") and in 2017 merged in the frame of Hayat Tahrir as-Sham (HTS)—a conglomeration of Salafi-Jihadi organizations in Syria.

Jaish al-Mahdi
'The Messiah's Army'an Iraqi Militia led by Iraqi cleric and politician Muqtada as-Sadr. The militia spearheaded the attack on US forces in Iraq during the 200's. The militia rebranded under the name Saraya al-salam (the Peace Companies).

Jamal (Gamal) Abdel Nasser (1918–1970)
Egyptian President from 1954 to 1970. He advocated for "Pan Arabism"—a political entity uniting all Arab countries under Egypt's Leadership.

Janjaweed

In 2003, rebels in Darfur (a predominantly Muslim region in western Sudan) launched an insurrection against the Sudanese government for oppressing Darfur's non-Arab population. The government responded by using Arab militias—later named Janjaweed—to carry out genocide and ethnic cleansing.

JCPOA

The Joint Comprehensive Plan of Action. Also called the "Vienna Agreement," "the Iran Nuclear Deal," or "the Iran Deal." An agreement was signed between Iran and the P5 +1 (the United States, the United Kingdom, France, Germany, the European Union, and China) in 2015 to limit the Iranian Nuclear Program. In May 2018, the US withdrew from the agreement.

Jerusalemite Palestinian

Jerusalem is the capitol of Israel. The city's population is about 940,000 people. About 563,000 are Jews, and 360,000 are Arabs, of whom 345,000 are Muslims. Most of the Arabs in the city are also known as Jerusalemite Palestinians. Most of the Jerusalemite Palestinians are permanent residents of the State of Israel.

Javad Zarif (1960–)

Iranian Foreign Minister

Jihad

The word Jihad in Arabic literally means "an effort." It comes from the widely known Arabic concept Jihad fi Sabil Allah, "an effort to implement Allah's way." In the very early days, Islam was on the run. Operating in a hostile environment, the prophet Muhammad and his first disciples had to exercise jihad—an intensive spiritual journey to reach a higher degree of inner purity in their beliefs and to try to be a purer worshiper of Allah. Throughout the evolution and expansion of Islam, jihad has become much more associated with the Muslim's willingness to sacrifice materially—including sacrificing their lives—for the glory of Islam and Allah. Salafi-jihadi ideology's core belief is that Islam will thrive again once it adopts the codes, laws, and values as they were in the time of the Prophet Muhammad and his first four successors. However, to achieve this goal, Salafi-jihadists violently impose their ideology and rules.

Jihad fi Sabil Allah
"An effort to implement Allah's way"

Joseph Robinette Biden Jr (1942–)
President of the United States (2021–). Vice President under Barack Obama (2009–2017).

Juba Peace Agreement
Signed on October 3, 2020, a peace agreement signed between the transitional government of Sudan and the "Sudan Revolutionary Front"—a coalition of militias operating in the provinces of Darfur, Blue Nile, and South Kordofan. These agreements are supposed to be the first step on the path to restoring peace in the Blue Nile, Darfur, and South Kordofan after many years of deadly conflicts. However, it should be noted that some of the militias in West and North Sudan did not join the agreement.

Kais Saied (1957–)
President of Tunisia (2019–)

Kafirun or Kuffar
Infidels

Karbala
A city in central Iraq and one of the holiest places for Shia. The burial site of Hussein Bin 'Ali Bin Abi Talib, the last male grandson of Prophet Muhammad through direct bloodline.

Kata'ib Hezbollah
Iranian-backed Iraqi proxy militia closely affiliated with the Iranian Revolutionary Guards.

Khalid bin Khalifa bin Abdulaziz Al Thani (1958–)
Prime Minister of Qatar (2020–)

Khaled Mashal (1956–)
Hamas senior leader

Khaled Yousef al-Jalahmah (1978–)
First Ambassador to Israel from Bahrain. Before his appointment in March 2021, he had served as Director of Operations of the Bahraini Foreign Office since 2017. He served as Deputy Ambassador of Bahrain to the United States (2009–2013).

Khalifa Haftar (1943–)
A Libyan general, the commander of the Tobruk-based Libyan National Army (LNA).

Khalifa bin Zayed bin Sultan Al Nahyan (1948–)
The second President of the United Arab Emirates (UAE) and the 16th Ruler of the Emirate of Abu Dhabi.

Jamal Khashoggi (1958–2018)
Saudi Arabian journalist assassinated at the Saudi Arabian consulate in Istanbul on October 2, 2018, by Saudi government agents.

Khorasan
A vast geographical area in Central Asia. The area includes northeast Iran, northwest Afghanistan, Tajikistan, Turkmenistan, and Uzbekistan. The militants of the Islamic Emirate of Khorasan are Afghans, Arabs, Kurds (from Iran), and recruits from Central Asian countries that border Afghanistan—Tajikistan, Turkmenistan, and Uzbekistan.

Khuzestan Province
A province in southwestern Iran on the Gulf nestled between Kuwait, Iraq, and Iran—its capitol is Ahvaz. Sunni and Shi'ite Arabs largely populate the area.

King Salman Causeway

Described as 'the biggest project in the world'—which, when completed, will connect Egypt and Saudi Arabia.

Kufr Billah

Heresy

Leviathan

A gas field in the territorial waters of Israel in the Mediterranean Sea.

Liwa Fatemiyoun

A Shi'ite militia consisting of Afghans living in Iran. Iran created the militia in 2014 to fight in Syria to support Assad's forces, keep him in power, and secure Iran's presence in Syria. In return for their service, militants receive monthly wages and are entitled to Iranian citizenship for themselves and their families.

Liwa Zainebiyoun

Zainebiyoun Brigade, an Iranian-backed Pakistani Shi'ite militia fighting in Syria. Iran created the militia in 2014 to fight in Syria to support Assad's forces, keep him in power, and secure Iran's presence in Syria. In return for their service, militants receive monthly wages and are entitled to Iranian citizenship for themselves and their families. The members are Shia Pakistanis living in Iran. Zaineb is one of two daughters of the fourth Caliph 'Ali Bin Abi Talib, and Fatimah, Prophet Muhammad's daughter. According to Islamic tradition, she is buried in Damascus.

Libyan National Army (LNA)

The civil war in Libya has resulted in the formation of two competing power centers. One is the Eastern Parliament, based in Tobruk. The other, an Islamist-affiliated government based in Tripoli. The government in Tobruk in eastern Libya and its military force—the Libyan National Army (LNA), are comprised of eastern Libyan tribes and Salafists. It is based in Benghazi (in eastern Libya) and led by General Haftar Khalifa.

Madaris
Islamic school

Mahdi
"The rightly guided one." A Messianic figure in the Shi'ite belief who, according to Islamic belief, will appear at the end of times to rid the world of evil and injustice.

Mahmoud Abbas (1935–)
"Abu Mazen," the President of the Palestinian Authority; Chairman of Palestinian Fath National Movement.

Majlis Shura al-Hashd
The Legislative Council of the PMU.

Marja'iyat Najaf (Marja'aiah)
Theological Shi'ite center in Iraq's home of four Iraqi-based grand Ayatollahs the most senior source for Shia religious jurisdiction.

Mashhad
Mashhad is a city in northeast Iran known as a place of religious pilgrimage and theological Shi'ite center.

Mavi Vatan Doctrine
Blue Homeland. The doctrine is presented to end Turkey's near-complete dependence on foreign energy sources and convert Turkey into a net energy exporter by controlling the surrounding waterways—the Black Sea, the Aegean Sea, and the Mediterranean Sea. However, in its essence, Mavi Vatan is a hegemonic strategy that Turkey has developed to exert its regional and international economic, political, and military superiority to aggressively assert a claim over the contested, potentially oil-rich regions of the Eastern Mediterranean.

Mecca

City in Saudi Arabia. Birthplace of prophet Muhammad. One of the three sacred places for Islam.

Michelle 'Aoun (1933–)

President of Lebanon (2016–). 'Aoun is a Christin Lebanese politician and the former Chief-of-Staff of the Lebanese military.

Militant Islam

An ideology committed to creating a global Caliphate through force and violence. The Caliphate they seek should be ruled by the strictest translation and application of the Islamic religious codex – the shari'ah law.

Mohamed Al Khaja (1980–)

First United Emirates Ambassador to Israel (2021–). Former chief of staff to the minister of Foreign Affairs and International Cooperation, to be the first Gulf ambassador to Israel.

IRGC Major General Mohammad Hossein Bagheri (1960–)

Armed Forces General Staff Chief (2016–). He is responsible for overseeing all Iranian military forces.

Major General Mohammad 'Ali Jafari (1957–)

Commander-in-Chief of the Islamic Revolutionary Guards Corps (IRGC) (2007–2019)

Mihwar al-Muqawama w'al Mummana'ah

"The Axis of Resistance and Defiance"

Mihwar al E'itidal

The "Alliance of Moderation"

Sheikh Mohammed bin Zayed al Nahyan (1961–)

The Crown Prince of the Abu Dhabi Emirate, Deputy Supreme Commander of the United Arab Emirates Armed Forces, de facto ruler of Abu Dhabi.

Mohammed Deif (1965–)
Palestinian chief of staff and supreme military commander of Izz ad-Din al-Qassam Brigades, the military wing of Hamas.

Mohamed Mahmoud Fateh Ali Abdulla Al Khaja (1980–)
The first UAE Ambassador to Israel. He began his position on February 14, 2021. Previously, Al Khaja was the Chief of Staff of the UAE Minister of Foreign Affairs and International Cooperation.

Mohammad Morsi (1951–2019)
Fifth President of Egypt (June 2012–July 2013). An Egyptian Islamist politician. Affiliated with the Muslim Brotherhood, though he ran as an independent candidate in the 2012 Egyptian elections. General Abdel Fattah el-Sisi removed him from office in a coup d'état after June 2013 protests.

Mohammed VI (1963–)
King of Morocco (1999–)

Ayatollah Mohammed Rida al-Sistani (1962–)
Iraqi cleric and the son of Grand Ayatollah, Ali al-Sistani.

Mohsen Fakhrizadeh (1958–2020)
A Brigadier General in Iran's Islamic Revolutionary Guards Corps. He was Iran's top nuclear scientist and the head of Iran's secret military nuclear program. He was killed in Iran on Friday, November 27, 2020.

Mossad
The National Intelligence Agency of Israel

Mostafa Madbouly (1966–)
Current Prime Minster of Egypt (2018–)

Muhammad bin Salman (1985–)
Muhammad bin Salman bin Abdulaziz Al-Saud, also known as MBS. The crown prince of Saudi Arabia.

Muhammad Dahlan (1961–)

Former Senior Fath member. Served as the head of Palestinian security forces in Gaza until Hamas coup (2007) and head of the Palestinian National Council.

Mujahedeen

Muslims who fight (jihad) on behalf of the faith or the Muslim community (ummah).

Muammar al-Ghaddafi (1942–2011)

Libyan dictator (1961–2011). Ousted following mass demonstrations and executed.

Haj Muhammad Amin al- Hosseini (1895–1974)

During the British Mandate rule over Palestine / the Land of Israel, he was the Grand Mufti of Palestine and the Supreme Arab Council's head. The Grand Mufti is the most senior position in the Islamic clerical order. He is also considered the first leader of the Palestinian National movement. He advocated for and incited severe violence against the Jewish communities in Palestine/ Land of Israel. He bitterly opposed the establishment of a state for the Jews in Palestine. During World War II, he cooperated with Nazi Germany.

Mullah

Iran is an Islamic Theocracy. Therefore, though there is a parliament and a president, the mullahs hold the power. A mullah is a Shi'ite clerical rank. Islam ranks its clerics—similar to the ranks in the Church or an army. The highest position is the 'Ayatollah Uzma' (The Grand Ayatollah). The highest spiritual center of the Shi'ites is located in Najaf and Karbala—cities in southern Iraq. Other major spiritual and theological centers of the Shi'a are located in Qom and Mashhad—cities in Iran. The Iraqi and Iranian Shi'ite theological centers have generated different, sometimes opposing, theological outlooks, resulting in a long history of rivalry over influence and prestige.

Mustafa al-Kadhimi (1967–)

Iraqi Prime Minister (2020–). Former head of Iraqi National Intelligence Services.

Muqtada al- Sadr (1974–)

A senior Shi'ite cleric in Iraq and the leader of the largest political coalition called "Saeroun." Al Sadr zig-zags between being a nationalist opposing Iranian involvement in Iraq and supporting Iranian involvement in Iraq. He is also the head of *Saraya al-Salam*, "The Peace Companies," a powerful Shi'ite militia.

The Muslim Brotherhood (MB)

Founded in 1929 in Egypt by Hassan al Bana. The MB adheres to the Political Islam school of thought and is the largest mass movement in the Sunni world. The MB is organized in a hierarchical structure. The Supreme Leader is called "the General Guide," An advisory board assists him called the Shurah. MB's slogan is "Islam is the Solution"Al-Islam hu al-hal in Arabic. The MB's goal is to establish a global Islamic framework—a Caliphate—that will be ruled according to the Islamic Shariah law. The MB rejects the concept of "Nation States." They argue that a nation state's vision is rooted in Western culture and values that contradict Islam and Islamic law (the Shariah) and therefore defy Allah's rule. The MB has chapters in every Muslim state in the world. The branches are hierarchically structured to reflect the global structure. The branches' structure is like the worldwide structure and is designed to promote the movement's ideology and values. However, each chapter has a certain degree of independence in its political position and political activities. Given that, one can indicate different—sometimes even opposing—positions of the branches regarding political issues. Against the backdrop of the Arab Spring events, the movement reached its climax. The MB won elections and thus ruled Egypt and Tunisia. And it gained power in other Arab states. However, the short-lived success—most significantly, the MB governments in Egypt and Tunisia failed and were replaced. The failure resulted in a political and ideological crisis within the MB, leading to inner splits in some of its chapters. As a result of this crisis, the pragmatic (pragmatic does not mean moderate) wing of the movement gained strength in places like Algeria, Egypt, Jordan, Tunisia, and Morocco at the expense of the more dogmatic wing.

Mustapha Adib (1972–)

On September 1, 2020, Lebanese President 'Aoun nominated the former Lebanese ambassador to Germany, Dr. Mustapha Adib, to be Lebanon's prime minister. But Adib failed to assemble a government, and on September 26, 2020, he resigned.

Nabih Berri (1938–)

Lebanese Shi'ite politician, Chairman of the Lebanese Parliament (1992–), leader of Lebanese Shi'ite Amal movement.

Naftali Bennett (1972–)

The current prime minister of Israel (2021–)

Najaf

A city in central Iraq. It is the Shi'ite world's spiritual capitol and the center of Shi'ite political power in Iraq. While Sunni Islam considers al-Quds (Jerusalem) as the third most sacred site in Islam, the Shi'ites consider Najaf as the third most sacred site (after Mecca and Medina). The holiest Shi'ite religious and pilgrimage sites are in Najaf and Karbala in Iraq and Qom and Mashhad in Iran. These cities are also home to the leading Shi'ite theological educational centers. The fourth Caliph, Ali Bin Abi Talib, is buried in Najaf.

Najib Mikati (1955–)

Prime Minister of Lebanon (2021–)

National Liberation Front

Erdoğan's strongest proxy is in north Syria: the National Liberation Front (NLF) is a Turkish-sponsored network of twenty-two rebel militias. The dominant militias in the NLF are a Salafi militia—Ahrar al-Sham and a Muslim Brotherhood militia—Faylak al-Sham. The NLF has approximately 70,000 militants.

Nawaf Al-Ahmad Al-Jaber Al-Sabah (1937–)

Emir of Kuwait (2020–)

Nayef bin Falah al-Hajraf
Secretary-General of the Cooperation Council for the Arab States of the Gulf (GCC)

NEOM
Saudi Arabia project, a futuristic city which will be in the northwestern part of the Kingdom.

Normalization
In the vernacular of the Middle East, the concept of 'Normalization' is a term that means recognizing Israel's existence in any manner or cooperating with Israel in any shape or form. The word describing 'Normalization' in Arabic is Tatb'ie. It is a word that can be translated as "making things natural," but also can be translated as "to stain," or to create something artificial.

Nouri al-Maliki (1950–)
Iraqi politician served as prime minister 2006–2014. In 2014 he was elected Iraq's third Vice President. He is known to be close to Iran.

Non-Proliferation Treaty (NPT)
1970 Non-Proliferation Treaty (NPT) banned all countries except the United States, Russia, China, Britain, and France from acquiring nuclear weapons. Non-nuclear signatories could develop peaceful nuclear programs for generating power and electricity.

NWFP (Northwestern Frontier Province)
An area in northwest Pakistan on the Afghan-Pakistani border. The area is dominated by Salafi-jihadi Taliban ideology, ruled by local tribal warlords, and housing a narcotic traffic corridor.

General Omar al-Bashir (1944–)
Ruler of Sudan from (1993–2019). In December 2018, protests began in Sudan. Sparked by a rise in bread prices, the disparate protests quickly evolved

into a wholesale revolution against the Sudanese government. And particularly Omar al-Bashir. On April 11, 2019, the Sudanese military overthrew al-Bashir.

OPEC—Organization of the Petroleum Exporting Countries

Founded in 1960. Its stated mission is to coordinate and unify the petroleum policies of its Member Countries and ensure the stabilization of oil markets in order to secure an efficient, economic, and regular supply of petroleum to consumers, a steady income to producers, and a fair return on capital for those investing in the petroleum industry. Its members are: Algeria, Congo, Equatorial Guinea, Gabon, Iran, Iraq, Kuwait, Libya, Nigeria, Saudi Arabia, the United Arab Emirates, and Venezuela.

Osama bin Laden (1957–2011)

Saudi-born founder and leader of Salafi-jihadi organization, al-Qaeda. Killed by the United States in 2011.

Oslo Process & Oslo Accords

A pair of agreements signed between the Government of Israel and the Palestine Liberation Organization (PLO). Oslo I (signed in Washington, DC, in 1993), Oslo II (signed in Taba, Egypt, in 1995). As part of the Oslo process, Israel recognized the PLO as the representative of the Palestinian people and as a partner in negotiations. The goal was to achieve a peace treaty based on United Nations Security Council Resolutions 242 and 338. The Oslo Accords also created the Palestinian National Authority (PA, PNA).

Otef Aza (Hebrew)

Meaning the 'Gaza's Envelope.' It refers to the Israeli communities (mostly agricultural communities—kibbutzim and moshavim, etc., and a couple of Israeli towns like Sderot, Netivot, and Ofaqim) around the Gaza Strip. Some of the communities are half a mile from the Israeli-Gaza border.

Particularism

An exclusive attachment to one's own group, party, or nation. The principle of leaving each state in an empire or federation free to govern itself and promote its own interests, without reference to those of the whole.

Particularistic Nationalism

The desire for national autonomy and sovereignty based on national characteristics and a distinct particular culture that evolves into the demand for political sovereignty. In Particularistic Nationalism, patriotism is linked to maintaining cultural integrity. It is patriotism based on cultural needs, which aims to secure and maintain a people's right to its own territory.

Statehood Model based on Particularism

A model of statehood that centers around the concept of "Watan" (the Homeland). In the "Watan" model, there is a sense of solidarity with all Arab states, and "Arab" as an ethnicity is a central (though not the only) component of the identity of the state. However, each state is independent and sovereign. The "Watan" model also emphasizes the state's unique characteristics (local history, traditions, societal fabric, etc.) and independence and sovereignty.

Pashtun

The Pashtun are native to the land comprising southern Afghanistan and northwestern Pakistan. In Afghanistan, the Pashtun are the largest ethnic group—comprising almost half of the population of Afghanistan; they live mainly in the south and the east of the country. In Pakistan, the Pashtun are the second-largest ethnic group—about 16 percent of its total population. The western and northwestern Pakistan area—the Federally Administered Tribal Area (FATA)—is populated by tribes, principally the Pashtun. FATA is inhabited by five and a half million people suffering from acute and persistent institutional neglect, poverty, ignorance, and Pakistan's most severe economic underdevelopment. The tribal areas in Pakistan are fertile ground for radical Islam.

Peace To Prosperity
A plan formally introduced in January 2020 by former US President Donald Trump to resolve the Israeli-Palestinian conflict.

Palestinian Liberation Organization (PLO)
A framework of different Palestinian organizations, established by Egypt in 1964. Its major pillar is the Fath movement, established in 1959. The PLO is the principal structure upon which the P.A. was established.

Palestinian National Authority/Palestinian Authority (P.A.)
A governing entity established as part of the Israeli-Palestinian Oslo Accords (1993–1995) to rule the Palestinians in the West Bank and Gaza Strip. The P.A. is based on the Palestinian Liberation Organization, and its central pillar is the Fath movement. The P.A.'s rule over Gaza ended in June 2007 when Hamas launched a violent coup.

People's Mojahedin Organization of Iran (PMOI/MEK)
Iranian opposition group

The Persian Civilization
The Persians are not Arabs. They do not come from the Arabian Peninsula. They come from Persia. They do not speak Arabic; they speak Farsi. Persians were pagans. As Islam rapidly spread, the Persian civilization adopted Sunni Islam. But in the Middle Ages, the Persian ruling dynasty adopted the Shi'ite orthodoxy, which has been the primary religion of Persia ever since.

Operation Northern Shield
The Israel Defense Forces launched Operation Northern Shield (December 2018–January 2019) to expose and neutralize cross-border attack tunnels that Hezbollah dug from Lebanon into Israel.

PKK
Kurdish Workers' Party militant Kurdish nationalist organization founded in the late 1970s. Although the group initially wanted to establish an

independent Kurdish state, its stated aims were later tempered to calls for a Kurdish autonomy.

Political Islam

A general name for Islamic political parties, movements, and organizations that participate in their countries' political domestic system. Political Islam wishes to advance an Islamist ideology centered around the vision of a global, pan-Islamist entity—the Caliphate through its political action. In the Caliphate, no other independent or sovereign state exists. The Caliphate should be governed & ruled by the sharī'ah. Islamist theologists believe the sharī'ah is the master plan given to humankind by Allah (God). Therefore, it is perfect and flawless. Any other political philosophy or political system—communism, democracy, socialism, etc.—is unacceptable to political Islam because it is human-made. And therefore, it is imperfect, unjust, and doomed to fail. Moreover, adopting any of these systems defies Allah's will.

Popular Resistance Committees

A Palestinian terrorist organization operating in the Gaza Strip. Supported mainly by Iran.

The Prophet Muhammad (570–632)

He founded Islam in the early seventh century.

Qais al-Khazali

Iraqi politician leader of the Iranian-backed Iraqi Shi'ite militia, Asa'ib Ahl Al-Haq (AAH).

General Qasem Soleimani (1957–2020)

He was the al-Quds Force commander. The al -Quds force is an elite unit of the Islamic Revolutionary Guards (IRG). The IRG reports directly to Iran's Supreme Leader Ali Khamenei. Soleimani was the mastermind, the spearhead, the lead strategist—in charge of designing, leading, and implementing Iran's hegemonic vision in the Middle East. His role was to spread Iran's reach and influence and make Iran the superpower in the region. And he did so primarily by creating, supporting, and nurturing a network of militias—agents and proxies—throughout the Middle East, including Hezbollah in Lebanon, Hamas, and Islamic Jihad in Gaza, Iraqi Shi'ite militias, Yemeni Houthi forces, Afghan and Pakistani Shi'ites militias, etc. Under Soleimani's command, Iran deepened its hold in Lebanon, Syria, Iraq, Yemen, and the Gaza Strip. He was killed by the United States in an air attack on January 3, 2020.

Qaum/Pan-Arabism

Pan-Arabism is committed to the creation of an entity with no physical borders that brings together all Arabs as one nation—a "Qaum." The Qaum model rejects the concept of a "particularistic" national statehood (Watan and Wataniya). Instead, it promotes a framework that there should be one united political entity for all Arabs as one nation.

Qom

A city in Iran sacred to Shi'ites. A major Shi'ite theological center.

Qur'an

The Sacred Book of the Muslims. The word means "what is read." The Muslims believe that the Qur'an is the word of Allah placed in the mouth of Muhammad.

Radwan

An Iranian-trained infantry elite Hezbollah ground force. In the Qur'an, Radwan is the name of the gatekeeper of heaven.

Ramadan

The ninth month of the Islamic (lunar) calendar. A month of prayer and fasting during the day and eating and celebrating at night. The holiday commemorates Muhammad's first revelation.

Rafik Al-Hariri (1944–2005)

Lebanese business tycoon and politician who served as the prime minister of Lebanon from 1992 to 1998, and again from 2000 to October 2004. He was murdered in Beirut in February 2005. The United Nations created the Special Tribunal for Lebanon (STL). On August 18, 2020, the STL presented its final verdict. The tribunal found a Lebanese citizen named Salim Jamil Ayyash guilty of al-Hariri's assassination. The STL identified Ayyash as a senior member of Lebanese Hezbollah.

Rashid al-Ghannouchi (1941–)
Tunisian politician, co-founder, and leader of the al-Nahdah Islamist Party Movement.

Recep Tayyip Erdoğan (1954–)
President of Turkey (2014–). Previously the Turkish Prime Minister (2003–2014) and the Mayor of Istanbul (1994–1998). He is the founder and leader of the Justice and Development Party (AKP)—an Islamist party.

Ruhollah Khomeini (1902–1989)
Islamic Shi'ite cleric, who held the rank of Ayatollah. Founder of the Islamic Revolution in Iran, Iran's Supreme Leader (1979–1989).

Sa'ad Al Din al-Hariri (1970–)
Lebanese Sunni politician. Leader of Sunni-based Al-Mustaqbal party. He served as Lebanon's Prime Minister (2009–2011 and 2016–2020). Son of Rafiq al-Hariri, Lebanese business tycoon and politician who served as the prime minister of Lebanon from 1992–1998, and again from 2000–October 2004.

Saddam Hussein (1937–2006)
Iraq's dictator between 1979–2003. Executed by Iraqi authorities after a trial in 2006.

Saed Eddin El-Othmani
Islamist Moroccan politician who has been prime minister of Morocco since 2017.

Sadiq al-Mahdi (1935–2020)
Sudanese politician and Islamist cleric served twice as Sudanese prime minister (1966–1967 and 1986–1989).

Saeroun
The meaning of the name is 'Marching On.' Iraq's largest political coalition, led by Muqtada al-Sadr.

Salaf
What has been previous.

Salafi/Salafism
Islamic ideology advocates for Muslims to live according to early Islamic core moral values.

Salafi-Jihadi
A militant Islamic ideology whose goal is to establish the Islamic Caliphate through violence. The Caliphate will be ruled according to the strict translation of the sharī 'ah—the Islamic religious codex.

Salim Jamil Ayyash
A senior member of Hezbollah, the STL found guilty of Rafik al-Hariri's assassination.

Salman bin Abdulaziz Al-Saud (1935–)
The King of Saudi Arabia (2015–).

Saraya al-Salam
Iraqi Shi'ite militia led by Iraqi politician and cleric Muqtada al-Sadr. In the 2000s, the militia was known by the name Jaish al-Mahdi.

Saraya al-Quds
"The Jerusalem Companies." The military arm/wing of the Islamic Jihad in Palestine. Supported mainly by Iran and affiliated with Hezbollah.

Saudi Peace Initiative/Arab Peace Initiative

Crown Prince Abdullah of Saudi Arabia announced the Arab Peace Initiative (API) at the Beirut Arab League Summit in March 2002. The Saudi Plan calls for Israel to withdraw from all the territories it controlled following the 1967 War, including East Jerusalem, Gaza, the Golan Heights, the West Bank, Gaza. It also calls for a solution to the Palestinian refugee situation, according to UNGA Resolution 194. And it calls for establishing a Palestinian state within the 1967 borders, with East Jerusalem as its capitol. If Israel respects these parameters, the Arab League promises to "consider the Arab-Israeli conflict ended" and enter into "normal relations" with Israel in a regional peace providing security for all states.

Sayyid Qutb (1906–1966)

An Egyptian intellectual, educator, and senior member of the Muslim Brotherhood. In the second half of the twentieth century, Qutb laid the foundation for the contemporary militant Islam ideology. Between 1948–1951 Qutb studied in the US. He earned his MA in Educational Methodology at the University of Northern Colorado's Teachers College. His encounter with Western culture caused him to be very hostile towards the West. He viewed the West as completely antithetical and a threat to Islam. This anger and resentment became one of the central tenets of his extreme ideology. In 1965 Egyptian authorities (Gamal Abdel Nasser was president) arrested and imprisoned him for his extremist positions. While in prison, he wrote his most famous book called "Landmarks on the Path." He was executed in Egypt in 1966 on charges of conspiring to overthrow the regime.

Shah Mohammad Reza Pahlavi (1919–1980)

Ruled Iran from 1941 to 1979. The Pahlavi dynasty had ruled the Imperial State of Iran since 1925.

Sharī'ah

Literally translated "a path." The sharī'ah is a codex of laws developed based on a combination of the 'Urfa (the Code of Laws of Tribes), the interpretation of the Qur'an (the Holy book of Islam), the Hadith (the oral book of Islam), and the interpretation of Islamic theologians. The Sunnis believe the Sharī 'ah codex was completed and sealed in the eleventh century. The Shi'ites believe the Sharī 'ah is dynamic and open to interpretation.

Shi'a/Shi'ite/Shi'at 'Ali

"The (Political) Faction of 'Ali." Shi'ites constitute approximately 15 percent of all Muslims in the world. Shi'ites believe that the leadership of the Islamic is a matter of inheritance. Sunnis believe it should be the most appropriate leader based on his skills. Shi'a was founded in the seventh century AD after the assassination of Hussein Bin 'Ali Bin Abi Talib ('Ali was the fourth Caliph of Islam) in the battle of Karbala (now a city in southern Iraq) in 680. Shi'ites claim that the leader of Islam should be a male descendant of 'Ali bin Abi Talib.

Shi'ite al-'Ataba

Shi'ite al-'Ataba established four military units to fight ISIS. Al-'Ataba are burial sites of key figures from Shi'ite history; there are five such sites in Iraq. These sites are a place of pilgrimage, centers for religious studies, and administrative and political centers of power. The collective name of these Shi'ite al-'Ataba units was al-'Atabat-al-Hashd al-Sha'abi. And they are known to be entirely loyal to al-Sistani.

The Shi'ite Crescent / The Iranian Crescent

In December 2004, King Abdullah II of Jordan warned that Iran was developing a Shi'ite Crescent—Lebanon, Syria, Iraq, Iran, and Yemen, to become the regional superpower. He warned that Iran would foment instability to achieve its objective and that it would be disastrous for the region if the Shi'ite Crescent were realized. As Iranian aggression has escalated, the king has used international forums, including the 2018 World Economic Forum in Davos, as a platform to express his concern. And in a January 2020 interview with France24, he changed the term "Shi'ite Crescent" to the "Iranian Crescent."

Sistan and Baluchistan Province

An Iranian province on the Hormuz Strait, on Iran's southeastern border with Afghanistan and Pakistan. The area is largely populated by Sunni and Shi'ite Arabs.

Southern Gas Corridor (SGC)

Slated to bring natural gas from the Caspian Sea to Europe. The planned SGC pipeline will cross seven countries. It will connect Azerbaijan to the Caspian Sea, Georgia, Turkey, Greece, and Albania. Then it crosses the Mediterranean to Italy.

Southern Transitional Council (STC)

A separatist movement that wants to create an independent entity in southern Yemen. The STC is supported by the UAE.

Special Tribunal for Lebanon (STL)

On February 14, 2005, former Lebanese Prime Minister Rafik al-Hariri was assassinated in Beirut. The United Nations Security Council created a special team and launched an investigation to determine who killed al-Hariri. Based on their findings, on May 30, 2007, the UNSC adopted Resolution 1757. UNSCR 1757 authorized the formation of an international tribunal to investigate the assassination. On August 18, 2020, the STL presented its final verdict. The tribunal found a Lebanese citizen named Salim Jamil Ayyash guilty of al-Hariri's assassination. The STL identified Ayyash as a senior member of Hezbollah.

Suez Canal

In Egypt, it connects the Red Sea and the Mediterranean Sea.

Sufism

A mystical form of Islam, a school of practice that emphasizes the inward search for God and shuns materialism.

Sunnah / Sunni

"Sunnat al-Nabi" (The Prophet's (Muhammad) Path/Way). About 85 percent of Muslims are Sunni. Sunnis believe that the leadership of the Islamic world is not a matter of inheritance but a choice of the most appropriate leader based on his skills. He does not rule alone. He rules side by side with and is advised by an advisory council called the "Shura"—whose role is to assist him in fulfilling his duties as a leader and in accordance with Islamic law.

Syrian National Army (SNA)

Also known as the Turkish-backed Free Syrian Army (TFSA). A militia of armed Syrian opposition groups consisting of 22,000-35,000 militants. Though 'officially' a Syrian army, it is armed, funded, and trained by Turkey. Turkey also pays their salaries. Turkey uses the SNA in Syria and uses them as militias abroad, specifically in Libya. It is a Syrian army commanded and controlled by Turkey.

Takfir

Rooted in the Arabic word 'kafer' meaning infidel. Takfir is a school of thought that has evolved within Salafi-jihadi militant Islam ideology. Takfir ideology argues that there are Muslims who do not fulfill the commandments of Islam in "the true and correct" manner. Therefore, they should not be considered Muslims. Instead, they should be viewed as enemies of Islam whose danger is even greater than those of the non-Muslim infidels. According to takfir ideology—the Muslim "infidels" are "corrupting" and "contaminating" Islam and its values from within. And as long as Islam is not "pure" from within, the ultimate vision of establishing Allah's dominion on earth cannot be realized. Therefore, takfir ideology believes that Islam must be "purified" of "Muslim impersonators."

Talb a-Shahada

The quest for martyrdom—a concept praised by militant Islam.

Taliban

Literally translated "students." Formed by young Afghan mujahedeen. They ruled Afghanistan from 1996 until 2011. They regained control of Afghanistan in August 2021 when the United States withdrew from Afghanistan. They are a Sunni militant Islam organization that follow a combination of Hanafi and Hanbali orthodoxy.

Sheikh Tamim bin Hamad al-Thani

The emir of Qatar

Tamar

A gas field in the territorial waters of Israel in the Mediterranean Sea.

Tatbi'e
Normalization

Temple Mount/Al-Haram al-Sharif/Har Habayit
In the heart of the Old City of Jerusalem is the Temple Mount Compound. It is called in Hebrew Har Ha-Bayit (the mountain of the two Jewish Temples). And, in Arabic, it is called Al-Haram al-Sharif (The Noble Sacred Compound). Two important symbols of Islam built during the Islamic conquests of the late seventh and early eighth centuries AD are located in Al-Haram al-Sharif. One is the Dome of the Rock, and the other is the Al-Aqsa Mosque.

Transitional Military Council (TMC)
After al-Bashir was ousted, a Transitional Military Council (TMC) was set up in Sudan to function as a transitional administrative government.

Trans-Anatolian Natural Gas Pipeline (TANAP)
Trans-Anatolian Natural Gas Pipeline (TANAP). Turkey, Azerbaijan, the State Oil Company of the Azerbaijan Republic (SOCAR), and British Petroleum (BP) own shares in TANAP. Turkey owns 30 percent, the Government of Azerbaijan and SOCAR (The State Oil Company of Azerbaijan Republic) own 58 percent, and British Petroleum (BP) owns 12 percent.

The Turkish Civilization
The Turks are neither Arabs nor Persians. Most Turks are Sunni. The Turkish Ottoman Empire ruled the Middle East for more than six hundred years, from about 1299 to 1922.

Twelver Shi'ite
The largest Shi'ite stream. Also called the "Imamiyyah." The Twelvers believe in a line of spiritual leaders called "Imam," starting with Ali bin Abi Taleb. The last in the line—number 12—was Muhammad bin Hassan al-Assakri, also known as the "Anticipated (or Disappeared) Imam." According to the Shi'ite belief, he disappeared as a small child in the tenth century. But he is not dead. He is waiting 'outside of history and time' until circumstances allow him to reappear as a Messiah—"Mahdi." When he returns, he will lead the salvation

of humanity through Armageddon. A process in which most people will be killed, and those who survive will receive the kingdom of eternal peace.

UAV
Unmanned aerial vehicle

Ummah
The Islamic collective community

Umrah
The Umrah is a pilgrimage to Islam's two holiest sites of Mecca and Medina. It can be undertaken at any time of the year.

UNAMI
United Nations Assistance Mission for Iraq

UNSC
United Nations Security Council

UNSCR 1696 (2006)
On July 31, 2006, the UNSC passed its first resolution regarding Iran's nuclear ambitions. UNSCR 1696 called on the regime to suspend its enrichment program and comply with the IAEA Board of Governor's requirements. Iran refused to cooperate and comply with UNSCR 1696 as well as subsequent demands of the international community, including additional UNSC requests and resolutions. Therefore, in December 2006, the UNSC passed UNSCR 1737.

UNSC Resolution 1701 (2006)
Ended the Second Lebanon War; ordered the deployment of the Lebanese army along the border with Israel and banned the armed presence of Hezbollah in the vicinity to the Israeli-Lebanese border. It also put an embargo on weapon shipments to Hezbollah.

UNSCR 1757 (2007)

On February 14, 2005, former Lebanese Prime Minister Rafik al-Hariri was assassinated in Beirut. The United Nations Security Council created a special team and launched an investigation to determine who killed al-Hariri. Based on their findings, on May 30, 2007, the UNSC adopted UNSCR 1757, authorizing an international tribunal's formation to investigate the assassination. The body was called the Special Tribunal for Lebanon (STL). Its mandate was to investigate people only. It did not have the authority to bring organizations or governments to trial. The tribunal was empowered to act under Chapter 7 of the UN Charter. Chapter 7 allows the use of force and sanctions against countries that do not cooperate with the STL's orders and demands.

UNSC 1737 (2006)

The first international resolution that imposed sanctions on Iran for not complying with previous demands and continuing its uranium enrichment program. UNSCR 1737 demanded that Iran halt its uranium enrichment program.

UNSC Resolution 2216 (2015)

Demands the Houthis withdraw from all areas seized during the conflict, relinquish the arms they took from military and security institutions, and restore the authority of the legitimate Government of Yemen. The Houthis ignored the resolution.

UNSCR 2231 (2015)

The Joint Comprehensive Plan of Action (JCPOA) was endorsed by UN Security Council Resolution 2231 and adopted on July 20, 2015. Iran's compliance with the nuclear-related provisions of the JCPOA was to be verified by the International Atomic Energy Agency (IAEA) according to certain requirements outlined in the agreement.

UNSCR 2259 (2015)

In December 2105, in an attempt to end the civil war in Libya and resolve the dispute between the eastern and western seats of government, the United Nations brokered an agreement known as the Libyan Political Agreement (LPA) or the Skihrat Agreement (since it was signed in Skihrat, Morocco). The LPA created a Presidency Council—a body tasked to form a unity government. UNSCR 2259 endorsed the agreement and called on the Presidency Council to form a Government of National Accord (GNA). The GNA was to be the official government of Libya, and it was to be based in Tripoli, which is in western Libya. The UNSCR also called on all member states to not support or contact any other entity outside of the GNA that claims to be the official representative or government of Libya.

UNSC Resolution 2451 (2018)

In December 2018, the UNSC unanimously passed Resolution 2451 endorsing the Yemenite Government and the Houthis agreement, known as the Stockholm Agreement or the Al-Hodeidah Agreement. The goal of the deal was to stop the violence and alleviate the escalating humanitarian crisis. According to the agreement, Hodeidah, occupied by the Houthis, and the surrounding area were to be demilitarized. And the UN was to monitor the al-Hodeidah ports. Thus far, the Stockholm Agreement and the UNSC Resolution 2451 have not been implemented.

UNSMIL

UN Envoy to Libya

Usuliyun/Usuliyah/Usuliyun

Ultra conservatives Muslims

Usuliyun mutashaddidun/al-mutashaddidun al-Islamiyyun

Supporters and militants of militant Islam groups.

Vladimir Putin (1952–)

President of Russia. In 2012 he was elected to his third term.

Wahabism

An ultra-conservative Sunni orthodoxy that originated in Saudi Arabia. Wahabism drew some of its core principles from the Hanbali orthodoxy.

Watan
The Homeland

Wataniya
Particularistic nationalism emphasizes the state's unique characteristics (local history, traditions, societal fabric, dialect, etc.) and its independence and sovereignty.

Wilayat al-Faqih
'The Rule of the Jurisprudent' in Shi'ite Islam. According to this ideology, the head of the system is the Jurisprudent. His rulings and decisions are absolute and must be obeyed without question. According to Shi'ite belief, he draws his knowledge from the divine providence and acts as a replacer of the 'anticipated Imam.' Therefore, he cannot be wrong, and his judgments and executive decisions cannot be wrong. The Supreme Leader can be ousted by order of the "Council of Experts"—a supervising council composed of eighty-six mullahs.

Yair Lapid (1963–)
Current Alternate Prime Minister of Israel and Minister of Foreign Affairs since 2021.

Yasser Arafat (1929–2004)
The Palestinian National movement's prominent leader was also known by his nickname - "Abu 'Ammar." He was one of the founders of the Fath Palestinian organization. He was the Palestinian Liberation Organization (PLO) Chairman and the Palestinian National Authority (P.A.).

Yazid bin Mua'awiya (645–683)
The seventh Caliph in Islam and the second Caliph of the Umayyad dynasty. Yazid's army slaughtered al-Hussein bin Ali bin Abi Talib and his family and supporters in 680.

YPG
An acronym for "the People's Protection Units." It is the central Kurdish military force in Syria. The YPG has an all-female brigade called the YPJ.

Sheikh Yussuf al-Qardawi

A senior Islamic theologist of Egyptian origin who serves as the chairman of the International Union of Islamist Scholars. Al-Qardawi is the unofficial higher spiritual authority of the Muslim Brotherhood.

Zaynab al-Kubra ("elder Zaynab") and Zaynab al-Sughra ("littler Zaynab" also known as Umm Kulthum)

The fourth caliph was 'Ali Bin Abi Talib, the son-in-law and cousin of Muhammad who ruled from 656 until he was assassinated in 661. 'Ali had nine wives and a total of twenty-one children. His first wife was Muhammad's daughter, Fatimah. Together they had four children—two boys, Hassan and Hussein, and two girls, Zaynab al-Kubra and Zaynab al-Sughra.

Ziad al-Nakhalah

Leader of the Islamic Jihad in Palestine organization (IJIP).

Zine el-Abidine Ben Ali (1936–2019)

The second president of Tunisia from 1987 until 2011. Zine el-Abidine Ben Ali was the first casualty of the Arab Spring. The autocratic ruler and his family fled to Saudi Arabia in January 2011.

Zionism

The Jews' return to their homeland and restoring Jewish sovereignty in their ancient Jewish homeland, known as Eretz Israel or Zion.

Zohr

Egypt's largest gas field in the Mediterranean Sea.

NOTES

Chapter 1

1. Raghida Dergham, "Adoption of Strategic Renaissance and Revival of Persian Nationalism," [in Arabic], *Elaph*, July 4, 2021, https://bit.ly/3wrtfyO.

Chapter 2

1. "Constitution of the Islamic Republic of Iran," United Nations High Commissioner for Refugees (UNHCR), https://bit.ly/3jTtoqh

2. Peter Martin and Tony Capaccio, "Iran Is a Daily Threat as U.S. Dominance Wanes, General Says," *Bloomberg*, April 20, 2021, https://bloom.bg/3lig6Xf.

3. Ian Williams and Shaan Shaikh, The Missile War in Yemen, June 9, 2020, https://bit.ly/2Nrmz33

4. "The Joint Comprehensive Plan of Action (JCPOA) at a Glance: Fact Sheets & Briefs," Arms Control Association, accessed September 3, 2021, https://bit.ly/3yO7AlM.

5. Avi Melamed, "Inside The Middle East: Making Sense of the Most Dangerous and Complicated Region on Earth," (New York: Skyhorse Publishing, 2016).

6. "Iran Military Power Ensuring Regime Survival and Securing Regional Dominance," US Defense Intelligence Agency, 2019 https://bit.ly/3rXCWDj

7. Iran Military Power "Ensuring."

8. David Adesnik, "Iran Spends $16 Billion Annually to Support Terrorists and Rogue Regimes," Foundation for Defense of Democracies, January 10, 2018, https://bit.ly/3yUuyZs

9. Adil al-Salmi, "IRGC Plans to Remain in Syria for 25 years," [in Arabic], *Asharq Al-Awsat*, August 19, 2016, https://bit.ly/34uLZlW.

10. Adil al-Salmi, "IRGC: We Will Never Compromise Our Hold in Bahrain, Yemen and Syria," [in Arabic] *Asharq Al-Awsat*, September 24, 2016 https://bit.ly/3jOiWQN

11. "Iranian Official Threatens Bahrain and Yemen after the Fall of Aleppo," [in Arabic], *JBC News*, December 14, 2016, http://bit.ly/2gDp3VY.

12. "Iran's Rouhani Warns Against the Collapse of the Regime in Iran," [in Arabic], *JBC News*, October 23, 2017, https://bit.ly/2J65hql.

13. "Khamenei's' advisor Says Iran is the Most Powerful Factor in the Region," [in Arabic], *Elaph*, February 2018 https://bit.ly/3balGUW.

14. "Gulf Cooperation Council Holds Iran Responsible for Violence in the Region," [in Arabic], *Middle East Online*, October 21, 2020, https://bit.ly/2HjlSFY.

15. David E. Sanger and Ronen Bergman, "How Israel, in Dark of Night, Torched Its Way to Iran's Nuclear Secrets," *The New York Times*, July 15, 2018, https://nyti.ms/2Ssk03x.

16. Kendall Siewert, "Acting Director General Urges Iran to Fully Cooperate with IAEA," IAEA: International Atomic Energy Agency, November 21, 2019, https://bit.ly/3qqlgjn

17. Siewert, "Acting Director General."

18. By: Kiyoko Metzler, David Rising, and Edith M. Lederer, "UN Agency Says Iran is Violating all Restrictions of Nuclear Deal," *Defense News*, June 5, 2020, https://bit.ly/2MgzJPJ.

19. "UN Rejects Iran's Explanations for Nuclear Material at Site Flagged by Israel," *The Times of Israel*, November 11, 2020, https://bit.ly/3rYzYyv

20. Patrick Pester, "Iran is enriching Uranium to 20%. What Does that Mean?" Foundation of Defense of Democracies, https://bit.ly/3aosZsI

21. Amos Yadlin, Ephraim Asculai, "How Close is Iran to a Nuclear Bomb?", January 13, 2021 Institute for National Security Studies (INSS) https://bit.ly/2ZgYTBb

22. Natasha Turak, "'Only Countries Making Bombs' are Enriching Uranium at Iran's Level, IAEA Chief Says," *CNBC*, MAY 26, 2021, https://cnb.cx/3wQQQcP.

23. "The Strait of Hormuz is the World's Most Important Oil Transit Checkpoint", *Today in Energy*, June 2019 https://bit.ly/2Nn9lo6

24. "Iran Conducts 'Provocative' Live Rockets Test Near US Ships", *BBC News*, December 30, 2015 https://bbc.in/3afaLd7

25. Iran Military Power", US Intelligence Defense Agency Report, 2019 https://bit.ly/3jUfJ2b

26. "Iran Guards Open New Naval Base for 'Dominance' over Hormuz," *The Arab Weekly*, September 25, 2020, https://bit.ly/2WyXzs1/

27. Jeff Seldin, "Iran Harasses US Ships, Submarine in Strait of Hormuz," *VOA News*, May 10, 2021, https://www.voanews.com/middle-east/iran-harasses-us-ships-submarine-strait-hormuz.

28. Ibid,, "Iran Guards Open New Naval Base for 'Dominance' over Hormuz", https://bit.ly/3ar1e2N

29. "G7 Condemns Mercer Street attack, Says Evidence Points to Iran," *Al-Monitor*, August 6, 2021, https://bit.ly/3g6wiHk.

30. Ariel Cohen, "Iran's Suspected Energy Terrorism: Persian Gulf Tanker Hijacking," *Forbes*, August 3, 2021, https://bit.ly/3jWSHIu

31. Nicholas Carl, "The Growing Iranian Threat Around the Strait of Hormuz", *Critical Threats*, September 22, 2020 https://bit.ly/3ddwB2O

32. Elizabeth White, "The Challenge of Guarding Bab el-Mandeb," *The Maritime Executive*, December 25, 2020, https://bit.ly/38sMtvN.

33. Missile Defense Project, "Missiles of Iran," *Missile Threat*, Center for Strategic and International Studies, June 14, 2018, last modified July 16, 2020, https://bit.ly/3pjaoTd

34. Williams and Shaikh.

35. Abdel Hadi al-Habtoor, "37 Houthi Strikes on Saudi Arabia since declaring its initiative," [in Arabic], *Asharq Al-Awsat*, April 16, 2021, https://bit.ly/32x7l0V

36. Jessica Kocan and Emily Estelle, "April 2021 Map Update: Al Houthi Attacks on Saudi Arabia," *Critical Threats*, April 16, 2021, https://bit.ly/3Cs6VJY.

37. Moaz Al-Omari, "Washington: Tehran Is Not Interested in Ending Conflict in Yemen," [in Arabic], *Asharq Al-Awsat*, April 22, 2021, https://bit.ly/2QKoEZJ.

38. "Arab States Condemn 'Blatant' Houthi Attacks on Saudi Arabia," *Arab News*, July 25, 2021, https://arab.news/rwtsj.

39. Omar Alawadhi and Nuha AlKhatib, "Tiger Team for Criminal Matters: Powers of the Arab Interior Ministers Council," Al Tamimi & Co., June 2020, https://bit.ly/2WZbPOy.

40. "Arab States Condemn 'Blatant'."

41. "Arab States Condemn 'Blatant'."

42. Houthis Military Escalation in Marib: Motivations, Consequences and Scenarios," Emirates Policy Center, February 28, 2021, https://bit.ly/33qO69A

43. "Egypt's Suez Canal Revenues up 4.7% In Last 5 Years – Chairman," *Reuters*, August 6, 2020, https://reut.rs/2N2Opmz; "Egypt's Suez Canal Revenues up 4.7% In Last 5 Years – Chairman," *Reuters*, August 6, 2020, https://reut.rs/2N2Opmz.

44. "Egypt's Suez Canal Reports Record Revenue Despite Blockage Crisis," *Al-Jazeera*, July 11, 2021, https://bit.ly/3jvaPc7.

45. Aaron Clark, Stephen Stapczynski, and Anna Shiryaevskaya, "The $9.6 Billion A Day Price Of A Suez Stuck Ship," *Captain*, March 25, 2021, https://bit.ly/3s0oFHa.

46. "100 Days Since Suez, the Global Supply Chain is yet to Recover," *Hellenic Shipping News*, June 7, 2021, https://www.hellenicshippingnews.com/100-days-since-suez-the-global-supply-chain-is-yet-to-recover/.

47. Carla Chahrour, "NEOM Aims to Be World's Most Competitive City," *Arab News*, July 19, 2021, https://bit.ly/3jttqWa.https://www.arabnews.com/node/1896596/business-economy

48. "Homepage," NEOM, accessed August 1, 2021, https://neom.com/en-us.

49. Jeremy M. Sharp, "Yemen: Recent Attack Against US Naval Vessels in the Red Sea", *CRS Insight*, October 21, 2016 https://bit.ly/2Zino0R

50. "The Coalition Destroyed Two explosive Speedboats and Two Drones Launched from Hodeidah by Houhti Terror Group", *Al-Sharq Al-Awsat*, March 17, 2020 https://bit.ly/3d95Mdi

51. Jack A. Kennedy, "Houthi Attacks on Saudi Arabia," *HIS Markit*, March 5, 2021, https://bit.ly/3AflOx6.

52. "King Abdullah II: Iran's Shia Crescent Poses Greatest Threat to Regional Countries," [in Arabic], *Al-Arab UK*, January 27, 2018, https://bit.ly/2HlpJIT.

53. "King Abdullah II Speaks about the Shia Crescent," [in Arabic], *Roya News*, January 13, 2020, https://bit.ly/3ofwyGu

54. Missile Defense Project, "Missiles of Iran," *Missile Threat*, Center for Strategic and International Studies, June 14, 2018, last modified July 16, 2020, https://bit.ly/37cKydw

55. "US to Review Troop Presence in Iraq," *Financial Times*, April 7, 2020, https://on.ft.com/2YWMZxw.

56. Mark Mazzetti and Eric Schmitt, "Pentagon Order to Plan for Escalation in Iraq Meets Warning from Top Commander," *The New York Times*, March 27, 2020, https://nyti.ms/3nD3KXI.

57. "Iranian Commander Urged Escalation Against US Forces at Iraq Meeting, Sources Say," *Reuters*, July 13, 2021, https://reut.rs/3CxYRYb.

58. Tal Beeri, "Hezbollah's 'Land of Tunnels': The North Korean-Iranian Connection," Alma Research and Education Center, July 2021, https://bit.ly/3xHGlc5.

59. "Haniyeh Thanks Iran for Supporting Hamas with 'Money, Arms, and Technologies'," [in Arabic], *An-Nahar*, May 21, 2021, https://bit.ly/3cHCXX2.

60. Ben Caspit, "Israeli Technology Exposes Gaza Attack Tunnel, Challenges Hamas," *Al-Monitor*, October 23, 2020, https://bit.ly/3e51pkG.

61. Ahmed Sake, "Following the Concrete, Why Egypt is Building a Steel Barrier Along Border with Gaza Strip?" [in Arabic], *Arabi 21*, April 29, 2020, https://bit.ly/2Yhf6XB.

62. Ali Bakeer, "US 'Maximum Pressure' on Iran is Empowering Russia in Syria," *Al-Jazeera*, May 30, 2019, https://bit.ly/38fN5nf.

63. "Iranian Militias Bring Surface-to-Surface Missiles into Syria," [in Arabic], *Elaph*, June 14, 2021, https://bit.ly/3cHV7rr.

64. "Map-Illustration... 477 Locations of Foreign Forces in Syria, Half of Which Belong to Iran and ''Hezbollah'," [in Arabic], *Enab Baladi*, January 6, 2021, https://bit.ly/2WS0SxJ.

65. "Iranian militias operating in Deir ez-Zor.. their elements.. their leaders.. their missions and subordination," [in Arabic], *Naher Media*, July 15, 2021, https://bit.ly/2Vsynq5.

66. Fabrice Balanche, "The Assad Regime Has Failed to Restore Full Sovereignty Over Syria," Policy Watch 3433, The Washington Institute for Near East Policy (WINEP), February 10, 2021.

67. "Iranian Militias Bring Surface-to-Surface Missiles into Syria," [in Arabic], *Elaph*, June 14, 2021, https://bit.ly/3cHV7rr.

68. Ido Yahel, "Iran in Syria: From Expansion to Entrenchment," Moshe Dayan Center for Middle Eastern and African Studies, June 17, 2021, https://bit.ly/3BWPDEm.

69. Avi Melamed, "A Growing Whirlpool of Violence: The Middle East Legacy of Barack Obama", January 17, 2017 https://bit.ly/3ack5OS

70. Avi Melamed, "A Prediction Materialized: Iranian Proxy Vows to "Fight to Liberate the Golan Heights", March 14,2017 https://bit.ly/2OsXXHD

71. Seth J. Frantzman, "Iran Vows to Liberate Golan Heights From Israel", *The Jerusalem Post*, October 28, 2020 https://bit.ly/3aWVH37

72. Iran's President Vows to Continue Supporting Syria", *AP News*, December 8, 2020 https://bit.ly/3qmdWWg

73. Ben Caspit, "Iran Seems to Reconsider Military Entrenchment in Syria," *Al-Monitor*, May 5, 2020, https://bit.ly/2YJYh8d.

74. Alex Fishman, "Stop Boasting, Iran has not Left Syria," *YnetNews*, May 6, 2020, https://www.ynetnews.com/article/ry8M8ZlqI.

75. "Israel Behind Cyberattack that Caused 'Total Disarray' at Iran Port – Report," *The Times of Israel*, May 19, 2020, https://bit.ly/2OIINOK

76. Judah Ari Gross, "Report: Israeli Cyberattack Caused Iran Nuclear Site Fire, F35s Hit Missile Base," *The Times of Israel*, July 3, 2020, https://bit.ly/3f8hzcr. https://bit.ly/3f8hzcr

77. "Iran Says Sabotage Caused Explosion at Natanz Nuclear Site," *Al Jazeera*, August 23, 2020, https://bit.ly/36s8MAU.

78. Iran's Top Nuclear Scientist Killed in Ambush State Media Say", *The New York Times*, November 27, 2020 https://nyti.ms/2KO62W8

79. Farnaz Fassihi and Ronen Bergman, "Iran Atomic Agency Says It Thwarted Attack on a Facility," *The New York Times*, June 23, 2021, https://www.nytimes.com/2021/06/23/world/middleeast/iran-atomic-agency-attack.html.

80. Ashraf Al-Falahi, "Houthi Threatens to Attack Israeli Targets in the Red Sea", *Arabi 21*, December 27, 2020 https://bit.ly/3aN42I7

81. Aurora Intel, "Report: Israel Has Been Attacking Iranian Tankers Since 2019," *The Maritime Executive*, March 12, 2021, https://bit.ly/3lEwfGk.

82. "Iran's Khamenei Denounces Israel as 'Tumor' that will be Eliminated", *The Times of India*, May 22. 2020 https://bit.ly/37aPNdx

83. Meir Elran, Carmit Padan, "Chief-of-Staff Aviv Kochavi on War and National Resilience", January 14, 2020, Institute for National Security Studies (INSS) https://bit.ly/3aIb7YF

84. "Iran Population," Worldometer, accessed January 1, 2021 https://bit.ly/2NxsPXb

85. Amir Taheri, "Iran – A National Uprising analysis", [in Arabic], *Al-Sharq al-Awsat*, January 12, 2108 https://bit.ly/2MGdgfD

86. "U.S. Views Election of Iran's Raisi as 'Pretty Manufactured'," *Reuters*, June 21, 2021, https://reut.rs/3x37QwY.

87. "Iran: Ebrahim Raisi Must Be Investigated for Crimes Against Humanity," Amnesty International, June 19, 2021, https://bit.ly/35P6kCV.

88. Michaela Abrams, "Iran's Water Crisis: Where to Begin?" *Iran Wire*, July 27, 2021, https://iranwire.com/en/blogs/1292/10020.

89. "A Year On Hezbollah Says Iran 'Doesn't Need Help' Avenging its Top General", January 3, 2021, *Times of Israel* https://bit.ly/3piD1Qv.

90. Maen Albayari, "Khaled Mashal on 'Al Arabiya'," [in Arabic], *The New Arab*, July 6, 2021, https://bit.ly/3dN1Ssx.

91. Sawsan al-Sha'er, "'Stay out, Iran!' Is the Motto of the Next Era," [in Arabic], *Asharq Al-Awsat*, October 6, 2019, https://bit.ly/2Wa6roD.

92. Farouk Yousuf, "Iran is a Cancer to be Eradicated, not Dialogued with," [in Arabic], *JBC News*, February 19, 2020, https://bit.ly/2uet53S.

93. Sulaiman Gouda, "Ambitions Lie in Wait on Borders with Cairo and Riyadh!" [in Arabic], *Asharq Al-Awsat*, December 5, 2019, https://bit.ly/3641pvR; Khattar Abo Diab, "Iranian Confusion after the Performance in Response to Solaimani's Killing," [in Arabic], *Middle East Transparent*, January 12, 2020, https://bit.ly/2NxOJGT; Yousuf Al-Dini, "From Syria

and Iraq to Lebanon: The Mullahs' Collapsed Walls," [in Arabic], *Asharq Al-Awsat*, October 22, 2019, https://bit.ly/2qB2xb7.https://bit.ly/3641pvR; https://bit.ly/2NxOJGT; https://bit.ly/2qB2xb7.

94. Ali Anouzla, "Iran's Gains and Arab Losses," [in Arabic], *The New Arab*, April 14, 2021, https://bit.ly/3g682FE.

95. "China Proposes Multilateral Dialogue Platform in the Middle East," [in Arabic], *Elaph*, October 11, 2020, https://bit.ly/3ktNKHh.

96. "A Source Close to Rouhani: China is not Interested in Resistance," [in Arabic], *Asharq Al-Awsat*, March 30, 2021, https://bit.ly/3dgpLI9.

97. Ibtihal Al-Khatib, "Smile for the Picture," [in Arabic], *Al-Quds Al-Arabi*, August 5, 2021, https://bit.ly/2TWCbPE.

98. "Sherman: Trump not Understanding that Iran won't Surrender," *Tehran Times*, July 29, 2018, https://bit.ly/3ffOpdy.

99. Barbara Slavin, "How the US Military Should Leave Iraq," Atlantic Council, April 23, 2020, https://bit.ly/2KXIL09

100. "Khamenei's Military Advisor Claims that Soleimani has Established 22 Regiments in Iraq and 60 in Syria", [in Arabic], January 12, 2021, *Iran International*, https://bit.ly/39vGvsX

101. Barbara Slavin, "The State of U.S.-Iran Relations: A Conversation with Barbara Slavin," *The Journal of International Affairs*, January 22, 2021, https://bit.ly/3irytqE.

102. Slavin

103. "Senators Urge Trump to Ease Iran Sanctions," *The Iran Primer*, March 27, 2020, https://bit.ly/2LSGveu..

104. Thomas Erdbrink, "US Remains the 'Great Satan,' Hard-Liners in Iran Say," *The New York Times*, September 1, 2015, https://nyti.ms/367bJ7P.

105. Andrew Hanna, "Iran's Ambitious Space Program," *The Iran Primer*, June 23, 2021, https://bit.ly/3yrdmcZ.

106. Nicholas Carl, "The Growing Iranian Threat Around the Strait of Hormuz", *Critical Threats*, September 22, 2020 https://bit.ly/3rMDvQo.

107. Iran Tests Fire Cruise Missiles Resistant to 'Electronic War' Says Naval Chief", *Defense News*, June 18, 2020 https://bit.ly/3aYShwN.

108. Farzin Nadimi, "Iran Applies Maximum Power to Annual IRGC Exercise", The Washington Institute for Near East Policy, August 10, 2020 https://bit.ly/3rHhIJY.

109. Farzin Nadimi, "Iran Flaunts New Missile and Jet Engine Technology", The Washington Institute for Near East Policy, August 28, 2020 https://bit.ly/3qk4FxH.

110. Maziar Motamedi, "Iran Holds Fifth Military Drill in Two Weeks Amid Tension With US," *AlJazeera*, January 19, 2021, https://bit.ly/2VFnXU0.

111. Turak, "'Only Countries Making Bombs."

112. 'Iran Has Drones With 7,000km Range, Says IRGC Leader," *The National News*, June 27, 2021, https://bit.ly/3hfciCo.

113. Joe Saballa, "Iran Unveils New Weapons, Equipment," *The Defense Post*, July 9, 2021, https://bit.ly/2VFnEsk.

114. "Iran: Overview," Corona Virus Resource Center, Johns Hopkins University, accessed August 1, 2021, https://coronavirus.jhu.edu/region/iran.

115. "Over 30,000 Covid Deaths In Tehran Cast Doubt On Iran's Official Numbers," *Iran International*, May 26, 2021, https://bit.ly/2WEUDh6; Uzi Rubin, "Iran's Space Program," The Jerusalem Institute for Strategy and Security, September 10, 2020, https://bit.ly/3yhDWFp; Zhanna Malekos Smith, "Iran's Space Program and the Wall Between 'Peaceful Purposes'," Center for Strategic & International Studies, October 1, 2020, https://bit.ly/389dUcK; Andrew Hanna, "Iran's Ambitious Space Program," *The Iran Primer*, June 23, 2020, https://bit.ly/2XMEmqw

116. Munqith Dagher, "The Iranian Islamic Revolutionary Guards (IRGC) from an Iraqi View- A Lost Roe or A Bright Future?", July 30, 2020 Center for Strategic and International Studies (CSIS) https://bit.ly/3u2EP3N

117. "Exclusive: IRGC Uses Iran's Central Bank Currency System to Fund Regional Proxies", December 11, 2020 Iran International https://bit.ly/2OyGm18.

118. "A Senior Commander of the IRGC: We Have Spent Seventeen Billion Dollars on our 'Defensive and Cultural Activities' in the Region", [in Arabic], January 3, 2021, *Iran International*, https://bit.ly/3piVfRE

119. David Adesnik, "Iran Spends $16 Billion Annually to Support Terrorists and Rogue Regimes," Foundation for Defense of Democracies, January 10, 2018, https://bit.ly/3kCFdBT.

120. US Mission Italy, "Secretary of State Pompeo on Supporting Iranian Voices," US Embassy & Consulates in Italy, July 22, 2018, https://bit.ly/3u3IXQT.

121. "This is How the US Moniotrs Hezbollah's Income Sources in Lebanon", [in Arabic], May 23, 2019 *JBC News*, https://bit.ly/3rYp8bE

122. Ibtahim Bayram, "Hezbollah's Financial Stress surfaces Nasrallah Says 'Trump is Sturving Us'", [in Arabic], *Beirut Observer*, February 28, 2019 https://bit.ly/3anXAXz

123. "Antony Blinken on Iran," *The Iran Primer*, Updated June 25, 2021, https://bit.ly/3sYuBkD.

124. "G7 leaders, NATO Members Vow to Prevent Iran from Getting Nuclear Weapons," *The Times of Israel*, June 15, 2021, https://bit.ly/3jiObVB.

125. Jacob Magid and Lazar Berman, "Austin tells Bennett: We'll Make Sure Israel Can Defend Itself against Iran," *The Times of Israel*, August 26, 2021, https://bit.ly/2Y1DwGF.

126. Mina al-Oraibi, "Al Kazemi in Washington… After a US Failure in the Security Council," [in Arabic], *Asharq Al-Awsat*, August 18, 2020, https://bit.ly/313GOIw; Tagel-Din Adel-Haq, "Hits to the Saudi Oil Installations: What is next? [in Arabic], *Eram News*, September 16, 2019, https://bit.ly/2kJxk2T; Abdulrahman Alrashed, "Iran is a Bigger Dilemma than Saudi Arabia ," [in Arabic], *Asharq Al-Awsat*, September 19, 2019, https://bit.ly/2mhAFq3; Salman Aldosery, "The solution with Iran," [in Arabic], *Asharq al-Awsat*, September 19, 2019, https://bit.ly/2mpJfDp; Muthana Abdullah, "Has bombing Iran from the inside started?" [in Arabic], *Arabi 21*, July 21, 2020, https://bit.ly/3eKzAMX.

127. "Saudi King's Annual Address: World Leaders Must Take Decisive Stance Against Iran," *The National News*, November 12, 2020, https://bit.ly/3xsRv53.

128. Susan Heavy, "No Sign Yet Iran Will Take Steps Needed to Remove Sanctions -U.S.'S Blinken," *Reuters*, May 23, 2021, https://reut.rs/3qrGZID.

129. "G7 Leaders, NATO Members Vow to Prevent Iran from Getting Nuclear Weapons," *The Times of Israel*, June 15, 2021, https://bit.ly/3xnu7p7.

130. Salem Al-Ketbi, "Hezbollah and the Abduction of Lebanon," [in Arabic], *Elaph*, June 14, 2021, https://bit.ly/35kjYNV.

Chapter 3

1. "US Lawsuit Against Qatar Islamic Bank Reveals Turkish Charity IHH's Link to Terrorist Groups", September 18, 2020 *Nordic Monitor*, https://bit.ly/3d9SDmM.

2. "Turkey Stays at the Gulf of Aden Despite Reconciliation with Saudi Arabia", [in Arabic], January 26, 2021 *Al- Arab*, https://bit.ly/2Yc8UPD.

3. Burak Bekdil, "Jihadis Are Becoming Turkey's Permanent Proxy Force," Begin-Sadat Center for Strategic Studies, March 31, 2021, https://bit.ly/3fGwEEv.

4. Hussein Abdul Aziz, "Where is the Free Syrian Army heading to?" [in Arabic], April 28, 2018 *Arabi 21*, https://bit.ly/39Ys81y.

5. Dr. Hay Eitan Cohen Yanrocak, and Dr. Jonathan Spyer "Turkish Militias and Proxies", January 27, 2021 The Jerusalem Institute for Strategy and Security (JISS) https://bit.ly/3tWAsXN.

6. Kübra Kara, "Turkey to Send 10 Truckloads of Aid to Gaza," *Anadolu Agency*, June 16, 2021, https://bit.ly/38edulq; "TİKA Provides Food Aid to 14,500 Families in Palestine During Ramadan," *Relief Web*, April 24, 2021, https://bit.ly/3BeEgpZ.

7. Furkan Abdula, "Only Turkey Can Protect Palestinian Children from Israel: Albanian Journalist," *Anadolu Agency*, May 14, 2021, https://bit.ly/3BGPGU3.

8. "Hamas Expands its Military Activities in Turkey by Setting Up Training Camps for its Members," [in Arabic], *Beirut Observer*, February 23, 2015, https://bit.ly/3gIWND5.

9. Raul Redondo, "Qatar Could Have Financed Hezbollah in Lebanon", July 19, 2020 *Atalayar*, https://bit.ly/3ahNTd3.

10. Meliha Benli Altunışık, "The End of The Gulf Rift May Not Signal The End of Turkey-Qatar Relations," Atlantic Council, April 5, 2021, https://bit.ly/3s6vyXO.

11. Esraa Ahmed Fuad," Turkish Occupation of Qatar. The Full Story of Tamim's Great Treason; Al-Hamdeen Organization Hands Erdogan the Keys to Doha; The Terror Prince Hosts 6,000 Soldiers in 'Rayyan' and 'Tariq' Bases to Protect Him. And the Result: An Occupied Emirate; A Loophole in Gulf Security," [in Arabic], *Youm7*, January 30, 2020, https://bit.ly/36xSiW4.

12. Hay Eitan Cohen Yanrocak, and Jonathan Spyer, Ibid, https://bit.ly/3alFu74

13. Altunışık, ""End of The Gulf Rift."

14. "Erdogan: Our Military Presence in Qatar Serves Stability in the Gulf Region," [in Arabic], *Al Modon*, October 8, 2020, https://bit.ly/2SyPQZ3.

15. "Cautious Turkish Moves."; "Southern Transitional Council Aborts Muslim Brotherhood Plans in Socotra," [in Arabic], *Alarab UK*, June 20, 2020, https://bit.ly/2YVH35V.

16. 'Alla 'Adel hansh, "What are the Similarities Between Shabwa's Port and Misrata Lybian Port"?, [in Arabic], November 10, 2020, *Al-Umanan*, https://bit.ly/3poy6NT

17. "An Agreement Signed by Shabwa's Governor Breaking the Siege Angers Saudi Arbia",[in Arabic], November 10, 2020 https://bit.ly/2OA2ech

18. "Saudi Arabia resentful with The Governor of Shabwah for Signing an Agreement Breaking the Coalition Siege", [in Arabic], November 10, 2020 *Al Awal Press*, https://bit.ly/3qm01z9 'Alla Adl Hanesh, "Qana Port in Shabwah – a pan of the Muslim Brotherhood to Establish a Special Region – Similarities between the Shabwah's Port and Misrata Libyan Port", [in Arabic], *Al-Omana*, November 10, 2020 https://bit.ly/3tWAP4D 'Alla Adl Hanesh, "Qana

Port in Shabwah – a pan of the Muslim Brotherhood to Establish a Special Region – Similarities between the Shabwah's Port and Misrata Libyan Port ", [in Arabic], *Al-Omana*, November 10, 2020 https://bit.ly/3tWAP4D. "Turkey Remains in the Gulf of Aden Despite the Truce with Saudi Arabia," [in Arabic], *Alarab UK*, January 26, 2021, https://bit.ly/3iYsY1z; "Breaking News: Shabwa Governor Breaks the Coalition-Imposed Siege by signing an Agreement that provokes Saudi Discontent (Detailed)," [in Arabic], *Alawal Press*, November 10, 2020, https://bit.ly/3t1CPIF; Alaa Adel Hanash, "Documented: "Ben Adyo" Signs an Agreement with Al-Essa to Establish a Sea Port," [in Arabic], *Al-Omana*, November 10, 2020, https://bit.ly/3jxBaaY.

19. "Cautious Turkish Moves to Secure a Position on the Yemeni Coasts," [in Arabic], *Alarab UK*, May 9, 2020, https://bit.ly/3fA3NzV.

20. Peter Fabricius, "Is Turkey's Expanding African Footprint Also a Proxy Battleground for Erdoğan's Middle East and European Rivalries?" Institute for Security Studies, March 12, 2021, https://bit.ly/2VoqeTO

21. Fabricius.

22. Harun Maruf, "Somalia Readies for Oil Exploration, Still Working on Petroleum Law", February 13, 2019 *Voa News*, https://bit.ly/3jN7p44.

23. Henri J. Barkey, "Turkey's Engagement with Somalia Offers a Window Into Its Strategy to Build Influence", January 27, 2021 *Times Now News*, https://bit.ly/2Or7ZZO

24. Ahmed Askar, Ibid

25. Carlos Lopes (@LopesInsights), "Turkish footprint in Africa is getting larger," Twitter, March 56, 2021, 12:32 a.m., https://bit.ly/3lEChXy.

26. Joseph V. Micallef, "The Geopolitics of Mediterranean Natural Gas," *Military News*, April 16, 2021, https://bit.ly/3A6gls4

27. Pat Davis Szymczak, "Chevron to Drill More Wells Sooner on Israel's Leviathan as East Med Gas Demand Soars," *Journal of Petroleum Technology*, July 19, 2021, https://bit.ly/38uW6c2.

28. "The Deal is Completed: Energy Giant Chevron Purchased Noble Energy." [in Hebrew], *ICE*, October 6, 2020, https://bit.ly/3sboEjk

29. Jennifer Hiller and Ron Bousso, "Chevron Bets on Middle East Gas Riches and Reconciliation," *Yahoo News*, October 26, 2020, https://yhoo.it/35J0jHt.

30. Jennifer Hiller and Ron Bousso, "Chevron Bets on Middle East Gas Riches and Reconciliation," *Yahoo News*, October 26, 2020, https://yhoo.it/35J0jHt.

31. Yaseen Al-Gohary, "Egyptian Zahr field: Huge Production Rate and Promising Investments," [in Arabic], *Sky News Arabia*, December 15, 2019, https://bit.ly/35VbVXi.

32. Yaacov Benmeleh, "Chevron to Invest in Pipelines to Send Israeli Gas to Egypt", January 19, 2021 *Bloomberg*, https://bloom.bg/3oGfY1P.

33. "US' Chevron Eyes New Investments in Egypt," *Zawya*, accessed August 30, 2021, https://bit.ly/3gNUleR.

34. Michael Harari, "Chevron's Regional Responsibility," *Globes*, July 5, 2021, https://bit.ly/3rWL9sV.

35. Ministry Of Foreign Affairs Egypt, "Joint Statement,"[in Arabic], Facebook, May 11, 2020, https://www.facebook.com/MFAEgypt/posts/3906141406124443

36. The Associated Press, "Egypt's President Signs Strategic Maritime Deal with Greece," *Yahoo News*, October 10, 2020, https://yhoo.it/2Fizvo8.

37. Avi Melamed, *Inside the Middle East: Making Sense of the Most Dangerous and Complicated Region on Earth* (New York: Skyhorse, 2016), 42.

38. Omar al-Murabbet, "Islamists of Morocco and Normalization…Between Clarity and Maneuvering," [in Arabic], *Al Arabi al Jadid*, December 20, 2020 https://bit.ly/2WyyT2I

39. "Saadeddine Othmani," [in Arabic], *Marefa*, accessed September 20, 2021, https://bit.ly/3z3BNNC.

40. Yasser al-Zaatreh, "About the Houthi, Hamas' imprisoned personnel, and the Yemenite Connection", [in Arabic] April 4,2020 *Arabi 21*, https://bit.ly/3ahdv9P

41. Yoni Ben Menachem, "Saudi Arabia Acts Against Hamas Terrorism," Jerusalem Center for Public Affairs, August 12, 2021, https://bit.ly/3sY2lig.

42. "Unofficial but Effective Saudi Boycott Strikes Blow at Turkey," [in Arabic], *The Arab Weekly*, October 15, 2020, https://bit.ly/2WyIWoG.

43. Yoni Ben Menachem, "Saudi Boycott on Turkey," [in Arabic], *News 1*, Octoe https://bit.ly/30TJLux

44. "Turkey, Concerned by Biden, Initiates Rapprochement with Egypt," [in Arabic], *Alarab UK*, March 4, 2021, https://bit.ly/3q9Iidu.

45. Mohamed Mghawr, "A Turkish Military Message to Egypt … Where Are Relations Going?" [in Arabic], *Arabi 21*, March 7, 2021, https://bit.ly/30nE5Za.

46. "Agreement between Jordan and Turkey for Trade and Economic Cooperation," [in Arabic], *Arabi 21*, August15, 2021, https://bit.ly/3iKtIZx.

47. Amal Abdulaziz Al–Hazani, "Dimensions of the Saudi Boycott of Turkish Goods," [in Arabic], *Asharq Al-Awsat*, October 20, 2020, https://bit.ly/2HjXJz0.

48. Ahmed Gamal. "Muslim Brotherhood Channels in Turkey Resume their Attack against Egypt after a Short Truce," *Alarab UK,* June 2, 2021, https://bit.ly/3uDfH2B.

49. Furkan Abdula, "Only Turkey Can Protect Palestinian Children from Israel: Albanian Journalist," *Anadolu Agency,* May 14, 2021, https://bit.ly/3BGPGU3.

50. "Cairo Appreciates Terminating Egyptian Media Programs in Turkey (Video)," [in Arabic], *Arabi 21,* July 4, 2021, https://bit.ly/2UktZZl.

51. Gallia Lindenstrauss and Remi Daniel, Operation Guardian of the Walls from the Turkish Perspective: Erdogan as the 'Defender of Palestine'? (INSS Insight No. 1483), June 7, 2021, https://bit.ly/3mKFsh2.

52. "The Economic Developments in Turkey at the Beginning of 2021", January 19, 2021 The Emirates Policy Center (EPC) https://bit.ly/36qFIZo

53. "Are you 'brain-dead'? Turkey's Erdogan raps Macron before NATO summit", November 29, 2019 *Reuters,* https://reut.rs/3rvSGNG

Chapter 4

1. Yossi Melman, "Israel's Little-Known Support for Haftar's War in Libya", April 15, 2020 *Middle East Eye,* https://bit.ly/3rS5MVY

2. Andreas Kluth, "Opinion: Law of the Sea Can't Solve the Greco-Turkish Island Problem," *gCaptain,* October 18, 2020, https://bit.ly/31i9U6s.

3. Joseph V. Micallef, Ibid

4. Saleh al-Qulab, "Erdogan and the Mavi Vatan and The Contol of Libya and the Engagement of Egypt," [in Arabic], *Al-Sharq al-Awsat,* January 16, 2020 https://bit.ly/2QYiwuw; "4700 Syrian Mercenaries Arrived in Tripli and 64 Flee to Europe," [in Arabic], *Al-Arabiya,* January 9, 2020 https://bit.ly/3sh661x; "Al Mismari, We Kill Turks and Erdogan Continues to Send Mercenaries to Libya," [in Arabic], *Arabi 21,* March 15, 2020, https://bit.ly/3aUBqJK.

5. "4700 Syrian Mercenaries arrived in Tripoli and 64 Flee to Europe", February 4, 2020 *Al-Arabiya* https://bit.ly/3qZoMRI.

6. Jason Pack and Wolfgang Pusztai, Turning the Tide How Turkey Won The War For Tripoli, Middle East Institute, November 2020, https://bit.ly/3jvOc8H.

7. Burak Bekdil, "Erdoğan's Libya Campaign: Another Neo-Ottoman Design", June 3 2020, Middle East Forum https://bit.ly/2N12DUR.

8. Muhammad Nabil Helmy, "Sisi Draws Red Lines for Turkey in Libya," [in Arabic], *Al Sharq al-Awsat,* October 18, 2020, https://bit.ly/2NgiNWX

9. "The War in Libya, The Government of National Accord Considers Abdel Fattah al-Sisi's Statements A Declaration of War," [in Arabic], *BBC Arabic*, June 22, 2020, https://bbc.in/3i4jAsz.

10. Dr. Hay Eitan Cohen Yanrocak, and Dr. Jonathan Spyer "Turkish Militias and Proxies", January 27, 2021 The Jerusalem Institute for Strategy and Security (JISS) https://bit.ly/39x3Ag3

11. Ahmed Askar, "Turkey's Expansion in the Sahel, the Sahara and West Africa: Motivations and Ramifications", August 24, 2020,The Emirates Policy Center (EPC) https://bit.ly/3tdFheP

12. Haftar:We will Confront Militarily Erdogan and the Turkish Occupation of Libya", [in Arabic], August 3,2020 *Al-Watan*, https://bit.ly/3rW71TJ

13. "Turkish-Egyptian understandings on Libya Behind the Scenes: Haftar is Begging for UAE and Russia Support for One of his Sons as the President," [in Arabic], *The New Arab*, May 4, 2021, https://bit.ly/3b3Osau; "Egypt Turns Haftar from a Major Ally into a Card when Necessary,"[in Arabic], *Alarab UK*, July 6, 2021, https://bit.ly/3AveyOA.

14. "Libya Repeats Demands to Turkey to Withdraw Its Mercenaries out of Libyan Land," [in Arabic], *Al Sharq al-Awsat*, May 4, 2021, https://bit.ly/3nJ5SON.

15. Multi-Billion-Dollar Reconstruction Projects Await in Post-War Libya," *France 24*, August 15, 2021, https://bit.ly/3BGDxhE; "Libya PM Plans to Establish Funds for Reconstruction," *Anadolu Agency*, April 28, 2021, https://bit.ly/2YnKLZw; Francesca Ebel, "Libya: Hopes for Reconstruction Boom Clash with Reality on the Ground," *Middle East Eye*, July 3, 2021, https://bit.ly/3DNSGQl; "Rebuilding Libya will Cost Nearly Half a Trillion Dollars," *Libyan Express*, March 22, 2021, https://bit.ly/3n8y6UA. $450 Billion," *Libya Consultancy*, March 23, 2021, https://www.libyaconsultancy.com/news/libyas-reconstruction-to-cost-450-billion/

16. Tayfun Ozberk, "Egypt Inaugurates a New Naval Base Near The Libyan Border," *Naval News*, July 7, 2021, https://bit.ly/3mVBguK.

17. Dan De Luce, "Nearly a Decade after Benghazi, the U.S. is Quietly Returning to Libya," *NBC News*, May 27, 2021, https://nbcnews.to/3yxRAow.

18. Rym Momtaz, "Macron Pitches Biden on Plan to Get foreign Fighters out of Libya," *Politico*, June 16, 2021, https://politi.co/3fDWvNp.

19. Rasheed Khashana, "Comprehensive Political Dialogue Forum: Saleh to Head the Presidency Council, Bashaga to Head the Government, and Elections Within 18 Months," [in Arabic], *Al-Quds al-Arabi*, November 7, 2020, https://bit.ly/2Iflida

20. Hoda al-Husseini, "The Real Face of the Gulf in Abu Dhabi Forum," [in Arabic], *Al-Sharq al-Awsat*, November 23, 2017, https://bit.ly/358dn9H.

Chapter 5

1. Emad El-Din Adib, "Some of us are More Unjust than 'Infidels of Quraish'!" [in Arabic], *Elaph*, August 22, 2020, https://bit.ly/37BiZuR.

2. FAO, IFAD, UNICEF, WFP, WHO and ESCWA, Near East and North Africa Regional Overview of Food Security and Nutrition (Cairo: FAO, 2020), https://bit.ly/3xvjXmb.

3. "Chapter 3: Agriculture and Water Sector," Arab Monetary Fund, accessed September 6, 2021, https://bit.ly/3mRezZ1.

4. Abdullah bin Bakhit, "Vision Should Rise Above the Sound of the Battle," [in Arabic], *Elaph,* June 20, 2019, https://bit.ly/3b7mCqU.

5. Saleh al-Qulab, "The Houthis Do Not Decide," [in Arabic], *Elaph*, July 14, 2020, https://bit.ly/3bb8C0b.

6. Magdi Khalil (@magdi_khalil), "What is Arabization?" [in Arabic], Twitter, April 26, 2020, 10:13 p.m., https://twitter.com/magdi_khalil/status/1254503988264947714?s=20.

7. Chaima Safi, "'The End' Series Screenwriter: Liberating Jerusalem is the Dream of Every Arab," [in Arabic], *Elaph*, April 28, 2020, https://bit.ly/2WRJiGr.

8. Abdel-Monem Sa'id, "The New Middle East," [in Arabic], *Asharq Al-Awsat*, August 22, 2018, https://bit.ly/2wgNCBS.

9. Khairallah Khairallah, "In Absence of Courage, Lebanon is on the Edge of a Precipice!" [in Arabic], *Alarab UK*, March 27, 2020, https://bit.ly/2yfle6O.

10. Maha Mohammed Alsharif, "Iran and Wreaking Havoc in the Arab World," [in Arabic], *Asharq Al-Awsat*, June 15, 2021, https://bit.ly/35n0OqM.

11. Melamed, *Inside the Middle East*, 42.

12. The Concluding Statement of Al-Nahda 10th Conference", [in Arabic] May 2016, https://bit.ly/2Zfqx1w

13. Hasan Salman, "Against the Background of power struggle over its Leadership Tunisian Al-Nahda Party Postpones its planned Conference", [in Arabic] November 16, 2020, *Al-Quds*, https://bit.ly/3nuzyxF

14. "The Islamic Group in Lebanon Presents its new Pact", [in Arabic], *JBC News*, May 14, 2017 https://bit.ly/2LsOpeA

15. Mohammed Al-Arsan, "The Islamic Movement in Jordan Introduces its Political Pact", June 17, 2019 *Arabi 21* https://bit.ly/3aYJJ9e

16. Omar al-Murabbet, "Islamists of Morocco and Normalization...Between Clarity and Maneuvering," [in Arabic], *Al Arabi al Jadid*, December 20, 2020 https://bit.ly/2WyyT2I

17. "Libya: Muslim Brotherhood Turns into 'Revival and Renewal' NGO," [in Arabic], *JBC News*, May 3, 2021, https://bit.ly/3gXtJsII

18. Adam Jezard, "Who and What is 'Civil Society?'," *World Economic Forum*, April 23, 2018, https://bit.ly/3rWUSzp.

19. "Civil Society Involvement in Drug Policy," Civil Society Involvement in Drug Policy, accessed August 30, 2021, https://csidp.eu/definitions/.

20. "Our Mission," Lawyers for Justice in Libya, accessed August 6, 2021, https://bit.ly/3ioUF4J.

21. "Selection of Libya's Interim Executive Authorities: LPDF Must Prioritise Human Rights, Justice and Accountability," Lawyers for Justice in Libya, February 1, 2021, https://bit.ly/3ip6WGq.

22. "The 20 List: Libyan Women You Must Know," Together We Build It Organization, accessed August 6, 2021, https://bit.ly/2X4QRNV.

23. "Landmark resolution on Women, Peace and Security," Office of the Special Adviser on Gender Issues and Advancement of Women, United Nations, October 31, 2000, https://bit.ly/37EERox.

24. "About Us," Together We Build It Organization, accessed August 6, 2021, https://bit.ly/3julVOL.

25. Aisha Jaffar, "Female Recruits in the Saudi Army for the First Time," [in Arabic], *Ashaq Al-Awsat*, October 3, 2019, https://bit.ly/3yxc2p3.

26. Natasha Turak, "Saudi Arabia Announces Major Legal Reforms, Paving the Way for Codified Law," *CNBC*, February 9, 2021, https://cnb.cx/3CmnhUj.

27. "Lebanon: Sexual Harassment Law Missing Key Protections," *Human Rights Watch*, March 5, 2021, https://bit.ly/3fkrXAd

28. "Egypt's New Amendments for Sexual Harassment Law Ends Different Forms of Violence against Women: UN Resident Coordinator," *Egypt Today*, August 19, 2021, https://bit.ly/3ky99yY.

29. Reem Leila, "Egypt's Railways: Safe Travels for Women," *Ahram Online*, January 15, 2021, https://bit.ly/3dbbXjQ.

30. "'Contrary to Nature': Lebanon Refuses to Pledge to Protect Gay Rights," [in Arabic], *Alhurra*, November 22, 2020, https://arbne.ws/3jbYwBk.

31. "Egypt's Railways."

32. Safwan Masri, "In The Arab Spring's Aftermath: An Emergent LGBTQ+ Movement?" at *The Brown Journal of World Affairs*, Fall/Winter 2020, xxvii, https://bit.ly/2NwwNiC

33. "First LGBT+ Organization Might be Set up in Kuwait, People Are Angry!,"*Al Bawaba*, July 10, 2019, https://bit.ly/2WyNRce.

34. "LGBT Rights in Lebanon," Equaldex, accessed September 3, 2021, https://bit.ly/3BM2Ejk.

35. Fatima Alsalem, "53% of Kuwaiti Women are Abused by Men," *AlQabas*, November 24, 2018, https://alqabas.com/article/607181.

36. Aljamey Kasimi and Mohamed Mamony Alalawy, "Moroccan King Pushes towards a Social Development Revolution in the Country," [in Arabic], *Alarab UK*, August 22, 2020, https://bit.ly/2LBToX2.

37. "The World Bank in Jordan: Overview," The World Bank, accessed August 6, 2021, https://bit.ly/3xujtfV.

38. "Jordan Economic Monitor: Uncertain and Long Trail Ahead," World Bank Group, Spring 2021, https://bit.ly/3howxi8.

39. "Prince Hamzah's Crisis and the Governing Impasse in Jordan," [in Arabic], *The New Arab*, April 8, 2021, https://bit.ly/3xqUpHr.

40. Melamed, *Inside the Middle East*, 166-167.

41. Daoud Kuttab, "Jordan to Become a Full Democracy within a Decade," *The Jerusalem Post*, August 6, 2021, https://bit.ly/3kB7vNh.

42. Jörg Gertel and Ralf Hexel, eds., *Coping with Uncertainty: Youth in the Middle East and North Africa* (London: Saqi Books, 2018), https://bit.ly/3gBWQ2Y.

43. Khawla Tomaleh, "The New Spiritualism: Would it steal Ramadan from Us?" [in Arabic], *Arabi 21*, April 17, 2021, https://bit.ly/3svJTLH.

44. Dr. Amal Moussa, "It is Rather the Second Nation State," [in Arabic], *Al-Sharq Al-Awsat*, July 17, 2020, https://bit.ly/2Wqkd6k.

45. Mohamed Hnid, "Tunisia: Struggle of Depth and Revolution," [in Arabic], *Arabi 21*, April 22, 2021, https://bit.ly/3tOibeQ.

46. "Officially In Video: A Landslide Victory for Sisi in the Egyptian Presidential Elections," [in Arabic], *JBC News*, April 2, 2018, https://bit.ly/3jlucp8.

47. "Egypt Announces the Results of the Constitutional Amendments Vote," [in Arabic], *Maan News*, April 23, 2019, https://www.maannews.net/news/982373.html.

48. Amr Mohamed Kandil, "6-year construction: housing projects executed under Egypt's El Sisi," *Egypt Today*, June 8, 2020, https://bit.ly/3zrEuJZ.

49. "Egypt Needs Civil Society Organizations, Economic Reform and Job Creation Inevitable: President Sisi," *Ahram Online*, August 14, 2021, https://bit.ly/2Yd7Del.

50. "Egypt's New Amendments for Sexual Harassment."

51. Abbas Maymoni, "Algeria: Why the "Society for Peace Movement" Refused to Participate in the Government (An Analysis)," [in Arabic], *Anadolu Agency*, June 30, 2021, https://bit.ly/3iribhv.

52. "Algeria Election Gets Low Turnout Amid Opposition Boycott," *Deutsche Welle*, June 13, 2021, https://bit.ly/38HXA2H.

53. Khairallah Khairallah, "Alarm Bell in Algeria," *JBC News*, November 4, 2020, https://bit.ly/3k3KP5L; Khalil Ibn Eldin, "Algeria and the de Facto Constitution," [in Arabic], *Al Araby Al Jadeed*, November 5, 2020; https://bit.ly/32wemzt.

54. Jewish Telegraphic Agency, "Sudan-Israel Announce Normalization," *Intermountain Jewish News*, October 29, 2020, https://bit.ly/3u2S4RV.

55. Abbey Ryan, "Sudan Rejoining The International Community," Organization of World Peace, July 10, 2021, https://bit.ly/3xEC3IT.

56. Basma Barakat, "In the House of Bouazizi's Grandfather, Mohamed's Cart is All That Remains," [in Arabic], *The New Arab*, January 14, 2021, https://bit.ly/3jbpzN7.

57. Kamal Ben Yonus, "Tunisia's Islamists and Organizational Democracy: A Quiet Review 1 of 2," [in Arabic], *Arabi 21*, November 16, 2020, https://bit.ly/3kCvWYs; Hassan Salman, "Tunisian 'Ennahda' Postpones its Next Conference, Amid Disagreements over the Movement's Presidency," [in Arabic], *Al-Quds Al-Arabi*, November 16, 2020, https://bit.ly/3nuzyxF

58. UNDP and International IDEA, The Constitution of the Tunisian Republic, adopted January 26, 2014, accessed August 30, 2021, https://bit.ly/38pcGu5.

59. Abdulrahman Yousuf, "The Road to the Gallows," [in Arabic], *Arabi 21*, August 1, 2021, https://bit.ly/3xi3XUt

60. "Ghannouchi: We Received the People's Message and are Ready to Sacrifice," [in Arabic], *Arabi 21*, August 11, 2021, https://bit.ly/3lTqPYb.

61. Dr. Amal Moussa, "It is Rather the Second Nation State," [in Arabic], *Al-Sharq Al-Awsat*, July 17, 2020, https://bit.ly/2Wqkd6k.

62. Mohammed Ahmad Bennis, "The Arab Spring and the Rule of Societies", [in Arabic] Jnauary21, 2021 *Al Arabi Al Jadid* https://bit.ly/3jIOEz0.

Chapter 6

1. "Syria Worst Man-Made Disaster since World War II – Zeid," Office of High Commissioner of Human Rights, March 14, 2017, https://bit.ly/37l5X4a.

2. Ali Bakeer, "US 'Maximum Pressure' on Iran is Empowering Russia in Syria," *Al Jazeera*, May 30, 2019, https://bit.ly/38fN5nf.

3. Bakeer, "US 'Maximum Pressure' on Iran." Thomas Schaffner, "Five Years After Russia Declared Victory in Syria: What Has Been Won?," *Russia Matters*, March 18, 2021, https://bit.ly/3sJOwnc; "Cost of Russia's Syrian Campaign Revealed as $480 Million," *The Moscow Times*, March 17, 2016, https://bit.ly/2UN1VP1

4. "The 'Assassination War' Continues... A Raging Conflict between Russia and Iran in Southern Syria!" [in Arabic], *Janoubia*, September 3, 2020, https://bit.ly/3gS8eWl; Ibrahim Hemaidy, "Two Years after the Southern Deal: A Worrisome Model for 'Future Syria'," [in Arabic], *Asharq Al-Awsat*, September 29, 2020, https://bit.ly/2Gp1QJv; "Unprecedented Tension in Daraa: Iranian-Russian Conflict under Ashes," [in Arabic], *JBC News*, November 9, 2020, https://bit.ly/2JG2WlR.

5. Ghassan Ibrahim, "The Conflict among Yesterday's Allies in Eastern Syria," [in Arabic], *Al-Arab UK*, April 24, 2021, https://bit.ly/3ew8ZoQ.

6. "Under the Microscope | Russia Mobilizes the 8th Brigade on the Fronts of the Deir ez-Zor Desert: Motives and Consequences," [in Arabic], Jusoor for Studies, April 28, 2021, https://bit.ly/3o06b7V

7. Melamed, *Inside the Middle East*, pp159-160

8. "After the Map with the 37 Locations, What does Turkey Want from Iraq?", [in Arabic], *Sky New Arabia*, July 9, 2020, https://bit.ly/3wweZ8a.

9. Dr. Hay Eitan Cohen Yanrocak, and Dr. Jonathan Spyer "Turkish Militias and Proxies".

10. Reuters, "Turkey Destroys Scores of Syrian Army Targets, Says Turkish Defense Minister," *The Moscow Times*, March 2, 2020, https://bit.ly/3bWP28h.

11. Saber Kul Anbari, "Iran's Approach to the Turkish Operation in Eastern Euphrates," [in Arabic], *Arabi 21*, October 12, 2019, https://bit.ly/2Mep6e5.

12. Abdullah ibn Begad Alotaiby, "Syria... Realistic Solutions and System Rehabilitation," [in Arabic], *Asharq Al- Awsat*, December 30, 2018, https://bit.ly/2CG69Mk; Sawsan Al-Sahaer, "To Protect our Interests, not Protect the Regime," [in Arabic], *Asharq Al-Awsat*, December 30, 2018, https://bit.ly/2Tg06n6; Ahmed Shantaf, "How will Hariri Deal with Syria? And What Worries Hezbollah?" [in Arabic], *Janoubia*, December 29, 2018, https://

bit.ly/2Vjs6s4; Mohamed Al-Dolimy, "Relations Must Continue with Damascus, Whatever the Hardships," [in Arabic], *Elaph*, December 30. 2018, https://bit.ly/3lyFBkg.

13. Saeid Abdel-Raziq, "The First Gulf AmbAssadAssadAssadAssadAssadAssadal-Assadal-Al-Assadal-Al-Al-Assador to Damascus since 2011," [in Arabic], *Asharq Al-Awsat*, October 5, 2020, https://bit.ly/36zZa72.

14. Ahmed Gomaa, "Egypt, UAE Call for Rethink of Syria's Expulsion from Arab League," *Al-Monitor*, March 15, 2021, https://bit.ly/3jdrCl9.

15. "Newspaper: A Saudi Delegation Meets Al-Assad and Mamlouk In Damascus... And an Agreement to Restore Relations," [in Arabic], *RT* Online, May 3, 2021, https://bit.ly/3l-HZZCn; "A Saudi Delegation Visits Damascus and Meets President Bashar Al-Assad," [in Arabic], *JBC News*, May 4, 2021, https://bit.ly/3y0Jqp4.

16. Ramzy Ezzeldin Ramzy, "Towards an Arab Initiative to Solve the Syrian Crisis," [in Arabic], *Asharq Al-Awsat*, December 13, 2019, https://bit.ly/36u8h5Z; Farouk Youssef, "An Arab Return to Syria or a Syrian Return to the Arabs," [in Arabic], *Al-Arab*, May 8, 2021, https://bit.ly/3ha8m7q; Salem al-Ketbi, "Syrian Elections and the Way Out from the Tunnel", [in Arabic], *Elaph*, May 30, 2020, https://bit.ly/2ZyuRg9.

17. "Syrian Regime Forces Bomb a Camp for the Displaced in Idlib... Qatar and Saudi Arabia: No Room for Normalization with Al-Assad," [in Arabic], *Al-Quds Al-Arabi*, June 9, 2021, https://bit.ly/3giB8Rg.

18. "The Iraqi Foreign Minister Explains Why Al-Assad was not Invited to the 'Baghdad Conference'," [in Arabic], *JBC News*, August 26, 2021, https://bit.ly/3BmpUUL.

19. "Arab Condemnation of Turkish Aggression and Hinting Possible Downscaling of Relations," [in Arabic], *Asharq Al-Awsat*, October 13, 2019, https://bit.ly/2OHQcf2.

20. "Mahdi's Lions" . . . Iran Establishes a New Militia in Syria," [in Arabic], *Yeni Safak*, January 25, 2020, https://bit.ly/3s8CoMj; "The Syrian Region Of Lajat, Stories of Control up to Establishing Iranian Militias Bases and Competing with Russia," [in Arabic], *Iran Wire Arabic*, June 30, 2021, https://bit.ly/2VsVdy4.

21. "After Heavy Losses, Iran is Strengthening its Influence West of the Euphrates," [in Arabic], *JBC News*, March 28, 2021, https://bit.ly/31zefSJ.

22. "Tehran Changes the Streets of "Sayeda Zainab" in Damascus," [in Arabic], *Ashaq Al-Awsat*, December 20, 2020, https://bit.ly/3rcPozC.

23. Ido Yahel, "Iran in Syria: From Expansion to Entrenchment," Moshe Dayan Center for Middle Eastern and African Studies, June 17, 2021, https://bit.ly/3yvWm5o.

24. Rokayya Al Abadi and Fatima Othman, "The Mahdi Scouts: A Chronicle of Child Recruitment into Iranian Militias," *Daraj*, May 6, 2021, https://daraj.com/en/71879/; The Meir Amit Intelligence and Terrorism Information Center, The Imam Al-Mahdi Scouts Association: Hezbollah's Youth Movement Which Indoctrinates Youth with Iranian Radical Shiite Islam and Serves as a Source of Youngsters who Join Hezbollah (Tel Aviv: Israeli Intelligence Heritage And Commemoration Center, 2019), https://bit.ly/3tS7l8i.

25. Anchal Vohra, "Iran Is Trying to Convert Syria to Shiism," *Foreign Policy*, March 15, 2021, https://bit.ly/3yvWxxA.

26. Vohra, "Iran Is Trying to Convert."

27. Navvar Saban, "Factbox: Iranian presence in Syria's Deir ez-Zor province," Atlantic Council, May 18, 2021, https://bit.ly/3Aqf3sC.

28. Tamara Abueish, "Iran-Backed Groups in Syria Recruit Locals to Buy Real Estate in Deir Ezzor: Report," *Al Arabiya English*, July 25, 2021, https://bit.ly/2Yct4MC.

29. Jonathan Spyer, "Iran Digs Deep in Hollowed-Out Syria," *The Jerusalem Post*, July 1, 2021, https://bit.ly/3fIX1cR.

30. Seth J. Frantzman, "Iranian-Backed Militias in Syria are Buying up Real Estate – Report," *The Jerusalem Post*, July 25, 2021, https://bit.ly/3AncKWZ.

31. Ido Yahel, "Iran in Syria: From Expansion to Entrenchment," *Tel Aviv Notes*, 15, no. 5 (June 2021): 1-6, https://bit.ly/2Xyfrre.

32. "Tehran Changes the Streets of "Sayeda Zainab" in Damascus," [in Arabic], *Ashaq Al-Awsat*, December 20, 2020, https://bit.ly/3rcPozC

33. "Tehran Changes the Streets of "Sayeda Zainab" Ibid

34. "Iran Constructing Power Plant in Syria' Latakia," *FARS News Agency*, August 9, 2021, http://fna.ir/3313b.

35. "Syrian Prime Minister: Interception of Seven Oil Tankers Bound for Syria, and a New Deal with Iran," [in Arabic], *Iran Wire Arabic*, January 17, 2021, https://iranwirearabic.com/archives/13050.

36. Anchal Vohra, "Iran Is Trying to Convert Syria to Shiism," *Foreign Policy*, March 15, 2021, https://bit.ly/3yvWxxA.

37. Hasan Ismaik, "The West and the Syrian-Iranian Alliance: A Card That Should Be Played," *Strategiecs*, December 12, 2020, https://bit.ly/3zz9Tdt.

38. Amir Buhbut, "Senior Security Official: To Achieve Peace, Al-Assad Halts Iranian Movement in Syria," [in Hebrew], *Walla News*, July 27, 2021, https://news.walla.co.il/item/3446385.

39. Sam Mansi, "The Cherry on the Iranian Cake," [in Arabic], *Asharq Al-Awsat*, June 14, 2021, https://bit.ly/3wmXLej

40. Khairallah Khairallah, "Which Syria Can Bet on Saving?," [in Arabic], *Alarab UK*, May 7, 2021, https://bit.ly/3xVRffu.

41. Ghazi Duhman, "AL-Tatbi'e (Normalization) is Al-Assad's Bridge Towards Rule", [in Arabic] January 28, 2021 *Al Arabi Al-Jadid* https://bit.ly/3r14BmG.

42. Ghazi Duhman, "Normalization is Hafez Bashar Al-Assad's Bridge Towards Ruling," [in Arabic], *The New Arab*, January 28, 2021, https://bit.ly/3r14BmG.

43. Adli Sadiq, "Indications of Israeli Bombings of Targets in Western Syria," [in Arabic], *Alarab UK*, May 8, 2021, https://bit.ly/33offde.

44. "Reports About an Israeli – Syrian Meeting Under Russian Hospice aimed to Push Iran Out of Syria" [in Arabic] January 17, 2021 *Al-Sharq al-Awsat* https://bit.ly/3dg0csp.

45. Ibrahim Al-Jabeen, "Damascus and the Next Deal of the Century," [in Arabic], *JBC News*, July 6, 2021, https://bit.ly/2VdxwZZ.

46. "Caesar Syria Civilian Protection Act," Office of the Spokesperson, US Dept of State, June 17, 2020, https://bit.ly/37msL3p.

47. Galia Lavi, "China and the Middle East: The Israeli-Palestinian Conflict on the Agenda," Institute for National Strategic Studies, August 18, 2021, https://bit.ly/3jeePik; Ian Williams, "China's Belt and Road to Damascus," *The Spectator*, July 24, 2021, https://bit.ly/3mA4csb; Sean Mathews, "Will China Save Syria's Economy after Years of Bloodshed and Turmoil?," *Middle East Eye*, August 3, 2021, https://bit.ly/3zjLIzC; "Foreign Ministry Spokesperson Zhao Lijian's Regular Press Conference on July 19, 2021," Ministry of Foreign Affairs of the People's Republic of China, July 19, 2021, https://bit.ly/3gsEMZS; "Syria Receives 150,000 Doses of Chinese COVID-19 Vaccines," *Xinhua Net*, July 30, 2021, https://bit.ly/3gtneMU; Samy Akil, "Why China Will Not Rebuild Syria," *East Asia Forum*, May 8, 2021, https://bit.ly/3jefksI.

48. Melamed, *Inside the Middle East.*

49. On the 9th Anniversary of the Popular Movement: Documenting the Killing of 226,247 Civilians (Syrian Network for Human Rights, 2020), https://bit.ly/3hNWDe9; Ibrahim Hemaidy, "Half a Trillion Dollars, 700,000 Dead: The Cost of the 'Syrian Disaster'," [in Arabic], *Asharq Al-Awsat*, May 27, 2020, https://bit.ly/2A6AWDf.

50. On the 9th Anniversary.

51. "12 Million Syrians Depend on Humanitarian Aid," [in Arabic], *JBC News*, April 25, 2019, https://bit.ly/3rd2mNO.

52. "UNICEF Syria Crisis - Humanitarian Situation Report (January – March 2021)," *Relief Web*, June 23, 2021, https://bit.ly/2VzyK25.

53. "The Syrian Center for Policy Research (SCPR)," SCPR, accessed January 1, 2021, Syrian Center for Policy Research https://www.scpr-syria.org.

54. "The Syrian Economic Scene in 2020," [in Arabic], Jusoor for Studies, December 30, 2020, https://bit.ly/37oY9y1

55. "Conflict Economies in Syria: Roots, Dynamics, and Pathways for Change," (Discussion Paper No.1, Development Policy Forum, Syrian Center for Policy Research, June 2020), https://bit.ly/35uqXoz.

56. "Aoun: The Lebanese Situation Resembles the "Titanic", No Time for the Luxury of Dissension," [in Arabic], *Lebanon 24*, June 18, 2019, https://bit.ly/2xHhDzw.

57. "President Aoun: Hezbollah's Role is Complementary to the Work of the Army," [in Arabic], *AlManar*, February 12, 2017, http://almanar.com.lb/1511574.

58. "The Lebanese President Opposes Hariri's Condition and Insists on Defending Hezbollah's Position in Syria," [in Arabic], *Eldorar Alshamia*, November 29, 2017, http://eldorar.com/node/116378.

59. George Shahen, "Al Hariri Accuses Hezbollah of Burning Lebanon in Exchange for Rescuing Al Asad," [in Arabic], *Lebanon Today*, May 1, 2013, https://bit.ly/2Yt5GIN.

60. "More than 220 Wounded in Protests in Tripoli Lebanon", [in Arabic], January 28, 2021 *Arabi 21*, https://bit.ly/2Yk5PNc.

61. Ali Al-Amin, "Lebanon: Be with the Resistance and Plunder Whatever you Like," [in Arabic], *Alarabiya*, March 10, 2020, https://bit.ly/2IweF6y.

62. "Does the Donors Conference Meet the Needs of the Beirut Port Disaster?" [in Arabic], *Al-Ghad*, August 11, 2020, https://bit.ly/2DPxy1q.

63. Enas Chery, "Chaos and Confusion in the Distributing Compensation to Port Explosion Victims," [in Arabic], *Asharq Al-Awsat*, November 8, 2020, https://bit.ly/3ldZb4Y.

64. Marawan Shlala, "Lebanese People Hang Hassan Nasrallah and Michel Aoun in Central Beirut," [in Arabic], *Elaph*, August 8, 2020, https://bit.ly/3ikFR3Q.

65. "Aoun Absolves his Ally Hezbollah from Beirut Bombing," [in Arabic], *Alarab UK*, August 19, 2020, https://bit.ly/34pNUrd.

66. Huda Al-Husseini, "Beirut will not Forgive those Responsible for its Bombings!" [in Arabic], *Asharq Al-Awsat*, August 13, 2020, https://bit.ly/31LSK0L.

67. Dawood Al-Farhan, "The Beirut Catastrophe was Planned in Advance," [in Arabic], *Asharq Al-Awsat*, August 11, 2020, https://bit.ly/3kzBiVC.

68. "Al-Assad "The Chemist" Blew up the Port of Beirut," [in Arabic], *Elaph*, February 22, 2021, https://bit.ly/2WZf3kD.

69. Dawood Al-Farhan, "Beirut's Disaster was "Orchestrated at Night," [in Arabic], *Asharq Al-Awsat*, August 11, 2020, https://bit.ly/3kzBiVC..

70. "Hezbollah's Missiles Cause Panic in Baabda, and Fears of a Repeat of the Port Explosion Scenario!" [in Arabic], *Janoubia*, August 17, 2020, https://bit.ly/34fYouO.

71. "Lebanon: Resignation of a Municipal Council after Investigations of 'Hezbollah's Missile Stores'," [in Arabic], *Al-Hurra*, August 20, 2020, https://arbne.ws/34iQgtw.

72. "The 14th Annual International Conference: New World Disorder, Redefining National Security," INSS, accessed August 31, 2021, https://bit.ly/3t3YMqt.

73. May Chidiac (@may_chidiac) "We (i.e., the Lebanese not Israel) were the ones hit in the head," [in Arabic], Twitter, August 5, 2020 https://bit.ly/3og8PWr.

74. Ibrahim Al-Amin, "The Great Collapse," [in Arabic], *Al-Akhbar*, August 5, 2020, https://bit.ly/30kOi9e.

75. "'Those Involved in the Blast in Beirut Port Are the Killers' The Body of a Retired Colonel Evokes Questions in Lebanon", [in Arabic] December 3, 2020 *Al-Hurra* https://arbne.ws/3pm1hkt

76. "Resolution 1757 (2007)," United Nations Security Council, May 30, 2007, https://bit.ly/3qqRpaP

77. "Home Page," The Special Tribunal for Lebanon, accessed January 1, 2021, https://bit.ly/3ljEEvN.

78. United Nations, "Chapter VII: Action with Respect to Threats to The Peace, Breaches of The Peace, and Acts of Aggression," Charter of the United Nations (1945), https://bit.ly/3n9PExi

79. "Nasrallah Rejects the Indictment and Excludes Handing over the Four Accused," [in Arabic], *Deutsche Welle*, July 2, 2011, https://bit.ly/37BjYv3

80. "Eisenkot: The Execution of Mustafa Badreddin has Completed the Integration of the Party's Forces into the Iranian Guard!" [in Arabic], *Middle East Transparent*, July 0, 2019, https://bit.ly/2XCVkC6.

81. Arthur Traldi, "Special Tribunal for Lebanon Hands Down Historic Verdict on Hariri Assassination Charges," *Law Fare*, August 20, 2020, https://bit.ly/2WDjAta.

82. "Hariri Assassination: UN-Backed Tribunal Finds One Guilty, Three Acquitted," United Nations, August 18, 2020, https://bit.ly/3sZDJ8N.

83. *The Prosecutor v. Ayyash et al.*, STL-11-01/T/TC (August 18, 2020), https://bit.ly/30tOPWn.

84. Omarslavin Nashaba, "The Court hearing the Assassination of RafiK Hariri and Others [7]: Why is the Court Concealing Information about Ahmed Abu Adass?" [in Arabic], *Al-Akhbar*, July 3, 2019, https://bit.ly/30ruq46.

85. "Lebanon Welcomes the International Tribunal Decision, and Calls to Preserve National Unity," [in Arabic], *Asharq Al-Awsat*, August 19, 2020, https://bit.ly/3ilsFvr.

86. Jeremy Bowen, "Rafik Hariri Tribunal: Guilty Verdict over Assassination of Lebanon ex-PM," *BBC*, August 18, 2020, https://bbc.in/3puyNGH.

87. "Lebanon Heading towards the Unknown after Rafik Al-Hariri's Court Decision," [in Arabic], *Beirut Observer*, August 18, 2020, https://bit.ly/2Sj3mQb.

88. "'Is it Possible to Live with Criminals?': Resistor Salim Ayyash's Sign Provokes the Lebanese," [in Arabic], *Beirut Observer*, August 19, 2020, https://bit.ly/3jjxwid.

89. Nicholas Blanford et al., "The Special Tribunal for Lebanon: What does its closure mean for Lebanon?," Atlantic Council, July 13, 2021, https://bit.ly/3zyD6Wa.

90. Stephanie Van Den Berg, "EXCLUSIVE U.N. Tribunal for Lebanon Runs out of Funds as Beirut's Crisis Spills Over," *Reuters*, May 25, 2021, https://reut.rs/3zz8sf9.

91. Najia Houssari, "Lebanon Officially Announces Default to Pay its Share for STL," *Arab News*, June 4, 2021, https://arab.news/wz6py

92. David Enders, "Lebanon's Economic Woes Threaten Terrorism Tribunal," *Foreign Policy*, June 9, 2021, https://bit.ly/3s4JVvq.

93. David Schenker, "In Lebanon, the Wheels of Justice Do Not Grind," The Washington Institute for Near East Policy, July 19, 2021, https://bit.ly/3ApgMif.

94. Raghida Dergham, "Lebanon's Lebanon in the Claws of Israel's and Iran's Lebanon," LinkedIn, August 16, 2020, https://bit.ly/2GvornM.

95. Amal Abdulaziz Al-Hazzani, "Why didn't Nasrallah get down to Streets?" [in Arabic], *Asharq Al-Awsat*, October 22, 2019, https://bit.ly/31AsCDR.

96. Dr. Mona Fayad, "Nasrallah! That is Enough!" [in Arabic], *Middle East Transparent*, August 16, 2020, https://bit.ly/2Ga1d7b.

97. Huda Al-Husseiny, "Lebanon! Change your Regime and you Shall Rest," [in Arabic], *Asharq Al-Awsat*, August 20, 2020, https://bit.ly/33nmm6r.

98. "Two Strikes in One Day: Saudi Arabia Writes off the Political Class, and the Banque du Liban Declares a Deficit," *Al-Arab UK*, August 12, 2021, https://bit.ly/2XpKLYN.

99. "Macron: Lebanese Parties Committed a Collective Treason," [in Arabic], *JBC News*, September 26, 2020, https://bit.ly/3mRNySJ.

100. AFP Published, "Fairuz: the Arab world's most Celebrated Living Voice," *Global Times*, September 1, 2020, https://bit.ly/3diHHU1

101. "Fairuz and Ziyad al-Rahbani: No Bad Feelings and Anger Over Hezbollah and Its Leader," [in Arabic], *RT Online*, June 3, 2018, https://bit.ly/38Evt4c.

102. "Does Fairuz Like Hezbollah? Ziyad Confirms While Rima Denies," [in Arabic], *Arabi21*, December 30, 2013, https://bit.ly/3q7ghUu.

103. "Macron Visits "Fayrouz" at her Home, amid Widespread Engagement," [in Arabic], *Arabi 21*, September 1, 2020, https://bit.ly/2UxhYMQ.

104. Abdel Rahman Shalgam, "Macron between Fayrouz and Hassan Nasrallah," [in Arabic], *Asharq Al-Awsat*, October 10, 2020, https://bit.ly/2FkhOVm.

105. "Sectarianism is Turkey's Card to Penetrate Lebanon," [in Arabic], *Al-Arab UK*, August 11, 2020, https://bit.ly/341JRTB.

106. "Foreign Minister Vows Turkish Citizenship for Lebanon's Turkmens Population", August 8, 2020 *Ahavl News* https://bit.ly/3cubh8A

107. "Erdogan Shocks Libyans as he Says Libya has a Million Turks," *218 News*, December 23, 2019, https://bit.ly/34BPyXS.

108. "Statement by Presidential Spokesperson Ambassador İbrahim Kalın," Presidency of the Republic of Turkey, November 1, 2020, https://bit.ly/2THm0lE.

109. "Who are the Turkmen and Where Do they Live?," Indiana University Bloomington, accessed August 31, 2021, https://bit.ly/2WEjVvg.

110. Yusra Ahmed, "Syrian Turkmen Refugees Face Double Suffering in Lebanon," *Zaman Al Wasl*, October 6, 2015, https://bit.ly/3gQpsWX.

111. Hamza Tekin, Safiye Karabacak, and Hacer Baser, "Refugee Turkmen Families in Lebanon Face Tough Fight for Life," [in Turkish], *Anadolu Ajansi*, November 11, 2015, https://bit.ly/3zLalpr.

112. Pierre-Axel Thüring, "Lebanon's Case in the Turkish Quest for Regional Leadership," *Strife*, March 19, 2021, https://bit.ly/3zpXacr.

113. Mohanad Hage Ali, "New Sultan on the Block," Carnegie Middle East Center, August 24, 2020, https://carnegie-mec.org/diwan/82554.

114. Joseph Haboush, "Security Fears in Lebanon After Reports of Turkish Weapons Shipments", August 19, 2020 *Al Arabiya* https://bit.ly/36tYorx

115. Dr. Ridwan al-Sayyid, "Before and After the International Tribunal," [in Arabic], *Asharq Al-Awsat*, August 21, 2020, https://bit.ly/3ne8a7F.

116. "Security Council Declares Support for Free, Fair Presidential Election in Lebanon; Calls for Withdrawal of Foreign Forces There," United Nations, September 2, 2004, https://bit.ly/3DBqG1W

117. "Security Council Calls for End to Hostilities Between Hizbollah, Israel, Unanimously Adopting Resolution 1701 (2006)," United Nations, August 11, 2006, https://bit.ly/3gNvO9o.

118. French President Plans Third Visit to Lebanon", January 31, 2021 *The Arab Weekly* https://bit.ly/2NP04Fj

119. Nadeem Koteich, "Price for the Fall of Hezbollah," [in Arabic], *Asharq Al-awsat*, December 10, 2019, https://bit.ly/2P8Rzn0.

120. "Aoun: We are Heading to Hell!" [in Arabic], *Lebanon Economy Files*, September 21, 2020, https://bit.ly/2M1VQda

121. "Human Rights Organization: 545 Killed in Protests in Iraq," [in Arabic], *Arabi 21*, February 19, 2020, https://bit.ly/2v2bUD9.

122. "Iraq: Karbala Mayor Shot Dead in the Street," *JBC News*, August 10, 2021, https://bit.ly/2U8LnAu.

123. Majid al-Samerai, "The Lie of The Military Coup Scenario in Iraq," [in Arabic], *Alarab UK*, March 28, 2020, https://bit.ly/2vUgunk.

124. Dr. Bahirah al-Shikhli, "The Split of the Shi'ite Camp Heralds Fighting in Iraq," [in Arabic], *JBC News*, March 24, 2020, https://bit.ly/2QJh2Uk.

125. Zyd Salem and Mohamed Ali, "The Number of "Popular Mobilization Forces" has Increased: 30,000 New Members," [in Arabic], *The New Arab*, April 6, 2021, https://bit.ly/3sUljVP.

126. "The Popular Mobilization is Losing its Social and Ideological Luster, and its Human Reservoir is Fading in Southern Iraq," [in Arabic], *Al-Arab*, April 16, 2021, https://bit.ly/3stIc1j.

127. Naher Media, "Learn about the Blue Lightning Operation that Led to the Killing of Qassem Soleimani," [in Arabic], YouTube video, 0:55, January 4, 2020, https://youtu.be/Ot-O7BpUbOA

128. "Iraq: Will Pro-Sistani and Pro-Iran 'Popular Mobilization Units' Split?," Emirates Policy Center, May 30, 2020, https://bit.ly/3DfDwD6.

129. A Sharp Controversy Within the PMU reflects the Controversy Between Al-Sistani and Khamenei", [in Arabic] December 23, 2020 *Iran Wire*, https://bit.ly/3rRUth8

130. Nab del Iraq, 2020 "Al Chaz Ali Says 'Al 'Atabat are Israeli and American backed," Facebook, September 21, 2020, https://bit.ly/2WJ5LcX

131. Osama Mahdi, "Iranian-backed Iraqi Militias argue Al Zurfi is an American Agent", [in Arabic] April 5, 2020 *Elaph* https://bit.ly/2Zfxfo1

132. "Al-Sistani: We Discused with The Pope the Wars and Violence that Peoples in our Region Suffer From," [in Arabic], *JBC News*, Mach 6, 2021, https://bit.ly/3ei4wYG.

133. "Muqtada al-Sadr Fabricates a controversy with Iran to Regain the Trust of the Iraqis", [in Arabic] January 14, 2021 *Al-Arab* https://bit.ly/3icSz6m

134. Mark Mazzetti and Eric Schmitt, "Pentagon Order to Plan for Escalation in Iraq Meets Warning from Top Commander," *The New York Times*, March 27, 2020, https://nyti.ms/3mAMKA7

135. Lara Seligman and Andrew Desiderio, "Biden Under Pressure to Respond to Escalating Attacks on U.S. Troops in Iraq and Syria," *Politico*, July 10, 2020, https://politi.co/3jsvpKl.

136. Fateen Al-Baddad, "Al-Kadhimi and Iran's Armed Militia," [in Arabic], *JBC News*, June 28, 2020, https://bit.ly/2VKebgx.

137. Fadil al Nashmi, "'Iranian Frictions' warn of Chaos....and Baghdad is Alarmed", [in Arabic] June 28, 2020 *Al-Sharq al-Awsat* Thttps://bit.ly/2NzyY1w

138. Waled Al-Khazraji, "Does Kadhimi Use Force to Disarm the Tribes in Southern Iraq?" [in Arabic], *Arabi 21*, July 17, 2020, https://bit.ly/2CnIH9n.

139. "The Release of QasemQasem Musleh is the Result of an Agreement that Obliges the Militias to Stop Bombing American Sites," [in Arabic], *Alarab UK*, June 10, 2021, https://bit.ly/3gaTzZu; Hasan Hamed Serdah, "How did Al-Kazemi fail?" [in Arabic], *Kitabat*, May 29, 2021, https://bit.ly/3uxj3nx.

140. Badr Alkahtani and Ali Rabei, "'Alshareyah' Eases the Humanitarian Crisis with Fuel Shipments to Hodeidah," [in Arabic], *Asharq Al-Awsat*, June 2, 2021, https://bit.ly/34DlKtd; "Al-Kazemi's Government is Serious in Warning the Popular Mobilization Against Repeating the Challenge with the State," [in Arabic], *Alarab UK*, May 31, 2021, https://bit.ly/34AUJXv; "The Iraqi Popular Mobilization: Its Leaders Fear its Disintegration," [in Arabic], *Elaph*, May 29, 2021, https://bit.ly/3q3LWHs.

141. Dr. Bahira al-Sheikhly, "Sectarian Powers in Iraq Change their Skin," [in Arabic], *JBC News*, October 20, 2020, https://bit.ly/2T9n4yf.

142. Al-Samerai, "Lie of the military coup."https://bit.ly/33Kfxfm

143. "Cairo Offers Baghdad Development for Oil", [in Arabic] November 1 2020, *Al Sharq al-Awsat* https://bit.ly/35WpUwu

144. "Final Statement of the Tripartite Summit in Baghdad," [in Arabic], *Al Ghad*, June 27, 2021, https://bit.ly/3DA7jGP.

145. Nasser Karimi, "Major Blackouts in Iran Prompt Rare Apology from President," The *Associated Press*, July 6, 2021, https://bit.ly/3DQHl1Q

146. "Iraq Signs 2-Year Deal to Continue Importing Electricity from Iran," *Xinhua Net*, June 6, 2020, https://bit.ly/3h5JyN0.

147. "Iraq to Import 400 Megawatts of GCC Electricity through Saudi Arabia," *The National News*, November 12, 2020, https://bit.ly/3r1D71h.

148. Kate Dourian, "Iraq Steps Up Solar Energy Plans With 2 GW Award to the UAE," The Arab Gulf States Institute in Washington, June 28, 2021, https://bit.ly/38NKcdD.

149. "Jordan, Iraq Sign Agreement to Connect Grids," *The Jordan Times*, September 28, 2020, https://bit.ly/38KM9Yo.

150. Joseph Haboush, "Iraq, US Companies Sign Deals Worth more than $8 Billion Before Kadhimi-Trump Meeting," *Al Arabiya English*, August 20, 2020, https://bit.ly/3zQCcEC.

151. Sinan Mahmoud, "Iraq Signs Major Energy Deal with France's Total," *The National*, March 29, 2021, https://bit.ly/2YyrC7p.

152. "Iraqi Government Signs Contract with Power China to Build Solar Plants," *Global Times*, August 26, 2021, https://bit.ly/3l1NVtA.

153. "Ambiguity Regarding the Goals of the "Energy Tower War" in Iraq," [in Arabic], *Asahrq Al-Awsat*, July 7, 2021, https://bit.ly/3hlRuud.

154. "Jordan-Iraq Oil Pipeline to Cost $5-7bn," *Iraq Business News*, March 24, 2017, https://bit.ly/3zVWIDW.

155. Iraq Cabinet Approves Plans to Build Jordan Pipeline and Island Port," *Oil & Gas*, July 11, 2019, https://bit.ly/3h6Yn1X.

156. "Energy Minister, Iraqi Oil Minister Discuss Basra-Aqaba Pipeline Developments," The Embassy of the Hashemite Kingdom of Jordan, July 11, 2019, https://bit.ly/3jJxO4x.

157. "Iraq-Jordan Oil Pipeline," Wikipedia, last edited April 30, 2021, https://bit.ly/386gY9h.

158. Simon Watkins, "A Controversial New Power Grid Divides the Middle East," *Oil Price*, December 22, 2020, https://bit.ly/3zeV7so.

159. "US to Help Lebanon Get Electricity from Jordan," *Saudi Gazette*, August 20, 2021, https://bit.ly/2Wf27r4.

160. Hussein Yassine, "The U.S. Will Help Lebanon Get Electricity from Jordan," *The 961*, August 19, 2021, https://bit.ly/3hJKoPJ.

161. Joseph Haboush, "US Talking to Egypt, Jordan to Help Lebanon's Fuel, Energy Needs: Senior US Diplomat," *Al Arabiya English*, August 19, 2021, https://bit.ly/3n5oKZZ.

162. "Hezbollah Says Iranian Fuel Oil Ship to Sail to Lebanon in Hours," *AlJazeera*, August 19, 2021, https://bit.ly/3yS4HjM.

163. Joseph Haboush, "US Urged to Allow Egypt, Jordan Gas Deal with Lebanon via Arab Gas Pipeline," *Al Arabiya English*, July 16, 2021, https://bit.ly/3DQyuNy.

Chapter 7

1. "COVID-19 Dashboard by the Center for Systems Science and Engineering (CSSE)," Corona Virus Resources Center: at Johns Hopkins University, accessed January 1, 2021, https://coronavirus.jhu.edu/map.html; Gaza and the Palestinian Territories data provided by the Palestinian Authority Ministry of Health.

2. Jordanian Society of Genetic Engineers: This is why Arabs are Resistant to Corona Virus," [in Arabic], *Almasry Alyoum*, April 20, 2020, https://bit.ly/339RQg4.

3. Ibid. "COVID-19 Dashboard."

4. Sadegh Pashm Foroush, "Iran Corona Virus Update: Over 203,800 Deaths, Alarms Sounding of a Fourth Covid-19 Wave", January 19, 2021 People's Mojahedin Organization of Iran (PMOI) https://bit.ly/3cyM8JZ

5. Shahriar Kia, "Iran's Coronavirus Crisis: After 117,000 Deaths the Real Catastrophe is Yet to Come," NCRI: National Council of Resistance of Iran, October 7, 2020, https://bit.ly/3duogWk.

6. Sadegh Pashm-Foroush, "Iran Coronavirus Update: Over 357,200 Deaths, "Tsunami of Death" Sweeping the Country," People's Mojahedin Organization of Iran, August 11, 2021, https://bit.ly/37ARocl.

7. Saleh Hemaid, "The Iranian Parliament: The Real Number of People Infected with COVID-19 is 750,000 and the Deaths are 8,600," [in Arabic], *AlArabiya*, May 20, 2020, https://bit.ly/2yU4tjb.

8. "US Pressure to Prevent Emergency Financing from the IMF for Iran," [in Arabic], *Middle East Online*, April 15, 2020, https://bit.ly/34FKCj7.

9. "Official Statistics of COVID-19 in Iran: 5,297 Deaths and Around 85,000 Infected," [in Arabic], *Iran International*, April 21, 2020, https://bit.ly/2LpCRVO.

10. "The Iranian Parliament Research Center Retracts its Report on COVID-19 Victims after its Media Coverage," [in Arabic], *Iran International*, April 16, 2020, https://bit.ly/2LqzXQB.

11. Shahed Alavi and Pouyan Khoshhal, "Lies, Misinformation and Makeshift Graves: A Chronology of Coronavirus in Iran," *IranWire*, April 19, 2020, https://bit.ly/3bu1nRa.

12. "Documents Exclusive to 'Iran International': The Iranian Regime was Aware of the COVID-19 Outbreak in the Country Long Before February 19," [in Arabic], *Iran International*, March 19, 2020, https://bit.ly/2xT5MhD.

13. Saleh Hemaid, "The Government Admits: COVID-19 has Spread in Iran since January," [in Arabic], *AlArabiya*, May 20, 2020, https://bit.ly/2UOFMvM.

14. "Khamenei's Advisor to the Iranian President: It is Time to Open Mosques and Shrines," [in Arabic], *Iran International*, April 21, 2020, https://bit.ly/3eHJ6So.

15. "Documents Exclusive to 'Iran International'."

16. Rohani: 25 Million COVID-19 Infections in Iran," [in Arabic], *Al-Araby Al-Jadeed*, July 18, 2020, https://bit.ly/2CgZR8N

17. Osama Mahdi, "Saleh: Our Battle Against Coronavirus has not Ended and we are Facing Challenges Confronting it," [in Arabic], *Elaph*, April 12, 2020, https://bit.ly/35xXyKk.

18. Ibrahim Saleh, "Iraq Reopens 3rd Border Crossing with Iran," *Anadolu Agency*, July 11, 2020, https://bit.ly/3fuYJgP.

19. "Is the Coronavirus Vaccine Halal or Haram? A Big Islamic State is Waiting for Verdict," , *Al-Hurra*, December 4, 2020, https://arbne.ws/3pJ20Ni.

20. "The Islamic Religious Ordinance Authority: There is No Objection to Use a Vaccine that Contains Pig," *CNN Arabic*, December 26, 2020, https://cnn.it/3neuahO.

Chapter 8

1. Melamed, "Inside The Middle East", (pp.266-267)

2. "Cautious Turkish Moves." https://bit.ly/3fA3NzV

3. Asaad Sulaiman, "Abu Dhabi Followers in Southern Yemen: We Extend our Hand to Israel and to Mars if Shall be," [in Arabic], *Al-Araby Al-Jadeed*, July 17, 2020, https://bit.ly/3fHGKmA.

4. Sulaiman.

5. Adnan Abo Amer, "Israel Welcomes the UAE's Control over Socotra in Yemen," [in Arabic], *Arabi 21*, July 12, 2020, https://bit.ly/2DuveN4.

6. "In Pictures: The UAE is Constructing a Runway at a Military Base on a Yemeni Island," [in Arabic], *Palestine Time*, April 6, 2021, https://bit.ly/3mo6hFy.

7. "Saudi-Led Coalition Confirms Military Presence on Red Sea Island," *The Arab Weekly*, May 28, 2021, https://bit.ly/2WbuvKF.

8. Ozberk, "Egypt Inaugurates A New Naval."

9. "Saudi Arabia and 7 Countries form Council to Secure Red Sea and Gulf of Aden," *Arab News*, January 6, 2020, https://arab.news/49exp.

10. ""Dubai Ports World - Soukhna" Continues to Operate the Port at Full Capacity," [in Arabic], *Albayan*, April 26, 2020, https://bit.ly/33OsDIA.

11. "Protesters Block the Port-Sudan Port in Objection to the Juba Agreement," [in Arabic], *JBC News*, October 5, 2020, https://bit.ly/30XYOn2.

12. Paul Wallace, "UAE and Israel Open Talks on Once-Secret Crude Oil Pipeline," *World Oil*, October 21, 2020, https://bit.ly/37h5r7a

13. "Saudi Arabia Facts and Figures," Organization of the Petroleum Exporting Countries, accessed January 1, 2021, https://bit.ly/3jVvOVj

14. Sue Surkes, "Israel partially freezes UAE oil pipeline deal over environmental concerns," *The Times of Israel*, July 25, 2021, https://bit.ly/30uqbIs.

15. "The Abraham Accords," US Dept of State, accessed January 1, 2021, https://bit.ly/3b96PtP

16. "The Abraham Accords."

17. "Joint Statement of the United States, the Republic of Sudan, and the State of Israel," The White House, October 23, 2020, https://www.whitehouse.gov/briefings-statements/joint-statement-united-states-republic-sudan-state-israel/.

18. "Israel Morocco Sign Direct Flight Agreement", January 21, 2021 *I24 News*, https://bit.ly/3ahi3gH

19. "Israel Announces the Establishment of a Full and Formal Peace between Israel and the UAE," Israel Ministry of Foreign Affairs, August 13, 2020, https://bit.ly/3trCnnu.

20. "Bahrain's First Ambal-Al-Al-Assador to Israel Arrives to Take Up Post," *Y Net News*, August 31, 2021, https://bit.ly/2WX88J2.

21. Lahav Harkov, "Bahrain-Israel Security Collab is no Secret - Top Diplomat," *The Jerusalem Post*, August 11, 2021, https://bit.ly/2WVl166.

22. Zev Stub, "One Year into Abraham Accords, Israel's Trade with UAE Tops $570m.," *The Jerusalem Post*, August 8, 2021, https://bit.ly/3tgh9ZC.

23. Danny Zaken, "Israel-Morocco Economic Ties Warming Up," *Globes*, August 10, 2021, https://bit.ly/3h2Iwl1.

24. "Rapprochement Between Israel and Arab Countries Set to Drive Economic Growth in MENA," *EU Reporter*, August 4, 2021, https://bit.ly/3DLBZVD.

25. "The Gulf-Israel Center for Social Entrepreneurship," Sharaka, accessed September 5, 2021, https://sharakango.com/.

26. "Home Page," Israel Is, accessed September 3, 2021, https://www.israel-is.org/en/.

27. David Kaminski-Morrow, "Israeli-Jordan Airspace Pact Set to Unlock More Middle Eastern Routes," *Flight Global*, October 8, 2020, https://bit.ly/3BJQCa2

28. "Israel and Jordan Sign Overflight Agreement," *Globes*, October 8, 2020, https://bit.ly/3h8ccwX.

29. Sabah Ibrahim, "Where is the Real Al-Aqsa Mosque Located?," [in Arabic], *Modern Discussion*, October 10, 2009, https://bit.ly/3xJWihZ; Wasfi Alkilany, "'Where is Al-Aqsa Mosque?' Refuting the Fallacies of Osama Yamani, Writer of the Okaz Newspaper," [in Arabic], *Amman Net*, November 17, 2021, https://bit.ly/3iJVQMu; "Fayyad: The Real Al-Aqsa Mosque Exists in Saudi Arabia, and the Current One did not Exist during the Time of the Prophet," [in Arabic], *Sputnik Arabic*, April 27, 2017, https://bit.ly/3CK2Qkl.

30. Essa Alqadome, "Where is Al-Aqsa Mosque Located?!!," [in Arabic], Bayt Al-Maqdis Center for Documentary Studies, November 20, 2020, https://bit.ly/2VUgsbW; "A Storm of Reactions on Social Media Regarding an Article in a Saudi Newspaper Questioning Al-Aqsa Mosque," [in Arabic], *Russia Today Online*, November 15, 2020, https://bit.ly/3ACKAY5.

31. Essa Alqadome, "Where is Al-Aqsa Mosque Located?!!," [in Arabic], Bayt Al-Maqdis Center for Documentary Studies, November 20, 2020, https://bit.ly/2VUgsbW.

32. Daoud Kuttab, "How Israel Passed the Most Dangerous Matters Related to the Temple Mount in the Normalization Agreement," [in Arabic], *Amman Net*, August 31, 2020, https://bit.ly/3jTZxNn.

33. Andisheh Azad, "Rebel Ayatollah: You Shouldn't Make Money from Religion", October 2013, *Iran Wire*, https://bit.ly/2NcF9fx

34. Erdogan Urges Muslims to Visit Al-Aqsa to Protect the Mosque's Islamic Identity", May 8, 2017, *Daily Sabah*, https://bit.ly/3aYbCzH

35. Seth J. Frantzman, "Turkey Vows to 'Liberate Al-Aqsa' After Turning Hagia Sophia to Mosque," *The Jerusalem Post*, July 11, 2020, https://bit.ly/37qmNhy.

36. "Ankara: We Are Keen to Carry the Palestinian Cause in International Forums," [in Arabic], *Arabi 21*, June 9, 2021, https://bit.ly/3pELizT.

37. Ankara says UAE has betrayed the Palestinian Cause and the nations will not forget UAE's Hypocrisy", [in Arabic], August 14, 2020 *Arabi 21* https://bit.ly/31Xe8Ai

38. "Arab Masses Reject the Israeli – UAE agreement....The Palestinian Authority defines the agreement as "treason", Iran views the Agreement as a 'Dangerous Step', Turkey Calls

the Agreement a Betray on the Palestinian Cause....The West and the Gulf Welcome the Agreement", [in Arabic], August 15, 2020, *Ad-Dayar*, https://bit.ly/3g31kgy

39. "Abbas in Factions' Meeting: It's Our People Who Thwarted the Annexation Plan," [in Arabic], *Arabi 21*, September 3, 2020, https://bit.ly/354hF2T.https://bit.ly/354hF2T

40. Palestinian Authority TV, "Leader of The Palestinian As-Sa'iqa Militant Faction Mu'in Hamed: Palestinians Have Taught the People of The Gulf How to Read and Write; Iran is Not Our Enemy, We Should Join Hands with It," *MEMRI TV*, September 3, 2020, https://bit.ly/2FpdSma.

41. "Alsab' to Moein Hamed: Conflict with the Arabs Turns you into a Spy," [in Arabic], *Al-Mashhad Al-Araby*, September 6, 2020, https://bit.ly/34UdZ1U.

42. Mashari Al-Thaidy, "The UAE-Israel Agreement: A Breach of the Barrier of Illusion," [in Arabic], *Asharq Al-Awsat*, August 14, 2020, https://bit.ly/3raVwZc.

43. Al-Thaidy, "The UAE-Israel Agreement."

44. Ben Gittleson, "Israel, UAE Agree to Normalize Ties in What Trump Calls 'Historic' Agreement," *ABC News*, August 14, 2020, https://abc7ne.ws/37iV8zs https://abc7ne.ws/3p7DFk3

45. Salem Al-Kutbi, "UAE Breaks Through the Troubled Regional Reality," [in Arabic], *Alarab UK*, August 16, 2020, https://bit.ly/3nLlRdI; "A Historic Emirati Achievement," [in Arabic], *Alwatan*, August 14, 2020, https://bit.ly/3354FId.

46. Suha al-Jundi, "UAE and Peace with Israel," [in Arabic], *Alarab UK*, August 15, 2020, https://bit.ly/3fWPMvf.

47. Ibid.

48. Nasr Al-Magaly, "Jordan: The Two-State Solution or the Conflict Continues," [in Arabic], *Elaph*, August 13, 2020, https://bit.ly/35etZ03https://bit.ly/35etZ03

49. Qatari Foreign Minister Talks about Normalization of Relations with Israel and the Gulf Reconciliation", January 8, 2021 *Arabi 21* https://bit.ly/3bj51A0

50. Abdulmalik ALmekhlafi (@almekhlafi59), "The Emirati Normalization with the Israeli Enemy is Unjustified and Condemned by All Arab Peoples," [in Arabic], Twitter, August 13, 2020, 11:06 p.m., https://bit.ly/3h41K8q.

Chapter 9

1. Jewish Virtual Library, "U.S. Foreign Relations Milestones: The Oslo Accords and the Arab-Israeli Peace Process (1993 - 2000)" https://bit.ly/3uJaUhF

2. Dr. Nasser Laham, "Syrian Style Reaction", [in Arabic], January 8, 2020, *Maan News* https://bit.ly/3pOZFQV

3. Elias Harfoush, "This 'Deal' Is a Consequence of the Region's Condition," *Asharq Al-Awsat*, January 31, 2020, https://bit.ly/35RLEuY.

4. Abdelmonem Saeid, "The Deal of the Century Returns Again!" [in Arabic], *Asharq Al-Awsat*, February 5, 2020, https://bit.ly/36XKdbt.

5. Khaled Al-Berry, "If I were Palestinian," [in Arabic], *Asharq Al-Awsat*, February 24, 2020, https://bit.ly/2SVQJvq.

6. Hussam Itani, "Trump's Plan: Imposing the Fait Accompli on Palestinians," [in Arabic], *Asharq Al-Awsat*, January 30, 2020, https://bit.ly/3mAzYlh.

7. Dr. Nagi Sadeq Sharab, "Biden, Palestine and the Palestinian State!," [in Arabic], *Elaph*, April 15, 2021, https://bit.ly/35SomEb.

8. Jerusalem Insitute for Policy Research, Statistical Yearbook of Jerusalem, Table III/10 - Population of Jerusalem, by Age, Religion and Geographical Spreading, 2019, https://bit.ly/2XBpqM1

9. "Mohammed Dahlan (Fatah – Democratic Reform Bloc)," Mapping Palestinian Politics, accessed August 6, 2021, https://bit.ly/2VCIzfz.

10. Ahmed Rafik Awad, "So the Elections Do not Turn into a Dismantling Tool," *Sama News*, February 22, 2021, https://bit.ly/3jpCM6p.

11. "Abbas Asks Erdogan to Stop Hamas Incitement Against PA," *Middle East Monitor*, July 12, 2021, https://bit.ly/37KAVCA.

12. *The Godfather*, 1972, Directed by Francis Ford Coppola

13. Mohsen Mohamed Saleh, "Map of the Palestinian Legislative Council Elections," [in Arabic], *Arabi 21*, April 2, 2021, https://bit.ly/3miaJp6; "After Meeting Head of Israeli 'Shin Bet': A Newspaper Reveals Abbas Received a New Message from an American Official Regarding Elections," [in Arabic], *Palestine Time*, March 20, 2021, https://bit.ly/3vMBUNa; "US Source to Palestinian Paper: Washington Will Understand Election Postponement ," *The Times of Israel*, April 17, 2021, https://bit.ly/3kcGgbN

14. "Homepage," The Meir Amit Intelligence and Terrorism Information Center, accessed August 6, 2021, https://www.terrorism-info.org.il/en/.

15. Last Week Tonight with John Oliver, "Israel v Palestine Conflict," YouTube Video, May16, 2021, https://youtu.be/PkQ4HZAepYc

16. Saleh Alqllab, "Why Hamas Staged the Gaza War under Iranian Directives!," [in Arabic], *Asharq Al-Awsat*, May 20, 2021, https://bit.ly/346wakS.

17. Majed Kayali, "Palestinian Struggle and Stubbornness, a Legend after a Legend," [in Arabic], *Alarab UK*, June 8, 2021, https://bit.ly/3g2DsNl.l

18. Muthni Abdullah, "Has Hamas Provoked its Supporters by Praising Iran?," [in Arabic], *Al-Quds Al-Arabi*, June 7, 2021, https://bit.ly/3gcleqs.

19. Khairallah Khairallah, "Hamas and the Need for Humility," [in Arabic], *Alarab UK*, June 11, 2021, https://bit.ly/3pOTZrE.

20. Mohammed Khalfan Al-Sawafi, "Investing in the Gaza War," [in Arabic], *Alarab UK*, June 11, 2021, https://bit.ly/2Y4RebQ.

21. Bakr Owaida, "Gaza is Calling, Who Will Respond?," [in Arabic], *Asharq Al-Awsat*, May 26, 2021, https://bit.ly/34hznOz; Tariq Alhomayed, "Gaza and Arab Negligence," [in Arabic], *Asharq Al-Awsat*, May 19. 2021, https://bit.ly/3ysSGKZP; Rajeh Al-khori," "Vienna Talks on the Fire of Gaza and Marib!," [in Arabic], *Asharq Al-Awsat*, June 6, 2021, https://bit. ly/2TAf0Kn; Fahim Alhamid, "Dealers of Treason and Coups: Hamas and Al-Houthi, Accomplices in Murder," [in Arabic], *Okaz*, June 8, 2021, https://bit.ly/3tgQPyy; Kyali, "Palestinian Struggle and Stubbornness."; Khairallah, "Hamas and the Need for Humility."; Alsawafi, "Investing in the Gaza War."; Hossam Kanafani, "Further Drowning in Dividing," [in Arabic], *The New Arab*, June 12, 2021, https://bit.ly/3zlKggJ.

22. "Press Release: Public Opinion Poll No (80)," Palestinian Center for Policy and Survey Research, June 15, 2021, https://pcpsr.org/en/node/843.

23. Majid Kayali, "The Palestinians in their struggle and stubbornness, from one myth to another," [in Arabic], *Al-Arab UK*, August 6, 2021, https://bit.ly/3g2DsNl; Nagi Sadek Shrab, "Israel and the gardener's strategy and mowing the lawn!" [in Arabic], *Elaph*, May 27, 2021, https://bit.ly/3vwyQnW

24. Kifah Mahmoud Karim, "Defeat Festivals!" [in Arabic], *Elaph*, June 6, 2021, https://bit. ly/3An3YbJ.

25. "Haniyeh Thanks Iran for Supporting Hamas with Money and Arms," [in Arabic], *Deutsche Welle*, May 21, 2021, https://bit.ly/3h2qDlF.

26. Mostafa Omara, "Hamas Representative in Iran, Praising its Support of the Resistance in Gaza, for Azzaman: We Need a Safety Net from the Arab, and We Still Have Strategic Weapons," [in Arabic], *Azzaman*, May 28, 2021, https://bit.ly/3c2g3ci.

27. Jack Khoury, "Hamas Leader Haniyeh Meets With Iran's Hardline President Raisi," *Haaretz*, August 6, 2021, https://bit.ly/3AHNdbh.

28. Nasr Almajali, "Raisi: Our Priority is Dialogue with Saudi Arabia," [in Arabic], *Elaph,* June 22, 2021, https://bit.ly/2Uwd3PC.

29. Ghassan Kanfani, "The hibernation season for the Palestinian cause," [in Arabic], *Al Arab UK*, January 16, 2021, https://bit.ly/38cuQNw

30. Dr. Amjad Ahmed Jibril, "The Role of Egypt and Hamas' Regional Relations," [in Arabic], *The New Arab*, July 7, 2021, https://bit.ly/3xmZJvJ.

31. Melamed

Chapter 10

1. Washington Examiner (@dcexaminer) "John Kerry in 2016: "There will be no separate peace between Israel and the Arab world. I want to make that very clear to all of you", Twitter, November 23, 2020 https://bit.ly/37ldnnZ

2. Ahmad Zeid Abadi, "Al-Quds Day: What Good Did it Do to Palestinians?," *Middle East Transparent*, May 22, 2020, https://middleeasttransparent.com/en/al-quds-day-what-good-did-it-do-to-palestinians/

3. Mishari al-Thaidy, "On the Deal of the Century and the Bidding Festival," [in Arabic], *Asharq Al-Awsat*, January 29, 2020, https://bit.ly/38L6rie.

4. Ibrahim Al-Zubeidi, "Death to Israel, the US, and 'Vicroty' to Iran", [in Arabic], *Al-Arab*, February 19, 2020 https://bit.ly/2uNcsNb

5. Ra'fat Al-Ghanem, "The Image of Transformed Israel in the Minds of Syrians," [in Arabic], *Elaph*, April 14, 2020, https://bit.ly/2N3aMbx

6. Faisal al-Qassem, "Captagon Party: for entrepreneurship, trade, abuse and promotion of all kinds of drugs", [in Arabic], December 25, 2020 *Al Quds Al Arabi* https://bit.ly/3hikCkl

7. Khaled Al-atrafi, "The Shaft of the Cartoon Resistance," [in Arabic], *Elaph*, May 31, 2021, https://bit.ly/2VX0KMR.

8. Maha Mohammed Al-Sharif, "Iran and Wreaking Havoc in the Arab World," [in Arabic], *Asharq Al-Awsat*, June 15, 2021, https://bit.ly/35n0OqM.

9. "Pentagon: Egypt Matters in Several Files, Including the Renaissance Dam, and Must Get Military Support," [in Arabic], *JBC News*, August 10, 2021, https://bit.ly/3CyYjB4.

Chapter 11

1. Al-Habib Al-Assoued, "What an American Defeat in Afghanistan?," [in Arabic], *Alarab UK*, August 17, 2021, https://bit.ly/3ATkZdP.

2. AlHabib AlAssoued, "What an American Defeat in Afghanistan?," [in Arabic], *Alarab UK*, August 17, 2021, https://bit.ly/3ATkZdP.

3. Abdulrahman Al-Rashed, "Is it the End or a Start of a New Afghan War?," [in Arabic], *Elaph*, June 17, 2021, https://bit.ly/3gNQjSy.

4. Jason W. Davidson, The Costs of War to United States Allies Since 9/11 (Providence, RI: Watson Institute for International and Public Affairs, 2021), https://bit.ly/3DV7gWb.

5. United Nations Assistance Mission in Afghanistan, Quarterly Report on The Protection of Civilians in Armed Conflict: 1 January to 30 September 2018, October 10, 2018, https://bit.ly/3yiA2Mp.

6. Nouri Al Hamza, "Afghanistan is an Open Combat Arena to Achieve Iran's Ambition," [in Arabic], *Al-Quds Al-Arabi*, August 21, 2021, https://bit.ly/2XDDN2a.

7. Arian Sharifi, "The Fatemiyoun Army: Iran's Afghan Crusaders in Syria," *The Diplomat*, April 23, 2021, https://bit.ly/3zpXFUC.

8. Kanishka Nawabi, "Fatemiyoun: Irans 'Good Taliban'," *Tolo News*, last edited February 10, 2021, https://bit.ly/3BgHauw.

9. Khaled al-Khateb, "Iranian forces form new groups to boost influence in east Syria," *Al-Monitor*, February 23, 2021,https://bit.ly/3sQAwZ2.

10. Fatemeh Aman, Water Dispute Escalating between Iran and Afghanistan (Washington, DC: Atlantic Council, South Asia Center, August 2016), https://bit.ly/38hntWW.

11. "Afghan Barter for Iran: Oil for Water," [in Arabic], *Alarab UK*, March 25, 2021, https://bit.ly/2PvcOlh.

12. United Nations office on Drugs and Crime, Drug Market Trends: Cannabis Opioids (Vienna: United Nations, June 2021), https://bit.ly/3kkxbgY.

13. Lynzy Billing, "Afghanistan's Crystal Meth Boom is Rooted in this Plant," *C&EN*, April 11, 2021, https://bit.ly/3n6NTDn.

14. Vanda Felbab-Brown, "Drugs, Security, and Counternarcotics Policies in Afghanistan," Brookings, October 29, 2020, https://brook.gs/3sXnoS2.

15. United Nations Office on Drugs and Crime, Afghanistan Opium Survey 2019: Socio-Economic Survey Report: Drivers, Causes and Consequences of Opium Poppy Cultivation (Vienna: United Nations, February 2021), https://bit.ly/3klyooe.

16. Felbab-Brown, "Drugs, Security, and Counternarcotics."https://brook.gs/2WvGe6q

17. European Monitoring Centre for Drugs and Drug Addiction, Methamphetamine Developments in South Asia: The Situation in Iran and the Implications for the EU And Its

Neighbours (Luxembourg: Publications Office of the European Union, 2021), https://bit.ly/3sDo92l.

18. Helen Fitzwilliam, "Middle East: A Drug Addict in the Family," Chatham House, August 1, 2021, https://bit.ly/3thcXso.

19. Abdorrahman Boroumand Center for Human Rights in Iran and Harm Reduction International, The Islamic Republic of Iran's Compliance with the International Covenant on Civil and Political Rights: Drug Offenses, https://bit.ly/3sEYV3t.

20. "Renewed Commitment Needed to Support Displaced Afghans and their Hosts," *Relief Web*, June 1, 2021, https://bit.ly/3jipN6r.

21. "Iran Afghan Refugees," ACAPS, accessed September 6, 2021, https://bit.ly/3sGekRh.

22. Golnar Motevalli Bloomberg, "Iran Braces for Life Next Door to the Taliban Once Again," *Union Leader*, August 19, 2021, https://bit.ly/3zah6jX.

23. Ahmed Ben Hassan Alshahri, "Can Afghanistan be a Gateway to Balances in East Asia?," [in Arabic], *Elaph*, August 15, 2021, https://bit.ly/3D9STN7.

24. Huda Alhusseini, "Iran Worried about Taliban Control of Afghanistan!," [in Arabic], *Asharq Al-Awsat*, August 12, 2021, https://bit.ly/37C01DC.

25. "Putin: The Situation in Afghanistan Directly Affects Russia's Security," [in Arabic], *Annahar*, August 22, 2021, https://bit.ly/3zkjLI9.

26. "Putin Warns Against 'Radical Islam' Spillover from Afghanistan," *AlJazeera*, August 23, 2021, https://bit.ly/3gAyojd.

27. Tsukasa Hadano, "China Extends Hand to Taliban for Rebuilding with Eye on Xinjiang," *Nikkei Asia*, August 27, 2021, https://s.nikkei.com/2X3ofoq.

28. Abdel Monem Said, "Exit from Afghanistan," [in Arabic], *Asharq Al-Awsat*, April 21, 2021, https://bit.ly/2QMdHGL.

29. Raghida Dergham, "U.S. Bids Farewell to Afghanistan and Leaves Concerns to China, Russia, Iran, India and Pakistan," [in Arabic], *Elaph*, July 18, 2021, https://bit.ly/2Wcnd9n.

30. Melamed, *Inside the Middle East*, pp 84

31. "Taliban Victory Encourages Iran to Go Further After the US Withdrawal from Iraq," [in Arabic], *Alarab UK*, August 17, 2021, https://bit.ly/3smY6w6.

32. Mark Fitzpatrick, "Whither US policy toward Iran?," *Al-Monitor*, August 17, 2021, https://bit.ly/3zf4HM0.

Chapter 12

1. Foreign Policy CAN (@CanadaFP), "Canada is Gravely Concerned about Additional Arrests of Civil Society and Women's Rights Activists in #SaudiArabia, including Samar Badawi," Twitter, August 3, 2018, 4:10 p.m., https://twitter.com/CanadaFP/status/1025383326960549889.

2. "Canada Declares Cancelling the Ban of Weapons Exporting to Saudi Arabia," [in Arabic], *Alkhaleej Online*, April 10, 2020, https://bit.ly/3bFVdwJ.

3. Dennis Horak, "Canada-Saudi Relations: Time to Get Back on Track," *Peace Diplomacy*, July 13, 2020, https://bit.ly/3dkeW9G

4. Joseph R. Biden, Jr., "Why America Must Lead Again," *Foreign Affairs*, March/April 2020, https://fam.ag/3qqfxtW

5. Stephanie Nebehay, "U.N. Expert Deems US Drone Strike on Iran's Soleimani an 'Unlawful' Killing," *Reuters*, July 6, 2020, https://reut.rs/3iFpeRW

6. "Iranian revenge for Soleimani.. Tehran talks about the killing of 80 American soldiers and monitors 100 targets to strike him in the region," [in Arabic], *Al-Jazeera*, January 8, 2020, https://bit.ly/2FrccF8

7. "A Dispute Between Al-Amiri And Khazali, or a Conflict Between the Revolutionary Guards and Iranian Intelligence?," [in Arabic], *Alarab UK*, April 24, 2021, https://bit.ly/32FE3x4; "Ali Al-Amin: Soleimani's Presence is More Important than Nasrallah's Presence... And The Iranian Project Has Reached Its End!," [in Arabic], *Janoubia*, February 16, 2020, https://bit.ly/38xgoQP; "Soleimani's killing: 'Hezbollah' Loses its 'Money House'!," [in Arabic], *Janoubia*, January 25, 2020, https://bit.ly/3kz5aCq.

8. Christopher Hamill-Stewart, "How QasemQasem Soleimani's killing diminished Iran's Middle East hegemony," *Arab News*, Updated August 12, 2020, https://arab.news/pb24n.

9. Charlie Rose, "Tom Friedman: How to Stop Iran from Getting Nukes," YouTube Video, 1:37, July 23, 2015, https://youtu.be/YThDt7MxNAI

10. "Al-Jubeir: Saudi Arabia Retains the Right of Nuclear Armament if Iran Becomes a Nuclear Power," [in Arabic], *Alquds Alarabi*, November 17, 2020, https://bit.ly/36OEffc.

11. Yadlin and Asculai

12. Elran and Padan

13. Anne Applebaum, "Liberal Democracy Is Worth a Fight," *The Atlantic*, August 20, 2021, https://bit.ly/2WDP6XC.

14. Daniel Benaim and Jake Sullivan, "America's Opportunity in the Middle East," *Foreign Affairs*, May 22, 2020, https://fam.ag/2Zx8l4P.

15. David M. Halbfinger, Ben Hubbard, and Farnaz Fassihi, "For Trump, Defying Mideast Truisms Produced Breakthroughs and Backfires," *The New York Times*, October 22, 2020, https://nyti.ms/2H0NZcQ.

16. Martin Indyk, "The Middle East Isn't Worth It Anymore," *The Wall Street Journal*, January 17, 2020, https://on.wsj.com/34eIoZG.

Chapter 13

1. Mina al-Oraibi, "The Middle East is Very Different Place from When Biden Was VP", November 16, 2020 The National News https://bit.ly/3rRHQC0

2. Dr. Essam Shaaban, "US Elections is an Egyptian Affair", [in Arabic], November 8, 2020 *Al-Arabi al-Jadid* https://bit.ly/36v5n2H

3. Emad El-Din Hussein, "The most Important is What Are We Going to Do with Biden?", [in Arabic], November 7, 2020 *Arabi 21* https://bit.ly/36ltfFx

4. Mamoun Fandi, "Will Biden Continue Obama's Way?" [in Arabic], November 9, 2020 *Al-Sharq Al-Awsat* https://bit.ly/36hdu2H

5. Ghassan Charbel , "Biden's America I in a Word That Has Changed", [in Arabic], November 9, 2020 *Al-Sharq Al-Awsat* https://bit.ly/36hzqdV

6. Turki Al-Faisal, "Biden is Well Aware of the US Interests in the Region", [in Arabic], November 9, 2020 *Arabi 21* https://bit.ly/3klHOhH

7. Hailah Al-Mushawah, "Who Will Stand Up to Iran?!," [in Arabic], *Elaph*, February 16, 2021, https://bit.ly/3qszoJd.

8. Abdul Rahman Al-Rashed, "Tehran Sees Biden Weak," [in Arabic], *Asharq Al-Awsat*, February 17, 2021, https://bit.ly/3gHlDDg.

9. Salem Al-Ketbi, "Biden and the 'Carrot' Without the Stick Policy," [in Aabic], *Elaph*, March 6, 2021, https://bit.ly/3A2MEJn.

10. Abdulah Bin Bijad Al- Otaibi, "Western Pampering of Iran," [in Arabic], *Asharq Al-Awsat*, March 7, 2021, https://bit.ly/2OvFGtq.

11. Raghida Dergham, "Twinning Diplomacy and Democracy in Biden's Security Strategy," [in Arabic], *Elaph*, March 7, 2021, https://bit.ly/3iRx39j.

12. Haitham El-Zobaidi, "Russia Coming to the Gulf: The West Left the Gulf, Not the Other Way Around," [in Arabic], *Alarab UK*, March 15, 2021, https://bit.ly/38Iy7GR.

13. Sam Mansi, "The Cherry on the Iranian Cake," [in Arabic], *Asharq Al-Awsat*, June 14, 2021, https://bit.ly/3wmXLej.

14. Emill Amin, "Saudi Arabia and Houthi Terror Missiles," [in Arabic], *Asharq Al-Awsat*, April 21, 2021, https://bit.ly/3tDMPaK; Ibrahim Al-Zubaidi, "The Solution is Only in Tehran," [in Arabic], *Alarab UK*, May 5, 2021, https://bit.ly/3ej3TNK; Khairallah Khairallah, "Marib: A test for Biden's Administration," [in Arabic], *Alarab UK*, May 10, 2021, https://bit.ly/3hetidF.

15. "Saudi Prince Visits Washington to Discuss Khashoggi Case," [in Arabic], *Arabi 21*, July 7, 2021, https://bit.ly/3xpuM9U; "Dinner Canceled and Conflict over Blinken Meeting at the Saudi Embassy," [in Arabic], *Arabi 21*, July 8, 2021, https://bit.ly/3yAtHMG.

16. Ali Khamenei (@Rahbar_Khamenei) "No matter who wins the #USElections2020, it won't affect our policy toward the US. Some people talk about what will happen if this or that one is elected. Yes, certain events may happen but they don't concern us. Our policy is calculated and clear", Tweeter, Nov 3, 2020 , 10:37 AM https://bit.ly/2JOFDqB

17. Willah Sai'id Al-Samerai "Iran's Withdrawal and the Renewal of the US Mandate in Iraq", [in Arabic], June 19, 2020 *Al-Arabi Al-Jadid* https://bit.ly/3hCuC7T

18. "Blinken Says Negotiations With Iran Cannot Go On Indefinitely," *Iran International*, July 29, 2021, https://bit.ly/3mN7NU1.

19. Alexander Ward And Quint Forgey, "Exclusive: Biden's Iran Envoy Calls Nuclear Deal's Fate 'One Big Question Mark'," *Politico*, August 19, 2021, https://politi.co/3zPMOna.

20. "JCPOA: Joint Statement by Spokespersons of The Foreign Ministries of France, Germany and the United Kingdom," Federal Foreign Office, August 19, 2021, https://bit.ly/3tfWqoM.

21. "France, Germany Urge Iran to Return Speedily to Nuclear Deal Talks, "*Reuters*, September 1, 2021, https://reut.rs/3n8eHn4.

22. "Iran Says Nuclear Talks Won't Resume for 2-3 Months," *The Times of Israel*, September 1, 2021, https://bit.ly/3jNN7Jr.

23. Peter Baker, "In Congress, Netanyahu Faults 'Bad Deal' on Iran Nuclear Program," *The New York Times*, March 3, 2015, https://nyti.ms/2VmebpW.

24. "Those are the Reasons for Palestinians Joy Over Trump's Defeat",[in Arabic], November 7, 2020, *Ma'an*, https://bit.ly/2MGNnfv

25. Palestine: Will Biden Fix what Trump has Damaged?", [in Arabic], November 8 2020, *Shehab news* https://bit.ly/38nv3kj

26. Karwan Faidhi Dri, "What can Syrian Kurds Expect from Biden?" *Rudaw*, November 12, 2020, https://bit.ly/3u6GwNm

27. Aykan Erdemir and Philip Kowalski, "Joe Biden Will Be America's Most Pro-Kurdish President," Foundation for Defense of Democracies, August 16, 2020, https://bit. ly/2USPPQG; Ruwayda Mustafah, "Biden Presidency Brings Hope for the Kurds," *Politics. CO.UK*, November 23, 2020, https://bit.ly/3pWIOg4.

28. Abdullah Bjad, "Iranian Elections and the 'Similarity Theory'," [in Arabic], *Asharq Al-Awsat*, June 20, 2021, https://bit.ly/3zEn0dQ.

29. Ali Alsarraf, "Robert Malley, Welcome," [in Arabic], *Alarab UK*, May 7, 2021, https://bit. ly/3vUbY1l.

Chapter 14

1. "India's ambitious plan: Rescue hundreds of thousands of migrant workers stuck without employment," [in Hebrew], May 5, 2020, https://bit.ly/3iItGAT; Manoj Kumar, "Israel-India Relations: Perceptions and Forecasts," Institute for National Security Studies, January 2017, https://bit.ly/39BrTss;

2. "The Business Opportunities Created in India for the Israeli Exporters Following the Corona Crisis," [in Hebrew], Ashr'a The Israeli Foreign Trade Risk Insurance Corporation, Ltd., May 26, 2020, https://bit.ly/2Wce7JG

3. Dergham, "Twinning Diplomacy and Democracy."

4. Michael Doran and Peter Rough, "China's Emerging Middle Eastern Kingdom," *Tablet*, August 03, 2020, https://bit.ly/2IeyiiG.

5. "The Economic and Strategic Issues in Trade and Investment Relations with China," [in Hebrew], The Information and Research Center of the Israeli Knesset, July 2021, https:// bit.ly/3aqGurj

6. John Calabrese, "China-Iraq Relations: Poised for a 'Quantum Leap'?" MEI: Middle East Institute, October 8, 2019, https://bit.ly/3l1MObg.

7. Diyari Salih, "Great Power Competition Comes to the Middle East: Iraq and the China-Iran Agreement," *Geopolitical Monitor*, April 7, 2021, https://bit.ly/3gQatwh.

8. Shira Efron, Howard J. Shatz, Arthur Chan, Emily Haskel, Lyle J. Morris, Andrew Scobell, "The Evolving Israel-China Relationship," The RAND Corporation, 2019, https://bit. ly/3a8AHGw

9. Efron et al, "The Evolving Israel-China Relationship"

10. Galia Lavi, "China and the Middle East: The Israeli-Palestinian Conflict on the Agenda," [in Hebrew], Institute for National Security Studies, August 18, 2021, https://bit.ly/3mzpBjA

Chapter 15

1. Huda Al-Husseini, "Raisi is just a President, But Decisions are up to Khamenei!," [in Arabic], *JBC News*, June 24, 2021, https://bit.ly/2SotLzK.

2. Saadia Mufarreh, "Yes...The Flowers of the Spring Have Not Yet Blossomed", January 28, 2021 *Al Arabi Al Jadid*

3. Daniel Egel, Shira Efron, Linda Robinson, "Abraham Accords Offer Historic Opportunity to Spur Mideast Growth," *RAND Blog*, March 25, 2021, https://bit.ly/3AocczK

4. Melamed (pp 43 - 84)

5. Melamed (pp 266 - 267)

6. "Maritime Chokepoints: The Backbone of International Trade, *Ship Technology*, October 3, 2017, https://bit.ly/3oKAjGU

7. Rasoul Sorkhabi, "How Much Oil in the Middle East?" *GEO Ex Pro*, 2014, https://bit.ly/3iLhRdo

8. Micallef, "The Geopolitics of Mediterranean Natural Gas"

9. Dalia Zeyada, "The End of the Middle East as We Know It," Liberal Democracy Institute, April 23, 2021, https://bit.ly/3vG0X3u.

INDEX

NOTES

NOTES

NOTES

NOTES

NOTES

NOTES

NOTES

NOTES

NOTES

NOTES

NOTES

NOTES

NOTES

NOTES

NOTES

NOTES

(FOUND ON PAGE 3)

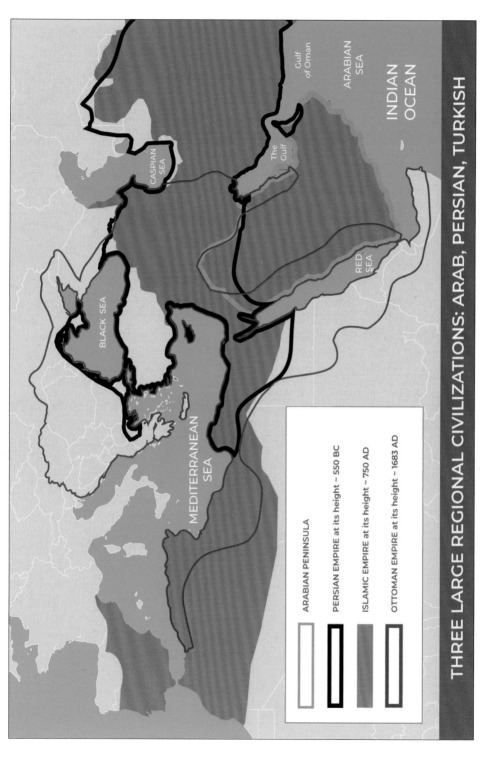

THREE LARGE REGIONAL CIVILIZATIONS: ARAB, PERSIAN, TURKISH

ARABIAN PENINSULA

PERSIAN EMPIRE at its height ~ 550 BC

ISLAMIC EMPIRE at its height ~ 750 AD

OTTOMAN EMPIRE at its height ~ 1683 AD

INDIAN OCEAN

ARABIAN SEA

Gulf of Oman

The Gulf

RED SEA

CASPIAN SEA

BLACK SEA

MEDITERRANEAN SEA

A

IRANIAN-BACKED SHI'ITE MILITANT GROUPS

CORE IDEOLOGY — The Shi'ites believe Islam's only legitimate leaders are a chain of twelve divinely appointed Imams (spiritual and religious leaders). The first divinely appointed Imam was the fourth Caliph, 'Ali Bin Abi Talib. Shi'ites believe that the last Imam in the chain (the twelfth Imam) disappeared in the 9th Century. He is therefore known as the Disappearing Imam. Shi'ites believe he is the Mahdi (messiah) and that he will come back and redeem humanity through a process in which most of humankind will die. The survivors will enjoy eternal justice, peace, and prosperity. Shi'ites are hostile to Western civilization and its values. They object to all political ideologies – Atheism, Communism, Democracy, Socialism, etc. Shi'ites are hostile to Sunnis. Shi'ites view Jews as impure. Shi'ite militias vow to eliminate the state of Israel.

IRANIAN AGENT OR PROXY — To further Iran's agenda, the Iranian Islamic Revolutionary Guards (IRG) and its elite unit, the al-Quds Force, support and nurture a network of Shi'ite and Sunni agents and proxies by providing them with military know-how, money, training, and weapons.

Agent — An existing entity that can help the Iranian regime further its goals. An agent's policy often prioritizes Iranian interests. However, an agent can often implement a policy that does not prioritize Iran's interests. An example of a Sunni Iranian agent is the Palestinian Sunni militant Islamic movement Hamas.

Proxy — If there is no existing Shi'ite or Sunni entity Iran can co-opt to help the regime further its goals, Iran creates one to act as a proxy. A proxy works and acts in close cooperation and coordination with the IRG and the al-Quds Force. Proxies almost always prioritize Iran's needs and interests. An example of a proxy is the Lebanese Hezbollah.

GROUPS	AREA OF OPERATION	PROXY / AGENT	POLITICAL PARTY	ADDITIONAL INFORMATION
HARAKAT AL-NUJABA	IRAQ / SYRIA	PROXY	YES	
HARAKAT AS-SABIREEN NASRAN LI-FILASTIN	GAZA	PROXY	NO	Consists of *Palestinians in Gaza who converted to Shi'ism. It is a minor militia.
ANSAR ALLAH	YEMEN	AGENT	YES	
'ASAIB AHL AL-HAQ (AAH)	IRAQ / SYRIA	PROXY	YES	
AL-BADR MILITIA	IRAQ	PROXY / AGENT	YES	
AL-FATEMIYOUN	SYRIA	PROXY	NO	Consists of Shi'ite Afghans recruited in Afghanistan or Iran.
HEZBOLLAH	AFRICA, EUROPE, MIDDLE EAST, SOUTH AMERICA	PROXY	YES	
IMAM 'ALI BRIGADES	IRAQ / SYRIA	PROXY	YES	
KATAIB HEZBOLLAH	IRAQ / SYRIA	PROXY	YES	
LIWA ABU AL-FADHAL AL-ABBAS	IRAQ / SYRIA	PROXY	YES	
LIWA ZAINEBIYOUN	SYRIA	PROXY	NO	Consists of Shi'ite Pakistanis recruited in Pakistan.

*Most Palestinians, like most Muslims, are Sunni

B

SUNNI ISLAM MILITANT GROUPS

CORE IDEOLOGY Sunni Militant Islam organizations are committed to creating a global Caliphate. They advocate for the implementation of shariʿah law - either in the strictest form (STR-SHARIʿA) or in a pragmatic / moderate form (PRAG-SHARIʿA). Militant Sunni Islam is hostile to Western civilization and its values. They object to all political ideologies – Atheism, Communism, democracy, Socialism, etc. Sunnis are hostile to Shiʿites. Militant Sunni Islam is hostile to Jews and vows to eliminate the state of Israel.

IDEOLOGICAL COMPONENTS

Muslim Brotherhood (MB) Committed to creating a global caliphate through education, preaching, serving the community, social service projects, economic initiatives, and political activities. The MB seeks to implement shariʿah law in a pragmatic form (PRAG-SHAR). The MB rejects the concept of takfir.

Salafi-Jihadi (SJ) Committed to creating a global Caliphate through violence. Salafi-Jihadi groups seek to implement the strictest form of shariʿah (STR-SHAR). A core component of their ideology is the concept of Takfir.

Takfir An ideology that argues that there are Muslims who do not fulfill the commandments of Islam in "the true and correct" manner. Therefore, they should not be seen as Muslims, but as enemies of Islam whose danger is even greater than those of non-Muslim infidels. Salafi-Jihadi groups believe that rulers in the Muslim world are "infidels" because they do not run their countries according to the strictest interpretation of the shariʿah law. Therefore, they are "fake" Muslims and should be overthrown.

GROUPS	AREA OF OPERATION	MB IDEOLOGY	SJ IDEOLOGY	TAKFIR IDEOLOGY	ADDITIONAL INFORMATION
AL QAEDA	AFRICA, CENTRAL ASIA, MIDDLE EAST, SOUTHEAST ASIA	NO	STR-SHAR	YES	
AL-SHABAB	SOMALIA	NO	STR-SHAR	YES	Governs part of Somalia
BOKO HARAM	AFRICA	NO	STR-SHAR	YES	
HAMAS	GAZA, WEST BANK	YES PRAG-SHAR	NO	NO	Governs Gaza by a moderate form of Shariah law
ISIS	AFRICA, CENTRAL ASIA, MIDDLE EAST, SOUTHEAST ASIA	NO	STR-SHAR	YES	
ISLAMIC JIHAD	GAZA, WEST BANK	YES	STR-SHAR	NO	
TALIBAN	AFGHANISTAN	YES	STR-SHAR with elements of Sufism*	NO	Created an Islamic Emirate and Governs most of Afghanistan

*Sufism, a mystical form of Islam. A school of practice that emphasizes the inner search for God through rituals and ceremonies, and shunning materialism.

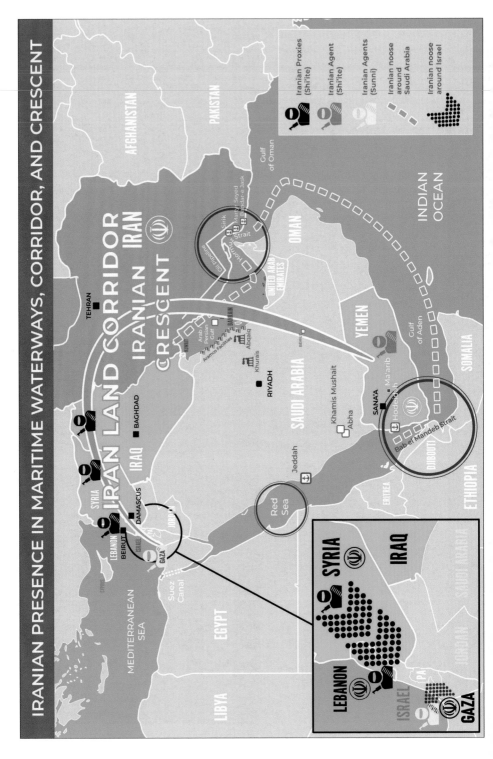

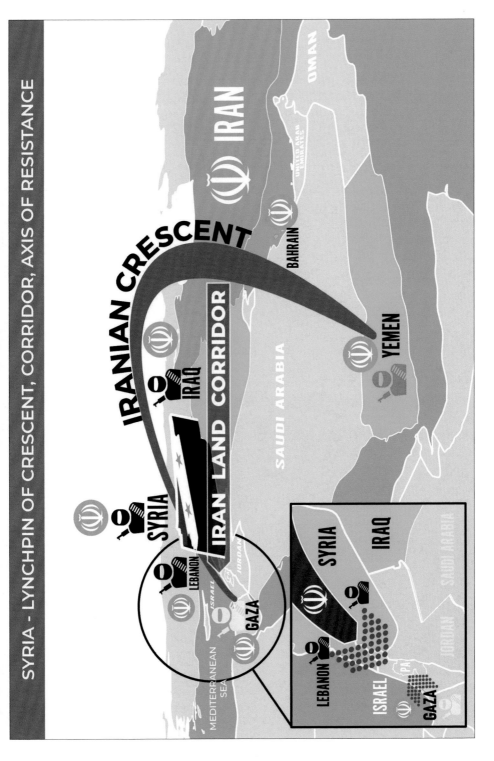

SYRIA - LYNCHPIN OF CRESCENT, CORRIDOR, AXIS OF RESISTANCE

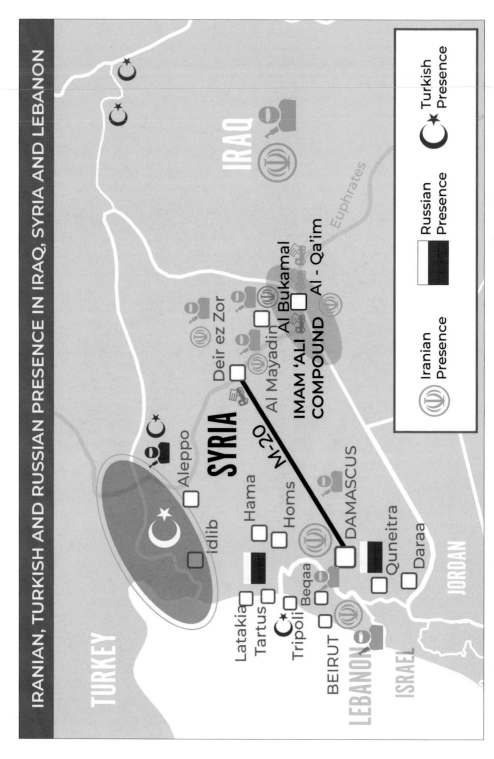

IRANIAN, TURKISH AND RUSSIAN PRESENCE IN IRAQ, SYRIA AND LEBANON

(FOUND ON PAGE 218)

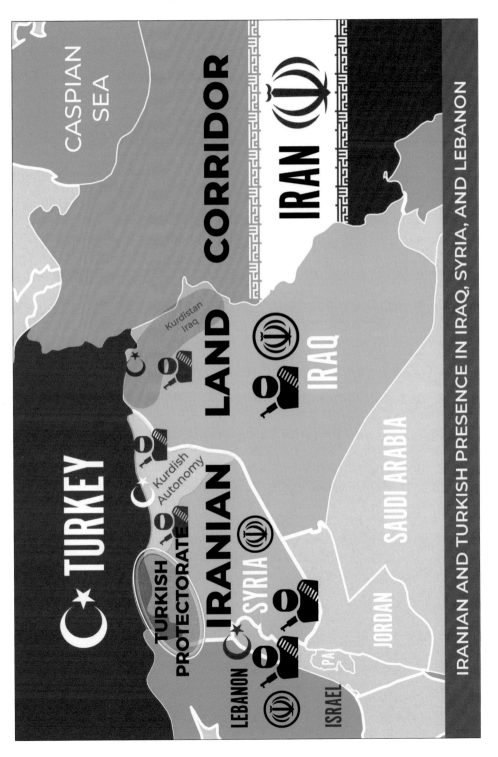

IRANIAN AND TURKISH PRESENCE IN IRAQ, SYRIA, AND LEBANON

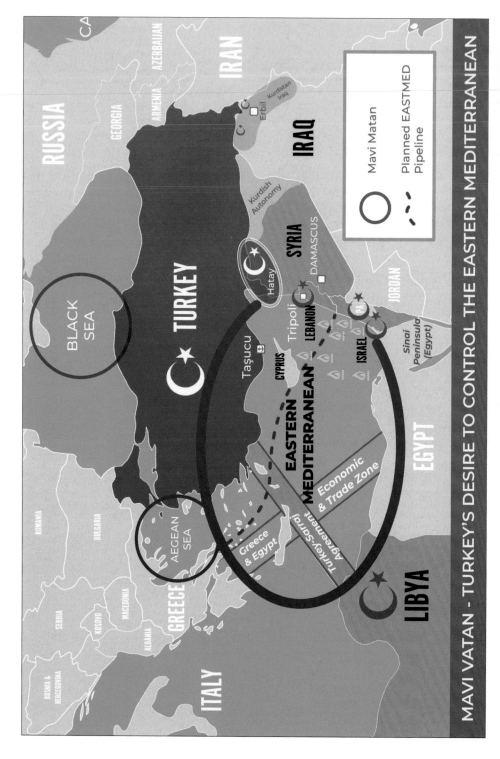

MAVI VATAN - TURKEY'S DESIRE TO CONTROL THE EASTERN MEDITERRANEAN

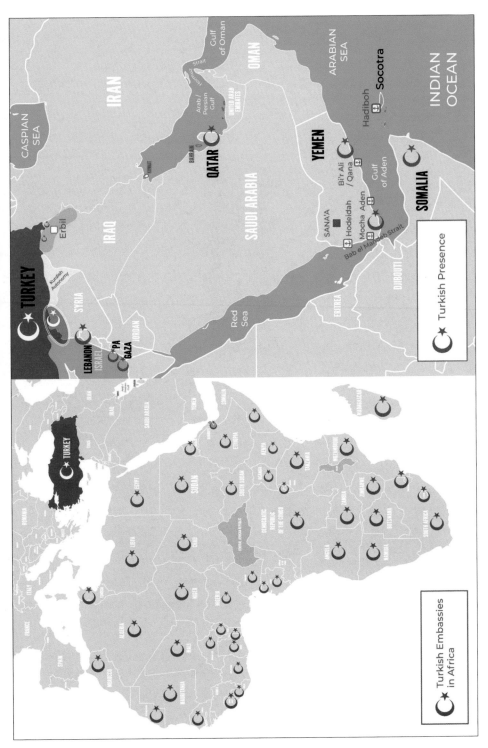

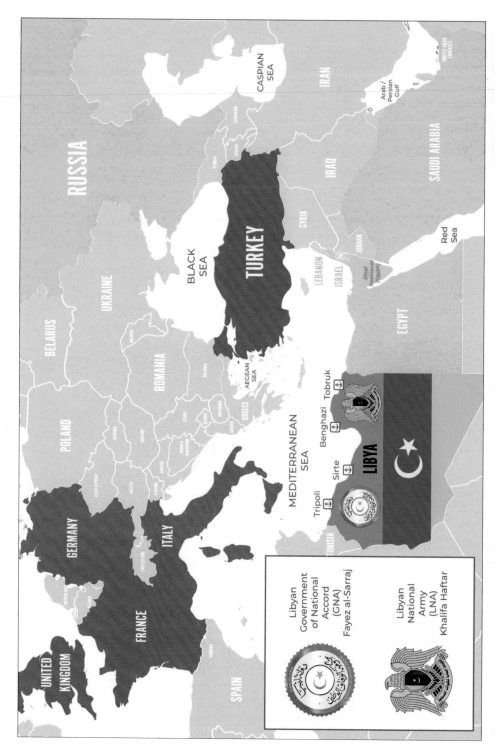

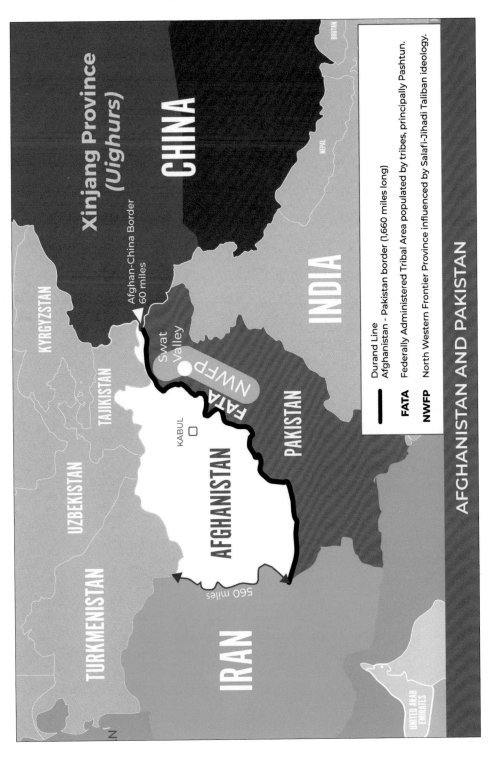

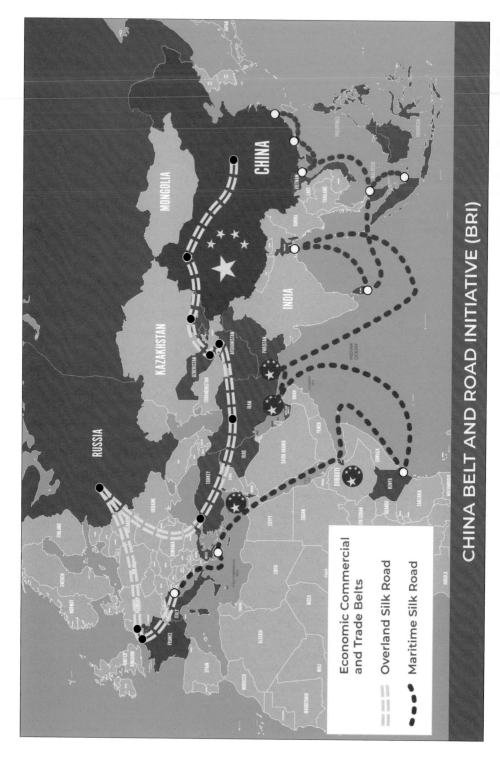

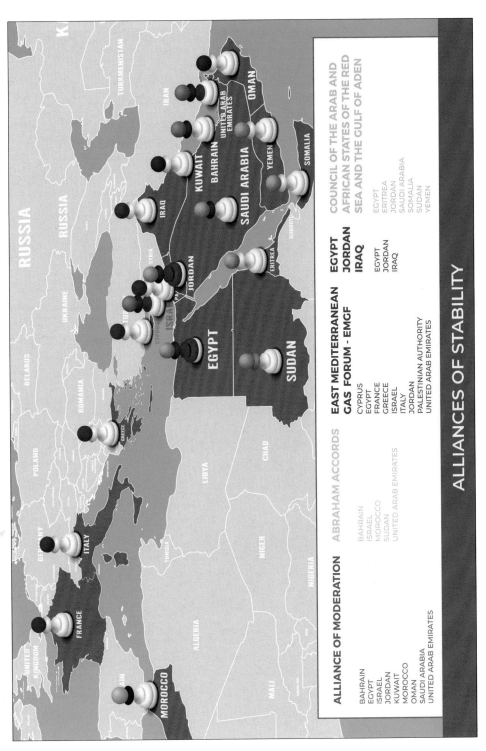

CHAPTER 4

ALLIANCES OF STABILITY

ALLIANCE OF MODERATION

BAHRAIN
EGYPT
ISRAEL
JORDAN
KUWAIT
MOROCCO
OMAN
SAUDI ARABIA
UNITED ARAB EMIRATES

ABRAHAM ACCORDS

BAHRAIN
ISRAEL
MOROCCO
SUDAN
UNITED ARAB EMIRATES

EAST MEDITERRANEAN GAS FORUM - EMGF

CYPRUS
EGYPT
FRANCE
GREECE
ISRAEL
ITALY
JORDAN
PALESTINIAN AUTHORITY
UNITED ARAB EMIRATES

EGYPT
JORDAN
IRAQ

EGYPT
JORDAN
IRAQ

COUNCIL OF THE ARAB AND AFRICAN STATES OF THE RED SEA AND THE GULF OF ADEN

EGYPT
ERITREA
JORDAN
SAUDI ARABIA
SOMALIA
SUDAN
YEMEN

M

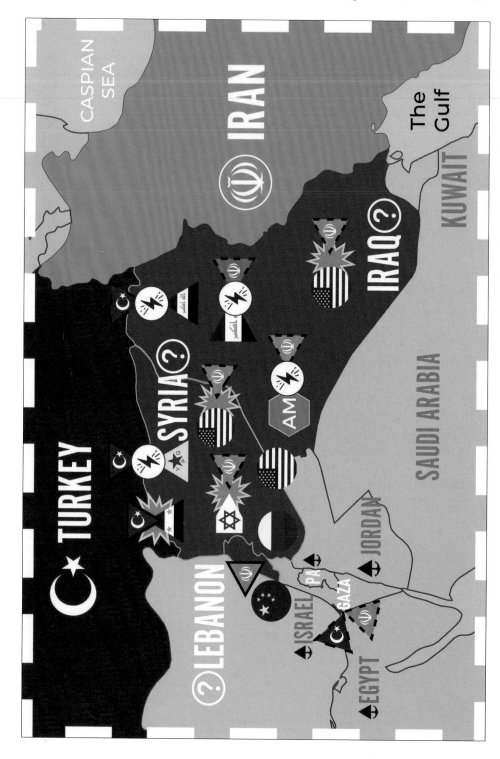

N

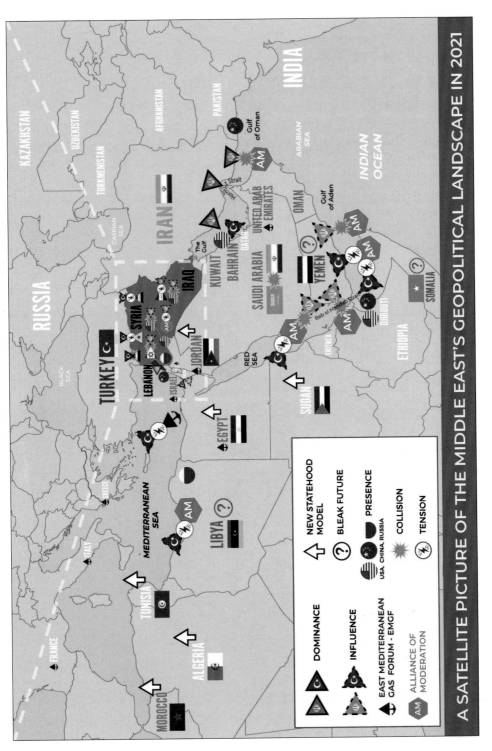

A SATELLITE PICTURE OF THE MIDDLE EAST'S GEOPOLITICAL LANDSCAPE IN 2021

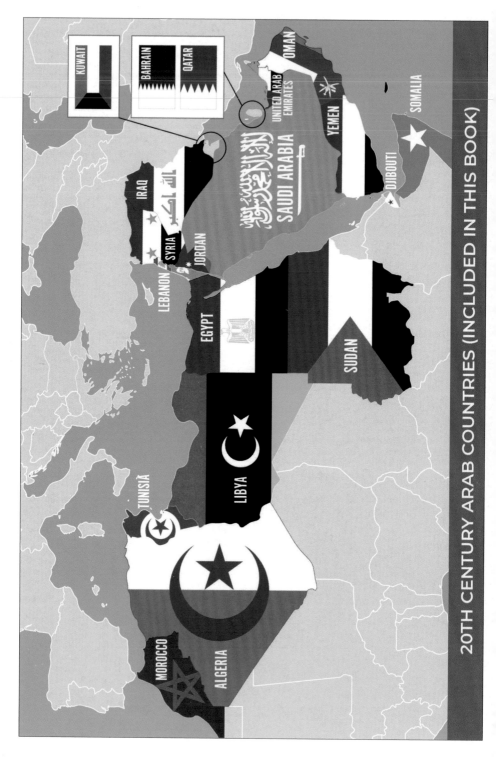

CHAPTER 5

20TH CENTURY ARAB COUNTRIES (INCLUDED IN THIS BOOK)